Information Systems and New Applications in the Service Sector:

Models and Methods

John Wang
Montclair State University, USA

BUSINESS SCIENCE REFERENCE
Hershey · New York

Director of Editorial Content: Kristin Klinger
Director of Book Publications: Julia Mosemann
Acquisitions Editor: Lindsay Johnston
Development Editor: Mike Killian
Typesetter: Keith Glazewski
Production Editor: Jamie Snavely
Cover Design: Lisa Tosheff

Published in the United States of America by
Business Science Reference (an imprint of IGI Global)
701 E. Chocolate Avenue
Hershey PA 17033
Tel: 717-533-8845
Fax: 717-533-8661
E-mail: cust@igi-global.com
Web site: http://www.igi-global.com/reference

Library of Congress Cataloging-in-Publication Data

Information systems and new applications in the service sector : models and methods / John Wang, editor.
p. cm.
Includes bibliographical references and index.
ISBN 978-1-60960-138-6 -- ISBN 978-1-60960-140-9 (ebook) 1. Service industries--Information technology. 2. Service industries--Technological innovations. 3. Web 2.0. 4. Web services. I. Wang, John, 1955-
HD30.2.I5235 2011
658.4'038011--dc22
2010047354

British Cataloguing in Publication Data
A Cataloguing in Publication record for this book is available from the British Library.

Table of Contents

Detailed Table of Contents

been selected as a widely used, already adopted service to seek for factors affecting consumer satisfaction. The second type of service was not currently widely adopted service in the market as opposed to already used SMS, which is called "Pocket Info&Enjoy" service in the paper. Pocket Info&Enjoy, which is information based service, had been described in the survey and asked questions to identify factors determining attitude to use this new service. Most of the findings were in line with literature, for an already adopted service, usefulness and attitude are direct factors influencing consumer satisfaction. On the other hand, usefulness and external influence are direct and personalization, image, content, mobility, entertainment are indirect determinants of consumer's attitude towards using new mobile services.

The continuing development and growth of the Internet imply that business and customers perceive that the Internet provides them with some kind of value. The Internet has also seen an increasing importance of user-generated content and utilisation of the Internet as a social medium often referred to as the Web 2.0. In this study the concept of customer value, based on the typology of consumer value (Holbrook, 1994; 1999) and the value hierarchy model (Woodruff & Gardial, 1996; Woodruff, 1997), is used to identify dimensions and expressions of what customer-perceived value is in travel and tourism web sites and how it is created. Moderately structured in-depth interviews are used to collect data. In the analysis connections between different types of value are presented and the lack of certain types of value is discussed.

The purpose of this study is to define generic service processes, their system, and a scope of service science developed originally by the author. In the presented approach, the main criterion is the class of serviced users, since this leads to the six kinds of process recognition and eventually helps in planning e-service systems' architecture. E-service system, e-SS is defined as a mission-goal-strategy-driven configuration of technology, organizational processes and networks designed to deliver HTservicesTH that satisfy the needs, wants, or aspirations of customers. Marketing, operations, and global environment considerations have significant implications for the design of an e-service system. Four criteria which impact e-service systems' architecture have been defined as: service business model, customer contact and level of involvement, Service User Interface, service provider's enterprise complexity, Enterprise Systems and Networks, and scope of goods involved in service. It was proved that the e-service system is the intermediary layer between Service User Interface and Enterprise Systems and Networks. Two examples of e-SS have been modeled.

Modern information systems are extending the traditional boundaries of organizations incorporating external recourses in the form of data and services. The need to support increasing client demands has led to dynamic and more complex business processes. Complex workflows in networked organizations are much more difficult to manage since traditional approaches are not suited for distributed environments. Service-Oriented approaches in the form of Web or Grid services bear the potential of increased performance and flexibility. In this work, we discuss the use of a relatively new computing paradigm that leverages distributed service-oriented business models: the Grid. We discuss how the Grid can facilitate efficient intra-business processes in highly dynamic virtual enterprises and present a high level architecture for managing complexity of business functions using Grid services.

Information Systems, IS effectiveness has been studied over the past three decades, with user satisfaction utilized as a key measure. However, very little attention has been given to the role of user-perceived cognitive value of IS in measuring the effectiveness of such systems. Therefore, this article defines and articulates user-perceived value of IS as an important construct for IS research, not from the financial or 'net benefit' perspective to the organization, rather from the cognitive perspective. Following literature review, a new taxonomy of IS effectiveness, Value-Satisfaction Taxonomy of IS Effectiveness, VSTISE, is presented. The VSTISE posits four quadrants to indicate level of user-perceived IS effectiveness: improvement, effective, misleading, and ineffective. A case study using the proposed VSTISE is discussed. Results based on the 192 responses identify several problematic system characteristics that warrant additional investigation for their limited IS effectiveness. Finally, recommendations for research and practice are provided.

Section 2

Semantic web services, SWS hold the promise of enabling dynamic discovery of candidate web services fitting a particular specified need. One interesting question is what impact this will have on software and systems engineering methods – will mainstream methods like RUP still be suitable, or will new or adapted methods be needed? This article surveys the state-of-the-art in methods specifically tailored for the engineering of SWS systems, looking at development methods trying to cover the entire lifecycle as well as methods covering only one or two phases. Some of the surveyed methods are specifically meant to deal with semantics, others are for the engineering of service-oriented systems in general. The survey reveals that there are many proposals being made in this area, some extensions of mainstream methods like RUP, others more experimental.

This paper proposes a framework for online service applications based on Service Science which identifies and enables a better understanding of the different issues faced by online service designers, engineers, and delivery personnel. The application of the Service Science framework is made possible by carefully distinguishing online service applications not only from traditional personal software applications but also from online information applications, such as the ones used by news and entertainment websites, through a process of specializing Pinhanez's definition of customer-intensive systems, Pinhanez, 2008 to online applications. To demonstrate the utility of the framework, we consider the six basic characteristics of services, as traditionally defined in Service Science — customer-as-input, heterogeneity, simultaneity, perishability, coproduction, and intangibility — and derive from these characteristics a list of 15 different issues that are highly important for the design and evaluation of the human-computer interface of online services.

Service and service systems concepts are fundamental constructs for the development of the emergent SSME, ITSM, and Service Oriented Software, SOS knowledge streams. A diversified literature has provided a richness of findings, but at the same time, the lack of standardized conceptualizations is a source of confusion to IT practitioners and academics. Given this problematic situation, we pose that a systems approach is useful to address it. In this article, we review and synthesize key studies in these knowledge streams to design:, i a framework to characterize both concepts under a system view and,, ii harmonized definitions, e.g. identification of shared and essential properties for such fundamental concepts. Our main contribution is scholastic, but we are confident that the posed conceptual artifacts can be further used to elaborate standardized definition for the IT service and IT service system constructs, as well as analysis tools for describe real service systems.

Historically, information systems, IS programs have taught two of the three areas of information technology, IT management: strategy and management, and applications development. Academic programs have ignored the third area, IT operations. IT operations management is becoming increasingly important as it is recognized as consuming as much as 90% of the IT budget and as acquisition of software becomes more prevalent than development of custom applications. Along with the shift of management focus to IT operations, standards such as the IT infrastructure library, ITIL have been adopted by businesses to guide the development of processes for IT operations that facilitate evolution to IT service management. This shift to servitizing IT management, creates an opportunity for IS programs to align with business practices by innovating in the teaching of IT service management. Several methods of incorporating ITSM material into educational programs are explored.

IT service management best practice frameworks such as the IT Infrastructure Library (ITIL) aim to improve the quality of service to customers. This study reports on recent surveys and case studies of organizations which have embarked on IT service management improvement. It highlights specific difficulties experienced by organizations in changing the orientation of staff to customer service rather than technology. Six factors were found to be critical in achieving an effective service-oriented philosophy. The factors are support from senior management; the threat or opportunity to outsource IT services; integration of processes to provide end-to-end service; involvement of business stakeholders; culture change of IT staff to service excellence; and the redesign of processes prior to investing in tools.

Section 3

The growth of the global service economy has led to a dramatic increase in our daily interactions with highly specialized service systems. Service, or value-cocreation interactions are both frequent and diverse, and may include retail, financial, healthcare, education, on-line, communications, technical support, entertainment, transportation, legal, professional, government, or many other types of specialized interactions. And yet surprisingly few students graduating from universities have studied anything about service or service systems. Service Science, Management, Engineering, and Design, SSMED,

This study compares the online services currently delivered by the official National Tourism Organizations, NTO portals of the 25 European Union states, to assess their capability in evolving into powerful marketing communication tools. A conceptual framework that identifies 129 online service quality attributes is developed based on the 2QCV3Q model, Mich et al., 2003 and on four different perspectives: marketing, customer, technical and information for the destination, So and Morrison, 2004. The 25 portals are compared by means of content analysis. Our rankings provide a first time assessment of the NTO online offerings and indicate high variability in their performance. Surprisingly, Greece and Italy, two of the most popular tourism destinations, underperformed with respect to all four perspectives examined. We provide out-of-sample evidence that affluence levels explain the variation in the observed scores, while e-readiness, popularity of tourism destination and cultural richness are not statistically significant.

This paper proposes a workflow and performance model for surgery patient identification using RFID (Radio Frequency Identification). Certain types of mistakes may be prevented by automatically identifying the patient before surgery. The proposed workflow is designed to ensure that both the correct site and patient are engaged in the surgical process. The performance model can be used to predict patient waiting time and service duration time with RFID implementation. A proof-of-concept system is developed to understand the information flow and to use information in RFID-based patient identification. Performance model indicates the response time to patients can be reduced to 38% after four hours using the proposed RFID based workflow.

Nonprofit organizations have been using the Internet for disseminating information about themselves, interacting with potential donors, and fundraising. In this chapter, we focus on online service providers for nonprofits (OSPNs) that bring donors and nonprofits together in an electronic environment to help them find a suitable match. We investigate the effects of OSPNs on the outcomes of fundraising markets by developing an economic model. We compare the total net revenues of nonprofits competing for donations in two different settings: while nonprofits in the first market use both the traditional fundraising techniques and the services provided by OSPNs, those in the second market implement the traditional method only. We derive analytical conditions under which the first setting provides better outcomes than the second one can generate.

This study compares consumer perceived risk between five e-service delivery systems and their traditional, non-Internet counterparts over each stage of the buying cycle. Using a survey methodology, the authors find that in general consumers perceive e-services as riskier than traditional services. The difference in perceived risk, which the authors define as the Internet risk premium, is significant for each service and each stage of the buying cycle. There is a spike in perceived risk at the purchase stage in the buying cycle for each of the five services. This pattern is also evident in the four services with traditional delivery systems. Perceived risk affects the consumer throughout the buying cycle and is not alleviated in the information search stage. Different risk factors drive perceived risk at various stages in the buying cycle. The authors provide both research and managerial implications of these findings.

The procurement as business discipline and function of equipping process has started the process of transformation from an administrative competence and necessity to a strategic capability (Kyte, 2006). To be efficient its processes have to be interoperable in the processing, semantic and technological way with other functions and processes of the business system; end-to-end process integration of the business system should be obtained. It is important to fully understand and document user requirements before development of the procurement (business) process. This results in the need for the development of a defined, articulated, communicated and managed model of procurement process. On the level of conceptual system modeling (business process owner's perspective) (ZIFA, 2010) this article shapes a new procurement model, in form of business service with appertaining processes, activities and other services necessary forits accomplishment. At logical and physical modeling level (designer's and builder's perspective) (ZIFA, 2010) service oriented perspective (SOA) has been considered, as well as Web services as technological concept for the implementation of the shaped procurement service model at the conceptual level of the system. Application of the shaped model requires organizational, process and system changes of the business system, that is, procurement function must develop the culture of service provider, avoiding the role of corporate purchasing controller. Event-Driven Business Process Management (EDBPM) is nowadays an enhancement of BPM by new concepts e.g. Event Driven Architecture (EDA). In this paper The position and the role of business service modeling within entire business process management (BPM) discipline has been established as well.

Preface

INFORMATION SYSTEMS AND NEW APPLICATIONS IN THE SERVICE SECTOR: CURRENT STATE AND FUTURE TRENDS

The computing era started in early 2000 and is highly present now and most likely will be in the near future (Benlian, Hess, & Buhmann, 2010). Cloud computing grows at a very fast pace. Cloud based computing and cloud based e-commerce are among the hottest topics in the IT industry. They are also two of the most widely discussed topics among IT professionals. Cloud based e-commerce is a relatively new and fast growing field.

Cloud computing is a way to increase the capacity or add capabilities dynamically without investing in new infrastructure, training new personnel, or licensing new software. It extends Information Technology's (IT) existing capabilities (Subashini & Kavitha, 2010). Cloud computing is a set of web-based applications that are stored on remote servers and accessed via the Internet using a standard Web browser. The word "cloud" is really used as metaphor for Internet. Typical cloud computing providers deliver common business applications online that are accessed from another Web service or software like a Web browser, while the software and data are stored on servers (LeClair, 2009). Consumers are able to access applications and data from a "cloud" anywhere in the world on demand. In other words, the cloud appears to be a single point of access for all the computing needs of consumers. The consumers are assured that the cloud infrastructure is very robust and will always be available at any time (Holtsnider & Jaffe, 2010).

There are three broad categories of clouds: public, private and hybrid. Public clouds provide standardized services on provider's cloud and access by subscription. Amazon and GAE are two well-known providers of public clouds (Campesto & Nilson, 2010). Public clouds are good if one needs lots of scaling and generally is not concerned with security. Private clouds provide the same services as public the only difference is that you are behind a firewall (McDonald, 2010). Private clouds are good if one wants to own everything and scaling is needed. The downsides of a private cloud are that it is the least flexible, plus it has higher operating cost.

Hybrid clouds are private clouds that also can access resources outside the firewall during period of high demand (Chandra Misra & Mondal, 2010). They maintain some data storage in-house plus rent bandwidth with a pay-as-you-go plan. Large companies may prefer hybrid clouds because they can lower their hardware cost, avoid a complexity of migrating data to a public data and avoid exposing sensitive data in public cloud.

Over the past few years, an increasing amount of both popular and scholarly attention has been focused on Web 2.0 and electronic government, or e-government. That tendency towards web based technology among government entities is stimulated by The E-Government Act of 2002 which was put in place to improve management and promote Internet-based services for citizens (Noyes, 2008). Defined as the electronic provision of information and services by governments 24 hours per day, seven days per week (Norris & Moon, 2008), e-government is said to expand and extend the ability of government organizations to serve their constituencies.

The phrase Web 2.0 has been used for over ten years now (Hinchcliffe, 2010). In its origins, no one could have imagined Web 2.0's reality today. This expression was first used to describe the second generation capability of the World Wide Web. It was meant to explain how the internet was expanding from basic web pages to a collaborative superpower which could penetrate the corporate world in many ways. Pellegrino and Eggers (2010) point out that before the term Web 2.0 was defined boundaries of Web 1.0 had to be delineated. Web 1.0 revolved around an idea of one-way communication, where information was displayed on static web-pages connected to limited research capabilities. With Web 2.0, communication turned into multi-direction and multi-level conversations as well as fast and secure channels for exchanging information. Based on that successful and collaborative platform, e-Government's goal is also to promote a host of other, mainly positive, benefits to both government and the private part of American society.

To certain extent, technology challenges are similar in public and private sectors. Both of those entities use technology for information sharing and collaboration, while consolidating infrastructure, information security and integrity. Despite similarities, government has different culture and approach to technology and such differences included lack of top-down technological leadership, focus on internal processes, not citizen outcomes and a belief that governments cannot be early adopters of latest technologies (Kumar, Mukerji, Butt, & Persaud, 2007). Consequently, what seemed to be a set of noble ideas in 2002 appeared to work well on national level, but it became a failure several years later, as state government system analysts and designers remained reluctant to adopt the E-Government Act or latest Web 2.0 technologies (Zhao, Zhao, & Zhao 2010). Fortunately, today, the Web 2.0 landscape looks much better on the state and local government levels.

Part of the emerging acceptance of Web 2.0 in today's government can be attributed to success of political campaign of the current president of the United States (Relly & Sabharwal, 2009; O'Donnell, 2010). The Obama-Biden campaign demonstrated that traditional top-down, presidential campaigns cannot compete against self-organizing armies of millions motivated by an inspiring candidate and empowered by a Web 2.0 savvy campaign team. The revolutionary changes in business, campaigning and collaboration driven by the new web technology have big implications for governance. O'Donnell (2010) adds that, with President Obama's commitment to bring his bottom-up, participatory model to the federal government—issuing a memorandum on transparency and openness in government to all executive department and agency heads on his first full day in office—government agencies are under intense pressure to keep up with the president.

CURRENT RESEARCH

Cloud Based E-Commerce Infrastructure & Services

Industry analysts have made optimistic projections on how cloud computing will transform the entire computing industry. Recently, several academic and industrial organizations have started investigating and developing technologies and infrastructure for cloud Computing. Cloud based computing worldwide spending was only 5 percent (17 billion) in 2009. However, in 2013 worldwide spending is going to be

10 percent, a whopping number 44 billion (Talbot, 2010). One International Data Corporation (IDC) report indicated that cloud-computing spending will increase from $16 billion in 2008 to $42 billion in 2012 (Rittinghouse & Ransome, 2010). According to Hewlett-Packard Co. Chairman and Chief Executive, Mark Hurd, cloud services revenues on pace to exceed $56 billion in 2010, an increase of 21% from a year ago. Overall, the cloud market is expected to reach $150.1 billion by 2013. These are very impressive numbers especially when we take into consideration the fact that there is a broader decline of more than 5% for the information-technology industry (Cheng, 2009). Those forecasts and statistical data indicate that cloud computing is going to grow and develop even further in near future because companies businesses are willing to invest money in these new technology.

Cloud E-Commerce is becoming so popular for many reasons. One of the major reasons is that it helps to reduce expenditure cost on hardware, software, and services substantially because users always pay only for what they use. Cloud computing is usually billed on pay-as-you-go basis and consumers can benefit from low barriers to entry, shared infrastructure and cost, low management overhead, and immediate access to broad range of applications (Holtsnider & Jaffe, 2010). Therefore, cloud computing is more immediately appealing to small and medium-size businesses that lack resources to purchase and own their own software and hardware. Especially it is beneficial for new businesses because time for a newly created company is extremely critical. With cloud based IT infrastructure one can immediately start his/her business operation which could in turn give you better chances to succeed. Plus any company could benefit from online data storage, which is major issue for any business. The company's essential data can be accessed from anywhere at any given moment. All you have to have is Internet connection. Not to mention that storage in the cloud can be less expensive than storing data yourself, and it can be more scalable, more efficient and more secure (Rash, 2010).

Due to so many advantages of cloud computing, every day more and more companies are trying to enter this field and become cloud providers. Let us take a closer look at a typical cloud computing company (cloud e-commerce company). Generally speaking, a cloud e-commerce company is a company that provides a service or product that belongs to the Software Platform Infrastructure (SPI) Model for cloud computing. Each SPI model addresses a specific business need. These are the SPI models: Software as a Service (SaaS), Platform as a Service (PaaS), and Infrastructure as a Service (IaaS) (Durkee, 2010). Software as a Service (SaaS) provides software application over the Internet. SaaS provides cloud – based software services such as customer resources management or enterprise resources management (Baer, 2008). A good example of SaaS would be a NetSuite's comprehensive business management suite.

Platform as a Service (PaaS) provides a development environment. It is actually very similar to SaaS, the only difference is that consumers use SaaS and developers use PaaS (McDonald, 2010). For instance, Coghead, one of a string of start-ups backed by SAP Ventures, offers a Web-based platform for enabling power users from the business—rather than developers—to compose applications using rebuilt components, such as rudimentary CRM and project management with contact management quote management, sales lead analysis, to-do lists, expense trackers, and others through a process akin to dragging and dropping widgets onto a form (Anonymous, 2008).

Infrastructure as a Service (IaaS) provides the physical hardware and software required by companies on the Internet. The basic requirement for the consumer is to send a provisioning request for the number of services with data storage requirements. The services are provisioned and the access to the services is granted by the service provider. IaaS provides a cloud-based platform for services, storage, memory, bandwidth and computing power on demand. Usually offerings of this type are delivered as an operating system on a server with some amount of storage and network transfer. These offerings can be delivered as a single server or as part of a collection of servers integrated into a virtual private data center (VPDC) (McDonald, 2010; Barman, 2009).

Although, there are many cloud computing vendors on the market the current major ones are: Amazon EC2, IBM Cloud labs, Google App Engine (GAE), and Microsoft Azure. Amazon Elastic Compute Cloud (EC2) provides a virtual computing environment that enables a user to run Linux-based applications. The user can either create a new Amazon Machine Image (AMI) containing the applications, libraries, data and associated configuration settings, or select from a library of globally available AMIs. The user then needs to upload the created or selected AMIs to Amazon Simple Storage Service (S3), before he can start, stop, and monitor instances of the uploaded AMIs. Amazon EC2 charges the user for the time when the instance is alive, while Amazon S3 charges for any data transfer (both upload and download) (Campesto & Nilson, 2010).

Google App Engine allows a user to run Web applications written using the Python programming language. Other than supporting the Python standard library, Google App Engine also supports Application Programming Interfaces (APIs) for the data store, Google Accounts, URL fetch, image manipulation, and email services. Google App Engine also provides a Web-based Administration Console for the user to easily manage his running Web applications. Currently, Google App Engine is free to use with up to 500MB of storage and about 5 million page views per month.

Generally available since January 2010, Windows Azure is essentially a cloud-based version of the Windows Server OS. Likewise, SQL Azure is a cloud-based version of the SQL Server 2008 relational database server. Unlike Windows Server, which is often used for file and print services, Windows Azure is an application platform. It runs the same types of web applications that run on Windows Server: C++, C#, and Visual Basic (VB). Pricing is structured on an as-used basis or by buying longer-term contracts at fixed prices. SQL Azure offers a subset of SQL Server's usual features (Otey, 2010).

While a lot of businesses embrace these relatively new trends towards cloud computing many of business executives are still hesitant to jump into the cloud. An issue of a security is a major concern for business owners. In February 2010 survey of 518 business technology pros, security concerns topped the list of reasons not to use cloud computing services (Shipley, 2010). The Internet has security issues, and since cloud computing is in the Internet, cloud computing will have those security issues. To demonstrate potential security shortfalls the study was done by three computer scientists at the University of California, San Diego, and one at MIT. They hired some virtual machines to serve as targets and others to serve as attackers—and tried to get both groups hosted on the same servers at Amazon's data centers. They succeeded in placing malicious virtual machines on the same servers as targets 40 percent of the time. This interesting experiment revealed the vulnerability and potential security exposure that cloud computing faces in every day operations (Talbot, 2010).

Another reason why businesses are hesitant to use cloud computing vendors is that they are afraid to store their internal data on the computer that is located externally in a cloud, especially, if the data are located in the other country. For instance, Asian companies have been concerned about data stored in USA because under jurisdiction of the U.S. Patriot Act, the U.S. Government can access that data very easily (Smith, 2009). Even more: depending on the nature of your business you might need to achieve and maintain data privacy requirements for Payment Card Industry Data Security Standards (PCI) compliance, Health Insurance Portability and Accountability Act (HIPAA) compliance, Sarbanes–Oxley Act (SOX) and so on, then use of cloud computing would increase risk of compromising sensitive data, because you have less control over data storage in a Cloud vendor facility (Barman, 2009). A possibility of power outage contributes to possible data loss issues. Even though it is a concern many of broadband providers guarantee 99.9% uptime and to increase system reliability even more you can also set up your system to 'failover' safely, with a router that uses a 3G wireless dongle as backup (Clark, 2010).

We mentioned earlier that one of the big advantages of cloud computing is cost control. However, it is not always the case. Sometimes even if you are unhappy with the services that you receive from your vendor you cannot change your vendor without some major changes to both your software and your data and that could significantly increase your cost (Smith, 2009). Once you select your cloud computing provider you depend on him. Since each cloud vendor offers unique service and unique ways to communicate with the computer your switching cost most likely to be very high.

Use of Web 2.0 Tools for E-Government & Service Sector

Many of us wonder why Web 2.0 approaches create more value more rapidly than other technological models. What we today observe as a multi-directional conversation appears to be the answer key. The reason for such success of Web 2.0 is something called architectures of participation, which, as Adebanjo and Roula (2010) add, is the combined network effect of pervasive two-way participation (blogging, wikis, media sharing, social networking, etc.) which allows value to be built quickly from a collective wave of contribution. A Web 2.0 application often consists of nothing but a framework to elicit widespread input from thousands or even millions of potential contributors.

Web 2.0's impact on the government has coined the new phrase "Government 2.0", also known as e-Government. Government 2.0 refers to a new style of government that makes information readily available to all citizens of the United States who have access to the internet. One of the key intentions behind this initiative is to make the government more transparent to the general public. In an age where information sharing is extremely popular, the government would like to participate as well. Sindelar, Mintz, & Hughes (2009) explain how the administration is "…making data available through multiple channels and developing policies that reflect an open government accessible by a growing list of Web 2.0 tools" (p.25). Ressler (2009) takes this idea one step further, adding another important element to that equation, by noting that Gov 2.0 is not only about "openness, transparency, and collaboration", but also promotes the idea that "the voices of the many are smarter than the voice of one" (p.10).

The genesis for this was the open source movement of the 1990's, which demonstrated that very complex and high-value outcomes could occur if anyone and everyone were encouraged to contribute and the community around the effort ensured that quality was maintained (Albors, Ramos,f & Hervas, 2008). As this decade closes, architectures of participation are now routinely embedded into product development, customer service, marketing, lines of business, and just about everywhere workers and government representatives must come together in teams (Adebanjo & Roula, 2010). This unfolding story is routinely found in the headlines of traditional media: virtually everyone in United States is familiar with the hugely popular, rapidly expanding social networking sites like Facebook and Twitter. As Scheir (2008) reports, government agencies such as the Army or U.S. Air Force use them as well, but as we observe today, Web 2.0 usage in e-government efforts and its services aren't limited to those large organizations.

What brings an exponential benefit to society is not so much the underlying technical software layer that makes Web 2.0 possible, but how it enables us to organize and work together as communities and how it allows the government to fulfill its new transparency initiatives (Bertot, Jaeger, & Grimes, 2010). The new technical vision of Web 2.0 includes re-use and "building on the shoulders of [Internet based] giants". With that core principle in mind, consumers, businesses and local governmental services can now build applications on top of existing applications, so-called software mashups, with relative ease

(Yang, Raskin, Goodchild, & Gahegan, 2010). They can remix data from multiple sources, creating ad hoc supply chains with business partners, harness user-generated content, participate in communities of individuals with similar affinities as well as aggregate global knowledge and much more. Web 2.0 has come to represent a set of best practices to get the most value from the Internet by taking advantage of its intrinsic power to reach people regardless of their physical location, time of day or type of a digital device (as long as some level of network connectivity is available) to then distribute and aggregate helpful services and fast information.

During the recent couple years, government agencies much smaller than the Army or U.S. Air Force have applied the concepts of mashups to accelerate the speed, accuracy and user-friendliness of their messages to and from local communities, states as well as entire regions (O'Donnell, 2010; Pellegrino & Eggers, 2010). For instance, the government of San Francisco, California, utilized Web 2.0 in a mashup of Google Maps, an online database of parking lots in the area and their existing web hosting solution to create dynamic Internet application that lists available accessible parking spaces within a customized radius from someone's current geo-location, near a specific address or along user defined route of travel. Washington, D.C. launched a mashup that, among other services, provides a Snow Response Reporting System, combining a web map interface, Google Maps database and live camera feeds to assure citizens' safety and share up-to-date information about road traffic conditions. Boston's Department of Transportation has become famous for its groundbreaking transparency in recent public sharing of scheduling data and geographic information; so that notoriously technical Bostonian crowds of software entrepreneurs could incorporate it in their latest community efforts. Osimo (2009) points out that such a 21st-century alternative to hiring consultants, who develop intelligent software at exorbitant costs, demonstrates a great success of local government Web 2.0 services.

In similar fashion to Web 2.0 implementations listed above, Miami, FL shows another impressive example of that is an insightful online application. The local government launched a service called Miami311Could App, which utilizes a cloud computing platform. Miami 311 is a public-facing, open government transparency application where the citizens of Miami can monitor and analyze non-emergency event information happening in their area. Citizens can report non-emergency requests, like pothole repair or missed trash pickup by dialing 3-1-1 on their telephone. They can then log on Miami 311 to monitor the progress of their request. Miami 311 also serves as a dashboard for City Commissioners to see and monitor citizen requests in their district. According to a Microsoft Case Study (2010) on the City of Miami, this system integrates with the larger Miami-Dade Motorola CSR system and will soon be extended to take service request input from citizens. Added combination of Microsoft Bing's public map database, MapDoNet service, Microsoft Azure cloud computing techniques and rich interactivity of Silverlight 3 web development platform allow the government of city of Miami, FL to provide a free and cutting-edge Web 2.0 mashup for its citizens.

Like all government initiatives, this has created a new problem. Because the United States Constitution deems equality for all men, the government must not discriminate against any citizen who cannot provide themselves or their families with internet access, either because of their geographical location, or because they cannot afford internet services. For Government 2.0 to work, our government must now find a way to provide internet access for people who cannot provide it for themselves, because one of the key factors in e-Government is allowing all citizens the ability to participate, if they so choose, in their own government.

FUTURE DIRECTION

Cloud Based E-Commerce Infrastructure & Services

Promising Outlook

Even though cloud computing has some disadvantages, according to IT experts the outlook of cloud computing is very promising for a number of reasons. Cloud computing provides an Internet-based platform that lays the foundation for a new generation of globally accessed, highly scalable cloud-based applications (Durkee, 2010). Cloud computing provides an opportunity for creation of a new type of businesses that were not possible only a few years before. It gives an access to unlimited IT resources at the modest cost of lowering barriers for entry. Your business's geographical location is becoming more and more irrelevant. Cloud computing is giving an opportunity for software product developed in the USA to be extended and supported by a developer in another continent, like Asia (Greengard, 2010). Some observers even believe businesses will eventually run no servers of their own, but simply rent access to a larger vendor's cloud of computer resources.

Strategic Tool

Cloud computing is playing a big role in the Obama Administration's new FY2011 budget. Federal CIO Vivek Kundra contends the U.S. government can acquire technology faster and at lower cost through cloud computing, leaders in the public and private sectors are more than ever working closely to use cloud computing as a strategic IT tool to help transform government and make them more effective and efficient, which means that government spending on cloud computing will increase significantly and that could stimulate cloud computing vendors to increase their R&D and capital investment on cloud computing infrastructure in order to get government contracts (PR Newswire, 2010).

Real Value

Corresponding to Chandra Misra & Mondal (2010), as the newest offering as service over the ubiquitous Web, cloud computing has been considered as a much hyped phenomenon in the IT and business world promising to deliver a host of benefits. Companies need to look beyond this hype and seriously consider the real value of incorporating the Cloud in their own businesses. Companies should analyze several characteristics of their own business as well as pre-existing IT resources to identify their favorability in the migration to the Cloud Architecture.

Trade-Off Balancing

Truong & Dustdar (2010) warn that scientists need to decide which parts of their applications should be executed in cloud computing systems in order to balance the trade-off between cost, time and resource requirements. They present a service for estimating, monitoring and analyzing costs associated with scientific applications in the cloud. This model could eventually be integrated into cloud resource management and execution services to support on-the-fly resource scheduling.

Potential Risks

Subashini & Kavitha (2010) claim that security is one of the major issues which reduce the growth of cloud computing and complications with data privacy and data protection continue to plague the market. Cloud service users need to be vigilant in understanding the risks of data breaches in this new environment. The advent of an advanced model should not negotiate with the required functionalities and capabilities present in a current model. A new model targeting at improving features of an existing model must not risk or threaten other important features of the current model.

Vertical Clouds

Nicholas Carr recently commented on the possibility of so-called vertical clouds that offer special resources or services to customers with specific needs. According to Mr. Carr, IT expert, vertical clouds would provide possible resources of addressing issues of information security crucial to industries such as health care and financial services. In simple words there is a high potential for growth and development of new modified specialized cloud computing services in industries such as financial industry and healthcare (Schick, 2009).

Grid Computing

As indicated by Schwiegelshohn et al. (2010), the underachievement of grid computing may have led to claims that the grid concept as a whole is on its way to being replaced by cloud computing and various X-as-a-Service approaches. Although there are shortcomings in current grid systems, they are convinced that the concept as a whole remains valid and can benefit from new developments, including cloud computing. Further research is required in order to turn this concept into reliable, efficient and user-friendly computing platforms.

New Abstraction Layer

Rodero-Merino, Vaquero, Gil, Galán, Fontán, Montero, & Llorente (2010) discovered that users are not fully realizing the implicit promise of clouds (leveraging them from the tasks related with infrastructure management). A reason for this is that current clouds offer interfaces too close to that infrastructure, while users demand functionalities that automate the management of their services as a whole unit. To overcome this limitation, Rodero-Merino et al. (2010) propose a new abstraction layer closer to the lifecycle of services that allows for their automatic deployment and escalation depending on the service status (not only on the infrastructure). This abstraction layer can sit on top of different cloud providers, hence mitigating the potential lock-in problem and allowing the transparent federation of clouds for the execution of services.

Based on the facts and data mentioned above we believe that cloud computing is here to stay. As you can see, a wide variety of E-Commerce companies offer solutions that range from user-oriented solutions to enterprise development platforms. At this point, cloud computing might not be for all businesses—and it is not going to replace all on-premise solutions in one day. However, we see that every day more and more private companies and government agency are moving to the cloud.

Use of Web 2.0 Tools for E-Government & Service Sector

More Involvement

Twenty years ago, people working for the Federal Government had access to the world's best technology. Today, many government employees have better technology at home than at work. In reaction to those ominous observations, Sproles (2010) sees great potential for the usage of Web 2.0 in e-government, but he does not omit possible points of failure. On the other hand, Meijer and Thaens (2010) state that with proper application of IT strategy and business strategic orientation can be applied towards operational success of Web 2.0 in government.

We agree with Shuler, Jaeger, & Bertot (2010) and believe that the Government Printing Office's Federal Depository Library Program (FDLP) is going to be affected the most. As technology and its security provide new presentation methods for various types of information, FDLP may need to transform from traditional printing plant to something else in the world of the Internet. Such a trend would have a drastically positive impact on the quality and accuracy of information available via public search engines, which could help us become better educated consumers and more influential contributors.

The future trend of e-Government may be leading our country into an age where the people can be more involved in politics than ever before. Their involvement can be both proactive and passive. Some citizens may choose to use e-Government tools as a platform to voice their opinions, while others may choose to quietly follow along what congress and their local governments are up to – as an alternative to watching the news on television. Overall, this seems like a great step in the right direction for our country.

New Tool (SBAT)

There is no doubt in our mind that Web 2.0 applications will continue to evolve and become more valuable to governments and their key stakeholders. However, government leaders must start down the collaborative path today to understand how these tools can drive their organization's desired outcomes in the future. Rowley (2010) points out the importance of various stakeholder groups in success of e-government in such an extensive organization as the government. Rowley also proposed a new stakeholder benefits analysis tool (SBAT), which can be used to map stakeholder roles to stakeholder benefits. That tool has been tested by an expert group, and revised, so we are hoping that the government body starts taking advantage of it to accelerate future acceptance of Web 2.0 for e-government. Some of the possible stakeholder groups to analyze using SBAT include educational institutions such as public universities and libraries. The availability of majority of government's information online, combined with the power of private search engines such as Google, ultimately allows every public or a university library to serve as an effective access point for e-government information.

Vulnerable Information

Personal privacy is also a cause for concern. The average internet user cannot fathom what happens to their information once they put it somewhere on the internet. Even the most knowledgeable and cautious users will, at some point, leave their information vulnerable. If even the most secure connection is hacked into, millions of people could be at risk of identity theft. After all is said and done, it will be the company who allowed this information to leak publicly that will incur the blame, not the individual who offered it. As Lyon (2010) describes "When customers do learn about privacy failings, they will not be mad at themselves. Instead, they will blame the company they feel should have protected them" (p.26). It is extremely important for individuals and companies alike to invest in the proper amount of security for their (or their customer's) private information.

In a much larger scale, if the government becomes too transparent, many security problems may arise, some of them as serious as national security. Probably the largest internet phenomenon is that once something is published on the internet, it will be there forever. The government will have to find a way to become more transparent while also closely censoring what becomes published information.

4-C Typology

Web 2.0 has also had a large impact on the service sector of our economy. Not only are product based companies required to use the internet to remain competitive in their respective industries, but service corporations now face the same obligation. Because services are not a tangible item, they become much more difficult to market on the internet. Everything from accounting services to consulting services to legal services must find a way to differentiate them from the competition.

In a marketplace that is constantly changing and evolving, sustainability becomes a firm's most important goal. Wirtz, Schilke and Ullrich (2010) have developed a Twenty-First Century business model typology which will help companies create value by using the internet to their advantage. Their basic model is known as the "4C Business Model Typology" consists of four business models that can prove to be successful in the era of Web 2.0 technology. The models are content-oriented (such as Wikipedia), commerce-oriented (such as Amazon), context-oriented (such as Google), and connection-oriented (such as Facebook) (pp.274-5). According to this structured set of online business practice, if a company can find themselves operating in one of these four areas, they have the opportunity to maintain sustainability and survive the Web 2.0 revolution while still turning a profit.

CONCLUSION

In the last few years, cloud computing has grown from being a promising business concept to one of the fast growing segments of the IT industry. Clouds have changed the way we think about IT infrastructure management. Cloud computing provides an opportunity for creation of a new type of businesses that were not possible only a few years before. It gives an access to unlimited IT resources at the modest cost lowering barriers for entry. Certainly, companies should analyze several characteristics of their own business as well as pre-existing IT resources to identify their favorability in the migration to the Cloud Architecture.

Web 2.0 does not only refer to a revolution in personal internet usage. There has also been a major shift that has affected businesses worldwide. Web 2.0 has changed the internet to an interactive information portal, where users proactively control their own experience. If corporations can harness and effectively implement what Web 2.0 technology has to offer, their potential competitive advantages will expand to a point previously unimaginable.

Web 2.0 technology is not just a trend. Web 2.0 is a shift in lifestyle, for people, companies, and government entities alike. To ignore its existence will leave you far behind society as a whole. It is imperative to embrace the technology available. The most difficult aspect to overcome about this behavioral shift will be the cultural changes. Our culture is changing, and change is hard for many people to understand

and cope with. Once they get their feet wet, Web 2.0 technology's offerings can have a profoundly positive impact on the way we do business, the way our government is run, and on how we live our lives.

REFERENCES

Adebanjo, D., & Roula, M. (2010, April). Analysis of Web 2.0 enabled e-clusters: A case study. *Technovation*, *30*(4), 238-248.

Albors, J., Ramos, J.C., & Hervas, J.L. (2008, June). New learning network paradigms: Communities of objectives, crowdsourcing, wikis and open source. *International Journal of Information Management*, *28*(3), 194-202.

Anonymous. (2008). Integration strategies - realize the full value of CRM. *CRM Magazine*, *12*(10), 18.

Baer, T. (2008). Platform as a service: Kerry Group extends enterprise apps into the cloud. *Manufacturing Business Technology*, *26*(7/8), 52-54.

Barman, B. (2009). Safe on the Cloud (a perspective into the security concerns of cloud computing). *Siliconindia*, *12*(4), 34-35.

Benlian, A., Hess, T., & Buhmann, P. (2010). *Software-as-a-service anbieterstrategien, kundenbedürfnisse und wertschöpfungsstrukturen. Kartoniert,* Germany: Gabler.

Bertot, J., Jaeger, P., & Grimes, J. (2010, July). Using ICTs to create a culture of transparency: E-government and social media as openness and anti-corruption tools for societies. *Government Information Quarterly*, *27*(3), 264-271.

Campesto, O., & Nilson, K. (2010). Web 2.0 fundamentals for developers. Sudbury, MA*: Johns and Bartlett Publishers.*

Chandra Misra, S., & Mondal, A. (2010). Identification of a company's suitability for the adoption of cloud computing and modelling its corresponding return on investment. *Mathematical and Computer Modelling*, in press. doi: 10.1016/j.mcm.2010.03.037

Cheng, R. (2009). Cloud computing, virtualization still strong- Companies continued to spend on these technologies even as they reduced other information outlays. *Wall Street Journal*, p.a.1.

Clark, T. (2010). Cloud cover. *Commercial Motor*, *212*(5367), 44-45.

Durkee, D. (2010). Why cloud computing will never be free. *Communications of the ACM*, *53*(5), 62-69.

Greengard, S. (2010). Cloud computing and developing nations. *Communications of the ACM*, *53*(5), 18-20.

Hinchcliffe, D. (2010). Why all the fuss about Web 2.0? *Infonomics*, *24*(1), 26-31.

Holtsnider, B., & Jaffe, B. (2010). IT manager's handbook: The business edition. Burlington, MA*: Morgan Kaufman Publishers*. 210-215.

Kumar, V., Mukerji, B., Butt, I., & Persaud, A. (2007). Factors for successful E-government adoption: A conceptual framework. *The Electronic Journal of e-Government*, *5*(1), 63-76.

LeClair, L. (2009). Here are the basics you need to know about cloud computing. *Inside Tucson Business, 19*(16), 13.

Lyon, S. (2010). Privacy lessons smart grid should take from WEB 2.0. *POWERGRID International, 15*(4), 24-26.

McDonald, K. (2010). Above the clouds: Managing risk in the world of cloud computing. *Cambridgeshire, United Kingdom: IT Governance Publishing*. 23-25.

Meijer, A., & Thaens, M. (2010, July). Alignment 2.0: Strategic use of new internet technologies in government. *Government Information Quarterly, 27*(2), 113-121.

Microsoft Case Studies. (2010, February). City government improves service offerings, cuts costs with "Cloud" services solution, Retrieved Jul. 30, 2010, from http://www.microsoft.com/casestudies/Case_Study_Detail.aspx?CaseStudyID=4000006568/

Norris, D., & Moon, J. (2008, January). Advancing E-government at the grassroots: Tortoise or hare? *Public Administration Review, 65*(1), 64-75.

Noyes, A. (2008, December). OMB, senators urge reauthorization of E-government act. *Congress Daily AM, 12*, 4.

O'Donnell, E. (2010, July). Web 2.0 and the federal government: A webinar sponsored by center for American progress, June 1, 2009, 12:00 pm–1:30 pm. *Government Information Quarterly, 27*(3), 305-306.

Osimo, D. (2009, August). Benchmarking eGovernment in the Web 2.0 era: What to measure, and how. *European Journal of ePractice, 4*, 5-10.

Otey, M. (2010). The rise of cloud computing. *Windows IT Pro*,10. Retrieved Jul. 30, 2010, from http://www.windowsitpro.com/print/cloud-computing2/The-Rise-of-Cloud-Computing.aspx

Pellegrino, G., & Eggers, W. D. (2010). National issues dialogues. *Web 2.0: The future of collaborative government,* 6.

PR Newswire. (2010). First-hand cloud computing government success stories and lessons learned to be showcased at Gov 2.0 Expo: NASA, State of California, City of Los Angeles, U.S. Army among featured government speakers. Retrieved Jul. 30, 2010, from http://www.prnewswire.com/news-releases/first-hand-cloud-computing-government-success-stories-and-lessons-learned-to-be-showcased-at-gov-20-expo-92175934.html

Rash, W. (2010). Cloud-based storage done right. *eWeek, 27*(3), 14-16.

Relly, J., & Sabharwal, M. (2009, January). Perceptions of transparency of government policymaking: A cross-national study, *Government Information Quarterly, 26*(1), 148-157.

Ressler, S. (2009). The rise of Gov 2.0- from govloop to the White House. *Public Manager, 38*(3), 10-13.

Rittinghouse, J., & Ransome, J. (2010). Cloud computing: implementation, management, and security. Boca Rayton, FL: CRC Press.

Rodero-Merino, L., Vaquero, L., Gil, V., Galan, F., Fontan, J., Montero, R., & Llorente, I. (2010). From infrastructure delivery to service management in clouds. *Future Generation Computer Systems*, in press. doi: 10.1016/j.future.2010.02.013

Rowley, J. (2010). E-government stakeholders—Who are they and what do they want? *International Journal of Information Management*, 2-10.

Scheir, N. (2008). The Air Force security cooperation knowledgebase: A critical enabler moves into the future., *DISAM Journal of International Security Assistance Management*, *30*(1), 99-101.

Schick, S. (2009). Head in the clouds? Welcome to the future. *The Globe and Mail*, 5. Retrieved Jul. 30, 2010, from http://www.theglobeandmail.com/news/technology/article137127

Schwiegelshohn, U., Badia, R., Bubak, M., Danelutto, M., Dustdar, S., Gagliardi, F., Yahyapour, R. (2010). *Perspectives on Grid Computing*, in press. doi: 10.1016/j.future.2010.05.010

Shipley, G. (2010). Cloud computing risk. *InformationWeek*, (1262), 20-24.

Shuler, J., Jaeger, P., & Bertot, J. (2010). Implications of harmonizing the future of the federal depository library program within e-government principles and policies. *Government Information Quarterly*, *27*(1), 9-16.

Sindelar, J., Mintz, D., & Hughes, T. (2009). The past is prologue: The Obama technology agenda. *Public Manager, 38(4),* 24-27.

Smith, R. (2009). Computing in the cloud. *Research Technology Manage*ment, *52*(5), 65-68.

Sproles, C. (2010, July). State of the eUnion: Government 2.0 and onwards*, Government Information Quarterly*, *27*(3), 308.

Subashini, S., & Kavitha, V. (2010). A survey on security issues in service delivery models of cloud computing. *Journal of Network and Computer Applications*, in press. doi: 10.1016/j.jnca.2010.07.006

Talbot, D. (2010). Security in the ether. *Technology Review*, *113*(1), 36-42.

Truong, H., & Dustdar, S. (2010). Composable cost estimation and monitoring for computational applications in cloud computing environments. *Procedia Computer Science*, *1*(1), 2169-2178.

Wirtz, B., Schilke, O., & Ullrich, S. (2010). Strategic development of business models:

Implications of the Web 2.0 for creating value on the internet. *Long Range Planning*, *43*(2/3), 272-290.

Yang, C., Raskin, R., Goodchild, M., & Gahegan, M. (2010, July). Geospatial cyberinfrastructure: Past, present and future. *Computers, Environment and Urban Systems, 34*(4), 264-277.

Zhao, J., Zhao, S., & Zhao, S. (2010, January). Opportunities and threats: A security assessment of state e-government websites. *Government Information Quarterly*, *27*(1), 49-56.

John Wang
Montclair State University, USA

Peijun Guo
Yokohama National University, Japan

Section 1

Chapter 1
Comparative Analysis of International Education Systems

John Wang
Montclair State University, USA

Jun Xia
Montclair State University, USA

Kimberly Hollister
Montclair State University, USA

Yawei Wang
Montclair State University, USA

ABSTRACT

International comparisons of educational systems are commonly practiced using subjective methods available in literature. The use of subjective methods can lead to non-standard ranking; each individual investigator inputs his or her own subjective judgment when assigning weights to measurements in each class. The complied results differ with large variations. A mathematical evaluation method based on concept of Pareto-optimal organization is proposed for this study. This method is easy to apply and uses linear programming model. The weights for various measurements are determined through an objective method. We illustrate our methodology in a comparison of the educational systems of twenty-one industrialized countries.

INTRODUCTION

In 1983, the *National Commission on Excellence in Education* released "A Nation at Risk." In this document, they warned the United States, "If only to keep and improve on the slim competitive edge we still retain in world markets, we must dedicate ourselves to the reform of our educational system for the benefit of all—old and young alike, affluent and poor, majority and minority" (Hanushek, Jamison, Jamison, & Woessmann, 2008, p.62). In this statement, the commission suggests that education plays a significant foundation in the economic success of a country. It also states that the investment and time devoted to education will not only increase the employment rate but also increase the graduation rate.

DOI: 10.4018/978-1-60960-138-6.ch001

In 2002, the United States passed the *No Child Left Behind Act* (NCLB), which focuses on improving the performance of U.S. primary and secondary schools. Through this act, the number of federal programs was reassessed. Education in the U.S. is primarily a State and local responsibility. With NCLB, the Department of Education (federal program) contributes a budget of $68.6 billion a year (U.S. Department of Education, 2008). However, the amount of educational investment varies from country to country.

Generally speaking, employment rates normally rise with educational attainment. For the most part, this is principally due to larger investment in human capital made by higher-educated individuals and the need for these individuals to recoup this investment. In our current global market, the level of skills demanded by industry is rising. The demand for increased skill comes not only from the changes in the employment share between occupations, but also the changing skill demands within occupations (OECD, 2007). For example, a mechanic can no longer succeed with only experience. He/She must know how to read, write, as well as know how to use computerized testing equipment. By recognizing these trends in globalization, countries face greater pressure to improve education and keep their competitive edge in the global economy. Globalization, together with skill-biased technology change, is shifting the composition of jobs in advanced economies. This has increased the importance of educating a larger proportion of the population to much higher standards than in the past (Hammod, 2008). In fact, illiteracy has declined worldwide over the past few decades. The percentage of the population without any schooling decreased from 36 percent in 1960 to 25 percent in 2000 (Wieczorek, 2008).

Higher education graduation rates have grown significantly in recent decades yet the question arises of whether the increasing supply of well-educated labor has been matched by the creation of an equivalent number of high-paying jobs? Governments in various countries including France, Germany and Japan, who are pursuing an expansion of tertiary education, have acknowledged the fact that more high-level skills are needed in an advanced knowledge economy. This requires a greater proportion of the workforce than in the past to be educated beyond the secondary school level. Dustmann, Fitzenberger, and Machin (2007) state that many countries have seen significant growth in the number of jobs and industries that are dependent on a having a skilled workforce. However, the question remains—what will be the effect increasing the supply of the well-educated on the labor market? Dustmann, Fitzenberger, and Machin (2006) note that one negative impact of increasing the supply of well-educated workers is a relative rise in unemployment among people with low qualifications (as high-qualified workers take their jobs); they also note the potential for a reduction in the pay premium associated with tertiary qualifications (as a rise in graduate supply outstrips any rise in demand for graduate skills).

Chan, Leung, and Wang (2006) found that the difference in unemployment rates between those with an upper secondary education and those with tertiary education decreased marginally, from 2.8% to 2.2% between 1995 and 2005. On the other hand, the difference between upper secondary and lower secondary unemployment rates increased from 3.4% to 5%. Since most countries started to attain upper secondary and tertiary schooling during this period, it suggests that these increases have been matched by demand for higher skills.

The purpose of this paper is to evaluate the international education system among 21 industrialized countries. As students are the future employees as well as the future customers of educational systems, this paper takes a look at how educational investment and the learning environment impacts graduation and employment rates. Educational investment is not only looked at by the annual expenditure per student but also the annual expenditure per student relative to GDP.

LITERATURE REVIEW

One may assume that the more money a country invests in education, the better the students. However, this may not be true. Higher spending on education does not automatically improve outcomes. Murray (2008) states the economic literature on the relationship between education spending and pupil achievement suggests a need to be very careful about how additional resources are spent. While different methodologies produce different findings, most reviews of the literature reach the same conclusion: some measurable school inputs do sometimes matter, but that the magnitude of the effects found are quite small. For example, people may argue that smaller class sizes yield higher test scores; yet some researchers conclude that smaller class sizes have no distinguishable effect on test scores. Others (Krueger, 2003) interpret the same literature differently and argue that class size reduction improves student achievement. It should be noted that the opinions of researchers do not imply that the level of educational resources is irrelevant in determining educational quality. There is significant evidence that high quality interventions in the early years can effectively promote learning (OECD, 2007). Studies have found that governments can maximize the return on education spending by directing a high proportion of spending towards ensuring the development of both cognitive and non-cognitive skills.

Hanushek et al. (2008) looked at the impact of average school attainment on the economic growth rate. They found when the average number of years of schooling in a country was higher; the economy grew at a higher annual rate over the following decades. In fact, over the 50 countries studied, they found that each additional year of average schooling in a country increased the average 40-year growth rate in GDP by about 0.37 percentage points. Nevertheless, the quality of education is important. While there are other factors that affect economic growth, there is a clear, strong relationship between cognitive skills and economic growth. In order to improve cognitive skills, countries should continue to invest in reform. However, the amount of money invested does not necessarily result in better outcomes.

Recent studies by the *United Nations International Children Educational Fund* (UNICEF 2002) indicate mediocre educational performance and achievement gaps when the educational system in the US is compared with the educational systems of other developed nations. The situation is so deplorable that in presenting indicators of risk facing the United States, poor performance of US students was cited as one of them. "It is thus believed that the United States might soon lose its economic power if it fails to move up the educational ranking" (Nickerson & Kritsonis, 2006, p.4).

On the contrary, Asian countries like Japan and South Korea rank the highest in the world when it comes to educational effectiveness. Researchers took the averages from five different categories and ranked the USA number 18 out of 24 nations in terms of relative effectiveness of its educational system (UNICEF, 2002). The above findings pose great challenge to the future human capital needs of the US. Another study analyzing global spending on education by the UNESCO Institute of Statistics (UIS) agreed that given its investment in education, the US is not getting the returns it expects when compared with the performance of other nations (Global Education Digest, 2007).

The same report shows that the United States is home to just 4% of the world's school-going age population of between 5 to 25 years and yet accounts for about 28% of the global education budget. This is mainly due to the large numbers of the university students and the relatively high costs associated with this level of education. The United States spends almost as much as that of all governments in six regions combined namely the Arab States, Central and Eastern Europe, Central Asia, Latin America and the Caribbean, South and West Asia and sub-Saharan Africa.

The United States fared better in reading literacy among fourth-graders, where it finished among the top scorers in 2001. But the declining performance as students grow older should serve as a wake-up call that the nation has two gaps to fill, one between it and other countries, and one between top performing and low achieving students in the nation (Associated Press 2003).

Educational Performance: Costs

In order to facilitate comparison among the quality assessment systems, we look at a few measurements. The empirical evidence on the determinants of educational performance overwhelmingly shows that at given levels of expenditures, an increase in the amount of resources used does not generally lead to an increase in educational performance. Cross-country resource differences do not help in understanding cross-country differences in educational performance. Based on Gonzales, Guzman, & Jocelyn's research (2004), the correlation coefficient between expenditure per student and average TIMSS test scores is 0.13 in primary education and 0.16 in secondary education. By implication, the level of schooling productivity - the ratio of educational performance to resources used - differs widely across schooling systems.

Educational System Management

School systems tend to be publicly managed all over the world, thereby often lacking incentives for improving students' performance or containing costs. Along the lines of Smyth (2008), while public provision of schooling may generally be associated with inefficiencies, the public schooling systems still differ substantially across countries in their institutional structure of educational decision-making processes. These institutional features include settings such as the centralization of examinations and of other decision-making powers, the distribution of responsibilities and influence between the administration, school principals, teachers, parents, and students, and the size of the private schooling sector. Institutional differences create different incentives for the agents involved in educational production, which should lead to different resource-allocation decisions and thereby ultimately to differences in the educational performance of students.

Student Characteristics

To determine the influence of student background, resources, and institutions on students' educational performance, the educational level achieved by the students' parents could possibly be strongly positively related to the students' educational performance. Students of schools located in geographically isolated communities performed worse than students from more urban areas. As a control for the overall level of development of the country in which the student lives, GDP per capita is positively related to mathematics achievement. All these effects of student and family characteristics are statistically highly significant (Harkness et al., 2007; Kao, 1994)). Also, Woessmann (2002) noticed that student and family background effects on science achievement are very similar to the case of mathematics achievement. While being qualitatively identical, the quantitative effect differs to some extent for some variables.

Distribution of Responsibilities between Schools and Administration

The evidence (Arambewela & Hall, 2006; Creemers, 2006) supports the hypothesis that the distribution of responsibilities between schools and administration impacts the overall educational performance of students. On the one hand, centralized decisions on standard setting, performance control, and the size of the school budget help to assure that the producers of education look for the performance of students. On the other hand, school autonomy seems to be the best way to guarantee high student performance in process and personnel-management decisions. Thus, the most conducive combination seems to be a mechanism of control from above to limit school-level opportunistic behavior combined with a high degree of freedom to decide at the school level on subjects where school-level knowledge is important.

Teachers' Influence

Overall, the findings on teachers' influence give a clear picture. If teachers can make use of their decentralized knowledge on which teaching method may be best for their students, this will help students to learn more. This conclusion is corroborated by the positive effects of individual teachers influencing the curriculum that is taught in the school and of teachers having responsibility for the purchase of supplies. However, if teachers can use their decision-making powers primarily to reduce their work-load, this will hurt students' learning opportunities. Other things to be considered may be the negative effects of teachers' responsibility for the school budget and an overwhelming teaching load (Smith, 2006; Crossley, 2007).

Students' Incentives

The incentives of students to learn should be influenced by the rules of the education system which determine the time a student spends studying and the benefits of studying as instruction time in school was positively related to students' performance (Harkness et al., 2007). As mentioned previously, centralized examinations, which should make students' learning efforts more visible to external observers, result in a positive impact on students' educational achievement. As another factor influencing the extent to which studying is rewarded and laziness penalized, the scrutiny with which teachers observe and mark students' achievement (i.e., preparing or grading exams) may also have a significantly effect on student performance.

Parents' Influence

Evidence was previously reported that parents' education and the number of books in a student's home were strongly positively related to the student's educational performance. Troman and Jeffery (2007) found that apart from the learning environment at home, the influence which parents exert on curricular matters and on teaching in the formal education system should also impact on students' learning opportunities. Accordingly, students in schools where parents had a lot of influence in determining the curriculum scored higher both in mathematics and science; however, these effects are not statistically significantly different from zero.

With regard to parents' influence on teaching, the class teacher reported whether parents uninterested in their children's learning and progress strongly limited how she teaches her class, e.g. because she then could not rely on parents in scrutinizing homework. Students in classes where uninterested parents strongly limited class teaching performed worse in mathematics and science (Nonoyama-Tarumi, 2008).

MODEL DEVELOPMENT

We develop a model to compare the education systems of twenty-one countries. Our multi-criteria model evaluates each educational system across five categorical areas: Expenditure on educational institutions as a percentage of GDP; Expenditure per student; Performance; Student achievement; and Post graduation performance. Each category is further broken down into subcategories allowing for multiple measurements to determine the score for each of the five main categories. The data for the comparison was all taken from the Organizations for Economic Co-operation and

Table 1.

	AU	BE	DE	FI	FR	GE	GR	HU	IC	IR	IT	JA	KO	ME	NE	NO	PO	SP	SN	SD	US
I.	4.44	6.05	6.83	5.89	5.69	4.44	3.88	5.01	6.77	4.1	4.59	3.5	4.18	5.12	4.64	6.66	5.46	4.34	6.69	5.7	5.33
	1.53	0.31	0.28	0.11	0.38	0.89	0.19	0.57	0.6	0.29	0.32	1.2	2.88	1.14	0.45	0.26	0.66	0.54	0.18	0.53	1.89
II.	5.169	5.665	7.727	5.087	5.033	4.537	3.803	3.016	7.171	4.180	7.231	6.117	3.553	1.467	5.568	7.508	2.585	4.592	7.143	7.776	8.049
	7.375	8.272	8.003	7.121	8.472	7.025	4.058	3.184	7.229	5.725	7.568	6.952	5.882	1.768	6.823	10.154	2111*	6.010	7.400	11.900	9.090
	12.416	12.019	15.183	11.768	9.276	10.999	4.731	8.205	8.251	9.809	8.636	11.716	6.047	6.074	13.101	13.739	4.834	8.020	15.715	23.714	20.545
III.	62.5	62.0	80.5	75.9	64.9	83.4	51.1	74.1	59.0	61.6	44.4	83.9	73.2	21.5	66.5	87.4	48.3	42.8	82.2	69.7	87.5
	72*	73*	85.8	84.3	80.9	96.9	95.9	87.4	78.7	90.7	80.8	91.1	85*	36.0	85*	91.7	85.6	66.9	75.9	90.1	73.3
	20.5	13.0	25.0	16.4	14.2	14.1	12.6	15.3	19.9	16.3	10.4	20.9	21.7	13.6	21.9	28.5	14.2	17.9	18.5	17.5	29.4
	49.0	18*	42.2	48.7	26.7	19.5	32.348	35.2	43.1	36.8	26.7	34.2	35*	41*	27*	39.8	44.1	32.1	35.4	21.6	32.9
IV.	525.4	507.0	492.3	543.5	496.2	491.4	472.3	481.9	491.7	515.5	475.7	498.1	534.1	399.7	513.1	499.7	496.6	480.5	514.3	499.1	495.2
	524.3	529.3	514.3	544.3	510.8	503.0	444.9	490.0	515.1	502.8	465.7	534.1	542.2	385.2	537.8	495.2	490.2	485.1	509.0	526.6	482.9
	525.1	508.8	475.2	548.2	511.2	502.3	481.0	503.3	494.7	505.4	486.5	547.6	538.4	404.9	524.4	484.2	497.8	487.1	506.1	513.0	491.3
V.	151	146	138	188	178	160	166.5*	274	271*	143	162	198*	138	138*	149*	139	217*	157	155	149	196
	158	147	126	171	167	155	156.17	208	205*	181	147	174*	201	201*	136*	141	201*	136	140	164	184
	2.9	3.6	4.1	3.3	6.7	4.5	3.7	1.3	1.2	2.4	3.8	3.1	2.7	2.8	2.1	2.6	6.6	5.6	4.7	3.7	3.2
	2.2	4.2	4.8	3.8	7.5	6.4	7.6	1.5	1.8	2.3	7.2	3.3	2.6	2.5	2.4	2.3	6.7	9.2	2.6	3.4	2.8

Source: Selected and compiled from Organization for Economic Co-Operation and Development (2007)

Note 1: AU - Australia, BE - Belgium, DE -Denmark, FI - Finland, FR -France, GE -Germany, GR -Greece, HU -Hungry, IC -Iceland, IR -Ireland, IT - Italy, JA - Japan, KO -Korea, ME -Mexico, NE - Nethelands, NO - Norway, PO - Poland, SP - Spain, SN - Sweeden, SD - Switzerland, US - United States

Note 2: I. Expenditures on Educational Institutions: % of GDP (Public, Private); II. Expenditure per student (Primary, Secondary, Tertiary); III. Performance (% Educational attainment of adult population (upper secondary or higher), Upper Secondary Graduation Rate, % of Tertiary-type A educational attainment, Tertiary-type A educational attainment Graduation Rate); IV. Student Achievement (Reading, Math, Science); V. Post graduation performance (Index of Earnings-Men, Index of Earnings-Women, Percentage unemployment ratio-Men, Percentage unemployment ratio-Women).

Note 3*: Information was not available for this cell. Information that was based on comparable countries is noted by an asterisk next to the number.

Development's Education at a Glance (OECD, 2007). Table 1 provides the raw data for each category and subcategory. In order to compare expenditures on education among different countries, we must first convert all expenditures to a common currency. In this paper, we use the United States Dollar (USD). It should be noted that, even after all currencies have been converted to a common unit it is still difficult to compare national expenditures because the data are dependent on other factors such as the size of the economy, the population, and enrollment rates (US Department of Education, 2000).

Most of the countries being analyzed are belong to the European Union. We could not obtain complete data sets for countries located in South America, Africa or some countries in the Asia-Pacific region. All countries included in the study can be considered industrialized.

Educational Investment

The following discussion will talk about each category and subcategory and discuss the reasons for including them as criteria for comparing educational systems in our study. The first category of educational investments consist of annual expenditure on education institution per student, annual expenditure per student on core services, annual expenditure of education institution per student relative to GDP per capita, expenditure on educational institutions as a percent of GDP, and total public expenditure on education as a percent of total public expenditure. All numbers used are based on purchasing power parities for GDP and reflect the amount of national currency required to produce the same basket of goods and services in a given country as that produced by the United States.

The first three subcategories assess investments made by the public and government into each student's school career. The main component of the investment is influenced by teacher salaries, pensions, teaching hours, and teaching material. It might be assumed that lower expenditures might mean lower achievements by students or lower quality in education, but Korea and the Netherlands are both below the average spending, but perform near the top in the PISA 2003 survey. The reason why this relationship between investment and quality does not occur is that those countries spend more per student relative to GDP per capita (OECD, 2007). As a result, we include the subcategory of educational spending relative to GDP as well as total expenditures by a country. The fourth subcategory shows the prioritization of a country's education in relation to the overall allocation of its resources; in other words, the final subcategory shows the value placed on education relative to other public investments made in such fields as health care, social security, defense, and security.

The five subcategories discussed above will be combined to account for our main category of educational investment; all an important role in assessing the quality of education by providing a measure of wealth invested in education. Investment in education helps foster economic growth, enhance productivity, contribute to social development, and reduce social inequality (Preus, 2007). For these reasons, we consider investment in schools as one of the most important factors for a country in rating their education system. By breaking down this category into five subcategories we believe that it enables us to paint a rounded picture of educational investment across countries.

The Learning Environment

Learning environment has a substantial impact on the experience students have while in school. We break the main category of learning environment down into two subcategories: time spent in school (hours per year).

The first subcategory, time spent in school, provides an indication of the social and economic importance of education in each country. Students need sufficient time spent in school to achieve positive learning outcomes. It should be noted that there is a direct relationship between time spent in school and the necessary public investment in education. Adding additional required time spent in school requires additional investment in education; as a result, it becomes important to optimize the way the time is used in schools. We note one problem with this indicator for learning environment; the quality of teaching and teaching materials is not included in this measurement (OECD, 2007). Despite this limitation, we conclude that measuring number of hours required in school gives some indication of how students are shaped by the education system. We believe that an increase in the number of contact hours will lead to better student outcomes and overall a better education system; therefore, countries are ranked higher when there are more required hours of school per year.

The second subcategory, average class size, provides an indication of the overall quality of learning in an educational system. Smaller classes allow teachers to focus on individuals and help them with their specific needs. There exists evidence in the literature supporting the claim that smaller class size leads to better outcomes in certain classes of students such as those from disadvantaged areas of students with special needs. The public also views smaller classes as an indicator of school system quality. We note that one problem with this subcategory is that there appears to be a non-linear relationship between student performance and class size which can make it difficult to estimate the effect of reduced class size. Despite this limitation, we conclude that students benefit from smaller class size; therefore countries are rated higher when their average class size is lower.

Overall, we felt that this category and its subcategories provide a good measure of leaning environment which can be used to compare educational systems. Including this category as an input helps add more to the equation that just how much money is put into each education systems; this category enables international educational systems to be compared on another level than just economics.

Together, the main categories of Educational Investment and Learning Environment provide the inputs to our model for comparing education systems. The next two sections discuss the two output measures used to rate each educational system.

Graduation Rates

The first output discussed is attainment or graduation rate. In this section we introduce graduation or attainment rates as a percent of the country's population as an output in our model. We consider two factors in this area: (1) the percent of the population that has attained at least upper secondary education and (2) the percent of population that has attained tertiary education. Combined, these indicators help characterize the educational attainment of the adult population in a country by capturing information on the knowledge and skills available to future national economies and societies.

Graduation or attainment rate is an important output of the educational system because a well-educated and well-trained population is needed in order to have a successful economy and society. Schools help contribute to the expansion of scientific and cultural knowledge. The term human capital is used to represent the skills acquired through the education systems that are available to the population and labor force (Ladd & Fiske, 2008).

The importance of secondary education is driven by today's labor markets; at a minimum, upper secondary education is a necessary foundation for advanced learning and training opportunities needed in order to be successful in the labor market. Individuals who leave school before reaching upper secondary education qualification face difficulty entering the job market. Attainment rate in secondary education plays a role in the overall economic success of a country. Therefore, we ranked the countries with a higher percent of population with upper secondary education attainment superior to countries with a lower percent.

Similarly, the rate of attainment in tertiary education is also an important output to measure in rating a successful education system. The term tertiary education covers many programs most of which can be classified as providing advanced knowledge to people. As attainment of secondary education becomes more common, the attainment rate of tertiary education plays a more significant role in determining the overall level of knowledge of a society. The skills and knowledge acquired from the tertiary education provide a source of innovation and growth in knowledge-based economies. Countries with high attainment and graduation rates of tertiary education are more likely to be creating and preserving a highly skilled labor force. Therefore, we feel that education systems are better if they create a population with a higher attainment of tertiary education; countries with a higher percent of population with tertiary education attainment are ranked as superior to countries with a lower tertiary attainment rates.

Together the two attainment rates in consideration, secondary and tertiary, help to characterize the output of each country's education systems. Furthermore, both rates capture the inherent benefits of education and its impact on the economy.

Economic Benefits

The second output category is the economic benefit and affect of education on the labor market in each country; we break this category into three subcategories: employment rate and educational attainment, unemployment rate and educational attainment, and relative earnings of the population with income from employment. In the first two subcategories we capture the relationship of education in the workplace, the third category examines the overall economic benefits of education.

The employment and unemployment rate examines the relationship between educational attainment and the labor force. As mentioned before, the economies of the various countries depend on a large supply of well-educated workers in order to improve the economic development of each country. We note two phenomena, as the required skill level of workers rises required educational attainment increases and as educational attainment rates rise the employment rate also increases. Employment rates increase because there is a large investment by educated people to find work that uses their abilities and to help recover their investment in higher education. The employment rate also signals information about the labor supply; as employment rate increases, there is a larger supply of well-educated workers.

One problem with using employment rate as an output is the employment limitations of female workers in some countries (OECD, 2007). Although we acknowledge this issue, we include it as a factor in our study because despite its limitations countries with higher employment rates will, in most cases, have higher rates of educational attainment which is attributable to the quality of the school system. In this study, the school system in countries with higher employment rates is rated higher than those with lower employment rates.

The second subcategory we consider for this factor is unemployment rate. Unemployment rates follow a similar pattern as employment rates; unemployment rates are lower for individuals with a higher education. Simply put there is a higher demand for individuals with higher levels of education. Unemployment rates are tied more to overall labor demand as opposed to labor supply as is the case with employment rates (*Anonymous, 2008*). In this study, the school system in countries with lower unemployment rates are rated higher than those with higher unemployment rates.

The final subcategory we consider is the relative earnings of the population with income from employment. This factor indicates the relative earnings of workers based on levels of educational attainment; it is important because one way in which the labor market creates motivation for individuals to improve, develop, and maintain skills by attain education is by providing the higher educated individuals with enhanced earnings. In this factor, we capture, by country, the relative earning potential of individuals based on their educational attainment; we can, in effect, capture which countries provide the most incentive for people to pursue higher education.

In summary, our model considers two main inputs: educational investment and the learning environment and two main outputs: graduation rates and economic benefits. When combined these inputs and outputs create a structure that takes into account many different factors allowing us to compare various countries' school systems and provide an unbiased analysis of these unbiased data.

MATHEMATICAL EVALUATION

In this section we discuss the development of our mathematical model aimed at comparing education systems among 21 countries. Our model is based upon the 2 main input and 2 main output categories discussed in the previous section. Table 1 presents the raw data for each country in each of the subcategories. Before we can use the unbiased data in our Pareto optimization model we must first convert the raw data into scaled data that can be used to rank each country on each input and output category.

In developing the ranking scale for each subcategory we convert each element of raw data into a scaled value between 1 and 10; a degree of subjectivity is input in the process of scaling the raw data for each subcategory. In Table 2 we present the final scaled data rankings for each country in each sub-category.

To provide the reader with insight into the process of transforming the raw data in Table 1 to the scaled data in Table 2, we provide the following example: In the first main category of educational investment, we create a 1 to 10 scale for each of the five subcategories. The lowest spending per student is assigned a scaled value near 10 and the highest spending per student is assigned a scaled value near 1; numbers in the middle of the range as assigned scaled values between 1 and 10. For educational investment we assigned a scaled rank of 1 to an investment of $13,100 and a scaled rank of 10 to an investment of $2,200; these values were chosen as they are slightly above and below the highest and lowest values reported for any country in educational investment. Similar ranges were formed for each of the remaining subcategories; in all cases a lower ranked score is desirable; for some subcategories, higher raw value is assigned a better rank,

Table 2.

	AU	BE	DE	FI	FR	GE	GR	HU	IC	IR	IT	JA	KO	ME	NE	NO	PO	SP	SN	SD	US
I. (A)	6.2	3.0	1.4	3.2	3.6	6.2	7.2	5.0	1.4	6.8	5.8	8.0	6.6	4.8	5.8	1.6	4.0	6.4	1.6	3.6	4.4
	7.0	9.4	9.4	9.8	9.2	8.2	9.6	8.8	8.8	9.4	9.4	7.6	4.2	7.8	9.0	9.4	8.6	9.0	9.6	9.0	6.2
II. (B)	5.4	6.8	3.8	6.4	5.0	6.0	6.7	3.5	3.3	6.2	3.2	4.4	7.0	8.0	5.0	3.0	8.0	6.1	3.4	2.8	2.5
	5.8	5.8	5.5	5.9	5.3	6.0	7.5	8.0	5.8	6.7	5.8	6.0	6.6	8.7	6.2	4.4	8.4	6.5	6.2	3.5	5.0
	5.1	5.5	4.3	5.6	6.3	5.9	7.6	6.7	6.7	6.1	6.5	5.7	7.3	7.3	5.0	4.7	7.7	6.8	4.1	1.4	2.8
III. (C)	6.2	6.2	8.1	7.6	6.5	8.3	5.1	7.4	5.9	6.2	4.4	8.4	7.3	2.2	6.7	8.7	4.8	4.3	8.2	7.0	8.8
	7.2	7.3	8.6	8.4	8.1	9.7	9.6	8.7	7.9	9.1	8.1	9.1	8.5	3.6	8.5	9.2	8.6	6.7	7.6	9.0	7.3
	4.2	2.6	5.0	3.2	2.8	2.8	2.6	3.0	4.0	3.2	2.0	4.2	4.4	2.8	4.4	5.8	2.8	3.6	3.8	3.6	5.8
	4.9	1.8	4.2	4.9	2.7	2.0	3.2	3.5	4.3	3.7	2.7	3.4	3.5	4.1	2.7	4.0	4.4	3.2	3.5	2.2	3.3
IV. (D)	9.0	8.1	7.8	8.7	7.9	7.8	5.9	7.2	7.7	8.5	7.0	8.0	9.5	4.0	8.5	8.0	7.9	7.3	8.7	8.0	7.9
	9.0	9.1	8.6	9.7	8.4	8.0	5.8	7.7	8.7	8.1	6.5	9.4	9.7	3.7	9.6	7.9	7.8	7.4	8.2	9.7	7.5
	9.0	8.2	7.0	9.9	8.4	8.1	7.2	8.1	7.9	7.2	7.6	9.9	8.5	4.2	9.0	7.5	8.0	7.5	8.1	8.6	7.7
V. (E)	2.0	2.9	2.5	4.5	4.1	3.4	3.2	8.0	7.9	2.8	3.5	5.0	2.5	2.5	3.0	2.6	5.6	3.2	3.2	3.0	5.0
	4.8	4.7	2.5	7.1	5.7	5.5	5.2	9.8	9.5	8.1	4.7	7.4	9.1	9.1	3.5	4.1	9.1	3.6	4.0	6.4	8.4
	6.1	5.4	4.9	6.7	2.3	4.5	4.3	6.7	6.8	6.6	4.4	5.9	6.3	5.2	6.9	5.5	2.4	3.4	4.3	5.3	5.8
	7.8	6.8	6.2	7.2	3.5	5.6	3.4	9.5	9.2	8.7	3.8	7.7	8.4	8.5	8.6	8.7	4.3	1.8	8.4	7.6	8.2

as in the case of relative earnings, but in other subcategories, a lower raw value is desirable, as in the case as unemployment rate. In all cases, the better the country scores in a subcategory, the higher the ranking, a scaled ranking closer to 10 and the worse a country scores a ranking closer to 1 is assigned. Table 2 presents the scaled rankings for each country in each subcategory.

PARETO OPTIMIZATION

The next step in our goal of ranking international education systems involves the use of the linear programming method Pareto optimization. Pareto optimization is a concept that helps describe a solution with multiple objectives. In a Pareto-optimal organization any change which improves the position of one person in turn diminishes the position of another. The underlying principle of Pareto optimization is that the Pareto optimal solution can only be improved by making another part of the solution worse (Petrie, 1995). An organization is Pareto-nonoptimal if an individual can improve their position without negatively impacting the position of another. Our model, each education system is considered an organization and each ranking in a subcategory are measures of the qualities of their educational system. When several education systems are compared, the systems with measurements dominated by other educations systems are not optimal. The comparison is relative not absolute, the score of each education system depends on the other education systems under consideration. When new education systems are added or old systems removed, the evaluated score of the remaining systems may change. The determination of the Pareto-optimal rankings is developed through the solution of a linear programming model.

In solving the linear program, each education system is assigned a weight with the goal of returning the highest possible score for that education system. The assigned weights are constrained by the requirement that the resulting weights within a category cannot exceed 100.

It is important to note that using this method of evaluation method an education system does not have to earn the highest ranking in every category to be optimal. It may be more advantageous to a systems final ranked position to concentrate on certain subcategory areas to achieve the optimal position.

Using technique of Pareto optimization we use the scaled subcategory rankings from Table 2 as parameters in our Pareto model; the output of the model is Table 3 which reduces the subcategory rankings for each country into one score with a maximum value of 100 for each main category. The maximum score a country can earn in each

Table 3.

Country	Expenditures on Educational Institutions (%of GDP)	Expenditure per Student	Performance	Student Achievement	Post Graduation Performance	Overall Ranking Score
Finland	100.00	72.73	100.00	100.00	97.99	94.144
Poland	88.35	100.00	98.08	85.63	92.86	92.984
Korea	82.50	94.81	91.55	100.00	93.65	92.502
Ireland	97.79	79.54	97.77	89.47	96.79	92.272
Iceland	89.90	87.01	93.59	90.00	100.00	92.100
Japan	100.00	74.02	97.63	100.00	86.56	91.642
Hungry	90.86	91.95	93.48	81.44	100.00	91.546
Netherlands	93.27	71.26	90.82	100.00	100.00	91.070
Sweden	97.96	71.26	93.84	91.58	88.42	88.612
Australia	81.52	67.90	100.00	97.01	88.81	87.048
Norway	95.92	61.04	100.00	86.23	91.58	86.954
Greece	100.00	98.70	100.00	70.00	63.04	86.348
Denmark	95.92	63.22	98.24	90.00	71.20	83.716
Germany	85.87	76.62	100.00	85.03	65.99	82.702
Belgium	95.92	72.50	76.07	90.00	78.73	82.644
Italy	97.29	84.41	84.43	80.24	64.36	82.146
Switzerland	92.17	40.23	94.43	100.00	80.00	81.366
France	94.18	81.82	85.57	85.63	58.16	81.072
Mexico	80.72	100.00	83.67	43.11	92.86	80.072
United States	64.46	57.47	100.00	85.63	86.49	78.810
Spain	93.57	88.31	74.83	82.04	49.78	77.706

main category is 100; the minimum score possible in a category approaches zero. The higher a score in each main category indicates the better the education system is compared to the other education systems in the study.

The rest of this section provides details into the mathematical formulation of the Pareto optimization linear programming model used for our study to generate the values for each country for each main category presented in Table 3.

Let

g = the number of categories considered for international comparison,

M_{ijr} = the j-th measurement of the i-th education system under category r,

Z_{kr} = the score of the k-th education system under category r,

W_{jr} = the weight to be assigned to measurement j under category r,

M_r = the number of measurements under category r,

n = the number of education system,

Z_k = the overall score of the k-th education system,

The score of the k-th education system under category r is calculated via the following linear program:

$$Z_{kr} = Max \sum_{j=1}^{Mr} W_{jr} M_{ijr}$$

Subject to the following constraints,

$$\sum_{j=1}^{Mr} W_{jr} M_{ijr} \leq 100 \qquad \forall i.$$

$$W_{jr} \geq 0 \qquad \forall j.$$

Again, after repeating the above linear program r times for r different categories,

$$Z_k = \sum_{r=1}^{g} Z_{kr}$$

Table 2 shows the measurements for each of the five categories for each country under consideration. The linear programming model discussed above has some restrictions regarding W_{jr}. The W_{jr} must be strictly positive and this way we can avoid assigning zero weight to unfavorable measurements. That is, $W_{jr} \geq € > 0$, where € is an infinitesabLy small quantity. Now, mathematical model is applied to calculate the scores of each grouping, with lower bound $W_{jr} \geq 0.005$. The scores are summarized in Table 3. Subsequently, the total scores Z_k are calculated using above equation and are shown in the fourth column of Table 3. If uniform weights are not acceptable, one can come up with differential weights for each category and the last equation can be changed to

$$Z_k = \sum_{r=1}^{g} W_r Z_{kr}$$

where W_r is the weight for category number r.

Once the optimal rankings are assigned for each country in each of the main categories the final step involves combining the rankings in the first four columns of Table 3 to calculate a final overall rank for each country's education system. To compute the final rankings of the selected education systems, we chose to calculate a simple average; the last column in Table 3 shows the final rankings for each educational system.

CONCLUDING REMARKS

It is very difficult to measure the quality of educational systems as there are multiple evaluation criteria to consider. Even the decision as to which aspects of educational systems are important is controversial importance weights varying among countries.

However, it is common to see comparisons of educational systems among countries; typically, these comparisons are done using subjective methods. Using a subjective method can lead to non-standard rankings as each individual investigator applies their own subjective judgment in assigning weights to measurements in each class. As a result, there are large variations in the results from various compiled studies. In this study, we employ the concept of Pareto optimization in the development of a mathematical model for evaluating educational systems; the methodology is a straightforward application of linear programming. The resulting model ranks educational systems based on objective data; avoiding the subjective problems of other comparative studies.

The results of this work can be directly used by each country to examine the effectiveness and efficiency of their substantial investments into their educational system; policy makers can use the results to examine practices from other countries as potential solutions for their own educational issues.,

The United States is ranked as second to the bottom while, Finland, Poland, and Korea hold the top three spots. The placement of the United States near the bottom was surprising; it seems that the United States lags behind most developed countries in the world in terms of their education systems. As noted towards the beginning of this paper, the United States accounts for almost 28% of the educational spending in the world; in contrast the United States accounts for only about 4% of the total population of school attendees. The results of this paper drive us to ask the question: "Are we really getting what we pay for?" Based on the above analysis it seems the United States is paying Bloomingdale prices, but getting a Wal-Mart product. The United States needs to focus on how to provide quality education at a price acceptable to the tax payers. If people monitored education statistics like Wall Street, education statistics would start to turn around. If institutes of higher education were asked to continually adjust their offerings based upon changing national or international societal circumstances, their performance rankings would also change over time.

REFERENCES

Anonymous.(2008). Improving education outcomes. *OECD Economic Surveys,* 2008(7), 93-132.

Arambewela, R., & Hall, J. (2006, July). A comparative analysis of international education satisfaction using Servqual. *Journal of Service Research*, *6*(special issue), 141–163.

Associated Press. (2003). U.S. tops the world in school spending but not test scores. *USA Today,* September 16.

Chan, J., Leung, M., & Wang, Z. (2006). Impact of school facilities on working behavior of teachers. *International Journal of Strategic Property Management*, *10*(2), 79–91.

Creemers, B. (2006, December). The importance and perspectives of international studies in educational effectiveness. *Educational Research and Evaluation*, *12*(6), 499–511. doi:10.1080/13803610600873978

Crossley, M. (2007, November). The political economy of cross-cultural educational research. *Comparative Education*, *43*(4), 469–470. doi:10.1080/03050060701611862

Dustmann, C., Fitzenberger, B., & Machin, S. (2007). The economics of education and training. *Empirical Economics*, *32*(2), 255–260. doi:10.1007/s00181-006-0113-2

Global Education Digest. (2007). UNESCO Institute for Statistics, Retrieved July 1, 2008, from www.uis.unesco.org/publications/GED2007

Gonzales, P., Guzman, J. C., & Jocelyn, L. (2004). Highlights from the Trends in International Mathematics and Science Study (TIMSS 2003). *United States Department of Education*. Retrieved July 1, 2008 from http://nces.ed.gov/pubs2005/2005005.pdf

Hammond, L. (2008, February). How they do it abroad. *Time*, *171*(8), 34.

Hanushek, E. A., Jamison, D. T., Jamison, E. A., & Woessmann, L. (2008, Spring). Education and economic growth: it's not just going to school, but learning something while there that matters. (Research). *Education Next*, *8*(2), 62–70.

Harkness, S., Blom, M., Oliva, A., Moscardino, U., Zylicz, P., & Bermudez, M. (2007). Teachers' ethno theories of the 'ideal student' in five western cultures. *Comparative Education*, *43*(1), 113–135. doi:10.1080/03050060601162438

Kao, C. (1994). Evaluation of Junior Colleges of Technology: The Taiwan Case. *European Journal of Operational Research*, *72*, 43–51. doi:10.1016/0377-2217(94)90328-X

Krueger, A. B. (2003). Economic considerations and class size. *The Economic Journal*, *113*(485), F34–F63. doi:10.1111/1468-0297.00098

Ladd, H., & Fiske, E. (2008). *Handbook of research in education finance and policy*. New York: Routledge.

Murray, S. (2008, January). Youthful force for change in society. FT.com, 1. Retrieved July 1, 2008, from ABI/INFORM Global database. (Document ID: 1418621681).

Nickerson, G. T., & Kritsonis, W. A. (2006). A global prospective: A comparison of Asian and American educational systems that impact student academic achievement. *National Journal for Publishing and Mentoring Doctoral Student Research*, *3*(1), 1–4.

Nonoyama-Tarumi, Y. (2008, January). Cross-national estimates of the effects of family background on student achievement: A sensitivity analysis. *International Review of Education*, *54*(1), 57–82. doi:10.1007/s11159-007-9069-5

OECD. (2007). Education at a glance 2007: OECD indicators. Retrieved July 1, 2008, from http://www.oecd.org/dataoecd/4/55/39313286.pdf

Petrie, C. (1995). Using Pareto optimality to coordinate distributed agents, *Stanford*. Retrieved July 1, 2008, from http://www-cdr.stanford.edu/nextlink/papers/pareto/pareto.html

Preus, B. (2007). Educational trends in China and the United States: proverbial pendulum or potential for balance? *Phi Delta Kappan*, *89*(2), 115–118.

Smith, P. (2006). Building a world of learning for all. *Prospects*, *36*, 5–7. doi:10.1007/s11125-006-8205-5

Smyth, J. A. (2008). The origins of the international standard classification of education. *Peabody Journal of Education*, *83*, 5–40.

Troman, G., & Jeffery, B. (2007). Qualitative data analysis in cross-cultural projects. *Comparative Education*, *43*(4), 511–525. doi:10.1080/03050060701611904

UNICEF. (2002, November). A league table of educational disadvantage in rich nations. Innocenti Report Card No.4. UNICEF Innocenti Research Centre, Florence.

U.S. Department of Education (2000). International comparisons of educational expenditures. Retrieved April 12, 2008, from Academic Search Premier. (Document ID: 3029268)

U.S. Department of Education. (2008). Budget Office—U.S. Department of Education. Retrieved July 1, 2008, from https://www.ed.gov/about/overview/budget/index.html?scr=gu

Wieczorek, C. C. (2008). Comparative analysis of educational systems of American and Japanese schools: views and visions. (Author abstract) (Report). *Educational Horizons*.

Woessmann, L. (2002). How central exams affected educational attainment: International evidence from TIMSS and TIMSS-repeat. *Harvard University Program on Education Policy and Governance Working Paper* No. PEPG.-02-10.

This work was previously published in International Journal of Information Systems in the Service Sector (IJISSS), edited by John Wang, pp. 1-14, copyright 2009 by IGI Publishing (an imprint of IGI Global).

Chapter 2
Customer Perspectives of Mobile Services

Banu Kargin
Turkcell, Turkey

Nuri Basoglu
Bogazici University, Turkey

Tugrul Daim
Portland State University, USA

ABSTRACT

This chapter addresses simple but effective framework for adoption factors of mobile services. The framework synthesizes, refines, and extends current approaches to explain adoption factors. The study started with a background research to identify factors determining the adoption of innovation and mobile services. Then, study is continued with a survey which had questions about two types of mobile services according to current adoption status of these services. For the first type of service, SMS had been selected as a widely used, already adopted service to seek for factors affecting consumer satisfaction. The second type of service was not currently widely adopted service in the market as opposed to already used SMS, which is called "Pocket Info&Enjoy" service in the paper. Pocket Info&Enjoy, which is information based service, had been described in the survey and asked questions to identify factors determining attitude to use this new service. Most of the findings were in line with literature, for an already adopted service, usefulness and attitude are direct factors influencing consumer satisfaction. On the other hand, usefulness and external influence are direct and personalization, image, content, mobility, entertainment are indirect determinants of consumer's attitude towards using new mobile services.

INTRODUCTION

The Mobile Industry, which is one of the most dynamic and growing industry in the world, is no longer just about the delivery of voice over phones. Introduction of new content services such as logo-melody or RBT (Ring Back Tone), and voting-contest services, data services, messaging services and java games make it more dynamic.

The future of mobile telephony is expected to rely on mobile services (Carlsson et al, 2006) due to saturation in voice. Therefore, operators try

DOI: 10.4018/978-1-60960-138-6.ch002

to find new and alternatives sources of revenue. To respond declining average revenue per user (ARPU) in telecommunication markets, mobile data services are seen as remediation (Knutsen et al., 2005). Bouwman et al. also underlines the importance of mobile services that the future of telecommunication sector will be depending on mobile internet services development in addition to voice services (Bouwman et al., 2006). The adoption of new mobile services disclaims this proposition as it has been much slower than expected, especially in Europe (Carlsson et al, 2006). However, basic services evolved rapidly. A good example is SMS, which became surprisingly popular after 1995 as users began sending messages to each other. Initially, it was introduced as an information service from operators to users. However, SMS became a greatly profitable business only when it became possible to send messages (P2P Messaging), which changed the communication world for users and contributed to creating a European mobile culture (Kaseniemi, 2003). Messaging services allows either the exchange of text messages or multimedia messages. However, the success of SMS can not be compared with MMS: MMS does not have a huge impact on total messaging market revenue. This may be result of acquired habits which have a strong affect on the choice of messaging (Bouwman et al., 2006). The transition from text to multimedia is an important change. Rau et al. (2006) say that this transition phase is similar to transition to DOS to Windows in PCs (Rau et al., 2006)

Although, some mobile services such as SMS, ring tones, icons and logos have either been adopted on a large scale or have at least been tried by a majority of users (Carlsson et al, 2005) but more advanced services have not yet found their ways into the everyday lives of consumers. This basic challenge is to understand how and why people adopt or do not adopt mobile services (Carlsson et al, 2006). Gilbert et al. is also tried to understand Mobile Data Services (MDS) adoption. According to Gilbert's study, decisions to use new services are innovation behaviors that change according to needs and perceptions of individual adopters. It also suggest to segment markets for MDS by combining demographic and psychographic data (Gilbert et al, 2004).

Hsu, Chin-Lung et al. made a study about adoption factors of MMS (Multimedia Message Service). MMS allows multimedia communication with entertainment effects (exchange pictures, sound clips, voice recording or animated pictures) than text-based short message service (SMS) (Hsu et al, 2006). In the study, it was seen that there is a significant difference between potential adopters and users. Apart from these studies many other reasons have been proposed for adoption factors.

This chapter also aims to discover these adoption factors by conducting surveys to service users and constructing a model for adoption pattern. The survey seeks to find adoption factors by focusing on SMS and Pocket Info&Enjoy services separately. Questions are categorized according to this separation. Pocket Info&Enjoy service is explained in the survey as follows: "When you query the closest hospital around you by Pocket Info&Enjoy service, the service provides phone number and address information and distance information and taxi fee to the hospital as well" or "When you ask phone number info of the closest Italian restaurant, the service provides the phone number info together with special meal information". One of the main characteristics of Pocket Info&Enjoy service is that there is an interaction between user and service provider. This service is similar to Location-Based information/directory service. However, there is no automation in Pocket Info&Enjoy service. Location-Based Information/Directory services automatically informs customer of location of nearest restaurants, facilities, parking areas, etc. More specifically, LBS automatically enable businesses to provide timely personalized services that are location-specific (Unni et al., 2005).

The reason to have a low level of demand and a slow diffusion may be user resistance, reliability concerns, price, social effects, or technical problems. On the other hand, some of the enablers of mobile services are improvements in network bandwidth and quality, ease of use, device or handset improvements, content richness or customer experiences may lead to development of new mobile services.

The purpose of this paper is to better understand adoption factors of mobile services. The remainder of the paper is organized as follows. The literature review section provides conceptual background including a brief review of the literature on the acceptance models, diffusion of innovations, and adoption research models to mobile services. In the third section, framework of a parsimonious model is presented. In the findings and discussion section, profile of the sample is analyzed and conceptual model and findings are explained deeply. In the final section, conclusions are presented.

LITERATURE SURVEY

Mobile service adoption can be attributed to several effective factors: personal, social or level of technology. Before exploring the mobile service adoption factors, foundation of theories and previous studies on technology adoption has been explored. A number of theories have been developed to help explain the concept of technology adoption (Mennecke and Strader, 2003; Kleijnen and de Ruyter, 2003). In summary, theoretical models that aims to clarify the relationship between consumer attitudes, intentions, and actual use include the Theory of Reasoned Action (TRA) (Ajzen & Fishbein, 1980), the Theory of Planned Behavior (TPB) (Ajzen, 1991), Innovation Diffusion Theory (Rogers, 1993; Agarwal & Prasad, 1997, 1998; Moore & Benbasat, 1991) and the Technology Acceptance Model (TAM) (Davis, 1989; Davis, Begossi, & Warshaw, 1989). One of the widely accepted and applied models is the Technology Acceptance Model (TAM) (Davis, 1989). TAM was proposed by Davis in 1989. TAM focuses on two particular constructs of perceived usefulness and perceived ease of use as drivers of technology acceptance. Perceived ease of use and perceived usefulness predicts attitude toward use of a technology. Then, attitude toward use predicts the behavioral intention to use. Finally, intention predicts the actual use of that technology (Davis, 1989). In summary, it includes five concepts: easy of use, usefulness, attitudes towards use, intention to use and actual use. Davis's original TAM is shown in Figure 1.

The model of TAM is a very useful theoretical model that has been tested in many empirical studies. The results and constructs of TAM are utilized in many studies. Especially, the study of Legris et al. (2003) summarizes and compares the findings of researches done with TAM (Legris et al., 2003)

Figure 1. Technology Acceptance Model (Davis et al. 1989)

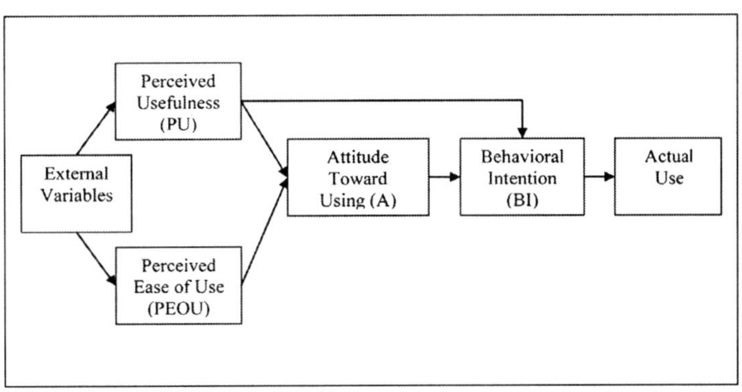

Lederer et al. investigated TAM for work related tasks involving the web. Their findings provided support for TAM and also corroborated that usefulness has a stronger effect than ease of use (Lederer, Maupin, Sena, Zhuang, 2000). Addition to this, some studies have shown that the perceived ease of use has little influence on acceptance. Sometimes, the influence could not even be proved. It is argued that it depends on the kind of task as to whether this influential factor is important for acceptance or not (Neudorfer, 2004). TAM may be seen as a special case of the TRA (Fishbein and Ajzen, 1975). TRA is used to explain behavior beyond the adoption of technology. The TRA-model includes four general concepts: behavioral attitudes, subjective norm, intention to use and actual use.

Diffusion of innovation is also useful to explain adoption factors. Practitioners and academics generally consider it as a useful way to study how innovations transform into consumer use (Carlsson, 2005). According to Rogers (1993), an innovation is more successful; the lower its complexity and the higher its relative advantage, compatibility, trialability, and communicability are. The Davis and Rogers models are both widely supported and complementary to each other. Specifically, Davis's usefulness is similar to Rogers's relative advantage factor and Davis's ease of use is similar to Rogers's factor of complexity (Keith, 2004). Few studies are found applying adoption research models to mobile services in general (Pedersen et al, 2004). Pedersen et al. say that because the users of mobile services are usually younger as well as skilful and experienced in technology use, the determinant of ease of use influences probably less their technology adoption behavior than could be expected on the basis of TAM. Plouffe et al. concluded that the TAM model may be too parsimonious and should successfully be supplemented and extended using more operational concepts, such as compatibility and image (Plouffe et al., 2001). Anckar et al. criticized the TAM model that it ignores the potential existence of perceived critical benefits and barriers to the use of technology (Anckar et al., 2003). Leung and Wei focus that a new generation of mobile telephony presents the telephone as a *content medium* as well as a *communication medium*. They identified the factors of sociability, mobility and instrumentality in addition to other factors (Leung and Wei, 2000). Malhotra et al. also tried to define social influence via "Psychological Attachment" construct. It can be defined as the degree of commitment of user toward system use based on the effects of social influences (Malhotra et al., 1999)

Kleinrock also explained the benefits provided by mobile technologies as "anytime and anywhere computing" and outlined the two most common dimensions of mobility as independence of time and place (Kleinrock, L, 1996). Mobility is definite contribution of mobile devices to our lives. Compared with traditional electronic commerce, mobile computing provides users with more freedom, as they can access information and services without having to find a physical place, such as, an office or an Internet cafe (May, 2001). However, Kakihara and Sorensen (2001) argued that mobility is not just being independent from place or geographical restrictions, but it is far more notably related to the interaction they perform. They suggest expanding the concept of mobility by looking at three distinct dimensions of human interaction, namely spatial, temporal and contextual mobility. In this research, we use the term mobility for independence from place, regardless of where people are, home or office; they can access information or use services (Kakihara et al., 2001). Höflich and Rössler (2001) also identified the gratifications of sociability, instrumentality and entertainment/enjoyment by conducting a uses study on text messaging. Of these gratifications, only *instrumentality* significantly predicted the use of text messaging services (Höflich and Rössler, 2001). Grinter and Eldridge (2001) studied the adoption of text messaging among teenagers and found that text messaging (SMS) were preferred to other media because it was considered quicker, cheaper,

Figure 2. Mobile Service Model Framework

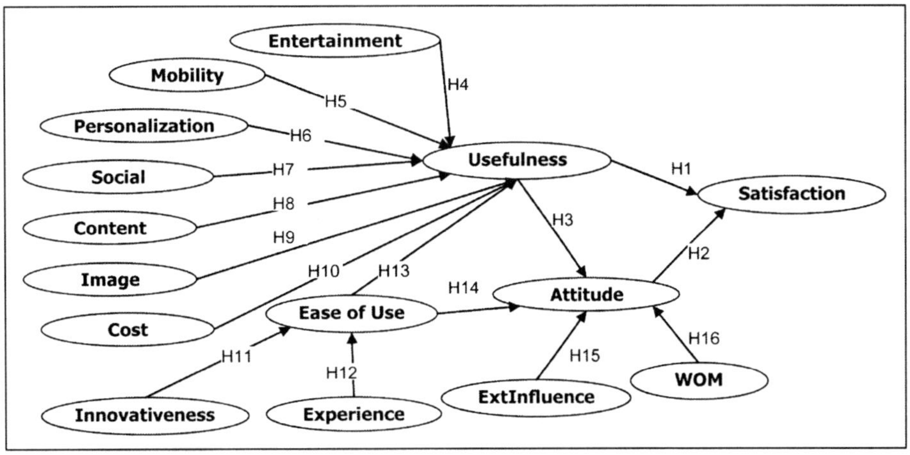

easier and more convenient to use (Grinter and Eldridge, 2001). These are helpful in explaining the factors of usefulness and ease of use. Pedersen et al. (2004) proposed a mobile service adoption model. The model clarifies the adopters' intention to use mobile services. They explained the factors of enjoyment and usefulness in addition to other factors such as expressiveness, subjective norm and behavioral control (Pedersen et al, 2004).

Another study is done by Turel et al. (2006) that used American Customer Satisfaction Model with mobile services. It is an adaptation of the ACSM to mobile services. According to results, perceived quality and perceived value (like usefulness) are the main factors for satisfaction with mobile services (Turel et al., 2006).

FRAMEWORK

In our research, the connection between satisfaction, attitude, usefulness, ease of use, entertainment, mobility, social factors, personalization, experience, content, image, external influences, WOM (Word of Mouth), cost and innovativeness are examined and hypotheses are built up accordingly. Figure 2 illustrates the research model for the factors affecting user satisfaction and attitude depending on services. The model was constructed based on concepts and the models that are discussed in literature survey section.

H1. Usefulness Significantly and Positively Influences Consumer Satisfaction

To study the adoption of mobile services, we suggest a model integrating many of the most essential models and researches and we propose sixteen hypotheses over this model. The proposed framework is pertinent for both services except the hypothetical service will not embrace satisfaction construct. The first two hypotheses of this study are as follows:

H2. Attitude Significantly and Positively Influences Consumer Satisfaction

Davis's (1989) usefulness is similar to Rogers's (1993) relative advantage factor which influence attitude to use and hence satisfaction. Relative Advantage means the degree to which an innovation is perceived as better than the idea it supersedes. Attitude toward use predicts the behavioral intention to use. Finally, intention predicts the actual use of that technology (Davis, 1989). Depending on Davis's (1989) and Rogers's (1993) models the following inference is made:

H3. Usefulness Significantly and Positively Influences Attitude

Many mobile services are entertainment services primarily. We expect entertainment to be more relevant when explaining service usefulness. Höflich and Rössler (2001) hence identified the entertainment/enjoyment as a gratification on text messaging (SMS). In addition to this, Zhu and Fui-Hoon (2002) identified enjoyment as an important construct that will affect users' intention to use a mobile device. Bouwman et al. (2006) also underlined the significance of perceived entertainment. In the study, they found that perceived entertainment plays an important role in future use of services. Davis et al. (1992) defined perceived enjoyment as the extent to which the activity of using the information technology is perceived to be enjoyable in its own right; different from any performance results that may be anticipated (Davis et al., 1992) Thong et al. (2006) also clarified the effect of Perceived enjoyment in their study. They have proposed expanded expectation-confirmation model (ECM) with perceived enjoyment and perceived ease of use (Thong et al., 2006). Based on the prior findings we propose the following hypothesis:

H4. Entertainment or Enjoyment Significantly and Positively Influences Usefulness

To have access real time information and communications (i.e., need for work, emergency, communication, and contact), mobility is significant. Mobile computing provides users more freedom, as they can access information and services without having to find a physical place, such as, an office or an Internet cafe (May, 2001). Kleinrock also explained the benefits provided by mobile technologies as "anytime and anywhere computing" and outlined the two most common dimensions of mobility as independence of time and place (Kleinrock, 1996). In addition to these findings, Mallat et al. (2006) used Mobility construct in their research model. Based on this prior finding, the following hypothesis has been constructed:

H5. Mobility Significantly and Positively Influences Usefulness

Personalization may be defined as a powerful tool that enables consumers to select the content, presentation and functionality of the service according to their unique needs and preferences. According to needs of consumers, personalization and customization seem to be desired features. This is also mentioned by Carlsson et al. (2006) such that dimensions of communication which involves personalization predict the use of some mobile services. Thus, the following is hypothesized;

H6. Personalization Significantly and Positively Influence Usefulness

Mobile communication services are important services for maintaining users' social networks, and consequently, social influence may explain adoption of services (Pedersen et al., 2004). Thus text messaging may be used for social influence reasons. Teo et al (2003) also explained the importance of social influence and significant others. The following hypothesis conducted about sociability;

H7. Social Factors Significantly and Positively Influence Usefulness

Content and content providers are significant factors for services. Especially, quality, correctness and delivery time of content of services are critical. In literature, Gilbert et al. also (2005) focuses on importance of content aspect of services. According to their findings, one key barrier to attracting a critical mass of adopters is the lack of compelling content (Gilbert et al., 2005). Thus, the following hypothesis has been constructed:

H8. Content of Services Significantly and Positively Influences Usefulness

The study of Hong et al. (2006) is exploring the service usage behavior. According to the findings, uniqueness motivation is an important factor in service adoption. Users feel themselves unique and recognizable in public with services and provide a distinctive image (Hong et al., 2006) In addition to these, high tech handset owners, who use only voice and SMS capabilities, try to obtain distinctive image by obtaining advanced high phones. This is an important research area. Based on the prior findings and common insight, the following hypothesis has been constructed:

H9. Image Positively and Significantly Affects Usefulness

Cost is another aspect of mobile services which can be compared with value of services. Users compare costs and benefits of services and try to find relative advantage over other services. Service costs are also researched by Carlsson et al. (2005). They found that financial costs are the significant barriers to the use of mobile services (Carlsson et al, 2005). The following hypothesis is defined;

H10. Cost Significantly and Negatively Influences Usefulness

Innovativeness is defined as the extent to which an individual is early in adopting new ideas relative to other members of a society (Rogers, 1993). Hung et al, 2003 also used the construct of innovativeness in research model as being Personal Innovativeness. According to results, users who adopt an innovation earlier than others have higher levels of personal innovativeness than others who do not (Hung et al., 2003). Ease of use may be affected by innovativeness thus the following hypothesis is constructed;

H11. Innovativeness Significantly and Positively Influences Ease of Use

Pedersen et al. (2004) state that "Attitudes may well have been developed towards a service, but attitudinal influence seemed to require user experience". The experienced users can compare services with other services' usage. Their attitude may be affected indirectly via EoU. Thus the following hypothesis has been used;

H12. Experience Significantly and Positively Affects Ease of Use

Perceived ease of use is defined as "the degree to which a person believes that using a particular system would be free of effort" (Davis, 1989). Davis and his colleagues (Davis, 1989; Davis et al., 1989) demonstrated that perceived ease of use affects perceived usefulness. So, we hypothesize that:

H13. Ease of Use Significantly and Positively Influences Usefulness

Perceived usefulness and perceived ease of use, the two constructs of Davis, are the drivers of technology acceptance. Perceived ease of use and perceived usefulness predicts attitude toward use of an innovative technology (Davis, 1989). Based on this evidence, we hypothesize that;

H14. Ease of Use Significantly and Positively Influence Attitude

Social influence plays a greater role when a behavior is new. Especially, when individuals have no or little experience on the related innovation, they will be affected by opinions of reference groups (Teo, T.S.H. et al, 2003). Similar to Teo (2003),

Hung et al. (2003) also used the social factors in their research model. They classified social factors as Peer Influence and External Influence (Hung et al., 2003). The following hypothesis has been constructed about external influence;

H15. External Influence Significantly and Positively Influences Attitude

Word of Mouth is a significant marketing concept. It is believed that this form of communication has valuable source credibility. According to studies, loyal customers tend to spend more and bring a steady stream of future customers by spreading positive word of mouth (Reichheld & Teal, 1996).

H16. Word of Mouth Significantly Influences Attitude

DATA COLLECTION

This is a pilot study. Therefore, the sample size is small but more than thirty. The data was collected by sending a questionnaire survey to 120 mobile service users via e-mail who use at least one mobile service including P2P SMS. The responses were collected by spreadsheet forms. 101 of targeted users returned valid answers. Collected data was analyzed using SPSS software. The questionnaire consisted of four sections. First section of the survey is formed to get information about profile of respondents. Second section contains items to measure our model constructs by asking general questions about mobile services. Third and fourth sections of the survey are used to collect information about SMS and Pocket Info&Enjoy services respectively. All items from part two were measured using a six-point Likert-type scale with anchors ranging from "strongly disagree" to "strongly agree". The constructs and their items are shown in Appendix A.

FINDINGS AND DISCUSSIONS

This section discusses the analysis results.

Profile of Respondents

The profile of survey respondents is presented in Table 1. The results indicate that our sample predominantly aged between 26 and 30. The gender distribution of the study subjects was 40.6% females and 59.4% males. 100% of the survey participants had at least one mobile device in use and used at least one mobile service including SMS. The sample consists of university students, university graduates or master graduates.

While studying the use of mobile services, all items in section 2, 3 and 4 of the questionnaire were measured using a six-point Likert-type scale where 1 equaled to "strongly disagree" and 6 to "strongly agree". Six-point Likert-type scale was used for the purpose of avoiding central tendency. The summated scale variables (constructs), their items and questions are shown in Appendix A. In order to prevent or diminish the potential floor effect, all variables in the questionnaire were randomly sequenced. In addition to this, some of the questions were worded reversely to ensure

Table 1. Profile of respondents

Variable	Frequency	Percentage (%)
Age		
21 – 25	33	32.7
26 – 30	49	48.5
31 and above	19	18.8
Gender		
Female	41	40.6
Male	60	59.4
Education		
University Student	18	17.8
University Degree	55	54.5
Master Degree	28	27.7

the desired balance. The internal consistency reliabilities of the summated scale variables (constructs) were tested with Cronbach's Alpha coefficient (α) that should not be below 0.60. Therefore, after the test items with Alpha coefficients lower than 0.60 have been dropped. Table 2 shows constructs in each section of questionnaire.

Descriptive Statistics

The results of the descriptive statistics are grouped in three sections: General Service Factors, SMS Factors and Pocket Info&Enjoy. The descriptive statistics are grouped then sorted based on mean value and depicted in Table 3

The results show that SMS users do not have difficulty in using the service. And they see SMS as a personal service and they are pleased about the level of personalization of SMS. They are satisfied with the overall system performance. Entertainment is also a significant factor for SMS users. Moreover, respondents find the service useful and their attitude to use the service is positive. However, users think that SMS does not contribute to personal image..

Table 2. Reliability Analysis of Constructs

Constructs	Section	# of items	Cronbach's α
Entertainment	Pocket Info&Enjoy	2	0.923
Personalization	Pocket Info&Enjoy	2	0.913
Usefulness	Pocket Info&Enjoy	3	0.861
Cost	Pocket Info&Enjoy	2	0.740
Satisfaction	SMS	2	0.956
Entertainment	SMS	2	0.919
Personalization	SMS	2	0.837
Usefulness	SMS	3	0.794
Cost	SMS	2	0.677

On the other hand, Pocket Info&Enjoy service which also uses SMS as the communication platform has different factors of adoption. In such an interactive information service, respondents gave higher value to personalization, cost and usefulness in comparison with ease of use. They find such a hypothetical service useful. However, the results show that they are guessing that the service will not be easy. Users distinguish SMS as an easy service, whereas Pocket Info&Enjoy service is believed to be complex.

Finally, ease of use, social factors and external influences are important general factors for mobile services. Another inference might be that these services are needed in order to be more mobile since mobility construct has relatively high value.

Conceptual Models

SMS Model

Result models explain the factors that are affecting consumer attitude and satisfaction for SMS and consumer attitude for Pocket Info&Enjoy service.

The results obtained by linear regression analysis are presented in Figure 3 and Figure 4. Research illustrates that six of the sixteen hypotheses for SMS were significantly supported. Figure 3 demonstrates all structural relationships in the model.

According to results, EoU (Ease of Use) does not have significant effect on attitude to use mobile services as opposed to TAM and our hypothesis. The model also reveals that for Short Messaging Service, mobility, social, content, image and cost do not have an impact on usefulness as opposed to our framework. In addition to these, innovativeness and experience has no influence on ease of use by contradicting to the framework model.

Figure 3 indicates that variance in consumer satisfaction explained by the model is 40%. This model shows that usefulness and attitude are direct determinants of consumer satisfaction.

Table 3. Descriptive Statistics

Constructs	Mean	S.D.	Min.	Max.	N
General Service Factors					
Ease of Use	4.99	1.09	1	6	101
Social	4.25	1.21	1	6	100
External Influence	4.25	1.31	1	6	100
Experience	4.23	1.27	1	6	101
Mobility	4.18	1.27	1	6	99
WOM	3.25	1.34	1	6	101
Innovativeness	3.21	1.40	1	6	101
SMS					
Ease of Use	5.26	0.94	2	6	100
Personalization	4.72	1.02	1	6	100
Satisfaction	4.57	1.06	1	6	100
Entertainment	4.26	0.96	1.5	6	101
Usefulness	4.24	1.06	2	6	101
Cost	4.15	1.23	1	6	101
Attitude	4.00	1.36	1	6	100
Content	3.96	1.24	1	6	100
Social	3.06	1.35	1	6	100
Image	2.36	1.20	1	6	101
Pocket Info&Enjoy					
Personalization	4.54	1.12	1	6	100
Cost	4.52	1.20	1	6	100
Usefulness	4.42	1.09	1.7	6	100
Content	4.13	1.07	1	6	100
Attitude	3.74	1.19	1	6	100
Entertainment	3.56	1.25	1	6	100
Image	3.40	1.46	1	6	100
Ease of Use	3.07	1.44	1	6	100
Social	2.92	1.34	1	6	100

Among them, usefulness has the strongest impact on consumer satisfaction. Earlier studies confirm the effect of usefulness on consumer satisfaction (Davis, 1989). The model also reveals that usefulness helps to build positive attitude toward use and these two give rise to satisfaction. An important aspect of this model is that entertainment has a strong indirect effect on consumer satisfaction via usefulness with a high beta coefficient (0.523). Entertainment also has a positive effect on EoU with a beta coefficient of 0.741.

In addition to these, personalization has a strong impact on usefulness and an indirect influence on consumer attitude and satisfaction. Depending on this finding, we understand that consumers perceive SMS as a personal service and feel that it is unique to them.

Figure 3. Results of the model of the factors that are affecting SMS adoption (Coefficients and significance symbols are shown on the lines)

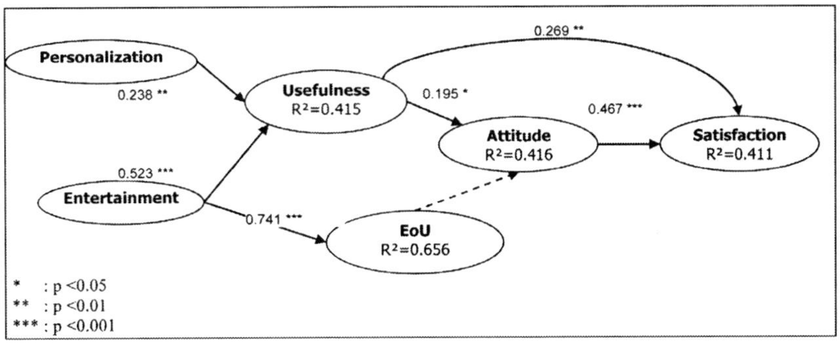

According to results, social factors do not have an impact on usefulness. As seen, social influences had no direct effects on attitude or satisfaction.

Ease of use is another construct used in framework to explain usefulness. However, contradicting to Davis and his colleagues' studies and in our study (Davis, 1989; Davis et al., 1989) perceived ease of use does not affect perceived usefulness according to our study results.

External Influence and word of mouth also do not have an effect on attitude and hence satisfaction as opposed to our framework (see Figure2).

The results of the model for Pocket Info&Enjoy Service are depicted in Figure 4.

Research illustrates that eight of the sixteen hypotheses for Pocket Info&Enjoy Service were significantly supported. Hypotheses on satisfaction had not been questioned in the survey for Pocket Info&Enjoy Service hence H1 and H2 are not applicable.

Pocket Info&Enjoy Model

Research indicates that the EoU does not definitely strengthen the perception of usefulness and does not have an impact on attitude to use mobile services in the case of Pocket Info&Enjoy Services. The results are similar to SMS Model.

Figure 4. Results of the model of the factors that are affecting mobile service adoption (Pocket Info & Enjoy) (Coefficients and significance symbols are shown on the lines)

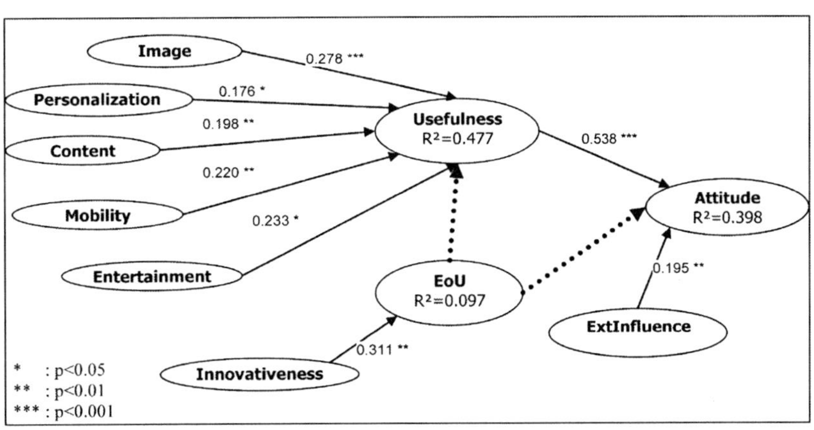

According to results, usefulness and external influence are direct determinants of attitude. As seen in Figure 4, among the constructs, usefulness has the strongest impact on consumer attitude to use the mobile services which is also confirmed by TAM. The most noticeable aspect of this model is that competency of users has no strong direct effect on consumer attitude to use mobile services as opposed to hypotheses. However, parallel to our hypothesis, in literature, Pedersen et al. states that "Attitudes may well have been developed towards a service, but attitudinal influence seemed to require user experience" (Pedersen et al., 2004).

As opposed to SMS Model, mobility, content and image have an impact on usefulness and an indirect influence on consumer attitude for Pocket Info&Enjoy service. Mobility has a strong impact on usefulness and an indirect influence on consumer attitude and satisfaction. The more mobile the user, the more valuable mobile computing is to the user (Pagani, 2004).

Content has a positive and direct effect on usefulness, and indirect effect on attitude via usefulness.

Similar to Hong et al.'s (2006) findings, image is an important factor in service usage. It positively and significantly affects the usefulness. According to our findings, uniqueness motivation is an important factor of service adoption. Users feel themselves unique and recognizable in public with services and provide a distinctive image (Hong et al., 2006).

Another significant finding of this model is that personalization has a direct impact on usefulness and indirect impact on attitude via usefulness similar to SMS Model. Making it exclusive to the individual in various ways is an important part of any service. Consumers should feel services are unique to them. As proposed in the framework, entertainment has a significant and positive impact on usefulness for Pocket Info&Enjoy. According to results, as entertainment increases, consumers find services more useful.

Innovativeness is another construct which has a direct impact on EoU with a beta coefficient of 0.311. In literature, innovativeness is defined as the extent to which an individual is early in adopting new ideas relative to other members of a society (Rogers, 1993). However, EoU does not affect attitude.

Based on the findings, external influence has a positive effect on attitude towards mobile services. For this type of information and entertainment services, ideas of opinions leaders, some advertisement materials, industry reports have a direct impact on Attitude. According to results, users are influenced by other people's ideas and usage behavior. Especially, when individuals have no or little experience on the related services, they will be affected by opinions of reference groups (Teo, et al, 2003).

CONCLUSION

Some technology forecast studies show that mobile systems will gain more popularity and will diffuse into different parts of our life. Better services will be best developed by understanding the requirements of the potential users. In this paper, our intention was to shed some light on the process of mobile service adoption by investigating two types of mobile service. For the adoption of SMS, we observed that usefulness and attitude are the key determinants. Personalization and entertainment through usefulness have the indirect impacts on consumer satisfaction. SMS is relatively matured in terms of diffusion among mobile phone users. For improving the satisfaction and diffusion, upgrades in personalization and entertainment capability of the SMS have to be searched. For short and asynchronous messaging SMS seems to be effective, however people may still have fun using different extensions of Multimedia Message Services. Even personalization potential of SMS seems to be limited; some creative ideas may be employed.

On the other hand, the results for Pocket Info & Enjoy service reveal that usefulness and external influence are the direct determinants whereas personalization, image, content, mobility, entertainment are the indirect factors of consumer attitude towards mobile services via usefulness. Besides entertainment and personalization improvements, establishing a rich and relevant content is very critical for providing a value. Mobility brings additional natural flavor and automatically beats its traditional competitors. Since potential users are open to external influences, an appropriate image has to be built and exposed to consumers.

The sample has been selected rather small (101) since this was a pilot study which will be followed by a comprehensive study that will have larger sample size. For future study, according to these findings, adoption pattern of value added services will be assessed. Additional information will be captured by conducting focus group studies, and user groups meetings.

Furthermore, prototypes will be generated, and tested by mobile service users. In order to capture the adoption pattern, mobile service users will be observed during the tests, and surveys will be applied to them about design of prototypes.

REFERENCES

Agarwal, R., & Prasad, J. (1997). The Role of Innovation Characteristics and Perceived Voluntariness in the Acceptance of Information Technologies. *Decision Sciences*, *28*(3), 557–581. doi:10.1111/j.1540-5915.1997.tb01322.x

Agarwal, R., & Prasad, J. (1998). A Conceptual and Operational Definition of Personal Innovativeness in the Domain of Information Technology. *Information Systems Research*, *9*(2), 204–215. doi:10.1287/isre.9.2.204

Ajzen, I. (1991). The Theory of Planned Behaviour. *Organizational Behavior and Human Decision Processes*, *50*(2), 179–211. doi:10.1016/0749-5978(91)90020-T

Ajzen, I., & Fishbein, M. (1980). *Understanding Attitudes and Predicting Social Behaviour*. Englewood Cliffs, NJ: Prentice-Hall.

Anckar, B., Carlsson, C., & Walden, P. (2003). Factors Affecting Adoption Decisions and Intents In *Mobile Commerce: Empirical Insights, 16th Bled eCommerce Conference. eTransformation*, 886- 900.

Bouwman, H., Carlsson, C., Moline-Castillo, F., Walden, P. (2006). Barriers and drivers in the adoption of current and future mobile services in Filland, Telematics and Informatics.

Carlsson, C., Carlsson, J., Hyvönen, K., Puhakainen, J., & Walden, P. (2006). *Adoption of Mobile Devices/Services – Searching for Answers with the UTAUT *Institute for Advanced Management Systems Research*. Finland: Åbo Akademi.

Carlsson, Christer, Hyvönen, Kaarina, Repo, Petteri and Walden, Pirkko, Asynchronous Adoption Patterns of Mobile Services. IAMSR/Abo Akademi University and National Consumer Research Centre, 2005

Davis, F. D., Bagozzi, R. P., & Warshaw, P. R. (1989). User Acceptance of Computer Technology: A Comparison of Two Theoretical Models. *Management Science*, *35*(8), 982–1003. doi:10.1287/mnsc.35.8.982

Davis, F.D., Bagozzi, R.P., & Warshaw, P.R., Extrinsic and intrinsic motivation to use computers in workplace, Journal of Applied Social Psychology, 1992

Davis, R. D. (1989). Perceived Usefulness, Perceived Ease of Use, and User Acceptance of Technology. *Management Information Systems Quarterly*, *13*(3), 319–340. doi:10.2307/249008

Dishaw, M.T, Strong, D.M, Extending The Technology Acceptance Model With Task-Technology Fit Constructs, Information Management, 1998.

Eastlick, M. A., & Lotz, S. (1999). Profiling Potential Adopters and Non-adopters of an Interactive Electronic, Shopping Medium. *International Journal of Retail and Distribution Management*, *26*(6), 209–223.

Fishbein, M., & Ajzen, I. (1975). *Belief, attitude, intention and behavior: an introduction to theory and research*. Reading, MA: Addison-Wesley.

Gilbert, A. Lee, Han, Hilda, Understanding mobile data services adoption: Demography, attitudes or needs?, 2004

Grinter, R. E., & Eldridge, M. (2001). *Y do tngrs luv 2 txt msg? K. Schmidt and V. Wilf. Dordrecht* (pp. 219–238). Dordrecht: Kluwer Academic Publishers.

Höflich, J. R., & Rössler, P. (2001). Mobile schriftliche Kommunikation oder: E -Mail für das Handy. *Medien & Kommunikationswissenschaft*, *49*, 437–461.

Hong, Se-Joon, Tam, Kar Yan, Kim, Jinwoo, Mobile Data Service Fuels the Desire for Uniqueness, Communication of the ACM, 2006

Hsu, Chin-Lung, Lu, His-Peng, Hsu, Huei-Hsia, Adoption f the mobile Internet: An empirical study of multimedia message service (MMS), Omega, 2006

Hung, Shin-Yuan, Ku, Cheng-Yuan, Chang, Chia-Ming, Critical Factors of Wap Services Adoption: an empirical study, 2003

Kakihara, M., & Sorensen, C. (2001). Expanding the 'Mobility' Concept. *SIGGROUP Bulletin*, *22*(3), 33–37.

Kaseniemi, E.-L. (2003). *Mobile Messages: Young People and a New Communication Culture*. Tampere: Tampere University Press.

Kleijnen, M., & de Ruyter, K. Factors Influencing the Adoption of Mobile Gaming Services, Mobile Commerce: Technology, Theory, and Applications, Hershey, Pennsylvania, Idea Group Publishing, 2003 Knutsen, Lars, Constantiou, Ioanna D., Damsgaard, Jan, Acceptance and Perceptions of advanced mobile services: Alterations during a field study

Kleinrock, L., Nomadicity: anytime, anywhere in a disconnected world, Mobile Networks and Applications, 1, 4, 1996, 351-357

Lederer, A. L., Maupin, D. J., Sena, M. P., & Zhuang, Y. (2000). The Technology Acceptance Model and the World Wide Web. *Decision Support Systems*, (29): 269–282. doi:10.1016/S0167-9236(00)00076-2

Leung, L., & Wei, R. (2000). More than just talk on the move: Uses and gratifications of the cellular phone. *J&MC Quarterly*, *77*, 308–320.

Malhotra, Yogesh, Galletta, Dennis F., Extending the Technology Acceptance Model to Account for Social Influence: Theoretical Bases and Emprical Validation, 1999

Mallat et al., The Impact of Use Situation and Mobility on the Acceptance of Mobile Ticketing Services, 2006

May, P. (2001). *Opportunities, Applications, and Technologies of Wireless Business*. Mobile, Commerce: Cambridge University Press. doi:10.1017/CBO9780511583919

Mennecke, B., & Strader, T. (2003). *Mobile Commerce Technology, Theory and Applications*. Hershey, Pennsylvania: Idea Group.

Moore, G., & Benbasat, I. (1991). Development of an Instrument to Measure the Perceptions of Adopting an Information Technology Innovation. *Information Systems Research*, *2*(3), 192–222. doi:10.1287/isre.2.3.192

Neudorfer, R. (2004). *Critical Success Factors for the Management of Innovative Mobile Business Models*. Evolaris Research Lab.

Pagani, Margherita, Determinants of Adoption of Third Generation Mobile Multimedia Services Journal of Interactive Marketing Volume 18, Number 3, 2004

Paul, L., Ingham, J., & Collerette, P. (2003). Why do people use information technology? A critical review of the technology acceptance model. *Information & Management*, *40*, 191–204. doi:10.1016/S0378-7206(01)00143-4

Pedersen, Per E., Nysveen, Herbjørn, Thorbjørnsen, Helge., Adoption of Mobile Services. Model Development and Cross-Service Study, 2004

Plouffe, C. R., Hulland, J. S., & Vandenbosh, M. (2001). 2001a. Richness versus parsimony in modeling technology adoption decisions, understanding merchant adoption of a smart card-based payment system. *Information Systems Research*, *12*, 208–222. doi:10.1287/isre.12.2.208.9697

Rau, Pei-Lun Patrick, Chen, Duye, Effects of watermark and music on mobile message advertisements, International Journal of Human-Computer Studies, 2006

(1996). *REICHHELD F and TEAL T., The Loyalty Effect*. Boston: Harvard Business School Press.

Roberts, Keith, James B. Pick G., Technology Factors in Corporate Adoption Mobile Cell Phones: A Case Study, 2004

Rogers, E. M., Diffusion of Innovations, 3rd edition, New York/London, 1993

Teo, T.S.H, Pok, Siau Heong, Adoption of WAP-enabled mobile phones among Internet users, 2003

Thong, James Y.L., Hong, Se-Joon, Tam, Kar Yan, The effects of post-adoption beliefs on the expectation-confirmation model for information technology continuance, International Journal of Human-Computer Studies, 2006

Turel, Ofir, Serenko, Alexander, Satisfaction with mobile services in Canada: An empirical investigation, Telecommunications Policy, 2006

Unni, R., & Harmon, R. Location Based Services: Models for Strategy Development in M-Commerce. Portland/usa, 2005]

Venkatesh, V., Morris, M. G., Davis, G. B., & Davis, F. D. (2003). User Acceptance of Information Technology: Toward a Unified View. *Management Information Systems Quarterly*, *27*(3).

Zhu, W., & Fui-Hoon, N. (2002). Factors Influencing Adoption of Mobile Computing. In *Proceedings of the Conference on Issues and Trends of IT Management in Contemporary Organizations* (IRMA). Hershey, PA: Idea Publishing Group.

APPENDIX A

Table 4. Items and Constructs

Construct	Items
SMS	
Attitude	I need to use this service
Content Image	I think that the content of this service is enough Using this service makes me different from others.
Cost	The price of this service is high I would use this service more if its price were lower
Ease of Use	This service is easy to use
Entertainment	I enjoy using this service I find using this service entertaining
Personalization	I like to personalize this service I find it important to customize some features of this service
Satisfaction	I am satisfied to use this service I recommend this service to everyone
Social	Using this service makes my relations better
Usefulness	This service helps me to get things done This service speeds up things to be done I find this service as useful as the Internet
Pocket Info&Enjoy Service	
Attitude	I need to use this service
Content	I find the content sent to me, insufficient, not timely and incorrect (R)
Cost	The price of this service is high I would use this service more if its price were lower
Ease of Use	Difficulty in using this service irritates me (R).
Entertainment	I enjoy using this service I find using this service entertaining
Social	Using this service makes my relations better
Personalization	I find it important to customize some features of this service I want to personalize this service
Image	Using this service makes me different from others.
Usefulness	This service helps me to get things done This service speeds up things to be done I find this service as useful as the Internet
General Service Factors	
EoU External Influence	Screen size, visual quality and key layout affects my usage of mobile services. Mobile service advertisements affects my usage decision
Experience	I am experienced in using mobile services.
Innovativeness	I prefer not to be first ones using the mobile services (R).
Mobility	Being out of office and home is an important reason to use mobile services.
Social	People around me affect my decisions to use mobile services.
Word of Mouth	I learned mobile services from people around me.

Chapter 3 Customer Perceived Value of Travel and Tourism Web Sites: An Outlook on Web 2.0 Developments

Maria Lexhagen
Mid Sweden University, Sweden

ABSTRACT

The continuing development and growth of the Internet imply that business and customers perceive that the Internet provides them with some kind of value. The Internet has also seen an increasing importance of user-generated content and utilisation of the Internet as a social medium often referred to as the Web 2.0. In this study the concept of customer value, based on the typology of consumer value (Holbrook, 1994; 1999) and the value hierarchy model (Woodruff & Gardial, 1996; Woodruff, 1997), is used to identify dimensions and expressions of what customer-perceived value is in travel and tourism web sites and how it is created. Moderately structured in-depth interviews are used to collect data. In the analysis connections between different types of value are presented and the lack of certain types of value is discussed.

INTRODUCTION

Today the Internet is an integral part of many people's daily lives. Twenty percent of the world population has access to the Internet: the penetration rate in Asia is 20%, in Europe it is 53% and in North America it is 76%. (Internet World Stats.com, 2010). The number of web sites increases by the minute, and the magnitude of services and information offered on the Internet is staggering. This development and growth imply that businesses and customers perceive that the Internet provides them with value.

Travel and tourism have, for a long time, been one of the top categories of web sites visited by Internet users. In Europe for instance, half of the online population visited a travel web site in March 2007 (ETC New Media, 2007). Internet users choose to visit travel and tourism web sites to search for information or to buy travel and tourism products such as airline tickets, accommodation, event tickets and packaged tours. Before booking

DOI: 10.4018/978-1-60960-138-6.ch003

a travel product 96% of Internet users' state that they search online for information and on average they visit 10 different web sites. Additionally, 62% of Internet users' book leisure trips and tourism services online (Phocuswright, 2009). Travel and tourism is the largest single business sector in e-commerce in Europe representing 25.7% (i.e. 65.2 Bn. €) of the total European online sales volume in 2009 (Marcussen, 2009). By 2012 it is expected to be worth €91 billion (ETC New Media, 2010). Furthermore, recent developments have shown that on many web sites user-generated content provides an important source of information. Some companies use this as a marketing strategy to increase trust and customer value.

For a business to attract and retain customers it is essential to provide customer value. From the perspective of a company's marketing strategy and investments it is important not to waste resources on developing web site features and content which customers do not desire (Verma, Iqbal & Plaschka, 2004). To ensure long-term profit of a business web site one needs to consider both advertising strategies to ensure increased visitation and strategies which enhance the customer experience in all phases of the purchase process. (Saeed, Hwang & Grover, 2002).

Customer-perceived value is a theoretical construct that is central within marketing and customer behavior research (Holbrook, 1994; 1996; 1999; Grewal, Iyer, Krisnan & Sharma, 2003; Parasuraman & Zinkhan, 2002; Woodruff & Gardial, 1996; Woodruff, 1997; Zeithaml, 1988). It is also significant for business success based on its importance as a customer outcome (Dodds, Monroe & Grewal, 1991; Holbrook, 1999; So & Sculli, 2002). Customer perceived value is an inclusive construct covering a number of factors such as convenience, time-saving, non-functional motives, and perceived utility (Lexhagen, 2009) As such it may be used to develop our knowledge of customer experiences gained from travel and tourism web sites.

Previous studies of customer perceived value have focused on both tangible products and services. Travel and tourism is a service industry that involves many businesses and organisations in producing what the customer perceive being the end product – the tourism product. However, production and consumption of tourism is to a large extent a simultaneous process involving the customer in the actual production of the tourism experience, hence business and customers are co-creating experiences. The Internet represents a marketing and distribution channel where the locus of control is with the customer rather than with the business. The customer is already interested in the product when he decides to view a web site, as opposed to being exposed to broadcasted marketing messages and then becoming interested. Though this is still a valid description, Internet developments have moved towards what is called the Web 2.0 (a term often used to describe the second generation of the World Wide Web and the transition from static HTML-based web pages to a more dynamic Internet). Web 2.0 refers to a more social dimension of the Internet where a large part of Internet content is user-generated and hence information is shared between customers rather than generated by businesses for customers. From a network perspective the Internet of today not only enables one-to-one communication and transactions, but also a many-to-many (Gummesson, 2006) functionality where many users distribute information to many other users. Hence, these networks of Internet users, where each individual is a node in a network connected to a node in another network have implications for how marketing strategies should be designed to be successful.

Research on Internet use is often not conclusive. However, research shows that, among other factors, convenience, time-saving, accessibility, previous usage or experience, price sensitivity, non-functional motives, perceived utility, perceived risk, product knowledge and type of product and product involvement are often factors that explain why people choose to use the Internet (Beatty & Smith, 1987; Beldona, Morrison & O'Leary, 2005; Breitenbach & Van Doren, 1998; Chang, Waiman & Lai, 2005; Cotte, Chowdhury, Ratneshwar & Ricci, 2006; Emmanouilides & Hammond, 2000; Goldsmith, 2002; Hansen, Jensen & Solgaard, 2004; Keen, Wetzels, de Ruyter & Feinberg, 2004; Mummalaneni, 2005; Parsons, 2002; Reibstein, 2002; Schlosser, Barnet-White & Lloyd, 2006; Schmidt & Spreng, 1996; Wang & Fesenmaier, 2004). Purchase decisions for Internet users are influenced by what they are exposed to while at a web site; and underlying utilitarian values influence how customers choose between different information and purchase channels and how they subsequently use them (Sismeiro & Bucklin, 2004; Noble, Griffith & Weinberger, 2005). Previous research also shows that emotional processes such as *flow* seem to be factors influencing and contributing to customers' Internet experience and on-line shopping experience (Rettie, 2001; Smith & Sivakumar, 2004). Adding to our understanding of the implications of web 2.0 on customer behavior research has shown that type of product differentiates between types of online behavior. For instance, Huang, Lurie and Mitra (2009) showed that reading product reviews provided by other customers has a greater effect on time spent on a web site for experience type of products compared to search goods (a product or service with features and characteristics more easily evaluated before purchase than for experience goods).

Purpose

In order to identify gaps in the ability of Internet technology to provide certain kinds of value, a holistic research approach is needed. The purpose of this research is to explore customer-perceived value in the context of travel and tourism web sites. Travel and tourism is used as an example of a type of service which has the potential to generate different kinds of customer perceived value in the customer search- and purchase process. For example, utility value in terms of saving time from more efficient information search and hedonic types of value from the products associations to pleasurable tourism experiences.

The research question for this study is:

How can customer-perceived value experienced from using travel and tourism web sites be described?

The aim of this study is twofold: (1) to identify dimensions and expressions of what customer perceived value is when travel and tourism web sites are used, and (2) to find indications of how customer value is created in customer web site interaction.

Two theoretical frameworks are used to collect and analyze the data: (1) *value hierarchies* in which customers define a product based on its attributes, its consequences, and the desired end-states (core value, purposes, and goals) associated with the product (Woodruff 1996; 1997) and (2) the *typology of consumer value* which is used to investigate different types of value (Holbrook, 1994; 1996; 1999).

These frameworks have been chosen based on the extent to which they have been used in literature within marketing and consumer behavior and in research studies focusing on customer value in an information technology context such as the Internet or other (Chen & Dubinsky, 2003; Kim, Chan & Gupta, 2007; Kleijnen, de Ruyter & Wetzels, 2007; Mathwick, Malhotra & Rigdon, 2001; 2002; Mäenpää, 2006; Overby & Lee, 2006; Saeed et al., 2002-3; Steenkamp & Geyskens, 2006; Verma et al., 2004; Yadav & Varadarajan, 2005). The value hierarchy represents how value is perceived and connected to indirect or direct effects for the customer, and the typology of consumer value is a useful framework for analysing different types of value.

LITERATURE REVIEW

In this section the concepts of customer perceived value, *value hierarchy* and *typology of consumer value,* and customer search mode will be reviewed.

Customer Value

One of the most cited definitions of perceived value is presented by Zeithaml (1988,). The author defines perceived value as "the consumer's overall assessment of the utility of a product based on what is received and what is given" (p. 142). Most research views costs in terms of a monetary price to be paid. However, other costs such as time, cognitive activity, and behavioral effort should be included when considering what customers have to give up in order to get something (Zeithaml, 1988). Value is, however, also something perceived to be more than merely the sum of all the costs, despite the fact that customers probably seldom carefully calculate each of the costs and benefits in making a decision about a product (Peter & Olson, 2002). Customer perceived value also refers to a "customer's meaning attached to product/service bundles relative to a use context" (Woodruff & Flint, 2006)

This research uses the term customer value rather than consumer value since it is believed to be a more inclusive term in that it not only involves the consumer's usage of a purchased product, but also the search for a product, the evaluation of a product, and the post-purchase experience.

Research focused on customer-perceived value in a context where information technology plays a significant role is scarce (Overby & Lee, 2006; Yadav & Varadarajan, 2005). Some previous research on customer value in an e-commerce context uses the concept of customer value as "the customers' perception of what they want to have happened in a specific use situation, with the help of a product or service, in order to accomplish a desired purpose or goal" (Woodruff & Gardial, 1996 p. 54) or as "an interactive relativistic preference experience" (Holbrook, 1999, p. 5). One example is a conceptual model on customer value in an e-commerce setting which explores a model of antecedents of perceived customer value, primarily in the pre-purchase stage, including the valence of on-line shopping experience, perceived product quality, perceived risk, and product price (Chen & Dubinsky, 2003).

Other research attempts to measure the hedonic (experiential benefits and sacrifices such as enjoyment and pleasure, e.g., shopping for the sake of shopping) and utilitarian (e.g., aspects and judgments of economic value, convenience and efficiency) sides of customer value and its effects on customer behavior and intention. Two research studies deal with perceived customer value focusing on utility value using mobile services (Kleijen et al., 2007; Kim et al., 2005). They point out the significance of time and efficiency dimensions in explaining customer behavior. Other studies (Mäenpää, 2000; Overby & Lee, 2006; Steenkamp & Geyskens, 2006) investigating perceptions of customer value in Internet banking services, online shopping, and web sites of consumer-packaged goods conclude that utilitarian value is the most important driver of perceived value. Some research even suggests that experiential features on a web site might be completely useless since they are not appreciated by customers and that utilitarian value is a stronger predictor of customer behavior than hedonic value (Overby & Lee, 2006). Recent research, which has complemented previous research on technology acceptance, has shown that both instrumental and hedonic factors affect individuals' intentions to explore a new technology but that performance expectancy increases over time (Magni, Taylor & Venkatesh, 2010). Customers seem to have a need for fun initially but later the need transfers to a more utility focused need where it is important to demonstrate the value of using the technology. Researchers have also acknowledged the frustration of customers in dealing with the massive range of information online. Grant, Clarke and Kyriazis (2010) propose a responsive real-time information system similar to how a salesperson identifies customer needs and motives during a face-to-face encounter and then acts to satisfy those needs. A system such as this would support a real-time value co-creation process.

These findings indicate that customer-perceived value in the context of information technology may consist of different kinds of value and be affected by factors such as customer motivation and previous experiences.

A Value-Hierarchy Model

In order to investigate how customers perceive value and what represents value for customers, this research uses a value-hierarchy model. Woodruff and Gardial (1996) claim that customer value must be seen as first different depending on whether the product or service is valued for contributing to a means-to-an-end value, or if its perceived value is based on the pure possession of the product or service. Second, customer value is a trade-off between positive and negative consequences of using a product or service. Third, customer value is highly dependent on the use situation. To structure the complexity of customer value the authors suggest a hierarchical model with three increasingly abstract and customer relevant levels. An important characteristic of the hierarchy is also the increasing stability over time at the higher levels.

At the lowest level of the hierarchy, *the attribute level,* customers are concerned with defining the product in terms of its attributes. It is how the customer would describe the product or, in the case of services, this would be what actually takes place during the service encounter. A product or a service may also be represented by bundles of attributes. It is important for a business to understand and improve attributes, but it is at the upper levels of the hierarchy that potential difficulties lie. At *the consequence level* customers define what the product can do for them. A consequence may be the result of a combination of many attributes. Consequences are the key to understanding why customers prefer certain attributes over others. It is then left to the business to decide which combination of attributes could produce the desired consequences. At the top of the hierarchy, *desired end-states*, are customers' core values, purposes and goals (i.e. the basic and fundamental motivators). These desired end-states are served by the product or service and they may be directly or indirectly related to the consumption (Woodruff & Gardial, 1996).

The hierarchical model suggests a utilitarian view on customer value where businesses provide products or services with attributes which are believed to support customers' wish to satisfy needs and wants. It also focuses on and assumes customer value is perceived from a process with a means-to-an-end perspective.

Typology of Consumer Value

To identify which types of value customers perceive, this research uses the typology of consumer value (Holbrook, 1999). This typology includes the means-to-an-end perspective, but also takes into account the intrinsic value of the consumption of a product or service in itself. As such, it offers a more holistic view of perceived customer value. Holbrooks' (1999) perspective on customer value is also evident from his definition of the concept "as an interactive relativistic preference experience" (p. 5). This implies customer value is interactive since customer value entails an interaction between a customer and a product; it is relativistic because it is comparative, personal, and situational; it is preferential because it involves a preference, or an evaluative, judgement; and it is an experience because customer value is derived from the consumption experience (Holbrook, 1994; 1999).

Holbrooks' typology of consumer value has three dimensions: extrinsic versus intrinsic, self-oriented versus other-oriented, and active versus reactive. Extrinsic value concerns a means-end relationship between the consumption and the purposes. The consumption is focused on its functional or utilitarian ability to serve this purpose. Intrinsic value, on the other hand, concerns the consumption experience as appreciated in and of itself. The self-oriented dimension relates to the act of consumption being prized according to how the consumer reacts to it or what effects it has on the consumer as an individual. Other-oriented is concerned with how the consumption process affects someone or something else. Lastly, the active dimension relates to the consumer actually doing something with the product as part of the consumption process, while the reactive dimension implies the product doing something to or with the consumer as part of the consumption process.

The eight different types of value presented in Holbrooks' (1999) typology are briefly explained below.

1. *Efficiency*: the extrinsic value that results from the active use of an object to achieve some self-oriented purpose, as measured by the ratio of outputs to inputs. A key example is often convenience where time is the denominator. Customers not only want to receive maximum convenience, but with minimum expenditures of time, energy, and money.
2. *Excellence*: a reactive appreciation of some object's or experience's potential ability to serve as an extrinsic means to some self-oriented end. It is related to satisfaction and quality which are concepts based on a comparison of performance with expectations. Customers may in this case perceive a value without actually using the object or experience in question.
3. *Status*: an active manipulation of the customer's own consumption as an extrinsic means toward some other-oriented end. The consumption is focused on how it affects ones image as perceived by other people. Customers may, for example, "dress for success" rather than just dress according to a functional requirement.
4. *Esteem*: a reactive appreciation of one's own consumption in a passive way as a potential extrinsic means to enhancing one's other-oriented public image. Resembles the concept of conspicuous consumption presented by Veblen in 1899. May be exemplified by customers who acquire possessions which shape and reflect their identity and hence provide them with a positive sense of self.
5. *Play*: a self-oriented experience intrinsically motivated and actively sought and enjoyed for its own sake. Play typically involves having fun, such as involvement in a leisure activity for pure pleasure.
6. *Aesthetics*: a reactive appreciation of some consumption experience valued intrinsically as a self-oriented end. One type of aesthetic value is beauty which is enjoyed purely for its own sake. Aesthetics involves a detachment from worldly concerns with practicality. Customers appreciate an object for its pleasing appearance rather than for utilitarian reasons.
7. *Ethics*: an active, other-oriented, intrinsically experienced value involving doing something for the sake of others. A concern for how the consumption will affect others or how they will react to it. Customers might choose to buy only environmentally friendly food or clothes since this will benefit future generations.
8. *Spirituality*: a reactive, other-oriented, intrinsically motivated value involving losing oneself in the Other (i.e. divine power, cosmic force, mystical entity, or an inner being) and thereby produce a sense of exaltation or magical experience. Spiritual value is pursued for its own sake and as an end in itself.

This typology includes experiential or hedonic types of value, as well as utility types of

Figure 1. A Typology of Consumer Value (Holbrook, 1999)

		Extrinsic	*Intrinsic*
Self-oriented	Active	**Efficiency**	**Play**
	Reactive	**Exellence**	**Aesthetics**
Other-oriented	Active	**Status**	**Ethics**
	Reactive	**Esteem**	**Spirituality**

value because it also acknowledges perceived value for its own sake or the way it might affect others in the value types: *play, aesthetics, ethics, spirituality, status,* and *esteem.*

Search Modes

Customers have different purposes when using web sites and this is believed to influence their perceived value. In previous research in marketing and new technology, Hoffman and Novak (1996) studied marketing communications and consumer psychology in a computerized environment. The researchers categorize consumers into two categories of behavior depending on their search mode when interacting with new technology. The categories are *goal-directed* and *experiential.* These categories are behavioral paths directed towards different types of value sought. Goal-directed behavior is characterized by extrinsic motivation, instrumental orientation, situational involvement, utilitarian benefits, directed search, and goal-directed choice. Experiential behavior, on the other hand, is characterized by intrinsic motivation, ritualized orientation, enduring involvement, hedonic benefits, non-directed search, and navigational choice.

These categories have also been used by researchers studying customer-perceived value from Internet shopping, the role of affective factors on perceived value in a tourism context, and in an attempt to develop an experiential value scale (Mathwick et al., 2002; Duman & Mattila, 2005; Mathwick et al., 2001). This research uses search mode to categorize web site user behaviors and hence search motives.

The experiential value scale presented by Mathwick et al. (2001) is largely based on Holbrooks' typology (1999). The scale was tested in an Internet and catalogue shopping context, and the results indicate that there was a strong link between customers with a preference for on-line shopping and those that perceived high levels of efficiency with this type of shopping. Catalogue shopping, on the other hand, was based on a much broader range of experiential value sources such as entertainment and visual appeal. The researchers suggest that this raises interesting questions: Does the Internet lack the ability to deliver aesthetic value, and do the users of different channels look for different value packages?

From a tourism perspective the concept of customer-perceived experiential value is investigated by Sigala (2004). Sigala (2004) argues that not only the traditional focus of value as a trade-off between quality and price should be considered, but also the more hedonic and experiential values which are believed to be important for Internet use. This is especially in tourism due to its service characteristics such as intangibility and inseparability. The relationship between customer perceived value and web site choice was studied. The results show that customers' shopping orientation (or purpose) is an important factor affecting their expectations of web sites and therefore their experience of using the web site. Furthermore,

Stangle and Dickinger (2010) present research results showing that utility focused and hedonic attributes of a website effect satisfaction levels differently for user groups with different preferred modes of communication (text or visual). Users who prefer text as communication mode are more strongly influenced by content quality and usefulness. While user groups who prefer visual content are more influence by web site design. Importantly, for increasing knowledge on the potentials and consequences of the developments of web 2.0 Guex (2010) present a somewhat different view on tourists' web usage. The author proposes that "tourist surfing involves social functions, especially because it has permitted an escape from social constraints, but also because it has favoured the creation of social links or bonds." (Guex, 2010 pp. 426) It is proposed that "the web has become for many a travel companion who gives good advice and has an attentive ear". (Guex, 2010 pp. 426) Although, Guexs research did not use the customer perceived value concept the results presented may be an indication of an increased importance of hedonic types of value in a web 2.0 context.

The present research builds on the previous studies by Mathwick et al. (2001; 2002) and Sigala (2004). Those studies both claim that customers' shopping orientation influences customer perceived value. However, both these studies have focused only on the self-oriented types of value. This research is an extension of the previous studies since it also includes the other-oriented types of value which are believed to potentially be important in adding value. Recent developments of the Internet into a more social and user focused medium make this even more important.

METHODOLOGY

A qualitative approach was used for this study. Personal interviews were carried out to collect data. Travel and tourism web sites were used in order to explore the relationship between customer perceived value and web site use.

The interviews for this research were designed according to two complementary techniques. Moderately structured in-depth interviews were carried out, using both a laddering technique (Woodruff & Gardial, 1996; Reynolds & Gutman,1988), and "the grand tour" (Woodruff & Gardial, 1996). Laddering is a one-on-one in-depth interviewing technique used to establish association networks of how customers' link product attributes to higher levels of abstract values following means-end theory. "The grand tour" is an interviewing technique which explores in detail how a product or service is experienced by a customer in a specific context through asking the customer to describe the situation in detail.

An interview guide was prepared for the interviews with topics drawn from the value hierarchy model (Woodruff & Gardial, 1996) and from the typology of consumer value (Holbrook, 1994; 1999). Also, questions on the typology of consumer value were extracted from Mathwick et al. (2001; 2002), since their study specifically focuses perceived value in an online environment, partly using Holbrooks' typology (1999).

Three pilot interviews were conducted in order to test the interview guide and to enable the interviewer to rehearse the interviewing techniques of laddering and "the grand tour." After finalizing the interview guide nine interviews were conducted during February and March 2007. The interviews focused on the interviewees' use of tourism web sites and the services offered at these web sites. The interviewees referred to web sites from several sections of the tourism industry such as destination web sites, travel agent and tour operator web sites, accommodation web sites, attraction and activity web sites, as well as transportation web sites (airline, train, and bus web sites). During the interview the interviewees were able to exemplify their statements by pointing to a specific web site. A computer with Internet connection was available to them during the interview. The interviews, which were recorded, lasted approximately 1.5 hours.

Based on the value hierarchy model (Woodruff & Gardial, 1996), the interviewees were asked to identify all attributes connected to a web site they had previously used, and the consequences of using the web site. Subsequently, the interviewees were asked to state what goals and motives they have in life as well as in connection to using travel and tourism web sites. Consequences and desired end-states were both investigated through explicit questions and through probing when a situation, context or attribute was described. Probes such as how, what, when, who, where and why were used, and interviewees were asked to elaborate on factors stated as important. The concepts described by the interviewees have been assigned to each level in the value hierarchy model based on either the interviewees' explicit description of the concept as belonging to a specific level (attribute, consequence, or desired end-state), or extracted from the interviewees' description of a context in which one level was specifically discussed.

Based on the typology of consumer value (Holbrook, 1994; 1999), the interviewees were also asked to elaborate on the different dimensions of this typology through explicit questions related to each dimension. Follow-up questions and probes were used in connection to these questions.

Analysis

All interview data was transcribed from the tape recordings. The data concerning the value hierarchy model was then qualitatively and quantitatively analysed using content analysis. Templates from Woodruff & Gardial (1996) were used to structure the interview data and develop content codes. This was done keeping as close to the explicit wordings of the interviewees as possible. However, in some cases when interviewees gave similar descriptions the researcher combined the data into a single term. A quantitative approach to content analysis, as presented by Reynolds & Gutman (1988) and Woodruff & Gardial (1996) was also used. This included counting content codes and linkages between codes. These templates were complemented with templates designed especially for this research (e.g. to structure value hierarchies from individual respondents into groups of respondents). The data concerning the typology of consumer value was qualitatively analysed summarizing the interviewees' descriptions of each dimension.

The analysis for this research employs a series of methods. Templates, figures, and tables, were used to structure the data in order to condense and extract information. Each interview was initially treated as one single case, and data was structured based on each case. This was then complemented with data structuring based on all the interviewees' descriptions of one factor, such as *attributes*, *consequences*, *use situation*, *internet experience*, or *travel experience*. Value hierarchies were constructed for each respondent.

In the analysis, data was also divided into three groups: the experiential group and then two groups showing lower and higher degrees of goal-directed search modes These groups are based on Hoffman and Novak's (1996) two consumer search modes': goal-directed and experiential. The groups were then used to construct summary value hierarchies and summary descriptions of the typology of customer value.

To avoid bias in the interpretation process transcripts of the interviews were distributed to three faculty colleagues who commented on the fit between the transcripts and the resulting analysis. Also, a draft of this research including results and analysis was presented at a faculty seminar where participants helped develop value-hierarchies for each interview and the interview groups (goal-directed and experiential).

In addition to the analysis of value-hierarchies and the typology of consumer value some indications from the results to the context of web 2.0 were made as a post-hoc analysis.

Sample

A convenience sample was used for this research. The sample was selected based on the difference between interviewees in terms of the experience of Internet use for travel and tourism purposes as well as the amount of on-line shopping.

The number of interviews for this research was decided based on the evaluation of the degree of saturation in the data collected as described by Glaser (1978) and Strauss and Corbin (1998). This study was considered saturated when no new information, such as new properties, dimensions, conditions, actions, or consequences appeared in the data and the range of variability was accounted for.

The sample consisted of four men and five women who were recruited from non-academic university staff (6) and students (3). The researcher did not previously know the interviewees. The ages in the sample range from 22 to 64.

All interviewees describe themselves as having much experience using the Internet. Some started using the Internet in the early 90's, and some started about five years ago. Based on how they answered various questions, six of the interviewees are classified as heavy users of the Internet. They use the Internet every day and for a variety of reasons such as e-mailing, Internet banking, information searching, communicating through chat, game playing, downloading music, distributing photos, and for shopping. They regularly buy a variety of things on the Internet.

The remaining three interviewees describe themselves as having little or medium experience of on-line shopping. They use the Internet once a week or less. In terms of purchases, only two of them have made Internet purchases. Their use of the Internet is more focused on e-mail and information retrieval, and one of them uses Internet banking.

Seven of the interviewees describe themselves as experienced travellers, including both individual travel and packaged tours to a variety of countries. Two of the interviewees, however, describe themselves as less experienced, since they have travelled mostly in Sweden or on packaged tours.

RESULTS

The interviewees in the study use a variety of tourism web sites such as tourist information sites, tour operator sites, travel agent sites, and transportation sites (i.e., airline, train, and bus). The interviewees also represent a variety of previous travel experiences, as well as previous Internet and on-line shopping experience.

The results are based on the interviewees' description of the last occasion prior to the time of the interview when they used one or more tourism web sites. Results are presented in terms of value-hierarchies including all interviewees. Additionally results are presented for each of the three groups (*experiential, goal-directed booking*, and *goal-directed information check*) used in the analysis in terms of both the *value hierarchy* and *the typology of consumer value*.

Value- Hierarchies

Results from analyzing the interview data in terms of the value-hierarchy model (Woodruff & Gardial, 1996) show that in total interviewees identified 44 attributes, 27 consequences, and 14 desired end-states when using travel and tourism web sites (see table 1).

Table 1 presents the attributes, consequences, and desired end-states expressed by the interviewees, with very little editing. The majority of these indicate positive experiences. However, some negative consequences are also included. They refer to instances where the interviewees expressed situations with more or less undesirable outcomes associated with their use of a tourism web site. For example, no personal contact, stress, frustration, and loosing trust. These instances represent

Table 1. Categories with content codes

Attributes	Consequences	Desired end-states
(1) **Simple and clear**	(45) **Got information**	(72) **Hassel-free**
(2) **Information**	(46) **Easy to do, no effort**	(73) Time to do other things
(3) **Booking**	(47) **Save time**	(74) Accomplishment
(4) Links	(48) No pressure to buy	(75) **Financial control**
(5) Functional	(49) **Flexibility and convenience**	(76) To feel secure
(6) Easy to use	(50) **Save money**	(77) Avoid stress
(7) Boring	(51) Decision involvement	(78) **Be in control**
(8) Easy access	(52) Enjoyment	(79) **Things to look forward to**
(9) Bad product/brand	(53) Reach travel decision	(80) Participation
(10) Good product/brand	(54) Booking	(81) Building self-esteem
(11) Lots of clicks	(55) **Achieve goal**	(82) Satisfaction
(12) **Few clicks**	(56) Relief	(83) To feel positive and happy
(13) **Comparison**	(57) Continue planning	(84) Learn new things
(14) Anonymous	(58) Print information	(85) To feel like an explorer
(15) **Logic**	(59) Positive feeling	
(16) Big company	(60) Complement other information	
(17) Check availability	(61) Personal contact	
(18) **Self-service**	(62) Forward information to others	
(19) **Quick**	*Negative consequences*	
(20) **Efficient**	(63) Problems lead to frustration	
(21) Nice colours	(64) Poor quality irritate	
(22) Photos and movie snaps	(65) More time	
(23) **Updated information**	(66) Big effort	
(24) Maps	(67) No personal contact	
(25) **Search**	(68) No sense of security and trust	
(26) Search options not relevant	(69) Loose trust	
(27) Aggregated information	(70) Stress	
(28) Atmosphere	(71) Give up personal principles	
(29) Newsletter subscription		
(30) Small site		
(31) Personalisation of information		
(32) Messy		
(33) Feels squeezed		
(34) Nice		
(35) **Attractive**		
(36) **Interactive**		
(37) Print documents/brochures		
(38) Reliable		
(39) **Means of payment**		
(40) Professional		
(41) Trustworthy		
(42) Order catalogue		
(43) You know what you get		
(44) **Useful**		

Note: Factors in bold signify the attributes, consequences, and desired end-state values that were explicitly, through wording or emotional expression, mentioned as important by one or more of the respondents. However, it might also be assumed that all the values mentioned at all the levels are somewhat important as opposed to those not mentioned. Also, the negative consequences are deemed negative on the basis of the interviewees' expression of them in negative terms.

a minority of the total number of consequences mentioned. Furthermore, *interactive* is the only attribute which may be considered to refer to a web 2.0 context. Also, *forward information to others* is a consequence which may indicate a connection to a web 2.0 context where the ease with which users can forward and distribute information to others is apparent in applications such as Facebook and Twitter. The desired end-state of *participation* may also be seen as a customer need with greater potentials in a web 2.0

context where social links and communication is central.

In order to find linkages between the three levels of the value-hierarchy model, and hence find indications that indeed customer-perceived value is hierarchical, a matrix of all the attributes, consequences, and desired-end states was constructed. The number of times each attribute was mentioned in connection to a consequence and/or a desired end-state was recorded. All attributes mentioned by the interviewees did not have any connections to higher levels of the model. Twenty out of 44 attributes are connected to higher levels in the hierarchy by the interviewees. Each of the interviewees expressed between two and seven attributes with linkages to higher levels in the value-hierarchy model.

The attribute most connected to higher levels was *simple and clear* which was connected to the consequence *save time* six times, four times to the consequence *easy to do/no effort*, three times to the consequence *positive feeling*. This attribute was also connected four times to the desired end-state of *accomplishment* and three times to *time to do other things*. However, overall most attributes show only single cases of connections to higher levels in the hierarchy, which might be seen as an indication either that most attributes seem to appeal differently to different individuals or that most attributes do not have a very strong link to specific consequences or desired end-states.

To highlight each desired end-state described by the interviewees and the consequences and attributes connected to these, a summary table was constructed. Table 2 presents all the complete value hierarchies (numbered 1-13) but since they focus on the desired end-states this means that one attribute may be connected to several consequences and desired end-states.

Table 2. Summary table of all value hierarchies

Hierarchy number	Attributes (lowest level)	Consequences (middle level)	Desired end-states (highest level)
1	- Simple and clear - Search - Easy to use	- Positive feeling - Got information	Satisfaction
2	- Simple and clear - Search - Easy to use - Booking	- Positive feeling - Easy to do, no effort - Booking	To feel positive and happy
3	- Simple and clear - Search - Information - Interactive	- Got information - Personal contact	Building self-esteem
4	- Comparison - Information - Search - Nice colours - Simple and clear - Booking	- Relief - Achieve goal - Easy to do, no effort - Save time - Continue planning - Save money - Booking	Accomplishment

continued on following page

Table 2. continued

Hierarchy number	Attributes (lowest level)	Consequences (middle level)	Desired end-states (highest level)
5	- Easy to use - Simple and clear - Information - Reliable - Means of payment - Photos and movie snaps - Comparison	- Save time - Got information Save money - Positive feeling	Financial control
6	- Simple and clear - Easy to use - Information	- Save time - Decision involvement	Be in control
7	- Information	- Got information	Learn new things
8	- Information - Booking	- Enjoyment - Booking	Things to look forward to
9	- Information	- Got information	Participation
10	- Information	- Enjoyment	To feel like an explorer
11	- Nice colours - Simple and clear - Booking	- Easy to do, no effort	Free of hassle
12	- Nice colours - Simple and clear - Booking	- Save time - Easy to do, no effort	Time to do other things
13	- Information - Reliable - Means of payment - Photos and movie snaps	- Positive feeling	To feel secure

Note: This table is based on each of the desired end-states mentioned and the consequences and attributes associated with it. Attributes which did not have any linkages to the highest level of the hierarchy are not included.

The desired end-state with the most consequences and attributes connected to it is *accomplishment* which might indicate that it is an important desired end-state, supported by a number of attributes and consequences. The desired end-states with the least consequences and attributes connected to them are *learn new things*, *participation*, and *to feel like an explorer*.

Experiential

Since customer value has been characterized as situational (Holbrook, 1994; 1999), interviewees have been categorized into three groups based on the situation and the main reasons for visiting the travel or tourism web site/s described in the interview. The first group, consisting of two interviewees, is named *experiential*. Their main purpose for visiting a tourism web site, as it is described in the interviews, was to have a look around. Their situation was characterized by unplanned visits to one or more web sites in an initial attempt to find information on such things as means of transportation and accommodation available for their loose plans or ideas about future travel. Interviewees in this group are experienced travellers and heavy users of the Internet. Table 3 presents the value hierarchies described by this group, and attributes and consequences are connected to desired end-states.

Table 3 shows that these customers, who do not have a clear purpose when using the travel or tourism web site, are mainly concerned with information processing at an early stage which in turn is connected to a number of consequences and desired end-states. Based on hierarchy number 6 it is likely that the experiential group will benefit from developments of web 2.0 applications since this hierarchy focuses on enjoyment from interaction and personal contact.

The results from the analysis of the experiential group in terms of Holbrooks' (1999) typology show that the value type *efficiency* is perceived as mainly focused on saving time and ease of use, and therefore it complements other sources of information. The value type *play* is described as tourism web sites which are inspiring and stimulate thoughts about future travel. Photos are perceived as important, and, if the web site is perceived as fun, the interviewees say it might stimulate them to go there. Also, the value type *excellence* shows that most tourism web sites are of good quality but that they may vary a lot and that frustration results when sites do not work or contain the information expected. The value type *aesthetics* is described as tourism web sites which are attractive. In reference to the value type *status*, none of the

Table 3. Value hierarchies for the experiential group

Hierarchy number	Attributes (lowest level)	Consequences (middle level)	Desired end-states (highest level)
1	Simple and clear	Easy to do, no effort	To feel positive and happy
2	Information	Got information	Financial control
3	Information	Got information	Learn new things
4	Information	Got information	Participation
5	Ínformation	Enjoyment	Things to look forward to
6	- Information - Interactive	- Got information - Enjoyment - Personal contact	Building self-esteem
7	Information	Enjoyment	To feel like an explorer

Note: This table is based on each of the desired end-states mentioned by this group and the consequences and attributes associated with it. Attributes which did not have any linkages to the highest level of the hierarchy are not included.

web sites were recommended to the interviewees. However, interviewees do know other users of the site/s. A typical description was: "I told some people about my use of the site and I have sent the link to them." In a web 2.0 context this type of expression has the potential to be greatly enhanced since it is so easy to share content using different types of applications available today.

In the value type *ethics* the environment is a third party affected by the interviewee's use of tourism web sites to increase travel to sensitive areas. The value type *esteem* is described differently by the interviewees where one is outgoing and socially active and the other is a curious daydreaming individualist living a family life. They are both interested in and spend their money on sports and travel. The value type *spirituality* is described by one of the interviewees as likely to happen on a tourism web site, while the other claims it has never happened.

Goal-Directed Booking

The second group, named *goal-directed booking*, consists of four interviewees. The main purpose for visiting a tourism web site described in the interviews was to make a booking. Thereby the interviewees finalise their plans to actually buy a product previously researched on the Internet and/or by other sources of information. This group consist of one inexperienced and three experienced travellers, and three low/medium users of the Internet and one experienced user.

The results indicate that the main concern for this group is to manage their time and money as well as to accomplish some kind of task with as little effort as possible (Table 4). Only marginally are *to feel positive and happy,* and *things to look forward to* mentioned as desired end-states. Also, they are connected to actually making a booking, which is a very goal-oriented type of consequence.

The results from the analysis of the goal-directed booking group show that the travel and tourism web site/s in reference to the value type *efficiency* is described by interviewees as saving time, being simple, being flexible and convenient, and saving money. Some negative experiences are also included such as using more time and effort compared to other ways of making a booking. Using a tourism web site in reference to the value type *play* is described by some of the interviewees as not being any fun at all. Some say however, that it is fun because they get something to look forward to and dream about. One interviewee describes this value type in these words, "I always have a purpose or motive for using the Internet." Interviewees in this group also think that tourism web sites are reasonable in terms of quality compared to other web sites (the value type *excellence*). They also perceive that expectations of the web site are met, but sometimes interviewees experience frustration with site layout. Tourism web sites are also believed to vary a lot in terms of *aesthetics*. Some are perceived as boring and unattractive and some as nice with photos and nice colours.

For the value type *status* the interviewees in this group state that they were not referred to the site, but that they know friends who use the site. They have also told others about using the site. One interviewee said "Most of my friends use the same web site." In a web 2.0 context strong communities are formed around the use of specific web sites and hence the *status* dimension of value is likely to become stronger. The comments by interviewees regarding the value type *ethics* vary. Some say their use of tourism web sites is good for the local community, because travel and tourism on the Internet develops travel to destinations previously unknown. Some say however, it is bad for society in general because Internet developments make the value of personal service disappear. Some also say it is good for the environment because Internet use makes less use of printed information, but, on the other hand some say it is bad for the environment because of toxic materials used in computers. In terms of the value type *esteem* interviewees claim to

Table 4. Value hierarchy for the group goal-directed booking

Hierarchy number	Attributes (lowest level)	Consequences (middle level)	Desired end-states (highest level)
1	• Booking	• Make a booking	To feel positive and happy
2	• Booking	• Make a booking	Things to look forward to
3	• Comparison • Means of payment • Information • Reliable • Booking • Simple and clear • Photos and movie snaps	• Positive feeling • Save money	Financial control
4	• Photos and movie snaps • Means of payment • Information • Reliable	• Positive feeling	To feel secure
5	• Search • Photos and movie snaps • Means of payment • Information • Reliable • Booking • Simple and clear • Nice colours	• Continue planning • Positive feeling • Save time • Save money • Easy to do/no effort	Accomplishment
6	• Booking • Simple and clear • Nice colours	• Save time • Easy to do/no effort	Time to do other things
7	• Booking • Simple and clear • Nice colours	• Easy to do/no effort	Free of hassle

Note: This table is based on each of the desired end-states mentioned by this group and the consequences and attributes associated with it. Attributes which did not have any linkages to the highest level of the hierarchy are not included.

have a variety of recreational interests ranging from sports and outdoor activities to culture and amateur radio. They all like to spend money on travel and/or entertainment such as restaurants and events. All, except one, like to try new things and all except one claim to have a vibrant social life with lots of friends and family. Everyone in this group agrees that they have not experienced any feelings of *spirituality* when using a tourism web site. Comments such as "Internet has nothing to do with feeling spiritual" or "visiting tourism web sites is for a practical reason not to get pleasure" exemplify the value type *spiritual* for this group.

Goal-Directed Information Check

The third group, *goal-directed information check*, consists of three interviewees. The main purpose for visiting a tourism web site for this group was to check information and, based on this information,

Table 5. Value-hierarchy for the group goal-directed information check

Hierarchy number	Attributes (lowest level)	Consequences (middle level)	Desired end-states (highest level)
1	- Information - Easy to use - Comparison - Simple and clear	- Decision involvement - Save time	Be in control
2	- Easy to use - Comparison - Simple and clear	- Save time	Financial control
3	- Easy to use - Comparison - Simple and clear - Information - Search	- Save time - Achieve goal - Relief - Easy to do/no effort	Accomplishment
4	- Search - Simple and clear	- Got information	Building self-esteem
5	- Easy to use - Search - Simple and clear	- Positive feeling	To feel positive and happy
6	- Search - Simple and clear - Easy to use	- Got information - Positive feeling	Satisfaction

Note: This table is based on each of the desired end-states mentioned by this group and the consequences and attributes associated with it. Attributes which did not have any linkages to the highest level of the hierarchy are not included.

reach a decision about travel. In this group there is one inexperienced traveller and two experienced travellers. All three are heavy users of the Internet.

Table 5 shows that this group is also, like the first group, concerned with information processing but at a later stage and therefore more focused on accomplishment. *Comparison* appears as an important attribute, and *save time* is an important consequence.

The results from analysing Holbrooks' typology (1999) for this group show that the value type *efficiency* is described by interviewees as the efficient use of time and with little effort expended. One of them also claims to have saved money. The value type *play* is described as the enjoyable content of the web site: "visiting a tourism web site makes me want to go there," or how a good site can make visiting that site a fun experience. Two of the interviewees claim to have had no expectations when visiting the site/s, while the other says expectations were met (the value type *excellence*). In terms of the comparison to other web sites one interviewee says tourism web sites are often unprofessional, while another says they are generally of good quality. The value type *aesthetics* also shows that two of the interviewees think the site/s, is boring or unattractive while the other likes the look of the site/s, and thinks it puts the user in a good mood. The sites were not recommended to the interviewees but they do know other users of the site/s. They have told others about using the site/s (the value type *status*). One interviewee describes this dimension saying, "Rumour says they have cheap trips." This type of expression is most likely much more common now in a web 2.0 context where users easily share reviews and comments online.

Interviewees describe the value type *ethics* saying, "Tourism information on the internet is good for local tourism development"; "Internet means easy availability and contact between people" and "Increased travel may lead to exploitation of sensitive areas." In terms of the value type *esteem*, the interviewees describe themselves as having open personalities and liking to try new things. They have a variety of interests such as sports, outdoor activities, and music. Two of them have a tight group of friends, while the third claims to know a lot of people, but seldom to have time to socialize. Money is spent on personal interests but not explicitly on travel and tourism. The value type *spiritual* is described: "I sometimes lose track of time if the site is good"; "If search is flowing and I find what I'm looking for then I'm very focused and I might feel a small sense of flow"; "Checking facts may lead to day dreaming" and "The thought of travelling is positive and enticing but not the site as such".

CONCLUSION

In response to the research question posed and earlier calls for more research on customer value and information technology (see for instance Parasuraman & Zinkhan, 2002; Grewal et al., 2003; Overby & Lee, 2006; Yadav & Varadarajan, 2005) the results of this research show that the interviewees identified 44 attributes, 27 consequences, and 14 desired end-states which describe their perceived customer value when using a travel and tourism web site. However, only 20 out of the 44 attributes identified had connections to higher levels in the value hierarchy. This indicates that customer value is hierarchical but that many attributes do not seem to connect to more deeply held goals or values.

Also, the findings indicate that utilitarian types of value, as opposed to hedonic or experiential types of value, are the ones most perceived by customers using travel and tourism web sites. This is supported by the results from the analysis of both the value hierarchies and the data analysed in the typology of customer value framework. The desired end-state factor (at the highest level of the value hierarchy) which had a link to most consequences was *accomplishment*. It was linked to consequences which almost solely can be described as utilitarian in character (such as achieve goal, save time, and save money). Also the desired end-state of *financial control* had links to most attributes, and again most of them might best be described as utilitarian in character (such as easy to use, simple and clear, means of payment, and comparison).

In terms of the typology of customer value, only very few interviewees could describe any cases of perceived value where the value could be connected to an intrinsic and reactive value such as *spirituality* (one interviewee) or *aesthetics* (two interviewees). Also, three could describe perceived value from using travel and tourism web sites which could be characterized as the intrinsic and active value of *play*. Hence, another indication that hedonic types of value do not seem to be perceived to any great extent by customers using travel and tourism web sites. From recent research we may however see a future change in perceptions of hedonic value. Huang, Backman and Backman (2010) investigated the impacts of virtual experiences of Second Life (an online virtual world game) on people's behavioral intentions to take an actual trip. The authors report that high levels of flow (the holistic sensation when acting with total involvement) for users participating in Second Life have a positive influence on their intentions to actually travel to the destination in real life.

Based on the need or motive (goal-directed or experiential) to use a travel and tourism web site, the results indicate that the group with primarily experiential motives identify consequences of their use (which was mainly focused on information processing) especially in terms of *enjoyment* and *personal contact*. Consequences such as these are not mentioned by the goal-directed groups which in turn focus on consequences such as *save time*, *save money*, *easy to do/no effort*, *achieve goal*, and *make plans*. This indicates how the need or motive to use a site influences the perceived customer value. The experiential group perceives experiential types of value, while the more goal-directed group perceives more utilitarian types of value. Based on measures of shopping frequency it has been suggested that experiential value is less likely to be perceived by experienced online shoppers as they will become more task oriented (Overby & Lee, 2006). However, the experiential group in this study consisted of experienced travellers and heavy users of the Internet, and still it appears that they perceive, to some extent, experiential types of value.

The main contribution of this research is the empirical exploration of the theoretical concepts of the value hierarchy model and the typology of consumer value, in one of the most popular areas of Internet use, namely travel and tourism. Also, the results identify a potentially important gap in travel and tourism companies' ability to provide customers with many different kinds of value. For an experience type of product such as travel and tourism and with the recent developments of the Internet and its capability to provide rich information and advanced services, customers still mainly perceive utility types of value. Utility types of value such as usefulness seem to also prevail in the increasing presence of firm-hosted travel communities which is an important area of web 2.0 in travel and tourism. Casaló, Flavián and Guinalíu (2010) have studied what motivates people to participate in such communities. They found that attitude toward participation, perceived behavioral control, perceived usefulness, and identification with the online community have positive influences on consumers' intentions to participate. However, the influence of identification on motivation to participate shows that also the value (such as belongingness) that the group itself represents, is important in this web 2.0 context.

In addition, the data and results provide a rich set of information which may be used to further research this topic. For instance, future research should address the issues of measuring the importance of different types of value in relation to the total perception of customer value when using web sites, as well as relationships between types of value. This research should also include moderating variables such as use situation (need/motive), type of product, and previous experience of the product and the Internet.

IMPLICATIONS

The findings of this research, that customers do not perceive hedonic types of value to any great extent, is important. The Internet has been suggested as an important marketing channel because of its interactive features and it has been suggested that interactivity would positively influence perceived value for customers (Yadav & Varadarajan, 2005). However, if this interactivity is mainly producing utilitarian types of customer perceived value it might imply that the Internet as a marketing channel is not fully utilizing its potential to generate value for customers. This being said, it is likely that the development of technology as such (increased speed of communication as well as increased capacity of computers, and access to the Internet through mobile platforms) and the development of web 2.0 with its focus on user-generated content will improve the opportunities for businesses to offer more experiential or hedonic types of customer value. The focus of management in the future should be to understand and address the issues of which customers perceive which types of value, in which use situations, and then consider this when developing marketing strategies. For example, travel blog users involvement level has been shown to influence advertising effect, and purchase intentions through the positive effect of brand attitude (Huang, Chou & Lin, 2010). This is important knowledge for businesses in travel and tourism who wish to better understand customer behavior in a web 2.0 context and improve their marketing communication.

Other managerial implications involve the value hierarchies. The value hierarchies described by the interviewees can be used to develop strategies to improve travel and tourism web sites so that they provide more value for customers. For instance, in the value hierarchies it is clear how customers' link attributes of a web site to explicit consequences and desired end-states. Therefore, managers gain a better understanding of what web site features to develop in order to support important customer outcomes. Also, the results based on the typology of consumer value are useful to further knowledge on what kinds of value customers perceive when using travel and tourism web sites and on which dimensions this value appears. Some examples are (1) if perceived value is something which is influenced by how the customers' interact with the web site, or (2) if the customers' are utility focused or experiential, or (3) if perceived value is mainly focused on the customer him/herself or if it also involves the customer's relationship with others. If these issues are better understood, then marketing strategies can be more effectively developed. Also, as Internet users and travellers become more experienced with the Web 2.0, customer perceived value needs further research in this context. As Phocuswright (2010) states in their newsletter: "Traveller reviews, photos, trip planning and sharing, and blogging are all influencing how travellers connect to and interact with suppliers, products and services." This implies that the market place has changed and that marketing and customer behaviour knowledge needs a better understanding of these phenomena.

REFERENCES

Beatty, S. E., & Smith, S. M. (1987). External search effort: An investigation across several product categories. *The Journal of Consumer Research*, *14*(June), 83–95. doi:10.1086/209095

Beldona, S., Morrison, A. M., & O'Leary, J. (2005). Online shopping motivations and pleasure travel products: A correspondence analysis. *Tourism Management*, *26*, 561–570. doi:10.1016/j.tourman.2004.03.008

Breitenbach, C. S., & Van Doren, D. C. (1998). Value-added marketing in the digital domain: enhancing the utility of the Internet. *Journal of Consumer Marketing*, *15*(6), 558–575. doi:10.1108/07363769810241436

Casaló, L. V., Flavián, C. & Guinalíu, M. (in press). Determinants of the intention to participate in firm-hosted online travel communities and effects on consumer behavioural intentions. *Tourism Management*, 2010, doi: 10.1016/j.tourman.2010.04.007.

Chang, M. K., Waiman, C., & Lai, V. S. (2005). Literature derived reference models for the adoption of online shopping. *Information & Management*, *42*, 543–559. doi:10.1016/S0378-7206(04)00051-5

Chen, Z., & Dubinsky, A. J. (2003). A conceptual model of perceived customer value in e-commerce: A preliminary investigation. *Psychology and Marketing*, *20*(4), 323–347. doi:10.1002/mar.10076

Cotte, J., Chowdhury, T. G., Ratneshwar, S., & Ricci, L. M. (2006). Pleasure or utility? Time planning style and web usage behaviours. *Journal of Interactive Marketing*, *20*(1), 45–57. doi:10.1002/dir.20055

Dodds, W. B., Monroe, K. B., & Grewal, D. (1991). Effects of price, brand and store information on buyers' product evaluations. *JMR, Journal of Marketing Research*, *28*(3), 307–319. doi:10.2307/3172866

Duman, T., & Mattila, A. S. (2005). The role of affective factors on perceived cruise vacation value. *Tourism Management*, *26*, 311–323. doi:10.1016/j.tourman.2003.11.014

Emmanouilides, C., & Hammond, K. (2000). Internet usage: predictors of active users and frequency of use. *Journal of Interactive Marketing*, *14*(2), 17–32. doi:10.1002/(SICI)1520-6653(200021)14:2<17::AID-DIR2>3.0.CO;2-E

Glaser, B. G. (1978). *Theoretical sensitivity – advances in the methodology of grounded theory*. San Francisco: The Sociology Press.

Goldsmith, R. E. (2002). Explaining and predicting consumer intention to purchase over the Internet: An exploratory study. *Journal of Marketing Theory and Practice*, Spring, 22-28.

Grant, R., Clarke, R. J., & Kyriazis, E. (2010). Research needs for assessing online value creation in complex consumer purchase process behaviour. *Journal of Retailing and Consumer Services*, *17*, 53–60. doi:10.1016/j.jretconser.2009.09.004

Grewal, D., Iyer, G. R., Krishnan, R., & Sharma, A. (2003). The Internet and the price-value- loyalty chain. *Journal of Business Research*, *56*, 391–398. doi:10.1016/S0148-2963(01)00227-2

Guex, V. (2010). A sociological view of the cybertourists. In Gretzel, U., Law, R. & Fuchs, M. (Eds.) *Information and Communication Technologies in Tourism 2010* (417-428). Proceedings of the ENTER conference Wien: Springer-Verlag.

Gummesson, E. (2006). Many-to-many marketing as grand theory In Lusch, R. F. & Vargo S. L. (Eds.) *The service-dominant logic of marketing – dialogue, debate, and directions* (339-353). New York: M.E. Sharpe.

Hansen, T., Jensen, J. M., & Solgaard, H. S. (2004). Predicting online grocery buying intention: a comparison of the theory of reasoned action and the theory of planned behaviour. *International Journal of Information Management*, *24*, 539–550. doi:10.1016/j.ijinfomgt.2004.08.004

Hoffman, D. L., & Novak, T. P. (1996). Marketing in hypermedia computer-mediated environments: Conceptual foundations. *Journal of Marketing*, *60*(July), 50–68. doi:10.2307/1251841

Holbrook, M. B. (1994). Defining service quality. In Rust, R. T. & Oliver, R. L. (Eds.) *Service Quality – New Directions in Theory and Practice* (21-71). Thousand Oaks, CA: Sage Publications.

Holbrook, M. B. (1996). Customer value – A framework for analysis and research. In Corfman, K. P., & Lynch, J. G. Jr., (Eds.), *Advances in Consumer Research, 23 (138-42)*. Provo, UT: Association for Consumer Research.

Holbrook, M. B. (1999). *Consumer value – A framework for analysis and research*. London: Routledge. doi:10.4324/9780203010679

Huang, C.-Y., Chour, C.-J., & Lin, P.-C. (2010). Involvment theory in constructing bloggers' intention to purchase travel products. *Tourism Management*, *31*, 513–526. doi:10.1016/j.tourman.2009.06.003

Huang, P., Lurie, N. H., & Mitra, S. (2009). Searching for experiences on the web: An empirical examination of consumer behavior for search and experience goods. *Journal of Marketing*, *73*(March), 55–69. doi:10.1509/jmkg.73.2.55

Huang, Y.-C., Backman, S. J., & Backman, K. F. (2010). The impacts of virtual experiences on people's travel intentions. In Gretzel, U., Law, R. & Fuchs, M. (Eds.) *Information and Communication Technologies in Tourism 2010* (555-566). Proceedings of the ENTER conference Wien: Springer-Verlag.

Internet World Stats. (n.d.). *Internet World Stats*. Retrieved June 24th, 2010, from Keen, C., Wetzels, M., de Ruyter, K. & Feinberg, R. (2004). E-tailers versus retailers: Which factors determine consumer preferences. *Journal of Business Research*, 57, 685-695. http://www.internetworldstats.com/stats.htm.

Kim, H. W., Chan, H. C., & Gupta, S. (2007). Value-based adoption of mobile Internet: An empirical investigation. *Decision Support Systems*, *43*, 111–126. doi:10.1016/j.dss.2005.05.009

Kleijnen, M., de Ruyter, K., & Wetzels, M. (2007). An assessment of value creation in mobile service delivery and the moderating role of time consciousness. *Journal of Retailing*, *83*(1), 33–46. doi:10.1016/j.jretai.2006.10.004

Lexhagen, M. (2009). E-marketing and customer perceived value in travel and tourism. [Östersund, Sweden: ETOUR.]. *ETOUR*, *2009*, 20.

Mäenpää, K. (2006). Clustering the consumer on the basis of their perceptions of the internet banking services. *Internet Research*, *16*(3), 304–322. doi:10.1108/10662240610673718

Magni, M., Taylor, M. S., & Venkatesh, V. (2010). To play or not to play: A cross-temporal investigation using hedonic and instrumental perspectives to explain user intentions to explore a technology. *International Journal of Human-Computer Studies*, *68*, 572–588. doi:10.1016/j.ijhcs.2010.03.004

Marcussen, C. H. (n.d.). *Marcussen*Retrieved June 20th, 2010, from http://wwwcrt.dk/UK/staff/chm/trends.htm.

Mathwick, C., Malhotra, N., & Rigdon, E. (2001). Experiential value: conceptualization, measurement and application in the catalogue and Internet shopping environment. *Journal of Retailing*, *77*, 39–56. doi:10.1016/S0022-4359(00)00045-2

Mathwick, C., Malhotra, N., & Rigdon, E. (2002). The effect of dynamic retail experiences on experiential perceptions of value: an Internet and catalogue comparison. *Journal of Retailing*, *78*, 51–60. doi:10.1016/S0022-4359(01)00066-5

Mummalaneni, V. (2005). An empirical investigation of web site characteristics, consumer emotional states and on-line shopping behaviours. *Journal of Business Research*, *58*, 526–532. doi:10.1016/S0148-2963(03)00143-7

New Media, E. T. C. (n.d.). *ETC New Media.* Retrieved June 24th, 2010, from http://www.newmediatrendwatch.com/world-overview/91-online-travel-market.

New Media, E. T. C. (n.d.). *ETC New Media. ETC New Media*, (n.d.). Retrieved June 8th, 2007, from http://www.etcnewmedia.com/review/default.asp?SectionID=3&uID=962&nnID=20/1173#1173.

Noble, S. M., Griffith, D. A., & Weinberger, M. G. (2005). Consumer derived utilitarian value and channel utilization in a multi-channel retail context. *Journal of Business Research*, *58*(12), 1643–1651. doi:10.1016/j.jbusres.2004.10.005

Overby, J. W., & Lee, E. J. (2006). The effects of utilitarian and hedonic online shopping value on consumer preferences and intentions. *Journal of Business Research*, *59*, 1160–1166. doi:10.1016/j.jbusres.2006.03.008

Parasuraman, A., & Zinkhan, G. M. (2002). Marketing to and service customers through the Internet: An overview and research agenda. *Journal of the Academy of Marketing Science*, *30*(4), 286–295. doi:10.1177/009207002236906

Parsons, A. G. (2002). Non-functional motives for online shoppers: Why we click. *Journal of Consumer Marketing*, *19*(5), 380–392. doi:10.1108/07363760210437614

Peter, J. P., & Olson, J. C. (2002). *Consumer Behaviour and Marketing Strategy* (6th ed.). New York: McGraw-Hill.

Phocuswright.com. (2010) *Phocuswright.com. Phocuswright*, (2010). FYI Newsletter., Retrievedreceived on the 5th of April 2010 from http://www.phocuswright.com.

Phocuswright.com. (n.d.) *Phocuswright.com.* Retrieved June 20th, 2010, from http://www.phocuswright.com.

Reibstein, D. J. (2002). What attracts customers to online stores, and what keeps them coming back? *Journal of the Academy of Marketing Science*, *30*(4), 465–473. doi:10.1177/009207002236918

Rettie, R. (2001). An exploration of flow during Internet use. *Internet Research: Electronic Networking Applications and Policy*, *11*(2), 103–113. doi:10.1108/10662240110695070

Reynolds, T. J., & Gutman, J. (1988). Laddering theory, method, analysis and interpretation. *Journal of Advertising Research*, *28*(February/March), 11–31.

Saeed, K. A., Hwang, Y., & Grover, V. (2002). Investigating the impact of web site value and advertising on firm performance in electronic commerce. *International Journal of Electronic Commerce*, *7*(2), 119–141.

Schlosser, A. E., Barnett-White, T., & Lloyd, S. M. (2006). Converting web site visitors into buyers: How web site investment increases consumer trusting beliefs and online purchase intentions. *Journal of Marketing*, *70*(April), 133–148. doi:10.1509/jmkg.70.2.133

Schmidt, J. B., & Spreng, R. A. (1996). A proposed model of external consumer information search. *Journal of the Academy of Marketing Science*, *24*(3), 246–256. doi:10.1177/0092070396243005

Sigala, M. (2004). Designing experiential web sites in tourism and hospitality: A customer-centric value approach. In Frew, A. (Eds.) *Information and Communication Technologies in Tourism 2004* (161-171). Proceedings of the ENTER conference. Vienna: Springer.

Sismeiro, C., & Bucklin, R. E. (2004). Modeling purchase behavior at an e-commerce web site: A task-completion approach. *JMR, Journal of Marketing Research*, *XLI*(August), 306–323. doi:10.1509/jmkr.41.3.306.35985

Smith, D. N., & Sivakumar, K. (2004). Flow and Internet shopping behaviour: A conceptual model and research propositions. *Journal of Business Research*, *57*, 1199–1208. doi:10.1016/S0148-2963(02)00330-2

So, M. W. C., & Sculli, D. (2002). The role of trust, quality, value and risk in conducting e-business. *Industrial Management & Data Systems*, *102*(9), 503–512. doi:10.1108/02635570210450181

Stangle, B., & Dickinger, A. (2010). How communication modes determine website satisfaction In Gretzel, U., Law, R. & Fuchs, M. (Eds.) *Information and Communication Technologies in Tourism 2010* (273-284). Proceedings of the ENTER conference. Wien: Springer-Verlag.

Steenkamp, J. B. E. M., & Geyskens, I. (2006). How country characteristics affect the perceived value of web sites. *Journal of Marketing*, *70*(July), 136–150. doi:10.1509/jmkg.70.3.136

Strauss, A., & Corbin, J. (1998). *Basics of qualitative research – techniques and procedures for developing grounded theory*. Thousand Oaks, CA: SAGE Publications.

Verma, R., Iqbal, Z., & Plaschka, G. (2004). Understanding customer choices in e-financial services. *California Management Review*, *46*(4), 43–67.

Wang, Y., & Fesenmaier, D. R. (2004). Towards understanding members' general participation in and active contribution to an online travel community. *Tourism Management*, *25*, 709–722. doi:10.1016/j.tourman.2003.09.011

Woodruff, R. B. (1997). Customer Value: The next source for competitive advantage. *Journal of the Academy of Marketing Science*, *25*(2), 139–153. doi:10.1007/BF02894350

Woodruff, R. B., & Flint, D. J. (2006). Marketing's service-dominant logic and customer value. In Lusch, R. F. & Vargo S. L. (Eds.) *The service-dominant logic of marketing – dialogue, debate, and directions* (183-195). New York: M.E. Sharpe.

Woodruff, R. B., & Gardial, S. F. (1996). *Know your customer – New approaches to understanding customer value and satisfaction.* Malden, MA: Blackwell Publishing.

Yadav, M. S., & Varadarajan, P. R. (2005). Understanding product migration to the electronic marketplace: A conceptual framework. *Journal of Retailing, 81*(2), 125–140. doi:10.1016/j.jretai.2005.03.006

Zeithaml, V. A. (1988). Consumer perceptions of price, quality, and value: A means-end model and synthesis of evidence. *Journal of Marketing, 52*(July), 2–22. doi:10.2307/1251446

Chapter 4
The Architecture of Service Systems as the Framework for the Definition of Service Science Scope

Andrew Targowski
Western Michigan University, USA

ABSTRACT

The purpose of this study is to define generic service processes, their system, and a scope of service science developed originally by the author. In the presented approach, the main criterion is the class of serviced users, since this leads to the six kinds of process recognition and eventually helps in planning e-service systems' architecture. E-service system (e-SS) is defined as a mission-goal-strategy-driven configuration of technology, organizational processes and networks designed to deliver HTservicesTH that satisfy the needs, wants, or aspirations of customers. Marketing, operations, and global environment considerations have significant implications for the design of an e-service system. Four criteria which impact e-service systems' architecture have been defined as: service business model, customer contact and level of involvement (Service User Interface), service provider's enterprise complexity (Enterprise Systems and Networks), and scope of goods involved in service. It was proved that the e-service system is the intermediary layer between Service User Interface and Enterprise Systems and Networks. Two examples of e-SS have been modeled.

INTRODUCTION

The purpose of this study is to define a scope of service science based on ideal generic service systems originally developed by the author. There are two goals of this study: 1) to develop generic service categories and their generic systems and 2) to define a scope of service science based upon the presented generic models of service systems, which determine the required support from emerging system science. The research methodology is based on the architectural modeling according the paradigm of enterprise-wide systems (Targowski 2003).

The architectural system approach is based on the philosophy of the system approach (Klir 1985),

DOI: 10.4018/978-1-60960-138-6.ch004

and management cybernetics (Beer 1981) which provide comprehensive and cohesive solutions to the problems of systems design, thus eliminating the fuziveness of the "application portfolio" and the "information archipelago" (McFarlan 1981), Targowski 1990). The mission of the architectural system approach is to find the ultimate synthesis of the whole system structure that involves appropriate logic, appropriate technological accommodation, operational quality, a positive user involvement, and coexistence with nature (Targowski 1990). In its nature, the architectural system approach is of deductive rather than inductive nature. It looks for the ideal model of a solution, which in practice is far away from its perfect level. The difference between the architectural system approach and the engineering approach is in the level of abstraction. The architectural models are more conceptual whereas engineering outcomes are more technical and specific. The architectural system approach is the response to the complexity of expected outcomes. Prior to spending a few million dollars for a new information system, one must provide its information architecture and the business and social implications associated with it (Targowski 2003). In this sense, this study will define service systems' architectures.

Service economy can refer to one or both of two recent economic developments. First is the increased importance of the Hsector in industrialized economies. Services account for a higher percentage of U.S. GDP than 20 years ago, since modern-day off-shore outsourcing of manufacturing contributes to the growing service sector of the American economy. The 2006 Fortune 500 companies list contains more service companies and fewer manufacturers than in previous decades. The service sector is classified as the tertiary sector of industry (also known as the service industry) and is one of the three main industrial categories of a developed economy, the others being the secondary industry (manufacturing, construction), and primary industry (extraction such as mining, agriculture and fishing). Services are defined in conventional literature as "intangible goods" (Drucker 1969, Rathmell 1974, Bell 1976, Shostack 1977). According to Laroche (2001), it is clear that intangibility has been cited by several authors as the fundamental factor differentiating services from goods (Breivik, Troye, and Olsson 1998; Lovelock 2001; Rust, Zahorik, and Keiningham 1996). All other differences emerge from this distinction (Bateson 1979; Zeithaml and Bitner 2000). According to evident practice, service tends to be wealth consuming, whereas manufacturing is wealth producing. The tertiary sector of industry involves the provision of services to businesses as well as final consumers and citizens (users of government services). Services may involve the transport, distribution and sale of goods from producer to a consumer as may happen in wholesaling and retailing, or may involve the provision of a service such as in pest control or Tentertainment. Goods may be transformed in the process of providing a service, as happens in the restaurant industry. However, the focus is on people interacting with people and serving the customer rather than transforming physical goods. Since the 1960s there has been a substantial shift from the other two industry sectors to the Tertiary Sector in industrialized countries. The service sector also consists of the "soft" parts of the economy such as insurance, government, tourism, banking, retail and education. In soft sector employment, people use time to deploy knowledge assets, collaboration assets, and process-engagement to create productivity (effectiveness), performance improvement potential (potential) and sustainability. Typically, the output of this time is content (information), service, attention, advice, experiences, and/or discussion ("intangible goods"). Other examples of service sector employment include public utilities, which are often considered part of the tertiary sector as they provide services to people. Creating the utility's infrastructure is often considered part of the secondary sector even though the same business may be involved in both aspects of the operation.

Economies tend to follow a developmental progression that takes them from a heavy reliance on agriculture and mining toward the development of industry (e.g. automobiles, textiles, shipbuilding, and steel) and finally toward a more service-based structure. For example, IBM treats its business as a service business. Although it still manufactures high-end computers, it sees the physical goods as a small part of the "business solutions" industry. They have found that the price elasticity of demand for "business solutions" is much less elastic than for hardware. There has been a corresponding shift to a subscription pricing model rather than receiving a single payment for a piece of manufactured equipment. Many manufacturers are now receiving a steady stream of revenue for ongoing contracts.

Manufacturing tends to be more open to international trade and competition than services. As a result, there has been a tendency for the first economies to industrialize to come under competitive attack by those seeking to industrialize later, e.g. because production, especially labor costs, are lower than in those industrializing later. The resultant shrinkage of manufacturing in the leading economies might explain their growing reliance on the service sector.

Service economy can refer to the relative importance of service in a product offering. That is, products today have a higher service component than in previous decades. In the management literature this is referred to as the servitization of products. Virtually every product today has a service component to it. The old dichotomy between product and service has been replaced by a service-product continuum. Many products are being transformed into services.

Figure 1 depicts the Contribution of the Service Sector to the U.S. Gross Domestic Product in 2005. Since government provides mostly services to its citizens, one can state that the Service Sector contributes 80% to the U.S. Gross Domestic product. This level of contribution must turn attention of

Figure 1. Contribution of sector to U.S. Gross Domestic Product 2005

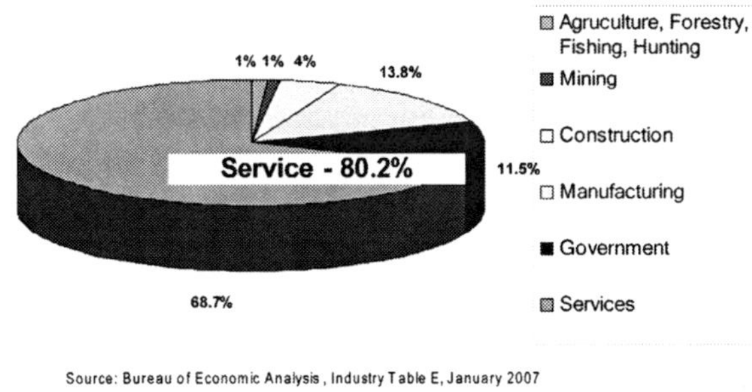

system developers, who up till now are mostly engaged in the production and commerce systems.

THE NATURE OF SERVICES

The first goal of this study will be pursued in defining first the nature of services and their categories. Later, comprehensive graphic models will be developed for generic systems, supporting major categories of service processes.

Service can be defined as follows:

Services are a diverse group of economic activities that include high-technology, knowledge-intensive sub-sectors as well as labor-intensive, low-skill areas. In many aspects, service sectors exhibit marked differences from manufacturing, although these distinctions may be blurring. (OECD Report-2000)

A good review of definitions of service provides Heskett (1990). Simply defined, services on demand are a diverse group of economic activities not directly associated with the manufacture of goods, mining or agriculture. They typically involve the provision of human value added in the form of labor, advice, managerial skill, entertainment, training, intermediation and the like, mostly after manufacturing or goods (such as natural resources and food) delivered to customers. They differ from other types of economic activities in a number of ways. Many, for example, cannot be inventoried and must be consumed ("customized") at the point of production. This could include trips to the doctor, enjoying a meal at a restaurant, flying from Chicago to Paris, or attending a concert. This is in marked contrast with manufactured products, whose tangible character allows them to be stored, distributed widely, and consumed without direct interaction with the entity that produced the good.

Technological advances are, however, narrowing the differences between services and other economic activities. While it has not reached the point where someone can enjoy the ambience of a good restaurant without physically going to one, information and communication technology (ICT) now enables people to participate in a growing number of service-related activities in real or deferred time without having to be physically present. Copies of movies and most other performances can be recorded and mass-produced for future consumption like manufactured products. Software is developed and boxed like any other manufactured product and is considered, for all intents and purposes, a good—albeit with a high service-related content. In these instances services have, in a sense, taken on the characteristics of commodities—one provider is mass-producing a common product for many people. Service providers are thus increasingly able to benefit from economies of scale. The benefits have not, however, been restricted to large enterprises as small firms can achieve similar gains through increased networking.

The relationship between service providers and consumers is also changing in other ways that may have significant implications for economies. Technology now allows providers to produce a single product which is not mass-produced but which is capable of being mass-consumed, either on a standardized or customized basis. Such is the case with online Internet access to dictionaries, encyclopedias, newspapers, museum collections, etc. It will also apparently be the case with key, basic operating software in the near future, as both Microsoft and Sun Microsystems have announced their intention to supplement distribution of "boxed" software with online versions (Taylor, 1999).

Technology is also affecting the relationship between providers and consumers in areas previously unthinkable such as health care, where the need for personal contact to diagnose and treat ailments is becoming less essential. Internet-based banking, real estate, retail and financial services provide other examples where personal or on-site contact with service providers is no longer essential for the services to be performed. In many instances such services can, in fact, be provided far more efficiently via the Internet.

Table 1 characterizes services in the developed economy.

Figure 2 illustrates the Processive Architecture of the U.S. National Economy, which also indicates that "service" dominates the economic activities of the American Society in term of its functionality, business, and pursuit for the complete life.

A CLASSIFICATION OF SERVICES IN A DEVELOPED ECONOMY

Once the developed economies moved to service economies in the second part of the 20th century (Bell 1973), the development of different kinds of services became almost endless. In order to grasp their realm it is necessary to classify them. One of the first who undertook this task were Malchup (1962) and Porat (1977) who wanted to address the rise of knowledge and information-based activities in national economy. They provoked Bell (1981) to emphasize that industrial economy is being transformed into information economy, which defined four criteria of his classification schema. All these tree classifications turned public attention to new economic activities and emerging people's knowledge and skills. Eventually, business strategies intercepted the torch of service classifications. The first was Lovelock

Table 1. Illustrative list of services

Service	Activities Related to the:
Wholesale and retail trade	Sale of goods
Information	Gathering and dissemination of written, audio or visual information, including films and records
Transportation and warehousing	Distribution of goods
Finance and insurance	Facilitation of financial transactions, including those related to risk management
Real estate, rental and leasing	Temporary transfer of property, and the temporary or definitive transfer of real estate
Professional, scientific and technical	Provision of specialized, generally "knowledge-based," expertise (e.g. legal, accountancy, and engineering)
Management of companies and enterprises	Management of holding companies
Heath care and social assistance	Provision of health care and social assistance (e.g. doctors, hospitals and clinics)
Education	Provision of instruction and training (e.g. schools and specialized training centers)
Arts, entertainment and recreation	Provision of entertainment in a broad sense (e.g. museums, opera, theatre, sports and gambling establishments)
Accommodation and food services	Provision of lodging, or the provision of meals, snacks or beverages
Public administration	Governing or administration of public entities and programs
Other	Provision of personal services, repair and maintenance activities, professional societies, religious institutions, etc.

Source: Based on US Bureau of Census, 1999.

Figure 2. The processive architecture of the US National Economy

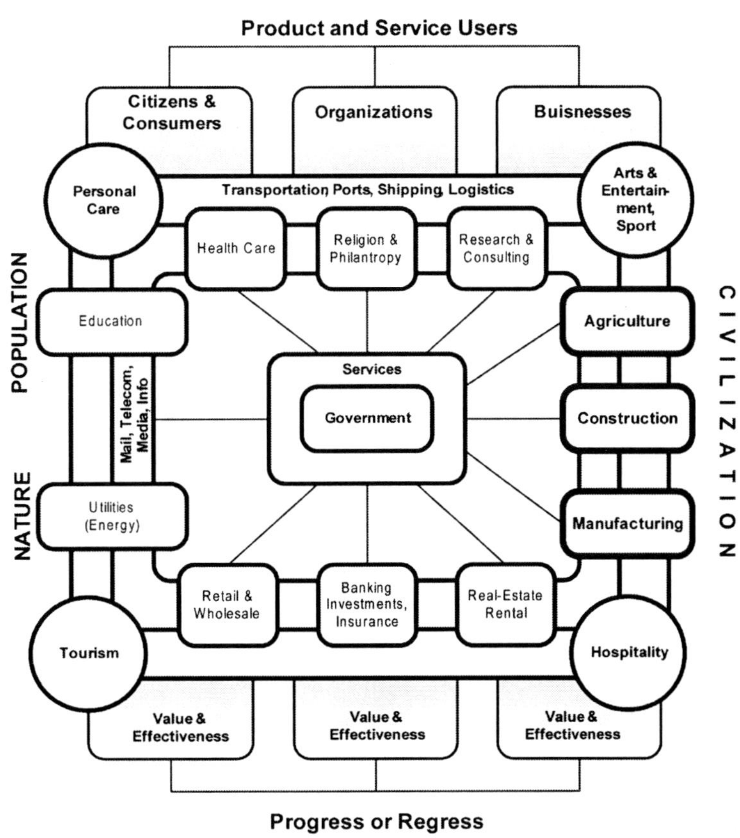

(1983), who defined classification of services from the point of view of how to gain strategic marketing internally. Later in his famous and very good textbook with Wirtz (2007) he extended this classification into the Four Categories of Service Classification.

A review of these service classifications is provided in Table 2

Every listed classification in Table 2 was defined according to a given purpose. The economic-orientation is the purpose of first seven classifications while the marketing orientation is the purpose of the last two classifications. Certainly these purposes served well in the broad context of national economy and marketing strategies, respectively.

In this investigation the e-service system architecture is the purpose of a new service classification. Three categories of service will be recognized as the main schema of the classification. Another three categories of services will be differentiated by applying a criterion of service intangibility, defined by Laroche (2001). In the post-industrial economy, more and more physically intangible products exist in our society, often called "information products" (Freiden et al. 1998), which are almost totally intangible. Laroche (2001) characterizes tangibility as more typical for "traditional" products and services. In a new service classification, services of six categories will be recognized either as "tangible" (traditional and "touchable") or as "intangible" (idea-information-oriented).

Figure 3 defines six categories of services applying the following criteria:

1. Society served:
   - Services directed at citizens and communities (tangible service)
   - Services directed at the nation (intangible service)
2. People served:
   - Services directed at a person (tangible service)
   - Services directed at a people's awareness (intangible service)
3. Possession served (criterion applied by Lovelock and Wirtz 2007):
   - Services directed at property (tangible service)
   - Services directed at info-communication handling (intangible service)

This classification is, to a certain degree, extending Lovelock & Wirtz's classification (2007) which is business-oriented. Their classification of

Table 2. A review of most popular classifications of service activities

Author	Purpose	Perspective of	Classification Schema	Classification Sub-schema
Smith ([1776] 1977)	To facilitate economic analysis	Economist	1.Productive activities (creating tangible product) 2.Nonproductive activities (creating intangible services)	
Clark (194)0	To analyze the transition of economy	Economist	1.Primary sector (extracting) 2.Secondary sector (manufacturing) 3.Tertiary sector (services)	
Gersuny and Rosengren (1973)	To analyze the economic activites	Economist	Tertiary sector	Quasi-domestic services (food and lodging) Business services "quinary" group including recreation, health care, and education

continued on following page

Table 2. continued

Author	Purpose	Perspective of	Classification Schema	Classification Sub-schema
Machlup (1962)	To emphasize the importance of knowledge production and distribution	Economist	1.Education 2.R & D 3.Communication media 4.Information machines 5.Information services	Expenditures made by: Government Business Consumers
Porat (1977)	To define what economic activities can be attributed to information activities	Economist	1.Markets for information	Media and educational institutions
			2.Information in markets	Advertising, insurance, finance, brokerages
			3.Information infrastructure	Printing, data processing, telecommunications, information goods
			4. Wholesale and retail trade in information goods	Bookstores, computer stores, theaters, and so on
			5.Support facilities for information activities	Buildings used by information industries, office furnishing, and so on
Bureau of Economic Analysis (2008)	To calculate GDP	Economist	1. Finance, insurance, Real estate 2. Retail trade 3. Wholesale Trade 4. Transportation and Public Utilities 5. Communications 6. Other services 7. Government and government enterprises	
Bell (1981)	To indicating the transfer from Industrial to Information Economy	Sociologist and Economist	1. Knowledge	Education, R &D, Libraries, Lawyers, Doctors, Accountants…
			2. Entertainment	Motion Picture Television, Music
			3. Economic Transactions and Records	Banking, Insurance, Brokerage
			4. Infrastructure Services	Telecommunications, Computers, and Programs
Lovelock (1983)	To gain strategic marketing inside	Business marketing strategist	1.Basic demand characteristics	Object served (persons vs, property), Extend of demand/supply imbalances, Discrete vs. continuous relationships between customers and providers,
			2. Service content and benefits	Extent of physical goods content, Extent of personal service content, Single service vs. bundle of service, Timing and duration of benefits
			3.Service delivery procedures	Multisite vs. single site delivery, Allocation of capacity (reservation vs. first come, first served
Bowen (1990a)	To integrate marketing with organizational behavior	Business marketing strategist	1. Service production 2. Service delivery 3. Service consumption	Focusing on service as a face-to-face game between persons.

service categories contains **four** major categories, such as tangible actions of people, tangible actions of possessions, intangible actions of people, and intangible actions of possessions. The presented classification in Figure 3 differentiates **six** major categories and differs in some titles of these categories and their content. For example, two new categories were added toreflect the whole national economy, andnot just business such as society served at the levels of citizens and communities and the nation; this includes 20 new kinds of services. Some titles in the presented classification looks perhaps similar but are more precise. For example, "information processing" is recognized as "info-communication handling," which incorporates many telecommunication-oriented services typical for the Information Age (1998+). In comparison, the older classification of"data processing" is more characteristic for the Computer Age (1980+) when technology-based services emerged as the main trend in the economy, but certainly not as e-services. The old classification's "mental stimulus processing" services sounds too freudelian. The new classification offers "services directed at people's awareness."

The new service classifications presented can be applied to modeling of the same type of services' systems. The service modeling approach by Dabholkar (1996) is mostly limited to technology-based self-service and testing customer attitude

Figure 3. Six categories of services

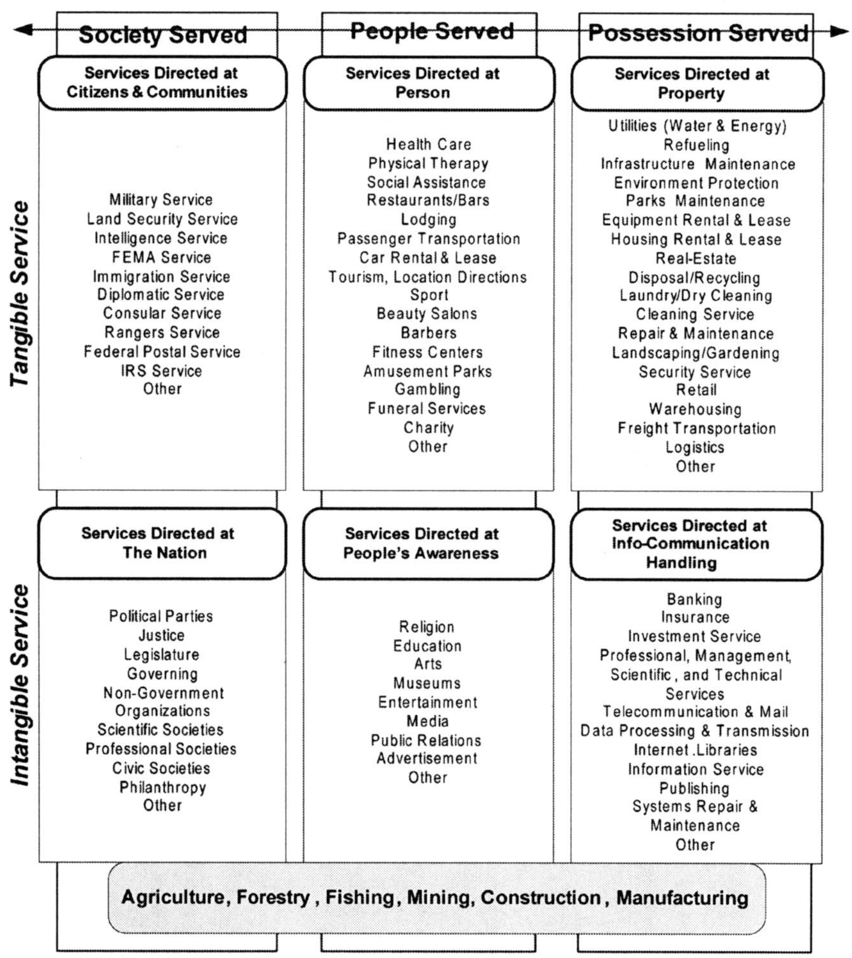

in the scope of cognitive attributes (e.g. speed of delivery, ease of use, reliability, enjoyment, control) and affective attributes (e.g. attitude toward using technological products and the need for interaction with a service employee). These attributes can be applied to many kinds of services classified in Figure 3 if they are delivered as a technology-based self-service.

Applying three main and six supportive criteria, it was possible to differentiate about 82 kinds of services. In practice, perhaps this table can accommodate about 1,000 kinds of services (e.g. copying, tanning, blacksmithing) which all cannot be listed here. Certainly one can apply many other criteria to classify services such as service substance, service output, service ownership, and so forth. In the presented approach, the main criterion is the kind of serviced users, since this leads to the processes recognition and eventually should help in e-service systems' architecture planning. On the other hand, one must state that e-service may not cover all needed services. In this approach a scope of services which can be globalized is not considered.

THE E-SERVICE SYSTEM REQUIREMENTS

E-service system (e-SS) is a mission-goal-strategy-driven configuration of technology, organizational processes and networks designed to deliver services that satisfy the needs, wants, or aspirations of customers, citizens, and users. Marketing, operations, and global environment considerations have significant implications for the design of an e-service system. Four criteria can impact e-service systems architecture:

- service business model
- customer contact and level of involvement (Service User Interface),
- service provider's enterprise complexity (Enterprise Systems and Networks)
- scope of goods involved in service

Properly designed e-service systems employ technology for organizational networks that can allow relatively inexperienced people to perform very sophisticated tasks quickly, vaulting them over normal learning curve delays. Ideally, empowerment of both service provider employees and customers (often via itself-service) results from well-designed e-service systems. Figure 4 illustrates the general architecture of IT-driven service systems.

E-service systems range from an individual person equipped with tools of the trade (e.g., architect, entrepreneur) to a portion of a government agency or business (e.g., branch office of a post office or bank) to complete multinational corporations and their information systems (e.g., Pizza Hut, UPS). Hospitals, universities, cities, and national governments are designed service systems. The language, norms, attitudes, and beliefs of the people that make up a service system may evolve over time as people adjust to new circumstances. In this sense, e-service systems are a type of complex system that is partially designed and partially evolving. E-service systems are designed to *deliver* or *provision* services but they often consume services as well.

The e-service system is both a service provider and a customer of multiple types of services. Because service systems are designed both in how they provision and consume services, services systems are often linked into a complex service value chain or value network where each link is a value proposition. Service systems may be nested inside of service systems, e.g. a staff and operating room unit inside a hospital that is part of a nationwide healthcare provider network.

E-service system developers and architects often seek to exploit economic complementarities or network effect to rapidly grow and scale up the service. For example, credit card usage is part of a service system in which the more people and businesses that use and accept the credit cards, the

Figure 4. The generic architecture of service-driven IT systems

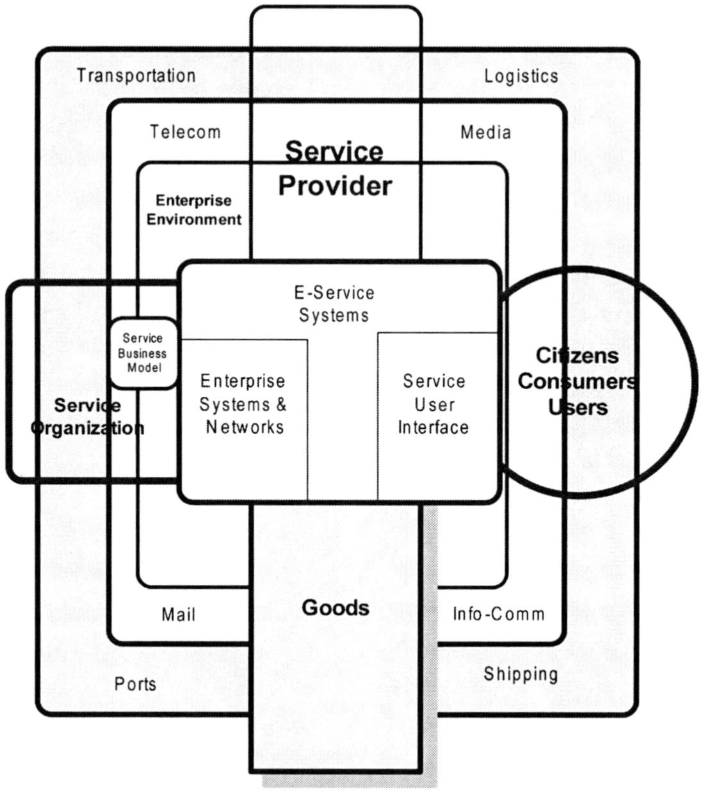

more value the credit cards system can eventually offer to the provider and all stakeholders in the e-service system. E-service system innovation often requires integrating technology innovation, business model (or value proposition) innovation, social-organizational innovation, and demand (new customer wants, needs, aspirations) innovation. For example, a national e-service system may be designed with policies that enable more citizens (the customers of the governments) to become an entrepreneur, and thereby create more innovation and wealth for the nation. E-service systems may include payment mechanisms for selecting a level of service to be provided (up-front or one-time payment) or payment based on downstream value sharing or taxation derived from customers who received the benefit of the service (downstream or ongoing payment). Payments may also be in the form of or other types of intangible value.

Table 3 provides application requirements for each of the six e-services systems categories. Its important to notice that in majority cases, the e-service system is the transition layer between Service User Interface and Enterprise Systems and Networks.

The architectures of web-driven services are quite well developed and widely described in the professional literature of the emerging 21st century (Rosenfeld and Morvil 2006, Felipe 2005, Erl 2004 and others). In this study, the main point is that the web-based service architectures should be an extension of enterprise-wide computing. Of course if the nature of e-service is based on relatively complex enterprise computing, which is called the "mortar and click" solution. If a solution is based on the modest "click and click" approach, then the enterprise-wide computing may be of limited application.

Table 3. The application requirements for e-service and enterprise systems

SERVICES DIRECTED at	BUSINESS MODEL (Service Organization)	SERVICE USER INTERFACE (Customer-Service Provider)	E-SERVICE SYSTEM	ENTERPRISE SYSTEMS & NETWORKS	GOODS INVOLVED
SOCIETY SERVED					
Citizens and communities	Efficiency & Value	Web-driven, Open Portal, Extranet	Citizens Orders, Licenses, Payments, Scheduling, News Letters, Citizens Service, Intranet	ERP, SCM, e-DMS, WFS, MIS, KMS, EUC, LAN, MAN, WAN	Highly
The nation	Value	Web-driven, Open Portal, Extranet	Polls, Blogs, Forums, News Letters, Memberships, Payments, Donations, Meetings, Membership Service, Intranet	e-DMS, WFS, MIS, FIS, AIS, KMS, EUC, LAN, MAN, WAN	Minimal
PEOPLE SERVED					
Person	Value & Profit	Web-driven, Open Portal & traditional, Extranet	Customer Orders, Scheduling, Payments, News Letters, Customer Service, Intranet	CRM, SCM, KMS, MIS, WFS, FIS, AIS, EUC LAN, MAN, WAN	Significantly
People's awareness	Value & Efficiency	Web-driven, Open Portal & traditional, Extranet	Blogs, Forums, News Letters, Customer Orders Payments, Donations, Meetings, Membership Service, Intranet	CRM, SCM, ERP for large organizations KMS, MIS, EUC, LAN, MAN, WAN, GAN	Significantly
POSSESION SERVED					
Property	Effectiveness	Web-driven, Open Portal & traditional Extranet	Customer/Citizens Orders, Payments, Scheduling, Forums, News Letters, Customer/Citizens Services, Intranet	CRM, SCM, ERP for large organizations KMS, MIS, WFS, EUC, LAN, MAN, WAN	Highly
Info-communication handling	Value & Effectiveness	Web-driven, Open Portal & traditional Extranet	Customer Orders, Payments, Scheduling, News Letters, Customer Service, Intranet	CRM, SCM, ERP for large organizations and KMS, WFS, MIS, FIS, AIS, EUC, LAN, MAN, WAN	Depends

The following components are included in the e-Service and Enterprise Systems Requirements (Targowski 2003):

- ERP as a set of Service Demand Planning (SDP), Service Resources Planning (SRP), Financial Information System (FIS),

Accounting Information System (AIS), and other
- SCM—Supply Chain Management
- CRM—Customer Relations Management
- WFS—Work Flow System
- E-DMS—Electronic Document Management System
- KMS–Knowledge Management System, composed of Data Warehouse and Data Mining
- MIS–Management Information System, composed of Transactions Processing System (TPS), Enterprise Data Base Management System (EDBMS), Enterprise Performance Management System (EPMS), and Executive Information System (EIS)
- EUC-End User Computing
- LAN-Local Area Network
- MAN-Metropolitan Network
- WAN-Wide Area Network
- GAN-Global Area Network
- Other

THE GENERIC ARCHITECTURES OF E-SERVICE SYSTEMS (E-SS)

Based on the application requirements provided in Table 2, two generic architectures are defined for the Citizen and Community e-Service System (Figure 5) and for the Person e-Service System (Figure 6). This is assumed that the Enterprise System and End-User-Computing are included in the e-SS.

Figure 5 illustrates the architecture of the Citizens and Community E-Service System category. It indicates that the e-Service System and

Figure 5. The architecture of citizens and community e-service system

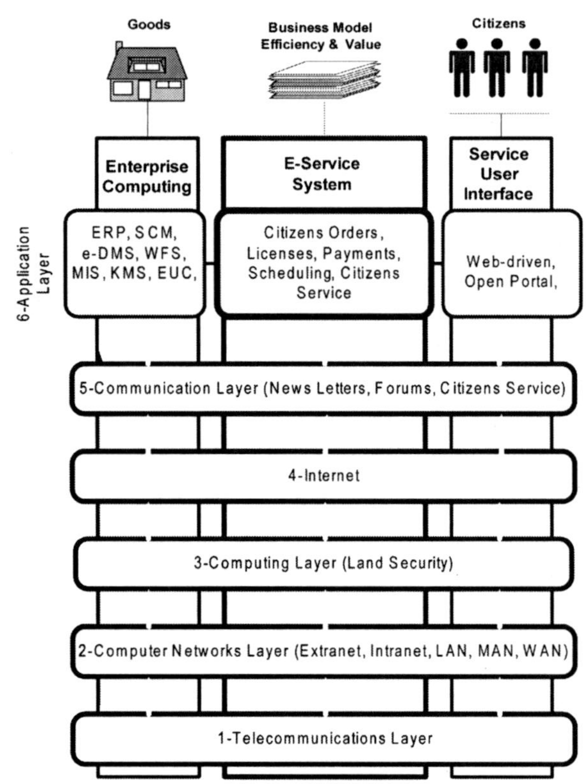

Figure 6. The architecture of person e-service system

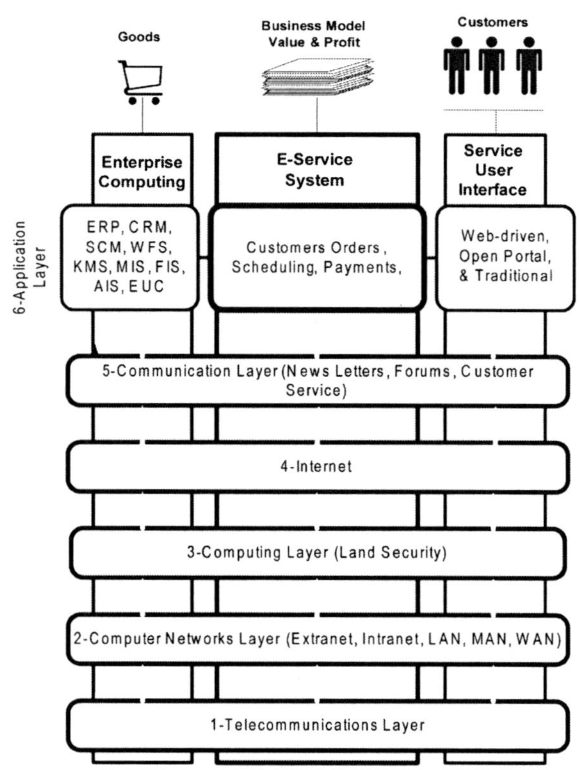

Service User Interface vertical segments are new additions to the Enterprise Computing vertical segment. Furthermore, these segments are built of six horizontal layers: telecommunication, computer networks, computing, Internet, communication, and applications. These six horizontal layers are typical for Enterprise Computing. It indicates that if possible, a successful e-Service System should be based on the previously developed Enterprise Computing.

Figure 6 illustrates the architecture of a Person E-Service System category. It also indicates the same regularities in the layer complexity as it was shown in Figure 5, reflecting a different e-service system category. However, the major difference between these two e-service system categories is in their application layers, where different kinds of services are provided in online processing.

The presented e-SS architectures are generic and their system/network components should be tailored for a given kind of e-SS. Based on the provided architectures and application requirements provided in Table 2, one can develop generic architectures for other four types of e-SS.

Technology also affect the relationship between service providers and consumers in areas previously unthinkable, such as health care, where the need for personal contact to diagnose and treat ailments is becoming less essential. Internet-based banking, real estate, retail and financial services provide other examples where personal, or onsite, contact with service providers is no longer essential for the services to be performed. In many instances such services can, in fact, be provided far more efficiently via the Internet or through other remote communication modes.

One of the most critical components of the e-SS is customer service,is the provision of HTTserviceTTH to customers before, during, and after a purchase. Its importance varies by product, industry and customer. For example, an expert customer might require less pre-purchase service (i.e., advice) than a novice customer.

In many cases customer service is more important if the purchase relates to a "service" as opposed to a "product." Customer service may be provided by a person (e.g., sales and service representative) or by automated means called self-service. Examples of self service are Internet sites. Customer service is normally an integral part of a company's HTTbusinessTTH model. An example of a service delivery system for the Best Buy chain is shown in Figure 7 (the Application Layer of previous models is expanded). This model indicates that if enterprise systems are well developed then e-service system is a natural addition to them. The most critical systems for e-service are: Portal, e-Catalog, e-Customer Orders, Supply Chain Management (SCM), Customer Relations Management (CRM) and Document Mangement System (DMS). Such subsystems of CRM not shown in Figure 7 are: e-Customer Service (web-driven), Call Center, e-Customer Support (web-driven), e-Store, e-Payment, e-Field Service, Contact Management, Internet Relationships Management, Telemarketing, and so forth.

TOWARD THE SERVICE SCIENCE SCOPE

The second goal of this study is to define a scope of service science based upon the generic service systems offered in the previous sections.

The key to defining service science is the understanding of the nature of service. Nowadays, *service* is a complex system which is characterized by the following attributes:

1. It is aimed to satisfy a customer/citizen/society
2. It is a system composed of customer/citizens, service providers, service-oriented technology, and control-oriented technology (IT)
3. It is driven by value, time, cost, and profit

Figure 7. A service delivery system of the Best Buy Chain (Aggregated)

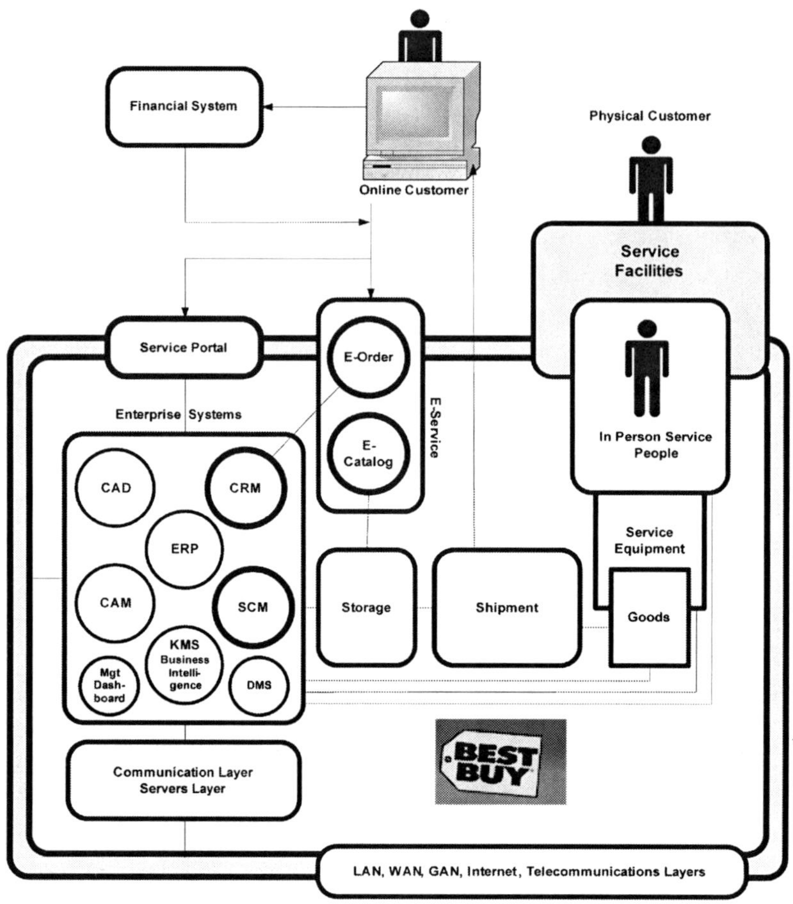

4. It is a "product," which is planned, designed, implemented ("produced"), operated, and managed.

Based upon these attributes one can define a matrix of developmental, operational, and management activities within a framework established by the IBM discipline named SSME (Glushko 2008). Supporting the IBM framework are theoretical disciplines which include a set of theories and approaches integrated and called service science (Figure 8).

Table 4 defines key outcomes of service science areas within the framework of service stages.

The discipline of *service science* is the systematic study of the theoretical foundations of service development, operations, and management. These foundations are perceived as complex systems which are service-technology-oriented and service managing technology-driven for the benefits of a society, person, and property in the scope of tangible and intangible services.

A *mission* of service science is to pursue the interdisciplinary theory (verified in practice) based on selected rules of business, system science, psychology, management science, operations research, service domain engineering, service economics, service law and ethics with info-communication science (ICS) in order to apply

Figure 8. The relationship among service science, management and engineering (SSME) approaches within the context of developmental and operational service stages

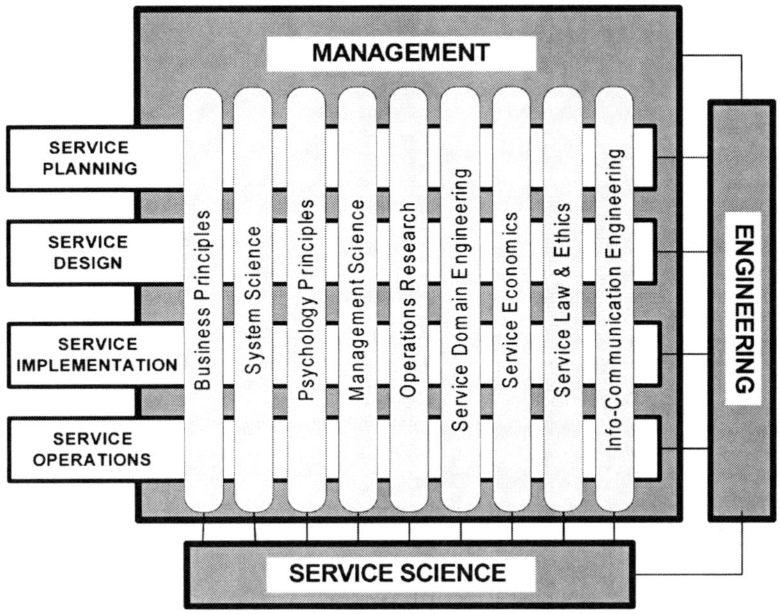

them in service, planning, design, implementation, operations, and management.

As such, service science's *aim* is to integrate these particular disciplines into a *coherent whole*. In fact, IBM relabeled its initiative in this area as"Service Sciences, Management, and Engineering" to highlight the interdisciplinary nature of the effort. Furthermore, HP created a Center for Service and Systems Science for the same reason. Universities have also begun to act on the need or service science (SSME) as well. For instance, UC Berkeley has created an SSME program. North Carolina State University created an MBA track for service and a computer engineering degree for services well. In both cases the schools recognize the interdisciplinary character of the field and incorporate content from a variety of disciplines. Other schools with interdisciplinary interests in SSME include University of Maryland, Arizona State University, Northern Illinois University, UC Santa Cruz, MIT, RPI, and others.

Academic publications in SSME are also starting to appear. For instance, one can recommend the special issue of the *Communications of the ACM* (July 2006) focused entirely on service science. *The International Journal of Services Operations and Informatics* issued its first volume in 2006. One can expect that the mentioned strong supporters and universities' faculty will pursue the interesting and inspiring task of supporting the U.S. Service Economy by theory-based service science.

THE SERVICE SCIENCE STARTEGY FOR INNOVATIONS

Perhaps the lack of academic involvement in systematization and innovation in the service economy put it in crisis. Gutek and Welsh (2000) write that "we are not thrilled with the quality of customer service today. Dissatisfaction with service has reached epidemic proportions in America—a sad state of affairs for a so-called 'service economy.'" According to authors Barbara Gutek and Theresa Welsh, this is because

Table 4. Key outcomes of service science

SERVICE SCIENCE AREAS	SERVICE STAGES				
	SERVICE PLANNING	SERVICE DESIGN	SERVICE IMPLEMENTATION	SERVICE OPERATIONS	SERVICE MANAGEMENT
Business Principles	Business Model	Business Model Revised	Business Model Implemented	Business Model Practiced	Service Project Defined
System Science	Service Model	Service Model Tested	Service Model Prototyped, Piloted, Implemented	Service Model Maintained & Improved	System Project Management
Psychology Principles	Customer Behavior Expected	Customer Behavior Updated	Customer Behavior Tested	Customer Behavior Updated	Customer Behavior Analyzed
Management Science	Decision Optimization Criteria	Decisions Optimized	Decisions Structured	Optimal Decisions Applied	CPM Applied
Operations Research	Service Optimization Criteria	Service Flow Optimized	Service Flow Established	Service Flow Operated	Service Flow Simulated
Service Domain Engineering	Service Processes Scopes	Service Processes Designed	Service Processes Implemented	Service Processes Maintained & Improved	Service Engineering Project Management
Service Economics	Expected Economic Impact	Economic Impact Verified	Economic Impact Tested	Economic Impact Updated	Local, National, Global Impact Managed
Service Law & Ethics	Ethics & Compliance	Ethics & Compliance Assured	Ethics & Compliance Observed	Ethics & Compliance Revised	Ethics & Compliance Controlled
Information-Communication Engineering	Architecture of CIS	CIS Tested	CIS Prototyped, Piloted, Implemented	CIS in Operations	CIS Project Management

service businesses are not adapting to the changing nature of service delivery. Instead they are trying to impose traditional aspects of customer service on completely new breeds of service. These tactics simply do not work and results in feelings of alienation, resentment, and cynicism in both customers and providers.

A role of universities in service innovation is to research the evolution of service delivery and teach students how to assure social and corporate responsibility in planning, developing, operating, and managing service systems. Figure 9 depicts a model of service evolution by six stages and their paradigms.

The *Collaborate Model* (1970s) is staffed with experts who can troubleshoot and easily explain to the service users all the problems with service since they created that particular service. Even today this is the case for start-up companies whose developers provide first-hand help to service recipients in areas such as software.

The *Augment Model* (1980s) applies service communication tools answering to the service users the most Frequently Asked Questions (FAQ). The first FAQ system was initiated by phone and later was applied to websites. A service user must still find out by how to use a service by him/her.

Figure 9. The paradigms of service evolution (the first four stages come from a model of J. Spohrer and P. Maglio from the IBM Almaden Research Center)

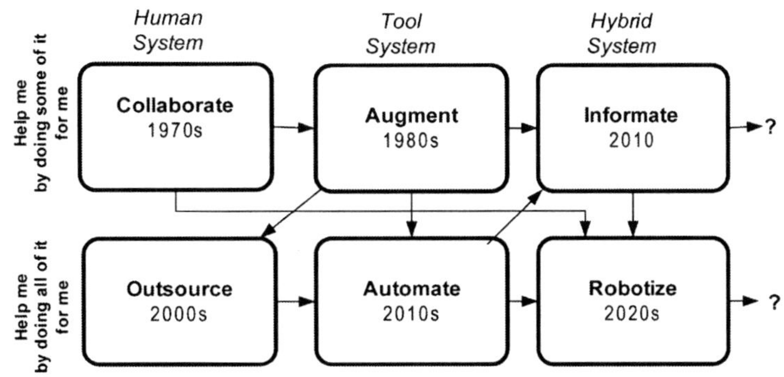

The *Outsource Model* (2000s) delegates servicing to a third party located on-shore or most frequently off-shore (e.g. India). This model was triggered by the strategy of restructuring and cost-cutting by allocating manufacturing to China and IT projects and customer service to India as both countries provide low-cost labor. This model leads to the decline of middle class in developed nations and as far as customer service is concerned, is not embraced by the American customers because the level of help and expertise provided is rather low, perhaps due to the physical distance from the places of action.

The *Automate Model* (2010s) is supported by high-tech companies which need to engage their available (idle?) resources in the next wave of technology development. This model eliminates humans from service processes and generates market demand for advanced technology. This is a very controversial strategy first, in terms of a right technical solution and second, in terms of the right social solution. As far as the former is concerned automation of *complex* service systems cannot be a reliable solution since many factors are not known for designers. For example, the FAA does not allow pilots to use an auto-pilot system in bad weather. If we look at the control rooms of many process installations we see a lot of instrumentation but operators who do nothing since the process control has been automated. In the case of an emergency these operators very often do not know what to do because they are without practice of how to handle crisis situations. As far as the latter is concerned, service automation should not lead to the drastic decline of employment as it has occurred in agriculture and manufacturing. People should have something to do and have the necessary income to support their lives and the society (including the demand creation for high-tech companies), even with the cost inefficiencies! Particularly if the population is constantly growing! Technology, particularly computers, may merely further automate blue- and white-collar jobs, achieving unprecedented speed and consistency, robbing workers of whatever skill and gratification they may retain, and increasing the impersonality and remoteness of management.

The *Informate* Model (2010) empowers ordinary working people with overall knowledge of service processes, making them capable of critical and collaborative judgment about service. This model assumes some sort of automated info-communication infrastructure. However, it is operated and supervised by humans supported by e-information which leaves room for the human to conceptualize status (change) and required decisions filtered by human knowledge (very often under the form of given business knowledge, coming from data mining) leading to wise decisions finally made ultimately by humans.

This model is particularly appropriate for semi-ill and ill-structured decisions under uncertainty. This model to a certain extent coexists with the Automate Model. A pilot who lands a plane by hand in a bad weather or a policeman who directs traffic when traffic lights fail (but is still in wireless communication with the command center) are good examples of this model.

The *Robotize Model* (2020) is a combination of the Collaborate, Automate, and Informate Models, particularly in a case of Japan. In some countries there is a shortage in the supply of labor for industrial work, which drives up investment in robotics. With the present demographic trends this shortage will be even more pronounced in years to come, which will further stimulate robotics investment in repetitive lifts involved in handling materials such as parts, beverage crates, and so forth. The number of robots is constantly increasing in manufacturing industry: Japan 280 per 10,000 people; Singapore 148; Rep. of Korea 116; Germany 102; Sweden 69; Italy 67; Finland 51; Benelux 49; United States 48; France 48; Switzerland 46; Austria 44; Spain 41 Australia 25; Denmark 24; United Kingdom 23; Norway 16 (UN/ECE NEWS, 2000). It is interesting that in Japan a robot does not replace a worker; rather the worker serves as its "master," taking care of it.

Organizations that take steps toward exclusively automating strategy can set a course that is not easily reversed. They are likely to find themselves crippled by antagonism from the work force and the depletion of knowledge that would be needed in value-adding activities. The absence of a self-conscious strategy to exploit the informating capacity of the new technology has tended to mean that managerial action flows along the path of least resistance—a path that, at least superficially, appears to serve only the interest of managerial hegemony. (Zuboff 1988, p. 391.)

The automation strategy of service creates the environment of jobbers, who are also required to act "automatically," leading in its conclusion again to deadliest, most sterile passivity history, which has been known since the fall of the Roman Empire (476 AD). This strategy will push humans into the bifurcation stage when complex systems designers will be very sophisticated people and the users of this systems will be very simple people. It has occurred in the history of the human race, when language-speaking *Cro Magnions* replaced the *Neanderthals*, who could only bark about 40,000 years ago in Europe.

The current role of universities is to launch service-oriented programs, whose systemic components to certain degrees are available and technologically are in the reach of the faculty and students. However, the most important role of the university is to research and teach the social, corporate, and personal responsibility in developing and managing ethical complex service systems!

In order to fulfill this noble task, the Three Laws of Service Systems cannot be violated by their developers and operators. These laws are similar to Isaac Asimov's approach to robotization but directed towards service automation and should be a subject of broader discussions among specialists in ethics, law, and other appropriate disciplines:

- Law I - Do not develop service systems without human presence.
- Law II - Do not develop service systems which harm society.
- Law III - Do not develop service systems which endanger human race.

The Law I protects people against passivity. Law II protects society against structured unemployment. Law III protects the human race against the bifurcation into two kinds of species. It would be necessary for governments, scientific, professional, trade and industrial associations to sign the Service Systems Agreement based on these laws to be sure that service systems are developed and managed in a responsible manner.

Figure 10. The developmental paradims of six catergories of services

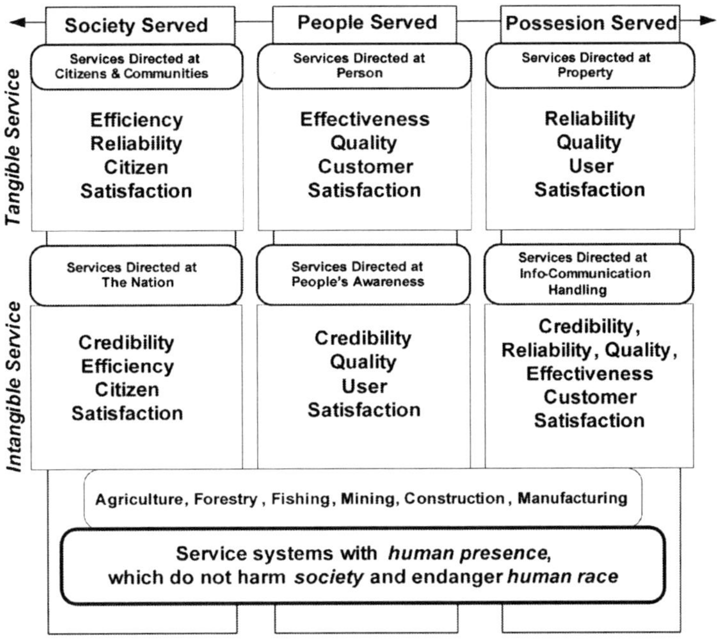

Figure 10 depicts a model of six service categories and their developmental paradigms. The role of Service Science is to constantly update these paradigms and implement into research, reaching, and consulting.

CONCLUSION

1. Service economy is a fact, which has not been yet noticed by IT developers and operators, which is still involved in enterprise systems, supporting steadily disappearing manufacturing systems, which are being outsourced off-shore.
2. The e-SS does not replace an enterprise system. Rather, it is the next layer above the layer of the enterprise system, and both layers are entered through the Service User Interface which is web-driven and can be open or entered by the Extranet.
3. Web technology is key solution for the e-SS, which has become an online-interactive info-communication tool for service users (citizens and customers).
4. Service science must support practical e-SS projects, which due to their complexity require a strong theoretical foundation.
5. The state of the art service systems' components are advanced which allows for the development of relatively complex service systems.
6. The development of service systems must comply with the Three Laws and with social, corporate, and personal responsibility.
7. To secure the right development of complex service systems, the *Service Systems Agreement* should be signed by appropriate stakeholders.
8. The future trends in e-service development will probably oscillate between fully automated and automated with human touch. The latter should be preferred trend.
9. Further research may focus on how the implemented e-service systems are complying with the ideal architecture-based solutions, sketched in this paper.

REFERENCES

Bateson, J. E. G. (1979). Why We Need Service Marketing. In Ferrell, O. C., Brown, S. W., & Lamb, C. W. (Eds.), *Conceptual and Theoretical Developments in Marketing* (pp. 131–146). Chicago: American Marketing Association.

Beer, S. (1981). *Brain of the Firm*. Chichester: John Wiley & Sons.

Bell, D. (1976). *The Coming of Post-Industrial Society*. New York: Basic Books.

Bell, D. (1981). The Social Framework of the Information Society. In Forester, T. (Ed.) *The Microelectronics Revolution*. Cambridge, MA: the MIT Press, 500-549.

Bowen, D. E. (1990a). Interdisciplinary Study of Service: Some Progress, Some Prospects. *Journal of Business Research*, *20*(1), 71–79. doi:10.1016/0148-2963(90)90044-E

Bowen, D. E., Chase, R. B., Cummings, Th. G., & Associates. (Edts). (1990). *Service Management Effectiveness, Balancing Strategy, Organization and Human Resources, Operations, and Marketing*. San Francisco: Jossey-Bass Publishers.

Breivik, E., Troye, S. V., & Olsson, U. H. (1998). *Dimensions of Intangibility and Their Impact on Product Evaluation,* working paper presented at the annual conference (October) of the Association for Consumer Research, Montreal, Canada.

Bureau of Economic Analysis. (2008). htpp//www.bea.gov/national, Retrieved 4-28-2008.

Clark, C. (1940). *The Conditions of Economic Progress*. London: Macmillan.

Dabholkar, P. A. (1994). *Technology-based Service Delivery, A Classification Scheme for Developing Marketing Strategies. Advances in Service Marketing and Management* (*Vol. 3*, pp. 241–271). Greenwich, CT: JAI Press.

Dabholkar, P. A. (1996). Consumer Evaluation of New Technology-Based Self-Service Options: An investigation of alternative models of service quality. *International Journal of Research in Marketing*, *13*(1), 29–51. doi:10.1016/0167-8116(95)00027-5

Drucker, P. (1969). *The Age of Discontinuity*. New York: Harper & Row.

Erl, Th. (2004). *Service-oriented Architecture: A Field Guide to Integrating XML and Web Services*. Upper Saddle River, NJ: Prentice Hall.

Felipe, L. (2005). *Web Services Architecture and Its Specifications: Essential for Understanding WS (Pro-Developer)*. Redwood, WA: Microsoft Press.

Freiden, J., Goldsmith, R., Takacs, S., & Hofacker, Ch. F. (1998). Information as a Product: Not Goods, Not Services. *Marketing Intelligence & Planning*, *16*(Fall), 210–220. doi:10.1108/02634509810217327

Gadrey, J., & Gallouj, F. (2002). *Productivity, Innovation and Knowledge in Services, New Economic and Socio-Economic Approaches*. Cheltenham, UK: Edward Elgar.

Gersuny, C., & Rosengren, W. R. (1973). *The Service Society*. Cambridge, MA: Schenkman.

Glushko, R. J. (2008). Design a Service Science Discipline with Disciple. *IBM Systems Journal*, *47*(1), 15–27. doi:10.1147/sj.471.0015

Gutek, B., & Welsh, Th. (2000). *The Brave New Service Strategy*. New York: AMA.

Hall, G. (1999), Presentation at the OECD Business and Industry Policy Forum on *Realizing the Potential of the Service Economy*, 28 September.

Heskett, J. L. (1990). Rethinking Strategy for Service Management.in Bowen, D. E., Chase, R. B., Cummings, Th. G. and Associates (Eds). (1990). *Service Management Effectiveness, Balancing Strategy, Organization and Human Resources, Operations, and Marketing*. San Francisco: Jossey-Bass Publishers.pp. 17-40.

Hsu, C. (Ed.). (2007) "Models of Cyberinfrastructure-based Enterprises and their Engineering" *Service Enterprise Integration: an Enterprise Engineering Perspective*, Springer Science, 2007

Klir, J. A. (1985). *Architect of System Problem Solving*. New York: Plenum Press.

Laroche, M., Bergerson, J., & Goutaland, Ch. (2001). A Three-Dimentional Scale of Intangibility. *Journal of Service Research*, *4*(1), 26–38. doi:10.1177/109467050141003

Lovelock, Ch. And J. Wirtz. (2007). *Service Marketing, People, Technology, Strategy*. Upper Saddle River, NJ: Pearson-Prentice Hall.

Lovelock, Ch. H. (1983). Classifying Services to Gain Strategic Marketing Insights. *Journal of Marketing*, *47*(Summer), 9–20. doi:10.2307/1251193

Lovelock, Ch. H. (2001). *Services Marketing: People, Technology, Strategy*. Upper Saddle River, NJ: Prentice Hall.

McFarlan, F. W. (1981). Portfolio Approach to Information Systems. *Harvard Business Review*, (September-October): 142–150.

OECD. (2000). *The Service Economy. Paris: OECD.Rathmell, John M. (1974), Marketing in the Service Sector*. Cambridge, MA: Winthrop.

Rosenfeld, L., & Morvile, P. (2006). *Information Architecture for the World Wide Web: Designing Large-Scale Web Sites*. Sebastopol, CA: O'Reilly Media, Inc.

Rust, R. T., Zahorik, A. J., & Keiningham, T. L. (1996). *Service Marketing*. New York: HarperCollins.

Sampson, S. E. (2001) "Understanding service businesses". John Wiley: New York Serving the Services, *ORMS Today* June 2006.

Shostack, G. L. (1977). Breaking Free from Product Marketing. *Journal of Marketing*, *41*(April), 73. doi:10.2307/1250637

Smith, A. (1977). *The Wealth of Nations*. New York: Dutton. (Original work published 1776)

Targowski, A. (1990). *The Architecture and Planning of Enterprise-wide Information Management Systems*. Harrisburg, PA: Idea group Publishing.

Targowski, A. (2003). *Electronic Enterprise*. Harrisburg, PA: The IRM Press.

Taylor, R. (1999), "Microsoft to Rent Software on the Internet", *WSJ Interactive*, 30 September.

Teboul, J. (2006). *Service is Front Stage*. INSEAD Business Press. doi:10.1057/9780230579477

Trends in Services Sciences in Japan and Abroad *Science and Technology Trends Quarterly Review*, April 2006

U.S. Bureau of The Census. (1999), *North American Industry Classification System*, http://www.census.gov/epcd/ www/naics.html.52

U.S. Council of Economic Advisers And The Us Department of Labor. (1999), "20 Million Jobs: January 1993 – November 1999", December, http://www.dol.gov.

World Services Congress 99 (1999), "Recommendations of the Global Services Network and Business Policy Forums for Services 2000 Trade Negotiations", November, http://www.worldservicescongress.com/home.cfm.

Zeithaml, V. A., & Bitner, M. J. M. J. (2000), *Services Marketing: Integrating Customer Focus across the Firms*. New York: McGraw-Hill.

This work was previously published in International Journal of Information Systems in the Service Sector (IJISSS), edited by John Wang, pp. 54-77, copyright 2009 by IGI Publishing (an imprint of IGI Global).

Chapter 5
The Grid as a Virtual Enterprise Enabler

Bill Vassiliadis
Hellenic Open University, Greece

ABSTRACT

Modern information systems are extending the traditional boundaries of organizations incorporating external recourses in the form of data and services. The need to support increasing client demands has led to dynamic and more complex business processes. Complex workflows in networked organizations are much more difficult to manage since traditional approaches are not suited for distributed environments. Service-Oriented approaches in the form of Web or Grid services bear the potential of increased performance and flexibility. In this work, we discuss the use of a relatively new computing paradigm that leverages distributed service-oriented business models: the Grid. We discuss how the Grid can facilitate efficient intra-business processes in highly dynamic virtual enterprises and present a high level architecture for managing complexity of business functions using Grid services.

INTRODUCTION

Future trends in Information Systems technology suggest that systems will be designed and driven by business and enterprise knowledge models supported by repeatable work processes and managed in open layered architectures. New business models favor the formation of dynamic alliances expanding the borders of the traditional enterprise to include resources (people, knowledge, processes) from other participants (Nilsson, 2005). In order to efficiently utilize networked business models, new paradigms that significantly increase connectivity, communication, coordination and collaboration must be adopted. Cooperation introduces communication in the form of information transfer between elements through data links (dataflow model) and method invocation (workflow model). Service-based operations will support the process enaction and automation inside and outside a company.

DOI: 10.4018/978-1-60960-138-6.ch005

Industrial R&D are in the business to develop new processes and services with an increasing use of computing power, the need to analyze large volumes of data, and a required synergy from geographically distributed groups. Company and site wise integration is an essential part behind the vision of sustainable enterprises. Grids can be employed to transform conventional manufacturing sites into virtual sites easy to manage, monitor, and understand. Grids can further support the development of novel products and services with means of visualization, better management of computer experiments, and decision support with the analysis and processing of data. The integration of industrial functions will take the form of virtual spaces for communication, management, and for designing computing environments that address complex industrial problems. Such problems account for industrial challenges in operations (scheduling, tactical and strategic planning, supply chain management and control), design (synthesis, integrated design, distributed computing experiments), and integrated workflow environments in R&D groups, operators and maintenance teams.

Grid Computing, or simply the Grid, is a new computing paradigm that enables access to distributed and heterogeneous computational resources (CPU cycles, storage, services, sensors, data) in a transparent, simple and on-demand way (Foster et al., 2001; Foster & Kesselman 2003). The basic vision of the Grid resembles that of the Electric Grid where resources (electric power) are offered to the users transparently, efficiently and cost effectively; the final goal is to enable the provision of computational resources as commodities. To enable this vision, several technologies have already been made available: coordination and virtualization of resources, management of heterogeneous resources, security, autonomy and others. Recent advances in Grid frameworks enable its application in many areas, especially e-science, enterprise computing, e-Commerce and e-learning. The use of Grid technology among large companies is not widespread, although several examples of efficient use are available: Wachovia is using Grid technology to speed up financial transaction processing (Wells, 2008), Shell Petroleum bases a part of its information workflow infrastructure on the Grid (Weidong et al., 2006) and Ford Motors performs fast 'what-if analysis' on Grid engine software.

Currently there is a lack of agreement among researchers on what a Grid really is (Stockinger, 2007). In the last few years, the Grid concept has borrowed some characteristics of the Service-Oriented model in order to be able to be applied to Business needs. The definition of Grid services that are actually extended web services is such a move. The Grid was supposed to have a profound impact on the way computing is used. Such a revolution did not take place since the success of this new technology relies not only on the definition of the appropriate technological standards but user acceptance as well. The latter depends on a combination of social, cultural, legal, ethical, organizational, political and economic parameters (Goyal & Lawande, 2007). However, the vision of using the Grid's Service-Oriented Architecture for the implementation of intra-enterprise communication has not died.

In this article the initial ideas presented in (Votis et al., 2004) are extended in order to present a Grid architecture for the implementation of large information systems that encompass several participants. We discuss how the Grid is emerging as a major enabler for networked organizations and relating technologies are used to support complex information systems. A three layered architecture is presented that uses workflow engines and Grid services to support the execution of complex business processes. A more holistic view of business infrastructures is supported where services are metadata enabled and ontologically principled. An Enterprise Resource Planning application is used to highlight in more detail the specific aspects of such a schema.

NETWORKED BUSINESS MODELS AND NEW COMPUTING PARADIGMS

The Virtual Enterprise

In recent years, the phenomenon of globalization has affected not only the economy but the way that enterprises are doing business as well. New business models for cooperation set forward by the recent advances in communications and computer networks have risen, like Virtual Enterprises, Extended Enterprises and Value Networks (Vanderhaeghen & Loos, 2007).

For most businesses, strategic partnerships have become central to competitive success in the fast changing global market. Since some of the knowledge and resources essential to an enterprise's prosperity may be located outside its boundaries, strategic partnerships are rather a necessity than an option especially in Supply Chain Management (Handy, 2000; Gunasekaran et al., 2008). Virtual Enterprises (VEs) are a special case of the Extended Enterprise (EE) business model: the organization's boundaries are shifted to include elements of other organizations, thus creating a "virtual organization" of much greater complexity. VE model aspects are under investigation and current research aims to gain a proper understanding of the complex environment within which this new model can reach the maximum of its efficiency.

Organizations involved in VE partnerships are held together because of perceived mutual benefit. VE partnerships such as supply chains provide flexibility and opportunities for innovation through a synergetic combination of previously separated resources, skills and knowledge. Although such business models respond to the great concern for adaptation to the fast changing market, there are several requirements to be fulfilled. Technical performance factors including reliability, safety and risk must be efficiently addressed since they have a direct impact on production costs and delays. The concept of "quicker, better and cheaper" is continuing to be a challenge in the first years of the third millennium and as a result, the VE business model must increase its reliability in order to assure a wider adoption.

VEs, are designed to overcome time-and-place constraints associated with rigid bureaucratic structuring and can be distinguished from existing organizations because they are based on a different design philosophy with regard to how, where and when work is done. Thus, workflow management remains an essential factor. In a VE, the problem of sequencing processes goes beyond the technical risks linked to the product development itself, but also the managerial risks expressed in terms of development delays and development and recurring costs. Resource optimization, sharing of infrastructure, market knowledge and R&D effort between partners, is a key strategic goal in order to manage processes in such a distributed environment. This requires the definition of reference architecture, information management, security prioritization and supporting tools for managing shared information originating from different sites. The concepts of dynamic networked organizations and VEs address these needs. A VE actually consists of partners acting as nodes in a network, connected via a high speed network VE infrastructure, sharing knowledge of processes, resources and business tasks.

Sequencing and coordination of business processes in distributed environment is difficult. Recent studies on the application of workflow management in VEs have showed promising results. Canavesio & Martinez (2007) present a conceptual model for SMEs organized in a virtual network to facilitate production. Chen (2008) uses ontology-driven mechanisms to enable knowledge sharing between organizations. Liu et al. (2005) present a workflow support system for supply chain management. Prodan et al. (2005) and Cavalcanti et al. (2005) discuss the experience of using the Grid for scientific workflow management. New trends in the field also include agent-based workflow enactment (Buhler et al., 2005; Yu et al., 2005) and web service standards such as BPEL (Fisteus et al., 2005). They all rely on Service-oriented architectures. The work of Yang et al. (2005) is one of the few efforts that focuses especially on the design of a workflow management system (WFMS) based on Grid services. Although the conceptual business model of networked schemes have been described, only recently appropriate technological solutions have appeared to overcome problems posed by distributed processes, security, heterogeneity and dynamic nature.

Grid Technology Revisited

The Grid started as a concept rather than a technology. Initially designed to support the processing of large e-Science data sets using heterogeneous computer sources, it was later promoted as promising technology for disciplines including Business, Economics and Life Sciences (Berman et al., 2003).

Grid technology relies on the dynamic coordination of highly distributed, heterogeneous resources (computer, storage, services) in order to support large scale computing and data management. Computation jobs can be distributed across several nodes in a Grid and executed in parallel, resulting in shorter execution times. The benefits of Grid computing extend to the provision of resource virtualization already supported by developing standards of the Open Grid Services Architecture (OGSA) (OGSA, 2008). The use of such models can shift the boundary of traditional networked models out to dynamically include/exclude elements of other organizations, thus increasing management and economical complexity. The use of Grid services permits the direct or indirect participation of enterprises in large vendor networks, which constitute very large dynamic systems. In this context, services are viewed as Grid- services that allow, amongst others, dynamic service instantiation and interaction, lifetime management and handling of complex activity requests from clients (Foster et al., 2001).

The Grid has already been proposed for supporting very large data processing tasks, efficient use of idle resources, and lately as a VE enabler. In this model, Grid technology is used for coordination, sharing and reuse of services, knowledge and data across the geographically dispersed nodes of the VE. VE nodes are mapped onto the physical Grid nodes (computers or clusters of computers) and predefined workflows are used for service execution and data management; the physical geographic distribution of an enterprises and its departments and/or partners (organizational level) is mapped to corresponding nodes of a VE (VE level) and then to the Grid (Grid level). The next generation of Grid solutions will increasingly adopt the service-oriented model for exploiting commodity technologies. Its goal is to enable, as well as facilitate the transformation of Information into Knowledge, by humans as well as – progressively – by software agents, providing the electronic underpinning for a global society in business, government, research, science, education and entertainment. The most important benefit of this technology is its ability to meet major bursts of CPU demand using existing resources. By decoupling the services from the underlying h/w, resources are automatically allocated/de-allocated as loads are increased / decreased (Foster & Tuecke, 2005). This increases Return On Investment (ROI) on h/w since idle computers are used instead of buying new ones.

From a VE point of view and in contradiction to Grid technology, traditional technologies such as virtual private networks (VPNs) and Intranets/Extranets based on HTTP provide just an infrastructure for their basic functionality. VEs need to be more dynamic, agile and able to extend automatically. The Grid reflects this philosophy by enabling on demand services, a step towards utility computing. A number of projects have proposed the use of Grid resources as computation utility include Globus (Foster et. al, 2002), NetSolve (Arnold et al., 2003) and Cactus (Allen et al., 2001).

In order to efficiently leverage a service oriented architecture for a VE, the concept of Grid services is available. The vision of integrating Grid and Web service concepts and technologies has been proposed as the WSRF. With efforts in OGSA implementation and standardization, application services are expected to be widely deployed and achieve higher interoperability (Foster et al., 2001). Conceptually, the Grid can be thought of in terms of three layers where different kinds of services are offered: the computational/data Grid, the information Grid and the knowledge Grid (figure 1).

Underlying everything is the computational and data grid: the computer hardware and data networks upon which the work will be conducted. Above this is the 'information grid': the databases of information to be accessed by the hardware, and systems for data manipulation. On top is the 'knowledge grid', where high-level applications mine the data for the knowledge that can form the basis of semantic understanding and intelligent decision making.

A data/computational grid forms the fabric of the Grid to provide raw computing power, high-speed bandwidth and associated data storage in a secure and auditable way. Diverse resources are represented as a single computer so the way that computational resources are allocated, scheduled and executed and the way that data is shipped between processing resources, is handled there.

A knowledge Grid using knowledge based methodologies and technologies for responding to high-level questions and finding the appropriate processes to deliver answers in the required form. This last layer may include data mining, machine learning, simulations, ontologies, intelligent portals, workflow reasoning and problem solving environments for supporting the way knowledge is acquired, used, retrieved, published and maintained. A knowledge Grid should provide intelligent guidance for decision makers and hypothesis generation.

Workflow in the Knowledge Grid may be supported through meta-models. Meta-models are object-type definitions that describe a view, a domain, a situation, content, a tool/method or a solution. The meta-model is the logical language of the situation or any of its aspects as mentioned. In the industry most users talk about descriptive knowledge rather than meta-knowledge, e.g. instructions of how to perform certain tasks. For computing systems to handle descriptive knowledge (how, why, what, where, when and who) the latter must be separated from the operational values as meta-models.

Figure 1. Three layered Grid abstraction (adapted from Chen-Burger, 2003)

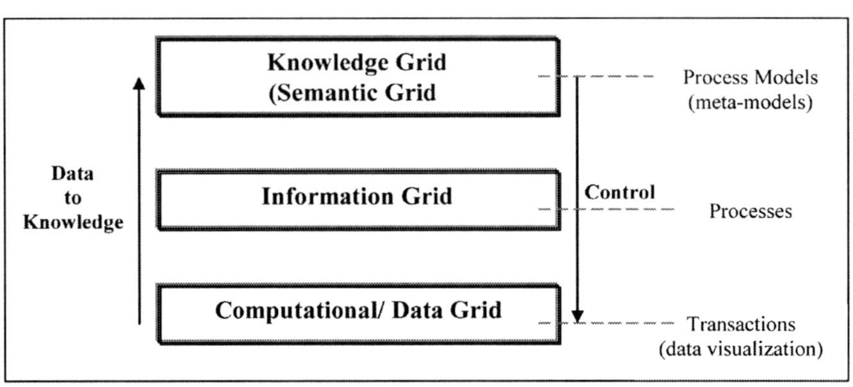

DISTRIBUTED BUSINESS MODELS

We envisage two distinct business models for the VE network configuration: the client-server and the point to point.

In the first model (depicted in figure 2), an enterprise extends its networks in order to include suppliers, customers and contractors to perform one or more operations. This creates a virtual network where the enterprise plays the major role and the other participants contribute. In order for this configuration to work efficiently, both the enterprise and the participants need to share information and resources. The name "client-server" does not refer to the technology per se but rather denotes a single enterprise is in the lead, and other enterprises contribute.

The 'point-to-point' model is highly distributable and more temporal in nature. Numerous enterprises cooperate (on equal terms more or less) to perform a function or functions. This kind of dynamic collaboration may end when the function is complete and take another form in the future, depending on business needs. Information and resources are shared without a specific central control, although in business terms an organization should be in charge of the function being performed. This business model resembles the Peer-to-Peer (P2P) computing model, a relatively new, highly distributed computing paradigm that enables sharing of resources and services through direct communication between peers. Extending the traditional model where most computers on a network act as clients, P2P introduces the concept of the simultaneous client/server mode: peers act both as clients and as servers. This form of collaborative networking is based on dynamic and failure-tolerant architectures. The characteristic of P2P is that a node does not necessarily has knowledge of the information of a neighbor node. Similarly, in the point-to-point business model, an enterprise shares only specific resources to other, specific nodes, not necessarily to all the others nodes that constitute this temporal VE. The difference with the 'client-server' model is that in the first, the leading enterprise shares much more resources and information to its peers. The latter is more tight in terms of sharing. Furthermore, nodes may cooperate with each other to perform a subset of an opera-

Figure 2. The 'client-server' model

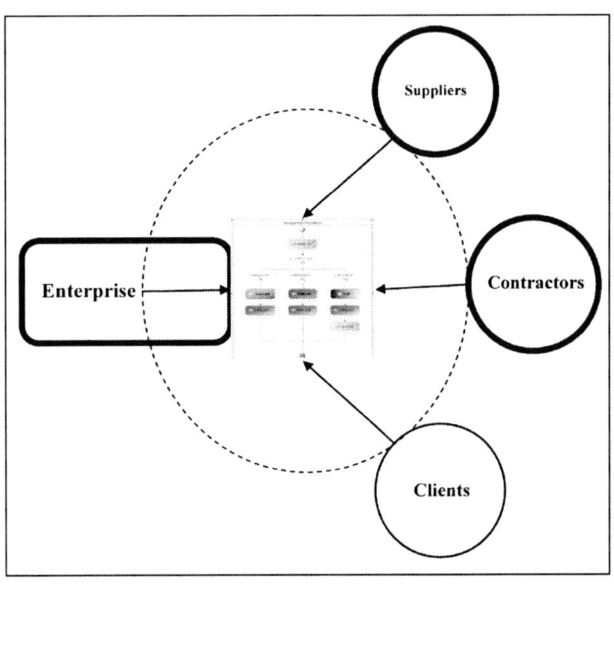

Figure 3. The 'point-to-point' model

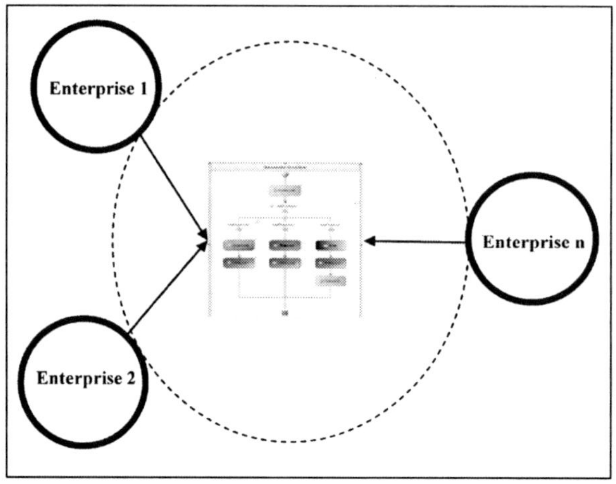

tion without any central supervision. This model can be mainly used by small and medium size companies. The 'point-to point' model is depicted in figure 3.

So, since business processes may encompass external partners either in an equal partnership or a contractor partnership, the information systems must support such operations. Let us consider a demanding application such as the Enterprise Resource Planning (ERP) system. A possible scenario that adheres to the 'client-server' model includes a large company that needs to include in its ERP system divisions of its subcontractors. In this case the EPR must be expanded to include these divisions. In another scenario that follows the 'point-to-point' model, an enterprise makes available ERP services to customers, that is smaller companies that do not have the capability to own an ERP solution. In the following sections the case of conventional use of an ERP system usage is examined in the light of these two scenarios and a new, high level architecture is proposed for their more efficient implementation.

Figure 4. Main ERP components

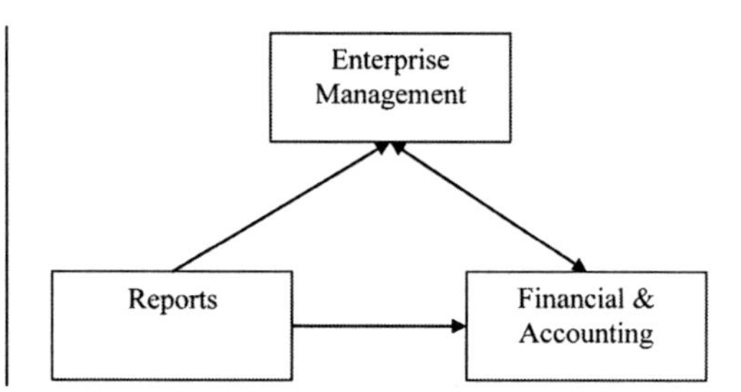

A CONVENTIONAL ERP SOLUTION

ERP systems are complex information systems that constitute a complete enterprise-wide business solution. They integrate all departments and functions of a company into a single information system. (Lee et al., 2003). An ERP system may consist of several software modules, one for each business areas such as marketing and sales, field service, product design and development, production and inventory control, procurement, distribution, industrial facilities management, process design and development, manufacturing, quality, human resources, finance and accounting, and information services.

The main set of services that can be provided by an ERP solution within distributed enterprises can be, however, identified in the following three main sectors (figure 4): Enterprise Management, Financial & Accounting and Reporting.

Figure 5. Business processes affecting various applications and processes within (light grey area) and outside an organization

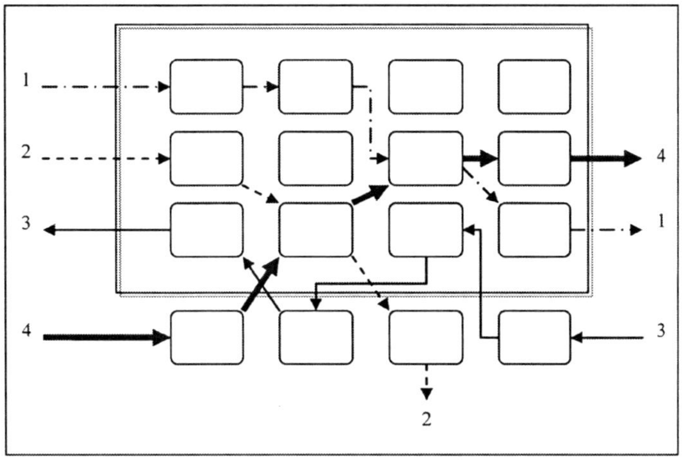

The aforementioned core components of the ERP constitute the minimum set of services for such a system. This is a typical example, in which an organization tries to optimize the complete set of activities – such as order entry, purchasing, production, and shipment – in order to minimize the lead time and costs for production, and at the same time maximize value for the customer. Figure 5 shows four business processes, each spanning a number of applications or sub processes. The grey area depicts the organization in question. Rectangles depict applications or sub processes. Process no. 1 takes place completely inside the organization. Process no. 2 starts inside and finishes outside. Process no. 3 starts outside and finishes inside. Process no. 4 leaves the organization at one point, but comes back before finishing, such as may be the case if a separate company takes care of delivery before the original company checks that the invoice has finally been paid. In the course of the process, queries and one-way messages are sent; answers and one-way messages are received, and timers are set and run out.

An overview of a simplified and reduced version of the ordering business process that needs to be executed when a new order is applied can be seen in the example depicted in figure 6. Upon the reception of an order by the sales department, an enterprise internal request is forwarded to the warehouse department. There, the availability of the ordered items is checked. If the stock in the warehouse cannot satisfy the order, the enterprise manufacturing chain needs to be activated. It is also mandatory to have an estimation of the availability of the resources involved in the manufac-

Figure 6. Order business processing

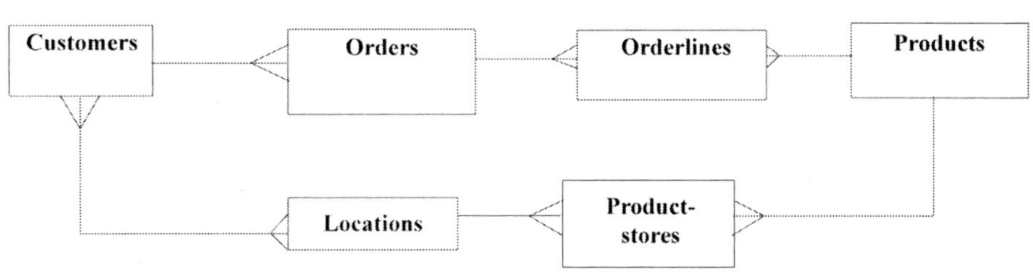

Figure 7. Provisioning of ERP tools through a web portal in a one-to-many model

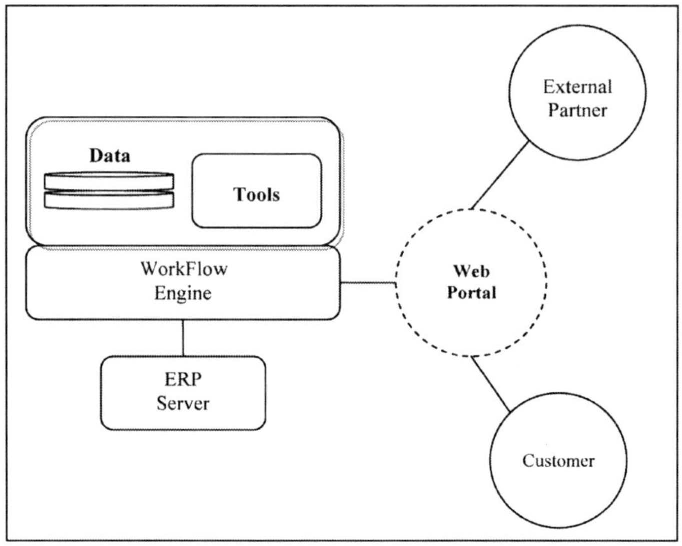

turing process before the manufacturing chain is activated.

In the traditional one-to-many ERP model, clients, partners and suppliers interact with a single provider (figure 7). Additional financial, data and content service provision is required in special cases.

This paradigm permits the integration and collaboration of provider and user resources using workflow engines that coordinate simple business processes. In this context, application intercommunication is necessary to carry out complex business workflows and reduce the overall load of the system. In order to execute businesses workflows, applications must be able to exchange data according to predetermined workflow rules. This is a challenge since many interoperability issues need to be solved. Repositories or services located in different sites (internal departments of the ERP provider or external partners) may have different configurations. Although certain interfaces between resources do exist, the need for supporting dynamic service provision requires flexible coordination of data and tasks. To solve this challenge, different approaches are possible. The first possible approach is to assume that all vendors' applications provide methods to exchange standardized business objects and are therefore able to exchange these objects directly. Another approach is to program all application interfaces according to customer requirements, a method which is often used by many ERP vendors.

GRID-ENABLED ERP AND VISUALIZATION OF THE SUPPLY CHAIN COMPONENTS

A High Level Architecture

The high cost of development and ownership has excluded industry-specific ERP products from the small and medium enterprise marketplace. The ERP software is expensive because the business logic is tightly linked to the user interface. This means that even relatively small changes, such as changing the terms presented on the screen to match those used in a particular industry, requires significant effort. The solution to this problem may lay in the adoption of new application architectures that separate the core functionality from the user interface. The basic principle of this architecture is that ERP applications as well as Customer Relationship Management (CRM) applications are for the most part transaction-based. The new approach involves the separation of transaction functionality or business logic from the presentation logic. This segregation is achieved by migrating business logic into database-stored procedures, triggers and views and using an engine to store the presentation logic consisting of rules, layouts and screens in the database as metadata. This configuration closely resamples Web service and Grid service functionality.

We propose a new VE high level architectural approach for scenario 1 that could also be used in a more distributed situation such as scenario 2. Different departments or geographically dispersed divisions of a company along with external partners comprise the nodes of a VE. Resources used by the ERP (including ERP servers, databases and services) are assigned to corresponding Grid nodes. Grid workflow engines are then responsible for handling coordination, security and unified access to heterogeneous resources. Complex queries are possible: for example the request for data mining from a client to the ERP system (reporting) triggers multiple data mining tasks to distributed, heterogeneous information repositories that may be internal or externally located.

External nodes use the Grid in order to rent services not available to them due to development costs. This configuration makes use of an earlier business idea, the one of renting software through networks to companies, the so called Application Service Providers (ASP). Although the concept "ASP" is not used anymore, terms such as Cloud Computing or Software as a Service use some of its core ideas. In the proposed configuration, the clients are small business and the provider a large company (or a coalition of large companies) that rent expensive software services. In order to facilitate a flexible and secure environment where dynamic requests for distributed resources take place, the Grid could be an approach worthwhile to investigate. Similar approaches have already been proposed by research projects like GRASP (GRASP, 2008).

Figure 8 illustrates the VE approach for a VEs ERP': components of the proposed solution are based on existing applications, traditional models and technologies in order to make them Grid-aware. In this general view, the main focus of the proposed solution in the ERP management domain is focused on assessing how workflow creation and management services can assist in handling different and complex business management tasks.

This involves task coordination on multiple set of distributed servers, different ERP components, different customization to suit different markets, different scheduling and optimization technologies, etc., in order to satisfy the numerous requests by the Clients/Users.

Overall, this is an integration architecture, bringing together multiple systems that require complex interactions. The current configuration is not a coherent architecture, but an integration of different standalone systems supported by Grid services.

Description of the Architecture

The abstract architecture is comprised of the following three layers:

First layer (data layer) - Data stores, which contains the data repositories such as relational databases, directories and files. These repositories include information stores that are used by ERP and other distributed enterprise applications. An enterprise stores lots of its vital information in databases – often there are many databases, each serving a single application. There is a need to effectively create views of all the relevant data for a given scenario – data stored (hidden) in databases are often very hard to visualize (get an overview of). The principle for visualizing the data is to use a mapping table that describes how to map the data in the database to the meta-model used by modeling tools.

Figure 8. Three layer abstract architecture and mapping to GRID layers

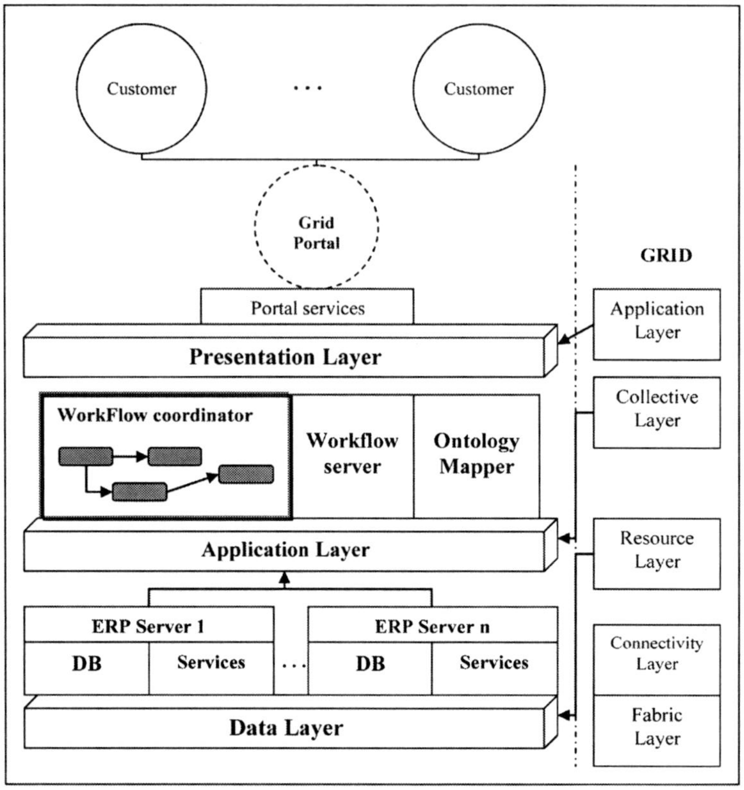

An information Grid provides homogeneous access to heterogeneous distributed information by dealing with the way that all forms of information are represented, stored, accessed, shared and maintained. This layer orchestrates data and applications to satisfy the request, including toolkits for composing workflows, accessing metadata, visualization, data management and instrumentation management. The web and other well-known and current middleware technologies are incorporated into one framework.

Second layer (middleware) –a workflow coordinator which manages the internal processes (workflow composition) between the different organizations (different ERP sites). This workflow coordinator comprises a workflow management system and also an Agent Engine that handles all the requests produced by the users of the Presentation Layer and forwards them to the modules interested. Each request is forwarded to the corresponding server while users are notified by a subscription service. Hence, users are notified when a particular event of interest occurs. Events can be produced by users' actions or automatically by the system when an activity or process state is modified.

The workflow coordinator service can be utilized as a server application that performs workflow management of work processes and project activities. The actual work management is based on a process definition as the representation of a business process in a form that supports automated manipulations, such as modeling, or enactment by a workflow management system. The process definition consists of a network of activities and their relationships, criteria to indicate the start and termination of the process, and information about the individual activities, such as participants, associated IT applications and data.

Workflow management is performed through the concept of work-lists. A work-list consists of a set of tasks to be performed with priorities, due dates etc. A task represents a piece of work that needs to be done. The task may be of different kinds – on the one end there are tasks that must follow a strict procedure and needs process support to carry out the task. On the other end, there are tasks that cannot be given any process support because of their nature as unstructured or emergent. Nevertheless, an overview of the context and the resources that may be relevant to the task may be supported.

Ontology Mapper - In order to cope with the heterogeneity of information (both in type and descriptions) that is stored in the various nodes of the VE (actually, the distributed ERP servers) an ontology mapper is used to facilitate workflow and searching tasks. These tasks are carried out in the metadata level, where information concerning information is published, managed and stored in the form of a scalable description of knowledge domains. A three layer semantic description of content is used: the Upper Search Ontology layer, describes the basic concepts of the domains of knowledge of the content, a set of Domain Description Ontology layer that represent a more detailed description of each domain and the Semantic Metadata layer where the different semantic description of the heterogeneous ERP servers lay. This scheme may include additional mapping information between the ontologies in the three layers providing the necessary information to search engines in order to navigate inside the ontology-based index. Also, the model utilizes a lexical ontology that comprises a set of lexical and notational synonyms reinforcing the searching among the various ontology instances of content representation.

Third-layer (presentation layer) - A front End Grid Portal, could be utilized as a java based customized portal for accessing services based on user needs, roles and permissions. It enables the virtual view of the data for knowledge navigation. A key concept behind this approach is the virtualization that making disparate resources appear and function as a single entity.

Grid vs. Web Services

The architecture presented in the previous section uses Grid Services (GS) instead of Web Services (WS). But where is the difference between the two. According to the definition given in OGSA (Open Grid Services Architecture), "a Grid service is a Web service that is designed to operate in a Grid environment, and meets the requirements of the Grid(s) in which it participates" (OGSA, 2006). So a GS is actually an extended WS and Grids are currently employing a service-oriented architecture described as OGSA-Web Service Resource Framework, which has actually replaced the older OGSI (OGSA-WSRF, 2006).

There are two main differences between the two kinds of services: Web services are stateless and non-transient while Grid Services are not. When a Web service is invoked, data from its previous execution are lost. In order to solve this problem in a sequence of invocations, where a web services calls other web services, intermediate data must be passed on as input parameters from one service to another. The use of Web Service containers to solve this problem creates a new one, the problem of keeping client data even when the client has stopped using the service. This means that there is a possibility that a new client of the service may access or alter another client's data. Grid services use factories as interfaces with the clients. Instances of a service instead of the service itself are invoked by the clients. This is actually a stateless implementation of a web service with the use of a stateful interface to resource (the factory). This "object-oriented" approach is suitable for business applications since there are increased security concerns and an equally increased need for individual nodes to access and manage remote resources.

CONCLUSION

The advent of networked business models has given rise to virtual enterprises, organizations comprised of geographically dispersed divisions and partners. In such situations, workflow management complexity has increased since processes use heterogeneous and dispersed resources. This situation entails the expansion of traditional workflow management practices, by taking into account the advantages of new computing paradigms such as the Grid and Service Oriented Computing.

In this article we discussed the importance of workflow processing for enabling networked business models. We proposed a mapping procedure that corresponds the different divisions of a coalition of distributed enterprises to VE nodes and then to the Grid. A high level architecture for enabling efficient workflow of a complex information system (namely an ERP) was presented. We argued that federated vendors may behave as virtual enterprises raising issues such as interoperability, distributed resource management and quality of service using Grid services.

Currently the Grid is being deployed mainly in research institutions but as technology matures the business sector can also benefit. As the Grid technology model evolves new service models that enable access of resources on-demand are proposed. Utility Computing is a service and not a leasing of infrastructure and/or applications and uses a pay-as-you- use policy. In order for such models to be operational, further specification of how the workflow model itself is affected by the use of Grid architecture is necessary.

REFERENCES

Allen, G., Dramlitsch, T., Foster, I., Karonis, N., Ripeanu, M., Seidel, E., and Toonen, B. (2001). Supporting Efficient Execution in Heterogeneous Distributed Computing Environments with Cactus and Globus. Supercomputing 2001.

Arnold, D., Casanova, H., and Dongarra, J. (2003). Innovation of the NetSolve Grid Computing System. Concurrency and Computation: Practice and Experience.

Berman, F., Fox, C. G., & Hey, A. (2003). *Grid Computing: Making the global infrastructure a reality*. Wiley Press.

Buhler, P. A., & Vidal, J. M. (2005). Towards Adaptive Workflow Enactment Using Multiagent Systems. *Information Technology Management*, *6*(1), 61–87. doi:10.1007/s10799-004-7775-2

Canavesio, M., & Martinez, E. (2007). Enterprise modeling of a project-oriented fractal company for SMEs networking. *Computers in Industry*, *58*(8-9), 794–813. doi:10.1016/j.compind.2007.02.005

Cavalcanti, M. C., Targino, R., Baião, F., Rössle, S. C., Bisch, P. M., & Pires, P. F. (2005). Managing structural genomic workflows using Web services. *Data & Knowledge Engineering*, *53*(1), 45–74. doi:10.1016/S0169-023X(04)00112-0

Chen, T. Y. (2008). Knowledge sharing in virtual enterprises via an ontology-based access control approach. *Computers in Industry*, *59*(5), 502–519. doi:10.1016/j.compind.2007.12.004

Chen-Burger, Y. H. (2003). A Semantic Based Workflow Management in a Virtual Organization. E-Science Workflow Workshop.

Fisteus, J. A., Fernández, L. S., & Kloos, C. D. (2005). Applying model checking to BPEL4WS business collaborations. ACM Symposium on Applied computing, 826- 830.

Foster, I., & Kesselman, C. (2003). *Grid 2: Blueprint for a New Computing Infrastructure*. The Elsevier Series in Grid Computing.

Foster, I., Kesselman, C., Nick, J., & Tuecke, S. (2002). The Physiology of the Grid: An Open Grid Services Architecture for Distributed Systems Integration. Open Grid Service Infrastructure WG, Global Grid Forum, [on line] http://www.ggf.org/

Foster, I., Kesselman, C., & Tuecke, S. (2001). The Anatomy of the Grid: Enabling Scalable Virtual Organizations. *International Journal of High Performance Computing Applications*, *15*(3), 200–222. doi:10.1177/109434200101500302

Foster, I., & Tuecke, S. (2005). The different faces of IT as a Service. *ACM Queue; Tomorrow's Computing Today*, *3*(6), 27–34.

Goyal, B., & Lawande, S. (2007). *Grid Revolution: An Introduction to Enterprise Grid Computing*. McGraw-Hill.

GRASP. (2008). Grid Application Service Provision Project Web Site. [on line] www.eu-grasp.net.

Gunasekaran, A., Lai, K., & Cheng, T. C. (2008). Responsive supply chain: A competitive strategy in a networked economy. *The International Journal of Management Science*, *36*(4), 549–564.

Handy, C. (2000). *Understanding Organizations*. Penguin.

Lee, J., Siau, K., & Hong, S. (2003). Enterprise integration with ERP and EAI. *Communications of the ACM*, *46*(2), 54–60. doi:10.1145/606272.606273

Liu, J., Zhang, S., & Hu, J. (2005). A case study of an inter-enterprise workflow-supported supply chain management system. *Information & Management*, *42*(3), 441–454. doi:10.1016/j.im.2004.01.010

Nilsson, A. G. (2005). Information Systems Development (ISD): Past, Present, Future. Information Systems Development: Advances in Theory, Practice and Education Edited by O. Vasilecas et al., Springer, 29-40. Open Grid Services Architecture (OGSA), [on line] http://www.ggf.org/ogsa-wg/

Open Grid Services Architecture (OGSA) Glossary of Terms v. 1.5 (2006). [on line] http://www.ogf.org/documents/GFD.81.pdf

Open Grid Services Architecture Web Services Reference Framework (OGSA WSRF). (2006) [on line] http://www.ogf.org/documents/GFD.72.pdf

Stockinger, H. (2007). Defining the grid: a snapshot on the current view. *The Journal of Supercomputing*, *42*, 3–17. doi:10.1007/s11227-006-0037-9

Vanderhaeghen, D., & Loos, P. (2007). Distributed model management platform for cross-enterprise business process management in virtual enterprise networks. *Journal of Intelligent Manufacturing*, *18*, 553–559. doi:10.1007/s10845-007-0060-6

Votis, K., Vassiliadis, B., Alexakos, Ch., Likothanassis, S., & Tsakalidis, A. (2004). Workflow Coordination in Grid Networks for Supporting Enterprise-wide Business Solutions. IADIS International Conference on E-Commerce, 253-260.

Weidong, L., Gaishan, Z., Hailiang, W., Xianghui, X., Yujing, W., Huiqing, Z., (2006). Application of Grid Computing in Petroleum Exploration. Grid and Cooperative Computing Workshops, 27 – 34.

Wells, A. J. (2008). *Grid Application System Design*. CRC Press.

Yang, M., Liang, H., & Xu, B. (2005). S-WFMS: A Service-Based Workflow Management System in Grid Environment. 19th International Conference on Advanced Information Networking and Applications, 293 – 297.

Yu, H., Bai, X., & Marinescu, D. C. (2005). Workflow management and resource discovery for an intelligent grid. *Parallel Computing*, *31*(7), 797–811. doi:10.1016/j.parco.2005.04.009

This work was previously published in International Journal of Information Systems in the Service Sector (IJISSS), edited by John Wang, pp. 78-92, copyright 2009 by IGI Publishing (an imprint of IGI Global).

Chapter 6
A Value-Satisfaction Taxonomy of IS Effectiveness (VSTISE):
A Case Study of User Satisfaction with IS and User-Perceived Value of IS

Yair Levy
Nova Southeastern University, USA

Kenneth E. Murphy
Willamette University, USA

Stelios H. Zanakis
Florida International University, USA

ABSTRACT

Information Systems (IS) effectiveness has been studied over the past three decades, with user satisfaction utilized as a key measure. However, very little attention has been given to the role of user-perceived cognitive value of IS in measuring the effectiveness of such systems. Therefore, this article defines and articulates user-perceived value of IS as an important construct for IS research, not from the financial or 'net benefit' perspective to the organization, rather from the cognitive perspective. Following literature review, a new taxonomy of IS effectiveness, Value-Satisfaction Taxonomy of IS Effectiveness (VSTISE), is presented. The VSTISE posits four quadrants to indicate level of user-perceived IS effectiveness: improvement, effective, misleading, and ineffective. A case study using the proposed VSTISE is discussed. Results based on the 192 responses identify several problematic system characteristics that warrant additional investigation for their limited IS effectiveness. Finally, recommendations for research and practice are provided.

INTRODUCTION

Nearly three decades scholars have suggested that effectiveness of Information Systems (IS) is "an important phenomenon for researchers and practitioners" (Scott, 1995, p. 43). Simultaneously, numerous scholars have noted the challenges for IS research in measuring IS effectiveness (Arnold, 1995; DeLone & McLean, 1992; Doll & Torkzadeh, 1988; Grover, Seung, & Segars,

DOI: 10.4018/978-1-60960-138-6.ch006

1996; Ives, Olson, & Baroudi, 1983; Kim, 1989; Stone, 1990; Yuthas & Eining, 1995). Grover et al. suggested that IS effectiveness depends on the unit of analysis, i.e., individual or organizational perspective. Although the organizational perspective is valid and critical, the focus of this article is on the individual (i.e., the user) perspective. There has been extensive investigation in the past three decades to assess IS effectiveness using *user satisfaction* as a surrogate measure (Bailey & Pearson, 1983; Baroudi & Orlikowski, 1988; Doll & Torkzadeh, 1988; 1991; 1994; Galletta & Lederer, 1989; Gelderman, 1998; Ives et al., 1983; Kettinger & Lee, 1994; Lee, Kim, & Lee, 1995; Torkzadeh & Doll, 1991). However, some IS scholars have voiced a concern about measures of user satisfaction with IS that do not take into account the "silent beliefs" of IS users (Etezadi-Amoli & Farhoomand, 1991, p. 1). Additionally, marketing scholars such as Chiou (2004) as well as Yang and Peterson (2004) also indicated the limitations of user satisfaction as a sole measure of effectiveness of customer loyalty. Chiou (2004) indicated that "more than half of the satisfied customers will defect eventually" (p. 686). According to Yang and Peterson (2004), "high value is one primary motivation for customer patronage" (p. 803). Moreover, IS scholars have noted that IS effectiveness is a multidimensional construct, and yet have used only user satisfaction as a surrogate predictor of that construct. Additionally, the significance of user-perceived value as a cognitive construct affecting human attitudes (and in turn affecting the construct of satisfaction) has been recognized by numerous scholars in a broad variety of fields (Rafaeli & Raban, 2003). Nevertheless, very little attention has been given in IS research to antecedent constructs such as the user's personal beliefs or perceived value. In this article, we attempt to fill this void by defining, articulating, and suggesting a specific measure, the *user-perceived value* construct. Moreover, we attempt to contribute to IS literature by providing the theoretical foundations to stimulate future research to use the perceived value construct in other models. We propose a new taxonomy of IS effectiveness that can be used as a benchmarking tool by practitioners and IS decision makers, especially in the service sector.

The majority of the work conducted in IS literature about the *value* construct has dealt with the economical or financial perspective of value (i.e., net benefit, return on investment, etc.; see (DeLone & McLean, 1992; 2003; Gefen & Ragowsky, 2005; Ragowsky, 1995; Ragowsky, Somers, & Adams, 2005; Ragowsky, Stern, & Adams, 2000)) as a dependent variable in IS models. The approach we advocate is to incorporate the user-perceived cognitive value construct as another variable in the measure of IS effectiveness. We define *user-perceived value* as a belief about the level of importance that users hold for IS characteristics. Figure 1 illustrates the conceptual model we propose. Interestingly enough, it was originally recognized in the IS literature that *user-perceived value* is relevant in understanding *user satisfaction* and *user-perceived IS effectiveness* with respect to a system's characteristics (Bailey & Pearson, 1983). However, much of the subsequent work on evaluating levels of user satisfaction concentrated primarily on attitudes towards IS (Doll & Torkzadeh, 1988; 1991; Ives et al., 1983; Torkzadeh & Doll, 1991). In part, this is because some scholars found that measuring user-perceived value (i.e., user-perceived importance level of system characteristics) provides very little additional information to the overall understanding of user satisfaction (Ives et al., 1983). However, some disagreement exists in the literature about such an approach, as measurement of user-perceived value can lead to a deeper understanding of the user-perceived IS effectiveness (Etezadi-Amoli & Farhoomand, 1991). Therefore, our primary objective in this article is to bring the attention of IS researchers to a new construct in the measurement of IS effectiveness. We present

Figure 1. Conceptual model of perceived value, satisfaction, and IS effectiveness

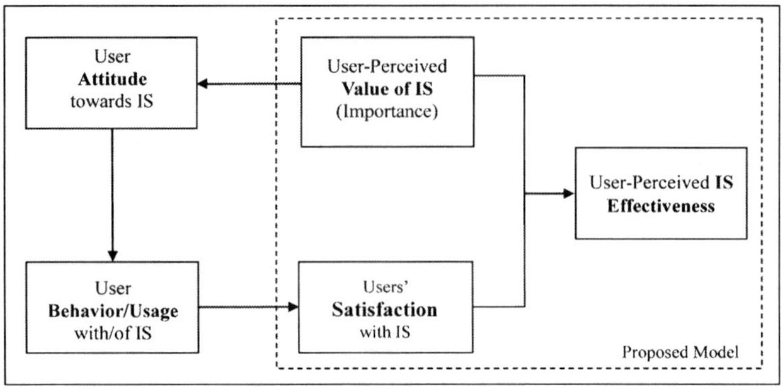

user-perceived value along with the previously used user satisfaction construct as measures to construct a new taxonomy of IS effectiveness from the user's cognitive perspective.

The organization of this article is as follows. Section II provides the theoretical background that serves as the foundation for this work. The section includes a review of the literature from the IS field on user satisfaction. The discussion provides a review of the IS measures developed and validated over the past three decades to measure user satisfaction with IS. Due to the nature of the review, we will attempt to present instrument development and maturation of constructs based on chronological order. This is followed by a similar review related to the construct of IS effectiveness. Additionally, a review of value theory from cognitive psychology and other fields is provided with an emphasis on the user as the unit of analysis. In section III, we propose a new taxonomy for IS effectiveness based on the combined measures of user satisfaction and user-perceived value of IS. A case study where the proposed new taxonomy was used is outlined in section IV. Finally, in section V, we offer discussion to articulate the implications of the user-perceived value construct for future IS research, and we offer IS decision makers and practitioners recommendations on using our new taxonomy as a benchmarking tool for IS effectiveness.

THEORETICAL BACKGROUND

User Satisfaction with IS

User satisfaction with IS has been dominating IS research for almost three decades as a central measure for IS effectiveness (DeLone & McLean, 1992; Ives et al., 1983; Kim, 1989). Extensive research in developing measures for user satisfaction with IS has evolved over time and researchers have debated definitions and validity of associated instruments (see e.g., Bailey & Pearson, 1983; Doll & Torkzadeh, 1988; Ives et al.). Early IS research in generating user satisfaction measures included Jenkins and Ricketts (1979) who examined user satisfaction with IS output reports. Bailey and Pearson were among the first IS scholars to successfully validate a widely accepted instrument to evaluate user satisfaction with IS. They provided a foundation for two major streams of research in a quest to develop sound measures of user satisfaction: user information satisfaction (Ives et al., 1983) and end-user computing satisfaction (Doll & Torkzadeh, 1988). Bailey and Pearson defined the overall measure of *user satisfaction* as the sum of the user's weighted reactions to a set of characteristics describing the IS. Bailey and Pearson's estimation of the overall user satisfaction with IS was a weighted average of the answers to a set of adjectives, while the level of importance of each characteristic was used as the weight in the estimation. Although the definition and validation of the associated instrument to measure user satisfaction was a clear contribution to the IS field, their survey with over 200 items was time consuming for users to complete. Ives et al. coined the term *user information satisfaction* (UIS) as "the extent to which users believe that the information system available to them meets their information requirements" (p. 785). They set out to improve internal consistency, reliability, and ease of administration of Bailey and Pearson's instrument. To accomplish this, they eliminated characteristics with the lowest correlations to the overall user satisfaction measure. They also eliminated the measures of importance. The latter was done for expediency, in part based on their observation that importance-weighted satisfaction and unweighted satisfaction scores were highly correlated in their study's data, making the importance items unnecessary.

Several scholars sought to reaffirm the reliability and validity of the UIS instrument of Ives et al. (1983), including Baroudi and Orlikowski (1988), who used the instrument in their survey of 358 IS users. Their results reaffirmed construct and convergent validity as well as reliability of the UIS instrument. Following Ives et al., Baroudi and Orlikowski's study also did not include any measure of the user-perceived importance (i.e., perceived value) for each characteristic. Galletta and Lederer (1989) questioned the usefulness and reliability of the 13-item instrument of Ives et al. at both the theoretical and measurement levels. They observed that when creating the UIS Ives et al. had removed potential items of interest like "confidence in systems" and "timeliness of information" as well as other items. They questioned estimating overall user satisfaction with IS by adding up heterogeneous items from broadly different IS characteristics (e.g., product and support) and with differences in scale, because even though the UIS analysis had resulted in validated reliability tests, the basic assumptions of those tests were not met (Galletta & Lederer, 1989). Kettinger and Lee (1994) noted that much of the previous work focused mostly on large centralized transaction systems, and because of changes in the nature of IS during the 1980s and 1990s, the IS as a service function had been overlooked. Galletta and Lederer used the results of Baroudi and Orlikowski and the prior research in service quality (SERVQUAL) by Parasuraman, Zeithaml, and Berry (1988) to revise the UIS. They surveyed 342 IS users at a major university by combining the UIS instrument and SERVQUAL. Their results indicate that IS service reliability and IS service empathy contribute to enhancing the prediction of user satisfaction with IS.

In response to the growth of end-user computing (Ahituv, Munro, & Wand, 1981; Benson, 1982), Doll and Torkzadeh (1988) created an instrument to measure the satisfaction of those users who deal directly with information systems or specific computer applications. They defined end-user computing satisfaction (EUCS) as "the affective attitude towards a specific computer application by someone who interacts with the application directly" (Doll & Torkzadeh, 1988, p. 261). They also argued that the existing user information satisfaction instruments (e.g., Bailey & Pearson, 1983; Ives et al., 1983) were evaluating general attitudes of managers towards IS rather than those of users of IS (i.e., computer end-users) specifically. They proposed to develop an instrument focusing on characteristics specific to computer applications affecting end-user satisfaction. A final revised instrument for EUCS with 12 items which comprised these five factors was produced. A test-retest study to validate the instrument, in which it was administered over three time intervals, was performed in a later study (Doll & Torkzadeh, 1991). Based on the second set of results, Torkzadeh and Doll (1991) concluded that the 12-item EUCS instrument is "internally consistent and stable" and that it does not "elicit a substantial reactivity effect" (p. 36), i.e., it does not cause inflation or deflation of results by respondents.

Etezadi-Amoli and Farhoomand (1991) voiced a number of concerns with Doll and Torkzadeh's (1988) EUCS instrument both from theoretical and methodological perspectives. One concern was the lack of a "scale evaluating the degree of importance of each item to the respondent" (p. 1), which prevents the EUCS instrument from measuring the "silent beliefs" of respondents' satisfaction with the IS. A second set of concerns has to do with the statistical techniques followed in the elimination of items and the analysis which led to the five factors underlying EUCS. In their study, Etezadi-Amoli and Farhoomand conducted confirmatory factor analysis using Doll and Torkzadeh's data. They found the fit to be "inadequate" and concluded that Doll and Torkzadeh's EUCS instrument "cannot be used unequivocally because of the. .. methodological and conceptual problems" (Etezadi-Amoli & Farhoomand, 1991, p. 3).

Doll, Xia, and Torkzadeh (1994) responded to Etezadi-Amoli and Farhoomand's (1991) criticism by conducting a confirmatory factor analysis in order to compare four proposed models to predict overall EUCS. The comparison of the different path analytic models predicting EUCS included three which incorporated the five factors found in their previous work, as well as a null model without the factors (Doll et al., 1994). New data was collected from 409 computer end users validating their original EUCS instrument. Hendrickson, Glorfeld, and Cronan (1994) conducted a study to further validate the test-retest findings of Doll and Torkzadeh (1991) over a 2-year time frame. The results were comparable to those reported by Doll and Torkzadeh, leading to the conclusion that the "reliability assessment over two years indicate[s] that the EUCS instrument is stable and reliable" (Hendrickson et al., 1994, p. 659). Lee et al. (1995) conducted a study to empirically test the relationship between end-user ability, EUCS, end-user IS acceptance, system utilization, and job satisfaction. They used the EUCS instrument to assess end-user satisfaction with IS. Data collection included a sample size of 236 end-users in the central US. Their results show strong reliability for EUCS, which provides additional validity for the instrument as a solid measure of the end-user computing satisfaction construct.

Palvia (1996) noted that both UIS and EUCS were developed for large organizations and he suggested adding other measures (such as productivity, hardware/software adequacy, system security/integrity, and so on) to the 12-item EUCS instrument to make it more appropriate for small businesses. He concluded that small businesses have significantly different factors associated with IS satisfaction than do end-users in large businesses (Palvia, 1996). McHanry and Cronan (1998) conducted a study to validate the EUCS instrument for simulation and decision support systems (DSS). Their results were comparable with those reported by Doll and Torkzadeh (1988). Additionally, they concluded that the EUCS instrument is valid and reliable also in measuring simulation systems and DSS settings. Seddon and Yip (1992) suggested that EUCS lacks newer aspects of IS satisfaction, such as technical support as well as user knowledge and involvement with system development. They observed that UIS and EUCS have some differences on the items to be measured and their relative importance. Studying user satisfaction with accounting information system, Seddon and Yip compared three types of IS user satisfaction instruments: UIS, EUCS, and a composite UIS/EUCS instrument. Their results show that Doll and Torkzadeh's EUCS provides the best predictor of overall user satisfaction.

In summary, extensive effort has been given to determining which characteristics of an IS are relevant for determination of satisfaction with IS, and the composition of the list of characteristics used has been affected both by definition of satisfaction and by the changing nature of IS over the past three decades. Scholars have made strides in reducing the list of characteristics to a manageable set for more expedient survey administration, which has, however, led to criticism on theoretical grounds on the exclusion of important measures. Finally, while the importance of a specific IS characteristic (i.e., user's perceived value) was originally a part of IS satisfaction surveys, because of early empirical observations it has largely been removed from most IS satisfaction instruments. It is our primary goal to build on the rich IS satisfaction work conducted over the past three decades by providing solid theoretical argumentation for the use of user-perceived value as an augmenting construct for our new taxonomy of IS effectiveness. As such, in the following section we will review literature associated with IS effectiveness.

IS Effectiveness

IS effectiveness has been defined in many ways including quality of system, quality of information provided by the system, impact on individuals and/or on the organization, as well as user satisfaction (Arnold, 1995; Grover et al., 1996; Kim, 1989; Seddon & Yip, 1992; Shannon & Weaver, 1949; Yuthas & Eining, 1995). After nearly three decades, IS scholars are still seeking a standard framework and instrument to evaluate IS effectiveness, and disagreement persists among researchers with respect to the composition of these constructs, frameworks, and measurement mechanisms (Kim, 1989; McHaney, Hightower, & Pearson, 2002; Seddon & Yip, 1992; Yuthas & Eining, 1995). However, it was noted that a single measure of IS effectiveness may not be applicable for all situations or systems (Seddon & Yip, 1992). In this section we provide a brief review of the literature in the area of IS effectiveness for the purposes of further demonstrating the centrality of user satisfaction in the endeavor to propose a new taxonomy of IS effectiveness.

Scott (1995) noted that "information system effectiveness is an important phenomenon for both researchers and practitioners" (p. 43). Moreover, she noted that user satisfaction with IS has been repeatedly used in literature as a measure of IS effectiveness. However, after conducting an analysis of data collected over 6 years from CEOs and IS managers Scott concluded that "we do not yet have an adequate measuring instrument for information system effectiveness" (Scott, 1995, p. 44). Accordingly, in this study we attempt to address this problem by augmenting the widely used *user satisfaction* construct with *user-perceived value of IS* for a new taxonomy of IS effectiveness.

Grover et al. (1996) suggested that there are many different definitions for IS effectiveness to be found in the literature, which depend on the basis for evaluation, the unit of analysis (individual or organization), and the type of evaluation that can occur at the process (system/technological), the response (communication), or the impact (outcome) level. The basis for evaluation can either be comparative, normative, or improvement based; where the comparative evaluates IS effectiveness between a system and peer systems, the normative defines IS effectiveness by the attainment of ideal state, and the improvement addresses changes in system effectiveness over time. Grover et al. also observed that mirroring technology's evolution there is a temporal effect on the definition of IS effectiveness; i.e., as the use of IS has changed so has the definition of IS effectiveness. In their seminal paper, Grover et al. classified over 100 papers from 14 top IS journals into one of six classes of definitions of IS effectiveness based on their classification. While financial and economical value of IS have been used as measures of IS effectiveness from the organizational unit of analysis (DeLone & McLean, 1992; 2003; Gefen & Ragowsky, 2005; Ragowsky, 1995; Ragowsky et al., 2005; Ragowsky et al., 2000), the main hypothesis we suggest deals with perceived value by the users (i.e., cognitive value). Moreover, Scott (1995) noted that future measures of IS effectiveness should not be related to financial performance, rather to individual users' perceptions related to the IS. Thus, the individual unit of analysis, as suggested by Grover et al., will be the focus of our IS effectiveness discussion from this point on.

IS usage has been broadly studied with respect to IS effectiveness. The fundamental argument is that a highly effective IS will be more often and more widely used than a system that is less effective (Baroudi, Olson, & Ives, 1986; Fuerst & Cheney, 1982; Ginzberg, 1981; Srinivasan, 1985). The classical Technology Acceptance Model (TAM) proposed by Davis (Davis, 1986; 1989) has been widely used in predicting antecedents constructs that influence intention to use and actual usage of IS. The TAM model is based on the Theory of Reasoned Action (TRA) proposed by Ajzen and Fishbein (1980). Accordingly, the TAM model proposes that perceived usefulness and ease of use impact attitude towards IS, acceptance behaviors or intention to use IS, and ultimately actual usage of an IS (Davis, 1989; Davis, Bagozzi, & Warshaw, 1989; Venkatesh, Morris, Davis, & Davis, 2003). However, research results on system use as a measure of IS effectiveness has been somewhat mixed. While some have argued that effective IS have increased system use, Srinivasan, for example, demonstrated that frequency of system use is not significantly correlated with user-perceived IS effectiveness. Srinavasan concluded that IS usage is not necessarily associated with IS effectiveness.

DeLone and McLean (1992) in their classical work identified system usage and user satisfaction with IS as key constructs to impact IS success (i.e., organizational impact and individual impact constructs). They noted that IS implementation success is synonymous with IS effectiveness as they maintained that a successful system is also an effective one. DeLone and McLean reviewed 180 empirical studies on IS success and categorized this body of research based on the constructs proposed in their framework. Their review leads to the conclusion that IS success/effectiveness is a multidimensional and interdependent phenomenon. Even within their general classification scheme for IS success there is a great deal of heterogeneity in the definitions and instruments to measure such a complex construct. Such heterogeneity led DeLone and McLean to argue for simplification of models to measure IS effectiveness and to move towards the development of a comprehensive instrument. Pitt, Watson, and Kavan (1995) observed that due to the changing nature of IS during the early 1990s, characteristics related to the service quality of IS should be included in any general framework for IS effectiveness. IS in industry had changed from being application centric to service centric, and hence the service component of IS should also be added to a model of IS effectiveness. They proposed applying service quality (i.e., SERVQUAL (Parasuraman et al., 1988)) as another construct that impacts IS success/effectiveness. In their 10-year recap following their original work, DeLone and McLean (2003) summarized the progress in the area of IS success/effectiveness since their highly cited 1992 study. Based on over 100 empirical studies, they revised their original IS success model, incorporating IS service quality as another construct in the model as proposed by Pitt et al. DeLone and McLean (2003) also collapsed organizational impact and individual impact into a single category which they called 'net benefits' depending on the unit of analysis used by a given study that utilizes their model. However, they note that "as a result of this 'use' and 'user satisfaction,' certain 'net benefits' will occur. If the IS or service is to be continued, it is assumed that the 'net benefits' from the perspective of the owner or sponsor of the system are positive, thus influencing and reinforcing subsequent 'use' and 'user satisfaction'" (DeLone & McLean, 2003, p. 23). Moreover, DeLone and McLean (2003) noted that "net benefit" measures should mainly be based on previously "developed and tested [measures] for IS investments" (p. 25). Thus, it appears that their measure of IS effectiveness is based on the financial benefit to the user or the owners of the system rather than a cognitive perceived benefit to the user. DeLone and McLean (2003) concluded that despite the complexity of the IS effectiveness construct, "an attempt should be made to reduce significantly the number of measures used to measure IS success [effectiveness] so that research results can be compared and findings validated" (p. 27). Consequently, in this study we attempt to address this exact issue by proposing a new approach to measure IS effectiveness based only on two constructs: *user satisfaction with IS* and *user-perceived value of IS*.

In summary, it appears that the IS effectiveness literature concludes that although both user satisfaction and IS usage have been used in various models that impact IS effectiveness, IS usage has been demonstrated to have mixed results as a predictor of IS effectiveness. However, user satisfaction with IS appears to have been widely employed as a key surrogate measure for IS effectiveness throughout the past three decades. Moreover, Zviran and Erlich (2003), after a substantial review of the literature of user satisfaction with IS and IS effectiveness, concluded that the "user satisfaction factor is an important criterion and the one most prevalent for measuring the success of information systems" (p. 83). Additionally, numerous researchers have noted that IS effectiveness is a multidimensional construct, while the actual measures of IS effectiveness in literature appear to concentrate only around one measure, i.e., user satisfaction with IS. Moreover, it appears that a measure of IS effectiveness from the user's perspective is still warranted, in particular based on user perceptions (Barki & Hartwick, 1994). Additionally, user satisfaction with IS is particularly important as a surrogate for effectiveness in contexts where the use of the IS is voluntary. However, satisfaction with IS as a sole measure of IS effectiveness may have some limitations. One such limitation may result from an aspect of human nature: some people do not want to admit a mistake, especially after heavy investment in time and resources. This human characteristic often drives an innate bias to argue for a system, especially in the early roll-out phase, on the part of those who championed or invested heavily in the system. Such users may indicate they are highly satisfied with the IS on a survey, even when it is not effective in their actual experience. In these cases, a normative comparison of the current state of a given system and ideal state of the system as perceived by the user would be very useful for the determination of IS effectiveness. Therefore, in this article we propose a new taxonomy of IS effectiveness following the work discussed here. Our approach, building on Grover et al.'s (1996) normative approach by introducing the user-perceived value construct along with the accepted key surrogate measure for IS effectiveness: user satisfaction with IS. Thus, a substantive review of value theory will follow this section to provide the theoretical background for using the user-perceived value construct in the proposed taxonomy.

Perceived Value Construct

The importance of research on value as a cognitive construct (i.e., human perceived value) affecting human attitudes has been recognized by numerous scholars in a broad variety of fields including psychology, sociology, anthropology, political science, and economics (Rafaeli & Raban, 2003). However, most work conducted so far in IS literature about the value construct has dealt with the economical value (i.e., net benefit, return on investment, etc.) rather than user-perceived cognitive value (Ragowsky et al., 2005). Nevertheless, some scholars outside the IS field including Allport, Vernon, and Lindzey (1951), Feather (1967; 1975), and Rokeach (1969; 1973; 1979) have argued that perceived value is fundamental and more stable in human cognition compared to attitudes (i.e., satisfaction), which can be altered based on one's experience over time. Management and education researchers have also recognized that the study of perceived value is vital for providing insight into their domains (Brown, 1976), as well as criticizing the neglect of the application of perceived value in their studies (e.g., see Brown; Durgee, O'Connor, & Veryzer, 1996; Kahle & Kennedy, 1988). In

IS literature, Doll and Torkzadeh (1991) divided research in IS effectiveness into two streams. The first ("downstream") investigates the causal link beginning with attitude and moves towards the social and economic impact of IS on individuals and organizations, while the second ("upstream") focuses on the linkage between those causal factors which affect beliefs (i.e., user-perceived value) and in turn affect attitude (i.e., user satisfaction). Doll and Torkzadeh (1991) observed that most IS research has concentrated on downstream analysis, while relatively little attention has been placed on those factors affecting attitudes towards IS. They noted that one reason that attitude research in the IS domain lacks clarity is that it "emphasizes the affective rather than the cognitive (e.g., beliefs,) dimension of attitude" (Doll & Torkzadeh, 1991, p. 5). Moreover, they noted that an "individual's attitude towards any object is a function of his or her beliefs about the objects. .. and the evaluative aspect [i.e., perceived value] of those beliefs" (Doll & Torkzadeh, 1991, p. 7). In the subsections below, we provide a definition for perceived value (as distinguished from economic value) from psychology literature and a discussion on cognitive value theory.

Definition of 'Perceived Value'

Literature beyond the IS field contained several definitions of perceived value (Barki & Hartwick, 1994; Brown, 1976; Chiou, 2004; Feather, 1975; Keeney & Raiffa, 1993; Kluckhohn, 1951; Rokeach, 1973; Williams, 1979; Yang & Peterson, 2004). In IS literature, Keeney and Raiffa (1993) defined value as a principle of importance. Additionally, Barki and Hartwick (1994) developed a measure of user involvement in which one of the user involvement's dimensions was importance. They defined it as "a psychological state reflecting the importance…of a new system to the user" (p. 62). Based on the definitions found in literature presented above, it appears that there is a consensus on the definition of perceived value. Such definition indicates that perceived value is an enduring core belief individuals use to evaluate the importance of objects, ideas, or behaviors. Henceforth, we propose a more narrow definition in the context of IS research of *users' perceived value of IS* as a combined set of enduring core beliefs that users incorporate to evaluate the importance of IS characteristics or attributes. For example, a user may believe that the quality of information of a given IS is very important, which indicates a very high perceived value of the system's characteristic believed by that given user. On the other hand, if that same user believes that quality of service of a given IS is not important, such a belief indicates a very low perceived value of the system's characteristic by that given user.

VALUE-SATISFACTION TAXONOMY OF IS EFFECTIVENESS (VSTISE)

IS researchers have incorporated user satisfaction in their understanding of IS effectiveness; however, the construct of *perceived value* has been given very little attention in such models. It appears that there is a great body of research conducted in fields other than IS, which suggests that perceived value is a highly relevant construct for any social science (Beatty, Kahle, Homer, & Misra, 1985; Durgee et al., 1996; Feather, 1967; 1975; Kahle & Kennedy, 1988; Prescott & Hopkins, 1984; Rokeach, 1969; 1973; 1979). In fact, Grover et al. (1996), in their review and categorization of over 100 articles on IS effectiveness, stated that noticeably missing are studies that deal with perceived value. Moreover, Barki and Hartwick (1994) noted that "systems deemed to be both important and personally relevant are likely to engender positive effective or evaluative feelings" (p. 62). Thus, the model we propose here will incorporate perceived value of IS as well as user satisfaction with IS and suggest a new taxonomy for user-perceived IS effectiveness. Our newly proposed taxonomy suggests that an IS will be considered *effective* when users perceive its characteristics as highly important (high perceived value) and are highly satisfied by those same characteristics (high satisfaction).

Galletta and Lederer (1989) suggested practitioners are interested in tools "to uncover user perception of strength and weaknesses [of systems' characteristics]" (p. 421). Thus, in this study we propose a new Value-Satisfaction taxonomy of 2×2 matrix to indicate user-perceived IS effectiveness based on user satisfaction with IS and perceived value of IS, noted as Value-Satisfaction Taxonomy of IS Effectiveness (VSTISE). In order to construct the taxonomy, decision makers can develop a list of characteristics for the system under investigation based on users' input and prior literature. A survey can be developed to measure users' perceptions for the level of satisfaction and the user-perceived value for that given IS characteristic. Figure 2 provides an example of survey item scales that should be used to construct the survey of measuring user satisfaction and user-perceived value of each IS characteristic for the purpose of constructing our proposed taxonomy of IS effectiveness. Similar item scales can be used for the list of characteristics suggested by the decision makers and users. Subsequently, assessment of the user satisfaction and perceived value can be made empirically using survey methodology that will yield dual scores for each IS characteristics and dual scores for the overall system (i.e., overall user satisfaction and overall perceived value). The data collected is then used to construct the 2×2 matrix of Value-Satisfaction taxonomy by positioning the mean score of the user satisfaction on the horizontal axis and positioning the mean score of the user-perceived value on the vertical axis (see Figure 3). Thus, each IS characteristic and the overall system will be represented as a point in the VSTISE taxonomy. Consequently, such a taxonomy can provide insight for actions and improvement priorities of

Figure 2. Proposed survey instrument item scales

Characteristic	Level of Satisfaction						Level of Perceived Value					
	Extremely unsatisfied	Very unsatisfied	Unsatisfied	Satisfied	Very satisfied	Extremely satisfied	Not Important	Not so Important	Slightly Important	Important	Very Important	Extremely Important
Quality of Information from the system	O	O	O	O	O	O	O	O	O	O	O	O

Figure 3. Value-satisfaction taxonomy of IS effectiveness (VSTISE)

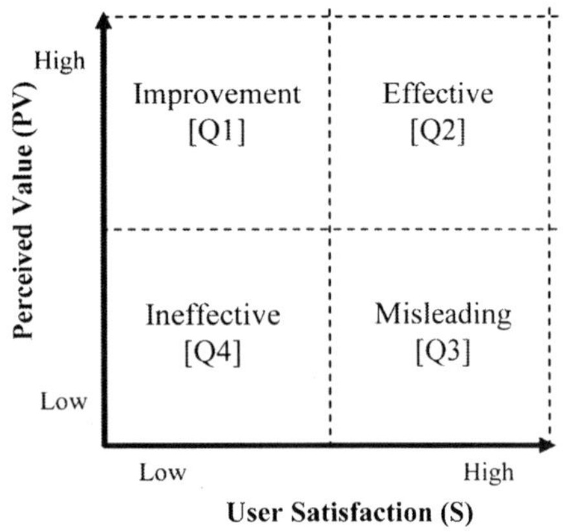

specific IS characteristics, thereby enabling decision makers to improve the overall effectiveness of an IS. The following discussion will elaborate on how such positioning of the IS characteristics in the taxonomy can enable decision makers to realize such effectiveness.

In Figure 3, the first quadrant, Q1, consists of low-satisfaction and high-value observations and is named '*improvement.*' IS characteristics positioned in this quadrant of the taxonomy provide the top opportunities for improvement in IS effectiveness. Improvement in such IS characteristics could occur by providing more resources in order to increase user satisfaction with the characteristics of the IS that are already perceived as highly important (i.e., high perceived value). The second quadrant, Q2, having high-satisfaction and high-value observations, is named '*effective.*' IS characteristics positioned in this quadrant of the taxonomy are considered to be effective as users are both highly satisfied with these IS characteristics and at the same time perceive them as highly important (i.e., high perceived value). No action is necessary for characteristics that fall in this quadrant. These IS characteristics are considered effective and can be considered as key characteristics of the system under study. The third quadrant, Q3, of characteristics with scores that are high-satisfaction and low-value is named '*misleading.*' IS characteristics positioned in this quadrant of the taxonomy suggest that the users are highly satisfied with characteristics that are simply not perceived as important (i.e., low perceived value). This may suggest that resources that are provided to such IS characteristics may be more appropriately used if transferred to other characteristics, e.g., those located in the 'improvement' quadrant (see Figure 4). The fourth quadrant, Q4, with low-satisfaction and low-value observations, is named '*ineffective.*' IS characteristics positioned in this quadrant of the taxonomy are perceived to have low value (importance) for users, while users express low satisfaction with them. Thus, such IS characteristics are ineffective and generally warrant a closer investigation to explore possibilities for increasing their perceived value and/or satisfaction. For example, IS characteristics in the 'ineffective' quadrant may have anticipated increases with respect to user-perceived value in the future, in which case these IS characteristics may demand improvement in satisfaction.

THE CASE STUDY: APPLYING VSTISE

The proposed Value-Satisfaction Taxonomy of IS effectiveness (VSTISE) is dependent on the specific industry and system being applied. This section discusses the methodology used to develop the IS effectiveness taxonomy in the context of online learning systems (OLSs). This case study included a two-phase approach: Phase I was a qualitative assessment of the characteristics to which users attribute value when using the system, while Phase II included quantitative assessment of the characteristics found in literature and those newly uncovered in Phase I of the study. Exploratory analysis of the data was made in order to clean up any irregularities such as multivariate outliers and response sets. This was followed by a

Figure 4. Summary of the value-satisfaction taxonomy of IS effectiveness (VSTISE) quadrants

VSTISE Quadrant		Description of IS Characteristics
Improvement	Q1	IS characteristics falling in this quadrant should be improved as users perceive them to have high value (highly important), however express low satisfaction from such attributes. ***Improvements*** can occur by providing additional resources to increase user satisfaction with such IS characteristics that are perceived to be of high value.
Effective	Q2	Users perceived high value for these IS characteristics as well as being highly satisfied, and hence performance on these IS characteristics can be considered ***effective***.
Misleading	Q3	Resources that are invested in these IS characteristics are wasted as users express high satisfaction from IS characteristics that are simply not as important to users, hence ***misleading***! Resources to support IS characteristics in this quadrant may be more appropriately used if transferred to other IS characteristics located, e.g., in the 'improvement' quadrant.
Ineffective	Q4	These IS characteristics are perceived to have low value (not important) and at the same time users are dissatisfied with them. Such IS characteristics are ***ineffective*** and generally warrant a closer investigation to explore possibilities for increasing their perceived value and/or user satisfaction.

reliability test of the instrument using Cronbach's α analysis of the instrument items.

Phase I of this study included qualitative research, following Keeney's (1999) methodology, in the pursuit of system characteristics to which users attribute value when using the system. The purpose of this phase was to augment the characteristics found in prior literature. A qualitative questionnaire was developed following Keeney's methodology, with open-ended questions. Appendix A includes the questionnaire used in this phase noted for a generic IS. Initially users were provided with the first section only (Section 1 of Appendix A) and were instructed to think about *all* the system's characteristics to which they attribute value (i.e., "that are important to them") when using the system. The second section of the qualitative questionnaire (Section 2 of Appendix A) includes open-ended questions to capture responses along four dimensions, noted in Appendix A for a generic IS. In the case study, due to the OLS context, the four system dimensions were following those proposed by Webster and Hackley (1997). The dimensions approach was employed in order to obtain more structured results focused on the four main dimensions. Four groups of OLS users participated in the focus group phase of this study, the first qualitative phase. Overall there were 75 responses out of 115 questionnaires, giving an overall response rate of over 65%. Responses from the users were grouped based on their similarities and categorized based on each of the four main dimensions proposed by Webster and Hackley. Similar terminologies were converted to a single characteristic and compared with the characteristics found in literature. Some of the terms did not correspond to existing system characteristics found in literature. As a result, six new characteristics were added to the list. Results of the qualitative process are presented in Appendix E and form the basis for the quantitative survey items used in Phase II of the study.

The second phase of this case study, Phase II, included a quantitative research using a survey instrument for the assessment of the characteristics found in literature and those newly uncovered in Phase I. A survey instrument was developed to assess the users' perceived cognitive value and satisfaction from each characteristic in the system's four dimensions and the overall system using the scale noted in Figure 5 above. Responses from 207 participants were submitted, represent-

Figure 5. VSTISE for Dimension A (technology, network, and technical support) (N=192)

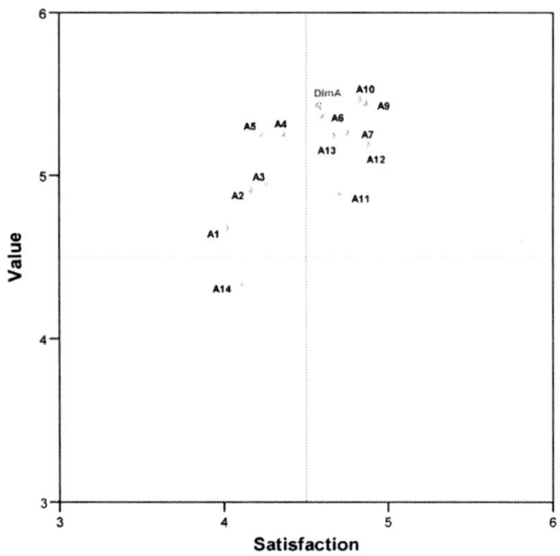

ing over 32% of the user sample. Subsequently, a pre-analysis data cleansing was conducted to ensure the reliability of the results following the guidance provided by Mertler and Vannatta (2001) for data cleansing based on various irregularities. Seven response-sets and eight multivariate outliers were observed in the data, resulting in a total of 192 usable cases.

Prior to the analyses of this data, an investigation was made of the correlation between the value (V) and satisfaction (S) constructs. This analysis included Pearson correlation, an indicator for linear association between two variables. Additionally, this analysis also included Eta (η) correlation, an indicator for non-linear association between two variables. Results of this analysis are provided in Table 1. These results suggest that there are no correlations (linear or non-linear) observed between value and satisfaction measures. These results are quite profound as they suggest that value and satisfaction are two distinct uncorrelated constructs. This adds to the overall validity of the current taxonomy as the approach for users' perceived IS effectiveness is noted to be based on these two distinct components. Hence, it also adds to the validity of the Value-Satisfaction Taxonomy of IS effectiveness.

A preliminary data analysis was done using the Principal Component Analysis (PCA) to explore the initial validity and reliability of the instrument. Four factors were extracted with a total cumulative variance explained of nearly 61% with Cronbach's α of over .83 for all four factors.

VSTISEs were developed in a similar manner to the SWOT proposed by marketing scholars (Andrews, 1987; Ansoff, 1965; Mintzberg, Ahlstrand, & Lampel, 1998; Porter, 1991). VSTISEs were based on aggregated user-perceived satisfaction with the system characteristics as well as aggregated user-perceived cognitive value of

Table 1. Eta & Pearson correlations for dimensions (A, B, C, & D) & Overall (O) Measures

Var 1 (Y) * Var 2 (X)	Eta	Pearson	Relationship
Sa_Act * Va_Act	0.228	0.228	No observed relationship
Va_Act * Sa_Act	0.390	0.228	No observed relationship
Sb_Act * Vb_Act	0.345	0.339	No observed relationship
Vb_Act * Sb_Act	0.499	0.339	No observed relationship
Sc_Act * Vc_Act	0.239	0.224	No observed relationship
Vc_Act * Sc_Act	0.434	0.224	No observed relationship
Sd_Act * Vd_Act	0.438	0.407	No observed relationship
Vd_Act * Sd_Act	0.486	0.407	No observed relationship
So_Act * Vo_Act	0.359	0.308	No observed relationship
Vo_Act * So_Act	0.419	0.308	No observed relationship

system characteristics. The taxonomy for each dimension was constructed by positioning all the system characteristics of that dimension in the taxonomy, where the *mean characteristics satisfaction* scores are positioned on the horizontal axis and the *mean characteristics value* scores are positioned on the vertical axis. The *dimension taxonomy* was developed for each of the four dimensions including the system characteristics as points in the taxonomy. Similarly, taxonomy for the overall system was constructed. The *overall taxonomy* also included the aggregated means of the four system dimensions as points in that taxonomy. One approach suggests that in the case of no user scores in the low-low quadrant, it is more appropriate to rescale the cut-off-point between the low and high quadrants on both axes to 75% of the maximum scale (EBI, 2002). In this study the measures scale ranges from 1 to 6, while no scores were noted below 3 in satisfaction and below 3 in value, resulting in the use of 4.5 as the cut-off point between low and high on both axes of the taxonomy.

Results of the VSTISE for dimension A (Figure 5) indicate that five system characteristics (A_1, A_2, A_3, A_4, and A_5) from the *Technology, Network, and Technical Support* dimension are in the high-value-low-satisfaction quadrant (Q1). This implies that support via phone, support via e-mail, quality of support, system up-time, and reduced system errors are of high importance to users but have low satisfaction, suggesting high priority for improvement in such system characteristics of dimension A (Technology, Network, and Technical Support). Results also indicate that seven system characteristics (A_6, A_7, A_9, A_{10}, A_{11}, A_{12}, and A_{13}) from the *Technology, Network, and Technical Support* dimension are in the high-value-high-satisfaction quadrant (Q2), implying that system security, access to content, access flexibility, submit files from anywhere, different system tools, access of all content from one area (portal), and remote access are high-effectiveness system characteristics that should be highlighted

Figure 6. VSTISE for Dimension B (information and content) (N=192)

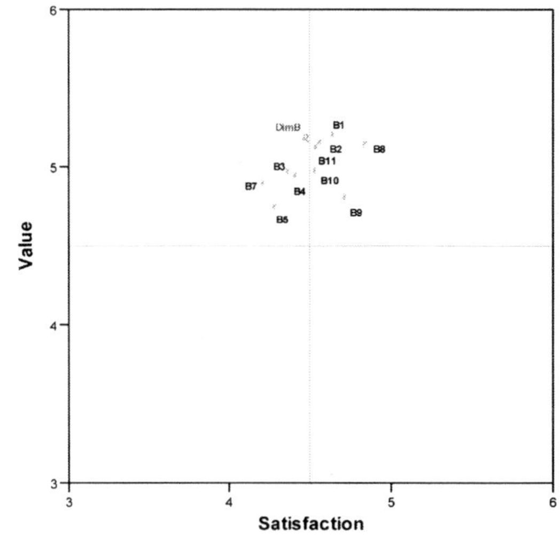

as part of the strengths of the system under study. One systems characteristic (A_{14}) from dimension A was found in the low-value-low-satisfaction quadrant (Q3), implying that content audios might not be needed as they are not important nor are users satisfied from them. No system characteristics from dimension A were found to be in the low-value-high-satisfaction quadrant (Q4), implying that no wasted resources were found among any of the systems characteristics of dimension A (Technology, Network, and Technical Support).

Results of the dimension B VSTISE (Figure 6) indicate four system characteristics (B_3, B_4, B_5, and B_7) from the *Information and Content* dimension in the high-value-low-satisfaction quadrant (Q1). This implies that content, interesting subject matter, difficulty of subject matter, and enjoyment from content are of high importance to students but have low satisfaction, suggesting these as first priority for improvement among the system characteristics of dimension B (*Information and Content*). Also, results of this taxonomy indicate that six system characteristics (B_1, B_2, B_8, B_9, B_{10}, and B_{11}) from the *Information and Content* dimension are in the high-value-high-satisfaction quadrant (Q2), implying that such characteristics are high-effectiveness system characteristics that should be highlighted among the strengths of the system under study. No system characteristic from dimension B was found in the low-value-low-satisfaction quadrant (Q3) and no system characteristic from dimension B was found in the low-value-high-satisfaction quadrant (Q4), implying no system characteristics from this dimension may need to be discarded and that no wasted resources were found for any of the system characteristics of dimension B.

Results of dimension C (Figure 7) indicate that five OLS characteristics (C_1, C_2, C_4, C_6, and C_7) from the *Developers and Managers* dimension are in the high-value-low-satisfaction quadrant (Q1). This implies that the amount of developers/managers-user interactions, developers'/managers' attitude, quality of developers/managers-user interactions, submission time window for files, and online workload are of high importance to users but have low satisfaction, suggesting these as first priority for improvement among the system characteristics of dimension C. Results of this taxonomy also indicate that one system characteristic (C_5) from dimension C is in the high-value-high-satisfaction quadrant (Q2), implying that freedom of usage (selective seeking and processing of information) should be highlighted as a strength of the system under study. No system characteristic from dimension C was found in the low-value-low-satisfaction quadrant (Q3) and no system characteristics from dimension C was found in the low-value-high-satisfaction quadrant (Q4), implying that no system characteristics from this dimension may need to be discarded and that no wasted resources were found among any of the system characteristics of dimension C.

Results of the VSTISE for dimension D (Figure 8) indicate that three system characteristics (D_1, D_9, and D_{10}) from the *User* dimension are in the high-value-low-satisfaction quadrant (Q1). Due to the very low satisfaction (2.85) of D_9, cost of courses, it was the only system characteristic not plotted in the taxonomy. This implies that extensive experiencing with the system, cost of using it, and cost of ISP and Internet access have high importance for users but have low satisfaction, suggesting these as first priority for improvement among the system characteristics of dimension D. Also, results of this taxonomy indicate that seven system characteristics (D_6, D_7, D_{11}, D_{12}, D_{13}, D_{14}, and D_{15}) from the *User* dimension are in the high-value-high-satisfaction quadrant (Q2),

Figure 7. VSTISE for Dimension C (developers & managers) (N=192)

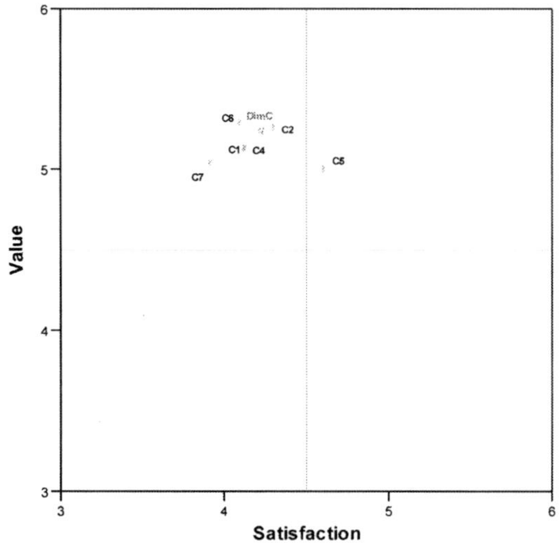

Figure 8. VSTISE for Dimension D (User) (N=192)

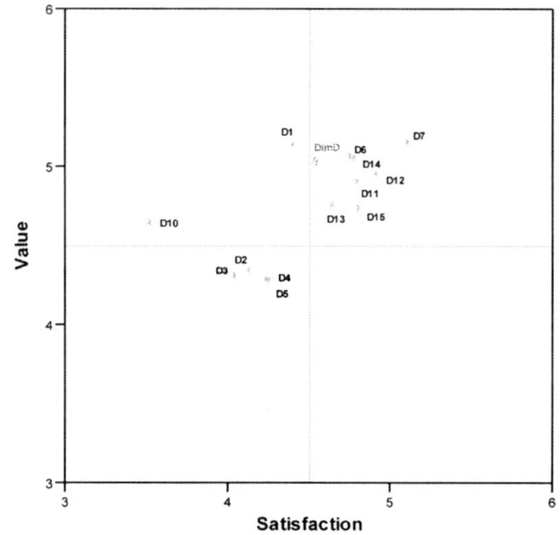

implying that users' comfort with online technology, users' perceived Internet and computer skills, reduced travel cost/time (to and from locations), ability to travel while using the system (for business or other), employer support, attendance to family responsibilities, and family support are high effectiveness system characteristics that should be highlighted as among the strengths of the system under study. Four systems characteristics (D_2, D_3, D_4, and D_5) from the *User* dimension were placed in the low-value-low-satisfaction quadrant (Q3), implying that these system characteristics do not seem to be effective as they are not important nor are users satisfied with them. These results suggest that the users of the system under study may not find co-users an effective part of the system. No system characteristic from the *User* dimension was found to be in the low-value-high-satisfaction quadrant (Q4), implying that no wasted resources were found among the system characteristics of dimension D.

Finally, results of the overall system VSTISE (Figure 9) indicate that system dimensions B (Information and Content) and C (Developers and Managers) are in the high-value-low-satisfaction quadrant (Q1), implying that overall both dimensions are of high importance for users but give low satisfaction. This suggests that higher management in charge of the system under study may need to focus their first attention on the improvement of characteristics in these two system dimensions. That may include enhancing content with games and adding some interactive features to the content. Moreover, it may also suggest that seminars and workshops are needed to improve developers' and managers' performances (such as the amount of developers/managers-user interaction, developers'/managers' attitude, quality of interaction, etc.). Results of this overall taxonomy also indicate that in general, system dimensions A (Technology, Network, and Technical Support) and D (User) are in the high-value-high-satisfaction quadrant (Q2), implying that both dimensions are effective and should be highlighted as among the strengths of the system under study. No system dimensions were found in the low-value-low-satisfaction quadrant (Q3) or the low-value-high-satisfaction quadrant (Q4).

Figure 9. VSTISE – Overall (N=192)

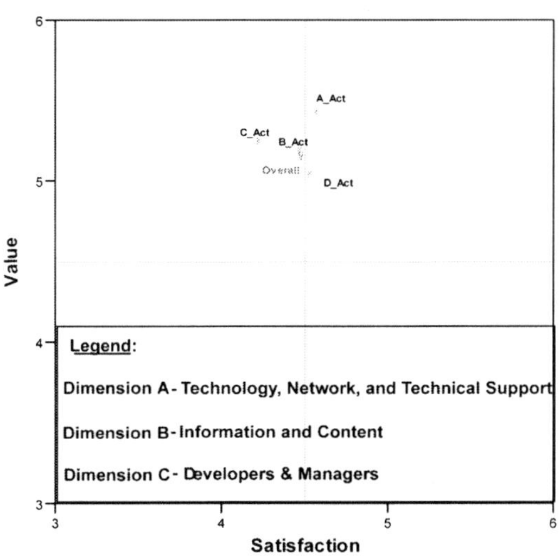

DISCUSSION AND CONCLUSION

Discussion

In this paper we provided a review of IS satisfaction, IS effectiveness, and perceived value literature. We extracted the definitions of *perceived value* construct from heterogeneous literature including psychology, marketing, operations research, information systems, and management to propose a definition of perceived value of IS. We consider IS as *effective* when users perceive its IS characteristics as highly important (i.e., high perceived value) and are highly satisfied by those same characteristics. Based on our definition, we propose a new taxonomy for incorporating the perceived value construct and the construct of user satisfaction with IS to the goal of obtaining a better understanding of user-perceived IS effectiveness. In this sense, we recommend that our definition of the perceived value construct and our new taxonomy, VSTISE, proposed here serve as a theoretical foundation for future empirical studies of IS effectiveness.

The rich and extensive IS satisfaction theory (UIS theory, EUCS theory, DeLone and McLean's classical IS success model, and Davis' classical TAM) provided the theoretical foundation for measures of user satisfaction with IS. We reviewed the extensive work done during the 1980s and early 1990s on IS user satisfaction and have provided and overview of several validated instruments in assessment of user satisfaction. However, some scholars suggest that IS research has omitted the measurements of the degree of importance (or user-perceived value), forgoing the opportunity for a deeper understanding of IS phenomena (Etezadi-Amoli & Farhoomand, 1991). Our review of definitions of value from psychology, marketing, IS, management science, and decision analysis suggests several synonymous terms for user-perceived value. Such synonyms might include importance, preference, and desirability. Our review of literature in the area of IS effectiveness suggests that there is little agreement on the definition of IS effectiveness, let alone how to measure it (Arnold, 1995; Grover et al., 1996; Kim, 1989; Seddon & Yip, 1992; Yuthas & Eining, 1995). Such inconsistencies have led to development of surrogate measures of IS effectiveness, rather than direct measures or taxonomies of IS effectiveness (Baroudi et al., 1986; Baroudi & Orlikowski, 1988; Ives et al., 1983). However, several scholars suggest that user satisfaction and system usage are not enough in the assessment of IS effectiveness (Arnold, 1995; Yuthas & Eining, 1995). Grover et al. present a clarifying framework of IS effectiveness. In this study, we follow such an approach by enabling decision makers and IS managers to develop the IS effectiveness taxonomy based on measurements of user satisfaction with the IS and user-perceived value of the IS as a benchmarking tool to assess such IS effectiveness. Constructing such VSTISEs will enable decision makers to visually see how all their IS characteristics fall into the four quadrants of the IS effectiveness taxonomy: improvement, effective, misleading, and ineffective. Moreover, the location that a given IS characteristic falls in the taxonomy can aid decision makers and IS managers in understanding additional actions needed in order to improve the effectiveness of the IS characteristic. For example, if *quality of service* measured in a given IS falls under the improvement quadrant (Q1) (i.e., low user satisfaction, high perceived value), decision makers should spend time understanding why users are unsatisfied with the quality of service provided. Clearly, users find the quality of service of that given IS to be highly important (i.e., high perceived value). Therefore, an attempt should be made to uncover ways to increase user satisfaction that may include, for example, better training for the IS service providers. On the other hand, if *ease of use* of a given IS falls under the misleading quadrant (Q3) (i.e., high user satisfaction, low perceived value), decision makers should understand that resources spent now on increasing or maintaining the system's ease of use may be unnecessary and funds spent on this effort may be better used on other IS characteristics, such as the quality of service in the example above. Our conclusion is noted based on the notion that users express high satisfaction with the current state of ease of use and it's not that important for them (i.e., low perceived value); thus, funds can be diverted from this IS characteristic (see Figure 7).

Implication for Research, Practice, and Future Research

The work proposed here is significant and beneficial both for researchers and practitioners. For researchers, the main theoretical contribution that this work provides is by integrating the construct of perceived value and the construct of user satisfaction in order to develop the taxonomy of IS effectiveness, VSTISE. However, additional work is needed to validate the taxonomy. Specifically, future research should attempt to empirical validate the proposed taxonomy in different IS services. Some examples for additional studies resulting from this work may include construction of VSTISE for electronic medical records (EMRs), e-government systems, flight reservation systems, customer relations management (CRM) systems, enterprise information systems or enterprise resource planning (ERP) systems, etc. Moreover, additional work is needed to fully understand the relationship of the user-perceived value construct and other key constructs in IS literature.

Practitioners (i.e., decision makers and IS managers) may use our proposed taxonomy in various types of systems as a benchmarking tool to assess the user-perceived IS effectiveness. Practitioners can use the VSTISE, following Grover et al.'s (1996) approach, to evaluate system effectiveness over time by seeing visually how the IS characteristics move in the taxonomy over time. Moreover, they can use the VSTISE to compare IS effectiveness among peer systems by comparing the results of the taxonomy measured by two or more IS. For example, a study could be done for the exploration of IS effectiveness of Web-based flight reservation systems. Such a study could follow the qualitative approaches proposed in the first phase of the case study to develop a list of characteristics and develop a survey to assess both user satisfaction and user-perceived value of the system. That data could then be used to develop the Value-Satisfaction grid of Web-based airline reservation systems. Such assessment can compare results of multiple systems as a comparative measure, or provide a longitudinal assessment and compare the same system or systems over time. Results of such VSTISEs can help managers and IS managers of such Web-based flight reservation systems to improve system characteristics with misleading effectiveness by channeling funding to these system characteristics and eliminate system characteristics that have high perceived value but low satisfaction.

Limitations

This study has several limitations. The first one is related to the definition of IS effectiveness. As discussed in the theoretical background section, the definition of IS effectiveness and ways to measure it has been a moving target for IS scholars for nearly three decades. In this work, we followed only one perspective proposed by Grover et al. (1996) to interpreting and measuring IS effectiveness, namely the individual user as the unit of analysis. However, Grover et al. (1996) indicated a second perspective of IS effectiveness, namely the organizational unit of analysis. Thus, additional research may be needed to investigate the use of VSTISE proposed here to indicate IS effectiveness from the organizational unit of analysis. The second study limitation is external validity. The results presented here are based exclusively on a single institution and one type of IS. Additional studies should attempt to validate the results in other institutions as well as other types of ISs. Finally, the nature of this study was an exploratory one attempting to develop the taxonomy, rather than test hypotheses. As such, additional validity and reliability measures are warranted. Straub (1989) suggested that sound measures of IS should be tested in multiple methodologies in order to provide evidence for construct validity. He defines construct validity as "measures [that] show stability across methodology" (Straub, 1989, p. 150). Although in this study, we have used both qualitative and qualitative approaches to develop and measure the constructs, additional validation is needed for the results presented here. Therefore, future studies may also use difference methodologies, e.g. confirmatory analysis, in order to provide further validity and reliability for the results.

Conclusion

The proposed taxonomy was highlighted for its validity with a case study of nearly 200 users. A two-phase study incorporating qualitative and quantitative methods was used to develop an instrument assessing users' perceived value and user satisfaction in the context of OLS. Prior to the development of the VSTISEs, empirical data validated that the construct of *perceived value* is indeed a fully independent construct from the construct of *user satisfaction*. Although previous IS literature suggested that the two constructs are highly correlated (i.e., user satisfaction and user-perceived value), results of this empirical case study suggest that the two constructs show no observed correlations (linear or non-linear), which is consistent with the findings by non-IS studies (Chiou, 2004; Yang & Peterson, 2004). Using aggregated data, VSTISEs were developed following four major system dimensions: (A) Technology, Network, and Technical Support; (B) Information and Content; (C) Developers and Managers; as well as (D) User. Results indicated several system characteristics that may need additional attention, while they also indicated several system characteristics that are perceived by the users as effective.

ACKNOWLEDGMENT

The authors would like to thank the accepting editor-in-chief Professor John Wang, as well as the anonymous referees, for their careful review and valuable suggestions. Additionally, the authors would like to thank the users for participating in this study.

REFERENCE

Ahituv, N., Munro, M. C., & Wand, Y. (1981). The value of information in information analysis. *Information & Management*, *4*(3), 143–150. doi:10.1016/0378-7206(81)90041-0

Ajzen, I., & Fishbein, M. (1980). *Understanding attitudes and predicting social behaviors*. Engelwood Cliffs, NJ: Prentice Hall.

Allport, G., Vernon, P., & Lindzey, G. (1951). *Study of values. Manual of directions*. Boston, MA: Houghton Mifflin.

Andrews, K. R. (1987). *The concept of corporate strategy*. Homewood, IL: Irwin.

Ansoff, H. I. (1965). *Corporate strategy*. New York: McGraw-Hill.

Arnold, V. (1995). Discussion of an experimental evaluation of measurements of information system effectiveness. *Journal of Information Systems*, *9*(2), 85–91.

Bailey, J. E., & Pearson, S. W. (1983). Development of a tool for measuring and analyzing computer user satisfaction. *Management Science*, *29*(5), 530–546. doi:10.1287/mnsc.29.5.530

Barki, H., & Hartwick, J. (1994). Measuring user participation, user involvement, and user attitude. *Management Information Systems Quarterly*, *18*(1), 59–82. doi:10.2307/249610

Baroudi, J. J., Olson, M. H., & Ives, B. (1986). An empirical study of the impact of user involvement on system usage and information satisfaction. *Communications of the ACM*, *29*(3), 232–238. doi:10.1145/5666.5669

Baroudi, J. J., & Orlikowski, W. J. (1988). A short-from measure of user information satisfaction: A psychometric evaluation and notes on use. *Journal of Management Information Systems*, *4*(4), 44–60.

Beatty, S. E., Kahle, L. R., Homer, P., & Misra, S. (1985). Alternative measurement approaches to consumer values: The list of values and the Rokeach value survey. *Psychology and Marketing*, *2*(3), 181–200. doi:10.1002/mar.4220020305

Benson, D. H. (1982). A field study of end-user computing: Findings and issues. *Management Information Systems Quarterly*, *6*(2), 11–31.

Brown, M. A. (1976). Values - a necessary but neglected ingredient of motivation on the job. *Academy of Management Review*, *1*(4), 15–23. doi:10.2307/257721

Chiou, J.-S. (2004). The antecedents of consumers' loyalty toward internet service providers. *Information & Management*, *41*(6), 685–695. doi:10.1016/j.im.2003.08.006

Davis, F. D. (1986). Technology acceptance model for empirically testing new end-user information systems: Theory and results. Dissertation abstracts international. (umi no. Aat 0374529). MA, USA: Massachusetts Institute of Technology.

Davis, F. D. (1989). Perceived usefulness, perceived ease of use, and user acceptance of information technology. *Management Information Systems Quarterly*, *13*(3), 319–339. doi:10.2307/249008

Davis, F. D., Bagozzi, R. P., & Warshaw, P. R. (1989). User acceptance of computer technology: A comparison of two theoretical models. *Management Science*, *35*(8), 982–1004. doi:10.1287/mnsc.35.8.982

DeLone, W. H., & McLean, E. R. (1992). Information system success: The quest for the dependent variable. *Information Systems Research*, *3*(1), 60–95. doi:10.1287/isre.3.1.60

DeLone, W. H., & McLean, E. R. (2003). The DeLone and McLean model of information systems success: A ten-year update. *Journal of Management Information Systems*, *19*(4), 9–30.

Doll, W., & Torkzadeh, G. (1988). The measurement of end-user computing satisfaction. *Management Information Systems Quarterly*, *12*(2), 259–274. doi:10.2307/248851

Doll, W. J., & Torkzadeh, G. (1991). The measurement of end-user computing satisfaction: Theoretical and methodological issues. *Management Information Systems Quarterly*, *15*(1), 5–9. doi:10.2307/249429

Doll, W. J., Xia, W., & Torkzadeh, G. (1994). A confirmatory factor analysis of the end-user computing satisfaction instrument. *Management Information Systems Quarterly*, *18*(4), 453–461. doi:10.2307/249524

Durgee, J. F., O'Connor, G. C., & Veryzer, R. W. (1996). Translating values into product wants. *Journal of Advertising Research*, *36*(6), 90–101.

Etezadi-Amoli, J., & Farhoomand, A. F. (1991). On end-user computing satisfaction. *Management Information Systems Quarterly*, *15*(1), 1–5. doi:10.2307/249428

Feather, N. T. (1967). An expectancy-value model of information-seeking behavior. *Psychological Review*, *74*(5), 242–360. doi:10.1037/h0024879

Feather, N. T. (1975). *Values in education and society*. New York, NY: The Free Press.

Fuerst, W. L., & Cheney, P. H. (1982). Factors affecting the perceived utilization of computer-based decision support systems in the oil industry. *Decision Sciences*, *13*(4), 554–569.

Galletta, D. F., & Lederer, A. L. (1989). Some cautions on the measurement of user information satisfaction. *Decision Sciences*, *20*(3), 419–439. doi:10.1111/j.1540-5915.1989.tb01558.x

Gefen, D., & Ragowsky, A. (2005). A multi-level approach to measuring the benefits of an erp system in manufacturing firms. *Information Systems Management*, *22*(1), 18–26. doi:10.1201/1078/44912.22.1.20051201/85735.3

Gelderman, M. (1998). The relation between user satisfaction, usage of information systems and performance. *Information & Management*, *34*(1), 11–18. doi:10.1016/S0378-7206(98)00044-5

Ginzberg, M. J. (1981). Early diagnosis of MIS implementation failure: Promising results and unanswered questions. *Management Science*, *27*(4), 459–478. doi:10.1287/mnsc.27.4.459

Grover, V., Seung, R. J., & Segars, A. H. (1996). Information systems effectiveness: The construct space and patters of application. *Information & Management*, *31*(4), 177–191. doi:10.1016/S0378-7206(96)01079-8

Hendrickson, A. R., Glorfeld, K., & Cronan, T. P. (1994). On the repeated test-retest reliability of the end-user computing satisfaction instrument: A comment. *Decision Sciences*, *25*(4), 655–668. doi:10.1111/j.1540-5915.1994.tb01864.x

Ives, B., Olson, M. H., & Baroudi, J. J. (1983). The measurement of user information satisfaction. *Communications of the ACM*, *26*(10), 785–793. doi:10.1145/358413.358430

Jenkins, A. M., & Ricketts, J. A. (1979). *Development of an instrument to measure user information satisfaction with management information systems* (pp. 1–27). Bloomington: Indiana University.

Kahle, L. R., & Kennedy, P. (1988). Using the list of values lov to understand consumers. *Journal of Services Marketing*, *2*(4), 49–56. doi:10.1108/eb024742

Keeney, R. L. (1999). The value of internet commerce to the customer. *Management Science*, *45*(4), 533–542. doi:10.1287/mnsc.45.4.533

Keeney, R. L., & Raiffa, H. (1993). *Decisions with multiple objectives: Preferences and value tradeoffs*. Cambridge, MA: Harvard University Press.

Kettinger, W. J., & Lee, C. C. (1994). Perceived service quality and user satisfaction with the information systems. *Decision Sciences*, *25*(5/6), 737–767. doi:10.1111/j.1540-5915.1994.tb01868.x

Kim, K. K. (1989). User satisfaction: A synthesis of three different perspectives. *Journal of Information Systems*, *4*(1), 1–12.

Kluckhohn, C. (1951). Values and value-orientations in the theory of action. In Parsons, T., & Shils, E. (Eds.), *Towards a general theory of action*. Cambridge, MA: Harvard University Press.

Lee, S. M., Kim, Y. R., & Lee, J. (1995). An empirical study of the relationships among end-user infor. *Journal of Management Information Systems*, *12*(2), 189–203.

McHaney, R., & Cronan, T. P. (1998). Computer simulation success: On the use of the end-user computing satisfaction instrument: A comment. *Decision Sciences*, *29*(2), 525–537. doi:10.1111/j.1540-5915.1998.tb01589.x

McHaney, R., Hightower, R., & Pearson, J. (2002). A validation of the end-user computing satisfaction instrument in Taiwan. *Information & Management*, *39*(6), 503–511. doi:10.1016/S0378-7206(01)00119-7

Mertler, C. A., & Vannatta, R. A. (2001). *Advanced and multivariate statistical methods: Practical application and interpretation*. Los Angeles, CA: Pyrczak Publishing.

Mintzberg, H., Ahlstrand, B., & Lampel, J. (1998). *Strategy safari: A guide through the wilds of strategic management*. New York: The Free Press.

Palvia, P. C. (1996). A model and instrument for measuring small business user satisfaction with information technology. *Information & Management*, *31*(3), 151–163. doi:10.1016/S0378-7206(96)01069-5

Parasuraman, A., Zeithaml, V. A., & Berry, L. L. (1988). SERVQUAL: A multiple-item scale for measuring consumer perceptions of service quality. *Journal of Retailing*, *64*(1), 12–40.

Pitt, L. F., Watson, R. T., & Kavan, C. B. (1995). Service quality: A measure of information systems effectiveness. *Management Information Systems Quarterly*, *19*(2), 173–187. doi:10.2307/249687

Porter, M. E. (1991). Toward a dynamic theory of strategy. *Strategic Management Journal*, *12*(1), 95–117. doi:10.1002/smj.4250121008

Prescott, S., & Hopkins, G. (1984). The value and attitude structure of special educators. *College Student Journal*, *18*(2), 56–59.

Rafaeli, S., & Raban, D. (2003). Experimental investigation of the subjective value of information in trading. *Journal of the AIS*, *4*(5), 119–137.

Ragowsky, A. (1995). Ranking the benefits of IS applications for manufacturing. *Journal of Systems Management*, *46*(2), 56–60.

Ragowsky, A., Somers, T. M., & Adams, D. A. (2005). Assessing the value provided by erp applications through organizational activities. *Communications of AIS*, *16*(18), 1–50.

Ragowsky, A., Stern, M., & Adams, D. A. (2000). Relating benefits from using IS to an organization's operating characteristics: Interpreting results from two countries. *Journal of Management Information Systems*, *16*(4), 175–195.

Rokeach, M. (1969). *Beliefs, attitudes, and values*. San Francisco, CA: Jossey-Bass Inc. Publishers.

Rokeach, M. (1973). *The nature of human values*. New York, NY: The Free Press.

Rokeach, M. (1979). *Understanding human values*. New York, NY: The Free Press.

Scott, J. E. (1995). The measurement of information systems effectiveness: Evaluating a measuring instrument. *The Data Base for Advances in Information Systems*, *26*(1), 43–61.

Seddon, P., & Yip, S. K. (1992). An empirical evaluation of user information satisfaction (UIS) measures for use with general ledger accounting software. *The Journal of Information Systems*, *6*(1), 75–93.

Shannon, C. E., & Weaver, W. (1949). *The mathematical theory of communication*. Urbana, IL: University of Illinois Press.

Srinivasan, A. (1985). Alternative measures of system effectiveness: Associations and implications. *Management Information Systems Quarterly*, *9*(3), 243–253. doi:10.2307/248951

Stone, D. N. (1990). Assumptions and values in the practice of information system evaluation. *The Journal of Information Systems*, *5*(1), 1–17.

Torkzadeh, G., & Doll, W. J. (1991). Test-retest reliability of the end-user computing satisfaction instrument. *Decision Sciences*, *22*(1), 26–38. doi:10.1111/j.1540-5915.1991.tb01259.x

Venkatesh, V., Morris, M. G., Davis, G. B., & Davis, F. D. (2003). User acceptance of information technology: Toward a unified view. *Management Information Systems Quarterly*, *27*(3), 425–478.

Webster, J., & Hackley, P. (1997). Teaching effectiveness in technology-mediated distance learning. *Academy of Management Journal*, *40*(6), 1282–1310. doi:10.2307/257034

Williams, R. M. (1979). Change and stability in values and value system: A sociological perspective. In Rokeach, M. (Ed.), *Understanding human values*. New York, NY: The Free Press.

Yang, Z., & Peterson, R. T. (2004). Customer perceived value, satisfaction, and loyalty: The role of switching costs. *Psychology and Marketing*, *21*(10), 799–822. doi:10.1002/mar.20030

Yuthas, K., & Eining, M. M. (1995). An experimental evaluation of measurements of information system effectiveness. *The Journal of Information Systems*, *9*(2), 69–84.

Zviran, M., & Erlich, Z. (2003). Measuring IS user satisfaction: Review and implications. *Communications of the Association for Information Systems*, *12*(1), 81–103.

APPENDIX A

Open Ended Questionnaire (Phase I)

Section 1:

Please identify five things that are important for you when using the information system:

1. _________________________
2. _________________________
3. _________________________
4. _________________________
5. _________________________

Section 2:

A. Technology, Network, and Technical Support

Now, please think about issues related to the ***Technology, Network and Technical Support*** and try to identify five more things that are important for you when using the information system:

1. _________________________
2. _________________________
3. _________________________
4. _________________________
5. _________________________

B. Information and Content

Now, please think about issues related to the ***Information and Content*** presented by the system and try to identify five more things that are important for you when using the information system:

1. _________________________
2. _________________________
3. _________________________
4. _________________________
5. _________________________

C. Developers & Managers

Now, please think about issues related to the ***Developers and Managers*** in charged of the system and try to identify five more things that are important for you when using the information system:

1. ____________________
2. ____________________
3. ____________________
4. ____________________
5. ____________________

D. User

Now, please think about issues related to the ***User*** and try to identify five more things that are important for you when using the information system:

1. ____________________
2. ____________________
3. ____________________
4. ____________________
5. ____________________

APPENDIX B

Resulted System Characteristics from Literature & Phase I in the Context of Online Learning Systems

Online Learning Systems Characteristics	
A1	Quick answer from technical support via phone
A2	Quick answer from technical support after-hours via e-mail
A3	Quality of technical support
A4	System operation time (up-time)
A5	Reduced system errors
A6	System security (discourage hacking, secure access, etc.)
A7	Access to courses from anywhere in the world (via the Internet)
A9	Learning at anytime of the day (schedule flexibility)
A10	Submit assignments from anywhere (via the Internet)
A11	Different system tools (chat, bulletin-board or discussion forums, etc.)
A12	Access of all courses from one area (My WebCT)
A13	Taking quizzes remotely (off-campus)
A14	Review course audios
B1	Availability of course content
B2	Quality content of courses
B3	Amount of material in courses
B4	Interesting subject matter
B5	Difficulty of subject matter
B7	Enjoyment from the courses/lessons
B8	Ease-of-use (with course content, navigation, interface, etc.)
B9	Similar of interface across all online courses
B10	Gathering information quickly
B11	Organization of courses (content of courses, organization of assignments, etc. across all courses)
B12	Taking practice tests prior to graded test
C1	Amount of professor-to-student interaction
C2	Professor's attitude (across all professors)
C4	Quality of professor-to-student interaction
C5	Freedom of learning (selective seeking and processing of information)
C6	Submission time window for assignments and quizzes
C7	Online workload of courses
D1	Learning a lot in these classes
D2	Amount of interaction with classmates
D3	Quality of interaction with classmates
D4	Classmates' attitude (across all courses)
D5	Being part of a 'class' although it was online

continued on following page

Appendix B. continued

Online Learning Systems Characteristics	
D6	Your comfort with online learning and technology
D7	Your Internet and computer skills
D8	Self-discipline and time management
D9	Cost of courses
D10	Cost of ISP and Internet access
D11	Reduced travel cost/time (to and from campus)
D12	Ability to travel while taking online courses (for business or other)
D13	Employer support and your ability to work while learning
D14	Attendance to family responsibilities
D15	Family support

This work was previously published in International Journal of Information Systems in the Service Sector (IJISSS), edited by John Wang, pp. 93-118, copyright 2009 by IGI Publishing (an imprint of IGI Global).

Section 2

Chapter 7
A Survey of Development Methods for Semantic Web Service Systems

Terje Wahl
Norwegian University of Science and Technology, Norway

Guttorm Sindre
Norwegian University of Science and Technology, Norway

ABSTRACT

Semantic web services (SWS) hold the promise of enabling dynamic discovery of candidate web services fitting a particular specified need. One interesting question is what impact this will have on software and systems engineering methods – will mainstream methods like RUP still be suitable, or will new or adapted methods be needed? This article surveys the state-of-the-art in methods specifically tailored for the engineering of SWS systems, looking at development methods trying to cover the entire lifecycle as well as methods covering only one or two phases. Some of the surveyed methods are specifically meant to deal with semantics, others are for the engineering of service-oriented systems in general. The survey reveals that there are many proposals being made in this area, some extensions of mainstream methods like RUP, others more experimental.

INTRODUCTION

During recent years, the software industry has increasingly acknowledged that using discrete building blocks of software provides an effective way of engineering such systems (Stojanovic & Dahanayake, 2005). The 1990's saw an increased use of component based development (CBD), but this is now giving way to the increasingly popular technologies of Web Services and Service Oriented Architectures (SOA) (Stojanovic & Dahanayake, 2005). In the future, Semantic Web Services (SWS) may provide an even more powerful way of rapidly building flexible and advanced Service Oriented Systems (SOS).

DOI: 10.4018/978-1-60960-138-6.ch007

Technology versus Development Methods

When information systems are developed based on some specific technology, this implies the use of some underlying basic concepts such as *ser-*

vice, *requester*, and *provider*, and a certain way of thinking about the structure and organization of the information systems. Hence, it is important that the system engineering methods match the underlying technology, to be able to create systems of high quality in a more effective manner. To effectively develop or adapt methods for engineering of SWS systems, there is a need for understanding what special concerns arise when engineering these systems. New engineering methods or adaptations of general methods may be desirable if special concerns are to be taken into consideration.

The service concept elevates the abstraction level and aims at empowering business users to create and execute software systems based on SOA (Erl, 2005; Stojanovic *et al.*, 2004). Many technology standards for SOS and Web Services-systems have emerged, but little attention has been given to methods for modeling and designing such systems (Cabral *et al.*, 2004). The amount of new technology is growing and it changes over time, making development complex and error-prone. As a result, increased application adaptability, widespread reuse and commercialization is slowed without proper support from methods and development tools (Cabral et al., 2004).

Motivation and Purpose

This article surveys the current state-of-the-art in engineering methods specifically tailored for the requirements specification, modeling, design and development of SWS systems. Methods may also be in the form of specially designed tools for supporting the development of SWS systems. The motivation for providing such a survey in terms of its utility for the reader is as follows:

- Giving an overview of methodological differences that have been envisioned between SWS systems development and current mainstream software development.
- Giving an overview of, and some comparison of, different methods and techniques that have been proposed to deal with the specific challenges of developing SWS systems, so that the reader can more easily navigate the plethora of existing proposals and possibly find a method which is useful in the reader's own context (whether this be research or practice).

We try to analyze what makes the development of SWS systems different and unique compared to the development of other kinds of information systems. From the survey we also try to identify what special concerns the methods take into consideration, and compare these concerns in the analysis. We perform a simple classification and comparison of the different methods and tools. In the end, we identify some suggested areas for future research into methods and tools supporting the engineering of SWS-based systems.

Scope

This article focuses on requirements specification, modeling, design / development, and testing / evaluation methods for creating SWS-based systems for end-users. It does not focus on methods for developing new technologies or frameworks for such systems, but rather attempts to look at what becomes important if assuming that the proper technical infrastructure is in place. As a result, we are focused on methods that involve users, with more or less technical skills, to see what systematic approach, actions, processes and tools are required to create a system for end-users based on an existing infrastructure framework.

Engineering of SWS systems may be seen from two perspectives: Engineering of individual SWS (as a service provider), or engineering of SOS utilizing SWS (SWS-based systems, as a service requester). When building the latter kinds of systems, there is often a need for simultaneously developing services - not only utilizing existing ones. This article tries to cover both these perspectives. On the other hand, the design, development and utilization of general domain ontologies are important aspects of developing SWS systems, but are considered beyond the scope of this article.

Many methods for engineering of information systems in general or SOS in general, e.g., (Stojanovic et al., 2004) might be useful for the engineering of SWS systems. This might especially be true for methods supporting modeling and elicitation of requirements, such as interviewing, workshops, etc. These methods are however considered beyond the scope of this article.

Research Questions and Methods

The research questions of this study are as follows: 1) What methods have been proposed specifically for the development of semantic web service systems? 2) How mature are these methods, e.g., in terms of empirical evaluations and tool support?

In the framework of (Glass *et al.*, 2004) the research method of this article would be classified as Literature Review / Analysis. In a more recent taxonomy by (Mora *et al.*, 2008) where IS research is divided into four quadrants according to the dimensions conceptual / empirical and behavioral / design, this article would fall into the category conceptual behavioral research, as it does not design anything new, rather reviewing existing proposals, and this review is on a conceptual level rather than performing empirical comparisons of various software engineering methods. As discussed by (Kitchenham, 2004) there are two types of reviews, the *traditional / conventional* and the *systematic*. Systematic reviews have several advantages in terms of the thoroughness of procedure and confidence in the final result, but also disadvantages in a much heavier workload due to its formality, therefore requiring much longer time. The review reported in this article would not fully satisfy all of the strict criteria for a systematic review as formulated by Kitchenham, but has many aspects of a systematic review in that it makes an unbiased analysis of a large collection of works rather than considering a more limited and biased collection of sources.

The literature search for this study was performed by searching in Thomson ISI, IEEE and ACM Digital Libraries, and Google Scholar with phrases "web service" and "service-oriented" combined with development stage terms such as "analysis", "requirements", "design", "development", "composition", and "testing". The sources that emerged from this search were quickly evaluated by reading the abstract or browsing through the full paper (if available) to determine its relevance to our study. The most relevant ones were then selected for further analysis, the inclusion/exclusion criterion being whether the paper really proposed or discussed a *method* for service-oriented systems development (rather than merely discussing advantages of service-orientation or proposing components or architecture of such systems). The reference list of found papers was also used to harvest further papers that for some reason did not pop up in the initial search.

Organization of this Article

Section 2 presents related work and explains how the current article is different from previous surveys in the field. Section 3 discusses the special challenges in the engineering of SWS systems, emphasizing how this is different from more traditional software development, and motivating why specific methods are needed although mainstream development methods can partially be used or adapted to this purpose. Section 4 presents the surveyed methods and tools, which are compared and discussed in section 5. Section 6 concludes and suggests further research directions.

RELATED WORK

Some work has been done on surveying the state of the art in SWS technologies and frameworks, e.g., (Cabral et al., 2004), and for the underlying technologies of service-oriented architecture, there is a thorough survey in (Papazoglou & van den Heuvel, 2007). (Küngas & Matskin, 2006) perform a survey of commercial and governmental web services to see which data they use, but this is more an investigation of the services as such, not of software development methods related to semantic web services.

(Srivastava & Koehler, 2003) have performed a survey of current solutions and open problems regarding web service composition. They focus on solutions used in industry vs. solutions proposed by academia. (Rao & Su, 2004) make a survey of automated approaches to service composition, referencing some of the same articles as this one, but of course missing those published after 2004. (Zimmermann *et al.*, 2005) discuss analysis and design techniques for service-oriented development in a survey-like manner, however, with fairly few references the paper is more a survey of issues than of sources in the field. (Ramollari *et al.*, 2007) present a survey of service-oriented development methodologies. The survey is most focused on the analysis and design stages, but does not focus specifically on semantic web services.

Hence, the main differences of the current survey compared to these previous ones is a more specific focus on engineering methods for SWS systems without restricting ourselves to any specific development stage, as well as looking at a broader range of methods.

SEMANTIC WEB SERVICES AND SOFTWARE ENGINEERING

Potential Benefits of Semantics

Existing technologies for traditional web services only allow descriptions at the syntactic level (Cabral *et al.*, 2004). This makes it difficult for requesters and providers to understand the meaning of the inputs and outputs and the real functionality of the service. This limitation may be overcome with the use of SWS. Semantic descriptions of web services are needed to enable automated discovery, composition and execution across heterogeneous users and domains (Cabral et al., 2004). Each SWS is described in a service ontology, enabling machines to understand its capabilities and reason over it related to other domain knowledge.

According to (Cabral et al., 2004), SWS infrastructures can be described along three different dimensions, as shown in Figure 1: *Usage activities*, *architecture* and *service ontology*. These dimensions are about the business, physical and conceptual level requirements for SWS respectively.

Special Lifecycle Concerns for SWS Systems

(Blake, 2007) discusses lifecycle issues in the development of service-oriented systems. Two different lifecycles are proposed. The development of single services is seen as similar to more traditional development, thus possible to do within mainstream lifecycles, for instance of RUP-like conceptualization and analysis, followed by iterative cycles of design, development, and testing, and finalized by deployment and retirement. However, the development of larger systems composed by such services, called service-centric software systems management, is seen as quite different, thus needing a new kind of lifecycle with several different roles participating. Business-process engineers will be responsible for business-process conceptualization and domain analysis. Software engineers will then be responsible for the subsequent design stage. This has an iterative cycle much similar to the previous lifecycle, but the nature of the steps is different: service discovery, service composition, and evaluation. Finally, the operation stage is also different in nature, with the steps on-demand composition and rebinding,

Figure 1. SWS infrastructure dimensions, adapted from (Cabral et al., 2004)

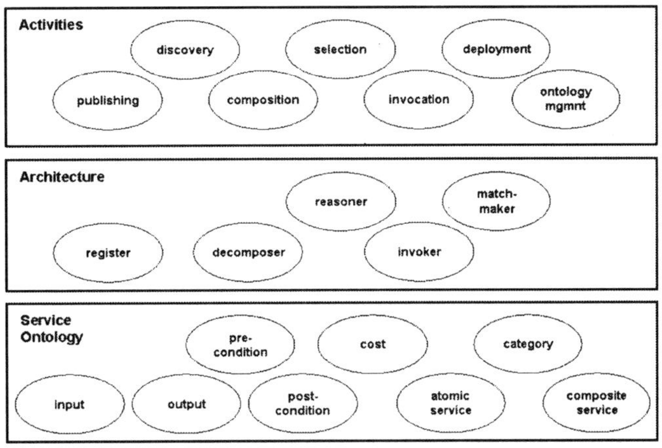

indicating a much higher dynamicity than for the traditional lifecycle.

(Gu & Lago, 2007) propose a more complex picture, illustrating the roles of several actors in one lifecycle picture. The main roles, however, are the service provider and application provider, which correspond to the two different kinds of lifecycle suggested by (Blake, 2007), and many similar aspects can be seen covered in both proposals. A somewhat more traditional lifecycle, much inspired by RUP, can be seen in (Papazoglou & van den Heuvel, 2006), identifying four different approaches to service-oriented applications: green-field, top-down, bottom-up, and meet-in-the-middle development.

(Tsai *et al.*, 2006) mention four challenges for service-oriented software engineering, namely decomposition challenge, utility challenge, quality challenge, and certification challenge, and state that service-oriented development has somewhat different methodological needs from the current mainstream focus on OOA / OOD with methods such as RUP and MSF. Yet, as pointed out by (Zimmermann et al., 2005) many of the general principles found in such mainstream methods still apply also in service-oriented software engineering, and extensions or adaptations of mainstream methods may therefore be one approach to better address service-oriented development. Some examples of RUP extensions are IBM's RUP for SOA (IBM, 2006) and the Service-Oriented Unified Process (Mittal, 2007). Sun's SOA RQ method (Sun, 2006) and the method proposed in (Papazoglou & van den Heuvel, 2006) are also partly based on or have many similarities with RUP. Another example of a relationship between mainstream and service-oriented software development is OMG's effort to combine MDA with SOA, and to provide a meta-model for defining ontologies to help the construction of semantic web applications in an MDA context (OMG, 2006). The UML SOA profile proposed by (Johnston, 2005) can be seen as a related effort to align service-oriented development with mainstream techniques.

Another view on lifecycle can be found in situations where the idea is not to build new software but to offer services to a customer, for instance in a sourcing situation. The Information Technology Infrastructure Library, version 3 (ITIL v3) has made an increasing focus on service-oriented approaches in IT service management (Greiner,

2007; Keel *et al.*, 2007). From the perspective of the service-provider, the following lifecycle activities are envisioned: Service Strategy, Service Design, Service Transition, Service Operation, and Continual Service Improvement (Greiner, 2007). ITIL provides a common vocabulary for these activities, as well as guidelines to how they should be conducted.

Special Phase Concerns for SWS Systems

To find suitable specialized engineering methods, there is a need for understanding what special concerns arise when engineering systems based on SWS. On the requirements level, service-orientation poses both challenges and opportunities. The introduction of a new architectural paradigm might mean that some traditional development methods are no longer appropriate, and that new methods are needed. On the other hand, the presence and possible reuse of existing services might make requirements engineering easier (Jones *et al.*, 2005) – for instance, functionality of available services might inspire stakeholders to become clear about requirements they were not aware of, and could also enable rapid prototyping for elicitation and validation purposes.

Moreover, requirements engineering challenges can be found on two different levels, requirements for single services (which should, for instance, be as generic as possible to make the service competitive for usage in a wide range of applications), and requirements for applications or systems composed of various services, where the goal is to satisfy the needs of the stakeholders of that particular application. This is quite similar to the old distinction between development for reuse and development with reuse (Sindre *et al.*, 1995).

To understand challenges in design and later development stages we need to know what parts of a system must be implemented if we assume that there already exists a suitable infrastructure framework on which to build the system? Answering this question requires us to analyze what components and functions of the system are (or are envisioned to be) fully automated elements that need no involvement from the (business) user or system developer that are creating the end-user system.

All the *architecture* components for SWS (as shown in Figure 1) are meant to be automatic functions in an SWS framework. For example, *reasoning* is supposed to be performed without human intervention. Regarding the *activities* performed in an SWS system, most of these are clearly desired to be automatically performed, e.g., *publishing* and *invocation* of services. However, some of the activities may need to be performed manually or at least semi-automatically, depending on the complexity and type of system. This especially applies to *composition* and *selection* of services (D. Martin *et al.*, 2004). A system performing simple tasks within a well known domain may perform fully automated service composition and selection if the underlying framework is sufficiently robust and advanced (D. Martin et al., 2004). But some tasks may be so complicated that they require a user to manually specify how different services are to be composed, or manually select desired services from lists of possible matches. In addition, sometimes users will want to be able to influence the composition process, e.g., if they only have a basic overall idea of their requirements for the system (Kim & Gil, 2004). One method of manually specifying a composition may be to define a process flow for the execution of a combination of different activities.

The *service ontology*, describing the service extensively, will usually have to be manually specified. This is done when implementing a service as a service provider, and must assure that the capabilities of the service are aligned with its service description (its service ontology). When specifying requirements for a SWS system, an overall service ontology may be created manually to specify the goal and requirements of the system, or a business process may be manually created and service ontologies defined for each of the activities in the process.

Service-oriented systems also have special challenges in the testing and evaluation phase. As pointed out by (Offutt & Xu, 2004) the testing of web service applications is difficult because they are distributed applications with runtime behaviors that differ from more traditional applications. For instance, the fact that service providers may change the implementation of a service at any time, introduces new challenges to regression testing (Ruth, 2008) and quality evaluation (Bianculli & Ghezzi, 2007).

Empowering the End User

Since the first software systems were created, systems have been developed at an increasing level of abstraction, making it easier for non-technical users to participate. SOS engineering (including SWS systems engineering) takes aim at providing modeling, design and development methods that map high-level business requirements to the technical implementation (Stojanovic & Dahanayake, 2005). Doing this will empower end-users to specify, design and develop their own systems, and thus "bridge the gap between business and IT" (Stojanovic & Dahanayake, 2005). Hence it is important that the methods and tools require as little technical skills as possible. Properly set up, and assuming an adequate supply of various services from providers, it could be possible for non-technical users to develop SWS systems in a fashion similar to Model Driven Development (MDD).

OVERVIEW OF METHODS AND TOOLS

In this section we survey methods and tools that support the engineering of SWS systems. We focus on methods and tools from the user perspective, i.e. involving user interaction.

Requirements for SWS systems

The EU-funded IP project "Service Centric Systems Engineering" (SeCSE) has addressed various aspects of the development of service-oriented applications, including the requirements process (Jones et al., 2005; Zachos *et al.*, 2007). This is envisioned as an iterative cycle between requirements formulation and searching for services. Starting with an incomplete requirements specification, some possible services may be found in a service repository, these may again provide ideas – either because of functionality they contain, or properties they are lacking – for more detailed requirements. Tool support is developed for the approach, including a requirements assistant (UCaRE), a service discovery tool (EDDiE), and a service exploration tool. An evaluation of UCaRE is presented in (Zachos et al., 2007), while the EDDiE tool is presented in more detail in (Dourdas *et al.*, 2006).

While the efforts around UCaRE have mainly addressed the requirements specification of larger systems (to be composed of services), another effort within SeCSE has addressed the specification of single services (Walkerdine *et al.*, 2007). A faceted specification approach is used to aid the later retrieval and comparison of services according to system specification. Also here, tool support has been developed and evaluated through a case study.

(Barn *et al.*, 2007) propose a tool workbench (SOA-MDK) for model-based development of service-oriented systems. The approach is inspired by component-based development, and the development method starts by developing business process models and information models, which can be considered RE activities on the system level. These models are then factored, and services allocated to the various parts. Finally, WSDL specifications are generated for the various services. A somewhat similar approach, but considering use cases plus non-functional requirements rather than business process models in the early stages, is proposed by (Dexter *et al.*, 2007).

Modeling and Design of SWS

(Timm & Gannod, 2005) recognize that the learning curve for the OWL-S descriptions language is steep, and that the current state of tool support is limited. They have created an automated software tool that uses model-driven architecture (MDA) techniques to generate OWL-S descriptions. The manual input to this tool is the description of an SWS in the form of a UML model specified in a standard UML modeling tool. Conversion to OWL-S is done via an XML representation of the UML model and XSLT.

(Jaeger *et al.*, 2005) propose a methodology for developing OWL-S descriptions that consists of three main steps: Generation of an OWL-S template, identification of available ontologies, and performing classification. Tasks in this methodology that must be performed manually are adapting or designing an ontology that describes the relevant domain, and classifications of the service, its inputs/outputs and any optional additions.

(Elenius *et al.*, 2005) have created a development tool for SWS, in the form of an OWL-S editor which aims to be easy and intuitive. The editor is implemented as a plug-in to the Protégé OWL ontology editor, and allows for engineering of all aspects of SWS by providing specialized views and design features wherever deemed necessary by the authors.

(Scicluna *et al.*, 2004) discuss how the difficult task of developing an OWL-S specification can result in incorrect specifications of the description or lead the user to rather utilize some other type of description language. They have created the OWL-S editor tool *OwlsWiz,* which enables creation of OWL-S ontologies from a WSDL description by presenting the user to a step-by-step process of inputting information. It allows a fast way of creating SWS descriptions while using well known standards such as WSDL and UML Activity Diagrams. Their main objective with the tool is to abstract away the underlying complexity of the OWL-S format and offer a relatively user-friendly way of building complex descriptions.

(Klein & Koenig-Ries, 2003) present an approach to improving the usability of DAML-S (now named OWL-S) by suggesting a process and a tool. The process guides through the activities needed to create adequate SWS descriptions by introducing a layered ontology of services, consisting of an upper service ontology, an ontology for the service category, and several domain ontologies. Their graphical tool *DINST* implements this process and claim to offer a comfortable way of editing SWS descriptions.

(Heß *et al.*, 2004) state that manually creating semantic metadata for services is tedious and error-prone. They propose a semi-automatic tool (*ASSAM*) for assisting a user in creating semantic metadata for SWS in the OWL-S format. *ASSAM* consists of two parts; a WSDL annotator application, and OATS (Operation Aggregation Tool for Web Services), a data aggregation/schema matching algorithm. The WSDL annotator application uses machine learning to provide the user with a point-and-click interface containing suggestions on how to semantically annotate a web service. The tools have been evaluated, and findings indicate their usefulness.

(Brambilla *et al.*, 2007) propose a framework for developing semantic web service systems cross-cutting several enterprises. The proposed approach utilizes several available techniques, such as BPMN for the specification of business process models and WebML for the development of web applications. WSMO ontologies are semi-automatically elicited from the design of the applications. Their model-driven design process is seen as consisting of four steps: process design, data design, hypertext design, and semantic description. For this approach, a CASE-tool has also been presented (Brambilla *et al.*, 2006).

Composition of Semantic Web Services

(Sirin *et al.*, 2004) have developed a goal-oriented and interactive composition approach that utilizes matchmaking algorithms to assist users in filtering and selecting services while building the composition. They have created a semi-automatic tool that uses OWL-S service descriptions and filters and selects services using matchmaking algorithms. The system has two separate components: One component is an inference engine that stores service requirements and processes match requests. The other is the composer that generates the service composition workflow. The composer communicates with the inference engine to discover possible matching services, and presents them to users that may create a workflow of services based on the choices presented at each step. Users enter constraints on the service parameters from a form generated by the system using the ontologies that define those parameters. Users make the final selection of the specific services at each step.

(Kim & Gil, 2004) have developed a framework for interactive composition of SWS that guide users in sketching a composition of services. They argue that users benefit when employing intelligent tools that help them specify complete and correct pathways, even if there is only a small number of services that need to be put together. Their approach is to first take existing service descriptions and extend them with domain ontologies and task ontologies that attend to various task types in the domain. Their analysis tool *CAT* (Composition Analysis Tool) then uses these ontologies when examining and giving specific suggestions regarding the user's solution. They demonstrate how *CAT* may be useful in a case study regarding the domain of earthquake science.

The Service Component Architecture (SCA) (Chappell, 2007) is a joint effort in by a number of American companies, defining a platform for how to program web services and how to assemble them. However, it focuses more on defining necessary standards and infrastructure, and less on software engineering methods.

IRS-III (Hakimpour *et al.*, 2005) is a framework for structured web service composition. Their approach is supported by a tool which automatically recommends candidate web services to satisfy the specified composition context.

Testing / Evaluation of Service-Oriented Systems

(Offutt & Xu, 2004) present an approach for automated generation of test cases for web service systems, based on data perturbation. Automated test generation is also the topic of (Sinha & Paradkar, 2006), proposing an approach based on finite state machines. In this approach, WSDL-S specifications are taken as input, hence utilizing some provided semantics of services.

(E. Martin *et al.*, 2007) presents a prototype tool for robustness testing of web service systems, but this is for web services in general, not specifically for semantic web services.

(Ruth, 2008) presents algorithms for safe test selection when performing regression testing on web service applications. (Penta *et al.*, 2007) propose the usage of genetic algorithms to produce test data for examining whether web services adhere to service level agreements.

As for evaluation, (Bianculli & Ghezzi, 2007) propose an approach for run-time quality monitoring of conversational web services, based on algebraic specifications. (Zhu *et al.*, 2006) present an approach for model-driven generation of benchmarks to evaluate service-oriented systems.

Methods Spanning Several Development Phases

(Gomez-Perez & González-Cabero, 2004) propose a framework for design and semi-automatic composition of SWS at a language-independent and knowledge level. The framework is directly based on the stack of ontologies that describe all the features of SWS. The framework specifies how to create SWS with the capabilities required by an external agent or user, focusing on three models: An instance model (specifying the SWS at the knowledge level), a checking model (utilizing design rules - called axioms - to check that there are no inconsistencies or errors in ontology instances) and a translation model (translating the service modeled at the knowledge level into an SWS-oriented language such as OWL-S combined with WDSL/SOAP). A prototype tool called *ODE SWS* has been implemented as an integrated part of *WebODE*, which is a platform for ontology development. The tool allows users to manually design descriptions and compositions of services at a conceptual level using a graphical user interface. The service model and composition is automatically checked for errors before performing an automatic translation into the OWL-S specification.

(Howard & Kerschberg, 2004) recognize the need for a comprehensive and overarching framework that deals with the processing and workflow requirements of Virtual Organizations, maps these into a group of service-oriented activities, dynamically configures these activities from available services and manages the choreography and execution of these services. They propose such a framework, which they call the Knowledge-based Dynamic Semantic Web Services (KDSWS) Framework. The framework deals with specification of service requirements, mapping of these requirements to composable services, and coordination of the execution of services conforming to enterprise workflow requirements. The KDSWS Framework has a functional architecture containing a user layer. The idea is that users would visit a portal of the e-enterprise, compose their request as a high-level task, and cooperate with a planning agent to decompose the task into a plan that is automatically processed further. A framework implementation is planned in the future.

(Papazoglou & van den Heuvel, 2006) propose a method which is inspired by RUP, combined with business process modeling and component-based development, covering all phases from planning to deployment and execution of the service-oriented system. However, while all phases are mentioned, some of them (e.g., testing) are discussed in rather general terms, not containing any suggestions of specific service-oriented techniques for that phase. The development of an integrated tool set supporting the approach is mentioned as future work in the article.

COMPARISON AND DISCUSSION

In this section we perform a simple classification and comparison of the different methods and tools, and discuss the result.

Table 1 gives an overview of the methods and tools identified in the survey dealing with stages before testing. It indicates what development phase the methods are intended for, whether tool support is documented for the method (the first Y/N in the Tool & Eval column), and if the usefulness of the method/tool is evaluated (the second Y/N in the Tool & Eval column). Note that an N in one of these columns does not necessarily mean that tool support or evaluations has not been established, only that this was not found documented in the publication. Furthermore, the "Lang" column indicates which modeling languages are utilized by the approach, and the final "Proc" column whether it makes any particular assumptions about the overall development process, e.g., being related to RUP or component-based development (CBD). Note here that a "no" does not necessarily mean that the approach could not be used together with, e.g., RUP, only that the publication does not make any particular assumption about this. Hence a "no" here may in some ways be a disadvantage (no overall process provided) but also in some ways an advantage (the proposed technique can potentially be used with many different larger-scale development methods).

Table 1. An overview of methods and tools supporting the engineering of SWS systems

Approach	Phase	Tool & eval		Lang	Proc
SOA-MDK (Barn et al., 2007; Dexter et al., 2007)	reqs	Y	Y	BPM, info.mod. Use cases	Inspired by CBD
SeCSE (Walkerdine et al., 2007; Zachos et al., 2007)	reqs, design, comp.	Y	Y	Use cases, Struct natural lang, WSDL	Extended RUP
(Timm & Gannod, 2005)	design	Y	N	UML, OWL-S	no
(Jaeger et al., 2005)	design	N	N	OWL-S	no
(Elenius et al., 2005)	design	Y	N	OWL-S	no
(Scicluna et al., 2004)	design	Y	N	OWL-S, WSDL, UML AD	no
(Klein & Koenig-Ries, 2003)	design	Y	N	OWL-S	no
(Heß et al., 2004)	design	Y	Y	OWL-S, WSDL	no
(Brambilla et al., 2007)	design	Y	Y	BPMN, WebML, WSMO	Own process
(Gomez-Perez & González-Cabero, 2004)	design, comp.	Y	N	OWL-S	no
(Sirin et al., 2004)	comp.	Y	N	OWL-S	no
(Kim & Gil, 2004)	comp.	Y	Y	WSDL	no
IRS-III (Hakimpour et al., 2005)	comp.	Y	Y	WSMO, UPML	no
(Howard & Kerschberg, 2004)	all	N	N	KDL, KDSPL	Own process
(Papazoglou & van den Heuvel, 2006)	all	N	N	BPEL	Inspired by RUP

Table 2 similarly gives an overview of the surveyed approaches to testing and evaluation of service-oriented systems. The columns indicate what kind of testing the technique supports, what kind of specifications it takes as input, what it delivers as output, and what approach is used for the intermediate processing.

The list of methods might not be comprehensive, but despite of this it may be argued that much more research has been done on the enabling technologies of SWS than research regarding methods for requirements engineering, modeling, design and composition of systems based on these technologies.

Most of the methods (all but two) are accompanied by a software tool. This might indicate that the need for tool support is recognized and reckoned with. However, most of the tools are at an early

Table 2. An overview of test and evaluation methods

Source	Kind of testing	input	output	approach
(Offutt & Xu, 2004)	functional	XML	test cases	Data perturbation
(Sinha & Paradkar, 2006)	functional	WSDL-S	Test cases	Extended finite state machines
(E. Martin et al., 2007)	robustness	WSDL	Test cases, test results	Java code generation
(Ruth, 2008)	regression	WSDL	Test selections	agents
(Penta et al., 2007)	Service level agreement	WS-BPEL	Test data	Genetic algorithms
(Bianculli & Ghezzi, 2007)	Perceived quality (run-time monitoring)	BPEL	Quality Evaluation	Algebraic specifications
(Zhu et al., 2006)	Performance / benchmarking	UML	benchmark	MDA

stage of development and undergoing continued development, showing that this research area is still somewhat experimental and immature. Yet, there is a positive trend that publications from the last 2-3 years tend to include evaluations of the proposed methods, while earlier publications did not.

Several methods focus on modeling & design or composition or both phases of development, but only two of the methods focus explicitly on requirements specification for SWS systems. This may be because this has not received a lot of attention in research, or because more general methods apply well to specifying requirements for SWS systems. Many methods talk about creating specifications of SWS systems, however it is important to note that a specification/description of a system is not the same as the system requirements.

Several of the suggested approaches underline the importance of user friendliness for the users that will make use of the methods and tools, by minimizing the needed amount of user input and the technical skills needed to provide it. This might point towards the underlying technologies being complex, and a wish for relatively non-technical business users to be able to create SWS systems in a fashion similar to Model Driven Development (MDD).

Most of the methods and tools utilize the OWL-S specification, indicating that it is very popular compared to other alternative technologies. Although most of the papers in this survey briefly rationalize the usefulness and argue the general benefits of their methods or correctness of their tools, only six of the methods have been evaluated for their usefulness. This hints at the relative immaturity of this research area, and a large potential for further research.

CONCLUSION AND SUGGESTIONS FOR FUTURE RESEARCH

Engineering of Semantic Web Services (SWS) systems include two important tasks that usually must be performed with input from a human user; requirements engineering, and modeling and design. In addition, manual input might often be needed when composing SWS into a workflow. Most of the other parts of SWS systems engineering are at least envisioned to be performed automatically. This indicates that engineering of SWS systems might become similar in fashion to Model Driven Development (MDD).

Our findings indicate that although some research have been done regarding methods for requirements engineering, modeling, design and composition of SWS systems, this research area is still somewhat experimental and immature. The need for tool support is recognized and reckoned with, and especially the approaches published in 2007 or later tend to come with working tool support, although this is often in the form of research prototypes that may not always be easily integrated with other mainstream software development tools. The OWL-S specification seems to be very popular in use compared to other alternative technologies. Methods for requirements engineering specifically aimed at SWS systems have not received a lot of attention. This might indicate that more general methods apply well to specifying requirements for SWS systems.

Research is being done to allow business users to be able to create SWS systems with as little technical knowledge as possible. This might also lead to engineering of SWS systems being performed in a fashion similar to MDD. There is also an evident convergence between business process modeling, enterprise application integration and service-orientation, for instance exemplified by the fact that many BPMS tools take a service-oriented approach. This convergence can also be seen in the survey, as languages such as BPMN and BPEL are included in several of the surveyed approaches in Table 1 and 2. The typical picture, however, is that the largest and most comprehensive tools tend to address service-oriented development in general, without any particular focus on semantics, while the tools that are ambitious on semantics tend to be smaller research prototypes with a more limited scope, dealing with only one or a few development phases. Hence, better tool support can be envisioned when ambitious semantic-based functionality also reaches the mainstream tools.

Future research is needed on methods for engineering of SWS systems. In particular, there is a need for further refinement of tools supporting the methods, and there is a strong need for research evaluating the usefulness of the proposed methods and tools. It will also prove valuable to do more research on requirements engineering for SWS systems, to examine if general requirements engineering methods are adequate, or if more suitable methods can be found when considering the distinctive character of SWS systems.

ACKNOWLEDGMENT

This work was performed in the context of the project WISEMOD, funded by the Norwegian Research Council.

REFERENCES

Barn, B., Dexter, H., Oussena, S., & Sparks, D. (2007). SOA-MDK: Towards a method development kit for service oriented system development. In Magyar, G., Knapp, G., Wojtkowski, W., Wojtkowski, W. G., & Zupančič, J. (Eds.), *Advances in information systems development: New methods and practice for the networked society* (pp. 191–201). Berlin: Springer.

Bianculli, D., & Ghezzi, C. (2007). *Monitoring conversational web services.* Paper presented at the 2nd International Workshop on Service Oriented Software Engineering (IW-SOSWE'07), Dubrovnik, Croatia. Retrieved 21.1., 2008, from http://www.selab.isti.cnr.it/IW-SOSWE07/program.html.

Blake, M. B. (2007). Decomposing composition: Service-oriented software engineers. *IEEE Software, 24*(6), 68–77. doi:10.1109/MS.2007.162

Brambilla, M., Ceri, S., Comai, S., & Fraternali, P. (2006). A CASE tool for modelling and automatically generating web service-enabled applications. *Int. J. Web Engineering and Technology, 2*(4).

Brambilla, M., Ceri, S., Facca, F. M., Celino, I., Cerizza, D., & Della Valle, E. (2007). Model-driven design and development of semantic web service applications. *ACM Transactions on Internet Technology, 8*(1), 3:1-3:31.

Cabral, L., Domingue, J., Motta, E., Payne, T. R., & Hakimpour, F. (2004). *Approaches to semantic web services: An overview and comparisons.* Paper presented at the ESWS'04.

Chappell, D. (2007). *Introducing sca.* Chappell & Associates.

Dexter, H., Petch, J., & Powley, D. (2007, 11-12 Jan). *Establishing an SOA composite applications development process for work-based learning and competency progression management.* Paper presented at the 2nd TENCompetence Open Workshop, Manchester, UK. Retrieved 20.1., 2008, from http://www.medicine.manchester.ac.uk/helm/TENCompPaper.pdf

Dourdas, N., Zhu, X., Maiden, N., Jones, S., & Zachos, K. (2006). Discovering remote software services that satisfy requirements: Patterns for query reformulation. In Dubois, E. & Pohl, K. (Eds.): *Advanced Information Systems Engineering, 18th International Conference*, CAiSE 2006, Luxembourg, June 5-9, 2006, Proceedings. Lecture Notes in Computer Science 4001 (pp. 239-254), Berlin: Springer.

Elenius, D., Denker, G., Martin, D., Gilham, F., Khouri, J., Sadaati, S., et al. (2005). The OWL-S editor: A development tool for semantic web services. In Gómez-Pérez, A. & Euzenat, J. (Eds.): *The Semantic Web: Research and Applications*, Second European Semantic Web Conference, ESWC 2005, Heraklion, Crete, Greece, May 29 - June 1, 2005, Proceedings. Lecture Notes in Computer Science 3532 (pp. 78-92). Berlin: Springer.

Erl, T. (2005). *Service-oriented architecture: Concepts, technology, and design*. Upper Saddle River, NJ: Prentice-Hall.

Glass, R. L., Ramesh, V., & Vessey, I. (2004). An analysis of research in computing disciplines. *Communications of the ACM*, *47*(6), 89–94. doi:10.1145/990680.990686

Gomez-Perez, A., & González-Cabero, R. (2004, 22-24 Mar). *A framework for design and composition of semantic web services*. Paper presented at the First International Semantic Web Services Symposium, Palo Alto, CA. Retrieved 22.4., 2007, from http://www.daml.ecs.soton.ac.uk/SSS-SWS04/44.pdf

Greiner, L. (2007). ITIL: The international repository of it wisdom. *Business: the 8th layer,* 9-11.

Gu, Q., & Lago, P. (2007). *A stakeholder-driven service life cycle model for soa*. Paper presented at the 2nd International Workshop on Service Oriented Software Engineering (IW-SOSWE'07), Dubrovnik, Croatia. Retrieved 21.1., 2008, from http://www.selab.isti.cnr.it/IW-SOSWE07/program.html.

Hakimpour, F., Sell, D., Cabral, L., Domingue, J., & Motta, E. (2005). *Semantic web service composition in IRS-III: The structured approach*. Paper presented at the 7th IEEE International Conference on E-Commerce Technology (CEC'05).

Heß, A., Johnston, E., & Kushmerick, N. (2004). *Assam: A tool for semi-automatically annotating semantic web services*. Paper presented at the International Semantic Web Conference (ISWC04), Hiroshima, Japan.

Howard, R., & Kerschberg, L. (2004). A framework for dynamic semantic web services management. *International Journal of Cooperative Information Systems*, *13*(4), 441–485. doi:10.1142/S0218843004001024

IBM. (2006). IBM RUP for service-oriented modeling and architecture v2.4. Retrieved 2.4., 2008, from http://www.ibm.com/developerworks/rational/downloads/06/rmc_soma/

Jaeger, M. C., Engel, L., & Geihs, K. (2005). *A methodology for developing OWL-S descriptions*. Paper presented at the Workshop on Web Services and Interoperability at First International Conference on Interoperability of Enterprise Software and Applications, Geneva, Switzerland.

Johnston, S. (2005). UML 2.0 profile for software services. Retrieved 4.4., 2008, from http://www-128.ibm.com/developerworks/rational/library/05/419_soa/

Jones, S. V., Maiden, N. A. M., Zachos, K., & Zhu, X. (2005). *How service-centric systems change the requirements process*. Paper presented at the 11th International Workshop on Requirements Engineering: Foundation for Software Quality (REFSQ'05), Porto, Portugal, 13-14 Jun.

Keel, A. J., Orr, M. A., Hernandez, R. R., Patrocinio, E. A., & Bouchard, J. (2007). From a technology-oriented to a service-oriented approach to IT management. *IBM Systems Journal*, *46*(3), 549–564. doi:10.1147/sj.463.0549

Kim, J., & Gil, Y. (2004). *Towards interactive composition of semantic web services*. Paper presented at the First International Semantic Web Services Symposium.

Kitchenham, B. (2004). *Procedures for performing systematic reviews* (Technical Report No. TR/SE-04-01). Keele, Staffordshire, UK: Keele University.

Klein, M., & Koenig-Ries, B. (2003). *A process and a tool for creating service descriptions based on DAML-S*. Paper presented at the 4th International Workshop Technologies for E-Services (TES 2003).

Küngas, P., & Matskin, M. (2006, 19-25 Feb). *Web services roadmap: The semantic web perspective.* Paper presented at the AICT/ICIW'06.

Martin, D., Paolucci, M., McIlraith, S., Burstein, M., McDermott, D., McGuinness, D., et al. (2004). *Bringing semantics to web services: The OWL-S approach.* Paper presented at the First International Workshop on Semantic Web Services and Web Process Composition.

Martin, E., Basu, S., & Xie, T. (2007). WebSob: A tool for robustness testing of web services. *29th International Conference on Software Engineering* (ICSE 2007), Minneapolis, MN, USA, May 20-26, 2007, *Companion Volume* (pp. 65-66). Los Vaqueros, CA: IEEE Computer Society.

Mittal, K. (2007). Service oriented unified process. Retrieved 3.3., 2008, from http://www.kunalmittal.com/html/soup.shtml

Mora, M., Gelman, O., Paradice, D., & Cervantes, F. (2008). The Case for Conceptual Research in Information Systems. In: Janczewski, L. & Gutierrez, J.: *Proceedings of the 2008 International Conference in Information Resources Management* (pp 1-10), Hershey, Pennsylvania: IRMA.

Offutt, J., & Xu, W. (2004). Generating test cases for web services using data perturbation. *ACM SIGSOFT Software Engineering Notes*, *29*(5), 1–10. doi:10.1145/1022494.1022529

OMG. (2006). Ontology definition metamodel. Retrieved 3.4., 2008, from http://www.omg.org/cgi-bin/doc?ad/06-05-01.pdf

Papazoglou, M. P., & van den Heuvel, W.-J. (2006). Service-oriented design and development methodology. *International Journal of Web Engineering and Technology*, *2*(4), 412–442. doi:10.1504/IJWET.2006.010423

Papazoglou, M. P., & van den Heuvel, W.-J. (2007). Service-oriented architectures: Approaches, technologies and research issues. *The VLDB Journal*, *16*, 389–415. doi:10.1007/s00778-007-0044-3

Penta, M. D., Canfora, G., Esposito, G., Mazza, V., & Bruno, M. (2007). *Search-based testing of service level agreements.* In Thierens, D. et al. (Eds.), *GECCO'07 - Genetic and Evolutionary Computation Conference*, (pp. 1090-1097), New York: ACM Press.

Ramollari, E., Dranidis, D., & Simons, A. J. H. (2007). *A survey of service oriented development methodologies.* Paper presented at the 2nd European Young Researchers Workshop on Service Oriented Computing, Leicester, UK. Retrieved 3.2., 2008, from http://www.dcs.shef.ac.uk/~ajhs/research/papers/soasurvey.pdf

Rao, J., & Su, X. (2004). A survey of automated web service composition methods. In J. Cardoso & A. Sheth (Eds.), *Semantic web services and web process composition* (pp. 43-54): Springer (LNCS 3387).

Ruth, M. E. (2008). *Concurrency in a decentralized automatic regression test selection framework for web services.* Paper presented at the 15th ACM Mardi Gras conference (MG'08), Baton Rouge, LA.

Scicluna, J., Abela, C., & Montebello, M. (2004). *Visual modeling of OWL-S services.* Paper presented at the IADIS International Conference WWW/Internet, Madrid, Spain.

Sindre, G., Conradi, R., & Karlsson, E.-A. (1995). The reboot approach to software reuse. *Journal of Systems and Software*, *30*(3), 201–212. doi:10.1016/0164-1212(94)00134-9

Sinha, A., & Paradkar, A. (2006). *Model-based functional conformance testing of web services operating on persistent data.* In *Proceedings of the 2006 workshop on Testing, analysis, and verification of web services and applications* (TAV-WEB'06), Portland, Maine (pp. 17-22). New York: ACM.

Sirin, E., & Parsia, B., & J., H. (2004). Filtering and selecting semantic web services with interactive composition techniques. *IEEE Intelligent Systems*, *19*(4), 42–49. doi:10.1109/MIS.2004.27

Srivastava, B., & Koehler, J. (2003). *Web service composition - current solutions and open problems.* Paper presented at the ICAPS 2003 Workshop on Planning for Web Services, Trento, Italy.

Stojanovic, Z., & Dahanayake, A. (2005). Service-oriented software system engineering: Challenges and practices: Preface. In Stojanovic, Z., & Dahanayake, A. (Eds.), *Service-oriented software system engineering: Challenges and practices* (pp. vii–xv). Hershey, PA: Idea Group.

Stojanovic, Z., Dahanayake, A., & Sol, H. (2004). *Modeling and design of service-oriented architecture.* In International Conference on Systems, Man and Cybernetics (pp. 4147 - 4152), IEEE.

Sun. (2006). SOA RQ methodology: A pragmatic approach. Retrieved 2.4., 2008, from http://www.sun.com/products/soa/soa_methodology.pdf

Timm, J. T. E., & Gannod, G. C. (2005, 11-15 Jul). *A model-d*riven *approach for specifying semantic web services.* Proceedings of the IEEE International Conference on Web Services (pp. 313-320), Los Vaqueros, CA: IEEE Computer Society Press.

Tsai, W. T., Malek, M., Chen, Y., & Bastani, F. (2006, May 27-28). *Perspectives on service-oriented computing and service-oriented system engineering.* In Proceedings International Workshop on Service Oriented Software Engineering (pp. 3-10), IEEE.

Walkerdine, J., Hutchinson, J., Sawyer, P., Dobson, G., & Onditi, V. (2007). *A faceted approach to service specification.* Paper presented at the Second International Conference on Internet and Web Applications and Services (ICIW'07).

Zachos, K., Maiden, N. A. M., Zhu, X., & Jones, S. (2007, Jun 11-15). *Discovering web services to specify more complete system requirements.* In Opdahl, A.L., Sindre, G. & Krogstie, J.: 19th Conference on Advanced Information Systems Engineering (CAiSE'07), Proceedings [Berlin: Springer.]. *Lecture Notes in Computer Science, 4495*, 142–157. doi:10.1007/978-3-540-72988-4_11

Zhu, L., Gorton, I., Liu, Y., & Bui, N. B. (2006). *Model driven benchmark generation for web services.* In *International Workshop on Service Oriented Software Engineering* (pp. 33-39), IEEE.

Zimmermann, O., Schlimm, N., Waller, G., & Pestel, M. (2005). Analysis and design techniques for service-oriented development and integration. *GI Jahrestagung*(2), 606-611.

This work was previously published in International Journal of Information Systems in the Service Sector (IJISSS), edited by John Wang, pp. 1-16, copyright 2009 by IGI Publishing (an imprint of IGI Global).

Chapter 8
A Service Science Perspective on Human-Computer Interface Issues of Online Service Applications

Claudio Pinhanez
IBM T.J. Watson Research Center, USA

ABSTRACT

This paper proposes a framework for online service applications based on Service Science which identifies and enables a better understanding of the different issues faced by online service designers, engineers, and delivery personnel. The application of the Service Science framework is made possible by carefully distinguishing online service applications not only from traditional personal software applications but also from online information applications, such as the ones used by news and entertainment websites, through a process of specializing Pinhanez's definition of customer-intensive systems (Pinhanez, 2008) to online applications. To demonstrate the utility of the framework, we consider the six basic characteristics of services, as traditionally defined in Service Science — customer-as-input, heterogeneity, simultaneity, perishability, coproduction, and intangibility — and derive from these characteristics a list of 15 different issues that are highly important for the design and evaluation of the human-computer interface of online services.

INTRODUCTION

In 1991, *Scientific American* published an extraordinary collection of essays about the upcoming era of integration of communications, computers, and networks (Dertouzos, 1991b). The issue included articles from technology visionaries such as Michael Dertouzos, Vinton Cerf, Nicholas Negroponte, Alan Kay, Mitchell Kapor, and then US Senator Al Gore. Among other things, the articles predicted the appearance of large scale broadband networks, the non-centralized structure of today's WWW, the ubiquity of e-mail, the telecommuting phenomenon, and the emergence of India as a software outsourcing powerhouse, as well as problems such as junk mail, cyber-crime, and identity theft.

DOI: 10.4018/978-1-60960-138-6.ch008

But notably, all authors failed to predict that the massive interconnection of users in cyberspace would open the space for large online service providers that could mediate the relationship between users and the vast amount of data. Among others, online service providers that collect, analyze, negotiate, process, filter public and private data, and provide simplified information access as services such as *Google*, *Yahoo*, and *Mapquest;* e-retailers such as *Travelocity*, *Amazon*, and others; and service providers based on social networking such as *eBay, Skype, Facebook, Orkut*, etc.

The common thinking 15 years ago seemed to be that the access to the myriad of computers in the network and the browsing and filtering of their data, as well as the bulk of the interpersonal connections, would be performed by personal tools or software agents that would scout and explore the Internet for information relevant to their users. A good exemplar of this view is the concept of *knowledge robots*, or *knowbots*, proposed by Robert Kahn and Vinton Cerf (Kahn & Cerf, 1988), *"...programs designed by their users to travel through a network, inspecting and understanding similar kinds of information..."* as described in (Dertouzos, 1991a, pg. 35). Knowbots were to be unleashed to fulfill specific user requests for information, moving *"...from machine to machine, possibly cloning themselves [...] dispatched to do our binding in a global landscape of networked computing and information resources."* (Cerf, 1991, pg. 44).

The problem with the agent-based vision of information search is that it does not scale up. In the current world of distributed information, this approach to information search would require each of us to run (and possibly store) the equivalent of *Google*'s operations of crawling the web, indexing, and search matching. What the authors of the *Scientific American* issue could not see is that, as networks and their users grow well beyond the academic, mostly engineering-minded users of the Internet in the early 90s, there are tremendous economies of scale when millions and millions of queries are handled by a central system that crawls and indexes all the information available (independent of specific queries) and provides information finding as an *online service application*.

But how different are such online service applications from traditional software applications? The goal of this article is to describe a framework for online service applications that differentiates them from traditional interactive software tools, so it can be used to explain and predict the differences between the two, particularly in issues related to the design of human-computer interface for online services. As a consequence software tools and online service applications are intrinsically different, even when used for similar tasks, and should be designed and engineered differently. There is, of course, an extensive body of practice and empirical knowledge about developing interfaces for online interactive applications — exemplified by all the knowledge built in the last decade and half about web applications, as, for example, described in (Nielsen, 2000). Also, there has been work examining HCI and usability issues in e-commerce (C.-M. Karat, Blom, & Karat, 2004; Nah & Davis, 2002; Voss, 2003), but we believe that these works suffer from not having an appropriate theoretical understanding of what an online service is and, therefore, miss an important part of the picture when reasoning about their findings.

We start by noticing that four assumptions base the understanding of how a traditional software tool is supposed to work: (1) a single user, (2) who controls the machine and data being used, (3) inputting data (4) to be automatically processed by the machine in order to produce some desired information output. In contrast, in online service applications, the usual architecture comprises a network of computer-based systems where (1) multiple, unrelated users, (2) who do not own or control the server machines and/or most of the data being used, (3) provide personal data or assets as input to an online provider (4) to receive some output, in the form of information or not, delivered automatically or with human assistance. For example, in *Google Web Search*, (1) thousands and thousands of people, virtually simultaneously, (2) who do not own or control *Google*'s machines or data, (3) type everything from trivial questions to their most intimate desires (4) to receive a list of web-links as determined by a mostly-automated process.

We take in this article a theoretical approach where we try to investigate such online service applications with concepts, ideas, and analytical tools from *Service Science*, which has been developed in the last 40 years mostly by researchers in business and management schools. (Fitzsimmons & Fitzsimmons, 2004; Lovelock & Wirtz, 2004; Zeithaml, Bitner, & Gremler, 2006) are good examples of textbooks in the area. This effort has been recently joined by computer scientists and engineers through the *SSME* initiative *(Service Science, Management, and Engineering)*, as detailed in (Spohrer, Maglio, Bailey, & Gruhl, 2007; Spohrer & Riecken, 2006).

However, to correctly apply concepts from Service Science to online service applications, we have to carefully identify which online applications have characteristics similar to traditional services. We start this process by agreeing with (Pinhanez, 2008) that one of the main differences between online applications and personal tools is that in the latter the user controls the means of production: when and how intensively to use it, where the information (often personal) is stored and who can access it, how much effort is put on a given task or goal, and even if the user is entitled and allowed to use the application. In other words, in the case of online service applications there is a high level of *user dependency* on the provider(s) of the means of production. This requires the online interface to deal with issues not usually even contemplated by a tool application, such as: trust creation and maintenance; privacy concerns when handling sensitive information; communication of user context; hard to predict interface response times due to fluctuations in demand; and many others.

Following, we argue that not all online applications are service applications, but that the online applications can be subdivided along the dimension of how fundamental user input is for the production process, or, borrowing from theoretical work on distinguishing services from goods by Sampson (Sampson & Froehle, 2006), how much *user intensity* they require,. It is important to distinguish between user intensity and personalization: the former quantifies the user input to the production process of the online application, while the latter refers to how to adapt the production process based on user's preference and information. Based on the level of *user intensity*, we draw a clear line between *online services providers* (*Google Web Search*, *Travelocity*) and *online information providers* (*cnn.com, Google finance*), similar to Pinhanez's concept of *customer-intensive systems* (Pinhanez, 2008).

We have been investigating how this framework can inform all aspects of online service applications, including design, development, testing, delivery, and evaluation. However, due to limitations in space, in this article we illustrate our approach by addressing only human-computer interface. We then how the Service Science framework reveals more clearly where and how interface design and evaluation is affected by traditional service ideas and how online service interfaces have an additional role as enablers of relationships between customers and service providers. Although there has been some work examining traditional Service Science concepts and how they apply in their counterparts in the online world — such as Ryan and Valverde's study on waiting in line effects on consumer behavior (Ryan & Valverde, 2006), and many works on service quality measurement of online services (Barnes & Vidgen, 2000; Loiacono, Watson, & Goodhue, 2007; Parasuraman, Zeithaml, & Malhotra, 2005; Szymanski & Hiseb, 2000; Webb & Webb, 2004; Wolfinbarger & Gilly, 2003; Yoo &

Donthu, 2001) — our approach here is to point out a much large number of candidate areas for future research. We conclude this article discussing issues related to the practical validation of this framework and examining future and possible developments of our ideas.

It is important to point out that there is an enormous amount of literature and practical knowledge on how to architect and develop *computer services* for online applications. The extensive work on *Service Oriented Architecture (SOA)*, described, for instance, in (Bieberstein, Sanjay, Fiammante, Jones, & Shah, 2006; Ferguson & Stockton, 2005) typifies this recent focus on understanding how computers can provide services. However, computer services, in the way addressed by SOA, are not to be consumed directly by human beings, but instead by computer applications. This feature changes, in our view, the essential nature of computer services dramatically, and makes the methods and techniques useful for their design and development radically different from the ones used on online services for humans. For instance, while establishing long-term relationships with their human customers is a key issue for online services, the key issue for computer services is likely more on the line of standardization. By constraining our discussion to online services applications as providers of services for people, we apply concepts and methods from Service Science which is traditionally focused on human customers.

A SPACE OF INFORMATION APPLICATIONS

The core of our framework relies on some recent work by Pinhanez (Pinhanez, 2008), building on some concepts from Sampson (Sampson, 2001), popularized in (Sampson & Froehle, 2006). According to Sampson's work, a necessary and sufficient condition for a production process to be a *service process* is that *"[...] the customer provides significant inputs into the production process."* (Sampson & Froehle, 2006, pg 331). This primacy of customer input is put in contrast to manufacturing processes, where *"groups of customers may contribute ideas to the design of the product, but individual customers' only participation is to select and consume the output."* (Sampson, 2001, pg 16). Figure 1 shows two diagrams depicting graphically the main differences between manufacturing and service processes.

Figure 1. Manufacturing and service processes according to Sampson's theory (Sampson, 2001)

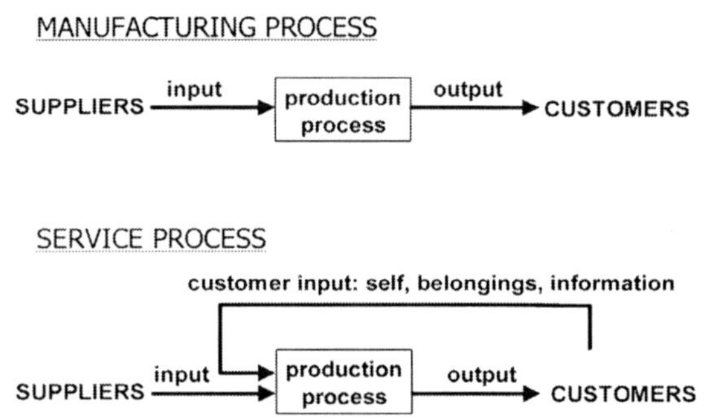

Notice that it is implicit in this definition — and discussed at length in (Sampson & Froehle, 2006) — that customers and service producer are separate entities. As proposed by Pinhanez (Pinhanez, 2008), a better way to make this distinction is to say that the customer does not control most of the means of production. (Pinhanez, 2008) then proposes the concept of *customer-intensive systems*, which comprises systems with high user intensity and user dependency and shows that not all services are customer-intensive.

Our framework uses Pinhanez's concept and applies it to online applications. We start by taking the two key concepts, *user input intensity* and *user dependency*, and consider them as two dimensions in the space of information applications as depicted in Figure 2.

The first dimension relates to **how much the user controls the means of production** (the horizontal axis of Figure 2), or the level of ***user***

Figure 2. The space of information applications as defined by two dimensions: user dependency on external providers and user input intensity. The positions of the applications shown here are illustrative and do not reflect specific coordinates

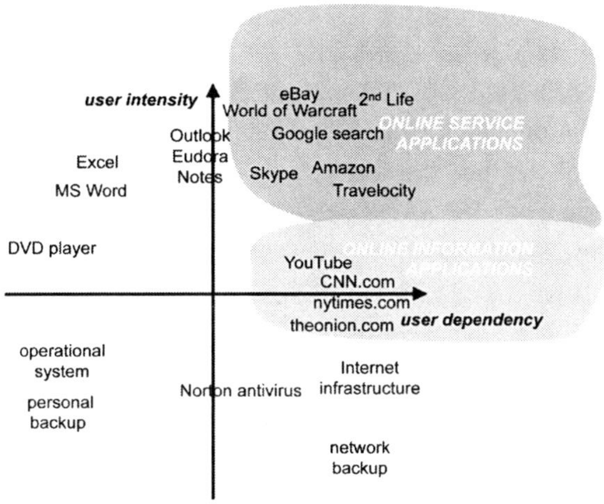

dependency on external providers. An application installed and able to run in a personal computer without network access such as traditional word processors (*MS Word*, LaTeX) is a typical example where the user controls most of the means of production. Other examples involve the basic core functions of the operational system, database applications using data stored in the user's machine, personal back-up systems, etc. As the user loses more and more control of the means of production, the closer the application gets to typical online applications such as web search and browsing, information and news provision, web retail, multiplayer online games, etc. Typical middle-point applications are e-mail applications such as *Eudora*, *Notes*, or *MS Outlook* which combine local processing and storage with extensive processing and data exchange with external servers; and local applications that depend on constant external updates such as most of today's anti-virus programs.

The second dimension tries to characterize **how much the user is an essential part of the input to the production process** (the vertical axis of Figure 2), or the level of user input ***intensity***, or simply, ***user intensity***. As described by Sampson in (Sampson, 2001; Sampson & Froehle, 2006), the user can be the input to the production process in different forms: as herself (body or mind) such as when the services of a doctor in a hospital are used; as her belongings, such as when the user's car is taken to a repair shop; or her information, as when giving financial information to get a loan from a bank. Notice that in all cases, the production process is unable to even start until the user provides her input. Typical information applications which require the user to be significant part of the input to the production process are most of the interactive software we use in our everyday work such as word processors, spreadsheets, e-mail clients, computer games, etc.; and many of the web applications available today.

However, not all web applications require the user to be an essential part of the input to the production process as pointed by (Pinhanez, 2008). Typical cases are online information providers such as *cnn.com, nytimes.com,* or *theonion.com*. Although the delivery of particular pieces of information or entertainment is trigguered by user input, a large part of the production process of the information is performed without any input from the user, through the manufacturing-like processes of news gathering and filtering, and entertainment production. Although the delivery of the information is interactive, the production of content is performed as free of user input as when cars are manufactured in an assembly line. Of course, *nytimes.com* is more dependent of user input than the *The New York Times* newspaper, but it clearly has a production process less dependent on user input than online services such as *Google Web Search*, *Travelocity*, or *Amazon*.

By taking these two dimensions spawning the space of information applications, we can draw the chart shown in Figure 2 that depicts different information applications as function of the level of user dependency, with the user being more dependent on external providers as we move from the left to right; and the level of user input intensity to the production process, with increasing user intensity from bottom to top. To illustrate our argument, we plotted some typical information applications and systems on this chart on approximate positions. No metric for the two dimensions has been precisely defined, so the chart in Figure 2 should be regarded more like a topological map showing only the relative displacement of typical applications and services.

ONLINE SERVICE APPLICATIONS

One way to understand the chart in Figure 2 is to consider the top half as the space of interactive (i.e., user intensive) applications; and the right half as the space of online (i.e. user dependent) applications. The top-right quadrant can then be seen as the one of online interactive applications which encompasses most interactive web applications. We observe here that not all the applications in this quadrant have enough similarity to traditional services, but only the top-right part of this quadrant where the user becomes a significant part of the input to the production process. As noticed before, traditional news and entertainment providers have a production process more similar to manufacturing than to services.

To take in account such issues, we propose the following definition. An *online service application*, or simply an *online service*, is an application where:

1. The user does not control most means of production.
2. The user (self, belongings, information) is a significant part of the input to the production process.

Part (1) of our definition states that the user does not control the basic factors of production — resources, capital, and labor — and therefore cannot determine when and how intensively resources are used: where her information is stored and who can access it; how much effort is put on a given task or goal; and what the price of the service is and how it changes through time. This definition contrasts with traditional tool applications, which tend to assume that the user communication with her data, other databases, the World Wide Web, or other users is not mediated through a service provider. To highlight the service vs. tool difference, we use the term *customer* instead of *user* whenever we are referring to a service application. We acknowledge here the importance of the discussion led by Don Norman (Norman, 2006) about the possible drawback of depersonalizing people by using the terms "customer" and "user", but we use the terms nonetheless because the distinction significantly contributes to highlight the difference contexts of online applications.

Part (2) of the online service application definition tries to differentiate between manufacturing and service production processes. The goal of this differentiation is to assure that we only apply service-related concepts and methods to online applications that actually behave as services. We argue here that even interactive online information providers such as *cnn.com* have characteristics closer to manufacturing systems than to services and therefore are not likely to be beneficiaries of traditional services ideas and methods. Notice that the distinction hangs a lot on the interpretation given to the term "significant part" of item (2) of our definition. We acknowledge this to be a possible source of future problems, but we consider premature at this point to establish a clearer metric to completely differentiate online service providers from information providers. It suffices to say that for the scope of this article, a commonsensical interpretation of the expression "significant part of the input" does not seem to create significant theoretical problems.

Having defined what we mean by an online service application, let us discuss typical characteristics of them.

Figure 3. Typical architecture of an online service application

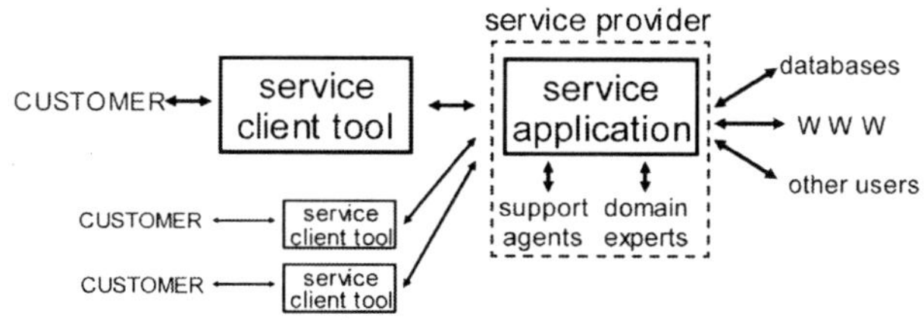

Figure 3 shows a typical architecture of an online service application. For example, a commonly found characteristic of an online service application is that the service provider has **a multitude of customers**, as shown diagrammatically in Figure 3. A service provider can exploit economies of scale to offer information provision at levels and cost that would be unfeasible in a tool-based approach.

Having a large number of users to share the costs also enables online service providers to employ more frequently expensive **human domain experts and contact agents** in hybrid production systems to accomplish tasks that are beyond today's computing abilities, such as situations involving common sense reasoning or ethical judgement. Also it allows the shared use of human support agents to handle situations too atypical to merit the construction of a dedicated piece of software or interface, or when there is a need of human contact, for example, to evaluate and address a customer complaint, or to detect and handle cases of customer negative or illegal behavior. This is hardly a possible solution in the context of tool software, where the user's machine has to automatically solve every task. We think that such human-machine hybrid architectures, possible mostly in the context of online services, are in fact a liberating idea for software engineering, traditionally submitted to the chains of full and complete automation, as more extensively discussed in the context of ubiquitous computing applications in (Pinhanez, 2007).

Finally, economies of scale are just one of the advantages of online service applications. An online service provider can also take the part of a **trusted and impartial intermediary** between two or more customers, enabling environments suitable to the establishment of relationships. For instance, consider *eBay* and how it mediates buyers and sellers in its auction environment. Similarly, **information about multiple users can be aggregated** and used to establish "cast of thousands" data handling methods such as collaborative filtering (Shardanand & Maes, 1995) and social matching (Terveen & McDonald, 2005).

HCI OF ONLINE SERVICE APPLICATIONS

There has been very little theoretical work in terms of establishing a framework to understand online applications that take the form of services in the way defined above and what is specific about how to architect, design, engineer, evaluate, deploy, and manage them. We are currently taking this approach in our research work, and so far our best insights have been related in the context of the design of the human-computer interface of online services.

In the HCI domain, most of the discussion about the design and evaluation of interfaces for online service applications tends to consider the broader class of online interactive applications — for instance, (Nielsen, 2000) — or the more restrictive class of online retailers (Loiacono et al., 2007; Nah & Davis, 2002; Voss, 2003). Our approach has to been to assure by construction, that our category of online service applications are services, at least according to Pinhanez's and Sampson's service theoretical frameworks (Pinhanez, 2008; Sampson, 2001), and to apply well-know concepts of Service Science in the context of HCI of online services.

Of course, there are many competing theories about how to characterize and classify services, as discussed, for example, in (Sampson & Froehle, 2006), especially in comparison to manufacturing. It is quite beyond the scope and need of this article to digress on the different views and to discuss how they may affect the HCI of online services.

Software production has traditionally been considered by economists in the services category of businesses. However, a more careful analysis under the light of the discussion of the previous sections reveals that many of the production processes for software in fact resemble more manufacturing than services. This is especially true for shrink-wrap software, such as popular tools like *Microsoft Office*, *Intuit Quicken*, *Adobe Photoshop*, as well as basic and middleware software such as operating systems and database programs.

Although there is user input during the design and implementation process of software, often from focus groups, individual user needs have hardly any impact on software development. Looking back into Figure 1, shrink-wrap software has traditionally followed production processes that resemble more the manufacturing of physical goods than typical service production processes. We believe that traditional HCI has thus been biased towards this model where tools are created for generic users to support a range of typical tasks. In terms of HCI evaluation and usability issues, a lot of effort is traditionally put in determining the typical individual usage scenarios of the tool and then to recreate in the laboratory meaningful test procedures. The different dynamics of web applications has required HCI practitioners to change their techniques to reflect some of the special needs of online applications as, for example, in the excellent handbook by Nielsen (Nielsen, 2000). Taking one step further, we believe that recognizing the specific characteristics of online service applications in contrast to generic online applications allows the development of more appropriate design and evaluation tools that also take in consideration the user dependency and the user intensity aspects.

We structured our discussion by considering the basic characteristics of services. We compiled and fused service characteristics listed by different authors (Fitzsimmons & Fitzsimmons, 2004; Lovelock & Wirtz, 2004; Sampson, 2001; Zeithaml et al., 2006), arriving to a "compromise" list which we believe most of them would agree to: *customer-as-input*, *heterogeneity*, *simultaneity*, *perishability*, *coproduction*, and *intangibility*. We have looked into these six characteristics and examined how concepts and techniques from Service Science related to each of them highlight some issues which are very relevant to the HCI design of online services. The result is the list of 15 important issues for the design of online service applications described below, organized by the prevailing service characteristic that best explain them.

Customer-as-Input Issues

Customer-as-input refers, as discussed before, to the fact that in services the production process significantly uses inputs from the customer, such as his body, his belongings, and/or his data. We believe an immediate consequence of customers' information as input in the context of an online service application is that trust, privacy, and security and authentication issues become key and strategic for the interface design.

Unlike in traditional tool software where the privacy of data is often taken for granted and trust on the tool is often assumed to be unlimited, dealing with a online service provider always involves an exchange of **trust** between the parties. Customers often entrust online service providers with very sensitive information about themselves, their health, their finances, their loved ones, even their most intimate desires. The HCI research community has looked into issues related to trust in many different ways. As pointed by Wang and Emurian's overview (Wang & Emurian, 2005) most research suggests that trust in online applications is a function of *"... a framework of trust-inducing interface design features, [...] namely (1) graphic design, (2) structure design, (3) content design, and (4) social-cue design. "* (Wang & Emurian, 2005, pg. 21). A study on websites creditbility by Fogg et al. (Fogg et al., 2001), as well as Brodie et al. study of e-commerce environments (Brodie, Karat, & Karat, 2004), share similar recommendations, also present in a well-known set of design guidelines for online experiences by Shneiderman (Shneiderman, 2000). (Featherman, Valacich, & Wells, 2006) tested similar hypothesises and found them true in their experiments, although other factors seem to influence the perceived risk of an online e-payment service, including the computational literacy of the customer and the generic class of the online service.

When we look into traditional services knowledge and practice, the focus of techniques for building trust often focus not only on front-end issues but also in making the back-end workings of services more "transparent" and visible to the customers. For example, a restaurant can improve the trust of their patrons in its cleanliness and service by having large windows to the kitchen area; or, in an online example, a shipping service may provide detailed real-time package tracking information (as most of them do now). The difference is paramount: instead of asking for trust by improving the form of the interface, the service provider elicites trust by making its internal workings more visible: "trust what I do" instead of "trust what I say". Interestingly, increasing the visibility of back-office operations in traditional services often improves also service quality, mostly due to the added pressure on the staff (Heskett, Sasser, & Schlesinger, 1997, pg. 160), but also by empowering the customer and transforming her into a quality inspector.

A services technique/tool that is often used to help identify the best candidates in the service process to be made visible to customers is a *service blueprint*, originally proposed by Shostack (Shostack, 1984) and further developed in (Zeithaml et al., 2006, pgs. 267-276). It is a map that portrays the service system, showing the whole process of service delivery, where customer contact happens, the roles of employees and customers, the visible elements of the service, and the overal flow of information. In particular, service blueprints depict clearly what is and is not visible to customers in a service process, by separating service components above and below a line called the *line of visibility*.

Dealing with *privacy* of information is also an issue that becomes fundamental in online services. Unlike in online information providers, private user information is often an essential part of the input to online services, for example, when applying to a bank loan. Traditional services often relied on the employees' judgment to decide which information to ask a customer, which part to actually record, and to decide the trustworthiness of the information provided. Also, often the privacy guarantees were part of the human relationship between customer and employee. Unfortunately designers are still trying to find ways to translate this human-based kind of privacy management to the online world. In the meantime, a general guideline is that, when an online service application asks for information that is particularly sensitive, the interface should clearly inform the customer why the system needs it, what the privacy policy is, for how long it will be kept, and whether there are alternatives to provide that particular information. Marking clearly which elements of personal information are mandatory and which are optional is a good practice often employed by websites. Notice that handling of private data issues are likely to be increasingly important given how common *phishing* attacks have become (Dhamija, Tygar, & Hearst, 2006).

It is interesting that many online services still resort to the long, legalese-full, license-agreement style of defining their privacy and data handling policies that are reminiscent of the never-read shrink-wrap software licenses. There have been efforts to simplify the establishment and negotiation between the customer and the service provider about privacy handling issues, for example in the *SPARCLE* project where privacy statements are machine-translated and automatically matched to customer-defined privacy standards (J. Karat, Karat, Brodie, & Feng, 2005).

Security is also a key issue for online service applications. There is a bias in computer science to look into security issues from a cryptology perspective, that is, by establishing complex mathematical mechanisms of encryption of information. Services, and in particular, sales, have found through the years that one of the most effective ways to provide a sense for security for their customers is through guarantees of satisfaction, such as return policies, and your-money-back, no-questions-asked mechanisms. Also, security is a two-way problem: the service provider also has to impose mechanisms to guarantee the payment for its services, often walking the thin line of not being perceived as distrusting of the customers.

Heterogeneity Issues

Heterogeneity is used in Service Science to address to the fact that in services customers tend to be very unique in their identity and requirements, so the execution of a service production process is usually highly tailored and quite unique to a customer request and input. One of the issues brought be heterogeneity is the need of *personalization*, which, unlike most of the issues discussed here, has been in fact extensively studied in HCI. In the HCI literature, personalization refers to the use of user-specific information to tailor the interaction process (J. Karat, Karat, & Brodie, 2004), often through the use of some sort of reasoning on top of a user model. For example, (C.-M. Karat et al., 2004) compiles several studies about personalizing e-commerce experiences.

But personalization of services is only one of the issues brought out by heterogeneity of input. Even if an online service does not allow interface personalization (such as *Google Search*), it still has to handle a high level of heterogeneity in its input, simply because people's lives, needs, and desires differ substantially, defying standardization at every corner. The effect of having highly heterogeneous input in the service production process is a traditional concern of Service Science. A key issue arising from heterogeneity of input is that it requires the service designer to consider all possible instances of the input and how to handle all specific cases, including those instances where the service is not delivered successfully. It is interesting how traditional HCI research rarely tries to understand how to handle tasks which are not achievable, or even how to inform the user about the limitations of a tool. In contrast, *service recovery*, or how to handle unsuccessful delivery of services, is a major theme of research in Service Science, given its known impact in service quality and customer loyalty. (Zeithaml et al., 2006, chapter 8) provides a good introduction to service recovery and to techniques used to alleviate the impact of failed delivery on customer satisfaction.

Another key issue that arises from customer input heterogeneity is ensuring *quality consistency* of the delivered services. It has been shown that heterogeneity of customer input, combined with the everyday fluctuations of the availability of human resources used in a service, create a vicious cycle that can drive service quality into a downwards spiral (Oliva & Sterman, 2001). This work also argued that to prevent erosion of service quality it is necessary to monitor it constantly and adequately, and that the most effective way to control it is to aim to delight the customer, not to please him.

We are starting to believe that this heterogeneity of input and output questions the very core foundations of the HCI practice. In particular, we have seen how difficult is to perform traditional user-centered design in the context of the lack of prototypical users and tasks created by heterogeneity. Not only it is extremely difficult to cover a reasonable spectrum of customers during usability tests but also it is hard to recreate in a laboratory the right context, diversity of tasks, and expectations. This is corroborated by the often common practice of web developers of tackling the heterogeneity issue by using extremely fast prototyping methods so they can *beta-test* the online application with a large number of actual customers instead of running in-laboratory usability experiments (a typical case are *Google labs* applications).

Simultaneity Issues

Simultaneity, also called inseparability, is the characteristic of service processes that refers to the fact that often services are produced and consumed at the same time. Production cannot start until the customer provides his share of the inputs, preventing inventory of output, a technique often used in manufacture to balance production. In other words, online services have to rely on a very unreliable input supplier, their own customers, and whether and when they need the services. Since demand for services is often very hard to predict, online service applications tend to exhibit fluctuations in performance, usually exhibiting the worst behavior when the largest number of customers uses them.

Performance consistency affects the perception and usefulness of an interface. Imagine a web search engine which, during peak times, takes 30 seconds to return the 10 best results of the search. This delay would make the customer very upset if the results returned were inappropriate. But most of us handle everyday hundreds of inappropriate search results from *Google*, for example, arguably because the results are given in 2-3 seconds. Traditional HCI tends to ignore performance issues or, simply assume that performance is constant through time and task. One way traditionally used in services to handle performance consistency issues is to have different processes, interfaces, and even content to handle differently the variations in performance. For example, sometimes news websites simplify radically the opening page when dealing with situations of extremely important news that generate levels of access beyond the delivery capabilities of the system.

Another aspect of online service software that interfaces have to take in account is **fairness** in situations involving multiple customers. For example, when multiple customers of an online auction try to post a bid almost at the same time, it is important to make it sure that their bids are processed in the exact order they are received. Unlike in a traditional auction where all bidders can see each other, it is very hard for the online bidder to evaluate whether the online auction is being fairly conducted, increasing the demands on trust and transparency of the interface.

At the same time, simultaneous customers accessing the same resource, for instance when buying the last pair of tickets for a concert, may require an interface design that clearly alerts them to the fact that even during the process the resource may be taken by other customer. While in brick-and-mortar service providers it is often possible for customers to understand that other customers are "ahead" of them in a line, it is unusual to provide the same kind of feedback in an online service. Nevertheless, service software interface designers should always try to make multiple customer resource access as much visible as possible for the sake of preserving the trust of the customers in the fairness of the service. After all, service visibility is one of the bastions of good quality service (Lovelock & Wirtz, 2004).

Perishability Issues

Perishability refers to the fact that often service production capacity is lost whenever there is no request for it. The capacity to host a guest in a hotel room is lost forever when the room is empty. Traditionally in services this issue is tackled with *demand management*, when, for instance, a service provider offer incentives (for example, lower prices) for customers to use the service in times of low demand.

Traditional HCI normally addresses only the situation of actual use of an application. Even the idea of marketing to increase the use of a tool, beyond what is needed for the purchase of the tool, tends to be the least of the concerns of designers. A similar situation occurs in highly automated service software where the only penalty for having a small number of customers may be relatively idle servers. The key challenges for HCI in this area refer to systems where the main benefit stems from multiple customers using the service at roughly the same time. For example, online chatting requires multiple users to be available at the same time to become valuable; online auctions need multiple bidders to be emotionally engaging and profitable for sellers; on-line multiplayer games tend to be boring when fewer enemies are around; and long distance VoIP systems such as *Skype* require each customer to have communication partners online to be useful.

How to make interfaces that incentives use in down times for those kinds of online services? We notice that *marketing* the use and need of an application is basically absent from interface design and evaluation of traditional tool software. Even in most situations of web design, the normal posture of HCI professionals is simply to consider that usability and elegance sell by itself and to avoid the integration of marketing concerns to the interface design, with a possible exception in the case of advertisement banners (which HCI types loath, anyway). Although there are potentially some ethical issues here, there are many situations where a large number of customers is beneficial to the individual customer as discussed before. So we advocate an increasing understanding and use of marketing techniques as a way to deal with perishability issues in online service software. For instance, an online auction system may include "live" chats with human experts during low traffic times to increase overall presence.

Another way to cope with perishability is to make the service provider invite customers to use the service when there are fewer than needed customers. The 1990s witnessed a lot of discussion about pull vs. push software, and in general, people have been very resistant to software which tries to push their usage. Nevertheless, the proliferation of viruses and mal-ware has made more common situations where computer software, such as antivirus and firewalls tools, interrupts the user and requests her attention. Similarly, instant messaging and VoIP systems also generate push-like interruptions, and a host of techniques have been created to manage them, such as "busy" flags.

We believe that this context is creating a situation where push techniques became more acceptable and usable in the context of online service applications. For example, auction customers may agree to install service daemons in their machines that may warn them, through a pop-up, that an auction is going to end soon and that there is a possible bargain given the current prices. For the service provider, the issuing of commands to generate pop-ups may be managed so it avoids auctions without sufficient customers but at the same time it does not importunate customers too often. This kind of concern has been largely studied in marketing and advertisement, but it is a rarity in interface design and evaluation. Also, for HCI practice, evaluating push software with laboratory techniques is particularly hard because it requires recreating situations where the customer has to be interrupted.

Coproduction Issues

Coproduction refers to the common practice in services to ask the customer to perform part of the production process, often doing the labor that otherwise would have to be performed by an employee of the service provider. The classical example is when customers help to clean up in fast food stores by taking their garbage to trash bins. Although coproduction is often introduced in a service process to decrease costs (for example, the airlines' self-service kiosks), many times coproduction has a desirable effect of empowering the customer and allowing more informative choices (for example, in the case of online travel services such as *Travelocity*), and even increasing customer satisfaction as described in (Zeithaml et al., 2006, chapter 13). Also, in many services coproduction is absolutely required, for example when a change in lifestyle or behavior is required in a medical treatment. When a doctor asks a patient to take some medication or quit smoking, the patient, for all purposes, is being invited to coproduce the cure.

Software developers are traditionally trained in a mindset where the goal of software is to automate a task, in the context of input from the user. In that framework, it is not a surprise that the user is often seen as an outsider of the production process. Notice that the word "interface" itself expresses an idea that the user is external to the system. Coproduction has often been used in online applications, though often disguised and many times misunderstood. *Google Web Search* is based on the notion that the customer can do a lot of information filtering herself as long as a reasonable summary is provided and the response time is fast. Similarly, online travel service providers such as *Travelocity* have pushed most of the travel agent's job to the customer. In many of these cases there is some loss of quality when part of the production process is moved to the customer, since less expert knowledge is brought to bear by human professionals. However, we should also recognize some key benefits of coproduction in those cases. Coproduction often tends to foster *customer empowerment*. For instance, direct access to information about travel gives the customer more time to reflect and weight options without the pressure of making a decision. As much as not having a waiter ready to clean up the table at a fast food restaurant allows customers to prolong their stay as they wish, coproduction in an online service application can be used to break down different steps of the production process in a pace that can be more convenient and pleasant for the customer.

However, HCI practitioners should be careful about how coproduction works and its impact in their evaluation techniques. For instance, the duration of a task, often used in usability studies, is not an appropriate measure when customers are taking time to decide among different options, gathering more information, or weighting risks. Also, coproduction often involves some level of *customer training*, so the interface design has to consider carefully how the customer is going to learn the skills needed to coproduce effectively. There are many interesting teaching techniques that have been developed by traditional services — see (Zeithaml et al., 2006) for some examples — and the HCI community can definitely learn from them.

Intangibility Issues

Intangibility refers to the fact that many of the key aspects related to customer satisfaction in services are very hard to quantify and measure, especially in a systematic and cost-effective way. Although in the past intangibility was often used as the distinguishing mark of services from goods, current services theorists tend to downplay or even negate intangibility as a defining characteristic of services (Sampson & Froehle, 2005).

One of the key distinctions between traditional tool applications and online service applications is the importance of service quality. How to create and maintain customer satisfaction cannot be an afterthought of interface design, but an essential part of the design and evaluation process. However, it is know in Service Science that customers tend to have strong *service expectations* about the quality of the service they are going to receive. Customers tend to incorporate into such expectations the price of the service, their prior experiences with the provider and with other providers, the location of the service, etc. An extensive body of literature in Service Science has examined the role of expectations when measuring service quality; a good summary can be found in (Schneider & White, 2004, chapter 2). As a consequence, the most commonly used service quality instrument by the services industry, *SERVQUAL* (Parasuraman, Zeithaml, & Berry, 1985), is in fact based on measuring the difference between service quality perceptions and expectations, or what is commonly known as the *gap-model approach*. There are many theoretical and statistical reasons to measure the gap between perception and expectation instead of simply determining the perceived quality of the service (Schneider & White, 2004, chapter 2). However, the most obvious advantage of using the gap-model approach is that it provides actionable information —which areas of the service are below what customers expect.

There is some strong evidence that, in fact, the gap-model is also the right way to measure service quality in online services (Trocchia & Janda, 2003; Zeithaml, Parasuraman, & Malhotra, 2002), giving rise to specific service quality instruments for web sites such as *WebQual, SiteQual,* and *eTailQ* (Barnes & Vidgen, 2000; Loiacono et al., 2007; Parasuraman et al., 2005; Szymanski & Hiseb, 2000; Webb & Webb, 2004; Wolfinbarger & Gilly, 2003; Yoo & Donthu, 2001). Interestingly, user expectations and gap measurement have been used very sporadically by the HCI community, for example in the work of (Bouch, Kuchinsky, & Bhatti, 2000). This kind of work which validates and adapts a traditional service tool, *SERVQUAL,* into online-specific versions is precisely the kind of approach we are advocating in this article.

Another important issue in services is *process satisfaction*. In many service situations the way the customer is treated during the service process may have a larger impact on customer satisfaction than the actual delivered service. For example, dieting clubs with great customer experiences tend to have a higher rate of customer loyalty, in spite of the fact that in most cases the customers do not achieve their actual goal of losing weight. Beyond the traditional goal of task completion used in HCI, process satisfaction of an online service has to do with many more intangible aspects of the experience such as fairness, politeness, aesthetics, speed, humor, etc.

Finally, the fact that the customer does not control the means of production increases the need for the online service interface designers to deal with issues of *anger and frustration management*. Unlike in the case of traditional applications, where users in many cases vent their frustration on themselves, in services the existence of the service provider as a separate, "conscious", humn-like entity enables the customer to transfer the anger or frustration to the service provider.

Online Service Interfaces as Relationship Maintainers

Service Science traditionally regards the interactions between service providers and customers as long-term relationships. We can argue that the need for relationships stems from both the users' lack of control of the means of production, therefore forcing them to connect to another entity, the service provider, and establish a relationship; and from the fact that in most cases there are a multitude of competing service providers, so it is also interesting for the service provider to seek long-term relationships.

Also, if we examine to the collection of 15 issues identified as very relevant to online service interfaces, it becomes apparent that most of

Figure 4. Important issues for interfaces of online services

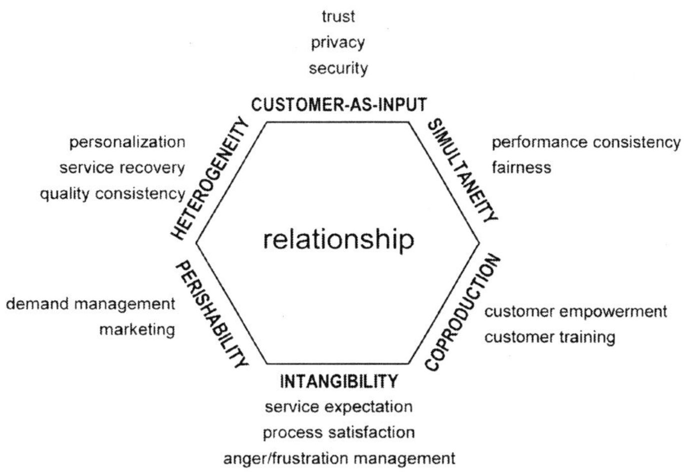

them are core issues when establishing and/or maintaining a relationship. For example, trust, privacy, security, fairness, consistency, recovery, empowerment, and anger/frustration management are clearly aspects of a healthy relationship.

Figure 4 summarizes the important new issues for interfaces of online services as identified through our Service Science framework and highlights the key aspect of an online service interface: being inductive to establish and maintain relationships.

This view of interfaces as relationship maintainers sharply contrasts to traditional understanding of software tool interfaces, which have been regarded as agents for *conversation* (Walker, 1990), *action* (Norman, 1988), *direct manipulation* (Shneiderman, 1987), or *representational action* (Laurel, 1991). Furthering the understanding the relationship aspect of services and online services, in particular, is currently a key part of our research efforts.

DISCUSSION AND FUTURE WORK

In this article we have proposed a definition of online service applications which allow the use Service Science as a reference framework to address their design, evaluation, and deployment issues. In our experience, designers and engineers of online services are mostly unaware of Service Science concepts, and therefore, by establishing this definition we are able to create a "safe" bridge which allows the use of techniques developed for traditional services in the realm of online services. We then exemplified how this merge of well-established concepts and a sound theoretical definition can be used by HCI practitioners to create a new reference framework for design and evaluation of online services based on the concept of relationship, in contrast with the traditional viewpoints of "action", "conversation", "representational action", "direct manipulation", etc.

At this point the reader can be understandably questioning where the evidence is that the Service Science framework and techniques are really important for online service applications. We have seen at least two documented cases — the line waiting study of Ryan and Valverde (Ryan & Valverde, 2006) and the application of *SERVQUAL*-like methods for evaluation of online services (Barnes & Vidgen, 2000; Loiacono et al., 2007; Parasuraman et al., 2005; Szymanski & Hiseb, 2000; Webb & Webb, 2004; Wolfinbarger

& Gilly, 2003; Yoo & Donthu, 2001)— where traditional services techniques are shown to be more appropriate to the online services domain than traditional HCI methods.

Said that, we have discussed here, notably in the previous section, many examples where simply by taking the six basic characteristics of services as a springboard, we were able to provide a better explanation for common difficulties facing online services interface design and evaluation and/or suggest new techniques and approaches to solve known HCI problems in the area. An example of the former is how input and output heterogeneity, a known and often studied issue in Service Science, seems to shed light onto the difficulties of online services evaluation. A typical example of the latter case is the discussion we had about *SERVQUAL* and how measuring service quality as the gap from expectations and perceptions are not only often more realistic but also more informative than simply measuring satisfaction.

As researchers with an HCI background, we were astonished when we realized the depth, breadth, and quality of the service quality literature, their relevance to online services, and how the HCI community is mostly unaware of it. Notice, however, that most of the literature in *SERVQUAL*-like evaluation methods (Barnes & Vidgen, 2000; Loiacono et al., 2007; Parasuraman et al., 2005; Szymanski & Hiseb, 2000; Webb & Webb, 2004; Wolfinbarger & Gilly, 2003; Yoo & Donthu, 2001) tends to look into usability issues in a very simplistic way: for instance, by asking the user whether a website has good usability. As well-known in the HCI community, it is not always the case that the user is aware of usability problems, which often need to be detected through direct observation of users working with the interface. Therefore, we see that there is a promising opportunity for the development of direct-observation evaluation techniques of the user experience of online services that integrate the concept of expectation gap of Service Science with the task-based evaluation methods traditionally used in HCI.

Though promising, those two examples of application of Service Science are more the exception than the rule in the practice of designing and building online services. Therefore, we believe there is an enormous opportunity to establish a framework for online service applications based on Service Science. In particular, we hope that this introductory discussion creates questioning and curiosity in the field and trigger further research. In our case, we are focusing efforts in codifying and adapting traditional services methodologies to the design and evaluation of online service applications. For instance, we have been trying to use *Service Design* methodologies (Shostack, 1984; Zeithaml et al., 2006, chapter 9) to reinvent the user experience in online technical support.

From online multiplayer games to web search, many of the new components of the online information landscape are structured as services, but they are still often designed and evaluated under the traditional "tool" view of computing. We hope we are contributing to change this mindset, towards increasing not only the quality of customer experience but also the efficiency and adequacy of online service applications.

REFERENCES

Barnes, S. J., & Vidgen, R. T. (2000, July 3-5). *WebQual: An Exploration of Web-Site Quality.* Paper presented at the Proceedings of the 8th European Conference on Information Systems, Trends in Information and Communication Systems for the 21st Century, ECIS 2000, Vienna, Austria.

Bieberstein, N., Sanjay, B., Fiammante, M., Jones, K., & Shah, R. (2006). *Service-Oriented Architecture Compass: Business Value, Planning, and Enterprise Roadmap*. Upper Saddle River, NJ: IBM Press.

Bouch, A., Kuchinsky, A., & Bhatti, N. (2000, April 1-6). *Quality is in the Eye of the Beholder: Meeting Users' Requirements for Internet Quality of Service*. Paper presented at the Proc. of CHI'00, The Hague, The Netherlands.

Brodie, C., Karat, C.-M., & Karat, J. (2004). Creating an e-Commerce Environment Where Consumers are Willing to Share Personal Information. In Karat, C.-M., Blom, J. O., & Karat, J. (Eds.), *Designing Personalized User Experiences in eCommerce* (pp. 185–206). Kluwer Academic Publishers. doi:10.1007/1-4020-2148-8_11

Cerf, V. G. (1991). Networks. *Scientific American, 265*(3), 42–51. doi:10.1038/scientificamerican0991-72

Dertouzos, M. L. (1991a). Communications, Computers and Networks. *Scientific American, 265*(3), 30–37. doi:10.1038/scientificamerican0991-62

Dertouzos, M. L. (Ed.). (1991b). *Scientific American* (*Vol. 265*, p. 3). Special Issue on Communications, Computers, and Networks.

Dhamija, R., Tygar, J. D., & Hearst, M. (2006). *Why Phishing Works*. Paper presented at the Proc. of CHI'06, Montreal, Canada.

Featherman, M. S., Valacich, J. S., & Wells, J. D. (2006). Is That Autentic or Artificial? Understanding Consumer Perceptions of Risk in e-Service Encounters. *Information Systems Journal, 16*(2), pgs. 107-134.

Ferguson, D. F., & Stockton, M. L. (2005). Service-Oriented Architecture: Programming Model and Product Architecture. *IBM Systems Journal, 44*(4), 753–780. doi:10.1147/sj.444.0753

Fitzsimmons, J. A., & Fitzsimmons, M. J. (2004). *Service Management: Operations*. Strategy, and Information Technology.

Fogg, B. J., Marshall, J., Laraki, O., Osipovich, A., Varma, C., Fang, N., et al. (2001, Mar 31-Apr 5). *What Makes Web Sites Credible? A Report on a Large Quantitative Study.* Paper presented at the Proc. of CHI'01, Seattle, Washington.

Heskett, J. L., Sasser, W. E., & Schlesinger, L. A. (1997). *The Service Profit Chain: How Leading Companies Link Profit and Growth to Loyalty, Satisfaction, and Value*. New York: Free Press.

Kahn, R. E., & Cerf, V. G. (1988). *The Digital Library Project, volume I: The World of Knowbots*. Unpublished manuscript, Reston, VA.

Karat, C.-M., Blom, J. O., & Karat, J. (Eds.). (2004). *Designing Personalized User Experiences in eCommerce*. Kluwer Academic Publishers. doi:10.1007/1-4020-2148-8

Karat, J., Karat, C.-M., & Brodie, C. (2004). Personalizing Interaction: Directions for HCI Research. In Karat, C.-M., Blom, J. O., & Karat, J. (Eds.), *Designing Personalized User Experiences in eCommerce* (pp. 7–17). Kluwer Academic Publishers. doi:10.1007/1-4020-2148-8_2

Karat, J., Karat, C.-M., Brodie, C., & Feng, J. (2005). Privacy in Information Technology: Designing to Enable Privacy Policy Management in Organizations. *International Journal of Human-Computer Studies, 63*, 153–174. doi:10.1016/j.ijhcs.2005.04.011

Laurel, B. (1991). *Computers as Theatre*. Reading, Massachusetts: Addison-Wesley.

Loiacono, E. T., Watson, R. T., & Goodhue, D. L. (2007). WebQual: An Instrument for Consumer Evaluations of Web Sites. *To appear in the Internation Journal of Electronic Commerce.*

Lovelock, C. H., & Wirtz, J. (2004). *Services Marketing: People, Technology, Strategy* (5th ed.). Upper Saddle River, N.J.: Pearson/Prentice Hall.

Nah, F. F.-H., & Davis, S. (2002). HCI Research Issues in Electronic Commerce. *Journal of Electronic Commerce Research*, *3*(3), 98–113.

Nielsen, J. (2000). *Designing Web Usability: The Practice of Simplicity*. Indianopolis, Indiana: New Riders Publishing.

Norman, D. A. (1988). *The Psychology of Everyday Things*. New York, New York: Basic Books.

Norman, D. A. (2006, Sep+Oct). Words Matter. Talk About People -- Not Customers, Not Consumers, Not Users. *Interactions, 13,* 49,63.

Oliva, R., & Sterman, J. D. (2001). Cutting Corners and Working Overtime: Quality Erosion in the Service Industry. *Management Science*, *47*(7), 894–914. doi:10.1287/mnsc.47.7.894.9807

Parasuraman, A., Zeithaml, V. A., & Berry, L. L. (1985, Fall). A Conceptual Model of Service Quality and Its Implications for Future Research. *Journal of Marketing*, *49*, 41–50. doi:10.2307/1251430

Parasuraman, A., Zeithaml, V. A., & Malhotra, A. (2005). E-S-QUAL: A Multiple-Item Scale for Assessing Electronic Service Quality. *Journal of Service Research*, *7*(3), 213–233. doi:10.1177/1094670504271156

Pinhanez, C. (2007, July 10-13). *Ubiquitous Services.* Paper presented at the Proc. of IEEE Services Computing Conference - SCC'07, Salt Lake City, Utah.

Pinhanez, C. (2008). *Service Systems as Customer-Intensive Systems and its Implications for Service Science and Engineering.* Paper presented at the Proc. of Hawaiian International Conference on System Sciences, HICSS-41, Big Island, Hawaii.

Ryan, G., & Valverde, M. (2006). Waiting in Line for Online Services: a Qualitative Study of the User's Perspective. *Information Systems Journal, 16*(2), pgs. 181-211.

Sampson, S. E. (2001). *Understanding Service Businesses* (2nd ed.). John Wiley & Sons.

Sampson, S. E., & Froehle, C. M. (2005). (Submitted to). [*Production and Operations Management.*]. *Foundations and Implications of a Proposed Unified Services Theory.*

Sampson, S. E., & Froehle, C. M. (2006). Foundations and Implications of a Proposed Unified Services Theory. *Production and Operations Management*, *15*(2), 329–343. doi:10.1111/j.1937-5956.2006.tb00248.x

Schneider, B., & White, S. S. (2004). *Service Quality: Research Perspectives*. Thousand Oaks, Calif.: Sage Publications.

Shardanand, U., & Maes, P. (1995, May 7-11). *Social Information Filtering: Algorithms for Automating Word of Mouth.* Paper presented at the Proc. of CHI'95, Denver, Colorado.

Shneiderman, B. (1987). *Designing the User Interface: Strategies for Effective Human-Computer Interaction.* Reading, Massachusetts: Addison-Wesley.

Shneiderman, B. (2000). Designing Trust into Online Experiences. *Communications of the ACM*, *43*(12), 57–59. doi:10.1145/355112.355124

Shostack, G. L. (1984). Designing Services that Deliver. *Harvard Business Review*, *62*(1), 133–139.

Spohrer, J., Maglio, P. P., Bailey, J., & Gruhl, D. (2007). Steps Toward a Science of Service Systems. *IEEE Computer*, 71-77.

Spohrer, J., & Riecken, D. (Eds.). (2006). *Communications of ACM: Special Issue on Services Science* (Vol. 49:7).

Szymanski, D. M., & Hiseb, R. T. (2000). E-satisfaction: An Initial Examination. *Journal of Retailing*, *76*(3), 309–322. doi:10.1016/S0022-4359(00)00035-X

Terveen, L., & McDonald, D. W. (2005). Social Matching: A Framework and Research Agenda. *ACM Transactions on Computer-Human Interaction*, *12*(3), 401–434. doi:10.1145/1096737.1096740

Trocchia, P. J., & Janda, S. (2003). How Do Consumers Evaluate Internet Retail Service Quality? *Journal of Services Marketing*, *17*(3), 243–253. doi:10.1108/08876040310474800

Voss, C. (2003). Rethinking Paradigms of Service: Service in a Virtual Environment. [IJOP]. *International Journal of Operations & Production Management*, *23*(1), 88–104. doi:10.1108/01443570310453271

Walker, J. (1990). Through the Looking Glass. In Laurel, B. (Ed.), *The Art of Human-Computer Interface Design*. Reading, Massachusetts: Addison-Wesley.

Wang, Y. D., & Emurian, H. H. (2005). An Overview of Online Trust: Concepts, Elements, and Implications. *Computers in Human Behavior*, *21*, 105–125. doi:10.1016/j.chb.2003.11.008

Webb, H. W., & Webb, L. A. (2004). SiteQual: An Integrated Measure of Web Site Quality. *Journal of Enterprise Information Management*, *17*(6), 430–440. doi:10.1108/17410390410566724

Wolfinbarger, M., & Gilly, M. C. (2003). eTailQ: Dimensionalizing, Measuring and Predicting etail Quality. *Journal of Retailing*, *79*(3), 183–198. doi:10.1016/S0022-4359(03)00034-4

Yoo, B., & Donthu, N. (2001). Developing a Scale to Measure the Perceived Quality of an Internet Shopping Site (SITEQUAL). *Quarterly Journal of Electronic Commerce*, *2*(1), 31–47.

Zeithaml, V. A., Bitner, M. J., & Gremler, D. D. (2006). *Services Marketing: Integrating Customer Focus Across the Firm* (4th ed.). Boston: McGraw-Hill/Irwin.

Zeithaml, V. A., Parasuraman, A., & Malhotra, A. (2002). Service Quality Delivery through Web Sites: A Critical Review of Extant Knowledge. *Journal of the Academy of Marketing Science*, *30*(4), 362–375. doi:10.1177/009207002236911

This work was previously published in International Journal of Information Systems in the Service Sector (IJISSS), edited by John Wang, pp. 17-35, copyright 2009 by IGI Publishing (an imprint of IGI Global).

Chapter 9
Toward an Integrated Conceptualization of the Service and Service System Concepts: A Systems Approach

Manuel Mora
Autonomous University of Aguascalientes, México

Mahesh S. Raisinghani
TWU School of Management, USA

Rory O'Connor
Dublin City University, Ireland

Ovsei Gelman
CCADET, Universidad Nacional Autónoma de México, México

ABSTRACT

Service and service systems concepts are fundamental constructs for the development of the emergent SSME, ITSM, and Service Oriented Software (SOS) knowledge streams. A diversified literature has provided a richness of findings, but at the same time, the lack of standardized conceptualizations is a source of confusion to IT practitioners and academics. Given this problematic situation, we pose that a systems approach is useful to address it. In this article, we review and synthesize key studies in these knowledge streams to design: (i) a framework to characterize both concepts under a system view and, (ii) harmonized definitions (e.g. identification of shared and essential properties) for such fundamental concepts. Our main contribution is scholastic, but we are confident that the posed conceptual artifacts can be further used to elaborate standardized definition for the IT service and IT service system constructs, as well as analysis tools for describe real service systems.

DOI: 10.4018/978-1-60960-138-6.ch009

INTRODUCTION

Service Science, Management and Engineering (SSME) (Chesbrough & Spohrer, 2006, Spohrer et al.. 2007), IT Service Management (ITSM) (OGC, 2007; Beachboard et al.. 2007), and Service-oriented Architecture/Software Engineering (SOA/SOSE) (Bieberstein et al.. 2005; Kontogiannis et al.. 2007), are knowledge streams focused on developing an emergent service system engineering and management paradigm founded in the concepts of service, service system and by extension upon: IT services, IT service systems, and Service Oriented Software (SOS) concepts.

Such a focus on services has been largely influenced by core marketing[1] and business researchers (Levitt, 1972, 1976; Heskett, 1987; Schlesinger & Heskett, 1991; Quinn, 1992), who independently have envisioned a high-valued and semantically richer concept of service than the traditional simple and low-valued one. In particular Quinn (1992) conceives a new service-based economy, through his studies of strategic re-definitions of product-oriented manufacturing organizations to service-oriented business organizations. At present, this service view has permeated so strongly in business organizations, that the business organizations focused on delivering "*help, utility, experience, information or other intellectual content ... account for more than 70% of total value added in the OECD*" (Sheehan, 2006). Thus the construct of service - as opposed to the product concept or the usual post-sale business activity - has experienced fundamental changes, and acquired a high business practical and theoretical relevance.

In particular since IT technology plays a critical role for the realization of such high-quality, cost-effective and trustworthy services provisioned by service systems (Zysman, 2006; Zhao et al.. 2007), we are motivated to provide practical assistance to help to IT stakeholders and to enlighten their understanding of such concepts. Academically we are interested in advancing our formal engineering and managerial knowledge on such systems. Such a diversified literature has provided a richness of findings on such concepts, however at the same time the lack of integrated and/or standardized conceptualizations has precluded a clear understanding to both IT practitioners and academics. For instance, the service concept has been used in the IT knowledge stream from the 1970's (Lewis, 1976; Olson & Chervany, 1980; Leitheiser & Wheteber, 1986) until today (Pitt et al.. 1997; Kettinger & Lee, 1997, 2005; OGC, 2007), but with different connotations.

Additionally, the current tight interrelationship of the ITSM and SOSE knowledge streams increases the conceptual variety and confusion on what are IT services and on how they can be engineered and managed efficiently and effectively. We consider that in the IT stream –and any knowledge stream- ambiguity and imprecision must be avoided by both IT stakeholders and academics. A vast literature of failed IT systems and the contrast of real user's needs versus the final capabilities implemented can be magnified for the multiple conceptualizations of what represents an IT service. For instance, an IT service can vary from a full ERP capability service priced in hundreds of dollars by hour to a single access to a laser printer priced at cents per sheet. Thus the available knowledge on services, service systems and IT services, is not harmonized: e.g. there are multiple definitions, with shared and unshared properties, and with different scope of referents, even though in the same knowledge stream as IT. Furthermore, no similar study on an integrated conceptualization of such concepts was located in the related business and SSME literatures.

We consider also that given the diverse nature of the above mentioned interrelated concepts, a system view (Ackoff, 1971; Gelman & Garcia, 1989) is useful to organize and integrate such diversified literature. Consequently, in this article, we use a systems approach to review and synthesize key studies on such knowledge streams to design: (i) an initial framework to characterize both concepts under a system view, and (ii) initial harmonized definitions (e.g. definitions based on the shared and essential properties of main sources) for such fundamental concepts.

The organization of our manuscript is as follows: we describe the systemic research method instanced as a conceptual design research (Mora et al.. 2008c; March & Smith, 1995). Next, we report the review of the set of selected studies - from business and SSME knowledge streams - and the design of the conceptual framework for service and service system constructs. We continue with an analysis of the conceptual evidences, and elaborate on an integrated definition for the constructs of service and service system. Finally, we conclude with a discussion on implications of such proposals for theory and practice, and on the limitations and cautions of our study.

DESCRIPTION OF THE CONCEPTUAL DESIGN RESEARCH METHOD UNDER A SYSTEMS APPROACH

The selection of the research method is based on two criteria: (i) adequacy to treat conceptual complex pieces to be analyzed and synthesized and (ii) method's familiarity to researchers. For the first case, we consider that the vast business and available SSME literature has provided a rich, but complex network of conceptual pieces for the constructs of service and service system. However, such a variety at the same time, adds a complexity dimension manifested for the lack of an agreement. Consequently, an adequate research method must provide tools for addressing and organizing such complex interrelationships. In this research, a systems approach (Ackoff, 1971; Gelman & Garcia, 1989) is used as a research meta-method[2] for such an aim. The specific instance is a conceptual design research method (Mora et al.. 2008c; March & Smith, 1995).

The systems approach assumes that the reality or conceptual situation under study can be mapped to a system comprised of interacting subsystems, and into a wider system, and environment, which affect it. Systems can be real or conceptual but all share the following properties: emergency, purposefulness, hierarchical organization, and control and communication information. A systems approach thus provides parsimonious but powerful concepts to organize disparate and complex elements as a hierarchical organization under a common purpose (Mora et al.., 2007).

The used specific conceptual design research method is reported in Mora et al. (2008c). Its five activities are[3]: CD.1 Knowledge Gap Identification, CD.2 Methodological Knowledge Selection, CD.3 Conceptual Design, CD.4 Design Data Collecting, and CD.5 Analysis and Synthesis. Activities CD.1 and CD.2 corresponds to first two sections of this article. Activities CD.3 and CD.5 are reported in forth one.

A conceptual design research method is used for designing a conceptual artifact through a systematic process. For March and Smith (1995) a design research approach is used to build and evaluate non-trivial, non-naturally created and non-existent artifacts needed for human-being purposes. Design research outcomes are constructs, models, methods, or instantiations. Build activity responses to the inquiry: is feasible to build X by using Y?, and evaluate activity to the inquiry: does the artifact X fulfill the design range of set M of expected metrics? March and Smith (1995) do not report guidelines for the build activity, but suggest strongly the development of metrics for the evaluation activity. Utility and value are the usual criteria suggested by March and Smith, in contrast to truthness for natural/behavioral sciences. Another core framework for research methods (Glass et al.. 2004) does not distinguish between natural and design research. However, from the reported three main research approaches (descriptive, formulative and evaluative), and 19 research methods, this research can be assessed as a formulative-framework/concept and evaluative-other approach, as well as an instance of conceptual research method. Under the Hevner et al.'s framework (2004), this research is a design research with two constructs and one model/framework as outputs. Seven design research guidelines are given by Hevner et al. (2004). Table A.4 in the appendix A, reports how these guidelines are addressed in this research.

CONCEPTUAL DESIGN OF THE SERVICE SYSTEM FRAMEWORK

SSME literature on services is new and limited, while the management science literature is vast. For our conceptual analysis with a design purpose we have identified five set of studies with theoretical sufficiency. This conceptual sampling procedure denominated theoretical sampling (Strauss & Corbin, 1990, p. 176) selects units of study by the relevance to build theory. This design research does not claim to elaborate on a theory of service systems, but we consider this criterion for selecting conceptual *ingredients* as highly adequate. The five set of studies are as follows: (i) Levitt (1972, 1976), (ii) Shostack (1984), Heskett (1987), and Schlesinger and Heskett (1991), (iii) Cook et. al (1999), (iv) Spohrer (2008) and Spohrer et al.. (2007), and (v) Mora et al.. (2008b).

Levitt (1972, 1976) is a pioneer in suggesting an engineering approach to design services process (e.g. a well-planned and industrialized process that reduces the employee's discretion, and assigns the adequate control level of employees on the service process). Shostack (1984), Heskett (1987), and Schlesinger and Heskett (1991) complement Levitt's industrialization approach to services with a focus on employee training, motivation and satisfaction features, but hold the premise that services can and must be engineered. Cook et al.'s study (1999) reviews 39 previous related studies on services published from 1964 to 1996 in the domain of business operations management. Spohrer (2008) and Spohrer' et al..'s (2007) studies are integrative studies on extensive service marketing and service business literature. These studies have also shaped the emergent SSME knowledge stream. Finally, Mora et al.'s study (2008b) poses concepts of service and service system by using the Theory of Systems (Ackoff, 1971; Gelman & Garcia, 1989). The main contribution of last study is the utilization of formal definitions of the concept system, in contrast to the typical but theoretically incomplete connotations widely used. A similar critique has been reported in the related domain of Information Systems (Alter, 2003; Mora et al.. 2003, 2008a; Gelman et al.. 2005).

For modeling a system (Gelman & Garcia, 1989; Mora et al.. 2003) it is necessary and sufficient to identify the following elements: (i) inner systems (subsystems), (ii) outer systems (suprasystem, environment), (iii) interrelationships with outer systems (inputs, outputs), (iv) interrelationships with inner systems, and (v) properties and actions.

Inner systems (called subsystems) are systems that compose the system under study, are mandatory for composing it and own their specific components. Outer systems (supra-system, and environment) are the immediate wider system that contains the system under description (suprasystem), and the outer setting that contains the supra-system (environment). Both affect the system and both can be affected by it. Interrelationships with outer systems are the transference of materials, energy and information that the system needs to fulfill its purpose (a fundamental emergent property). The system's inputs are the flows of materials, energy and/or information that the system needs to have a useful purpose. The system's outputs are flows of materials, energy and/or information that the system generates to the supra-system for accomplishing its purpose. The interrelationships with inner systems can be considered inner inputs and outputs. Finally the system's properties are substantial features with the potential to exhibit an effect/product or cause/producer, while that the system's actions are acts

Table 1. The essential system framework

ELEMENT 1: INNER SYSTEMS
1.1 Subsystem A
1.1.1 Process/activities
1.1.2 People (employees)
1.1.3 Resources
1.2 Subsystem B
1.2.1 Process/activities
1.2.2 People (employees)
1.2.3 Resources
1.X Subsystem …
ELEMENT 2: OUTER SYSTEMS
2.1 Suprasystem
2.1.1 Beneficiaries/Customers
2.1.2 Competitors
2.1.3 Suppliers
2.1.4 Regulators
2.1.5 Partnerships
2.2 Environment
2.2.1 Economic Influences
2.2.2 Legal Influences
2.2.3 Social Influences
2.2.4 Technological Influences
2.2.5 Physical Influences
ELEMENT 3: INTERRELATIONSHIPS WITH OUTER SYSTEMS
3.1 INPUTS
3.1.1 Customer's needs/wants
3.1.2 User's needs/wants
3.1.3 Extent of beneficiaries' contact (presence/participation)
3.2 OUTPUTS
3.2.1 Service actions' attributes
ELEMENT 4: INTERRELATIONSHIPS WITH INNER SYSTEMS
4.1 INNER INPUTS
4.1.1 Inner Customer's needs/wants
4.1.2 Inner User's needs/wants
4.1.3 Inner Extent of beneficiaries' contact (presence/participation)
4.2 INNER OUTPUTS
4.2.1 Inner Service actions' attributes
ELEMENT 5: PROPERTIES & ACTIONS
5.1 Emergency
5.1.1 Purposefulness
5.1.2 Hierarchical organization
5.1.3 Control and communication information
5.1.4 Outcomes
5.1.5 Other properties
5.2 Actions

performed by the exercise of properties, and these (actions) can be realized on itself (e.g. the system) or on other external systems.

Systems own some mandatory properties: emergency, purposefulness, hierarchical organization, control and communication information, and outcomes. Emergency is a generic name for any property owned by the whole system but not by a subset of parts. Purposefulness is the implicit general and long-term aim searching by the system. This can be self-defined or imposed by an external system. Hierarchical organization is a property that is manifested by the system per se through its composition by subsystems and its inner interrelationships. Control and communication information property is manifested through the exchange of information for controlling and/or communicating aims. The system's outcomes are properties that affect the wider system called supra-system. These effects are usually measured through system's effectiveness metrics. Additional system's metrics are of efficiency to evaluate the rate of outputs to inputs (including other resources), and of efficacy to evaluate the rightness of the real achieved outputs versus the expected ones. Of all these properties, emergency can be considered the root one, and the remainders as a subset. For instance, purposefulness is an emergent property as it is own by the whole entity, and not for a particular part. This view is exhibited in Table 1.

Consequently to design the service systems framework the following steps were undertaken: (I) we selected a previous theoretically valid conceptual framework of what is a system (Mora et al.. 2003) and it was updated with generic knowledge on services by two lead authors. (II) Each core study was reviewed by two lead authors for identifying conceptual pieces that fit in some of the five elements that comprise a system. Each time a new conceptual element was identified (and agreed to be included by at least two authors that acted as codifiers), previous studies were analyzed again to assess the extent to which that element is: explicitly (●), implicitly (◉) or not posed (○) in such studies. Thus, the assessment of elements exhibited in Table 2 was built iteratively. (III) Authors qualitatively assessed the elements identified in the five studies to pose the final non-redundant and essential ones to be included in the harmonized view of the construct: service system. The triple symbol (ΔΔΔ) stands by for an essential/mandatory element for the harmonized view of service system, two symbols (ΔΔ) stands by for a sub-item of a mandatory element, and a single symbol (Δ) for a sub-item of a mandatory element but few reported. Finally, (IV) the other three co-authors conduct a face validity test on the rationale of such element in the service system framework. Table 1 exhibits the essential system framework, and Table 2 the new designed service system framework.

The main insights from the set of five core studies are used to design and theoretically support the service system framework exhibited in Table 2. We remark the essential ones. From Levitt's studies (1972, 1976), suggests that we must avoid a discretionary and casual human-intensive approach for services and we must design, deploy and control services similar to the standards and quality of products that are manufactured. Thus, components (1.1.1, and 1.1.3) are remarked.

Subsequent studies (Shostack, 1984; Heskett, 1987; Schlesinger & Heskett, 1991) have complemented Levitt's view for services with employees' satisfaction and motivation. Schelesinger and Heskett (1991, p. 73), while defending the need of employee motivation and satisfaction, admit that implicitly these issues are insufficient when asserting that " ... *service failures are not failures, they have been designed into the system by the choices senior management have done*". Thus from a systems view, service failures must be assigned to the overall system and trust only in highly motivated employees is insufficient to guarantee a stable and predictable quality of service. Thus from this set of studies, the systemic element (1.1.2) is justified as essential.

The next study (Cook et al. 1999) is one of the most complete in the business operations management literature. While the authors conclude that a service definition is not adequate, we believe that while an individual proposal for defining such a construct can be disparate, an integrative definition from shared and essential attributes can be helpful. Cook et al. (1999) identify marketing-oriented and operations-oriented service attributes. In the former case, these attributes are tangibility-intangibility, differentiation, object of service (people or people's possessions), type of customer (individual or institutional), and commitment. In the latter case, these attributes are customer contact, capital-people intensity, customer involvement, production process, and employee discretion. Additional attributes such as customization, quality and socio-economic environment issues are also identified. From this extensive study, as illustrated in Table 2, several elements can be remarked (1.1.1, 1.1.3, 3.1, 3.2, 2.2.1, and 2.2.3).

We review Spohrer's (2008) and Spohrer et al.'s (2007) studies by their comprehensiveness in the SSME knowledge stream. While several partial definitions for the construct service are elaborated, we consider that the following one (Spohrer, 2008): "*... the application of resources (including competences, skills, and knowledge) to make changes that have value for another*

Table 2. The service system framework

	Levitt (1972, 1976)	Shostack (1984,), Heskett (1987), Schelesinger & Heskett (1991)	Cook et al. (1999)	Spohrer (2007), Spohrer et al. (2008)	Mora et al. (2008b)	Level of Inclusion
ELEMENT 1: INNER SYSTEMS	◉	◉	◉	●	●	ΔΔΔ
1.1 Subsystem A	◉	◉	◉	●	●	ΔΔΔ
1.1.1 Process/activities	●	●	●	●	●	ΔΔΔ
2.1.1 Well-defined/designed process	●	●	◉	●	●	ΔΔΔ
2.1.2 Procedures (routinized, standardized)	●	●	◉	●	●	ΔΔΔ
1.1.2 People (employees)	●	●	●	●	●	ΔΔΔ
2.2.1 Discretion-Divergence controllability	●	◉	●	◉	◉	ΔΔ
2.2.2 Unskilled, skilled or professional	◉	◉	●	◉	◉	Δ
2.2.3 Motivation/ Satisfaction	○	●	○	○	○	ΔΔ
1.2.3 Resources	●	●	●	●	●	ΔΔΔ
2.3.1 Materials and Machines	●	●	●	●	●	ΔΔ
2.3.2 Information and knowledge	◉	●	◉	●	●	ΔΔ
2.3.3 Capital (hard, soft, hybrid)-people intensity levels	●	●	●	●	◉	ΔΔ
1.2 Subsystem B …						Δ
ELEMENT 2: OUTER SYSTEMS	◉	◉	●	●	●	ΔΔΔ
2.1 Suprasystem	◉	◉	●	●	●	ΔΔΔ
2.1.1 Beneficiaries	◉	◉	●	●	●	ΔΔΔ
2.1.1.1 People (individual vs collective consumption)	◉	◉	●	●	◉	ΔΔ
2.1.1.2 Things (people's possessions)	●	●	●	●	●	ΔΔ
2.1.1.3 Organizations (virtual people's possessions)	◉	◉	●	◉	◉	ΔΔ
2.1.2 Competitors	◉	◉	◉	●	●	Δ
2.1.3 Suppliers	◉	◉	◉	●	●	Δ
2.1.4 Regulators	◉	◉	◉	●	●	Δ
2.1.5 Partnerships	◉	◉	◉	●	●	Δ
2.2 Environment	◉	◉	●	●	●	ΔΔΔ
2.2.1 Economic Influences	◉	◉	●	●	●	ΔΔ
2.2.2 Legal Influences	◉	◉	●	●	●	ΔΔ
2.2.3 Social Influences	◉	●	●	●	●	ΔΔ
2.2.4 Technological Influences	●	◉	●	●	●	ΔΔ
2.2.5 Physical Influences	◉	◉	●	◉	◉	ΔΔ
ELEMENT 3: INTERRELATIONSHIPS WITH OUTER SYSTEMS	◉	◉	◉	●	●	ΔΔΔ
3.1 Inputs	◉	◉	◉	●	●	ΔΔΔ
3.1.1 Customer's needs/wants	●	●	●	●	◉	ΔΔ
3.1.2 User's needs/wants	●	●	●	●	◉	ΔΔ

continued on following page

Table 2. continued

	Levitt (1972, 1976)	Shostack (1984,), Heskett (1987), Schelesinger & Heskett (1991)	Cook et al. (1999)	Spohrer (2007), Spohrer et al. (2008)	Mora et al. (2008b)	Level of Inclusion
3.1.3 Extent of beneficiaries' contact (presence/participation)	◉	◉	●	●	◉	ΔΔ
3.2 Outputs	◉	◉	◉	●	●	ΔΔΔ
3.2 Service actions' attributes	●	●	●	●	●	ΔΔΔ
3.2.1.1 Intangibility	●	●	●	●	●	ΔΔ
3.2.1.2 Quality features (ordered, uniform, predictable, reliable, standard, cost-effective)	●	●	●	●	●	ΔΔ
3.2.1.3 Simultaneous production -consumption time	◉	●	●	●	●	ΔΔ
3.2.1.4 Co-manufacturing between customer-service system	●	●	◉	●	●	ΔΔ
3.2.1.5 Perishability of effects	○	○	●	◉	○	Δ
3.2.1.6 Reversibility of effects	○	○	●	◉	○	Δ
3.2.1.7 Extent of customization, differentiation and specialization (unique/generic)	●	●	●	●	◉	Δ
3.2.1.8 Financial evaluation (cost, economic value)	●	●	◉	●	◉	ΔΔ
ELEMENT 4: INTERRELATIONSHIPS WITH INNER SYSTEMS	○	○	○	◉	◉	ΔΔΔ
4.1 Inner Inputs	○	○	○	◉	◉	Δ
4.2 Inner Outputs	○	○	○	◉	◉	Δ
ELEMENT 5: PROPERTIES & ACTIONS	○	○	○	●	●	ΔΔΔ
5.1 Emergency	○	○	○	●	●	Δ
5.1.1 Purposefulness	○	○	○	●	●	Δ
5.1.2 Hierarchical organization	○	○	○	●	●	Δ
5.1.3 Control and communication information	○	○	○	●	●	Δ
5.1.4 Outcomes	◉	◉	◉	●	●	ΔΔΔ
5.1.4.1 Generic added value only assessed by beneficiaries	●	●	●	●	●	ΔΔΔ
5.1.4.2 Physical-Temporal added value (time, place, form) only assessed by beneficiaries	◉	●	●	◉	●	ΔΔ
5.1.4.3 Mental added value (psychological, cognitive) only assessed by beneficiaries	◉	●	●	◉	●	ΔΔ
5.1.4.4 Financial/economic added value only assessed by beneficiaries	●	●	◉	●	◉	ΔΔ
5.1.5 Other properties	◉	◉	◉	●	●	ΔΔΔ
5.6.1 Complexity	●	◉	●	●	●	Δ
5.6.2 Sustainability / Survivability	○	○	○	●	◉	Δ
5.6.3 Efficiency/internal service system's metrics	◉	◉	●	●	●	ΔΔ
5.6.4 Efficacy, Ethical and Aesthetical metrics	◉	◉	◉	◉	●	Δ
5.7 Actions	◉	◉	◉	●	●	Δ

(system)", as well as the postulation of the service system construct as "*... a value coproduction configuration of people, technology, other internal and external service systems, and shared information (such as language, processes, metrics, prices, policies, and laws*." (idem, p. 72), as the core two contributions related to this research. Spohrer et al. (2007, p. 76) indicates that " *... service systems are complex adaptive systems made up of people, and people are complex and adaptive themselves. Service systems are dynamic and open, rather than simple and optimized. And there are many different kinds of value, including financial, relationship, and reputation*." Spohrer's study (2008) is mainly built up on Lusch and Vargo's (2006) service-dominant logic, where each "*service system engages in three main activities that make up the service interaction: (1) proposing a value co-creation interaction to another service system (proposal), (2) agreeing to a proposal (agreement), and (3) realizing the proposal (realization)*". Spohrer (2008) study endorses Lusch and Vargo's (2006) core proposition that "*value is always uniquely and phenomenologically determined by the beneficiary*." Service system's efficiency (how well the system is performing its processes) and effectiveness (how much the system's outcomes are valuable to its supra-system) emerge as value-oriented natural attributes. The remaining systemic metrics, i.e., efficacy, ethical, and aesthetical measurements (Checkland, 2000) are implicitly addressed. Efficacy refers to how well the system is generating the expected outputs. The Ethical category assesses how well the system is acting in conformity with the legal, social and the cultural de facto and de jure norms in its supra-system. In turn, aesthetical issues measures how pleasant are the system's actions. Thus, the five elements are justified, and in particular the element 5.5 (outcome), emerges as an essential feature through the added-value premise that each service system must fulfill.

Finally, from Mora et al.'s (2008b) study, the concepts of business organization, business organizational subsystem, business process and sub-process, business activity, and product and service, are considered from a systems perspective. For Mora et al. (2008b) a service can be defined as an expected and intangible system's people-oriented and valued outcome from a system's outputs (acts), where a system can be a business activity, business process, business organizational subsystem or business organization. In contrast, a product (or good) is defined as an expected and tangible system's machine-oriented valued outcome from system's outputs (matter), where a system can be a business activity, business process, business organizational subsystem or business organization. Accordingly based on the Theory of Systems, generic system's outputs can be classified as a flux of matter, energy, and/or information. Mora et al. (2008b) extends such a classification to include a flux of acts and knowledge, where acts can be considered a special kind of energy, and knowledge a special kind of interpreted information about - how- and why-based information pieces. Such definitions are abstract. Specific attributes are responsibility of the system's modeler. Main distinction between the service and product concepts, is the type of element that can assess the value received (subjective or intra-subjective). In the former case, this can only be conducted by a single person or a group of people, and in the latter case, by automated machines (objective assessment). However, machine-oriented value metrics can be incorporated into an overall service valuation (e.g. for adding objective metrics).

Hence, from these last studies, the five main elements are justified. However, despite the definition a system as subsystems and inner interrelationships, no study reports such elements. For theoretical consistency these elements are kept in Table 2 and assessed with the single symbol (Δ) as few reported.

THE HARMONIZED DEFINITIONS FOR SERVICE AND SERVICE SYSTEMS CONSTRUCTS

The review of these five set of studies covers the most relevant conceptual pieces to assemble the service system framework (exhibited in Table 2). We consider this useful to elaborate on a harmonized view of the service and service system constructs. The main theoretical implication that contrasts with the previous disparate definitions for the service construct, is a holistic multidimensional conceptualization. From a systems view, a service can be initially mapped to: (i) an agreed integrated flux of actions (outputs' system) delivered by a provider system to a customer system to co-create value (Spohrer et al. 2007 view), and to (ii) a status property in the customer service that is affected by the delivered provider's system actions.

However, given the core characteristic on the co-responsibility of both parties (provider and customer systems) to generate the expected value, by applying a systems view again, this characteristic can be assessed as an emergent property. Thus, both the service provider and the service customer are co-producers (e.g. single necessary elements but not sufficient ones by separate) for this expected value realization. This last implication carries out to derive from a systems approach an innovative and challenger re-conceptualization for both service and service system constructs. Instead to consider the service system like uniquely the provider system, and the users being external to the system, we can re-conceptualize it with the following two core components: (i) a *service facilitator* sub-system (e.g. the original service provider), and (ii) a *service appraiser* subsystem (e.g. the initial user's system). This re-conceptualization implies that services failures can be caused by deviations on the agreed behaviors not only from the *service facilitator* subsystem -as at present is usually accepted-, but also from mistakes into the *service appraiser* subsystem. We pose denote this system as ***service-fα system*** to distinguish it from its current connotation, and for the *service facilitator and service appraiser* subsystems as ***service-f*** and ***service-α*** subsystems.

With this new view of system, the initial two-dimensional mappings for the concept service must be updated to be consistent with the systems approach. Thus, we pose the following mappings for the concept of service: (i) an agreed integrated flux of actions delivered by a *facilitator sub-system* to an *sub-appraiser system*, complemented with a flux of actions of the latter, to co-create an expected value outcome, and affect positively the predetermined status properties in both systems (extended Spohrer et al.'s 2007 view), (ii) status properties in the *facilitator* and *appraiser* subsystems that are affected by the service interactions between both subsystems, and (iii) an value outcome (e.g. an emergent property, thus co-generated) that affects to the suprasystem.

To distinguish these three dimensions of a service, we pose the following notation: (i) ***service-f(f1,f2,...)*** and ***service-α(α1, α2,...)*** stand by service as a flux of actions, (ii), ***service-f(sf)*** and ***service-α(sα)*** stand by service as properties, and (iii) ***service-fα**** stand by service as the system's outcome. Based in derived findings, we define:

- a ***service-f system*** as a system designed for delivering ***service-f(f1,f2,...)*** actions toward, and receiving ***service-α(α1, α2,...)*** actions from, a *service-α system*, with the purpose to mutually generate an expected outcome called ***service-fα**** and affect positively two properties called ***service-f(sf)*** and ***service-α(sα)***.
- a ***service- α system*** as a system existent for receiving ***service-f(f1,f2,...)*** actions from, and delivering ***service-α(α1, α2,...)*** actions toward, a *service-f system*, with the purpose to mutually generate an expected outcome called ***service-fα**** and affect positively two properties called ***service-f(sf)*** and ***service-α(sα)***.

- **a *service-fα system*** is a system comprised of a *service-f sub-system* and a *service-α sub-system*, with the purpose to mutually generate an expected value outcome called *service-fα**, and which operates into a suprasystem and an environment.
- **a *service-fα**** is an expected people-oriented and valued outcome (which can be complemented by objective machines-oriented metrics), from a ***service-fα system,*** under an implicit or explicit agreement of its *service-f* and *service-α* sub-systems during a well-delimited period.
- **a *service-α(sα)*** is a *service-α system's* property expected to be positively affected by the ***service-f(f1,f2,...)*** and its ***service-α(α1, α2,...)*** actions, under an implicit or explicit agreement of such *service-f* and *service-α* sub-systems during a well-delimited period.
- **a *service-f(sf)*** is a *service-f system's* property expected to be positively affected by the ***service-α(α1, α2,...)*** and its ***service-f(f1,f2,...)*** actions, under an implicit or explicit agreement of such *service-f* and *service-α* sub-systems during a well-delimited period.

Figure 1 illustrates a diagram of such constructs. This definition incorporates the most relevant and shared properties from previous studies but introduces a new connotation on the service concept: by using Theory of Systems, the service is mapped to three systemic constructs: system's actions, properties, and outcomes (special emergent properties). In Figure 1, it is illustrated that the expected valued outcome (e.g. the ***service-fα****) is not experienced only by the *appraisal subsystem* (e.g. the traditional customer or user entities that receive the service) but for all systemic elements: the *facilitator system*, the provider supra-system and finally its environment by the co-creation of value that has interdependencies. The distinction between the appraisal and facilitator system is further elaborated in tables 3.1, 3.2 and 3.3 below.

Figure 1, also illustrates the systemic view of the remainders systems in the suprasystem: system of service regulators, system of service partner-

Figure 1. Diagram of the service system and service constructs

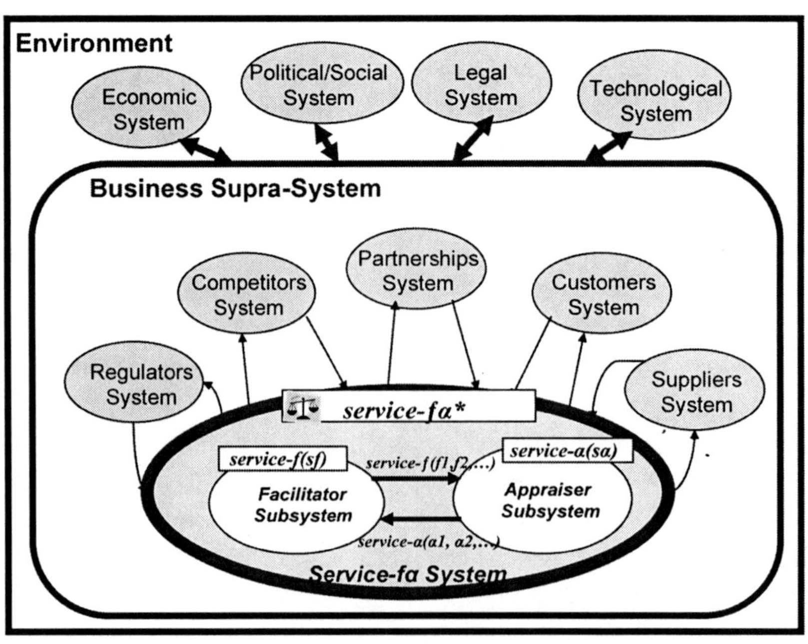

Table 3a. Examples of the Service System Categorizations: a facilitator-oriented service system

Service-fa: service system name	Air transportation for passengers service system.
Service-fa*: expected value outcome	A trustworthy, cost-effective, and on-time transportation by aircraft from a planned origin to a destination.
service-f: service facilitator sub-system (●)	Airline company.
service-f(sf): service facilitator status properties	-Availability of schedule flights for most expected traveling cities. - Operational conditions of aircrafts. - Enjoyable/pleasant flight environment. - Competitive air tickets prices. - Availability of loyalty rewards programs. - Code-share with other airlines to offer more routes and destinations
service-f(f1,f2,...): service facilitator actions	- Ticket reservation. - Passenger check-ins and check-outs. - Luggage handling. - Flight operation. - Background pre-flight operations. - Background post-flight operations.
service-α: service appraiser sub-system (◉)	A passenger.
service- α(sa): service appraiser status properties	- Pleasant (secure, enjoyable and on-time) arrival to planned destination by plane. - Pleasant check-out of flight (luggage is not missed)
service- α(α1, α2,...): service appraiser actions	- On time arrival to airport/airline offices - To respect and abide by the airline/federal aviation authority (FAA)/Transportation Security Administration (TSA) rules & regulations.
Supra-System	International air transportation service system.
Environment	Air and legal space macro-system

ships, system of appraiser's competitors, and the system of service facilitators. It is clear that from a service facilitator system's view, some elements change (e.g. competitors become customers for instance). However, Figure 1, exhibits these supra-system's elements from the ***service-fa*** system, that provides to it an expected outcome (***service-fa****) and which interacts and it is finally affected by the following suprasystem elements: regulators, partnerships, suppliers, competitors and customers.

Additionally by incorporating the fourth and fifth systemic metrics for any kind of systems (Checkland, 2000) of ethics and aesthetic, it is clear that a high quality and valued service (e.g. the outcome) as well as its co-generative service system, must comply also the legal, environmental and social regulations toward its supra-system and environment. Aesthetic issues can be also incorporated by including comparative metrics on how pleasant are the actions experienced by the appraiser and facilitator subsystem in two competitive service systems. Thus, for instance, a high quality service is not more when employees are stressed for unpleasant acts, or when the service system is damaging its environment. With this innovative conceptualization of a service system, we support the Quinn's (1992) notion of a service as the building block for a new trading and business economy, which affects no only to customers, but to all involved systems. In addition, because a service is also an expected outcome, it lasts more, equal, or less than the service period of co-generation (e.g. application of actions).

An additional implication that can be derivable from both these harmonized connotations is an innovative initial taxonomy of three categories of service systems according to their intensity of responsibility of each sub-system. This is as follows:

i. Facilitator-oriented service systems - are service systems when the commitments asked to the service facilitators exceed relevantly to the ones asked to service appraisers.
ii. Appraiser-oriented service systems - are service systems when the commitments asked to the service appraisers exceed relevantly to the ones asked to service facilitators.
iii. Balance-oriented service systems - are service systems when the commitments from both parties are relatively of similar intensity.

We estimate that most service systems at present in business and governmental organizations belong to the categories (i) and (iii). Tables 3.1, 3.2 and 3.3 illustrate such a classification of service systems with three examples. In these tables the symbols (●,▾,◉) indicate respectively a strong, similar and sufficient intensity of responsibility for the expected value co-generation. In the first case, an air transportation system seeks to serve through a reliable transportation by aircraft from one city to another one. In the second case, a tax declaration system seeks to serve through timely satisfied tax obligations. Finally, in the third case, a graduate educational system seeks to serve through the development of high-quality competences in a specific knowledge domain.

As illustrated in table 3a, an air transportation systems serves as a facilitator-oriented service system to provide a comprehensive service that meets and hopefully exceeds the needs, wants and expectations of the passenger from a service perspective. A strategic alliance with another airline allows code sharing so that passengers have a wider variety of routes (i.e., origins and destinations) to choose from and receive frequent flier miles from code-share partner airlines (e.g., the One World alliance among American Airlines, British Airways, Air Mexico, Cathay Pacific, and so forth). This *service-fa system* is classified as facilitator-oriented, because the responsibilities of the passengers (e.g the appraiser subsystem), are simple and low cost when these are compared with the assigned ones to the facilitator subsystem (e.g. complex and high cost).

As illustrated in table 3b, an e-Tax citizen declaration service system serves as *an appraiser service-oriented system* to provide a timely and cost effective service to the taxpayers and the government's treasury department/internal revenue service (IRS). The up-to-date tax code/rules/regulations can be implemented by this transaction system to facilitate the fair and accurate collection of taxes. Web 2.0 technologies (e.g., avatars in Second Life) can be used as supplementary services to assist the taxpayers with their queries and reduce human resources costs for the government. In this case, the *service-fa system* is classified as appraisal-oriented, because while there are relevant responsibilities from the facilitator system, the taxpayers (citizens and business) (e.g the appraiser subsystem), are asked to provide and execute a series of actions ranging from simple to very complex actions, with high cost implicated by wrong actions. In this type of systems, the cost of involuntary mistakes done from the appraiser system is high compared with the first type.

As illustrated in table 3c, a graduate education service system serves as a balanced service-oriented system to provide a valuable service that contributes to the development of the students' lifelong learning activities and helps them earn a living in an ethical and responsible manner. The co-creation of value by the learning facilitator and the student not only enhances the learning experience but also contributes to the development of the individual, society and economy. This *service-fa* system is classified as a balanced facilitator-appraisal system, because the non-accomplishment of responsibilities of any of the two systems will reduce the expected value outcome.

Table 3b. Examples of the service system categorizations: an appraiser-oriented service system

Service-fα: service system name	e-Tax citizen declaration service system.
Service-fα*: expected value outcome	Timely satisfied fiscal obligations.
service-f: service facilitator sub-system (◉)	Government tax office and online tax declaration system.
service-f(sf): service facilitator status properties	- Status of collected taxes. - Status of availability of e-offices
service-f(f1,f2,…): service facilitator actions	- To notify timely the tax payment obligations. - To make available office or e-systems to receive the tax declarations. - To processing tax declarations.
service-α: service appraiser sub-system (●)	A tax contributor.
service- α(sα): service appraiser status properties	- Correctness and timeliness of tax declaration (with potential assistance of other service systems).
service- α(α1, α2,…): service appraiser actions	- To be aware of the tax declarations deadlines. - To present timely the tax declaration, - To keep the fiscal records for further auditing procedures.
Supra-System	Governmental e-service system
Environment	A country tax regulation macro-system

Table 3c. Examples of the service system categorizations: a balance-oriented service system

Service-fα: service system name	Graduate education service system.
Service-fα*: expected value outcome	Development of high-quality competences in a specific knowledge domain.
service-f: service facilitator sub-system (◒)	Graduate system (faculty, curriculum, infrastructure)
service-f(sf): service facilitator status properties	- Innovative knowledge transference status - Relevance of knowledge generated
service-f(f1,f2,…): service facilitator actions	-To teach high-quality knowledge. -To assess students in an unbiased manner. -To encourage students for their maximum performance. -To instill a love/passion for lifelong learning
service-α: service appraiser sub-system (◒)	Graduate student (as a single human being system).
service- α(sα): service appraiser status properties	- Knowledge level - Stress level
service- α(α1, α2,…): service appraiser actions	- To achieve high grade-point-average (GPA). - To fulfill the academic regulations -To apply the learned knowledge in an ethical and responsible manner with sound judgment.
Supra-System	Regional educational service system (e.g., SACS)
Environment	A countrywide and worldwide educational macro-system

Hence, we can pose as three initial criteria for assessing a *service-fα* system as facilitator, appraiser or balanced one, as follows: (i) the cost of mistakes, (ii) the complexity of actions, and (iii) the legal responsibility for achieving the expected outputs.

From these conceptual systemic designs, we can conclude that these new definitions: (i) include previous main shared properties from key/seminal studies in three knowledge streams, (ii) endorse and enhance two of the best and updated definitions for such constructs (from Spohrer (2008) and Spohrer et al. 2007)), and (iii) are build up on more elaborated concepts of Theory of Systems. Table 1 reports a generic framework of a system. Table 2 exhibits a framework based in Table 1's framework, populated with essential as well as few reported but important elements posed to be considered to characterize a service system and a service. From these findings, the definitions of such fundamental concepts have been reported. In particular, both definitions are highly innovative and challenger to the current ones, but are theoretically consistent with most important elements suggested. Additionally, given the innovative definition of a service system as a whole system comprised of the facilitator and the appraiser subsystems, an initial taxonomy of three types of service systems is reported in Table 3.

We finally argue that from these definitions, more detailed definitions can be generated if the interrelationships and properties of the system under study (e.g. the service system) are considered. These particularizations are suggested for further research.

CONCLUSION

In this conceptual design study, we have reviewed key/seminal studies on two highly related knowledge streams to design: (i) an initial framework to characterize the concepts of service system and service, under a system view, and (ii) initial harmonized definitions (e.g. identification of shared and essential properties) for such fundamental concepts. This article reports also an innovative concept of service as a multidimensional concept: service as actions, service as a property, and service as an expected. For instance, when a person is operated, the service acts are all medical and patient actions for achieving the "be operated" goal, service status properties for patient and doctor can be "health status" and "work satisfaction" respectively, and service as expected value outcome can be "efficient utilization of medical resources" and "recovering a productive person". It must be noted that expected value are strongly influenced during the application of service acts, but it can last after a long period..

We believe this is a challenger and innovative idea based in Theory of Systems. Furthermore, most service studies have used a limited conceptualization of what is a system or have omitted seminal references. For instance, Lovelock & Gummesson (2004) do not cite papers from Quinn (1992) and Levitt's (1972, 74). Furthermore, these authors (Lovelock & Gummesson, 2004, p. 38) suggest that "*in particular, we believe there is a need for systematic field research in services*" (pp. 38) but no seminal reference/s on Theory of Systems is/are cited.

Furthermore, despite there is a growing body of research on isolated aspects of operations services; still there is little research that is explicitly IT Service Management (ITSM) related. Consequently, while there is a significant growth of ITSM practice in industry, there is no academic work or community of scholars that shares a common mission to understand how to advance it. This article serves as a good foundation to build this stream of research using the systems theory as a theoretical foundation. Services are emerging in separate areas of academic, industry and government but few attempts have been made to integrate them. Since the early versions of ITIL lacked truly quantifiable business values, IT organizations are not interested in and supportive of ITSM processes. ITIL faces an uphill battle for acceptance and creditability that needs to be won across the entire organization.

The facilitator and the appraisal system are measurement-driven and outcome-based approach to continuous process improvement that focuses on reduction of variation, consistency and high service quality. Therefore, in terms of IT service oriented industry, combining the ideas from this article with established frameworks such as ITIL, ITSM, Capability Maturity Model Integrative (CMMI) can migrate current processes toward usable, measurable processes that can help enhance and sustain competitive advantage.

In terms of future research directions, more research needs to take place specifically relating to how measures from the framework described in this article contribute to organizational performance and service quality. Furthermore, what are the most appropriate and effective ways to measure the variables illustrated in Figure 1, and on the trade-offs between the various performance measures. Research should also be performed on ways to make the measure/s evolve to keep up with the dynamic changes in the system and needs of each field/industry taking into consideration various factors such as cost, scope, value and timeliness.

Hence, while the primary contribution of this article can be considered scholastic, we claim that these initial framework and definitions for service system can be useful to integrate the disparate current views of IT services, and to advance the knowledge demanded for IT service stakeholders for a better understanding on how to engineering and manage IT service and IT service systems. However, further research is encouraged for such aims.

REFERENCES

Ackoff, R. (1971). Towards a system of systems concepts. *Management Science*, *17*(11), 661–671. doi:10.1287/mnsc.17.11.661

Alter, S. (2003). 18 Reasons Why IT-Reliant Work Systems Should Replace "The IT Artifact" as the Core Subject Matter of the IS Field. *Communications of AIS*, *12*, 366–395.

Beachboard, J., Conger, S., Galup, S., Hernandez, A., Probst, J., & Venkataraman, R. (2007). AMCIS 2007 Panel on IT Service Management: IT Service Management in the IS Curriculum. *CAIS,* 20(35).

Bieberstein, N., Bose, S., Walker, L., & Lynch, A. (2005). Impact of service-oriented architecture on enterprise systems, organizational structures, and individuals. *IBM Systems Journal*, *44*(4), 691–708. doi:10.1147/sj.444.0691

Checkland, P. (2000). Soft Systems Methodology: a 30-year Retrospective. In Checkland, P. (Ed.), *Systems Thinking, Systems Practice* (pp. A1–A65). Chichester: Wiley.

Chesbrough, H., & Spohrer, J. (2006). A Research Manifesto for Services Sciences. *Communications of the ACM*, *49*(7), 35–40. doi:10.1145/1139922.1139945

Cook, D., Goh, C., & Chung, C. (1999). Service Typologies: a State of the Art Survey. *Production and Operations Management*, *8*(3), 318–338. doi:10.1111/j.1937-5956.1999.tb00311.x

Gelman, O., & Garcia, J. (1989). Formulation and axiomatization of the concept of general system. *Outlet of the Mexican Institute of Planning and Systems Operation*, *19*(92), 1–81.

Gelman, O., Mora, M., Forgionne, G., & Cervantes, F. (2005). *Information Systems and Systems Theory. Encyclopedia of Information Science and Technology* (pp. 1491–1496). Hershey, PA: Idea Group.

Glass, R., Armes, V., & Vessey, I. (2004). An Analysis of Research in Computing Disciplines. *Communications of the ACM*, *47*(6), 89–94. doi:10.1145/990680.990686

Heskett, J. (1987). Lessons in the service sector. *Harvard Business Review*, (Mar-Apr): 118–126.

Hevner, A. R., March, S. T., Park, J., & Ram, S. (2004). Design Science in Information Systems Research. *Management Information Systems Quarterly*, *28*(1), 75–105.

Kettinger, W., & Lee, C. (1997). Pragmatic Perspectives on the Measurement of Information Systems Service Quality. *Management Information Systems Quarterly*, *21*(2), 223–240. doi:10.2307/249421

Kettinger, W., & Lee, C. (2005). Zones of Tolerance: Alternatives Scales for Measuring Information Systems Service Quality. *Management Information Systems Quarterly*, *29*(4), 607–623.

Kontogiannis, K., Lewis, G., Smith, D., Litoiu, M., Müller, H., Schuster, S., & Stroulia, E. (2007). The Landscape of Service-Oriented Systems: A Research Perspective. In: *International Workshop on Systems Development in SOA Environments* ((SDSOA'07: ICSE Workshops 2007). IEEE, 1-6.

Leitheiser, R., & Wheteber, J. (1986). Service-Support Levels: an Organized Approach to End-user Computing. *Management Information Systems Quarterly*, (December): 337–349. doi:10.2307/249187

Levitt, T. (1972). Production-line approach to service. *Harvard Business Review*, (Sep-Oct): 41–52.

Levitt, T. (1976). The Industrialization of Service. *Harvard Business Review*, (Sep-Oct): 63–74.

Lewis, L. (1976). Service level: a concept of the user and the computer center. *IBM Systems Journal*, *4*, 328–357. doi:10.1147/sj.154.0328

Lovelock, C., & Gummesson, E. (2004). Whither services marketing? In search of a new paradigm and fresh perspectives. *Journal of Service Research*, *7*(1), 20–41. doi:10.1177/1094670504266131

Lusch, R., & Vargo, S. (2006). (Eds.). *The Service-Dominant Logic of Marketing: Dialog, Debate, and Directions*. M.E. Sharpe: New York.

March, S., & Smith, G. (1995). Design and natural science research on information technology. *Decision Support Systems*, *15*, 251–266. doi:10.1016/0167-9236(94)00041-2

Mora, M., Gelman, O., & Cervantes, F. (2003). A systemic approach for the formalization of the information system concept: why information systems are systems? In Cano, J. (Ed.), *Critical reflections of Information systems: a systemic approach* (pp. 1–29). Hershey, PA: Idea Group.

Mora, M., Gelman, O., Forgionne, G., Petkov, D., & Cano, J. (2007). Integrating the Fragmented Pieces of Is research Paradigms and Frameworks: A systems Approach. *Information Resources Management Journal*, *20*(2), 1–12.

Mora, M., Gelman, O., Frank, M., Cervantes, F., & Forgionne, G. (2008a). Toward an Interdisciplinary Engineering and Management of Complex IT-intensive Organizational Systems: a Systems View. *International Journal of Information Technologies and Systems Approach*, *1*(1), 1–24.

Mora, M., Gelman, O., O'Connor, R., Alvarez, F., & Macias-Luevano, J. (2008b). A Conceptual Descriptive-Comparative Study of Models and Standards of Processes in SE, SwE and IT disciplines using the Theory of Systems. *International Journal of Information Technologies and Systems Approach*, *1*(2).

Mora, M., Gelman, O., Paradice, D., & Cervantes, F. (2008c). The Case for Conceptual Research in Information Systems. In: G. Grant & F. Tan (Eds), e-Proceedings of the 2008 International Conference on Information Resources Management (Conf-IRM), May 18-20, 2008, Niagara Falls, Ontario, Canada, 1-10.

OGC. (2007). *The Official Introduction to the ITIL Service Lifecycle*. London: TSO.

Olson, M., & Chervany, N. (1980). The relationship between organizational characteristics and the structure of the information service function. *Management Information Systems Quarterly*, (June): 57–68. doi:10.2307/249337

Parasuraman, A., Zeithaml, V., & Berry, L. (1988). SERVQUAL: a Multiple-item Scale for Measuring Consumer Perceptions in Service Quality. *Journal of Retailing*, *64*(1), 12–40.

Parasuraman, A., Zeithaml, V. A., & Berry, L. (1994). Alternative Scales for Measuring Service Quality: A Comparative Assessment Based on Psychometric and Diagnostic Criteria. *Journal of Retailing*, *70*(3), 201–229. doi:10.1016/0022-4359(94)90033-7

Pitt, L., Watson, R., & Kavan, C. (1997). Measuring Information Systems Service Quality: Concerns for a Complete Canvas. *Management Information Systems Quarterly*, *21*(2), 209–221. doi:10.2307/249420

Quinn, J. (1992). *Intelligent Enterprise*. New York: The Free Press.

Sargent, R. (1999). Validation and Verification of Simulation Models. In: P. A. Farrington, H. B. Nembhard, D. T. Sturrock, and G. W. Evans (Eds), *Proceedings of the 1999 Winter Simulation Conference,* Phoenix, Arizona, USA, 39-48.

Schlesinger, L., & Heskett, J. (1991). The Service-driven Service Company. *Harvard Business Review*, (Sep-Oct): 71–81.

Sheehan, J. (2006). Understanding Service Sector and Innovation. *Communications of the ACM*, *49*(7), 43–47. doi:10.1145/1139922.1139946

Shostack, G. (1984). Designing services that deliver. *Harvard Business Review*, Jan-Feb issue, 133-139.

Spohrer, J. (2008). (in press). [Draft version provided from author by email.]. *The Service Systems as the Basic Abstraction of Service Science.*

Spohrer, J., Maglio, P., Bailey, J., & Gruhl, D. (2007). Steps Toward a Science of Service Systems, *IEEE Computer*, January, 71-77.

Straus, A., & Corbin, J. (1990). *Basics of Qualitative Research: Grounded Theory Procedures and Techniques*. Newbury Park: SAGE Publications.

van Bon, J., Pieper, M., & van deer Veen, A. (2006). *Foundations of IT service management, based in ITIL*. San Antonio, TX: Van Haren.

Zhao, J., Hsu, C., Jain, H., Spohrer, J., & Tanniru, M. (2007). Panel on: Bridging service computing and service management: how MIS contributes to service orientation. *Twenty Eighth International Conference on Information Systems*, Montreal, CA, 1-4.

Zysman, J. (2006). The Algorithmic Revolution –The Fourth Service Transformation. *Communications of the ACM*, *49*(7), 48–48. doi:10.1145/1139922.1139947

ENDNOTES

1. The studies considered in this article are theoretically different from classic marketing studies focused on the quality of services measurement (Parasuraman, Zeithaml, & Berry, 1988; 1994).
2. We define a research meta-method as a research generic process that can be particularized with multiple specific research methods, under a systemic philosophical stance and a multi-methodology research approach.
3. Appendix A presents complementary information on the research method employed. Face validation is based on Sargent (1999) recommendations.

APPENDIX A. THE CONCEPTUAL DESIGN RESEARCH METHOD

Table A.1 Research activities of conceptual design research

Research activity	Inputs	Process	Outputs
CD.1 Knowledge Gap Identification.	* Initial research goals. * Conceptual units of study.	1.1 Selection of studies by (i) recognition of authors; and (ii) comprehensibility of studies. 1.2 Identification of contributions and limitations in studies regarding the research goals. 1.3 Relevance validity assessment of the knowledge gaps.	* The confirmed and refined research goals. * The relevant knowledge gaps.
CD. 2 Methodological Knowledge Selection.	* Confirmed and refined research goals. * Relevant knowledge gaps. * Conceptual units of study.	2.1 Definition of the research purpose (conceptual exploratory or full design). 2.2 Assignation of unit of studies between researchers. 2.3 Selection of the design approach (heuristic or axiomatic).	* The research purpose. * The work plan.
CD. 3 Conceptual Design.	* Conceptual units of study.	3.1 Designing of the construct, framework/model/theory, method, or system/component (not instanced in a real object) by applying the selected design approach.	* The conceptual designed artifact.
CD. 4 Design Data Collecting.	* Conceptual designed artifact. .	4.1 Identification of conceptual units for testing. 4.2 Application of conceptual units for testing. 4.3 Face validity from a panel of experts (not involved in the design team).	* The conceptual designed and tested artifact (initially used with test data). 2. The face validity assessment.
CD. 5 Analysis and Synthesis.	* Conceptual designed artifact tested (initially used with test data). * Face validity assessment.	5.1 Analysis (direct insights) and synthesis (emergent insights) of findings derivable from the designed conceptual artifact.	* The contributions from the conceptual designed artifact.

Table A.2. Results from the model face validation 4.3 Activity (version 1.0)

CONCEPTUAL INSTRUMENT FOR MODEL FACE VALIDATION						PANEL OF EXPERTS						RESULTS	
	Total disagreement				Total agreement	Academic 01	Academic 02	Academic 03	Academic 04	Consultant 01	Consultant 02	Mean	Deviation Std.
I.1 The designed conceptual model is supported by core theoretical foundations regarding the topic under study.	1	2	3	4	5	4	5	4	5	4	4	4.3	0.52
I.2 The theoretical foundations used for developing the designed conceptual model are relevant to the topic under study.	1	2	3	4	5	4	5	4	5	4	4	4.3	0.52
I.3 There are no critical omissions in the literature used for developing the designed conceptual model.	1	2	3	4	5	*	*	4	5	4	5	4.0	0.58
I.4 The designed conceptual model is logically coherent to the purpose to the reality of study.	1	2	3	4	5	3	5	5	5	4	4	4.0	0.82
I.5 The designed conceptual model is adequate to the purpose of study.	1	2	3	4	5	4	*	5	5	4	*	4.0	0.58
I.6 The outcome (i.e. the designed conceptual model) is congruent with the underlying epistemological philosophy used for its development among positivist, interpretative, critical or critical realism.	1	2	3	4	5	*	4	5	5	4	4	4.0	0.55
I.7 The designed conceptual model reports strong innovative original findings.	1	2	3	4	5	2	4	4	4	4	5	3.5	0.98
I.8 The designed conceptual model reports findings that contribute to the knowledge discipline.	1	2	3	4	5	4	5	4	5	4	5	4.3	0.55
I.9 The designed conceptual model is reported using an appropriate scientific style of writing.	1	2	3	4	5	2	4	5	4	4	4	3.8	0.98
Mean						3.3	4.6	4.4	4.8	4.0	4.4	4.27	
Deviation Standard						0.95	0.53	0.53	0.44	0.29	0.52	0.70	

Table A.3. Demography of the panel of experts for the face validation 4.3 activity

Academic 01	Academic 02 (member of the research team)	Academic 03
• PhD in CSc • 15 years in graduate teaching and research activities in SwE • Assoc. Professor in a top European University • Expert in IT Standards • EiC of a Journal related with Standards	• PhD in CSc • 8 years in graduate teaching and research activities in Sw • Senior Lecture in a top European University	• PhD in Education • 5 years in graduate teaching and research activities in Sw • Expert in SwE standards • Assoc. Professor in a top ten state Mexican University
Academic 04	Consultant 01	Consultant 02
• PhD in MIS • 15 years in graduate teaching and research activities in MIS • Full Professor in a top three private Mexican University	• PhD in CSc • 5 years research activities in Service Science • Lead Principal Researcher in a worldwide USA Research Center focused in Service Science	• MSc in MIS • 5 years in graduate teaching and research activities in MIS • Assoc. Professor in a top ten state Mexican University

Table A.4. Compliance to Hevner's et al. design research guidelines

Id	Hevner's et al. Guideline	Addressing by this research
1	*"Design as an Artifact"*	A new framework and two integrative constructs are generated.
2	*"Problem Relevance"*	The need of having standardized/integrated definitions for the constructs of service and service system is reported. These concepts are fundamental for the development of three knowledge streams: SSME, ITSM and SOSE.
3	*"Design Evaluation"*	Given the scarcity of similar frameworks, the evaluation is realized through the descriptive category by using an informed argument from a panel of experts. This validation is usual in conceptual design of simulation models (e.g. face validation).
4	*"Research Contributions"*	Research contributions are satisfied by the (i) designed artifact itself, and (ii) the foundations for designing service systems. It is not claimed a contribution to category iii: design methodologies.
5	*"Research Rigor"*	Methodological rigor is satisfied through the utilization of the Systems Approach instanced in the design conceptual research method based in Mora et al. (2008c), March and Smith (1995), and Glass et al. (2004). It satisfies also Hevner's et al. (2004, p. 81) criterion for that a problem be considered for design research versus routine design: "*Design-science research in IS addresses what are considered to be wicked problems …That is, those problems characterized by … complex interactions among subcomponents of the problem and its solution*".
6	*"Design as a Search Process"*	Design as a process - based in Artificial Intelligence discipline- can be defined as the time-space-economical feasible localization/generation of a feasible node in the solution space under the satisfaction of the goal and related constrain set. For complex problems, this an iterative process guided by axioms –if exist them- or heuristics. This research, given the complexity of the conceptual pieces to be used required such a process.
7	*"Communication of Research"*	Design research is presented for engineering audience (the service system framework), and it is also explained its usefulness for managerial audience.

This work was previously published in International Journal of Information Systems in the Service Sector (IJISSS), edited by John Wang, pp. 36-57, copyright 2009 by IGI Publishing (an imprint of IGI Global).

Chapter 10
Information Technology Service Management and Opportunities for Information Systems Curricula

Sue Conger
University of Dallas, USA

ABSTRACT

Historically, information systems (IS) programs have taught two of the three areas of information technology (IT) management: strategy and management, and applications development. Academic programs have ignored the third area, IT operations. IT operations management is becoming increasingly important as it is recognized as consuming as much as 90% of the IT budget and as acquisition of software becomes more prevalent than development of custom applications. Along with the shift of management focus to IT operations, standards such as the IT infrastructure library (ITIL) have been adopted by businesses to guide the development of processes for IT operations that facilitate evolution to IT service management. This shift to servitizing IT management, creates an opportunity for IS programs to align with business practices by innovating in the teaching of IT service management. Several methods of incorporating ITSM material into educational programs are explored.

INTRODUCTION

With increasing frequency, disruptive technology-related innovations cause a paradigm shift in IT practice and management. In the 1950s and 1960s, methodologies codified best practices in application development for analyzing and computerizing complex processes (De Marco, 1979; Yourdon, 1988). Subsequent generations of methodologies evolved to include data orientation, then object orientation, and most recently, event orientation. Relational database technology, introduced by Codd and Date, similarly disrupted data management in the 1970s (Codd, 1970; Date, 1999). The development of personal computers disrupted both industry and academia in the 1980s. Object orientation changed methods of teaching application development and programming in the 1990s (Jacobson et al., 1998). The Internet changed business conduct beginning with its privatization

DOI: 10.4018/978-1-60960-138-6.ch010

in 1993 but accelerating with technology maturity in the late 1990s and early 2000s. This decade is witnessing two disruptions relating to the servitizing of IT organizations, one technical in the form of service-oriented architecture (SOA) (Durvasula et al., 2008), and one process and management oriented in the form of IT Service Management (ITSM) (itSMF, 2007).

This article addresses the changes in the conduct of IT in business and the related need for academic programs to address those changes. Alternative approaches for developing academic programs are presented and discussed.

THE CONDUCT OF IT IN BUSINESS

In the last century, Information Technology (IT) and the Chief Information Office (CIO) often were separated from the business strategy-development team. Business strategy was developed and possibly discussed with the CIO, who developed an IT strategy, to the extent possible, that fit the business strategy. Enlightened organizations might allow the CIO to sit in the meetings so the later discussion was circumvented. Enlightened organizations might also conduct their critical decision making to prioritize and select projects for development or acquisition through an IT steering committee comprised of the CIO plus other executives who represented critical stakeholders to the decision process (cf. King, 1985). The outcome of a successful matching exercise should align the business and the IT strategy.

IT in Business: The Academic View

More recently, the need for more seamless integration of business and IT strategies has been described (Weill & Ross, 2004). Under the newer scheme, IT moves away from responding to single requests in a never-ending queue toward architecture-driven IT decisions that ensure improved organizational support and, eventually, improved organizational response to changing environmental conditions (Ross et al., 2006; Broadbent & Kitzis, 2005; Ross et al., 2006). Under these more recent schemes, the responsibility for alignment is shared between the C-level executives and the CIO, with successful organizations being those that most closely align IT with business strategy. However, alignment activities apply to matching applications to strategy and does not extend to operations, help desk, or other types of services.

One key issue in these writings and others like them is that the prescriptions give little guidance on how to actually conduct business within the IT department that mirrors and fulfills the alignment objectives decided. Frameworks, such as the IT Infrastructure Library (ITIL), Control Objectives for Information and related Technology (CobiT) or the Capability Maturity Model - Integrated (CMMI) might be alluded to with an implicit assumption that their application will provide the needed IT discipline for IT organizations to act as desired (SEI, 2006; ITGI, 2007; OGC, 2008).

These ways of thinking, rather than avoiding the issues of IT management, either assume that the important actions take place in the decision process or that day to day operation of the IT organization is not relevant to discussions of strategy. Further, books and academic programs that *do* address daily functioning of IT focus on applications development, such as object orientation, or technology, such as telecommunications with little regard to how they are configured and managed in a production environment.

IT in Business: Business Practice

Business organizations, whether public, private, profit, or non-profit, have realized that undisciplined, non-repeatable work can undermine the best governance architecture. To develop a process discipline along with a culture of service, organizations of all types are rapidly servitizing the IT organization and its offerings. Adoption of the IT Infrastructure Library (ITIL) has spread to about

70% of non-US organizations and about 60% of US organizations (Dubie, 2008). In the U.S., 87% of companies with more than 10,000 employees have adopted ITIL (All, 2008). ITIL is chosen over or in concert with Cobit, CMMI, and Six Sigma because as Evelyn Huber of Forrester Research says, "there is nothing else" (Anthes, 2008, pg 2.)

The adoption of service management tenets is idiosyncratic to each organization with significant contextualization of each adopted process and function (Conger & Schultze, 2008). In addition to the high global adoption rate for ITSM tenets and ITIL, in particular, the adopting companies generate a significant number of new jobs requiring service management and process understanding. One U.S. study of itSMF-USA (a practitioner organization) member companies found that about 15,000 jobs requiring ITIL knowledge and skills are created annually (Conger et al., 2008).

The combination of adoption rate and job growth has not gone completely unnoticed with about 15 programs in Australia, Europe, Africa, Mexico, and New Zealand (Cater-Steel & Toleman, 2007). By contrast there are two undergraduate and one graduate ITSM program in the U.S. These adopting universities are bucking established programs and courses to bridge the gap between business and academia. However, the gap is firmly institutionalized in academic program guidelines that hinder broad adoption. The divide between business practice and academic practice is an important one for it permeates IT education. The nature of the divide is explored in the next section.

IT IN EDUCATION

The Model Curriculum guidelines for undergraduate IS/IT education in the U.S. exemplify the business-IS/IT curriculum divide. U.S. curriculum is developed by the Joint Task Force on Computing Curricula, comprised of mostly academics through the Association for Computing Machinery (ACM), Association for Information Systems (AIS), and Institute for Electrical and Electronics Engineers (IEEE). While the 2005, currently official, version is discussed here, an update for 2008 was let for review recently. This discussion applies equally to the 2008 update which only uses the term 'service' in terms of student *service* projects, not mentioning IT management, IT operations, process, or service in any pedagogical discussion (The Joint Task Force, 2008).

The computing curriculum guidelines are summarized with weights applied to knowledge areas as shown in Table 1. Degree types and abbreviations include Computer Engineering (CE), Computer Science (CS), Information Systems (IS), Information Technology (IT), and Software Engineering (SE). The numbers ranges from zero to five and represent the relative emphasis at which program coverage is recommended (The Joint Task Force, 2005). Figure 1 shows the "organization" emphasis for information systems. These figures imply that there should be a preponderance of organizational information in IS programs. In fact, the Joint Task Force report says:

"The meaningful question is: 'Has an IS program broadened its scope to include an integrated view of the enterprise with complex information needs and high-level dependency on IT-enabled business processes?' ... IS students must learn how to assess and evaluate organizational information needs, specify information requirements, and design practical systems to satisfy these requirements" (ACM/AIS/IEEE The Joint Task Force on Computing Curricula, 2005, p. 32).

The lower half of Table 1 lists 'business' knowledge to be included in undergraduate curricula, including organization models, theory, structures, and functions along with system concepts and theories, skills in benchmarking, value chain analysis, quality concepts, valuation concepts, and evaluation of investment performance (ACM/AIS/AITP Joint Task Force on Computing Curricula, 2002, p. 14; The Joint Task Force, 2005).

Table 1. Comparative weights of program components

Knowledge Area	CE		CS		IS		IT		SE	
	Min	Max	Min	Max	Min	Max	Min	Max	Min	Max
Programming Fundamentals	4	4	4	5	2	4	2	4	5	5
Integrative Programming	0	2	1	3	2	4	3	5	1	3
Algorithms and Complexity	2	4	4	5	1	2	1	2	3	4
Computer Architecture and Organization	5	5	2	4	1	2	1	2	2	4
Operating Systems Principles & Design	2	5	3	5	1	1	1	2	3	4
Operating Systems Configuration & Use	2	3	2	4	2	3	3	5	2	4
Net Centric Principles and Design	1	3	2	4	1	3	3	4	2	4
Net Centric Use and configuration	1	2	2	3	2	4	4	5	2	3
Platform technologies	0	1	0	2	1	3	2	4	0	3
Theory of Programming Languages	1	2	3	5	0	1	0	1	2	4
Human-Computer Interaction	2	5	2	4	2	5	4	5	3	5
Graphics and Visualization	1	3	1	5	1	1	0	1	1	3
Intelligent Systems (AI)	1	3	2	5	1	1	0	0	0	0
Information Management (DB) Theory	1	3	2	5	1	3	1	1	2	5
Information Management (DB) Practice	1	2	1	4	4	5	3	4	1	4
Scientific computer (Numerical methods)	0	2	0	5	0	0	0	0	0	0
Legal / Professional / Ethics / Society	2	5	2	4	2	5	2	4	2	5
Information Systems Development	0	2	0	2	5	5	1	3	2	4
Analysis of Business Requirements	0	1	0	1	5	5	1	2	1	3
E-business	0	0	0	0	4	5	1	2	0	3
Analysis of Technical Requirements	2	5	2	4	2	4	3	5	3	5
Engineering Foundations for SW	1	2	1	2	1	1	0	0	2	5
Engineering Economics for SW	1	3	0	1	1	2	0	1	2	3
Software Modeling and Analysis	1	3	2	3	3	3	1	3	4	5
Software Design	2	4	3	5	1	3	1	2	5	5
Software Verification and Validation	1	3	1	2	1	2	1	2	4	5
Software Evolution (maintenance)	1	3	1	1	1	2	1	2	2	4
Software Process	1	1	1	2	1	2	1	1	2	5
Software Quality	1	2	1	2	1	2	1	2	2	4
Comp Systems Engineering	5	5	1	2	0	0	0	0	2	3
Digital logic	5	5	2	3	1	1	1	1	0	3
Embedded Systems	2	5	0	3	0	0	0	1	0	4
Distributed Systems	3	5	1	3	2	4	1	3	2	4
Security: Issues and principles	2	3	1	4	2	3	1	3	1	3
Security: implementation and mgt	1	2	1	3	1	3	3	5	1	3
Systems administration	1	2	1	1	1	3	3	5	1	2
Management of Info Systems org.	0	0	0	0	3	5	0	0	0	0
Systems integration	1	4	1	2	1	4	4	5	1	4

continued on following page

Table 21. continued

Knowledge Area	CE		CS		IS		IT		SE	
	Min	Max	Min	Max	Min	Max	Min	Max	Min	Max
Digital media development	0	2	0	1	1	2	3	5	0	1
Technical support	0	1	0	1	1	3	5	5	0	1
Non-Computing Topics										
Organizational Theory	0	0	0	0	1	4	1	2	0	0
Decision Theory	0	0	0	0	3	3	0	1	0	0
Organizational Behavior	0	0	0	0	3	5	1	2	0	0
Organizational Change Management	0	0	0	0	2	2	1	2	0	0
General Systems Theory	0	0	0	0	2	2	1	2	0	0
Risk Management (Project, safety risk)	2	4	1	1	2	3	1	4	2	4
Project Management	2	4	1	2	3	5	2	3	4	5
Business Models	0	0	0	0	4	5	0	0	0	0
Functional Business Areas	0	0	0	0	4	5	0	0	0	0
Evaluation of Business performance	0	0	0	0	4	5	0	0	0	0
Circuits and Systems	5	5	0	2	0	0	0	1	0	0
Electronics	5	5	0	0	0	0	0	1	0	0
Digital Signal Processing	3	5	0	2	0	0	0	0	0	2
VLSI design	2	5	0	1	0	0	0	0	0	1
HW testing and fault tolerance	3	5	0	0	0	0	0	2	0	0
Mathematical foundations	4	5	4	5	2	4	2	4	3	5
Interpersonal communication	3	4	1	4	3	5	3	4	3	4

(ACM/AIS/IEEE The Joint Task Force on Computing Curricula, 2005, p. 24-25)

Figure 1. Information systems profile of topic coverage (ACM/AIS/IEEE The Joint Task Force on Computing Curricula, 2005, p. 19)

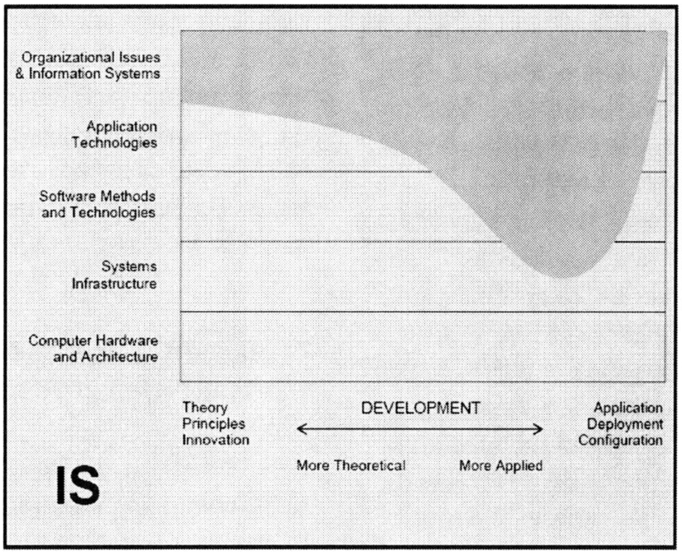

Figure 2. IT in education with operations and ITSM as the missing links

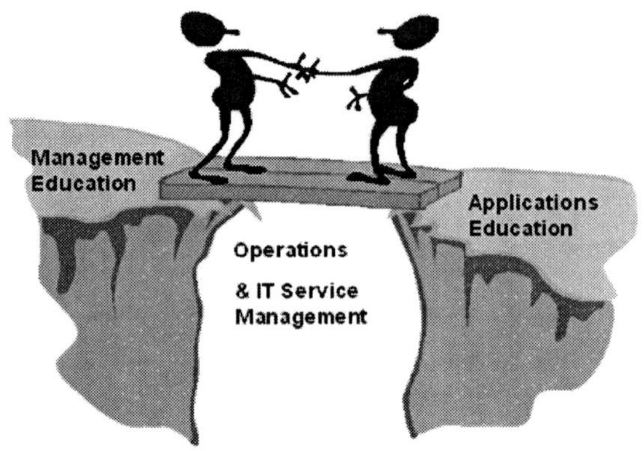

For graduate students, recommended 'business' knowledge includes financial accounting, organizational behavior, and marketing (ACM/IEEE The Joint Task Force on Computing Curricula, 2000, p. 18) in courses with no ties to or even discussion of information technology or its relationship to the topic area. That is, the emphasis, even in programs with a focus on organizational issues does not actually attend to the daily operation of an IT organization.

Neither undergraduates nor graduates in IS programs are required to learn basic information such as how to define, recognize, or analyze a process, let alone how to determine whether or not a process can be improved through automation. Process modeling is confined to creation of data flow diagrams, not process maps that include non-automated activities. Further, the specific management processes applied to the management of IS/IT organizations are missing.

There is nothing in IS/IT curricula about IT Operations or how this function delivers IT resources to organizational customers. This gap is depicted in Figure 2 in which the three key aspects of IT academic program gaps are depicted. On the one hand, IT management, discussing topics recommended in the curriculum guidelines, describes business functions (e.g., Marketing), information levels, and how information is used in organizations. From a service perspective, this discussion is lacking in discussion of the non-functional requirements that must come from business users, for instance, criticality of an application to the organization, and requirements for security, privacy, and recoverability. On the other side of the divide is the application development function for which academic programs discuss programming, requirements modeling, and use case development.

In the gap are Operations, which manages the organization's IT infrastructure and IT Service Management, the discipline that provides process maturity to the entire IT organization. Scant infrastructure organization knowledge or its tasks are recommended in any programs (see Table 1). Further, what infrastructure topics are discussed tend to be 'silo' technology topics such as telecommunications or operating systems. There is no discussion of how the product an applications group delivers actually is placed into production or how it is managed in a production environment. There is no discussion of how to size an application, let alone capacity modeling or planning for a data center. There is no discussion of any of the processes involved in running a data center such as availability management, finance management, incident management, change management, continuity management, and so on. These areas of knowledge are the focus for IT Service Management, the emerging, disruptive IT-related set of management best practices that promises to bridge the gaps between applications and management. ITSM is the first step to servitizing an IT organization and thus, facilitating alignment of IT with its related business strategy.

IT SERVICE MANAGEMENT EDUCATION OPPORTUNITIES

Since infrastructure represents a significant gap in all computing education programs, and since management of IT is articulated within the IS academic discipline, IS curricula are the most likely place for ITSM programs. In this section, ITSM is briefly explained and linked to IT strategy. Then, three options for incorporating ITSM concepts into IS curricula are described.

IT Service Management

IT Service Management is generally used to refer to the management of processes within IT Operations so that, through efficient and effective execution of the processes, value accrues to the organization. Thus, companies can create value through application of best practices to IT Operations (Nieves & Iqbal, 2007). IT operations are critical to organizational effectiveness since as much as 90% of IT budgets is used to manage operations (Fleming, 2005).

The term "service" has no single definition and ranges from a change in condition or state of an entity caused by another to a set of deeds, processes, and resulting performances (Zeithaml & Bitner, 1996). From the ITIL perspective, a service is "a means of delivering value to customers by facilitating outcomes customers want to achieve without the ownership of specific costs and risks" (TSO, 2007, p. 45).

IT service management begins with business strategy, which when new or changed, causes reflection on the existing IT service offerings in the form of applications, computing resources and user services. The heart of service management is a series of processes and functions (e.g., service/help desk) where a "process is the set of activities (repeated steps or tasks) that accomplishes some business function" (Conger & Schultze, 2008, pg. 4). Thus, students of ITSM need to understand how business strategy is reciprocally created with IT strategy, and how the development of strategy can cause changes in any IT resources – human, financial, or capital (e.g., hardware), and how the changes are embodied in processes that ensure repeatability and quality.

The processes in ITIL relate to keeping an operations organization functional. The main ITIL processes relate to management of incidents, problems, changes, releases, configuration, availability, capacity planning, financial planning, continuity, and service levels. While the processes apply to any size organization, the benefits of scale are best attained in global organizations, such as Unilever or Proctor and Gamble. One important body of knowledge relates to the scaling of process management from small to large organizations.

ITIL tends to be implemented in the infrastructure organization first. However, many ITIL processes, for instance, incident and change management, though initiated within operations, are actually remedied or executed within another organization usually within IT, such as applications maintenance. Thus, service management processes have tendrils that permeate other organizational processes and coordination of activities throughout an organization is needed to ensure successful and encompassing ITIL implementation. This integration of operations with all other IT organizational activities includes a need for operational process understanding for applications, database, security, and all technology areas.

While ITIL is the only best practice framework that principally addresses IT Operations, there are many valuable alternatives to ITIL that a company might adopt. For instance, the Control Objectives for Information and Technology (CobiT©), the framework most closely related to financial reporting compliance (e.g., Sarbanes-Oxley in the U.S.), was initiated in the auditing world but has crossed over to management of the IT organization (ITGI, 2007). Another often-used framework is the Capability Maturity Model – Integrated (CMMI©), which was originally developed to support application development management has crossed over to use by operations organizations for such areas as project management (SEI, 2006).

Similarly, there are customized versions of ITIL by Microsoft – the Microsoft Operations Framework (MOF©), Hewlett-Packard, IBM, and others. These frameworks adopt ITIL as their base and build on them by customizing for a suite of support software that imbeds the process within the operational framework of software for help desk, network monitoring and the like.

For all of these frameworks, and for service management in general, the goal is creation of value to the organization through its IT operations function. A secondary goal and outcome of successful service management implementation is alignment with the strategy of the business since strategy is the starting point for the development of all service offerings.

Curricular Alternatives Incorporating IT Service Management

The three alternatives for incorporating ITSM into IS academic programs include the following:

- Part of an existing course(s)
- A single course
- A concentration or major set of courses (Beachboard et al., 2007).

Each of these alternatives is briefly discussed.

ITSM as Part of Existing Course(s)

If ITSM were incorporated into a single existing course, one likely course would be an IS Foundations course because it serves the broadest audience. A module on ITSM could discuss concepts of process and service, providing definitions and examples of each. In addition, a brief overview of IT Operations and its criticality to organizational functioning could be provided. Finally, a high level discussion defining various operational processes, such as capacity management, and describing their relationship to other operational processes could be included.

Other existing courses into which ITSM concepts could be interjected include any applications development, database, or telecommunications courses. For instance, during systems analysis and design (SAD), risk analysis and related security mitigations should be discussed. Also in an SAD class, the need for early capacity planning to ensure adequacy of testing and production facilities for hardware, data storage, and telecommunications could be included. A partial list of non-functional requirements and the need for their articulation and sharing with IT Operations would include, for example, transaction volumes and peaks, number of users and locations, security and privacy, compliance requirements, data integrity, organizational criticality, recoverability, help desk, and access requirements (Conger, 2008). Also in SAD, change management, both for users in terms of using a new application and for the developers in terms of moving the application from testing into a production environment and the work that such a move entails could be included.

Single Course in ITSM

A single course could address Fundamentals of ITSM. This course could discuss alignment of business strategy and IT strategy with the need for demand management driving the creation and presentation of services to the organization. If ITIL were the basis for the course, the five main areas of the framework, relating to strategy, planning, transition, operations, and continuous improvement could be structured into one to three sessions each with case studies and practical exercises for students to apply the concepts.

Concentration or Major in ITSM

A concentration in ITSM requires decisions on content and purpose of the major. If the goal of the program is to obtain the highest possible certifications for students, then alignment with ISO/IEC 20000 would allow students to obtain master's level certification (EXIN, 2008). The ITIL v3 certification scheme now requires over 10 courses and takes more than five years to obtain and is thus beyond the scope of most academic programs (Taylor, 2007). Under the EXIN scheme, the courses relate to ITIL version 2 (the basis for the international standard ISO/IEC 20000) and include Foundations of Service Management, Advanced Services Support and Advanced Service Delivery. One or two other courses could be electives, for instance, Systems Analysis and Design, Process Management, and/or Managing the IT Function.

One issue with a program based on the ITIL framework is that ITIL, per se, does not guarantee 'service management' (Conger & Schultze, 2008). Ultimately, servitizing requires proactive demand management. As in manufacturing operations, IT demand management is used to plan and deploy resources (i.e., applications, computing resources and user services). Once deployed, demand management concentrates on delivering a product that meets a contracted level of service. Under this more 'service management' approach, courses might include some combination of Foundations of Service Management, IT Service Management, Process and Service Design, Service Delivery, Demand Management, and IT Governance.

CONCLUSION

This article argues that IS academic programs are incomplete because of the absence of any content dealing with servitizing the IT function. This absence has caused a widening gap between business conduct and IT academic programs. Servitization includes not only the management of IT Operations but also courses on the processes required to actually manage an IT function. IT Service Management, in the form of ITIL, has become a significant activity in many organizations, and its body of knowledge directly addresses both the gap between IT academic programs and business practice and provides the 'how' to aligning business strategy with IT service delivery. Therefore, ITSM provides an opportunity to move toward explaining *how* to align IT with business strategy, provide students with an understanding of process and service orientations, and move toward developing courseware that comprehends the servitizing of IT.

REFERENCES

ACM/AIS/AITP Joint Task Force on Computing Curricula. (2002). *IS 2002: Model Curriculum Guidelines for Undergraduate Degree Programs in Information Systems*. New York: Association for Computing Machinery.

ACM/AIS/IEEE The Joint Task Force on Computing Curricula. (2005). *Computing Curricula 2005: The Overview Report*. New York: Association for Computing Machinery.

ACM/IEEE The Joint Task Force on Computing Curricula. (2000). *Computing Curricula 2000: Graduate IS Curricula*. New York: Association for Computing Machinery.

All, A. (2008). ITIL's Popularity Continues to Grow. http://www.itbusinessedge.com/blogs/tve/?p=286 [On-line].

Anthes, G. H. (2008). ITIL v3: Five ways to make it work for you. http://www.computerworld.com/action/article.do?command=printArticleBasic&articleId=9077960 [On-line].

Beachboard, J., Conger, S., Galup, S., Venkataraman, R., Probst, J., & Hernandez, A. (2007). *A roadmap*. IT Service Managementin the IS Curriculum.

Broadbent, M., & Kitzis, E. S. (2005). *The New CIO Leader*. Harvard Business School Press.

Cater-Steel, A., & Toleman, M. (2007). Education for IT service management standards. *International Journal of IT Standards and Standardization Research*, *5*, 27–41.

Codd, E. F. (1970). A Relational Model of Data for Large Shared Data Banks. *Communications of the ACM*, *13*, 377–387. doi:10.1145/362384.362685

Conger, S. (2008). *Tech 7370 Requirements and Sourcing Course (Rep. No. Unit 4)*. Irving, TX: University of Dallas.

Conger, S., & Schultze, U. (2008). *IT Governance and Control: Making sense of Standards, Guidelines, and Frameworks*. Chicago, IL: The Society for Information Management Advanced Practices Council.

Conger, S., Venkataraman, R., Hernandez, A., & Probst, J. (2008). (Forthcoming). Market Potential for ITSM Students. *Survey (London, England)*.

Date, C. J. (1999). *An Introduction to Database Systems* (8th ed.). NY: Addison-Wesley Longman.

De Marco, T. P. P. J. (1979). *Structured Analysis and System Specification*. Prentice Hall.

Dubie, D. (2008). ITIL adoption increases in U.S., proficiency still lacking. *NetworkWorld.com*.

Durvasula, S., Guttmann, M., Kumar, A., Lamb, J., Mitchell, T., Oral, B., et al. (2008). *SOA Practitioners Guide Part 2: SOA Reference Architecture*http://www.soablueprint.com/whitepapers/SOAPGPart2.pdf.

EXIN. (2008). ISO/IEC 20000 Certification Exams. Examination Board Ref Type: Internet Communication

Fleming, W. (2005). *Using Cost of Service to Align IT* Presentation at itSMF-USA, Chicago, IL.

ITGI. (2007). *Control Objectives for IT and related Technologies 4.1. Rolling Meadows, IL: IT Governance Institute (ITGI). itSMF (2007). An Introductory Overview of ITIL V3*. London: IT Service Management Forum.

Jacobson, I., & Booch, G. Rumbaugh, & James (1998). *Unified Software Development Process*. (Unified Software Development Process ed.) Addison Wesley Longman.

King, W. R. (1985). Information Technology and Corporate Growth. *The Columbia Journal of World Business*, *20*, 29–34.

Nieves, M., & Iqbal, M. (2007). *ITIL v3 Core Practice Book 1: Service Strategy* (3rd ed.). London, UK: The Stationary Office of the Office of Government Commerce.

OGC. (2008). ITIL. http://www.itil.co.uk/ [Online].

Ross, J., Weill, P., Ross, J., & Robertson, D. C. (2006). *Enterprise Architecture as Strategy*. Harvard Business School Press.

SEI. (2006). *CMMI for Development 1.2*. Pittsburgh, PA: Software Engineering Institute (SEI), Inc.

Taylor, S. (2007). *ITIL Service Management Practices: V3 Qualifications Scheme* London, UK: Office of General Commerce (OGC).

The Joint Task Force. (2005). *Computing Curricula 2005* New York: Association for Computing Machinery (ACM).

The Joint Task Force. (2008). *Computing Curricula: Information Technology Volume* New York: Association for Computing Machinery (ACM).

TSO. (2007). *ITIL® V3 Glossary v01*. London: Office of Government Commerce.

Weill, P., & Ross, J. (2004). *IT Governance*. Harvard Business School Press.

Yourdon, E. (1988). *Modern Structured Analysis*. Prentice Hall.

Zeithaml, V. A., & Bitner, M. J. (1996). *Service Marketing*. New York, NY: McGraw-Hill.

This work was previously published in International Journal of Information Systems in the Service Sector (IJISSS), edited by John Wang, pp. 58-68, copyright 2009 by IGI Publishing (an imprint of IGI Global).

Chapter 11
IT Service Personnel:
Changing the Culture from Technology to Service

Aileen Cater-Steel
University of Southern Queensland, Australia

ABSTRACT

IT service management best practice frameworks such as the IT Infrastructure Library® (ITIL®) aim to improve the quality of service to customers. This study reports on recent surveys and case studies of organizations which have embarked on IT service management improvement. It highlights specific difficulties experienced by organizations in changing the orientation of staff to customer service rather than technology. Six factors were found to be critical in achieving an effective service-oriented philosophy. The factors are support from senior management; the threat or opportunity to outsource IT services; integration of processes to provide end-to-end service; involvement of business stakeholders; culture change of IT staff to service excellence; and the redesign of processes prior to investing in tools.

INTRODUCTION

Providers of IT services now have to consider the quality of the services they provide and focus on the relationship with their customers. No longer can they afford to focus on technology (Van Bon, 2007). It is becoming increasingly recognised that the provision of high quality and competitive service requires organizations to adopt a customer-centric, service-oriented philosophy. The growth of the service economy has seen a paradigm shift which has moved the focus from goods to services, and impacts the business processes, management practices, employee policies, engineering knowledge, and culture of organizations (Rust & Kannan, 2003; Rust & Miu, 2006). After analysing a large financial service provider in the Netherlands as an example of a service-oriented enterprise, Janssen and Joha determined that the main critical management issues, apart from a carefully executed strategy, are the 'redesign and reorganization of activities and roles, the standardization of processes, applications and the underlying IT architecture, and management of

DOI: 10.4018/978-1-60960-138-6.ch011

the transformation by involving all stakeholders.' (2008, p. 35).

Information technology (IT) is considered to be the 'critical enabler' for transforming service industries (Chesbrough & Spohrer, 2006). As IT systems become more powerful and cost-effective they provide the potential to efficiently gather and analyse data, and to codify and transmit knowledge to the far corners of the globe (Bitner & Brown, 2006; Chesbrough & Spohrer, 2006). Although IT service providers are constituents in the service sector, their total contribution to the service sector can only be grasped by considering that private businesses in the USA spend in excess of 50 percent of all invested capital on IT – hardware, software and communications equipment (Laudon & Laudon, 2010). Specifically within the service sector, IT plays an important role in helping organizations provide better customer service, create new products and services, enhance relationships with suppliers, and improve decision making.

It has been noted by Johnson et al. (2007) that businesses are demanding more from their IT organizations than ever before. As well as 'better and more disciplined provisioning of IT services to ensure smooth operation' (p. 595), IT is expected to respond with agility in light of new business opportunities, to demonstrate responsible financial management and to satisfy internal staff and external customers. This level of service can only be achieved with effective relationships and communication between IT and lines of business.

However, despite the fact that organizations are increasingly reliant on IT and the increasing awareness of the need to become service-oriented and customer-focussed, many IT service providers are struggling to change the culture and processes within their own departments or organizations. Many IT service providers are still characterised by a culture which is technology-focused rather than customer-centric. This may be due to the fact that many of the IT line managers are 'predominately ex-technologists' (Bruton, 2004, p. 4).

This paper considers the people, process and technology issues related to improving IT service management. Although there is growing adoption of existing frameworks and standards, such as the IT Infrastructure Library (ITIL) and the IT Service management standard (ISO/IEC 20000), and development of new frameworks such as CMMI-SVC®, many IT service providers find it an almost insurmountable challenge to achieve effective end-to-end service. This paper strives to answer the research question: what factors inhibit the transformation of IT service providers when seeking to adopt a service-oriented philosophy? The paper is structured as follows. The background provides a summary of popular and emerging standards for IT service management. Then, the research methodology is briefly explained, followed by a discussion of challenges identified through surveys and case studies. The conclusion includes directions for future research.

BACKGROUND

Recently, there has been a concerted effort to develop, refine and promulgate frameworks for IT service management. In this section, the current and emerging frameworks are described.

ITIL: IT Infrastructure Library

IT Service management standards such as the IT Infrastructure Library (ITIL) are of increasing importance to organizations around the globe. The current version, ITIL version 3 was released in 2007 and comprises five core texts: Service Strategy; Service Design; Service Transition; Service Operation; and Continual Service Improvement (OGC, 2007). This version focuses on the lifecycle of services and attempts to remove process silos. It is recognised that ITIL requires a devoted focus on IT services and customers' needs, which more technically oriented organizations may find challenging (Iden & Langeland, 2010).

Figure 1. Cumulative Total of ITIL Foundation Certificates awarded Oct 2008-Nov 2009 (Derived from statistics provided by S. Campbell, personal communication, February2, 2010)

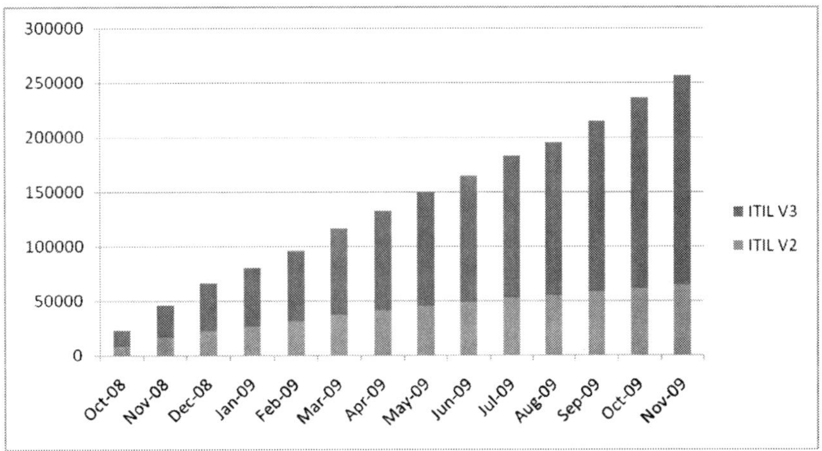

Although the actual number of organizations adopting ITIL is not known, there are many indicators of the growing awareness and adoption of ITIL. For example, there are now 46 national chapters of the IT Service Management Forum (itSMF) with in excess of 100,000 members worldwide (itSMFI); itSMF conferences are enjoying robust attendances; the demand for ITIL-qualified staff is increasing, accompanied by an exponential rise in the number of people qualifying for the ITIL Foundation certificate.

As shown in Figure 1, worldwide the number of ITIL Foundation certificates awarded has risen steadily during 2009 and more than one quarter of a million people have obtained ITIL Foundation certificates in the 14 months depicted. This graph does not include the ISO/IEC 20000 Foundation certificates or the more advanced certificates for v2 Practitioner, v2 Service Manager, or v3 Intermediate.

ISO/IEC 20000 IT Service Management Standard

In December 2005, ISO member countries adopted a standard for IT service management - ISO/IEC 20000, based on BS 15000 which was derived from ITILv2. ISO/IEC 20000 comprises five groups of processes: service delivery processes (service level management, service reporting, service continuity and availability, budgeting and accounting for IT services, capacity management, information security management); relationship processes (business relationship management, supplier management); resolution processes (incident management, problem management); control processes (configuration management, change management); and release management (ISO/IEC, 2005).

The international standard for IT service management provides a formal and universal standard for organizations seeking to have their service management capabilities audited. Since it was ratified in December 2005 by the International Organization for Standardization (ISO), growth in its adoption has accelerated. As of November 2010, 572 organizations in 49 countries have registered their certification details on the itSMF International site (itSMF, 2010). The ITIL resources provide a useful body of knowledge for organizations interested in achieving ISO/IEC 20000.

ISO/IEC 15504 – IT Process Assessment Standard

In 2005, a team of researchers at the Public Research Centre Henri Tudor in Luxembourg developed a process reference model (PRM) and process assessment model (PAM) consistent with ITIL and compliant with the IT Assessment Standard ISO/IEC 15504 (Di Renzo, Barafort, Lejeune, Prime, & Simon, 2005). The Assessment and Improvement integrateD Approach (AIDA) project developed the PAM based on the ISO/IEC 15504-5 assessment model (ISO/IEC, 2003) and includes process performance indicators for base practices and work products, and process capability indicators. The PRM includes the five ITILv2 service support processes (incident management, problem management, configuration management, change management and release management) and the five ITILv2 service delivery processes (service level management, IT financial management, capacity management, IT service continuity management and availability management). The ITIL books were used to identify input and output work products which were then classified according to relevant processes.

In June 2007, two new work items were proposed to the ISO/IEC Standards Working Group responsible for IT Service and Operations Management (JTC 1/SC7 WG25). To form a bridge between the IT service management standard and the IT process assessment standard, an exemplar process assessment model for IT service management is proposed as Part 8 of ISO/IEC 15504, and a process reference model is proposed as Part 4 of ISO/IEC 20000. The completion of these parts will enable compliant assessments of process capability to be conducted on IT service management processes.

RESEARCH METHODOLOGY

Since August 2005, researchers at the University of Southern Queensland have undertaken a project in collaboration with the Australian chapter of itSMF. The project aims to investigate the adoption of frameworks for improving IT service management. The project has taken on international significance with the collaboration of academics and researchers from many other universities including St Gallen (Switzerland), De Montford (UK), Appalachian State (USA), Carlton (Canada), George-August (Germany), NHH (Norway), and members of itSMF USA and itSMF Thailand.

The IT service management research project has surveyed delegates at the itSMF Australia Conferences each year since 2005. The survey has been replicated at itSMF conferences in Thailand and Norway. Over the past five years, IT Service Managers from 22 organizations in the public and private sector have been interviewed to gain a deeper understanding of the benefits and challenges of improving IT service management through ITIL adoption. The interview instrument is based on that developed by Hochstein et al. (2005) for interviews with six German firms. The interviews, conducted in Australia, United Kingdom, New Zealand and United States of America, have been transcribed, checked for accuracy and analysed to extract themes pertaining to the implementation of ITIL and ISO/IEC 20000.

This paper draws on the findings from the surveys and case studies to investigate factors which inhibit the transformation to a service-orientation as an objective of ITIL adoption.

DISCUSSION

All the organizations who responded to the Australian itSMF surveys had adopted ITIL and were making substantial progress in implementing this framework. To date, organizations have given priority to implementing the service desk function, incident management and change management processes. The strongest motivating factor to implement IT service management improvement is to improve the focus on IT service, followed by a desire to improve IT/business process integration, and to a lesser degree, internal compliance, cost reduction, and external compliance.

The 2009 itSMF Australian survey results confirmed that IT service management can help to promote a service-orientation: the highest rating benefit was that IT service management provides improved customer satisfaction (Cater-Steel, Tan, & Toleman, 2009). Half of the respondents selected improved response and resolution, closely followed by clarity in identification of roles and responsibilities. The fourth ranked benefit was reduction in cost per incident, followed by improved IT employee productivity. In contrast, the survey of the participants of the 2007 Thai itSMF Conference revealed less than half the respondents were adopting ITIL, although many had internally developed IT service management initiatives (Lawkobkit, 2008). It would appear that ITIL is more established in Australia: 2007 saw Thailand's first itSMF conference but Australia's tenth.

The interviews with IT Service Managers demonstrate that implementing ITIL can transform IT service management and provide benefits to organizations such as a more predictable infrastructure from improved rigour in testing and system changes, improved consultation with IT groups within the organization, smoother negotiation of service level agreements (SLAs), reduced server faults, seamless end-to-end service, documented and consistent IT service management processes across the organization, and consistent logging of incidents.

Many of the IT Service Managers interviewed reported that they have not made as much progress with ITIL implementation as they desired, due to problems such as lack of management support, cultural change in terms of resistance from technical staff, and delays in establishing an appropriate tool set.

To provide a more detailed discussion of the factors impeding the shift to a service orientation, the four-level IT-service performance management framework developed by Praeg and Schnabel (2006) is used to review the data collected. The rationale underlying the framework is based on the understanding that the strategic level and process levels determine the performance requirements while the tool level secures the sustainability of the performance.

Strategic Level: Executive Support and Outsourcing Trend

It was no surprise that the surveys revealed that commitment from senior management is regarded as the most critical factor for successful IT service management implementation. Managers interviewed also stressed the importance of support from senior management. As well as being necessary to guarantee funding for resources such as training, hardware and software, senior management support is essential to endorse policy and enforce compliance to the standard processes across the entire organization. Effective culture change is not possible without support from the highest level. To gain executive support most of the organizations interviewed sought approval by presenting a business case. However, there was a tendency by some organizations to view ITIL as 'business as usual' rather than as a project. Some view ITIL as an ongoing process improvement program (Cater-Steel & Pollard, 2008). This tendency to adopt 'standards by stealth' contradicts a basic tenet of IT governance: projects should not commence without an approved business case setting out all known and foreseeable risks, specification, benefits and costs of the project (Musson & Jordan, 2006).

Many of the Service Managers interviewed commented on the practice of outsourcing IT services. Increasingly, organizations are outsourcing all or part of their IT infrastructure services. According to Bitner and Brown (2006), standardised processes stimulate growth in off-shoring and will accelerate the trend to source service IT provision from developing nations.

The Gartner group has estimated that the worldwide IT outsourcing market will grow from the US$180 billion revenues in 2003 to US$253 billion in 2008 at a compound annual growth rate of 7 percent (Gonzalez, Gasco, & Llopis, 2006). The IT Service Manager of a large government department stated that the organization wanted to outsource some services but could not as the processes were not adequately documented. In this case, improving IT service management was seen as the pre-cursor to outsourcing. A large financial company reported that ITIL adoption facilitated outsourcing of infrastructure support. This view is consistent with that of Janssen and Joha (2008) who claim that shared service centres based on service level agreements are often a first step towards outsourcing. On the other hand, a large organization in the financial sector saw certification to ISO/IEC 20000 as a defence against outsourcing. This firm successfully changed the culture of the organization by urging IT staff to adopt a service-centric focus to enable the IT department to become the 'supplier of choice' for other departments in the organization (Cater-Steel & McBride, 2007).

Business Process Level: End-to-End Service

As part of ITILadoption, many organizations found it effective to appoint process owners for each of the ITIL core processes. This certainly provided impetus to define and implement each process but raised the difficulty of integrating these processes to enable a seamless end-to-end provision of service. A large government department reported that each section was performing their processes well but that the users had 'fallen down the sink in this great big hole between two processes'. Other organizations explained the importance of involving all stakeholders in integration mapping workshops. A significant effort is required to ensure the interfaces between processes are effective. Steinberg warns of the risks of only implementing selected processes and insists that all processes need to be developed simultaneously (2005).

It is evident that ITIL is providing the means to compensate for the four gaps between users' expectations and their perceptions of the service provided by the IT department as identified by Pitt et al. (1998). Through better communication and a stronger business and strategic focus, IT managers can understand what the users want. Rather than the time consuming and onerous task of developing their own standards, ITIL provides a convenient starting point for IT Service Managers to set and monitor achievable service quality standards. With the help of effective SLAs, delivery of a structured and integrated service can deliver on the promises made by the IT department.

IT-Service Level

The most difficult aspect of ITIL implementation was evident at the IT service level with new terminology, policies, procedures, and employee performance evaluations modified to include ITIL.

Managers who reported successful implementation of ITIL stressed the importance of identifying stakeholders and especially gaining the commitment of all IT staff. In one large financial company, the external consultants who were contracted to implement and enforce the new processes were referred to as 'ITIL Nazis'. A university found it very difficult to persuade technical staff to complete documentation of their activities. This challenge was overcome by a charismatic 'Doctor ITIL' who conducted fun-filled workshops and training seminars to engage with the IT staff as well as corporate users.

One of the difficulties in transforming IT culture is due to the practice of promoting people with good technical skills to management positions (Bruton, 2004). Unfortunately, these people often do not have expertise in customer service management or relationship management. For example, some firms interviewed were grappling with changing their IT service metrics to collect and report statistics that were meaningful to the customer rather than the technology. As stressed by Ghayekhloo et al. (2009), most IT monitoring activities concentrate on performance, while ignoring quality and processes. They give the example that most Service Desks can report how quickly they escalate incidents, but few can report how often they escalate incidents to the wrong person.

Most of the managers interviewed reported that one of the most effective change management activities was the simulation game included in the ITIL Foundations training course. Each training provider has a variation on the experiential learning exercise which might be set, for example in a busy shipping port, railway or space shuttle launch site. During the game, players become aware that delays in providing work-arounds for incidents or solving problems will have dire consequences. As well, the importance of building up a knowledge base of solutions becomes apparent. Feedback from interviewees repeatedly indicated that the game resulted in a change of attitude of many technical staff. They realised how their work impacted on the profitability and reputation of the business.

Tool Level

According to Praeg and Schnabel (2006), the tool level encompasses methods and instruments. Tools vendors have responded to the increased popularity of ITIL by developing sophisticated, integrated tools. These tools facilitate the end-to-end and life-cycle view by integrating the recording of incidents with the configuration management database and change management. Discovery tools are used to monitor the performance of network components and assist in diagnosis, reconfiguration and recovery. However, many managers interviewed described that their initial attempt to adopt ITIL failed because they purchased a tool before understanding and developing their processes. A large government department were many months through a tender process before they realised their specification was totally inadequate. Another government department explained the tool selection process totally derailed the ITIL project. Two of the large finance companies interviewed reported they had a history of purchasing expensive IT service management systems which were never implemented. There is evidence that many organizations focus on acquiring tools without first designing IT service management processes. The mistake of premature purchase of tools is symptomatic of the culture of focussing on technology as a panacea, instead of first considering the processes the tools are meant to support.

Although ITSM tools have been identified as problematic, Iden and Langeland's Delphi study to determine factors of ITIL adoption found that factors related to technology and methods are considered to have less importance compared to senior management's role, competence, information, stakeholder involvement and cultural change (2010).

CONCLUSION

From the analysis of recent literature, surveys and case studies, six factors are identified as critical for IT departments to transform to a service orientation:

- Support from senior management is essential to provide resources and enforce compliance to new processes. As in most initiatives involving organizational change and technology, the key is effective engagement of personnel affected coupled with support from senior management. Senior management does not need an in-depth understanding of ITIL but must provide support in terms of resources and authority to enforce new policies.
- The threat or opportunity to outsource IT service management needs to be considered.

- Process silos need to be overcome by integration to provide end-to-end service. Each process has critical dependencies with other processes.
- Business staff and customers need to be identified as stakeholders and involved in process redesign. Effective use of one-on-one communication with key stakeholders, backed up with newsletters and workshops helps to promote ITIL to the wider group of stakeholders.
- The culture of IT staff needs to change in terms of focus from technology to service excellence by understanding how IT contributes value to the business and customers.
- Processes should be redesigned prior to investing in tools.

IT Service Managers need to consider these factors when implementing IT service improvements. If IT service providers fail to provide a reliable customer-centric focus, it will impact on their organizations by limiting the potential for IT to add value. This view is reinforced by Mohamed et al. (2008) who state that ITIL implementation should be viewed as a reflection of a dramatic shift as the convergence of IT and business visions call for better collaboration, cooperation, and coordination for knowledge sharing. They go on to warn that this convergence requires the IT department to shed its 'self-centred attitude, build mutual symbiotic relationships with business and participate in culture of trust and sharing' (2008).

The ITIL phenomenon has radically changed the discipline of IT service management. Emerging standards such as ISO/IEC 15504 and ISO/IEC 20000 will extend the impact, and in the future, it is likely that providers will be selected based on capability assessments or certification. Future research will analyse certification records to perform an international comparison of the up-take rate of the international standard.

ACKNOWLEGMENT

I would like to acknowledge the other members of the USQ IT service management research team: Dr Wui-Gee Tan and Professor Mark Toleman. Special thanks also to others who have contributed to this research effort: Mr Peter Cross (Chair of itSMF Australia), Dr Neil McBride (De Montford University), Dr Carol Pollard (Appelachian State University), Montri Lawkobkit (itSMF Thailand).

ITIL® is a Registered Trade Mark of the Office of Government Commerce in the United Kingdom and other countries

IT Infrastructure Library® is a Registered Trade Mark of the Office of Government Commerce in the United Kingdom and other countries

®CMMI is registered in the U.S. Patent and Trademark Office by Carnegie Mellon University

REFERENCES

Bitner, M. J., & Brown, S. W. (2006). The Evolution and Discovery of Services Science in Business Schools. *Communications of the ACM*, *49*(7), 73–78. doi:10.1145/1139922.1139952

Bruton, N. (2004). *Managing the IT services process*. Oxford: Butterworth-Heinemann.

Cater-Steel, A. P., & McBride, N. (2007). *IT Service Management Improvement – an Actor Network Perspective*. Paper presented at the European Conference on Information Systems.

Cater-Steel, A. P., & Pollard, C. (2008). *Conflicting views on ITIL implementation: managed as a project – or business as usual?* Paper presented at the International Conference on Information Resources Management (Conf-IRM).

Cater-Steel, A. P., Tan, W., & Toleman, M. (2009). itSMF Australia 2009 Conference: Summary of Report of ITSM Standards and Frameworks Survey.

Chesbrough, H., & Spohrer, J. (2006). A Research Manifesto for Services Science. *Communications of the ACM*, *49*(7), 35–40. doi:10.1145/1139922.1139945

Di Renzo, B., Barafort, B., Lejeune, V., Prime, S., & Simon, J. M. (2005, April). *ITIL based service management measurement and ISO/IEC 15504 process assessment: A win-win opportunity.* Paper presented at the SPICE 2005 Conference, Klagenfurt, Austria.

Ghayekhloo, G., Sedighi, M., Nassiri, R., Latif Shabgahi, G., & Khodadadi Tirkolaei, H. (2009). *Pathology of organizations currently implementing ITIL in developing countries.* Paper presented at the Second International Conference on Computer and Electrical Engineering.

Gonzalez, R., Gasco, J., & Llopis, J. (2006). Information Systems Outsourcing: a literature analysis. *Information & Management*, *43*(7), 821–834. doi:10.1016/j.im.2006.07.002

Hochstein, A., Tamm, G., & Brenner, W. (2005). *Service-Oriented IT Management: Benefit, Cost and Success Factors.* Paper presented at the 15th European Conference on Information Systems.

Iden, J., & Langeland, L. (2010). Setting the Stage for a Successful ITIL Adoption: A Delphi Study of IT Experts in the Norwegian Armed Forces. *Information Systems Management*, (27): 103–112. doi:10.1080/10580531003708378

ISO/IEC. (2003). *ISO/IEC 15504.5:2004 Information technology - Process assessment - an exemplar Process Assessment Model o.* Document Number.

ISO/IEC. (2005). ISO/IEC 20000:2005 Information technology - Service management - Part 2: Code of practice [Electronic Version]

itSMF. (2010). Certified Organisations. Retrieved 8 March, 2010, from http://www.isoiec20000certification.com/lookuplist.asp?Type=9

itSMFI. itSMF International: the IT Service Management Forum. Retrieved 31 October, 2008, from http://www.itsmfi.org/content/chapters

Janssen, M., & Joha, A. (2008). Emerging shared service organizations and the service-oriented enterprise: critical management issues. *Outsourcing: an International Journal*, *1*(1), 35–49. doi:10.1108/17538290810857466

Johnson, M. W., Hately, A., Miller, B. A., & Orr, R. (2007). Evolving standards for IT service management. *IBM Systems Journal*, *46*(3), 583–597. doi:10.1147/sj.463.0583

Laudon, K. C., & Laudon, J. P. (2010). *Management Information Systems: Managing the Digital Firm* (11 ed.). Upper Saddle River, New Jersey: Prentice Hall.

Lawkobkit, M. (2008). *Thailand IT Service Management Adoption.* Thailand: itSMFo. Document Number)

Mohamed, M. S., Ribière, V. M., O'Sullivan, K. J., & Mohamed, M. A. (2008). The re-structuring of the information technology infrastructure library (ITIL) implementation using knowledge management framework. *Vine*, *38*(3). doi:10.1108/03055720810904835

Musson, D., & Jordan, E. (2006). *The Benefits of IT Governance.* Paper presented at the European Conference on Information Systems Goteborg, Sweden.

OGC. (2007). *Service Strategy.* London: TSO for the Office of Government Commerce.

Pitt, L., Berthon, P., & Lane, N. (1998). Gaps within the IS department: barriers to service quality. *Journal of Information Technology*, *13*(3), 191–200. doi:10.1080/026839698344837

Praeg, C.-P., & Schnabel, U. (2006, 4-7 Jan). *IT-Service Cachet - managing IT-service performance and IT-service quality.* Paper presented at the 39th Annual Hawaii International Conference on System Sciences (HICSS'06), Kauai.

Rust, R. T., & Kannan, P. K. (2003). E-service: a new paradigm for business in the electronic environment. *Communications of the ACM*, *43*(6), 37–42.

Rust, R. T., & Miu, C. (2006). What Academic Research Tells us about Service. *Communications of the ACM*, *49*(7), 49–54. doi:10.1145/1139922.1139948

Steinberg, R. A. (2005). *Implementing ITIL: adapting your organization to the coming revolution in IT service management*. Victoria, BC: Trafford.

Van Bon, J. (2007). *IT Service Management based on ITIL v3*. Saltbommel: Van Haren.

Section 3

Chapter 12
Service Science, Management, Engineering, and Design (SSMED): An Emerging Discipline – Outline & References[1]

Jim Spohrer
IBM Research

Stephen K. Kwan
San José State University, USA

ABSTRACT

The growth of the global service economy has led to a dramatic increase in our daily interactions with highly specialized service systems. Service (or value-cocreation) interactions are both frequent and diverse, and may include retail, financial, healthcare, education, on-line, communications, technical support, entertainment, transportation, legal, professional, government, or many other types of specialized interactions. And yet surprisingly few students graduating from universities have studied anything about service or service systems. Service Science, Management, Engineering, and Design (SSMED), or service science for short, is an emerging discipline aimed at understanding service and innovating service systems. This article sketches an outline and provides an extensive, yet preliminary, set of references to provoke discussions about the interdisciplinary nature of SSMED. One difficult challenge remaining is to integrate multiple disciplines to create a new and unique service science.

THEORETICAL AND PRACTICAL FOUNDATIONS

The emerging discipline of Service Science, Management, Engineering, and Design (SSMED) or service science, for short, is outlined in this article (IBM Research 2004; Chesbrough, 2005; Horn, 2005; Chesbrough & Spohrer, 2006; Hidaka, 2006; Monahan, Pym, Taylor, Tofts, & Yearworth 2006; Spohrer, Maglio, Bailey, & Gruhl, 2007; IfM & IBM, 2008; Spohrer & Maglio, 2008). This section provides some of the key theoretical and practical foundations of service science. What is truly new

DOI: 10.4018/978-1-60960-138-6.ch012

and unique about service science? Haven't people been doing service research for over thirty years? What's changed? The next section provides the primary connections to existing disciplines. How does service science relate to existing academic disciplines? Does every service scientist need to know about all these disciplines?

How is service science changing and being changed by these disciplines? The last section provides the primary connections to existing professions. How does service science relate to existing professions? Which professions are likely to benefit from the rise of service science?

Concepts and Questions

Why now? The International Labor Organization released a report[2] in January 2007 that stated there are, for the first time in human history, more service jobs (40%) than agricultural jobs (39.6%) and nearly doubles those of manufacturing jobs (20.4%). Nowadays most people survive (and some thrive) even though they do not create new physical things, such as food or tangible products, in their jobs. Over the past thirty years, a growing number of academics and practitioners have begun to study "service" as a distinct phenomenon, with its own body of knowledge and rules of practice. The growth of service value in society is undeniable.

However, aside from the statistics is there really anything new in this "growth of service" phenomenon, and is there anything worthy of a new science? And what is service? From von Mises (1998), we see that service relates to increasing value from more and more sophisticated forms of cooperation, or what we term *value-cocreation mechanisms*. Many have begun to observe that over time, service-for-service exchanges not only dominate in an economy, but become more specialized and knowledge-intensive, and further increase the value creation density of societies (Normann 2001). The growth of service also means interacting more with strangers (Seabright 2005); even though we know the role someone is playing in a service system, we do not always know the person. So what is going on? What is behind the growth of service? Ludwig von Mises (1998) wrote, near the middle of the last century, about the fundamental understanding of value and cooperation: "Within society, cooperation substitutes interpersonal or social exchange for autistic exchange. Man gives to other men in order to receive from them. Mutuality emerges. Man serves in order to be served. (Pg. 194)"

More recently, Vargo & Lusch (2004, 2006, and 2008) in their Service-Dominant Logic *define service as the application of competence (e.g., knowledge, resources, etc.) for the benefit of another entity*. They point out that most people today use a Product-Dominant Logic that has arisen from two centuries of measuring value as increases in physical output. For example, bushels of wheat or palettes of consumer goods are physical output. This focus on the physical products is quite understandable, in part, given that manufacturing production efficiencies have lead to enormous improvements in material wealth (Beinhocker, 2006). However, now with the rise of the internet and low-cost global communications, information and knowledge as a contributor in value-cocreation is becoming more quantifiable. Foray (2004) points out that information is easy to copy (known digital encoding in machines), while knowledge is hard to copy (unknown neural encoding in people). The growth of service is truly tied to the growth of information and knowledge.

What's new? While division-of-labor and cooperation are not new thoughts, the growth of service provides a new lens through which to see the world. The growth of service, seen as the evolution of value-cocreation mechanisms between service system entities, becomes a way to view human history and understand future change. Perhaps it is even true, as some writers suggest that people in modern societies are getting better at playing win-win games (Wright 2000). People are starting to understand that value-cocreation is the best game in town.

Service is in fact becoming the lens through which many disparate areas of study can be viewed within a common framework. For example, the increased focus on service in recent years is in large part due to the growing dominance of service activities in national economic accounts of jobs, GDP, exports, and productivity (Triplett & Bosworth 2004; Lewis 2004; Herzenberg, Alic, & Wial 2000). In everyday business and government, service is most strongly associated with the growth of high-value, knowledge-intensive types of customer-provider interactions, between entities such as people, organizations, agencies, machines, or infrastructure, in which taxes, advertising fees, subscription fees, usage fees, annual enrollment fees, or the scarce resource of human attention are typically exchanged for the actions, experiences, assurances, or access privileges of service providers. In computer science, service refers to computational resources (as in web service or grid service) that can be discovered, accessed, and applied using standard protocols (Spohrer, Anderson, Pass, Ager, & Gruhl, 2008). In the public sector and social sciences, service is often associated with intangible value from selfless acts of loyalty, courage, or ethical/religious convictions about what is right and good in human society. For example, the removal of *unfreedoms* (i.e., unhealthy, uneducated, unprotected, uninformed, etc.) from the billions of underserved people around the world is one view on the importance of service activities that connect economic, political, and social thinkers (Sen, 1998; Lewis, 2004). Also, one-time service encounters are very different from long-term or life-time service relationships (Gutek, 1995), and the application of knowledge-based assets is very different from the application of physical assets (Boisot, 2002). Manufacturing businesses are increasingly driven to understand service innovation, as they seek to transform themselves to higher levels of value-cocreation with their customers and other stakeholders (IfM & IBM, 2008). All these views contribute to an increasing need to understand the phenomenon of service as the evolution of and the design of value-cocreation mechanisms between entities – the business of society is becoming value-cocreation.

Basic Concepts. If we are to understand human history as the evolution and design of value-cocreation mechanisms between entities, then where should we begin? Let's start by understanding the following ten basic concepts: resources, service system entities, access rights, value-proposition-based interactions (a more traditional, business-oriented name for value-cocreation mechanism), governance mechanisms, service system networks, service system ecology, stakeholders, measures, and outcomes.

Resources: "Things come and go, and we name them in order to communicate about them." Every nameable physical and non-physical thing is a resource. For example, an instance of an apple is a physical resource, and the concept of a right triangle is a non-physical resource. As von Mises (1998) observed: "Thinking man sees the serviceableness of things, i.e., their ability to minister to his ends, and acting man makes them means." (Pg. 92); Legal man attributes rights to certain types of physical and non-physical resources. For example, adult people are physical resources with rights, and businesses, that have properly incorporated, paid their taxes on time, and fulfill other obligations, are non-physical resources with rights. Businesses may own physical resources or contract for physical resources, but as a type of resource they are themselves not physical, but instead a conceptual-legal construct. So in the end, all resources fall into one of four types: *physical-with-rights, not-physical-with-rights, physical-with-no-rights, and not-physical-with-rights*. In modern society, physicists are the professional authorities who tell us which resources are or are not physical. Judges are the professional authorities who tell us which resources have or do not have rights within their jurisdictions. Physicists and judges are types of authority stakeholders (a concept introduced below). As we will see later, communities of authority stakeholders establish and uphold the rules of the game. Thus, the concept of resource and the four logical types is socially constructed (Berger & Luckmann, 1967).

Different types of resources are governed by different types of laws (Maglio, Kreulen, Srinivasan, & Spohrer, 2006). Physical resources are governed by the laws of nature. Conceptual or information resources are governed by the laws of logic-and-mathematics. Both physical and conceptual resources, in a modern human culture, are governed by human law (e.g., property rights). This notion of four types of resources is one of the first fundamental insights from service science, and is part of the service systems worldview.

Latour (2007) in "Reassembling the Social: An Introduction to Actor Network Theory" provides the term 'actant' to describe what we have termed 'resources' in this article. Vargo & Lusch (2004) make the distinction between operant (actor) and operand (object) resources, and note that all resources, depending on the context and event, may be of either category (e.g., when considering people, the surgeon may be operant and the patient on the table operand).

Service system entities. "Together we can change the world to our mutual benefit." Service system entities are *dynamic configurations of resources*, including at least one resource with rights (and responsibilities, as these come in pairs for legal man), including some type of access rights to all the resources in the configuration, either directly or indirectly through relationships with other service system entities. Recall, within a jurisdiction, an authority stakeholder is required to determine which resources have rights and the nature of the rights. Some dynamic configurations of resources are service system entities (a business or a city, including the people that make them up), and other configurations of resources are not service system entities (an automobile, without a resource with rights, such as the owner person or driver person included). The most common types of service system entities are people and organizations. New types of service system entities are constantly emerging and disappearing. Recently, open-source and on-line communities have emerged as service systems entities. The concept of service system entity is evolving rapidly (Spohrer, Maglio, Bailey, & Gruhl, 2007; Spohrer, Vargo, Maglio, & Caswell, 2008).

Access rights. "By what authority, do you use that resource?" Service system entities have four main types of access rights to the resources within their configuration: *owned outright, leased/contracted, shared access, and privileged access*. Shared access resources include resources such as air, roads, natural language, and internet web sites. Privileged access resources include resources such as thoughts, individual histories, and family relationships.

Value-proposition-based interactions. "I'll do this, if you'll do that." Service system entities interact (normatively) via value propositions. Normative behavior is behavior that "ought to happen according to an ideal model of one or more stakeholders," but in fact may not always occur. Interactions via value propositions are intended to cocreate-value for both interacting entities. Both interacting entities must agree, explicitly or tacitly, to the value proposition. A value proposition communicates a mutually agreeable plan to collaborate and cocreate-value, most often by reconfiguring resources or access rights to resources. A value proposition is a value-cocreation mechanism (Anderson, Narus, & Rossu, 2006; Lovelock& Gummesson 2004; Kim & Mauborgne, 2005; Slywotzky, Wise, & Weber, 2003; Afuah, 2004; Gummesson 2007; Normann 2001). For example, an installment payment plan can allow customers to pay over time for items they get to use in advance of completing payment, while increasing short-term sales for the provider. The value proposition creates a win-win relationship.

Governance mechanisms. "Here's what will happen if things go wrong." Service system entities may not realize the value expected from a previously (mutually) agreed to value proposition. If value is not realized as expected, this may result in a dispute between the entities. Governance mechanisms reduce the uncertainty in these situations by prescribing a mutually agreed to process for resolving the dispute. Governance mechanisms are also known as dispute resolution or conflict resolution mechanisms (Williamson, 1999; Adams, 2000; March 1991; Omerod, 2005; Bernstein, 1998).

Service system networks. "Here's how we can all link up." Service systems entities interact with other service system entities (normatively) via value propositions. Over time, for a population of entities, the patterns of interaction can be viewed as networks with direct and indirect connectivity strengths. A service system network is an abstraction that only emerges when one assumes a particular analysis overlay on the history of interactions amongst service system entities.

Service system ecology. "Populations of entities, changing the ways they interact." Different types of service systems entities exist in populations, and the universe of all service system entities forms the service system ecology or service world (Bryson, Daniels, and Warf, 2004). The ecology is characterized both by the diversity of types of service system entities and their relative numbers, as well as the dynamics resulting from value-cocreation mechanisms and governance mechanisms.

Stakeholders. "When it comes to value, perspective really matters." The four primary types of stakeholders are *customer, provider, authority, and competitor.* Reasoning about multiple stakeholders and their perspectives on resource access is necessary to design new and improved value-cocreation mechanisms and governance mechanisms, as well as to design new and improved types of service system entities. In addition to the four fundamental stakeholder perspectives (customer, provider, authority, competition), other stakeholder perspectives include employee, partner, entrepreneur, criminal, victim, underserved, citizen, manager, children, aged, and many others. Designing business and societal systems that address more than the four fundamental stakeholder perspectives is sometimes considered to be the difference between having a society that is merely 'prosperous' and having a society that is truly 'great' (Collins, 2005).

Measures. "Without standardized measures, it is hard to agree and harder to trust." The four primary types of measures are *quality, productivity, compliance, and sustainable innovation.* Each of these corresponds to a stakeholder perspective: customers evaluate quality, providers evaluate productivity, authorities evaluate compliance, and, in a very real sense, competitors evaluate sustainable innovation. With regard to sustainable innovation, von Mises (1998) states: "Competitors aim at excellence and preeminence in accomplishments within a system of mutual cooperation" (Pp. 116-117). The ongoing challenge that service system entities (e.g., people) perceive is 'self competition' to sustain a balance between too much challenge (anxiety and risk of failure, if skills are lacking) and too little challenge (boredom and risk of meaningless success). A dynamic balance between anxiety and boredom helps to ensure a sense that change has meaning and value (Csiksezntmihalyi, 1990).

Outcomes. "How did we do? Can this become a new routine or long-term relationship?" In a two player game, there are four possible outcomes: win-win, lose-lose, win-lose, and lose-win. Win-win corresponds to value-cocreation, and the other three are likely to lead to disputes. However, only four outcomes, relative to real world complexity, is too impoverished to be of much use. To create a more realistic model we developed ISPAR with ten possible outcomes (Spohrer, Vargo, Maglio, & Caswell, 2008). ISPAR (Interact-Service-Propose-Agree-Realize) includes outcomes in which: (1) value is realized, (2) the proposal (value proposition) is not understood, (3) the proposal is not agreed to, (4) value is not realized and disputes do not arise, (5) value-cocreation disputes are resolved in a manner that is OK for all stakeholders, (6) value-cocreation disputes are resolved in manner that is not OK for all stakeholder (7) an interaction is not a service interaction and is welcomed, (8) an unwelcomed non-service interaction is not criminal, (9) an unwelcomed non-service interaction is criminal and justice results, (10) an unwelcome non-service interaction is criminal and justice does not result. Beyond a standard two player game, with a customer player and a provider player, ISPAR assumes there exists both an authority player as well as a competitor-criminal player. By admitting the notion of non-service interactions and competitor-criminal stakeholders, ISPAR goes beyond the normative view of service system entity interactions. Service system entities have the competence to make decisions about *relationships* over a life time of interaction, not only the history of past interactions but also reason about the possible future *customer life time value* of service interactions (Rust, 2000).

Service systems worldview. These ten basic concepts underlie the *service systems worldview*: The view that the world is made up of populations of service system entities that interact (normatively) via value propositions to cocreate-value, but often disputes arise and so governance mechanisms are invoked to resolve disputes. In the service systems worldview, people, businesses, government agencies, nations, cities, hospitals, universities, and many other entities are instances of formal service systems.

Formal service system entities are types of legal entities with rights and responsibilities, that can own property, and with named identities that can create contracts with other legal entities. Formal service system entities are legal entities (Williamson, 1999; Roberts, 2004). Formal service systems exist within a legal and economic framework of contracts and expectations.

Informal service system entities include families (though households are formal from a tax law perspective), open source communities (that have not created a formal non-profit entity for governance or charitable giving purposes), and many other societal or social systems that are governed typically by unwritten cultural and behavioral norms (social systems with rudimentary political systems). A service scientist seeks to understand the fossilized value propositions that underlie these informal routines and norms. Informal service systems exist within a social and political framework of promises and expectations.

Natural history of service system entities. Service science seeks to create an understanding of the formal and informal nature of service in terms of entities, interactions, and outcomes, and how these evolve (or are designed) over time. An initial premise is that the entities, which are sophisticated enough to engage in rationally designed service interactions that can consistently lead to win-win value cocreation outcomes, must be able to build models of the past (reputation, trust), present, and future (options, risk-reward, opportunities, hopes and aspirations) possible worlds, including models of themselves and others, and reason about knowledge value (Fagin et al, 2003). The foundations for a natural history of service systems can be found in the anthropology literature, and the foundations for a natural history of value propositions and governance mechanisms can be found in the economics and law literature. The challenge of service science, as we see even more below, is the integration of these and other disciplines, centered on the service research literature.

Basic questions. A general theory of service system entities and networks formed through value-proposition-based interactions has four parts, which directly lead to the four basic types of questions that SSMED seeks to answer:

Science (improve understanding, map natural history, validate mechanisms, make predictions). What are service system entities, how have they naturally evolved to present, and how might they evolve in the future? What can we know about their interactions, how the interactions are shaped (value propositions, governance mechanisms), and the possible outcomes of those interactions both short-term and long-term?

Management (improve capabilities, define progress measures, optimize investment strategy). How should one invest to create, improve, and scale service system networks? How do the four measures of quality, productivity, compliance, and sustainable innovation relate to numerous key performance indicators (KPIs) of business and societal systems? Is there a "Moore's Law" of service system investment? Can doubling information lead to a doubling of capabilities (performance) on a predictable basis?

Engineering (improve control, optimize resources). How can the performance of service system entities and scaling of service system networks be improved by the invention of new technologies (and environmental infrastructures) or the reconfiguration of existing ones? What is required to develop a CAD (Computer-Aided Design) tool for service system entity and service system network design?

Design (improve experience, explore possibilities). How can one best improve the experience of people in service system entities and networks? How can the experience of service system creation, improvement, and scaling be enhanced by better design? Can the space of possible value propositions and governance mechanisms be explored systematically?

Sciences of the artificial. Sciences of the artificial are different from natural sciences, and so it becomes especially important to consider these four parts – science, management, engineering, and design – as important knowledge components. In "The Sciences of the Artificial" (Simon 1996), Simon reflects "The world we live in today is much more man-made, or artificial, world than it is a natural world… …we must be careful about equating 'biological' with 'natural.' A forest may be a phenomenon of nature; a farm certainly is not. …A plowed field is no more part of nature than an asphalted street – and no less. These examples set the terms of our problem, for those things we call artifacts are not apart from nature. They have no dispensation to ignore or violate natural law. At the same time they are adapted to human goals and purposes. …Natural science is knowledge about natural objects and phenomena. We ask whether there cannot also be 'artificial' science – knowledge about artificial objects and phenomena. Unfortunately the term 'artificial' has a pejorative air about it that we must dispel before we can proceed." (Pp. 2-3). We note that some say 'service' with a pejorative air.

Service Science, Management, Engineering, and Design (SSMED) is emerging as one of the sciences of the artificial. Service science is knowledge about service system entities, value-proposition-based interactions (or value-cocreation mechanisms), governance mechanisms, and the other seven basic concepts. Following Simon even further, one could argue that service system entities are physical symbol systems, dealing with symbols that are named resources, and grounded in physical routines for carrying out the symbolic manipulations related to named resources. "A physical symbol system is a machine that, as it moves through time, produces an evolving collection of symbol structures." (*ibid*, Pg. 22). In our parlance, service system entities move through time and produce an evolving configuration of resources that are shaped by interactions with other service system entities. In a well working society, the interactions are based primarily on mutually agreed to value propositions. Service science seeks to improve our understanding by mapping the natural history (growth of service), discovering the mechanisms of change, and predicting future types of service system entities, value-cocreation mechanisms, and governance mechanisms.

Tools and Methods

B2C service. "When the customer is a person." James Teboul (2006) provides an easily accessible introduction to a few of the basic tools and methods that researchers and practitioners have created to both understand service and design new service offerings. The design of business to consumer (B2C) service offerings has especially benefited from two basic tools, the *service intensity matrix and service blueprinting.*

The service intensity matrix can be used to show how different businesses create different value-cocreation mechanisms that populate all the design niches, ranging from highly customized and high interaction service offerings to highly standardized and low interaction service offerings.

The service blueprint tool (see examples from (Fitzsimmons 2008) and Bitner et al (2007)) is used to describe and improve customer-provider interactions in service processes. The service blueprint is particularly useful in helping management test out concepts, identify potential failure points and/or opportunities for innovation. Many variations of service blueprinting tools and methods exist, including one recently developed by Womack & Jones (2005) in their book "Lean Solutions." Heskett, Sasser and Schlesinger (1997) (p. 40) provided a method of calculating value from the perspective of the customer. The simple formula provides a good basis for formulating the win-win value proposition between the customer and the service provider. Gutek and Welsh (2000) proposed a COP model of encounters and relationships. The model described the linkages among Customer, Organization and Provider in a "Service Triangle". The tightness/looseness of the linkage among the components represents the type of and sustainability of the service encounter and relationship. ServeLab at Germany's Fraunhofer Institute provides a disciplined approach to new service product designs (Ganz, 2006). More and more service offerings are designed to be accessed on the web, via mobile phones, or via self-service kiosks. The design of these service systems has benefited from an explosion of development tools and methods.

B2B service. "When the customer is a complex organization." The design of business to business (B2B) service offerings has a growing number of tools and methods such as IBM's Component Business Model (CBM) approach. The CBM approach provides a business architecture view of the customer's business components, the key performance indicators (KPIs) that underlie business performance in that industry, and approaches to outsourcing or otherwise transforming the performance of components. Glushko & McGrath (2005) in "Document Engineering" provide a disciplined approach to business process design. Alter (2006) has developed the work system method and customized it for the design of service systems. Alter (2008) also developed the Service Responsibility Table (SRT) as a tool to bring the customer into the preliminary stages of analyzing and transforming a work system/service system. The advantage of using SRT is that it is intuitive and could be used by a customer who is not trained in heavy-duty systems analysis and design.

DISCIPLINES AND EXPERT THINKING

In this section, the ten academic discipline pillars of service science are presented. Service scientists may specialize in one of these ten areas (expert thinking skills, also known as contributory expertise), but must also be, to some degree, well versed in all ten areas in order to work effectively on multidisciplinary teams of professionals (complex communication skills, also known as interactional expertise) (Collins, Evans, & Gorman, 2007; Collins & Kusch, 1999; Levy 2005). Service scientists should be *T-shaped professionals* (the vertical of the *T* - deep in their home discipline area and appropriately broad to work well in teams – the horizontal of the *T*). We also suggest that T-shaped professionals can learn and adapt more rapidly to the changing needs of business. For this reason, we also refer to T-shaped professionals as *adaptive innovators* (IfM and IBM, 2008). In what follows, the rationale for selecting these ten pillar disciplines will be presented as well as some of the key concepts from each of them. Because students start with a great deal of commonsense and prewired cultural knowledge about the service system worldview, even though they do not have the formal vocabulary, there is good reason to believe material outlined below is not too much knowledge for students to learn (Richardson & Boyd, 2005).

In the following subsections, we briefly introduce the ten disciplines that can provide an understanding of the past (***a***), present (***b-i***), and future (***j***) of service systems, while highlighting the key types of resources/stakeholders (***b-e***) and measures/access rights (***f-i***) needed to understand service systems, value-cocreation mechanisms, and governance mechanisms. The reader should note that the knowledge in each of the discipline areas (clusters really) are expansive and growing rapidly. Our aim is to show how all ten might integrate into a service science framework.

A. History: Economics and Law Evolving

Evolution of trust. Service science, like biology, must ultimately explain the origins and evolutionary paths that lead to today's service system ecology. Wright (2001) in "Non-Zero" provides an accessible version of the history of the evolution of human cooperation and win-win relationship formation. More recently, Beinhocker (2006) in "Origin of Wealth" provides an introduction to evolutionary economics, including a summary of the works of many scholars on the evolution of cooperation. Seabright (2005) in "The Company of Strangers" provides an exposition of the evolution of trust in early human groups (informal service systems), and explores the physical and cultural change in humans that bridge from nomadic hunter-gatherers to the rise of agriculture and early cities. In cities, division of labor reached new heights as population density increased, and communication and transportation costs dropped in what Hawley (1986) called the human ecology.

Division of labor. Adam Smith wrote about the wealth of nations as created by division-of-labor that can lead to an increase in productive capacity (Smith 1776/1904). Smith also wrote about the importance of markets ('markets' as the 'the invisible hand') for coordinating prices based on supply and demand. Ricardo, another early political economist, addressed the issue of optimal import-export strategies for nations to maximize individual and collective productive capacities by appropriately dividing production tasks between nations (Ricardo 1817/2004). Paradoxically, even when one nation can do everything 'better' (i.e., more productively, profitably) than another nation, as long as 'comparative advantages' exist (i.e., relative differences in productivity), then there is often a mathematical, and therefore economic and social, advantage to interactions and exchange. The implications of Ricardo's insight are profound and go well beyond the notion of division of labor.

Learning curves. The evolution of service system interactions in a population of service systems can be seen, in part, as each service system entity 'doing a little bit more of what they do best, a little bit less of what they do worse, and a little bit more interacting with not just complementary service systems ('specialization', 'division of labor,' 'opposites attract'). Diversity creates the conditions for coevolution and complementary improvements of service system entities. Learning or experience curves (Argote 2005) provide further and on-going mathematical advantage to interactions ('practice makes perfect').

Value-cocreation mechanisms. Barnard provides one of the early attempts by a business practitioner to outline a theory of "cooperative systems," including a discussion of formal and informal cooperative systems (Barnard 1938/1968). Richard Normann's (2001) "Reframing Business" is a more modern treatment of many of the same issues, more from a service networks and value propositions rather than an internal organization perspective, and outlines a framework for 'value creating systems' that are very close to our notion of service system entities and networks. Normann identifies three fundamental sources of value: new technological innovation, legal and regulatory changes, and reconfigurations of resources and value propositions from existing value creating systems. Alfred Chandler (1977) provides the historical account of the rise of industrial age business organizations ('managers' as the 'visible hand'). The creation of new roles in existing or new types of service systems often means that individual service systems (people) must step up to new levels of multitasking in their lives. Milgrom & Robert (1992) in "Economics, Organization, and Management" provide a quite comprehensive view of the value (economic advantage) of alternative organizational and management forms.

Governance mechanisms. Williamson (1999) in "The Mechanisms of Governance" refines views on transaction costs and the new institutional economics that provide the foundations for empirical comparisons in context of alternative governance mechanisms. Williamson's notion of "incomplete contracting in its entirety" speaks to rational design attempts to safeguard against both opportunism and bounded rationality when creating value propositions (contracts) with others. In many ways, contract diversity is to service providers as product diversity is to manufacturers. North (2005) in "Understanding the Process of Economic Change" writes about the success of human attempts to gain some measure of control over the physical world with science and engineering, and the limited success of human attempts to control or even guide the evolution of economic growth through the creation of institutions (combined social, political, economic, legal, linguistic systems).

Evolving perspectives on service. Bastiat (1848; 1850), a French political economist in the early 19th century, provided one of the first and most prescient analyses of value as service instead of value in things. With the exception of Bastiat, it is worth noting that most of the accounts above have focused on the growth of productive capacity through manufacturing activities (i.e., the production of things). Colin Clark (1957) in his seminal work "Conditions of Economic Growth" was the first to systematically document the dramatic growth of service activities in national value creation. William Baumol (2007) also drew attention to the growth of the service sector in the latter half of the 20th century, as a drag on the productivity gains of nations. Gadrey and Gallouj (2002) have drawn attention to the difficulty in measuring productivity and quality for service activities compared to manufacturing activities that lead to tangible output. Triplett & Bosworth (2004) provide a modern account of attempts to measure productivity gains in service industries, showing recent periods of time in the US economy where service productivity gains have actually outpaced gains in productivity in extractive and manufacturing sectors. Baumol (2002) has also written about the importance of R&D services ("the leader of the services") to counteract the so called *Baumol's Disease* (asymptotically static service productivity), and provide continuous improvement and even discontinuous jumps in service productivity.

B. Marketing: Customers and the Quality Measure

Marketing and the customer stakeholder. Marketing, as a function within a business firm, has the responsibility to understand the existing and (potential) future customers of that business. Analyzing the relationships and interactions with existing customers, understanding the quality of the customer experience, and working to communicate the appropriate image of the provider firm to attract new customers and improve the customer experience is part of the marketing function of the firm.

Service is different. Service marketing is different from product marketing according to a leading textbook on this subject (Zeithaml, Bitner,

& Gremler, 2006). Traditional product marketing deals with the four P's of product, place, promotion, and price. However, service marketing adds three additional P's: people, physical evidence, and process, because in many service provisioning situations, the service employees and customers interact directly. The service experience in these cases of simultaneous production and consumption is determined by the people, the physical evidence where the interactions happen, and process that guides the customer-provider interactions. Of eleven challenges and questions for service marketers highlighted in this textbook (Pp. 24-25), three mention quality: How can service quality be defined and improved? How does the firm communicate the quality and value to the consumer? How can the organization ensure the delivery of consistent quality service?

Case studies are a common tool in textbooks and business books in the service marketing, relationship marketing, and customer lifetime value areas (Lovelock & Gummesson 2004, Rust et al 2000). These books provide methods for pricing services, communicating service value propositions (including by word of mouth from satisfied customers), recovering from service failure, estimating customer lifetime value, demand forecasting, segmenting markets, using CRM (customer relationships management) technology and systems effectively in organizations, and many other topics related to demand innovation and revenue growth from customers.

Measuring quality. Zeithaml, Bitner, & Gremler (2006) advance the Customer Quality Gaps Model as a way to understand the factors that contribute to service quality. Ben Schneider (Schneider and Bowen 1995, Schneider, & White 2003) has performed a number of empirical studies that show service quality levels inside the firm (as rated by employees) are reflected outside the firm in the experience of quality (as rated by customers). This finding is often used to emphasize the importance of business culture and cultural factors when implementing quality improvement initiatives (Moulton Reger 2006). Pine & Gilmore (1999) and Chase (Chase, Jacobs, & Aquilano, 2004) provide simple formula that help reason about improving quality measures. For example, Pine & Gilmore suggest two rules of thumb for estimating customer satisfaction (what customer expect to get – what customer perceives he gets) and customer sacrifice (what customer wants exactly - what customer settles for).

Quality in B2C and B2B interactions. In B2C service interactions, quality of service is often both a major focus of employee selection and training, as well as an 'unconditional guarantee' made to customers as part of the value proposition used to attract and retain customers. Customer lifetime value is part of the calculation of how "generous" failure recovery offers can be, and still remain profitable over the expected lifetime of the relationship. In B2B and IT-enabled service provisioning, contracts may explicitly call out Service Level Agreements (SLAs) with specific objective measures and penalty clauses in case the SLAs are violated.

C. Operations: Providers and the Productivity Measure

Operations and the provider stakeholder. A leading Operations Management textbook (Chase, Jacobs, & Aquilano, 2004, Pp 6-7) states: *"Operations Management (OM) is defined as the design, operation, and improvement of the systems that create and deliver the firm's primary products and services... while operations managers use decision-making tools of OR/MS (such as critical path scheduling) and are concerned with many of the same issues as IE (such as factory automation), OM's distinct management role distinguishes it from these other disciplines."*

Service is different. Scott Sampson's (2001) "Unified Theory of Services" extends Chase's customer-interaction model of service production processes as distinct from traditional manufacturing production processes. Sampson is advancing a view of service operations as a distinct scientific field (Sampson & Frohle, 2006). The vocabulary of operations and operations management centers on the concept of *process*. The history of operations is primarily associated with the industrial revolution (processes with standard parts and economics of scale) and the rise of scientific management (processes with routine and repetitive human performance). More recently operations has sought an appropriate balancing between investments aimed at optimizing a process (queuing theory to eliminate waiting and inventory bottlenecks) and those aimed at maintaining an increasing flexibility of a process (capacity and demand matching, agility for rapid change). A good overview of these perspectives on operations, including some basics of the human element in processes, is provided in the book "Factory Physics" by Hopp & Spearman (1996). Fitzsimmons & Fitzsimmons (2007) is the author of one of top selling service operations textbooks, "Service Management: Operations, Strategy, and Information Technology." While originally primarily focused on B2C service activities, recent editions have expanded the B2B and IT-delivered service sections.

Measuring productivity. Productivity, broadly defined, is a ratio of output to input from the provider stakeholder perspective. Productivity is a relative measure, typically used to compare a previous time period to a current time period to get a sense of either efficiency gains (reducing costs of inputs) or revenue gains (increasing demand for and hence value of outputs). Partial productivity measures, measure output to labor or output to capital or output to energy. Multi-factor productivity measures, measure output in relation to the sum of a set of input factors. Total productivity measures combine all outputs and all inputs. In operations the emphasis is on efficiency while doing things at the lowest possible cost. The tradeoff most commonly perceived is not to lower the quality of the output of a process as the cost of performing the process is reduced – in fact, ideally the quality should increase as the cost is reduced. The standardization of processes by removing waste (Lean methods), removing variance (Six Sigma method), and then automating to achieve superior quality at the lowest cost is a typical operations worldview approach. Increasingly, operations add a final step of global sourcing (see subsection ***i***) to obtain the lowest cost labor resources required to operate the process. Pigou's Paradox demonstrates that the productive capacity of a system can be increased by adding a simple law to a service system with appropriate governance mechanisms (see subsection ***d***), while adding an advanced technology (i.e., zero cost network linkages) to the same service system could decrease the productivity capacity (Roughgarden 2005).

Back stage and front stage processes. Operations as a function of the firm seeks to understand provider processes and productivity, both those that do not directly involve the customer (back stage processes) and those that directly involve the customer (front stage processes). By understanding the value providers derive from a process as well as the value that customers derive from a process, appropriate operations techniques can be used to reconfigure activities, information, risk, etc. between people and technology, between organizations, and between employees and customers to improve productivity and quality of experience (Womack & Jones 2005). By segmenting types of processes into *front-stage* and *back-stage* processes, appropriate techniques can be used to optimize productivity as well as improve flexible responsiveness (Levitt 1976; Teboul 2006). By decomposing processes into reconfigurable components, service activities can be industrialized as technological capabilities advance to improve quality and economies of scale (Levitt 1976, Quinn & Paquette, 1990).

Industrial engineering compared to service science. The easiest way to appreciate the difference is to compare Hopp & Spearman's "Factory Physics" to Fitzsimmons' "Service Management." The key difference is the focus shift from factory systems, products, and processes to service systems, value, and interactions. That is, from systems governed by physical laws to systems governed by human-made laws.

D. Governance: Authorities and the Compliance Measure

Governance and the authority stakeholder. Political science, legal theory, contract law, all relate to governance. Principal-agent theory in economics also relates to governance (Roberts, 2004). Management mechanisms and administrative science are associated with top down control of resources in a hierarchy, while governance mechanisms are associated with agents or organizations (service system entities in our vocabulary) interacting in the context of markets, organizations, and institutions, and preferring the efficiency and freedoms associated with self governance wherever possible. Williams (1999) in "The Mechanisms of Governance" provides theoretical and empirical investigations of alternative governance mechanisms. Computer scientists, mathematicians, game theorists, and economist have also worked to create the area known as mechanism design. Mechanism design provides a formalization of the properties of different types of auction mechanisms as well as algorithms to repeatedly exchange resources among agents in a system.

Service is different. Violating the laws of physics is impossible; violating the laws of logic is folly; violating the laws of man is either criminal or an innovation (e.g. "Declaration of Independence"). While service system interactions (normatively) are proposals to cocreate-value via win-win value propositions, many things can go wrong. For example, even if the value proposition succeeds, third-party stakeholders (victims) can step forward with grievances and claims against the primary stakeholders (providers-customers). Also, stakeholders known as criminals may act in the role of customer or provider with the intention to deceive and act opportunistically, thus they seek a win-lose outcome. Stakeholders known as authorities may act to bring criminals to justice, and legitimately use coercive capabilities to realize value propositions between authorities and citizens. The ISPAR model of service system interactions provides a description of the ten most common outcomes of service system interactions (Spohrer, Vargo, Maglio, & Caswell, 2008).

Measuring compliance. The overall level of regulatory compliance and the cost of maintaining or improving those levels vary considerably among the many nations around the world. Regulatory compliance is a factor in the transaction costs associated with doing business in different regions of the world (or even districts in a single city). For example, see the Rule of Law Index described in (Kaufmann, Kraay, & Mastruzzi, 2003). The Federalist Papers provide an example of a famous historical effort to design and advocate for a particular form of self governance – which led to the United States.

One measure of the success of a governance structure is its ability to align incentives and overcome opportunism. Langlois & Robertson (1995) in "Firms, Markets, and Economic Change" provide a dynamic theory of the boundaries of the firm that complements much of the work by Coase, North, and Williamson on transaction costs, new institutional economics, and governance structures.

100% compliance may not be optimal. The service systems worldview does not make the assumption that 100% win-win interactions are optimal. An ecology of interacting service systems with 100% win-win interactions could be achieved with 100% compliant service systems. For example, if people were as predictable as technological components in their performance, then success rates approaching 100% might be possible. However, in the case of 100% compliance, the ecology of service systems might not be very innovative.

Risk, rewards, and learning rates. Non-compliance may be risky. John Adams (2000), the UK scholar, in his recent book "Risk" describes the way in which people self-govern risk levels to balance risk and reward. By accepting some amount of risk, service system entities (people, businesses, nations) are able to take actions in a much wider range of situations and learn more rapidly than otherwise might be possible. Adams also describes four models of rationality that describe alternative worldviews about risk taking behavior in society. Systems that tolerate risk taking can also (under certain assumptions) be demonstrated to convert *unknown unknowns* to *known unknowns* and sometimes to *known knowns* to improve future performance. Governance, compliance, risk, trust, privacy, fairness, and learning are all interrelated. Governance mechanisms can also be designed to adjust the learning rates of service system entities in service system ecologies with many unknowns and dynamic properties. For example, the prime interest rate acts as a single parameter related to the cost of capital and is used by the chairman of U.S. Federal Reserve Bank to curb inflationary tendencies (raise interest rate) or curb recessionary tendencies (lower interest rate). Investing in R&D and innovation (risk taking) in an economy tends to diminish when the prime rate is high, and increase when the prime rate is lower.

E. Design: Competitors and the Sustainable Innovation Measure

Design and the competitor stakeholder. Alternative designs compete. Unlike evolutionary change, design relates to conscious exploration of possibilities (changing resource configurations), while remaining sensitive to subjective and objective human response (changing experiences). Hunt (2000) in "A General Theory of Competition" outlines resource advantage theory, and warns that reducing competition in national economic systems has resulted in decreased innovation capacity over time. The design of new products, interfaces, processes, spaces, and systems are all related, but different. For example, the boundaries of a design task are often determined by considerations of who are the people involved: Are the people involved users of physical products? Are they users of information interfaces? Are they participants in a process? Are they participants in using a physical or virtual space? Or are they stakeholder/roleholders in a system with rights and responsibilities? What is the likely duration of the lifecycle of the product, interface, process, space, or system? Design is a conscious change that will compete with an alternative design, and may win or lose for reasons that are subjective, not objective.

Service is different.Gustafsson & Johnson (2003) in "Competing in a Service Economy: How to Create Competitive Advantage Through Service Development and Innovation" state *"As an executive, your job is to set a service strategy and enable your people to both innovate and continuously improve your services."* They outline a progression from product value, to service value, to solution value, to experience value.

Measuring sustainable innovation. Innovation is a measure of value created for populations. Innovation in a service system ecology (multiple populations of interacting types of service system entities) is a relative measure of the value-cocreation increase both short-term and long-term (sustainability). Standard examples of service system innovation include: (1) a loyalty program for an airline, (2) a self-service system at a bank (ATMs), airport (tickets), or retail outlet (checkout scanning), (3) creating a financial services offering, (4) creating a new franchise model, (5) creating a new type of business or organizational structure, (6) specializing and streamlining a medical procedure to expand the number of patients that can afford and hence seek treatment, etc.

Experience design. Experience design is often seen as a balancing act. Csikseztmihalyi (1990) in "Flow" describes the design of optimal experience as balancing anxiety (too much challenge, and not enough skill) with boredom (not enough challenge, and too much unutilized skill).

Csiksezntmihalyi also describes the balancing act between differentiation (more unique individual experiences) and integration (more standardized collective experiences). Pine & Gilmore (1999) in "The Experience Economy" provide a perspective on economic evolution from commodities to goods to services to experience and then to transformations, as balancing more customization (customer satisfaction) with commoditization (customer sacrifice).

F. Anthropology: Privileged Access and People Resources

Anthropology and the people resource. Anthropology is the discipline that is concerned with the study of humanity – all people across all places, times, and dimensions of analysis. The "four fields" approach to anthropology encompasses physical anthropology (based on physical data of biological and human evolution), archeology (based on physical artifacts and environmental data), cultural anthropology or social anthropology (based on data of past and present organized groups of people who share learning contexts or culture), and linguistics (based on language data). It is worth noting the rough correspondence between the "four fields" and the four fundamental categories of resources in service science (people, technology, organizations, and shared information).

Service is different. Dawson (2004) in "Developing Knowledge-based Client Relationships: Leadership in Professional Services" states that it is important to remember that ultimately knowledge and relationships are about people. He identifies seven drivers shaping the evolution of the professional services industries: client sophistication, governance, connectivity, transparency, modularization, globalization, and commoditization. One of four strategies for dealing with commoditization of knowledge proposed by Dawson is to automate ahead of the competition. This shifts the knowledge value from the people who deliver the professional service to the people who deliver the technology, and the people and systems that keep the necessary dynamic information and content up to date. One important knowledge value information flow in service systems is from frontline people who deliver service to customers to technology people who automate and operate/maintain technology systems to deliver the related service to customers. Ensuring the sustainability of this type of information flow over time is a requirement of sustainable innovation in most professional service firms.

Privileged access. People are special. They have unique and privileged access to their own thoughts. Also, kinship relations and historical facts are unique for individuals. Important properties of people as individual service systems include: they have finite lifecycles (e.g., time is a limited resource), identities (e.g., stakeholders and roleholders in many service systems with associated histories and future expectations), legal rights and responsibilities (e.g., ownership of property or assets, authority to perform certain acts, and this varies over the lifecycle from child to adult), perform multitasking as a way to increase individual productive output in a finite time, and engage in division-of-labor with others to increase collective productive output in finite time.

Life cycles. One view of service science is that it is the emerging theory of the lifecycles of resources (people, technology, shared information and organizations) as they are dynamically configured into service systems that interact via value propositions to cocreate-value (as mutually measured or judged by various stakeholders; "mutually" meaning they can reason about each other's reasoning processes – or step into each other's shoes temporarily). The value of knowledge, which is sometime thought of as embedded in resources, changes over their life cycles depending on the context of use (Boisot 1995).

G. Engineering: Owned Outright and Technological/ Environmental Resources

Engineering and physical resources. Fundamentally, engineering is concerned with the translation of knowledge to value, by manifesting the knowledge in some physical and useful form. Engineering approaches have been broadly applied to areas relevant to service science, including industrial and systems engineering, industrialization of services, engineering economics (Woods & Degarmo, 1953/1959; Park 2004; Newman, Lavelle, & Eschenbach, 2003; Sepulveda, Souder, & Gottfried, 1984), activity-based costing (ABC), incentive engineering, human performance engineering (Gilbert 2007), financial engineering (Neftci 2004), process engineering and statistical process control, product engineering, document engineering (Glushko & McGrath 2005), and of course service engineering (Ganz 2006; Spath 2007; Mandelbaum and Zeltyn, 2008). ***Service is different.*** Engineering problems are solved in order to create solutions that help realize a value proposition between service systems. Engineering of sustainable service systems seeks to economize on scarce resources (individual people's time, attention, and capital as well as environmental resources, societal and business resources, etc.). Engineering in close collaboration with their underlying science areas also seeks to create new abundant resources and infrastructures that can enable the translation of desired possibilities into reality.

Owned outright. Physical property can be owned outright. Since property does not have rights, it can be completely controlled at the whim of the owner. A good general introduction to the role of engineering in modern society is Beniger's (1986) "The Control Revolution: Technological and Economic Origins of the Information Society." North (2005) wrote about gaining control and predictability in economic systems by using knowledge to remove uncertainty first from physical systems and then social systems. h. Computing: Shared Access and Information Resources ***Computing and information resources.*** The area of services computing and web services (Zhang 2007) is one of the most fundamental of the emerging disciplines relevant to the design and engineering of scalable and sustainable service systems. Marks & Bell (2006) in "Service-Oriented Architecture: A Planning and Implementation Guide for Business and Technology" wrote that *"Many organizations wrestle with the semantic and linguistic barriers between the business community and the IT community... SOA offers the potential to create a unified language of business based on a unit of analysis known as a service."* As businesses embrace SOA, a service system worldview is catching on slowly, and both business practitioners and IT specialist have begun to converge on a common service-oriented language. Checkland & Howell (1998/2005) developed the notion that all information systems are in fact service systems: *"A consequence of the nature of the process, in which intentions are formed and purposeful action is undertaken by people who are supported by information, is that 'information system' has to be seen as a service system: one which serves those taking the action."*

Service is different. A key trend in service interactions is self-service. The provider that had empowered employees with a special information infrastructure opens up that infrastructure to sophisticated customers who engage in self-service interactions. Honebein & Cammarano (2005) in "Creating Do-It-Yourself Customers" examine this trend, starting with the rise of the sophisticated customer.

Shared access. The internet and world-wide-web have greatly expanded the shared information in the world. Effective customer-provider interactions are based on shared access to information. Value propositions (one type of shared information) can be communicated (a proposal), agreed to (a promise or contract), and realized (an event or assurance of a future event). The value of shared information is central to all service system entities. Information is used to update models of all stakeholders (customers, providers, authority, competitors) in the world (*world model fidelity*), which is essential to creating new value propositions, realizing value propositions that are part of existing relationships, as well as fairly and transparently resolving disputes. Customers 'own' the knowledge assets related to the problems they need solved. Providers 'own' the knowledge assets related to the capabilities that can be brought to bear to solve those problems. However, without somehow sharing the information, it is of little value. Castells (2004) in "The Network Society" describes *"A network society is a society whose social structure is made of networks powered by microelectronics-based information and communication technologies."* ***Money as shared information.*** In the service system worldview, money and capital are primarily information (for example, see "The Shape of Actions: What Humans and Machines Can Do" by Collins & Kusch (1999)). The growth of on-line or virtual worlds with artificial currencies, makes the notion of "money as information" even more apparent. The connection between information accumulation and culture is a strong one (see the definition of culture and its relation to information in "Not By Genes Alone" by Richardson & Boyd (2005)).

i. Sourcing: Leasing/Contracts and Organization Resources

Sourcing and organizations as resources. Sourcing is also known as the discipline of procurement. Scott (1981/2003) in "Organizations: Rational, Natural, and Open Systems" observed that *"Today's organizations are vigorously pursuing a strategy of externalization, outsourcing functions and relying on alliances or contracts for essential goods and services..."* A single person can run a sole-proprietorship business, and so an organization can consist of a single individual. Clearly, a lot of functions would be outsourced in this situation. However, while most individual people are not considered organizations, all people are considered to be a service system. So 'service system' is a more general concept than 'organization,' as service system includes people, open source communities, and markets, as well as all organizations. Moving beyond outsourcing, some authors and practitioners have begun talking about the notion of multisourcing (Cohen & Young, 2006): *"The disciplined provisioning and blending of business and IT services from the optimal set of internal and external providers in the pursuit of business goals."* Building a sourcing strategy requires a deep understanding of the short-term and long-term nature of the need for custom or standard, business outcome driven (value) or operational outcome driven (cost) service for every component of a business and service value network of partners.

Service is different. While oil and iron ore may only exist in specific geographies, people exist everywhere. Sourcing can redistributes jobs and expertise on a global scale. Friedman (2005) in "The World is Flat" fueled the growing concern that expertise, hence services, can be sourced from anywhere. These concerns have lead to the US report "Rising above the Gathering Storm" (COSEPUP, 2007) which provides recommendations for US policy aimed at ensuring a strong high-skill innovation economy in the US. ***Leasing/Contracts.*** Access to resource via leasing and other types of contracts. The fundamental generalization of make-buy from early manufacturing is the concern in sourcing. Sourcing creates more interdependence and less independence. ***Organizational intelligence.*** March (1999) in "The Pursuit of Organizational Intelligence" wrote *"Organizations pursue intelligence... In particular, organizations (like other adaptive systems) are plagued by the difficulty of balancing exploration and exploitation. By exploration is meant such things as search, discovery, novelty, and innovation. It involves variation, risk taking, and experimentation. It commonly leads to disasters but occasionally leads to important new directions and discoveries. By exploitation is* *meant refinement, routinization, production, and implementation of knowledge. It involves choice, efficiency, selection, and reliability. It usually leads to improvement but often is blind to major redirections."* This is a very fundamental observation. Organizations, and in general service system entities, are dynamic configurations of resources in a constant process of change. However, to continue to exist that organizational change must balance two types of activities – exploration and exploitation – in order to both exist in and adapt to a changing environment. This balance is not unlike the balance that individual people seek in optimal learning, in which too much challenge can lead to anxiety and too little challenge can lead to boredom. Balance is the key to sustainable change.

Open innovation and boundaries of the firm. Historically in large firms, common perceptions were that (1) internal sourcing (central R&D) is best to create innovations, and (2) external sourcing (partnership) is best for cost reductions and industry standardizations. However, open innovation models (Chesbrough 2006) may challenge the former perspective, and increasingly standardized approaches to leaning and automating processes may challenge the latter perspective. Moore (2005) in his book "Dealing with Darwin" states that *"The formula for tackling innovation and overcoming inertia in tandem is simple: Extract resources from context and repurpose them for core."* What is context (can be outsourced) and what is core (should not be outsourced) changes over time, and must be constantly reassessed and is at the heart of business discipline. j. Futures: Strategic Investment & Management

Strategy. Learning from the future is akin to what chess experts do when they 'look ahead' to possible worlds, and then invest their efforts in trying to realize the possible worlds that are more favorable to their ambitions. The challenge is to understand the likely responses of others. Nevertheless, strategy can be viewed as the art of learning from possible futures. Management then seeks to make wise investments to realize favorable possible futures.

Servitization strategy. Many enterprises which had successes in product development and manufacturing processes are facing growth pressures, and are seeking new revenue models through innovation and *servitization*. For example, this led to Toyota to declare itself a "service company". Servitization includes strategies of providing *customer solutions* combining products and service options with active customer and community participation in creating value. The impact of these actions is dramatic in some industries.

Investment. A key responsibility of management is to provide strategic direction to the firm, and allocate resources and investment wisely to ensure the future of the firm. Fitzsimmons & Fitzsimmons (2008) in "Service Management" provide an overview of the types of operational and strategic investment decisions typical of service firms, including mergers and acquisitions, divestitures, shifting to a franchise business model, etc. Mendelson & Ziegler (1999) in "Survival of the Smartest" identify the five characteristics (external information awareness, effective decision architecture, internal knowledge dissemination, organizational focus, and information age business network) of High-IQ versus Low-IQ companies, and show a correlation with superior growth rate for High-IQ companies..

Management. Management of information systems (MIS), project management (PM), innovation and management of technology (IMOT), operations management (OM), financial management (FM), supply chain management (SCM), enterprise resource management (ERP), customer relation management (CRM), human resource management (HRM), intellectual property management, contract management (CM), risk management, as well as strategy and organizational change management (S&OCM) are well developed fields of knowledge related to improving decision making and the performance of complex business and societal systems.

PROFESSIONS AND COMPLEX COMMUNICATIONS

Before students choose to study service science, they will surely ask about future jobs and professions. Is this a good career choice? Yes, from the perspective of flexibility. Service scientists must possess complex communication skills (interactional expertise) across multiple academic disciplines and areas of practice. Entrepreneurs and business consultants are in high demand, but it has been difficult to specify curriculum beyond exposure to technology change and management practice. SSMED offers a new opportunity to create curriculum relevant to those who aspire to entrepreneurship and business consulting. Scientists and engineers are also in high demand, but demand constantly shifts to new areas. We expect more students who aspire to be system scientists and system engineers will seek a solid understanding of service science for many different career paths in academics, government, and business.

Entrepreneurs, Business Consultants, and Mindset

Entrepreneurs. Entrepreneurial capitalism (Baumol, Litan, Schramm, 2007) is "a type of capitalism where entrepreneurs, who continue to provide radical ideas that meet the test of the marketplace, play a central role in the system." The rise of entrepreneurial capitalism is a relatively recent phenomenon fueled in part by increasing global wealth. Simultaneously, more and more students aspire to have their own business. Student surveys at a number of universities indicate the growing importance of flexibility and personal growth, as well as open career paths, behind their interest in entrepreneurship.

Business Consultants. According to the US Bureau of Labor Statistics job growth will be strongest in business and professional services, even stronger than growth in healthcare, which is second strongest. Business consulting, which relates to global supply chains, organizational change, information technology-driven business transformation, mergers and acquisitions, as well as divestitures, are high demand areas. McKenna (2006) in "The World's Newest Profession: Management Consulting in the Twentieth Century." speaks to the cyclic focus on creating a more technical and advanced tool-based form of consulting. Service science seeks to provide the foundation for the growing technical and systematic approaches to consulting.

Mindset. A service mindset is based in part on empathy for customers, as well as a sense of empowerment that comes from understanding how things are likely to change in the future. Understanding the life time value of a customer is essential, and responding in ways that have the potential to scale beyond the customer to create whole new markets. A successful service mindset, like successful entrepreneurship, comes from creating new markets. Berry (1995) states, "Great service is a matter of mentality. The quest to improve is unrelenting; ideas are part of the job; the spirit of entrepreneurship is strong." (Pg. 16).

Service System Design Lab Network: Beyond lectures and textbooks, to help ensure that students gain practical experience from realistic assignments, service science laboratories (also known as service systems design lab networks) are being envisioned by a number of academics (Kwan & Freund 2007). The goals of service system labs include: support of service science curriculum and research; engage industry and government partners; develop and disseminate service science curriculum materials; create collaborative opportunities among universities involved in the service science initiative; establish an entrepreneurial service mindset in students based on empathy for customers, and a sense of empowerment that can lead to establishing new markets. Service system design lab networks will connect academics, government, and business around challenge-based, project-based instruction aimed at real world, virtual world, and simulated world solutions to service system and value proposition design challenges.

Scientists, Engineers, and Leadership

System scientists. John Sterman (2000) in "Business Dynamics: Systems Thinking for a Complex World" wrote: *"The dizzying effects of accelerating change are not new. Henry Adams, a perceptive observer of the great changes wrought by the industrial revolution, formulated the Law of Acceleration to describe the exponential growth of technology, production, and population... A steady stream of philosophers, scientists, and management gurus have since echoed Adams, lamenting the acceleration and calling for similar leaps to fundamental new ways of thinking and acting. Many advocate the development of systems thinking – the ability to see the world as a complex system, in which we understand that 'you can't just do one thing' and that 'everything is connected to everything else.'"* Sterman then goes on to develop vocabulary, tools, and examples to enable systems thinking. Fortunately for our efforts, many of his examples are examples of complex service systems. Sterman contrasts the event-oriented view of the world and its vocabulary (goals + situation, problem, decision, results) with the feedback (double loop learning) view of the world and its vocabulary (real world, information feedback, decisions, mental models, strategy, structure, decision rules). He goes on to identify the impediments to learning that make even the feedback view of the world problematic for dealing with the dynamic complexity of the real world. He concludes, and we agree, that simulations are an essential tool for professionals who want to approach systems thinking rigorously and seriously. Sawyer (2005) in "Social Emergence: Societies as Complex Systems" describes third wave systems theory and ever growing importance of simulations tools for thinking about emergence in complex societal systems.

Weinberg (1975/2001) in his classic "An Introduction to General Systems Theory" provides a distillation of many concepts from system theorists such as von Bertalanffy (1976) and many others. While general systems theorists seek to understand the general principles that underlie all systems (physical, chemical, biological, computational, social, etc.), service science aims to be descriptive, explanatory, and predictive of business and societal evolution. Within this more limited context of complex service systems, Wright (2001) in "Non-Zero: History, Evolution, Human Cooperation" provides insights into systems that establish and evolve win-win value propositions. Buchanan (2001) in "Ubiquity: The Science of History" and more recently in his (2007) "The Social Atom" provides insights into the path-dependent evolution of complex systems where, to understand the evolution, the properties of the parts are less important than organization of those parts.

System engineers. Bell Laboratories provided the foundational work for both systems engineering and stochastic service system analysis almost a half century ago. Hall (1962) in "A Methodology for Systems Engineers" laid the foundation for the field of system engineering. Riordin (1962) in "Stochastic Service Systems" drew on and then extended queuing theory for what he argued where more general types of service systems.

Science challenge: Confidential data. The best science depends on improved measurement and access to data. Businesses are service system entities, so much of the data that would inform service science are considered proprietary and hence not easily shared. For example, details of successful and unsuccessful contract negotiations and executions would be of enormous value in understanding learning curves for service interactions. However, most business would be reluctant to share the details of successful, much less, unsuccessful contracting attempts. One implication is that developments in service science will likely be much more dependent on simulated data as a result. The properties of simulated worlds will be more transparent and repeatable, and allow cumulative progress that might not otherwise be possible. As techniques for modeling and measuring simulated ecologies of service systems advance, these efforts may someday lead to the equivalent of a CAD (computer-aided design) tool for service system design and engineering. Ultimately, service scientists will have deep competence in using service system simulations tools.

Engineering challenge: Patent incentives. The best engineers create a lot of patents. This is personally motivating to the engineers, and highly beneficial to their employers. Just as many business method and software patents are challenged on the grounds of "technicity" (technical contribution - this area is already a major difference between US and EU patent law), the invention of new types of service systems entities, value-cocreation mechanisms, and governance mechanisms may be difficult or impossible to patent. Without the ability to patent inventions, a major incentive for innovation is removed. Nevertheless, the continuous innovation in this area may confer significant advantages to providers of service over their competitors, or even their own previous business approaches, and hence be a significant driver of investment. As the ability to design new service systems entities and networks (CAD for service) increases, along with the ability to drop them into simulation of existing ecologies, the technicity requirement may become easier to achieve, allowing innovative designs to become patentable.

National economic leadership. History provides evidence that emerging sciences and their associated engineering and management disciplines can provide the basis for national economic leadership. For example, Murmann (2006) describes the rise of chemistry in Germany in the 19th century, Bush (1945) foresaw the rise of computing in the US in the mid 20th century, and finally, the product quality and innovation management movements in Japan provides a more recent example. In these cases, the key to success was government, industry, and academic collaboration. Today, nanotechnology, biochemistry, computational biology, and service science offer the possibilities for such collaborations around emerging areas of science. However, of these four, only service science seeks to understand in general the complex sociotechnical dimensions of using new knowledge to enable new value creating systems. The full benefits of technological inventions cannot be realized without the development of new service system networks that carry the invention into the market. Understanding the science of service systems holds the potential to rapidly realize the value potential inherent in technological inventions, as well as to help prioritize which technological inventions might be poised to provide the most benefit to business and society.

SUMMARY

In sum, this article has attempted to provide an outline and set of preliminary references to better understand the emergence of Service Science, Management, Engineering, and Design (SSMED). Service science is at the beginning of the beginning, and a great deal of work remains to integrate across the disciplines. As a next step, we invite others to use the ten basic concepts to create a more integrated view of existing disciplines. Finally, we invite academics around the world to establish service system design lab networks in conjunction with practitioner partners from business, government, and non-profit agencies, and seek answers to the foundational questions in the context of specific service systems in which they live and work.

Categorization of the References

Each of the references below has been given a primary mapping key number (1-14) as well as a list of secondary mapping key numbers (1-14) into each section of this article. The 15th category number indicates a "must read reference." We hope to encourage this *interdisciplinary service science reference categorization* to stimulate important connections in the emerging service science community.

1. service science researchers and students of service
2. service science practitioners and other practitioners
3. economists, historians, mathematicians
4. marketing professionals
5. operations professionals
6. political scientist, legal professionals
7. designers, artists, innovators
8. social scientists, anthropologists, cognitive scientists
9. engineers, technologists
10. computer scientists, linguists
11. organization theorists, procurement specialists
12. managers, investors, strategists, mathematicians
13. entrepreneurs, professors, lab instructors
14. systems theorists, leaders, general scientists

For example, consider the reference to the book that is of primary interest to economists (3), as well as organization theorists (11) and managers (12):

Milgrom, P. & Roberts, J. (1992) Economics, Organization, and Management. Upper Saddle River, NJ: Prentice Hall. [3 (11 12)]

An online version of all references (with quotations) is maintained at: http://www.cob.sjsu.edu/ssme/refmenu.asp

ACKNOWLEDGMENT

Support from IBM, San José State University, and NSF grant IIS-0527770 2006-09 is gratefully acknowledged.

REFERENCES

Abbot, A. (2001). *Chaos of Disciplines*. Chicago, IL: University of Chicago Press. 14 (3 8)

Adams, J. (1995/2000). *Risk*. London, UK: Routledge. 1 (12 15)

Afuh, A. (2004). *Business Models: A Strategic Management Approach*. New York, NY: McGraw-Hill Irwin. 1, (12)

Albrecht, K., & Zemke, R. (1985). *Service America!* New York, NY: Warner Books. 12 (3)

Alter, S. (2002). *Information Systems: The Foundations of e-Business*. Upper Saddle River, NJ: Prentice Hall. 10, (12)

Alter, S. (2006). *The Work System Method: Connecting People, Processes, and IT for Business Results*. Larkspur, CA: Work Systems Press. 2 (10 15)

Alter, S. (2008). Service Systems Fundamentals: Work systems, value chains and life cycle. *IBM Systems Journal*, 47(1). 1 (11)

Anderson, C. (2006). *The Long Tail: Why the Future of Business Is Selling Less of More*. New York, NY: Hyperion. 12 (4)

Anderson, J. C., Narus, J. A. Narus, & van Rossum, W. (2006). Customer Value Propositions in Business Markets. *Harvard Business Review*, 84(3), 90-99. 1 (4 15)

Argote, L. (2005). *Organizational Learning: Creating, Retaining and Transferring Knowledge*. New York, NY: Springer. 11 (1 15)

Argyris, C. (1992/1999). *On Organizational Learning*. Second Edition. Malden, MA: Blackwell. 11 (8 12)

Argyris, C., & Schon, D. A. (1996). Organizational *Learning II: Theory, Method, Practice*. New York, NY: Addison-Wesley. 11 (12)

Arrow, K. J. (1974). *The Limits of Organization*. New York, NY: W.W. Norton & Company. 3 (6)

Arthur, W. B. (1994). *Increasing Returns and Path Dependence in the Economy.* Ann Arbor, MI: University of Michigan Press. 3 (1)

Baldwin, C. Y., & Clark, K. B. (2000). *Design Rules: Volume 1. The Power of Modularity.* Cambridge, MA: MIT Press. 7 (3)

Barley, S. R., & Orr, J. E. (1997). Introduction: The Neglected Workforce. In S. R. Barley & J. E. Orr (Ed.), *Between Craft and Science: Technical Work in U.S. Settings.* Ithaca, NY: Cornell University Press. 8 (3)

Barlow, S., Parry, S., & Faulkner, M. (2005). *Sense and Respond: The Journey to Customer Purpose*. New York, NY: Palgrave/MacMillan. 4 (11)

Barnard, C. I. (1938/1968). *The Functions of the Executive*. Thirtieth Anniversary Edition. Boston, MA: Harvard University Press. 1 (11 12)

Bastiat, F. (1848/1964). *Selected Essays on Political Economy*, Patrick S. Sterling, trans, G. B. de Huzar (Ed.). Princeton, NJ: D. Van Nordstrand. 3 (6 8 11)

Bastiat, F. (1850/1979). Economic *Harmonies.* Irvington-on-Hudson, NY: The Foundation for Economics Education. 3 (6 8 11)

Baumol, W. J. (2002). Services as Leaders and the Leader of the Services. In J. Gadrey, & F. Gallouj (Ed.), *Productivity, Innovation and Knowledge in Services: New Economic & Socio-Economic Approaches,* (pp. 147-163). Cheltenham, UK: Edward Elgar, 3 (1)

Baumol, W. J., Litan, R. E., & Schramm, C. J. (2007). *Good Capitalism, Bad Capitalism, and the Economies of Growth and Prosperity*. New Haven, CT: Yale University Press. 11 (3)

Bausch, K. C. (2001). *The Emerging Consensus in Social Systems Theory*. New York, NY: Kluwer. 14 (1)

Becker, G. S. (1976/1990). *The Economic Approach to Human Behavior*. Chicago, IL: University of Chicago Press. 3 (8 15)

Beinhocker, E. D. (2006). *The Origin of Wealth: Evolution, Complexity, and the Radical Remaking of Economics*. Cambridge, MA: Harvard Business School Press. 3 (8 1 14 15)

Bell, D. (1973/1999). The *Coming of the Post-Industrial Society: A Venture in Social Forecasting.* New York, NY: Basic. 12 (3)

Beniger, J. R. (1986). *The Control Revolution: Technological and Economic Origins of the Information Society.* Cambridge, MA: Harvard University Press. 9 (3 10)

Benkler, Y. (2007). *The Wealth of Networks: How Social Production Transforms Markets and Freedom*. New Haven, CT: Yale University Press. 3 (10 8)

Berger, P. L., & Luckmann, T. (1967). *The Social Construction of Reality: A Treatise in the Sociology of Knowledge*. New York, NY: Anchor. 8 (1 15)

Bernstein, P. L. (1998). *Against the Gods: The Remarkable Story of Risk*. New York, NY: Wiley. 12 (3)

Berry, L. L. (1995). *On Great Service: A Framework for Action*. New York, NY: Free Press. 4 (12)

Bitner, M. J., Ostrom, A. L., & Morgan, F. N. (2007). Service Blueprinting: A Practical Tool for Service Innovation. Working Paper, Center for Services Leadership, Arizona State University.

Bohn, R., & Jaikumar, R. (2005). *From Filing and Fitting to Flexible Manufacturing*. Hanover, MA: Now Publishers Inc. 3 (9 5)

Boisot, M. H. (2002). *Knowledge Assets: Securing Competitive Advantage in the Information Economy*. Oxford, UK: Oxford University Press. 1 (10 15)

Bryson, J. R., Daniels, P. W., & Warf, B. (2004). *Service Worlds: People, Organizations, and Technology.* New York, NY: Routledge. 3 (8 9 10 11)

Buchanan, M. (2001). *Ubiquity: Why Catastrophes Happen.* New York, NY: Three River Press. 14 (3)

Buchanan, M. (2007). *The Social Atom: Why the rich get richer, cheaters get caught, and your neighbors usually look like you.* New York, NY: Bloomsbury. 8 (14)

Bush, V. (1945). As We May Think. *The Atlantic Monthly,* 176(1), 101-108 (July). 10 (12)

Castells, M. (2004). *The Network Society: A Cross-cultural Perspective*. Cheltenham, UK: Edward Elger. 8 (3 10 11 12)

Chandler, A. D. (1977). *The Visible Hand: The Managerial Revolution in American Business*. Cambridge, MA: Belknap/Harvard University Press. 3 (11 12)

Chase, R. B., Jacobs, F. R., & Aquilano, N. J. (2004). *Operations Management for Competitive Advantage.* Instructor's Edition. Tenth Edition. New York, NY: McGraw Hill Irwin. 2 (5 15)

Checkland, P., & Holwell, S. (1998/2005). *Information, Systems, and Information Systems: Making Sense of the Field.* Chichester, UK: Wiley. 10 (1 14 15)

Chesbrough, H. (2005). Toward a science of services (in Breakthrough Ideas of 2005). *Harvard Business Review*, 83(2), 17-54. 1 (14)

Chesbrough, H. (2006). *Open Business Models: How to thrive in the New Innovation Landscape*. Boston, MA: Harvard Business School Press. 7 (12)

Chesbrough, H., & Spohrer, J. (2006). A research manifesto for services science. *Communications of the ACM*, 49(7), 35-40. 1 (14)

Childe, V. G. (1936/2003). *Man Makes Himself.* Nottingham, UK: Spokesman/Watts. 3 (8)

Christopher, M., Payne, A., & Ballantyne, D. (1991). *Relationship Marketing: Bringing quality, customer service, and marketing together.* London, UK: Butterworth-Heinemann. 4 (12)

Christopher, W. F. (2007). *Holistic Management: Managing What Matters for Company Success.* Hoboken, NJ: Wiley-Interscience. 14 (1 11 12 15)

Clark, C. (1940/1957). *Conditions of Economic Progress*. Third Edition. New York, NY: Macmillan. 3 (11)

Clippinger, J. H., III. (1999). *The Biology of Business: Decoding the Natural Laws of Enterprise*. Jossey-Bass. 14 (3 11)

Coase, R. H. (1937). The Nature of the Firm. *Economica*, 4, 386-405. 3 (11)

Coase, R. H. (1990). *The Firm, the Market, and the Law*. Chicago, IL: University of Chicago Press. 3 (6 11)

Cohen, L., & Young, A. (2006). *Multisourcing: Moving Beyond Outsourcing to Achieve Growth and Agility*. Boston, MA: Harvard Business School Press. 11 (6 12 15)

Cohen, S. S., & Zysman, J. (1988). *Manufacturing Matters: The Myth of the Post-Industrial Economy*. New York, NY: Basic. 3 (10 13)

Collins, H., Evans, R., & Gorman, M. (2007). Trading zones and interactional expertise. *Studies in History and Philosophy of Science*, 39(1). 13 (8)

Collins, H., & Kusch, M. (1999). The *Shape of Actions: What Humans and Machines Can Do*. Cambridge, MA: MIT Press. 8 (10 Collins, J (2005). Why Business Thinking is Not the Answer: Good to Great and the Social Sector: A monograph to Accompany *Good to Great. Why Some Companies Make the Leap... and Others Don't*. ISBN-10: 0-9773264-0-3. 12 (13)

Cooper, R. G., & Edgett, S. J. (1999). *Product Development for the Service Sector: Lessons from Market Leaders*. Cambridge, MA: Basic Books. 7 (12)

COSEPUP. (2007). Rising Above the Gathering Storm: Energizing and Employing America for a Brighter Economic Future. Committee on Science, Engineering, and Public Policy (COSEPUP), US National Academies Press. 13 (14)

Csikszentmihalyi, M. (1990). Flow: *The Psychology of Optimal Experience: Steps Toward Enhancing The Quality of Life*. New York, NY: Harper/Perennial. 7 (4 8 13)

Darr, A. (2006). *Selling Technology: The Changing Shape of Sales in an Information Economy*. Ithaca. NY: Cornell University Press. 8 (3 9)

Davis, M. M., & Heineke, J. (2005). *Operations Management: Integrating Manufacturing and Services*. Fifth Edition. Boston, MA: McGraw-Hill Irwin. 2 (5 15)

Dawson, R. (2005). Developing Knowledge-Based Client Relationships: Leadership in Professional Services. New York, NY: Elsevier. 12 (4 8 10)

Deacon, T. W. (1997). *The Symbolic Species: The Co-Evolution of Language and the Brain*. New York, NY: Norton. 10 (3)

Diamond, J. (2005). *Collapse: How Societies Choose to Fail or Succeed*. New York, NY: Viking. 3 (12)

Dixit, A. K. (2004). *Lawlessness and Economics: Alternative Models of Governance*. Princeton, NJ: Princeton University Press. 6 (1 3 11 12 15)

Drucker, P. F. (1993). *Post-Capitalist Society*. New York, NY: Harper Business. 12 (3)

Durkheim, E. (1893/1997). *The Division of Labor in Society*. New York, NY: Free Press. 3 (8)

Fagin, R., Halpern, J. Y., Moses, Y., & Vardi, M. Y. (2003). *Reasoning About Knowledge*. Cambridge, MA: MIT Press. 1 (10 15)

Fitzsimmons, J. A., & Fitzsimmons, M. J. (2007). *Service management: Operations, Strategy, Information Technology*. Sixth Edition. New York, NY: McGraw-Hill Irwin. 2 (5 12 15)

Foster, I., Kesselman, C., & Tuecke, S. (2001). The Anatomy of the Grid: Enabling Scalable Virtual Organizations. *International J. Supercomputer Applications*, 15(3). 10 (6 11)

Freidson, E. (2001). *Professionalism: The Third Logic/On the Practice of Knowledge*. Chicago, IL: University of Chicago Press. 14 (13)

Friedman, D. (1996/2007). A little manifesto on Learning and Economics. URL http://leeps.ucsc.edu/leeps/manifesto. 3 (12)

Friedman, T. L. (2005). *The World is Flat*. Farrar Straus & Giroux. 11 (3)

Gadrey, J., & Gallouj, F. (2002). *Productivity, Innovation and Knowledge in Services: New Economic & Socio-Economic Approaches*. Cheltenham, U.K: Edward Elgar. 3 (5 7)

Ganz, W. (2006). Germany: service engineering. *Communications of the ACM*, 49(7), 79. 9 (2)

Garud, R., Kumaraswamy, A., & Langlois, R. N. (2003). *Managing in the Modular Age: Architectures, Networks, and Organizations*. New York, NY: Blackwell Publishing. 14 (10 11)

Gershuny, J. (2000). Changing *Times: Work and Leisure in Postindustrial Society*. Oxford, UK: Oxford University Press. 3 (8)

Gilbert, T. F. (1978). *Human Competence: Engineering Worthy Performance.* New York, NY: McGraw Hill. 9 (8)

Glushko, R., & McGrath, T. (2005). *Document Engineering: Analyzing and Designing Documents for Business Informatics and Web Services.* Cambridge, MA: MIT Press. 10 (9 15)

Goldratt, E. M. (1990). *Theory of Constraints*. Great Barrington, MA: North River Press. 11 (14)

Guba, E. G., & Lincoln, Y. S. (1989). *Fourth Generation Evaluation*. London, UK: Sage. 2 (3 4 5 6 7 8 9 12)

Guile, B. R., & Quinn, J. B. (1988). *Technology in Services: Policies for Growth, Trade, and Employment*. Washington, DC: National Academy Press. 9 (6)

Gummesson, E. (2001). Are current research approaches in marketing leading us astray? *Marketing Theory,* 1(1), 27-48. 2 (4 11 13 14)

Gummesson, E. (2003). All research is interpretive! *Journal of Business & Industrial Marketing*, (18)6/7, 482-492. 2 (4 11 13 14)

Gummesson, E. (2007). Exit Services Marketing – Enter Service Marketing. *The Journal of Customer Behaviour,* 6(2), 113-141. 4 (12)

Gummesson, E. (2007). Case study research and network theory: birds of a feather. *Qualitative Research in Organizations and Management: An International Journal,* 2(3), 226-248. 2 (4 11 14)

Gustafsson, A., & Johnson, M. D. (2003). *Competing in a Service Economy: How to Create Competitive Advantage Through Service Development and Innovation*. San Francisco, CA: Wiley/ Jossey-Bass. 7 (12)

Gutek, B., & Welsh, T. (2000). *The Brave New Service Strategy – Aligning Customer Relationships, Market Strategies, and Business Structure.* New York, NY: AMACOM. 12 (3 4 8 11)

Gutek, B. A. (1995). *The Dynamics of Service: Reflections on the Changing Nature of Customer/ Provider Interactions*. San Francico, CA: Jossey-Bass Publishers. 1 (3 4 8 10 11 12 15)

Hall, A. D. (1962). *A Methodology for Systems Engineering*. Princeton, NJ: D. Van Nostrand Company. 14 (9 15)

Handy, C. (1989). *The Age of Unreason*. Cambridge, MA: Harvard Business School Press. 12 (8 11)

Hawley, A. H. (1986). *Human Ecology: A Theoretical Essay*. Chicago, IL: University of Chicago Press. 14 (3 8 11)

Heizer, J., & Render, B. (2004). *Principles of Operations Management*. Upper Saddle Creek, NJ: Pearson Education. 5 (2)

Helpman, E. (2004). *The Mystery of Economic Growth.* Cambridge, MA: Harvard University Press. 3 (5)

Heritage, J. (1984/1989). *Garfinkel and Enthnomethodology.* Cambridge, UK: Polity Press. 8 (2 11)

Herzenberg, S. A., Alic, J. A., & Wial, H. (2000). *New Rules for a New Economy: Employment and Opportunity in Postindustrial America*. Ithaca, NY: ILR Press Books, Cornell University Press. 3 (6 12)

Heskett, J. L., Sasser, W. E., Jr., & Schlesinger, L. A. (1997). *The Service Profit Chain*. New York, NY: The Free Press. 2 (12)

Hidaka, K. (2006). Trends in services sciences in Japan and abroad. *Science & Technology Trends: Quarterly Review*, 19, 35-47 (April). 1 (10)

Honebein, P. C., & Cammarano, R. F. (2005). *Creating Do-It-Yourself Customers: How Great Customer Experiences Build Great Companies*. Mason, OH: Thomson. 4 (7)

Hoopes, J. (2003). *False Prophets: The Gurus Who Created Modern Management and Why Their Ideas are Bad for Business Today*. Cambridge, MA: Perseus Books. 3 (12)

Hopp, W. J., & Spearman, M. L. (1996). *Factory Physics: Foundations of Manufacturing Management*. Boston, MA: Irwin McGraw-Hill. 5 (2 14)

Horn, P. (2005). The New Discipline of Services Science. *BusinessWeek*, January 21, 2005. 14 (10)

Hunt, S. D. (2000). *A General Theory of Competition: Resources, Competences, Productivity, Economic Growth*. Thousand Oaks, CA: Sage Publications. 3 (1 11)

Huntzinger, J. R. (2007). *Lean Cost Management: Accounting for Lean by Establishing Flow.* Fort Lauderdale, FL: Ross Publishing. 12 (2 9)

IfM & IBM. (2007). Succeeding through Service Innovation: A Discussion Paper. Cambridge, United Kingdom: University of Cambridge Institute for Manufacturing. ISBN: 978-1-902546-59-8. 1 (14)

Johansson, F. (2006). *The Medici Effect: What Elephants and Epidemics Can Teach Us About Innovation*. Boston, MA: Harvard Business School Press. 13 (7)

Johnson, S. (2001). *Emergence: The connected lives of ants, brains, cities, and software.* New York, NY: Scribner. 14 (11)

Johnston, D. C. (2007). *Free Lunch: How The Wealthiest Americans Enrich Themselves At Government Expense (And Stick You With The Bill)*. New York, NY: Portfolio. 6 (3)

Kaufmann, D., Kraay, A., & Mastruzzi, M. (2003). Governance Matters III: Governance Indicators for 1996–2002. World Bank, World Bank Policy Research Working Paper 3106. Available at: http://www.worldbank.org/wbi/governance/pubs/govmatters2001.htm 6 (12)

Kessler, A. (2005). *How We Got Here: A Slightly Irreverent History of Technology and Markets.* New York, NY: Harper Collins. 3 (6 9 11 12)

Khalil, T. (2000). *Management of Technology: The Key to Competitiveness and Wealth Creation.* Boston, MA: McGraw-Hill. 9 (7 12)

Kim, W. C., & Mauborgne, R. (2005). *Blue Ocean Strategy: How to Create Uncontested Market Space and Make the Competition Irrelevant.* Boston, MA: Harvard Business School Press. 7 (12)

Kwan, S. K., & Freund, L. (2007). Developing a Service Science, Management and Engineering (SSME) Program at SJSU. 13 (14)

Langlois, R. N., & Robertson, P. L. (1995). *Firms, Markets, and Economic Change*. London, UK: Routledge. 3 (6 11)

Laszlo, E. (2002). *The Systems View of the World.* Cresskill, NJ: Hampton Press. 14 (13)

Laszlo, E. (2007). *Science and the Akashic Field: An Integrated Theory of Everything*. Rochester, VT: Inner Traditions. 14 (13)

Latour, B. (2007). *Reassembling the Social: An Introduction to Actor-Network-Theory* (Clarendon Lectures in Management Studies). Oxford, UK: Oxford University. 8 (11)

Levinson, M. (2006). *The Box: How the Shipping Container Made the World Smaller and the World Economy Bigger.* Princeton, NJ: Princeton University Press. 5 (3 9 11)

Levitt, T. (1976). The Industrialization of Service. *Harvard Business Review*. 54(5), 63-74. 12 (9)

Levy, F., & Murnane, R. J. (2005). *The New Division of Labor: How Computers Are Creating the Next Job Market*. Princeton, NJ: Princeton University Press. 3 (11)

Lewis, W. W. (2004). *The Power of Productivity: Wealth, Poverty, and the Threat to Global Stability.* Chicago, IL: University of Chicago Press. 5 (3 6)

Lovelock, C. (2007). *Services Marketing: People, Technology, Strategy*. Sixth Edition. Upper Saddle River, NJ: Pearson Education. 4 (2 8 9 10 11 12 15)

Lovelock, C., & Gummesson, E. (2004). Whither service marketing? In search of a new paradigm and fresh perspectives. *Journal of Service Research*, 7(1), 20-41. 4 (12)

Lusch, R. F., & Vargo, S. L. (2006). *The Service-Dominant Logic of Marketing: Dialog, Debate and Directions*. Armonk, NY: M.E. Sharpe. 4 (12 15)

Maglio, P. P., Kreulen, J., Srinivasan, S., & Spohrer, J. (2006). Service systems, service scientists, SSME, and innovation. *Communications of the ACM*, 49(7), 81 – 85. 14 (1)

Maglio, P. P., & Spohrer, J. (2006). (in press). SSME. *Production and Operations Management*, *14*(13).

Malone, T. W. (2004). *The Future of Work: How the New Order of Business Will Shape Your Organization, Your Management Style, and Your Life*. Cambridge, MA: Harvard Business School Press. 11 (3 6 8 10 12)

Mandelbaum, A., & Zeltyn, S. (2008). Service engineering of call centers; Research, Teaching, and Practice. In Hefly, B., & Murphy W. (Ed.), *Service Science Management and Engineer: Education for the 21st Century,* (pp. 317-328). New York, NY: Springer. 9 (10)

March, J., & Simon, H. (1958/2003). *Organizations*. Second Edition. Cambridge, MA: Blackwell. 11 (6 8 12 14)

March, J. G. (1988). *Decisions and Organizations*. New York, NY: Basil Blackwell. 6 (11 12)

March, J. G. (1991). Exploration and exploitation in organizational learning. *Organizational Science*, 2(1), 71-87. 11 (5 7 12)

March, J. G. (1999). *The Pursuit of Organizational Intelligence*. Malden, MA: Blackwell. 11 (14)

Marks, E. A., & Bell, M. (2006). *Service-Oriented Architecture: A Planning and Implementation Guide for Business and Technology.* Hoboken, NJ: Wiley. 10 (12)

Marshall, A. (1890/2006). *Principles of Economics*. Abridged Edition. New York, NY: Cosimo. 3 (6 8)

McGahan, A. M. (2004). *How Industries Evolve: Principles for Achieving and Sustaining Superior Performance*. Boston, MA: Harvard Business School Press. 7 (3 11)

McKenna, C. D. (2006). *The World's Newest Profession: Management Consulting in the Twentieth Century* (Cambridge Studies in the Emergence of Global Enterprise). Cambridge, UK: Cambridge University Press. 13 (8 11 12 14 15)

Mendelson, H., & Ziegler, J. (1999). *Survival of the Smartest: Managing Information for Rapid Action and World-Class Performance*. New York, NY: Wiley. 12 (10 11)

Milgrom, P., & Roberts, J. (1992). *Economics, Organization, and Management*. Upper Saddle River, NJ: Prentice Hall. 3 (11 12)

Mill, J. S. (1929). *Principles of the Political Economy*. London, UK: Longmans Green. (Available on Google Books) 3 (6 8)

Monahan, B., Pym, D., Taylor, R., Tofts, C., & Yearworth, M. (2006). Grand Challenges for Systems and Services Sciences. Paper prepared for FET/FP7 Workshop, Brussels (January 31, 2006). Available as HP Labs Technical Report, HPL-2006-99, from http://www.hpl.hp.com/techreports/2006/HPL-2006-99.pdf 14 (9 10)

Moore, G. (2005). *Dealing with Darwin: How Great Companies Innovate at Every Phase of Their Evolution.* New York, NY: Portfolio/Penguin Group. 7 (11 12)

Morgan, G. (1997). *Images of Organization.* Thousand Oaks, CA. *Sage (Atlanta, Ga.), 11*(8).

Moulton Reger, S. J. (2006). *Can Two Rights Make a Wrong? Insights from IBM's Tangible Culture Approach.* Upper Saddle River, NJ: Pearson/IBM Press. 8 (10 11)

Mulgan, G. (2006). The Process of Social Innovation. Innovations, 145-162 (Spring). URL: http://www.youngfoundation.org 13 (6 7)

Murmann, J. P. (2006). *Knowledge and Competitive Advantage: The Coevolution of Firms, Technology, and National Institutions* (Cambridge Studies in the Emergence of Global Enterprise). Cambridge, UK: Cambridge University Press. 3 (6 7 8 9 10 11)

Nagle, T. T., & Holden, R. K. (1987/2002). *The Strategy and Tactics of Pricing: A Guide to Profitable Decision Making.* Third Edition. Upper Saddle River. NJ: Prentice Hall. 12 (4)

Nambisan, S., & Sawhney, M. (2008). *The Global Brain: Your Roadmap for Innovating Faster and Smarter in a Networked World.* Saddle River, NJ: Pearson Education, Wharton School Publishing. 7 (6 11 12)

Neftci, S. N. (2004). *Principles of Financial Engineering.* New York, NY: Elsevier. 9 (12 15)

Nelson, R. R., & Winter, S. G. (1982). *An Evolutionary Theory of Economic Change.* Cambridge, MA: Harvard University Press. 3 (8 14)

Newnan, D. G., Lavelle, J. P., & Eschenbach, T. G. (2003). *Essentials of Engineering Economics.* Second Edition. Oxford, UK: Oxford University Press. 9 (3 12)

Norman, D. A. (1993). *Things That Make Us Smart: Defending Human Attributes in the Age of the Machine.* New York, NY: Addison Wesley. 7 (8 9)

Normann, R. (2001). *Reframing Business: When the Map Changes the Landscape.* Chichester, New Sussex: Wiley. 1 (2 4 6 7 8 12 13 14 15)

North, D. C. (2005). *Understanding the process of economic change.* Princeton, NJ: Princeton University Press. 1 (3 6 11 15)

Ormerod, P. (2005). *Why Most Things Fail: Evolution, Extinction, and Economics.* London, UK: Faber and Faber. 3 (11 12)

Palmisano, S.J. (2006). The Globally Integrated Enterprise. *Foreign Affairs*, 127-136 (May/June). 11 (12)

Park, C. S. (2004). *Fundamentals of Engineering Economics.* Upper Saddle River, NJ: Pearson. 9 (2 3 12)

Penrose, E. (1959/1995). *The Theory of the Growth of the Firm.* Third Edition. Oxford, UK: Oxford University Press. 3 (8 11 12)

Pine, B. J., II, & Gilmore, J. H. (1999). *The Experience Economy: Work is Theatre and Every Business a Stage.* Boston, MA: Harvard Business School Press. 7 (3 4 8 12)

Porat, M. U. (1977). The Information Economy: Definition and Measurement. US Department of Commerce, Office of Telecommunications, OT Special Publication, 77-12(1). 3 (8 10 11)

Prahalad, C. K. (2004). *The Future of Competition. Co-Creating Unique Value with Customers*. Boston, MA: Harvard Business School Press. 7 (4)

Prencipe, A., Davies, A., & Hobday, M. (2005). *The Business of Systems Integration*. Oxford, UK: Oxford University Press. 9 (3 11 12)

Quinn, J. B., Baruch, J. J., & Paquette, P. C. (1987). Technology in Services. *Scientific American*, 257(2) (December). 9 (4 10 11 12)

Quinn, J. B., & Paquette, P. C. (1990). Technology in services: Creating organizational revolutions. *Sloan Management Review*, 31(2), 67-78. 11 (4 9 10 12)

Research, I. B. M. (2004). "Services science: a new academic discipline?" A 120-page report of a two-day summit entitled Architecture of On-Demand Business, May 17-18, 2004. 14 (10 11 12)

Ricardo, D. (1817/2004). *The Principles of Political Economy and Taxation*. Mineola, NY: Dover Publications. 1 (3 6 8 9 12)

Richardson, P. J., & Boyd, R. (2005). *Not By Genes Alone: How Culture Transformed Human Evolution*. Chicago, IL: University of Chicago Press. 8 (3 10)

Riordin, J. (1962). *Stochastic Service Systems*. New York, NY: Wiley. 14 (1 5 9)

Roberts, J. (2004). *The Modern Firm: Organizational Design for Performance and Growth*. Oxford, UK: Oxford University Press. 11 (3 6 8 12 15)

Roughgarden, T. (2005). *Selfish Routing and the Price of Anarchy*. Cambridge, MA: MIT Press. 1 (3 5 6 8 9 10 11)

Rouse, W. B. (2006). *Enterprise Transformation: Understanding and Enabling Fundamental Change*. Hoboken, NJ: Wiley. 14 (2 8 9 10 11 12)

Rust, R., Zeithaml, V., & Lemon, K. (2000). *Driving Customer Equity: How Customer Lifetime Value is Reshaping Corporate Strategy*. New York, NY: Free Press. 4 (12 15)

Sampson, S. E. (2001). *Understanding Service Businesses: Applying Principles of the Unified Services Theory*. Second Edition. Wiley. 2 (4 5 12 14 15)

Sampson, S. E., & Froehle, C. M. (2006). Foundations and Implications of a Proposed Unified Services Theory. *Production and Operations Management*, 15(2), 329-343. 14 (4 5 12)

Sawyer, R. K. (2005). *Social Emergence: Societies as Complex Systems*. Cambridge, UK: Cambridge University Press. 14 (6 8 11)

Say, J. B. (1821). *A Treatise on the Political Economy*. Boston, MA: Wells and Lilly. (In Google Books) 6 (3)

Scheer, A., & Spath, D. (2004). *Computer-Aided Service Engineering*. Berlin, Germany: Springer. In German 9 (7)

Schmenner, R. W. (1986). How Can Service Businesses Survive and Prosper? *Sloan Management Review*, 27(3). 2 (4 5 12)

Schmitt, B. H. (2003). *Customer Experience Management: A Revolutionary Approach to Connecting With Your Customers*. Hoboken, NJ: Wiley. 4 (7 12)

Schneider, B., & Bowen, D. E. (1995). *Winning the Service Game*. Boston, MA: Harvard Business School Press. 4 (8 11 12)

Schneider, B., & White, S. S. (2003). *Service Quality: Research Perspectives*. Thousand Oaks, CA: Sage. 4 (8 11 12)

Scott, W. R. (1981/2003). *Organizations: Rational, Natural, and Open Systems*. Fifth Edition. Upper Saddle River, NJ: Prentice Hall. 11 (6 12)

Seabright, P. (2005). *The Company of Strangers: A Natural History of Economic Life.* Princeton, NJ: Princeton University. 3 (8 11)

Sen, A. (2000). *Development As Freedom.* New York, NY: Anchor/Random House. 3 (6 8 11 13 15)

Sepulveda, J. A., Souder, W. E., & Gottfried, B. S. (1984). *Theory and Problems of Engineering Economics.* New York, NY: McGraw Hill/ Schaum's Outline Series. 9 (2 3 12)

Shostack, G.L. (1982). How to Design a Service. *European Journal of Marketing,* 16(1), 49-63. 7 (2 4 8 15)

Simon, H. A. (1945/1997). *Administrative Behavior: A study of decision-making processes in administrative organizations.* New York, NY: Free Press. 11 (3 6 8 10 12 14)

Slywotzky, A., Wise, W., & Weber, K. (2003). *How to Grow When Markets Don't.* New York, NY: Warner Business Books. 7 (4 11 12)

Smith, A. (1776/1904). *An Inquiry into the Nature and Causes of the Wealth of Nations.* London, UK: W. Strahan & T, Cadell, 3 (1 5 8 11)

Solow, R. (1956). A Contribution to the Theory of Economic Growth. *Quarterly Journal of Economics,* February. 3 (5 6 7 8 9 10 11 12)

Spath, D. (2007). *Advances in Services Innovations.* New York, NY: Springer. 7 (2 9)

Spitzer, D. R. (2007). *Transforming Performance Measurement: Rethinking the Way We Measure and Drive Organizational Success.* New York, NY: American Management Association. 1 (4 5 6 7 8 11 12)

Spohrer, J., Anderson, L., Pass, N., & Gruhl, D. (Submitted). Service Science. *The Journal of Grid Computing.* 10 (1)

Spohrer, J., & Kwan, S. K. (2008forthcoming). Service Science, Management, Engineering, and Design (SSMED): Outline & References. In Ganz, W., & Spath, D. (Eds.), *The Future of Services – Trends and Perspectives.* Stuttgart, Germany: Frunhofer-Institut Arbeitswirtschaft und Organisation.

Spohrer, J., & Maglio, P. P. (In Press). The emergence of service science. *Production and Operations Management.* 14 (13)

Spohrer, J, Maglio, P. P., Bailey, J., & Gruhl, D. (2007). Towards a Science of Service Systems. *Computer,* 40(1), 71-77. 1 (14 15)

Spohrer, J., Maglio, P. P., McDavid, D., & Cortada, D. (2006). NBIC Convergence and Coevolution: Towards a Services Science to Increase Productivity Capacity. In W. S. Bainbridge & M. C. Roco (Ed.), *Managing Nano-Bio-Info-Cogno Innovations.* The Netherlands: Springer. 14 (3 9)

Spohrer, J., & Riecken, D. (2006). Special Issue: Services science. *Communications of the ACM.* 49(7), 30 – 87 (July). 14 (3 4 5 6 7 8 9 10 11 12 13)

Spohrer, J., Vargo, S., Maglio, P. M., & Caswell, N. (submitted). The service system is the basic abstraction of service science. HICSS Conference. 1 (14)

Stacey, R. D. (2003). *Strategic Management and Organizational Dynamics: The Challenge of Complexity.* Fourth Edition. Harlow, England: Prentice Hall/Pearson Education. 12 (11 14)

Sterman, J. D. (2000). *Business Dynamics: Systems Thinking and Modeling for a Complex World.* Irwin Boston, MA: McGraw-Hill. 13 (1 2 3 4 5 6 7 8 9 10 11 12 14 15)

Subramanian, K. (Subbu) (2000). *The System Approach: A Strategy to Survive and Succeed in the Global Economy.* Cincinnati, OH: Modern Machine Shop/Hanser Gardner Publications. 14 (12)

Taleb, N. N. (2004). *Fooled by Randomness: The Hidden Role of Chance in Life and in the Markets.* Second Edition. New York, NY: Texere/Thomson. 12 (8)

Tapscott, D. (2003). *The Naked Corporation: How the Age of Transparency Will Revolutionize Business.* New York, NY: Free Press. 11 (2 6 10 12)

Tapscott, D., & Williams, A. D. (2006). *Wikinomics: How Mass Collaboration Changes Everything.* New York, NY: Portfolio/Penguin. 6 (3 4 8 10 11 12)

Teboul, J. (2006). *Service Is Front Stage: Positioning Services for Value Advantage.* INSEAD Business Press, Palgrave MacMillan. 2 (4 5 12 15)

Tien, J. M., & Berg, D. (2007). A Calculus for Services Innovation. *J Sys Sci Syst Eng*, 16(2), 129-165. 7 (13 14)

Tien, J. M., & Berg, D. (under review). On Services Research and Education. *Journal of Systems Science and Systems Engineering.* 14 (13)

Triplett, J. E., & Bosworth, B. P. (2004). *Productivity in the U.S. Services Sector: New Sources of Economic Growth.* Washington, DC: The Brookings Institute. 5 (3 8 11)

Vargo, S. L. (In Press). On A Theory of Markets And Marketing: From Positively Normative To Normatively Positive. *Australasian Marketing Journal.* 4 (3)

Vargo, S. L., & Lusch, R.F. (2004). Evolving to a New Dominant Logic for Marketing. *Journal of Marketing*, 68, 1-17. 1 (3 4)

Vargo, S. L., & Lusch, R. F. (2006). Service-Dominant Logic: What It Is, What It Is Not, What It Might Be. In R.F. Lusch & S. L. Vargo, S. L. (Ed.) *The Service-Dominant Logic of Marketing: Dialog, Debate, and Directions.* Armonk, NY: M.E. Sharpe. 4 (1 3)

Vargo, S. L., & Lusch, R. F. (In Press a). From Goods To Service(s): Divergences And Convergences Of Logics. *Industrial Marketing Management.* 4 (1 3)

Vargo, S. L., & Lusch, R. F. (In Press b). Service-Dominant Logic: Further Evolution. *Journal of the Academy of Marketing Science.* 4 (1 3)

Vargo, S. L., & Morgan, F. W. (2005). An Historical Reexamination of the Nature of Exchange: The Service-Dominant Perspective. *Journal of Macromarketing*, 25 (1), 42-53. 4 (1 3)

von Bertalanffy, L. (1976). *General System Theory: Foundation, Development, Applications.* George Braziller. 14 (11)

von Mises, L. (1998). *Human Action: A Treatise on Economics* (Scholars Edition). Ludwig Von Mises Institute. 3 (1 8 15)

Wallin, J. (2006). *Business Orchestration: Strategic Leadership in the Era of Digital Convergence.* Hoboken, NJ: Wiley. 12 (6 9 10 11)

Watts, D. J. (2003). *Six Degrees: The Science of a Connected Age.* New York, NY: W.W. Norton & Company. 14 (1 15)

Weber, M. (1978). *Economy and Society.* Berkeley, CA: University of California Press. 3 (6 8 11)

Weber, S. (2004). *The Success of Open Source.* Cambridge, MA: Harvard Business Press. 6 (10)

Weinberg, G. M. (1975/2001). *An Introduction to General Systems Thinking* (Silver Anniversary Edition). Dorset House Publishing. 14 (13 15)

Williamson, O. E. (1985). *The Economic Institutions of Capitalism.* New York, NY: Free Press. 6 (3 8 12)

Williamson, O. E. (1999). *The Mechanisms of Governance.* Oxford, UK: Oxford University Press. 6 (1 3 11 12 15)

Wilson, E. O. (1998). *Consilience: The Unity of Knowledge*. New York, NY: Borzoi/Knopf. 14 (8)

Womack, J. P., & Jones, D. T. (2005). *Lean Solutions: How Companies and Customers Can Create Value and Wealth Together*. New York, NY: Free Press. 5 (2 4 8 11 12 15)

Woods, B. M., & Degarmo, E. P. (1953/1959). *Introduction to Engineering Economy.* Second Edition. New York, NY: Macmillan. 9 (2 3 12)

Wooldridge, M. (2002). *An Introduction to MultiAgent Systems*. Chichester, UK: John Wiley. 10 (1 2 6 8 11 13 14 15)

Wright, R. (2000). *Non-Zero: The Logic of Human Destiny*. New York, NY: Vintage/Random House. 3 (6 1)

Young, H. P. (1998/2001). *Individual Strategy and Social Structure: An Evolutionary Theory of Institutions*. Princeton, NJ: Princeton University Press. 11 (1 3 6 8 12 14 15)

Zeithaml, V. A., Bitner, M. J., & Gremler, D. D. (2006). *Services Marketing: Integrating Customer Focus Across the Firm*. 4th Edition. New York, NY: McGraw-Hill Irwin. 4 (2 15)

Zhang, L. (2007). Modern *Technologies in Web Services Research*. Hershey, PA: IGI Publishing. 10 (9 15)

Zuboff, S., & Maxmin, J. (2002). *The Support Economy: Why Corporations are Failing Individuals and the Next Episode of Capitalism*. New York, NY: Penguin. 3 (4 8 12)

ENDNOTES

1. An earlier version of this paper containing quotations accompanying the extensive set of references will appear in (Spohrer & Kwan 2008).
2. See URL http://www.ilo.org/public/english/region/asro/bangkok/public/releases/yr2007/pr07_02sa.htm.

This work was previously published in International Journal of Information Systems in the Service Sector (IJISSS), edited by John Wang, pp. 1-31, copyright 2009 by IGI Publishing (an imprint of IGI Global).

Chapter 13
Access Control Method with XML Databases

Lili Sun
University of Southern Queensland, Australia

Yan Li
University of Southern Queensland, Australia

Hua Wang
University of Southern Queensland, Australia

ABSTRACT

XML documents usually contain private information that cannot be shared by every user communities. It is widely used in web environment. XML database is becoming increasingly important since it consists of XML documents. Several applications for supporting selective access to data are available over the web. Usage control has been considered as the next generation access control model with distinguishing properties of decision continuity. It has been proven efficient to improve security administration with flexible authorization management. Object-oriented database systems represent complex data structure and XML databases may be stored in the objects-oriented database system. Therefore authorization models for XML databases could be used the same the models as object-oriented databases. In this paper, we propose usage control models to access XML databases and compare with an authorization model designed for object-oriented databases. We have analysed the characteristics of various access authorizations and presented detailed models for different kinds of authorizations. Finally, comparisons with related works are analysed.

INTRODUCTION

The extensible markup language (XML) is a standard for describing the structure of information and content on the Internet over the past several years. XML has recently emerged as the most relevant standardization in the area of document representation through markup language (Bertion, 2002). XML is used to store and exchange data in the Internet environment that may include private messages of customers. It overcomes the complexity of Standard Generalized Markup Language (SGML) and the user can define document structures, removing the limit of the fixed

DOI: 10.4018/978-1-60960-138-6.ch013

tags in Hypertext Markup Language (HTML). XML documents support storage of information at different degrees of sensitivity and varying granularity levels.

We identified two levels of authorization, instance level and the Document Type Definition (DTD) level are with which authorizations on XML documents can be defined (Bertion, Castano, Ferrari & Mesiti, 1999; Damiani, Capitani & Samarati, 2002). A DTD is a file which contains a formal definition of a particular type of XML documents. A DTD consists of the element declarations and the attributes declarations. Instance level authorizations denote privileges that are relevant only to a specific document. DTD level authorizations specify the privileges of all documents following a given DTD. XML Schema is an XML-based alternative to DTD (Kudo & Hada, 2000). It supports complex constraints for XML components, such as elements, attributes, datatypes and groups. A well-validated XML document must follow the format specified by one or more schemas. In the access control model the central authority uses XML schemas to specify the format of information to be changed. With the features of XML Schema, a flexible and easy-customized access control model can be achieved.

Access control has been considered as a major issue in information security community since the beginning of the information security discipline (Park & Sandhu, 2002). Through access control, the system can restrict unauthorized access to the resources in the system and guarantees the confidentiality and integrity of the resources. Manage access control for database or other collections of structured data, the traditional access control models, the discretionary and mandatory access control (Damiani, Paraboschi & Samarati, 2002; Damiani, Samarati, Vimercati & Paraboschi, 2001; Kudo & Hada, 2000) have been augmented by various research groups. Usage control is a new access control model which extends traditional access control models and other access control models in many aspects. The term "usage" means usage of rights on digital objects. The main difference between usage control and traditional access control models are the continuity of access decision and the mutability of subject attributes and object attributes (Sandhu & Park, 2003).

A recent development in the database field has been the introduction of semi-structured and self-describing data, collection of the data in XML format called XML Databases (Wang & Osborn, 2004). Some work (Roshan & Ravi, 1993; Wang & Osborn, 2004) on the relationship between securing XML documents and object oriented databases (OODB) has been done. However, we have not found a detailed discussion of how the usage access model can be applied to XML databases. In this paper, we propose authorization models which adopt usage control to manage access XML based databases. Traditional access control, such as the discretionary and mandatory access control, focused on the control of access to server-side objects. They use an algorithm to compute a view of the target XML document based on the user's requirement rights. They make authorization decisions on a subject's access request to target resources before access. However, in usage access control, authorization decisions are not only made before access, but are also repeatly checked during the access period. Meanwhile obligations and conditions become decision factors for the authorization management of XML documents.

The remainder of this paper is organized as follows: Section 2 illustrates the background of XML and XML databases. The usage control model and continuity properties are also introduced in this section. Section 3 is a review of the OODB authorization model. In section 4 we proposed our authorization models for usage control of XML databases. The models include *pre-Authorizations, ongoing-Authorizations, pre-Obligations, ongoing-Obligations, pre-Conditions and ongoing-Conditions*. The differences between this works in this paper from others are discussed in section 5. Finally, Section 6 concludes the paper.

BACKGROUND

XML

XML (Bray, Paoli, Sperberg & Maler, 2000) is a markup language for describing semi-structured information. Semi-structured data is just data that does not fit neatly into the relational model. In XML, data can have an elaborate and intricate structure that is significantly richer and more complex than a table of rows and columns. XML makes possible capturing and expressing data structure as we understand it, without forcing it into an oversimplified structure. XML documents can be classified into two categories: well-formed and valid. A document is said to be well-formed if it follows the grammatical rules of XML. For example, there is exactly one XML element that completely contains all other elements or elements may nest but not overlapped, *etc*. A well-formed document is valid only if it contains a proper DTD in the source and if the document obeys the constraints of that declaration. On the other hand, since XML is a structural transformation, it can transform data represented with one structure to another structure. An example of XML document containing staff information of a company is shown in Example 1.

XML documents not only records the contents of data but also the constraints and relationships between data referring to in Example 1. The element *GeneralInfo* includes *Name, address,* and *email* elements, and *GeneralInfo* element is a sub-element of *staff*. Since an XML document can express complex relationship between data, it can satisfy with various security requirements. XML is used to store and exchange data in the Internet including private messages. Some users may like to access some particular parts of an XML document. In the example shown in Example 1, for *staff* objects everyone can read general information such as *name*, *address*, and *email*. However, the sub-element financial information will be restricted. Therefore user access permission has to be limited according to security policies. This

Example 1. XML Document Example

```
<?xml version= "1.0" encoding= "UTF8"?>
   <StaffInfo xmlns=
      "http://www.company.com/StaffInfo">
     <company name= "computer company">
      <staff StaffId="12345">
       <GeneralInfo>
           <name> Tony Mahanee </name>
           <address> 1 Smart Street </address>
           <email> Tony@hotmail.com</email>
       </GeneralInfo>
       <WorkInfo>
            <workarea>implement</workarea>
            <developarea>research</developarea>
       </WorkInfo>
       <FinancialInfo>$3800</FinancialInfo>
      </staff>
    </staffInfo>
```

example shows that securing XML document is a significant topic for research.

Document Type Definition (DTD) and XML Schema are two main validation specification mechanisms (Bertion & Ferrari, 2002; Sun & Li, 2006). They can be attached to XML documents, specifying the rules that XML documents may follow. An XML Schema is an XML-based alternative to DTD (Zhang, Park & Sandhu, 2003). XML Schemas provide means for defining the structures, contents and semantics of XML documents. XML Schemas are extensible to future additions and are richer and more powerful than DTDs. The example shown in Example 2 displays an XML Schema for a corresponding valid XML instance in Example 1.

XML and Databases

An XML document is a collection of data. It is a self-describable, exchangeable and a tree graphic structure description data set. XML documents fall

Example 2. XML Schema Example

```
<?xml version= "1.0"  encoding= "UTF-8"? >
  <xs:schema
         targetNamespace= "http://www.company.com/StaffInfo"
         xmlns:xs="http://www.w3.org/2001/XMLSchema"
         elementFormDefault= "qualified">
        <xs:annotation>
               <xs:documentation>
                    Staff Information Instance
               </xs:documentation>
        </xs:annotation>
     <xs:element name= "StaffInfo">
       <xs:sequence>
            <xs:element name= "staff"  type= "xs:string"/>
                  <xs:complexType name= "GeneralInfo"/>
                    <xs:sequence>
                         <xs:element name= "name" type= "xs:string"/>
                          <xs:element name= "address"  type= "xs:string"/>
                            <xs:element name= "email"  type= "xs:string"/>
                          </xs:sequence>
                     </xs:complexType>
                <xs:complexType name= "WorkInfo"/>
                  <xs:sequence>
                        <xs:element name="workarea"  type= "xs:string"/>
                       <xs:element name= "developarea"  type= "xs:string"/>
                 </xs:sequence>
               </xs:complexType>
       <xs:element name= "FinancialInfo"  type= "xs:string"/>
       <xs:attribute name= "StaffId"  type= "xs:string"/>
</xs:schema>
```

into two categories: *data-centric* and *document-centric* (Gabillon, 2004; Wang & Tan, 2001). Data-centric documents are those where XML is used as a data transport. For example, dynamic Web pages are a special case of data-centric documents. Document-centric documents are designed for human reading. Examples are books, emails and advertisements. They are characterized by irregular structures and mixed contents.

To store and retrieve data in data-centric documents, you need to know how well structured your data is. For highly structured data, you will use an XML-enabled database for data storage, such as a relational or object-oriented database, and some sort of data transfer software such as middleware (Bourret, 2003). If your data is semi-structured, you may have two choices. You can fit your data into a well-structured database, such as a relational database, or you can store it in a native XML database. The native XML database is specialized for storing XML data and stores all components of the XML model intact (Damiani, Capitani & Samarati, 2002; Park, Sandhu & Schifalacqua 2003). To store and retrieve document-centric documents, you will need a native XML database. Some native XML database models are stored in the relational and object-oriented databases. For example, in the relational database storage Document Object Model (DOM), there are elements, attributes, entity, and other entities cited forms. As traditional databases add native XML capabilities and native XML databases support the storage of document fragments in external (usually relational) databases, the access control models for traditional databases, such as a relational or object-oriented databases and native XML databases could be used in the same way.

Usage Access Control

The usage control is a generalization of access control. It enriches and refines the access control areas in its definition and covers obligations, conditions, continuity (ongoing controls) and mutability (Cao, Sun & Wang, 2005; Park & Sandhu, 2002; Wang, Zhang & Cao 2006; Zhang, Park & Parisi, 2004). Eight core components of the usage control model are subjects, subject attributes, objects, object attributes, rights, authorizations, obligations, and conditions (see Figure 1). Subjects and objects are familiar concepts with the tradition access control. A right is used when a subject access an object in a mode, such as read or write. Subject and object attributes can be used during the access decision process. Subject attributes are identities, group names, roles, memberships, security clearance, and so on. Objects are entities that subjects hold rights on, whereby the subjects can access or use

Figure 1. Components of usage control model

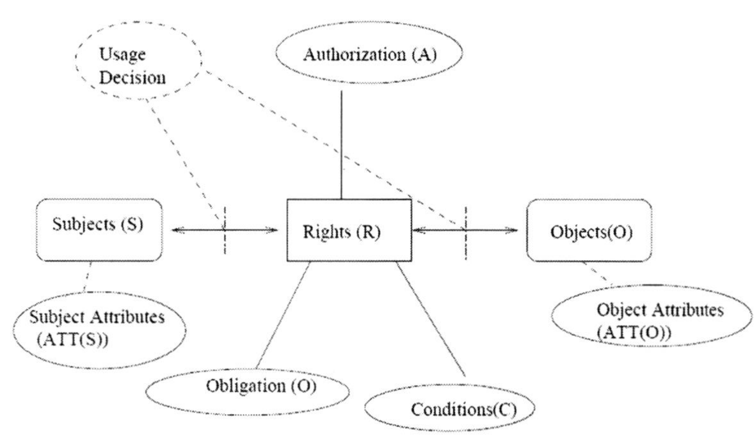

objects. For instance, in an on-line shopping store, a customer can be subject. Price could be an attribute of a book object. Rights are privileges that subjects can hold on objects. The authorizations of rights require associations with subjects and objects. A right represents a mode of access of a subject to an object, such as read or write.

The authorization, obligations and conditions are main components of usage control decisions. In the usage control model, the authorization rule permits or denies the access of a subject to an object based on subject and object attributes. Obligations are performed by subjects or by the system. Conditions are not related to subject or object attributes. They are system environment restrictions.

Authorizations, obligations and conditions are decision factors used to check and determine whether a subject should be allowed to access an object. Obligations and conditions are new concepts that can resolve certain shortcomings that have been in traditional access controls. In general, the authorization of most traditional access controls, such as mandatory, discretionary and role based access control are assumed to be done before access is allowed (Sandhu & Park, 2003). However in the usage control model it extends this for continuous enforcement. Authorizations may require updates on subject and object attributes. The process of continuity properties in usage control model consists of three phrases: before usage, ongoing usage and after usage. To enforce control decisions, we have two different types: pre-decision and ongoing-decision. For mutability, there are three kinds of updates: pre-update, ongoing-update, and post-update. Therefore, Authorizations can be either pre-authorization (preA) or ongoing-authorization (onA). Pre-authorization is performed before authorization is required to the access. But ongoing authorization may be performed during the access, such as when a book stocking list in a bookstore is periodically checked while the access is in progress. Obligations are requirements that a subject must perform before (pre) or during (ongoing) accesses. Conditions are decision factors that depend on environmental and system-oriented requirements. Subject and object attributes can be used to select which condition requirements have to be used for a request.

Based on the involvement of three decision factors: authorizations, obligations, and conditions, we focus on developing usage control models for XML databases. This involves XML Schemas and XML documents. We assume that a usage request exists on an XML target object. Decision-making can be done before (pre), during (ongoing) or after the exercise of the requested right. Based on the requirements we have six possible cases as a model for usage control: pre-Authorizations, ongoing-Authorizations, pre-Obligations, ongoing-Obligations, pre-Conditions and ongoing-Conditions.

THE OODB AUTHORIZATION MODEL

Object-oriented database systems (OODB) (Rabitti, Bertino, Kim & Woelk 1991) are an important emerging technology for applications in business, industry, and many other areas. OODB is the most popular data model to represent complex data structure (Kakeshita & Murata, 2003). XML database is a standard for representing semi-structured data. Schemas of XML databases can represent dynamic data structure, such as list, tree and graph. Since OODB and XML databases are suitable to represent complex objects, They may have the same authorization models. Therefore, the OODB authorization model can be applied to XML Schema and documents (Kakeshita & Murata, 2003 ; Zhang, Park & Sandhu, 2003). The OODB authorization model presented by Rabitti et al (Rabitti, Bertino, Kim & Woelk, 1991) is a discretionary access control model for object-oriented database. It models an authorization as a triple:

$$f: S \times O \times A \rightarrow (\text{True, False})$$

Figure 2. Authorization object schema

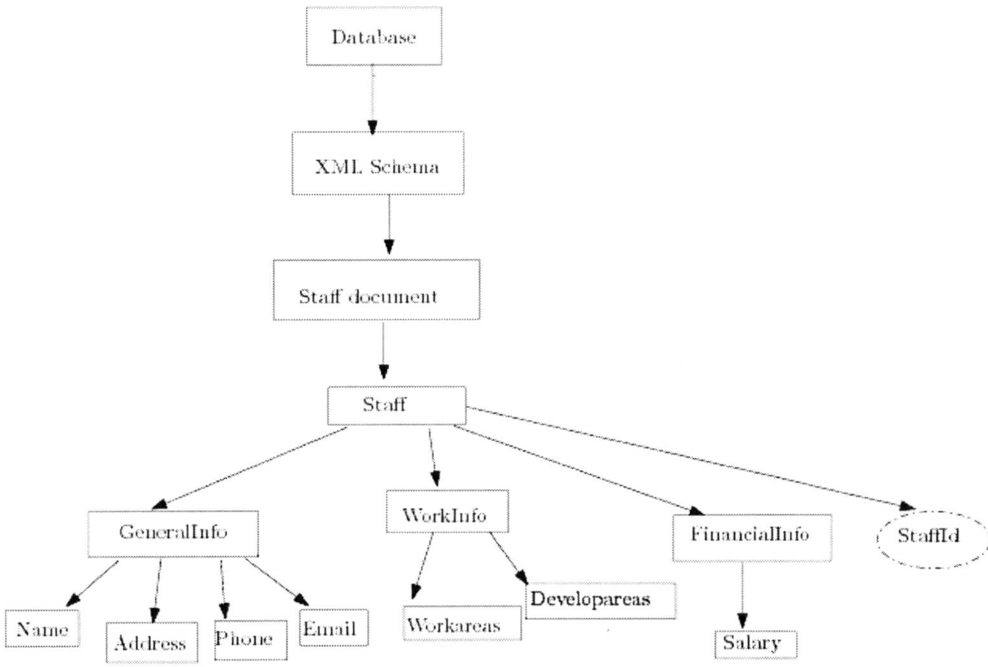

Where *S* represents the set of subjects, *O* represents the set of objects and *A* is the possible authorization types (access modes) in a system. The models of authorization supported in existing database systems are all designed for relational, hierarchical, or network models of data.

The basic idea of access control model is to group subjects into access control groups and to grant authorizations in terms of access types, such as read, write, and delete (Roshan & Ravi, 1993). These access types are usually ordered such that the authorization for one right may include others. Thus authorization for a delete may imply authorization for a write, which in turn may imply authorization for a read. Database systems usually define authorizations for the schema entities, such as classes, attributes, and indexes (Roshan & Ravi, 1993). In the database object part of the authorization, Rabitti et al. discusses two graphs: the authorization object schema (AOS) and the authorization object graph (AOG). Figures 2 and 3 show examples of AOS and AOG, respectively. The edges in the AOG represent relationships between objects. The nodes in both the AOS and AOG deal with collections of objects of a given type depending on how OODB handles sets of objects. AOS looks at the possible granules defined by the schema for OODB; AOG considers actual object instances on the database. All access control problems ultimately point at a fundamental question: subjects allowed to access of type on object *o*. The answer to any access control request can now be obtained by utilizing a function *f* that determines if the corresponding authorization *(s, o, a)* is true or false.

XML schema defines XML documents with a hierarchical structure, containing attributes and elements. Elements can have sub-elements nested to any level. In this paper we assume that the objects using access control consist of documents which conform to an XML Schema. For Rabitti model (Rabitti, Bertino, Kim & Woelk, 1991) the XML Schema can be used to construct the AOS, and the XML documents make up the

Figure 3. Authorization object graph

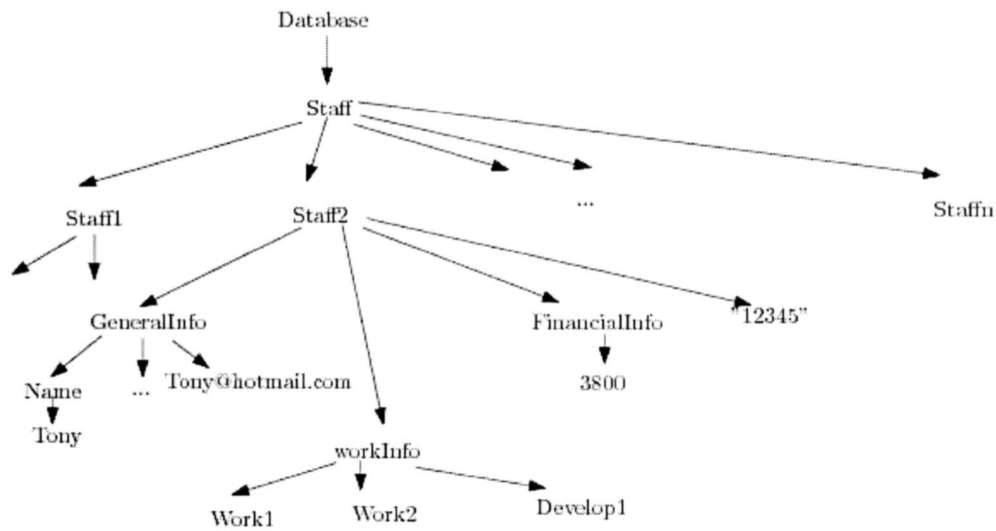

AOG. An AOS and AOG, for our example in Section 2, are shown in Figures 2 and 3, respectively. In the AOS of Figure 2, we have indicated elements by rectangles, attributes by ovals. So *Staff, GeneralInfo, WorkInfo,* and *FinancialInfo* are elements, *StaffId* is attribute of element *Staff.* In the AOG of Figure 3, the element values are shown as their string value and attribute values are in quotes. *Tony, Tony@hotmail.com* and *3800* are string values of elements and "*12345*" is the value of an attribute.

USAGE CONTROL MODELS WITH XML DATABASES (UCMXMLDB)

For the XML databases with the usage control model, the concepts of subjects and objects are similar to OODB authorization models. A right represents the access of a subject to an object, such as read or write. Operations on parts or all of an XML document, such as reading, changing the contents (update), adding sub-elements or attributes (extend) and following a pointer and applying XLS transformations are possible. This is similar to component authorization types in discretionary access control model for object-oriented database. In a real life environment, XML objects may originate from different XML Schemas from various servers and organizations. Therefore there will be vast number of schema components. On the other hand, a number of users can make subjects complex. With all these features, the security administration will be very complex in both centralized and decentralized deployments.

We now discuss authorization models for XML database adopting usage control in this section. XML documents provide the information structure and semantics in a web environment and XML documents will be stored in a relational, object-oriented database or XML Native database. The authorization models for XML Native database model are the same as the OODB model. Based on the three usage control components: *Authorization, Obligations* and *Conditions*, we develop six possible cases as core models: pre-Authorization, ongoing-Authorization, pre-Obligations, ongoing-Obligations, pre-Conditions, ongoing-Conditions using XML database. Meanwhile, to apply the modularity, extensibility information is stored in the XML databases. All the components in our models, such as subjects, subject attributes, objects, object attributes, rights, authorizations, obligations, and conditions are specified in an XML format.

1. pre-Authorization Model (UCMpreA) with XML databases

In *UCMpreA* model, the decision process is performed before the access is allowed. The *UCMpreA* model provides an authorization method on whether a subject can access the XML database. It consists of the following components: *S, XO, R, ATT(S), ATT(XO)* and usage decision functions *preA*, respectively. *S, XO, R,* represent Subject, XML object, Rights required on XML object access modes, respectively. While *ATT(S), ATT(XO),* represent attributes of a subject and attribute of an XML object, respectively. In usage control, authorization decision is made based on subject attributes and object attributes. In the *UCMpreA* model the decision process is

$allowed\ (s, xo, r) \Rightarrow preA(ATT(s), ATT(xo), r),$

This predicate indicates that if subject *s* is allowed to access XML object *xo* with right *r,* then the indicated condition *preA* must be true. This corresponds roughly to the discretionary access control model. *preA* is very similar as the triple relationship *f* in OODB authorization model mentioned in previous section. The three components *ATT(s), ATT(xo)* and *r* replace *S, O, A* in OODB authorization model. For example, applying *UCMpreA* to Figures 2 and 3, for the element staff *Tony*, his financial records can only be accessed by himself and financial administrators. Before they want to access this information, they have to give a username (subject) and a password (subject attribute). In the meantime they need to know *Tony*'s (object) staffId (object attribute). Then they are able to read (right) Tony's financial records.

2. ongoing-Authorizations Model (UCMonA) with XML databases

A usage control model for ongoing-Authorizations is used to check ongoing authorization during an access process. In this model, usage requests are allowed without any 'pre' decision making. With XML database, *UCMonA* model has the same components: *S, XO, XD, R, ATT(S), ATT(XO)* as UCMpreA. The ongoing usage decision functions *onA* is used to check whether *S* can continue to access or not. It includes two processes:

$allowed\ (s, xo, r) \Rightarrow true,$

$stopped\ (s, xo,r) \Leftarrow \neg\ onA(ATT(s), ATT(xo), r),$

The *allowed (s, xo, r)* is a prerequisite for ongoing authorization on XML object *xo*. Comparing with OODB authorization model, *onA* is similar to the triple relationship *f. ATT(s), ATT(xo), r* also replace *S, O, A* in OODB authorization model. The access of subject *s* to *xo* is terminated if the ongoing authorization *onA* fails. During this process the requested access is always allowed as there is no pre-authorization at any time. *allowed (s, xo, r)* is required to be *true*, otherwise ongoing authorization can not be initiated. Ongoing authorizations are active throughout the usage of the requested right, and some requirements are repeatedly checked for a continued access. These checks are performed periodically based on time or event. During the process *stopped* will be started when attributes are changed and requirements are no longer satisfied. *Stopped (s, xo, r)* indicates that rights *r* of subject *s* on object XML database are revoked and the ongoing access is terminated. For example, in a limited number of simultaneous usages, suppose only any two of financial staff and Tony himself are able to access the information about his salary. If a third financial staff requests the access and passed the pre-authorization, the staff with the earliest time access would be terminated. *onA* monitors the number of current usages on *xo(ATT(xo))*, records which access is the earliest start, and terminates it. While this is a case of ongoing authorization, it is important that the certificate should be evaluated in a *pre* decision.

3. pre-Obligations Model (UCMpreB) with XML databases

UCMpreB introduces pre-obligations that have to be fulfilled before access is permitted. It will return *true* or *false* for usage decision depending on whether obligation actions have been fulfilled or not. For example, an administrator is required to register by filling forms before accessing one staff financial information. Pre-obligation action may also be done by some other subjects. When using *UCMpreB* model to access XML database documents, the *UCMpreB* model has the same components: *S*, *XO*, *R*, *ATT(S)*, and *ATT (XO)* as UCMpreA. *OBS, OBO* and *OB* represent obligation subjects, objects, and actions respectively. The decision function *preObfilled*: $OBS \times OBO \times OB \rightarrow \{true, false\}$ checks if obligations are obeyed or not before the subject(s) accesses the object(xo). *preObfilled*: $OBS \times OBO \times OB \rightarrow \{true, false\}$ is the same as the triple relationship *f*: $S \times O \times A \rightarrow (true, false)$ in OODB authorization model. The preObfilled function must be true if subject(*s*) is allowed to access XML object *xo* with right *r*.

4. ongoing-Obligations Model (UCMonB) with XML databases

Different from the pre-Obligations model, Ongoing-obligations model may have to be fulfilled periodically or continuously. For example, when an administrator accesses the financial information through the Internet for 15 continuous days, she/he may have to input a password repeatedly. The model concerns whether obligations are fulfilled or not. Using the *UCMonB* model with XML databases it has the same components: *S, XO, R, ATT(S)* and *ATT(XO)* as UCMpreA and an ongoing decision function *onObfilled*: $OBS \times OBO \times OB \rightarrow \{true, false\}$. *OBS, OBO*, and *OB* represent obligation subjects, objects, and actions, respectively. The ongoing function *onObfilled* is used to check if obligations are continually obeyed or not while *subject(s)* is accessing *object(xo)* in an XML database document. *onObfilled:* $OBS \times OBO \times OB \rightarrow \{true, false\}$ is the same as the triple relationship *f*: $S \times O \times A \rightarrow (true, false)$ in OODB authorization model. *allowed*(s, xo, r) is a prerequisite for *UCMonB*. It means that *s* can access XML database documents. Where *stopped (s, xo, r)* indicates that the access of *s* on *xo* with *r* is revoked if any of the ongoing obligations fails.

5. pre-Conditions Model (UCMpreC) with XML databases

Condition is a very important component in the usage control model. Conditions define that certain restrictions have to be satisfied for usage. By using conditions in usage decision process, it can provide fine-grain controls on usage. Usually the pre-conditions model has to be used before requested rights can be exercised. An example of pre-conditions is time restriction for accessing information. You should check them before a usage allowed. The *UCMpreC* model with XML databases has the same components *S, XO, R, ATT(S)*, and *ATT(XO)* as UCMpreA and *preCON* (a set of pre-conditions) is for verifying conditions, $preCON \rightarrow \{true, false\}$. The function *preConSatisfied*: $S \times O \times R \rightarrow 2^{preCON}$ is used to check whether the pre-conditions are satisfied or not.

$$allowed(s, xo, r) \Rightarrow preC(s, xo, r)$$

preC is very similar as the triple relationship *f* in OODB authorization model. *s, xo, r* replace *S, O, A* in OODB authorization model. *allowed*(s, xo, r) expresses that all conditions which have to be satisfied before access is approved. Unlike other models, condition models cannot have updated procedures. All pre-conditions have to be checked if there are more than two conditions.

6. ongoing-Conditions Model (*UCMonC*) with XML databases

UCMonC model requires conditions to be satisfied while rights are in active use. If any of the conditions is not satisfied, the allowed right is revoked and the exercise is stopped. For example, if the staff information system status changes to "special mode", accesses from certain users may be terminated.

For the usage access control with XML databases the six models all include some functions. These functions, such as *preA*, *onA*, *preObfilled*, *onObfilled*, *preC, etc* are very similar to *f*: $(S \times O \times A)$ in the OODB authorization model. But usage authorization method for XML database focuses on checking users' (subjects') authorizations, obligations and conditions with continuity properties. It can also be used for different processes. In practice, two or more of the six models of pre-Authorizations, ongoing-Authorizations, pre-Obligations, ongoing-Obligations, pre-Conditions and ongoing-Conditions may need to be combined for access control.

DISCUSSION

Jingzhu and Sylvia (Wang & Osborn, 2004) introduced a role based approach to access control for XML database. In their model, they provide a general access control methodology for parts of XML documents, combining role based access control as found in the Role Graph Model, with a methodology originally designed for object-oriented databases. Several constraints are included in the model. Their protocol is based on RBAC and hence it focuses on permissions-role assignment, objects hierarchies and constrains. Our approach is based on usage access control; we have analysed the characteristics of various access authorizations and presented six detailed models for different kinds of authorizations. It is an important improvement for access control of XML documents in the Internet since users always alter their conditions or obligations. By contrast, users in our scheme have to pass pre-Authorizations, ongoing-Authorizations, pre-Obligations, pre-Conditions and ongoing-Obligations as well as ongoing-Conditions. This indicates that our method is much more secure and powerful in dynamic environments.

Elisa and Elena (Bertino & Ferrari, 2002) presented an access control system supporting selective distribution of XML documents among possible large user communities by using a range of key distribution methods. In their papers, a formal model of access control policies for XML documents is given. It focuses on key distribution methods to protect XML documents. The approach consists of encrypting different portions of the same document according to different encryption keys, and selectively distributing these keys to the various users. By contrast, our work provides a rich variety of options that can deal with XML database documents. Users can access XML documents with their keys at any time, even when their properties are updated. In our scheme, users have to satisfy pre-Authorizations, pre-Obligations, pre-Conditions ongoing-Authorizations, ongoing-Obligations and ongoing-Conditions.

CONCLUSION

In this paper we reviewed XML, XML databases, usage control and OODB authorization model. We discussed access control models for XML databases by using usage control. OODB authorization control is used in database system access control. It only has an authorization component, it doesn't include obligation and condition components. Usage control encompasses traditional access control, trust management and provide an approach for the next generation of access control. It covers both security and privacy issues of current business and information systems. Comparing with the OODB authorization model, usage control model for accessing XML databases has a wide scope of application. We developed six core models for XML databases using usage access control. In these models we analyse not only decision factors, such as authorizations, obligations and conditions, but also the continuity properties. In this paper we have provided a foundation for further research and development on usage control model with XML databases. It is a new application of usage control. However, much work is needed to be done before these models can be used in practice.

REFERENCES

Bertion, E. (2002). Protecting XML documents. In *Proceedings of Computer Software and Applications Conference* (pp.132-133), Taiwan.

Bertion, E., Castano, S., Ferrari, E., & Mesiti, E. (1999). Controlled access and dissemination of xml documents. In *Processings of the second international workshop on Web information and data management* (pp. 22–27). ACM Press. doi:10.1145/319759.319770

Bertion, E., & Ferrari, E. (2002). Secure and selective dis-semination of xml documents. *ACM Transactions on Information and System Security*, *5*(3), 290–331. doi:10.1145/545186.545190

Bourret, R. (2003). XML Database Products.

Bray, T., Paoli, J., Sperberg, M., & Maler, E. (2000). Extensible Markup Language (XML) 1.1 (Second Edition). World Wide Web Consortium (W3C), Cambridge, MA, USA.

Cao, J., Sun, L., & Wang, H. (2005). Towards secure XML document with usage control, *Proceedings of The 7th Asia Pacific Web Conference, Lecture Notes in Computer Science, Springer* (pp.296-307), Shanghai, China.

Damiani, E., Capitani, S., & Samarati, P. (2002). Towards securing xml web services. *In Proc. of the 2002 ACM Workshop on XML Security*, Washington, DC, USA.

Damiani, E., Paraboschi, S., & Samarati, P. (2002). A fine-grained access control system for XML documents. *ACM Transactions on Information and System Security*, *5*(2), 169–202. doi:10.1145/505586.505590

Damiani, E., & Samarati, S., Vimercati, di., & Paraboschi, S. (2001). Controlling access to XML documents. *IEEE Internet Computing*, *5*(6), 18–28. doi:10.1109/4236.968827

Gabillon, A. (2004) An authorization model for xml databases. *In Proceedings of the 11th ACM conference on Computer Security.*

Kakeshita, T., & Murata, M. (2003). *A declarative manipulation for OODB and XML DB having cyclic schema.* IEEE.

Kudo, M., & Hada, S. (2000). Xml access control. Retrieved October 24, 2000, from http://www.trl.ibm.com/projects/xml/xacl/xmlac-proposal.html

Kudo, M., & Hada, S. (2000) XML document security based on provisional authorization. *In Proc. 7tth ACM Conference on Computer and Communications Security* (pp.87-96).

Kuper, G., Massacci, F., & Rassadko, N. (2005). Generalized xml security views. In *Proceedings of the 10th ACM sysposium on Access control models and technologies* (pp. 77-84). ACM Press.

Park, J., & Sandhu, R. (2002). Towards usage control models: beyond traditional access control. In *Proceedings of the seventh ACM symposium on Access control models and technologies* (pp. 57-64). ACM Press.

Park, J., Sandhu, R., & Schifalacqua, J. (2003). Security architectures for controlled digital information dissemination. *In Proceedings of 16th Annual Computer Security Application Conference.*

Rabitti, F., Bertino, E., Kim, W., & Woelk, D. (1991). A model of authorization for next-generation database systems. *ACM Transactions on Database Systems*, *16*(1), 88–131. doi:10.1145/103140.103144

Roshan, K. T., & Ravi, S. S. (1993). Discretionary access control in Object-Oriented databases issues and research directions. *Proc. Of the 16th NIST_NCSC National Computer Security conference* (pp. 63-74).

Sandhu, R., & Park, J. (2003). Usage control: A vision for next generation access control. In *MMM-ACNS 2003* (pp. 17-31). Springer-Verlag Berlin Heideberg.

Sun, L., & Li, Y. (2006). DTD level authorization in xml documents with usage control. In. *International Journal of Science Network Security*, *6*, 244–250.

Wang, H., Zhang, Y., & Cao, J. (2006). Ubiquitous computing environments and its usage access control. *The First International Conference on Scalable Information Systems (INFOSCALE 2006)*, IEEE CS Society, Hong Kong.

Wang, J., & Osborn, S. L. (2004) A role-based approach to access control for XML databases. *SACMAT'04*.

Wang, Y., & Tan, K. (2001). A scalable xml access control system. In *Proceedings of the 10th international WWW conference*, Poster.

Zhang, X., Park, J., & Parisi-Presicce, F. (2004). A logical specification for usage control. In *SACMAT'4*. ACM Press.

Zhang, X., Park, J., & Sandhu, R. (2003). Schema based xml security: Rbac approach. In *Proceedings of the IFIP WG*. ACM Press.

Chapter 14
IT Services Offshoring: Opportunities and Critical Factors from a Strategic Perspective

Paolo Popoli
Parthenope University of Naples, Italy

ABSTRACT

In light of new changes in the market, in supply as well as demand, IT offshore outsourcing may be interpreted as an articulate and complex tool for pursuing strategic goals which go well beyond the traditional objective of cost saving. Indeed, IT services today are required not only to make management processes more efficient and economical, but also to help increase a company's capacity to create value, and thus gain a greater competitive advantage. From a strategic point of view, IT structures are increasingly crucial in the implementation of business, and are no longer mere support factors in value chain activities. At the same time, the increased potential of this tool has also led to a greater complexity of management, which can only be properly matched by a flexible, dynamic governing model. This paper will identify some critical elements in managing offshoring relationships aimed at the innovation and improvement of the value creation processes.

INTRODUCTION

In the era of globalization, offshoring IT services aim to improve economic conditions and organizational systems to carry out activities or processes previously performed within the company. Since the nineties, there has been a remarkable global expansion of high-level IT skills, taking place mainly in countries with emerging economies. These countries have been able to reap the benefits of a considerable amount of research and development investment and human resources training in the IT field, thereby developing their own economies and GNP, and in turn attracting foreign investment, thereby increasing their own competitive position in respect to the U.S.A. and European countries (Leonard, 2006).

Consequently, India, the Philippines, China, Canada, Brazil, Ireland, and many eastern European countries have become the real protagonists

DOI: 10.4018/978-1-60960-138-6.ch014

of IT services, basing their competiveness not only on significant advantages in production costs (especially human resources), but also on their well known, high-level information technology skills. Today, these countries can count on a high level of professionalism and specialization that, in many cases, proves to be superior to that in the U.S. or Europe.

Take, for example, companies like Tata Consultancy, Infosys, Wipro Technologies, HCL Technologies, which operate in Electronics City in Bangalore, India; Flextronics in Singapore, or Celestina in Canada. These companies hold the top positions in the global arena of highly qualified IT providers. With the quality of IT service they offer, these companies have been able to earn a position of excellence in one of the most prestigious systems of international certification, the "CMMI: Capability Maturity Model Integration for Software", developed by the Software Engineering Institute (SEI) of Carnegie Mellon University. This is a set of rigorous standards for assessing the "level of maturity" companies demonstrate in the organization and management of their software process. The CMMI system has five levels of certification[1]; 50 to 60% of the companies who have earned the highest levels of certification (the fourth or fifth level) are Indian.

Consider also that, as Popoli A. (2009, p. 59) shows, "many of the players from emerging countries – if this term makes sense any more – have opened branches in Europe, for not only commercial but also traditional on-site consulting services. At the same time, the main players in the global market such as IT, Accenture, IBM, HP and EDS have long included in their offer *delivery centres of excellence* in countries such as India, Brazil, Russia, China and the Philippines, with highly qualified personnel dealing with all the most innovative platforms and technologies. In this way the major holdings can resist global competition since they are able to combine the best of their more traditional onsite activities with the need for industrialization and efficiency offered by the delivery centres of excellence".

From these brief considerations, we see that what was once the domain of European countries and the U.S., is no longer (Garner, 2004; Pfannenstein and Tsai, 2004; Kedia and Lahiri, 2007; Lewin and Couto, 2007). It is this changed geography in the global arena of high-level IT services which is at the base of not only of the widely diffused practice of offshoring, but also the change in the content itself, which today goes beyond mere cost advantages to incorporate business development systems based on medium-long term partnerships with IT service providers. If, in the past, the principal motivation for opting for offshoring was the possibility of cost savings, today the appeal of offshoring lies in obtaining highly specialized IT capability, which increases the capacity to create value, and therefore, to gain competitive advantage.

Phenomena emerging from recent empirical studies confirm a shift in the IT offshoring paradigm. Once economy and efficiency were the main concerns of businesses considering IT offshoring. Now, businesses are more interested in the strategic innovation and development resources and knowledge that IT offshoring firms have to offer resources and knowledge that complement and can be integrated with internal resources the company already possesses. Recent research shows that first, dissatisfaction with the services offered by IT providers increases with quality requirements and levels of innovation, compared to expectations of cost savings. Secondly, IT outsourcing is becoming increasingly *selective,* regarding information system components, as opposed to *full outsourcing,* regarding a company's entire IT system. Thirdly, IT service suppliers are becoming increasingly specialized, based on research of competitive advantage in differentiation rather than cost leadership obtainable through an approach of standardization.

In conclusion, the analysis of changes in the market and the identification of some critical elements of discontinuity with respect to the past support our thesis that IT offshoring must be considered with new conceptual paradigms. We can name this new way "*IT offshoring for value creation*": it identifies new purposes and new contents for outsourcing options, increasingly aimed at obtain specialized IT services and tailored on specific development plans.

The growing complexity of both market environment and technologies determines the need for the companies to "open" their value chain to relevant contributions from external agents. As a consequence, the main decisive factor for achieving a competitive advantage is to develop a strong capability to manage and coordinate a series of business relationships with the partners who integrate the own core competencies with complementary and integrative skills.

We start by confuting two traditional concepts: first, that the advantage to be derived from offshore outsourcing is above all a matter of costs, and secondly that only activities which are not directly involved in the core-business can be candidates for outsourcing. Our approach is framed within the principles and contents of *strategic outsourcing*, analysed with specific reference to IT offshoring.

THE OLD CONCEPTUAL FRAMEWORKS FOR IT SERVICE OFFSHORING

The traditional paradigm of choices in the IT outsourcing field pivots on the twin objectives of reducing cost and dedicating a greater amount of organizational, financial, and human resources to core business activities (Quinn and Hilmer, 1994). The first objective represents the traditional driver of choice of *make or buy,* assessing alternative solutions from a purely economic perspective.

The theoretic framework that guided such choices was the *transaction cost economics theory* of Williamson (1986), which was developed from the earlier propositions of Coase (1937), whereby the choice among market, hierarchy, and intermediate solutions must be aimed at minimizing the combined costs of production and transaction. And, in this regard, it is undeniable that the industrialization of processes that characterize the larger and more qualified IT providers can achieve economies of scale of production and management that significantly reduce the cost of IT services. This choice was based on the dual assumption of being able to maintain full control over the provider through detailed specifications of required performance standards, and still maintaining an adequate cognitive grasp on the externalized activity, without running excessive financial and operational risks. A second objective in outsourcing non core-business activities is to enable the company to streamline, thereby rendering the organizational structure more flexible, and freeing up human and financial resources for the development of the core-business.

Given these two objectives, based on the traditional paradigm of outsourcing in the IT industry that dominated the scene in the eighties and nineties, we have seen two different, historical phases:

- I phase: IT "*on-shore and near-shore outsourcing for commodities*";
- II phase: IT "*offshoring for cost saving*".

In the first phase, which can be placed in the eighties, companies resorted to IT outsourcing for economic efficiency and productivity, initially turning to specialized operators working in their home country (on-shoring), and subsequently different countries, geographically, culturally, and institutionally similar (near-shoring).

The nineties witnessed the second phase of IT outsourcing, offshoring, meaning the outsourcing of activities and systems to companies operating in countries geographically distant, especially those with emerging economies[2] (Mol, van Tulder and Beije, 2005). In this phase, the imperative of cost saving still dominated the choice of outsourcing, due to significant increases in efficiency and relative opportunities for companies to change their cost structures through varying previously fixed costs. The difference from the first phase lies in the fact that research in cost advantage turned towards countries defined as *low cost,* but was still aimed at achieving competitive differentials in economy (Jilovec, 2005).

In this regard, there are many studies that have provided a quantitative indication of the cost savings derived from offshoring practices. For instance, Pfannenstein and Tsai (2004) have shown that in the area of IT services, hourly rates for workers in Asia and other emerging markets are reported to be anywhere from 30 to 75% lower than they are in the United States, generating close to 50% savings for offshoring an activity; Dossani and Kennedy (2004) point out that firms offshoring IT enabled services to India claimed that savings on a given activity had to be at least 40% for them to offshore and that in practice these savings could be as high as 80%.

In the second phase, outsourcing to low cost countries became possible because companies could acquire the same level of service, the same technologies, and the same professionalism available in Europe and the U.S. at a decidedly lower cost. Indeed, in some cases, offshore vendors may provide a better level of service at a lower cost than is available in-house (Barthélemy and Dominique, 2004).

Low cost countries started to reap the rewards of their investment in information technology, providing a growing number of services and closing the initial gap with the U.S. and European countries. Therefore, the cost effectiveness of outsourcing IT functions and services, already tested in local markets (on-shoring) or neighboring countries (near-shoring), led companies to increasingly broaden the search for satisfactory performance quality, but at costs well lower than those experienced in previous solutions. At this point, the demand for services still pertained to mere support functions or activities, not activities related to core-business processes.

Offshore service providers, meanwhile, developed their business around the prevailing logic of standardization that fulfilled the demand for basic services, rendered even from great distances without the necessity to carry out management processes face-to-face.

THE HIDDEN COSTS OF IT OFFSHORING

The limits of the traditional approach to offshoring for cost saving and the need for a new approach to offshoring strategies become clear when considering that cost advantage expectations are not always satisfied by moving IT activities and functions abroad. First, all outsourcing deals, including those on-shore and near-shore, have a number of additional costs that relate to the management and control of the transaction, known in literature as "hidden costs". These costs trace back to several factors that can't always be predetermined with accuracy, but which arise during the course of the outsourcing relationship (Barthélemy, 2001; Lampel and Bhalla, 2008; Stringfellow, Teagarden and Nie, 2008; Kedia and Mukherjee, 2009). In summary, a trade relationship involves "coordination costs" (related to the management and control of the transaction) which consist of:

- the cost of researching, evaluating, and selecting potential providers;
- the cost of negotiating terms and conditions of the contract;
- the cost of monitoring and controlling the execution of contractual obligations, and in broader terms, the supplier's behavior;
- the cost of revising terms and conditions of contracts required by changes in the internal/external environmental context to the cooperative relationship between the parties;
- the cost of coordinating outsourced activities, functions and processes with those

carried out internally with a company, as well as harmonizing and integrating interfacing processes.

In general terms, to this list can be added the costs of managing any disputes that may occur between parties, and in the event of termination of contract, costs of substituting suppliers or reintroducing activities, functions or processes back into the company (back-sourcing). These management costs can be predicted only to a certain degree, and can manifest depending on how the relationship unfolds, according to changing circumstances in the external environment that could generate adaptation costs. Even the most prominent exponent of the *transaction-cost economics theory*, Williamson (1986) was aware that an analysis of transactional costs was possible, *ex ante*, only for certain kinds of costs, while other costs could only be estimated. In the case of offshore outsourcing, the factors leading to hidden costs are even more numerous and are related, in particular, to the following aspects.

The first aspect is the political instability of some countries involved in offshore projects. When companies move operations abroad, insurance premiums may increase due to additional risks incurred.

The second aspect is less control of production processes when interacting with people and structures that are geographically distant. Coping with problems of geographic distance, a company is bound to meet additional costs. For example, human resources may be employed inside national boundaries to act as a link between internal and external operations. Adding the normal cost of human resources to any costs of infrastructures abroad and travel, the cost of human resources may very well be higher than originally calculated.

It should also be considered that some methods of coordinating work that require face-to-face contact, such as stand-up meetings or sharing the same workspace, are lost in international relationships. This problem is due to both geographical distance and time-zone differences.

A third aspect has to do with the protection of data and business information, software piracy, and the protection of intellectual property. National laws do not always apply to other countries, and even if the contract with the supplier provides rules governing this matter, some contracts cannot be contested outside national borders. Despite the recent emphasis being given to the matter of privacy and data protection, there remains an undefined area that is left to interpretation when crossing national borders. This requires the presence of legal consultant expert in international law, and therefore also the costs associated with legal activities may be more than budgeted.

The issue of intellectual property protection is also relevant considering the great capacity for learning demonstrated by the low cost countries. The phenomenon of appropriation of knowledge and expertise by foreign operators should be considered not only from the perspective of the different legal regimes that govern these matters, but also in light of the fact that the confidentiality clauses included in contracts are not always effective in achieving full protection of intellectual property (Renard, 2003).

Other factors to consider when choosing offshoring which may add costs relate to differences in culture (Gefen and Carmel, 2008; Levina and Vaast, 2008; Metters, 2008), including managerial culture, between the client's country and that of the provider. Still today, language differences can create obstacles for effective communication at all levels of operation (Ellram, Tate and Billington, 2008).

Stringfellow, Teagarden and Nie (2008) analyzed in depth the relevance of these factors. In particular, they highlighted that geographic distance (travel distance and time-zone differences), language distance (speech intelligibility) and cultural distance (individualism *versus* collectivism; universalism *versus* particularism; communication style) are important drivers of the invisible costs associated with offshoring. Also Head, Mayer and Ries (2009) in their empirical analysis performed on data from 65 Countries over the period 1992-2006 on offshoring professional services – as IT and communication services – confirm that the physical distance, differences in time-zone, languages and legal systems generate extra costs for businesses. One of the results of this study is that very often firms are willing to pay "a wage premium to avoid the costs associated with remote provision of services" (Head, Mayer and Ries, 2009, p. 430). Referring specifically to the offshoring of services, Hahn and Bunyaratavej (2010) emphasized the impact of cultural dimensions on offshoring location choices, using four out of five dimensions of culture indentified by Hofstede (2001): uncertainty avoidance, power distance, individualism *versus* collectivism, masculinity *versus* feminility.

Finally, one last consideration is the differential pay rates that exist in the world, which is one of the main reasons for outsourcing activities and functions abroad. From a medium-long term perspective, globalization will eventually result in a convergence of wage levels for distinct professional levels, which will reduce the gap that now exists in the world. One factor that will contribute in the future to this leveling of salary is the growing importance and diffusion of expectations of all stakeholders regarding moral and ethical aspects of business. Indeed, behind low wage levels, there are very often circumstances of questionable morality and ethics, and it is reasonable to expect that social control over these aspects will be increasingly important in the future. Already evident is the fact that the salaries of IT professionals have decreased all over the world in respect to the boom era of net-economy (Jilovec, 2005).

WHY A NEW APPROACH FROM A STRATEGIC PERSPECTIVE?

The need to rethink a new approach to offshoring decisions from a strategic perspective comes from two main factors. First, in many cases of offshoring expectations of cost reduction, the principal motive for outsourcing, have not been met. Second, new competitive challenges presented by globalization and continuous technological research in the field of IT have lead to the loss of the "self sufficient" capacity of companies. Companies, therefore, must require their IT service providers to be increasingly involved in value creation processes.

In regards to the first factor, we have already indicated the reasons that offshoring can prove more costly than originally estimated. Furthermore, according to Di Romualdo and Gurbaxani (1998) cost reduction is "only one of three kinds of strategic intent for IT outsourcing (*IS Improvement*); there are other two strategic intent of it: '*Outsourcing for Business Impact*', focused on improving IT's contribution to company performance within its existing lines of business, and '*Outsourcing for Commercial Exploitation*', focused on leveraging technology in the marketplace through the development and marketing of new technology-based products and services".

In regards to the second factor, the *resource-based theory* and the *core-competence theory* of the nineties indicated that the search for competitive advantage must be based on the possession of distinctive skills (Prahalad and Hamel, 1990) which, being difficult to imitate by competitors (Teece, Pisano and Shuen, 1990), will generate competitive differentials. In today's economic context, we find that these distinctive competences are built not only from within a company, but through the contribution of knowledge and skills by third parties. As Kedia and Mukherjee (2009) argue, an enlightened relationship between provider and client firm leads to two types of externalization advantages:

1. co-specialization by harnessing the specialized resources and capabilities of the provider;
2. organizational learning by harnessing information/resources, through socially embedded relationship.

It can be asserted, therefore, that the emerging distinctive skill that can help a business gain competitive advantage is the ability to manage relationships with other companies, from the perspective of gaining knowledge reciprocal to both parties. Companies should prime internal learning processes while being open to innovations that external partners can bring, rendering their specialized competence available for the company's client. Dyer and Singh (1998) define "a relational rent as a supernormal profit jointly generated in an exchange relationship that cannot be generated by either firm in isolation".

In the IT sector, the increasing difficulty for companies to control the variability and the variety of the technological environment and market has imposed the search for a partner able to offer cognitive and complementary technologically integrative resources, with whom to establish a partnership and carry out a *competence building strategy*.

As Lampel and Bhalla (2008, p. 431) argue, "what has changed the character of current offshoring is the advent of new information technologies, which have allowed firms to create new value chain capabilities, specifically in the provision of so-called IT-enabled services, and develop value chain configurations that open new strategic opportunities". For instance, Popoli A. (2009, p. 57) points out that, in the telecommunications market, "the continuous introduction of new services based on the availability of broadband networks, the need for fixed-mobile convergence involving *service orchestration*, the increasing importance of *content management* and *digital asset management*, and the recent launch of IP television services, are just some examples of areas representing challenges and requirements for operators that are quite new with respect to the past:

- the need for multi-layer competences, at various levels of technical expertise: management of the new generation of network infrastructures, personalisation of packages, system building, service assurance, network protocols, etc.;
- the problem of the rapid obsolescence of such skills and the corresponding need for new competences;
- the impossibility of finding all the required competences in a single partner/provider.

These new requirements have in fact already generated new relations of IT outsourcing aiming at guaranteeing essential market elements: availability of state-of-the-art technology skills, possibility of up-grading resources at short notice, stability and predictability of operating costs (and not necessarily, it must be stressed, reduction of such costs)". As a consequence, IT service providers are more and more requested to be directly engaged in development and innovation objectives rather than to be only providers of innovative skills (Kotabe and Murray, 2004).

The transition from pure cost criteria to higher expectations of service quality and requests for the provider to participate in value creation explain the growing phenomena of back-sourcing, of the prematurely terminated contracts, and selective outsourcing. These failures are the result of an over-enthusiastic initial push towards offshoring (even more than what took place in near-shoring or on-shoring) that was not always supported by adequate skills in governing the relationship, neither before, through a careful identification and evaluation of outsourcing costs as a whole, or during, through adequate management of the relationship with the supplier (Brandes, Lilliecreutz and Brege, 1997) still seen, mainly from a contractual perspective rather than from a partnership point of view.

It is not surprising, therefore, that many companies have felt unsatisfied by the quality of service from their providers, and that there have been many organizational and cultural coordination problems between client and provider. In this context, Dyer and Singh (1998) affirm that "the ability of alliance partners to generate relational rents from complementary strategic resources increases with the degree of compatibility in their organizational systems, processes and cultures".

In conclusion, the necessity for companies to consider IT offshoring from a new strategic perspective arises from the observation of numerous causes of failure which companies have, in many cases, experienced the hard way: poor customer service, greater than expected outsourcing costs, the provider's lack of understanding of the company's business logic, poor adaptability and flexibility to the needs of the company by the IT provider, technological changeovers which were more difficult than expected, provider's lack of respect for the level of service agreed upon, and, in fewer cases, the client company's lack of competent and qualified human resources.

THE NEW PHASE OF OFFSHORING FROM A STRATEGIC PERSPECTIVE

The paradigm shift from IT "offshoring for cost savings" to IT "offshoring for value creation" marks the birth of a new phase of IT service offshoring strategies. This third phase, which began in the early 21st century, is characterized by the decreasing importance of cost differentials as a source of competitive advantage, and the ensuing search of high-quality IT services which are differentiated and closely related to the specific needs of the company.

It should also be considered that the shift of outsourcing activities as commodities to outsourcing activities with greater quality and content strategy has also been helped by experiences of offshoring. As Lampel and Bhalla (2008) show, firms learn how to negotiate, how to set up operations, how to understand their providers, how to evaluate their partners, and their previous experiences represent an opportunity to engage with a strategic option that has considerable upside potential. Also Rottman and Lacity (2004), observing IT offshoring practices followed by large U.S. firms, talk of a phased approach in the sense that the accumulation of experience in the management of offshoring allows firms to move from a simple search of cost advantages and flexibility to the research phase of qualitative results with more impact on the processes of value creation.

The demand that companies make to their providers no longer have to do merely with support services or functions, but increasingly address the acquisition of resources and highly specialized skills that can increase the company's ability to create value through process innovation and expansion of opportunities to develop business. From this perspective, IT service providers should prove adaptable to the logic and business needs of the company, provide tools to elevate the quality level of both material and immaterial components of the company's offering, and help raise the strategic and operational flexibility of management processes.

The point that we want to emphasize here is that, in our opinion, the idea that the goal of outsourcing can be limited only to non core-business functions or processes is definitely to be refuted. According to Venkatraman (1997), it is the character of the pervasiveness of IT in the value chain that makes it difficult to distinguish between mere support activities and those that participate in creating value.

If one accepts the idea that the new key skill for achieving competitive advantage is the ability to manage and coordinate the network of relations which the firm is able to put in place, and which can become "distinctive" with respect to competitors, then one must also be prepared to go beyond the traditional distinction between core and non-core activities in deciding which activities can be outsourced. In other words, limiting outsourcing to non-core activities or processes while maintaining the core counterparts in-house is based on two apparently axiomatic elements which must be called into questions.

The first concerns the possibility of clearly separating what is "core" from what is not, and

Figure 1. "What" to outsource

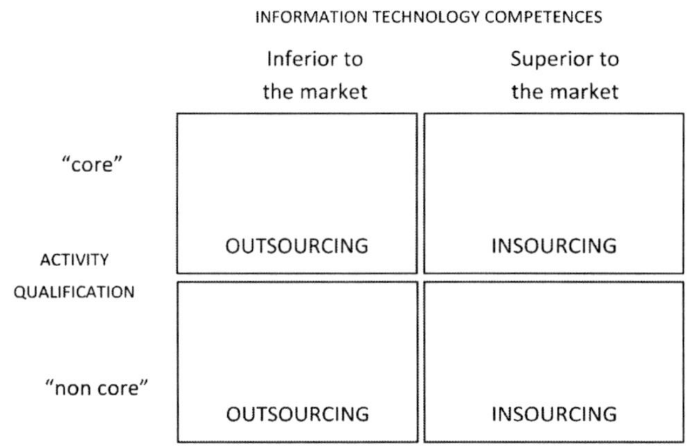

this is by no means always straightforward[3]; the second concerns the restrictions of distinctive skills, based on the traditional evaluation of *make or buy*, to the management of activities which are critical for the value chain; this restriction does not include the most important distinctive competence skill, meaning the management of the inter-organizational relations network, and more concretely, the coordination and control of the cognitive and functional input of external operators specialized in certain activities or processes.

The problem, therefore, is no longer to identify outsourcing opportunities using degrees of closeness to "core-business" activities as the criteria; rather, the problem is evaluating if the skills possessed by the company are superior or not to those on the market (Figure1).

It must be emphasized that until the recent past, virtually all business management literature or the subject held that only non-core business activities would be subject to outsourcing. There were few exceptions that recognized the possibility of outsourcing core business activities as well (Accabi and Lopez, 1995; Hinterhuber and Stuhec, 1996; Quinn and Hilmer, 1994). More recently there have been diverse opinions regarding the aims, content, and nature (tactical or strategically) of outsourcing which attribute a large potential for business innovation and development to outsourcing (Kedia, Lahiri and Lovvorn, 2005; Lewin and Peeters, 2006; Kedia and Lahiri, 2007).

New doctrinal positions based on the *resource-based view*, *knowledge management* theories, *core competency* theories and *network* theories, address the outsourcing process literature in terms of key strategies, and also extend the scope of outsourcing from simple activity commodities to processes involved in creating value (*Business Process Outsourcing*[4] and *Transformational Outsourcing*[5]).

The problem, therefore, consists in evaluating the contribution the external IT service provider can make to improve the company's overall business system, and evaluating how that potential contribution could be carried out while reducing the risks (loss of control, resource and innovative capability depletion, strategic dependence on provider) traditionally associated with core-business strategic activities. In this regard, we believe that the risks perceived by the company, often impeding the choice of outsourcing, such as "loss of control over strategic assets", "cognitive dependence on the provider", and "depletion of internal innovative capacity", represent only the incapacity or the insecurity of the company to accept that its business system and its competitive advantage sources are outside of the company, out of its "possession" and "control hierarchy", and therefore, almost inevitably destined to create dangerous conditions leading to strategic impoverishment that could effect the company's capacity for survival.

In 2005, Sirmi S.p.A, an Italian organization that carries out market research, analysis and consultancy in ICT, conducted a survey of about 250 companies. From this research, it was confirmed that the fear of the "supplier dependence" and "loss of know-how technology" was perceived by companies who had never experienced outsourcing, with little relevance for those who do use this option. In fact, research shows that the gap between companies who implement outsourcing and companies who do not is very significant: supplier dependence is feared by 35.1% of companies that do not implement outsourcing, compared to 15.1% by those implementing it; the "loss of technological know-how" is feared by 21.7% of companies that do not implement outsourcing, while feared by only 9.6% from those implementing it.

This empirical evidence reinforces the idea that emerging distinctive competence made up of the ability to coordinate and manage the "innovation network" presupposes accepting the fragmentation of the company's business system (Quinn and Hilmer, 1994; Di Romualdo and Gurbaxani, 1998; Domberger, 1998; Dyer and Singh, 1998; Baden-Fuller, Targett and Hunt, 2000; Sambamurthy and Zmud, 2000; Mahnke, 2001; Lee, 2001; Kedia and Mukherjee, 2009) and the involvement of third parties in the development of the company's innovative capacity, and therefore its competitive capacity. These organizational design changes are essential in the face of macro-environmental changes, such as rapid technological development, globalization and the consequent hypercompetition, the new geography in the world of expertise (Lou, 2007; Holcomb and Hitt, 2007).

From the supply side of IT services, that which once prevented outsourcing to be a suitable solution for managing processes of value creation was the difficulty of finding qualified experts on the market who were able to understand the business needs of clients and identify appropriate IT solution that completely integrated with the specific processes with on which individual companies built their competitive capacities.

This difficulty was also due to the approach of standardization that characterized the providers' traditional offering. This standardization allowed IT companies to achieve economy of scale and therefore base their business strategy on cost leadership. Recently, providers have realized that their business costumers' needs are no longer only linked to obtaining cost advantage, but are increasing links to improving performance quality and acquiring differentiated services tailored to the company's needs. Therefore, also the competitive strategies of providers, from being predominantly based on cost leadership, have gradually shifted towards differentiation. This was made possible by the considerable development of their information technology skills, and more pronounced *marketing oriented* approach. For example, the striking aspect of many Indian providers is the strong sense of commitment and the elevated operative flexibility in regards to the needs of their business clients. These companies take a *client satisfaction* approach that translates into availability for relationships and long-term partnerships.

Finally, what characterizes this third phase of development of the IT services market is the phenomenon of the polarization of knowledge and information skills. IT providers are increasingly specialized and able to offer clients solutions for business development. In fact, during the nineties, there was a geographic dispersion of skills in the IT field, which, however, also showed the limit of qualitative growth. Since then, some countries, not all, have succeeded in planning the development of knowledge through coordinating and finalizing IT investments, giving birth to actual innovative "poles".

The emerging phenomenon of *selective outsourcing* is the actual effect of the polarization of knowledge and differentiation of services specialized to serve companies' specific problems. Selective outsourcing, in fact, consists in externalizing parts of information systems or specific segments of the company's activities (Lacity and Wilcox, 1998). Whatever the specific object of selective outsourcing, the primary goal is to directly access a particular resource (Aiea-Clusit, 2006): specific professional skills, targeted application solutions, particularly innovative technology or niche technology.

Furthermore, the evolution of the "*utility on demand*" market follows the logic of turning to those firms who can best satisfy a company's present and changing needs, not necessarily a single provider[6]. The demand for "*managed service*" from the point of view of selective outsourcing is linked to companies' needs for the most advance technologies to increase their capacity to react in the environment (greater flexibility), and to have the highest level of security and computing capacity for their information systems. The diverse and changing business needs of companies, especially companies who work in the global arena, render *full outsourcing*, in which the IT service provider, bound by a long term contract, handles all the activities and IT processes for a company, inadequate. Moreover, by acquiring skills through offshoring, companies can avoid transferring parts of business operations abroad to acquire specialization from around the world (Al Najjari, 2003): in this sense, this business model has been defined by some as "metanational" (Doz, Santos and Williamson, 2004).

CRITICAL FACTORS OF IT OFFSHORING FOR VALUE CREATION

We have so far described how the overview of outsourcing is highlighting new trends and imposing new logical interpretations of the phenomenon, both in strategies and management models. Moreover, the change of perspective shown in this work does not only relate to the objectives that companies are gradually expanding and differentiating with respect to the past, but also to the gradual realization that the Sourcing Strategy should be seen as a whole and in its dynamics (Popoli A., 2009): as a whole, i.e. not limited to a single sector or project, but as a management integrated system of alliances; in its dynamics, i.e. its volatility resulting from the evolution of skill inquiry, the volumes of activity, a change of priority targets, etc..

This openness to third parties allows companies to seek the "best skills" around the world, but calls for a change of approach, an approach that transcends the logic of trade and contracts, and adopts a logic of "sharing" and "reciprocal integration" (Madhok, 2006; Vivek, Shankar and Banwet, 2008; Vivek, Glenn Richey and Dalela, 2009).

If the aim of the relationship is the co-generation of new common knowledge, it is no longer enough to define contractual rules to coordinate the action of the parties; it is necessary to create the organizational conditions for facilitating the sharing of knowledge and the integration of the respective value chains: of the client firm and of the provider firm. In particular, we can say that we will achieve real success in the relationship if and only if we are able to integrate the value chains of both the parties or, in other words, if and only if activities, processes or functions assigned to the service provider are totally aligned to his business strategy and development plans. The successful inter-firm collaborations are a product of both partners achieving their goals (Lee and Kim, 1999; Hitt, Dacin, Levitas, Arregle and Borza, 2000; Dyer, Kale and Singh, 2001).

Moreover, Di Romualdo and Gurbaxani (1998) affirm that "for a successful outsourcing relationship, the operating styles and cultures of both organizations, client and vendor, must be compatible at all levels". Sambamurthy and Zmud (2000) argue that flexibility is the essential element for a firm's interorganizational IT arrangements. In a relational view, highly specified and formalized contracts may have severe limitations, and relationship between provider and client may be better based on mutual trust (Lee and Kim, 1999; Poppo and Zenger, 2002). Mahnke, Overby and Vang (2003) point out that today outsourcing contracts are less defined *ex ante* and tend to be more relationship based.

In conclusion, it's possible for a company to develop new skills and innovation by means of a partner, if and only if, there is a corresponding development plan for the partner that can be "translated" in a win-win contract. In this way, "offshoring relationship are a moving target in terms of governance of relationship from transactional to resource complementary to a phase where trust and long-term orientation governs the offshored process or processes" (Vivek, Glenn Richey and Dalela, 2009).

From these considerations, it follows fully that the contract is central as a critical success factor, both in the drafting and negotiation phase, and the contract management phase. As Popoli A. (2009, p. 59) points out, the contract, being the instrument of connection between business strategies, is critical for various reasons:

a. "the contract has legal validity between the parties, which makes it not *apriori* adaptable to changes in scenario and requirements. Thus it is essential for it to include explicitly the possibility of modifications and integrations, as well as the procedures of *change management* enabling it to be modified while in course;
b. *service level agreements* should be linked to the real company's business goals, avoiding strict obligations to respect the numerous indicators which all too often ensure not required (and sometimes not useful) levels of quality and responsiveness. The definition of SLAs drawn up only on the basis of technical/operative criteria or parameters introduces not only the risk of an excessive rigidity for the provider but also the impossibility of being able to overcome this. It may be helpful to give an example. A standard indicator in services of bug fixing in the context of Application Outsourcing contracts is *resolution time*, meaning the time taken to solve an application error measured from when it was reported to its release in the operative environment. An SLA which required for all errors a very short resolution time would mean a continuous and onerous installation activity in production, with a consequent interruption in operative availability for end users. A more suitable solution, frequently adopted nowadays, can instead be to base the resolution time on a classification of errors according to severity and priority, leaving less serious errors to be dealt with in production and programmed "patches";
c. it is fairly clear that a contract should meet (or seek to meet) the needs and expectations of the client. It is less obvious or usual for the needs and expectations of the provider to be examined in detail. Making the contract central helps to focus attention on the provider's standpoint, laying the foundations for a genuine partnership rather than leaving this to be only a declaration of intent or a purely commercial matter".

In practice, very often the negotiation phase is conceived instead as merely aimed at finding a balance between Terms and Conditions to protect the parties against negative events or occurrence of conflicts. It also follows that "the definition and formalization phase of a contract often only comes after a business agreement is considered to have been entered into by buyer and vendor. Thus the phase of drawing up the contract becomes merely a negotiation concerning general terms and conditions which all too often introduce elements of extreme rigidity into the relationship" (Popoli A., 2009, p. 58).

Another critical success factor of offshoring – but this may apply generally to the choice of outsourcing – is the management of choice within the company. This regards internal communication, and in particular relates to the fact that there is awareness at all levels of organizational goals and objectives to achieve through this choice. There needs to be full alignment between business strategy and sourcing strategy, i.e. between top management and middle management. Otherwise, inadequate communication between the various levels of management can determine both the effect of reactive or obstructionist conduct within the company with respect to new organizational and operational model, and a different interpretation of the benefits and risks associated with choice outsourcing. Consequently, for these reasons during the life of the outsourcing relationship, factors may arise that cause friction or impede the desired results.

In conclusion, the organizational risk of outsourcing is not only the lack of integration between structures, cultures, and operating procedures between customer and its providers, but also an underestimation of the internal dynamics of the organization, with particular reference to issues of human resource management. In this respect, top management must be able to identify the right way, the right time and the right content for internal communication of this organizational change. It should be carefully planned and detailed, so the choice is the least traumatic as possible within the organization. As Greaver (1999) noted, "the true measure of their success will be how quickly the employees accept the change and move forward".

CONCLUSION AND FUTURE DEVELOPMENTS

We have tried to show how the IT offshore outsourcing may be interpreted, increasingly in the future, as an articulate and complex tool for pursuing strategic goals which go well beyond the traditional objectives of cost saving. In the past, the traditional analysis of IT offshoring was focused on evaluating the affordability of the options to make or buy, in light of the *transaction cost theory*. Diversely, from a strategic perspective, IT offshoring represents a way for companies to acquire resources and skills for business innovation and development. In many cases, it is a forced choice: the growing competiveness of global markets and the continued development of technologies require companies to "open" their value chains to the contributions in innovation and development that third parties can offer. Thus, the new interpretative keys of the phenomenon lie in the most recent approaches to strategic management, combined with contributions from several other theories: *resource based view, knowledge management, core competences, relational view.* These theoretic frameworks attribute particular importance to cooperative relationships aimed at increasing resources and skills to be used in business innovation and development.

At the same time, greater potential in IT offshoring has made it more difficult to manage relations with providers, because increasing the strategic dimensions of this option corresponds with increased economic and strategic risks. The success of offshoring depends on a variety of factors which, however, act interdependently. The fact that in many cases the choice of offshoring has not produced the desired benefits, allows for the assertion, according to Bhalla, Sodhi and Son (2008), that it is not possible to theorize a positive relationship between offshoring and improving business performance.

From our analysis arise critical factors in managing outsourcing relationships aimed at the innovation and improvement of value creation processes.

1. The approach to IT offshoring must move from a transaction-based to a relationship-

based or partnership-based approach. This means, above all, that the main tool for the relationship, the contract, should allow an adequate level of flexibility and dynamism needed to maintain the relationship between the two partners always aligned to their strategic goals, according to a "win-win" logic. From this point of view, we believe that a true partnership between two entities can only operate if their value chains integrate both the strategic and operational profile.

2. Another very important aspect related to the relational dimension is the change of parameters and criteria for selecting a provider. In the past, the evaluation criteria for providers was focused mainly on a set of "*subjective requirements*", including economic and financial solidity, expertise, customer portfolios, experience in the sector, and available material and immaterial resources. Little consideration was given to the "*relational requirements*" of the provider, or rather the propensity for partnership, sharing of objectives and risk, the possibility of organizational integration, the availability of effectuating shard investment, the compatibility of value systems, etc.. These requirements are now central in evaluating the choice of provider, in that they constitute the necessary conditions to enable an outsourcing relationship to evolve towards a partnership and shared goals. In particular, it is necessary that the provider's value chain and capabilities be evaluated in terms of structural and strategic compatibility with respect to the client company.
3. To align strategic objectives between the provider and client, it is necessary to use organizational tools for managing the relationship. These relationships will no longer be based merely on contractual obligations but will involve coordination mechanisms, both formal and informal, to facilitate the joint undertaking of programming and operative activities. In practice the rationale of networking, which for some time could be seen as modifying exchanges between client and provider, in strategic decisions regarding offshoring reaches its full affirmation in a sector like IT, in which the knowledge factor dominates the production processes.

As regards, finally, some directions for future research on the IT offshoring processes, in traditional empirical research much attention was given to economic evaluation aspects, even if there is still much to be investigated on identifying and quantifying hidden costs of offshoring. Little attention was given to analyzing offshoring processes from a strategic perspective, as an instrument for value creation. Studies still need to be done to investigate how the "on time" availability of strategic skills from external sources can quickly be used in the value chain processes.

In our opinion, future empirical researches should be based on this kind of analysis and aimed to validate the proposed new paradigm for IT outsourcing. In particular, future research should provide answers as to how IT outsourcing can improve the innovation capability of a company and how it works in value creation. For example, the communication industry provides a wide set of case studies where the acquisition from external sources of new core skills is no longer a choice, being necessary to ensure a constant and rapid update of technologies and software platforms.

A further direction for future empiric researches should be found in investigating key factors both in success and failure cases of relevant outsourcing contracts within innovation programs. Indeed, very few cases of failure are usually available in literature, basically for the natural difficulty in gathering the information with enough level of transparency and details. Moreover, the analysis of both success and failure key factors should be aimed to confirm (or refute) that governance of relationship and expectations management play fundamental roles not only in the planning and contracting phases but – especially – in the ongoing management and for the entire duration of the contract.

Finally, further research development should be focused on offshoring models, aimed to investigate how companies are able to control the increased complexity in managing geographically distributed providers – with different cultures and languages – by means of a fine balancing among offshoring, near-shoring and on-shoring options. In this context, further empirical research could investigate more deeply the problem of hidden costs associated with offshoring choices, especially in terms of their quantification, and how the different offshoring models differ in terms of balance between opportunity, on one hand, and economic, strategic and organizational risks on the other.

REFERENCES

Accabi, R., & Lopez, L. (1995). Outsourcing estremo per situazioni complesse. *L'Impresa, 10.*

AIEA & CLUSIT. (2006). *The IT outsourcing: best practice and auditing*. Milano: Aiea-Clusit.

Al Najjari, N. (2005). Le Pmi tra delocalizzazione e neo protezionismo: quali opzioni per chi va, quali scelte per chi resta. [Electronic version]. *PMI*, *4*, 31–37.

Baden-Fuller, C., Targett, D., & Hunt, B. (2000). Outsourcing to outmanoeuvre: outsourcing redefines competitive strategy and structure. *European Management Journal*, *18*(3), 285–295. doi:10.1016/S0263-2373(00)00010-4

Barthélemy, J. (2001). The hidden costs of IT outsourcing. *Sloan Management Review, Spring.*

Barthélemy, J., & Dominique, G. (2004). The determinants of total IT outsourcing: An empirical investigation of French and German firms. *Journal of Computer Information Systems*, *44*(3), 91–98.

Bhalla, A., Sodhi, M. S., & Son, B. (2008). Is more IT offshoring better? An exploratory study of western companies offshoring to South East Asia. *Journal of Operations Management*, *26*, 322–335. doi:10.1016/j.jom.2007.02.005

Brandes, H., Lilliecreutz, J., & Brege, S. (1997). Outsourcing: success or failure? *European Journal of Purchasing & Supply Management*, *3*, 63–75. doi:10.1016/S0969-7012(97)00001-4

Di Romualdo, A., & Gurbaxani, V. (1998). Strategic intent for IT outsourcing. *Sloan Management Review, Summer*.

Domberger, S. (1998). *The contracting organization. A guide to strategic outsourcing. Oxford.* UK: Oxford University Press.

Dossani, R., & Kenney, M. (2004). *The next wave of globalization: Exploring the relocation of service provision to India*. Working paper. Stanford, CA: Asia Pacific Research Center, Stanford University.

Doz, Y., Santos, R., & Williamson, O. (2004). *Da globale a metanazionale*. Bologna: Il Mulino.

Dyer, J. K., Kale, P., & Singh, H. (2001). How to make strategic alliances work. *Sloan Management Review*, (Summer): 37–44.

Dyer, J. K., & Singh, H. (1998). The relational view: cooperative strategy and sources of interorganizational competitive advantage. *Academy of Management Review*, *23*(4), 660–679. doi:10.2307/259056

Ellram, L. M., Tate, W. L., & Billington, C. (2008). Offshore outsourcing of professional services: A transaction cost economics perspective. *Journal of Operations Management*, *26*, 148–163. doi:10.1016/j.jom.2007.02.008

Garner, C.A. (2004). Offshoring in the service sector: economic impact and policy issues. *Federal Reserve Bank of Kansas City Economic Review, third-quarter.*

Gefen, D., & Carmel, E. (2008). Is the world really flat? A look at offshoring at an online programming marketplace. *Management Information Systems Quarterly*, *32*(2), 367–384.

Greaver, M. F. (1999). *Strategic outsourcing. A structured approach to outsourcing decisions and initiatives*. New York: Amacom.

Hahn, E. D., & Bunyaratavej, K. (2010). Services cultural alignment in offshoring: The impact of cultural dimensions on offshoring location choices. *Journal of Operations Management*, *28*, 186–193. doi:10.1016/j.jom.2009.10.005

Head, K., Mayer, T., & Ries, J. (2009). How remote is the offshoring threat? *European Economic Review*, *53*, 429–444. doi:10.1016/j.euroecorev.2008.08.001

Hinterhuber, H. & Stuhec, U. (1996). Competenze distintive e outsourcing strategico. *Finanza, Marketing e Produzione, 4.*

Hitt, M., Dacin, M. T., Levitas, E., Arregle, J. L., & Borza, A. (2000). Partner selection in emerging and developed market contexts: resource-based and organizational learning perspective. *Academy of Management Journal*, *43*, 449–467. doi:10.2307/1556404

Hofstede, G. H. (2001). *Culture's consequences: Comparing values, behaviors, institutions and organizations across nations*. CA: Thousand Oaks.

Holcomb, R. T., & Hitt, M. A. (2007). Toward a model of strategic outsourcing. *Journal of Operations Management*, *25*, 464–481. doi:10.1016/j.jom.2006.05.003

Jilovec, N. (2005). L'offshoring delle risorse IT. *I-Series News, marzo* 22-26.

Kedia, B. L., & Lahiri, S. (2007). International outsourcing of services: A partnership model. *Journal of International Management*, *13*, 22–37. doi:10.1016/j.intman.2006.09.006

Kedia, B. L., Lahiri, S., & Lovvorn, A. (2005). Seeking competitive advantage on distant shores. *European Business Forum*, *21*, 37–40.

Kedia, B. L., & Mukherjee, D. (2009). Understanding offshoring: A research framework based on disintegration, location and externalization advantages. *Journal of World Business*, *44*, 250–261. doi:10.1016/j.jwb.2008.08.005

Kotabe, M., & Murray, J. Y. (2004). Global sourcing strategy and sustainable competitive advantage. *Industrial Marketing Management*, *33*, 7–14. doi:10.1016/j.indmarman.2003.08.004

Lacity, M., & Willcocks, L. (1998). An empirical investigation of information technology sourcing practices: lessons from experience. *Management Information Systems Quarterly*, (September): 363–409. doi:10.2307/249670

Lampel, J., & Bhalla, A. (2008). Embracing realism and recognizing choice in IT offshoring initiatives. *Business Horizons*, *51*, 429–440. doi:10.1016/j.bushor.2008.03.007

Lee, J. N. (2001). The impact of knowledge sharing, organizational capability and partnership quality in IS outsourcing success. *Information & Management*, *38*, 323–335. doi:10.1016/S0378-7206(00)00074-4

Lee, J. N., & Kim, Y. G. (1999). Effects of partnership quality on IS outsourcing success: conceptual framework and empirical evidence. *Journal of Management Information Systems*, (Spring): 15, 29–61.

Leonard, J. (2006). Offshoring of information technology jobs: myths and realities. *American Sentinel University, May.*

Levina, N., & Vaast, E. (2008). Innovating or doing as told? Status differences and overlapping boundaries in offshore collaboration. *Management Information Systems Quarterly*, *32*(2), 307–332.

Lewin, A.Y. & Couto, V. (2007). *Next generation offshoring: The globalization of innovation*. Durkham: Duke University Ciber/Booz Allen Hamilton Report.

Lewin, A. Y., & Peeters, C. (2006). The top-line allure of offshoring. *Harvard Business Review*, *84*, 22–24.

Luo, Y. (2007). A coopetition perspective of global competition. *Journal of World Business*, *42*, 129–144. doi:10.1016/j.jwb.2006.08.007

Madhoc, A. (2006). How much does ownership really matter? Equity and trust relations in joint venture relationship. *Journal of International Business Studies*, *37*, 4–11. doi:10.1057/palgrave.jibs.8400182

Mahnke, V. (2001). The process of vertical dis-integration: an evolutionary perspective on outsourcing. *Journal of Management and Governance*, *5*, 353–379. doi:10.1023/A:1014003229386

Mahnke, V., Overby, M. L., & Vang, J. (2003). Strategic IT outsourcing: what do we know and need to know? *Paper presented at the Druid Conference 2003 on Creating, sharing and transferring knowledge*. Copenhagen, June 12-14.

Metters, R. (2008). A case study of national culture and offshoring services. *International Journal of Operations & Production Management*, *28*(8), 727–747. doi:10.1108/01443570810888616

Mol, M. J., van Tulder, R. J. M., & Beije, P. R. (2005). Antecedents and performance consequences of international outsourcing. *International Business Review*, *14*, 599–617. doi:10.1016/j.ibusrev.2005.05.004

Pfannenstein, L. L., & Tsai, R. J. (2004). Offshoring outsourcing: Current and future effect on American IT industry. *Information Systems Management*, *21*(4), 72–80. doi:10.1201/1078/44705.21.4.20040901/84190.9

Popoli, P., & Popoli, A. (2009). Old and new paradigms for IT services offshoring. *International Journal of Information Systems in the Service Sector*, *1*(3), 47–64.

Poppo, L., & Zenger, T. (2002). Do formal contracts and relational governance function as substitutes or complements? *Strategic Management Journal*, *23*, 707–725. doi:10.1002/smj.249

Prahalad, C. K., & Hamel, G. (1990). *The core competence of the corporation*. Harvard Business Review, May-June.

Quinn, J.B. (1999). Strategic outsourcing: leveraging knowledge capabilities. *Sloan Management Review, Summer.*

Quinn, J. B., & Hilmer, F. G. (1994). Strategic outsourcing. *Sloan Management Review*, 35.

Renard, I. (2003, December 8). L'outsourcing vers les low cost. L'angle Juridique. [Electronic version]. *Edhec Business et Technologie – Télécom Bretagne – Club France Amériques.*

Rottman, J., & Lacity, M. (2004). Twenty practices for offshore sourcing. *MIS Quarterly Executive*, *3*(3), 117–130.

Sambamurthy, V., & Zmud, R. (2000). Research commentary: the organizing logic for an enterprise's IT activities in the digital era. A prognosis of practice and a call for research. *Information Systems Research*, *11*(2), 105–114. doi:10.1287/isre.11.2.105.11780

Stringfellow, A., Teagarden, M., & Nie, W. (2008). Invisible costs in offshoring services worl. *Journal of Operations Management*, *26*, 164–179. doi:10.1016/j.jom.2007.02.009

Teece, D. J., Pisano, G., & Shuen, A. (1990). *Firm capabilities, resources and concept of strategy: four paradigms of strategic management*. Berkeley: University of California, Center for Research in Management.

Venkatraman, N. (1997). Beyond outsourcing: managing IT resource as a value center. *Research Policy*, *26*, 51–63.

Vivek, S. D., Glenn Richey, R., & Dalela, V. (2009). A longitudinal examination of partnership governance in offshoring: A moving target. *Journal of World Business*, *44*, 16–30. doi:10.1016/j.jwb.2008.03.017

Vivek, S. D., Shankar, R., & Banwet, D. K. (2008). Analysis of interactions among core, transaction and relationship-specific investments: The case of offshoring. *Journal of Operations Management*, *26*(2), 180–197. doi:10.1016/j.jom.2007.02.010

Williamson, O. E. (1986). *Economic organization. Firms, markets and policy control*. London: Harverster Wheatsheaf.

ENDNOTES

1 The CMMI defines the evolution of an organization as follows: Level 1: *Initial*. The process is characterized by a set of ad hoc activities. The process is not defined and success depends heavily on individual efforts and acts of "heroism". Level 2: *Managed*. At this level you put into practice the elementary processes of management to track costs, time activities and define functions. Discipline is somehow available to repeat the initial successes in similar projects. Level 3: *Defined*. The process is documented for both managerial and technical activities and is based on defined standards. All projects use an approved and customized (if necessary) version of the standard business model for the development and maintenance of software. Level 4: *Quantitatively Managed*. Detailed information on the quality of software process and product are collected. Both process and product are assessed and monitored from a quantitative point of view. Level 5: *Optimizing*. Continuous improvement of the process is enabled by quantitative feedback from the metric system applied to the process itself and the technological innovation initiatives and processes related to the critical areas monitored.

2 Offshore projects can be divided up into two main categories: "fixed-price projects", in which the client does not participate in the developmental phase but merely outlines the requisite aims; "collaborative projects", in which the offshore team participates in developing the project together with the insite team, in a *co-sourced* approach, requiring adequate processes of communication and interaction between client company and provider.

3 Lampel and Bhalla (2008) mentioning the outsourcing experience of Sainsbury's, British food retailers, who in 2000 decided to outsource IT activities because the company considered it as a mere cost center. Next, Sainsbury's reintroduced these activities in-house because the top management realized that IT activities represented a "strategic differentiator". In particular, automation of the logistics system had an important impact on the availability of goods within the stores, and that this was a very important component of the value created for consumers.

4 *Business Process Outsourcing* involves outsourcing management processes in their entirety, such as human resources, supply chain, logistics, training, financial services, and also R&D.

5 *Transformational Outsourcing* involves engaging a provider to operate a radical transformation of the company's whole informatic system, and manage the associated changeover both of organizational and managerial processes and of business characteristics and rationale.

6 The added value which now characterises the offers of "outsourcing on demand" is

flexibility, thanks to the ability of the provider to offer personalised solutions and increase or diminish the calculating capacity of computer systems according to the client's business needs (e.g. for phenomena of seasonal variation or concerning new, specific initiatives), on the basis of "*sense and respond*", feasible only in the presence of a strong partnership.

Chapter 15
Online Services Delivered by NTO Portals:
A Cross-Country Examination

Marco Papa
University of Bari, Italy

Marina Avgeri
Monte dei Paschi di Siena Bank, Italy

ABSTRACT

This study compares the online services currently delivered by the official National Tourism Organizations (NTO) portals of the 25 European Union states, to assess their capability in evolving into powerful marketing communication tools. A conceptual framework that identifies 129 online service quality attributes is developed based on the 2QCV3Q model (Mich et al., 2003) and on four different perspectives: marketing, customer, technical and information for the destination (So and Morrison, 2004). The 25 portals are compared by means of content analysis. Our rankings provide a first time assessment of the NTO online offerings and indicate high variability in their performance. Surprisingly, Greece and Italy, two of the most popular tourism destinations, underperformed with respect to all four perspectives examined. We provide out-of-sample evidence that affluence levels explain the variation in the observed scores, while e-readiness, popularity of tourism destination and cultural richness are not statistically significant.

INTRODUCTION: THE ROLE OF NATIONAL TOURISM ORGANIZATIONS' PORTALS

Among the Destination Management Organizations (DMOs), prominent is the role of the National Tourism Organizations (NTOs[1]) in marketing a destination at a national level. Prior to the Internet era the DMOs have been rather passive and limited to the distribution of printed tourist promotional material on demand (So and Morrison, 2004; King, 2002). However, the adoption and the diffusion of e-commerce applications have provoked unprecedented changes (Wöber, 2003). All European Union (EU) members have invested in the development of websites with different levels of interactivity (Morgan et al., 2002). Essentially, these portals undertake the management of "content information" relating to a tourist destination, arriving from a wide variety of different sources

DOI: 10.4018/978-1-60960-138-6.ch015

(Turban et al., 2004: 322). By assuming the role of on line brokers of information providers, they become responsible for matching cross cultural demand of individual tourists with the destinations' tourism service supply (Scharl et al., 2004).

Different studies indicate that NTO portals should not be perceived exclusively as information seeking facilitators (Morgan et al., 2002). Instead, they should aim to evolve into powerful interactive marketing communication tools (Sainaghi, 2006; Griff and Palmer, 1999[2]; Cano and Prentice, 1998) that have the potential to enhance the overall attractiveness of a travel destination and to evoke an optimal experience for their on line users, offering superior value to different customer groups (Nysveen et al., 2003). However, while the trend of internet being the first point of embarkation for prospect tourists is gaining *momentum* (Buhalis and Licata, 2002) and the presence of NTOs through internet is becoming better established (Feng et al., 2002), there is still a *paucity* of empirical research regarding the online offerings and the internet marketing strategies undertaken from them.

Under the recognition that it is important to examine NTOs in an *exploratory way*, where the dimensions of online quality from a customer perspective will serve as a framework, this study compares the official European NTO portals online offerings. The aim is to examine *what* information and services of value added each of the 25 EU portals is offering and *why* their offerings differ. To this end, as first objective, there were identified the online services that may facilitate the tourist search, evaluation of information and purchase of services via the NTO sites, based on a deep inspection of the e-Service Quality (e-SQ) and the DMO empirical literature. Secondly, these portals were compared by means of content analysis in order to study the service quality attributes provided and to investigate the extent to which four country context variables explain differences in the NTOs' performance.

E-SERVICE QUALITY AND DMO OFFERINGS

The way e-SQ is conceptualized is still at an exploratory stage. Researchers not only have tried to combine known dimensions that influence product quality and Service Quality (SQ), but also to discover some unique factors, relevant to the virtual operations only. The e-SQ attributes seem to depend on the level of web-based technology readiness of the different users (Zhu et al., 2002) and do not to demonstrate a linear relationship, since "more" of an attribute is not necessarily perceived as better (O'Neill et al., 2001).

In order to define e-SQ, some authors take into account both the *pre* and *post* web sites services aspects (Santos, 2003; Liu and Arnett, 2000), while others consider only the interaction with the site itself (Zeithaml et al., 2002). Additionally, in contrast to the traditional service offerings, online users tend to regard e-SQ more as a universal concept, deriving from their overall online experience, rather than from sub-processes (Van Riel et al., 2001).[3] The *focus* of each individual research (e.g., consumer buying procedure), as well as the *types of web sites* used (e.g., portals, retailing sites, etc.) determine how the definition of e-SQ may be conceptualised (Kim et al., 2006). Given that the NTO portals' core activity is to help customers at different stages in the information search process, the definition of website quality used in this study is based on the concept of value added services as provided by Nysveen (2003) and Lexhagen (2004): "Services giving access to various forms of information about the tourism products offered on a website", disregarding approaches tailored for e-commerce shopping (Zeithaml et al., 2002), or based on an ex-ante definition of e-services (Santos, 2003: 235).

Not only defining, but also measuring the multidimensional construct of e-SQ continues to generate increased academic debate. Many different scales have been proposed during the last eight years based on different classifications of quality dimensions and attributes (O'Neill et al., 2001; Madu and Madu, 2002; Zhu et al., 2002; Yoo and Donthu 2001; Santos, 2003; Zeithmal et al., 2002; Parasuraman et al., 2005, etc.), either emphasizing the *human and soft* elements of service quality or the *technical dimensions* of on line efficiency, or both (Sigala, 2004).

An extended framework, which incorporates many of the e-SQ dimensions proposed by previous approaches, has been developed by Madu and Madu (2002). Their model included some of the product quality dimensions according to Garvin (1984), as well as the 5 quality dimensions of the SERVQUAL scale (Parasuraman et al., 1988), while it identified some unique, new dimensions, appropriate only for virtual contexts. Even if the proposed dimensions have never been tested empirically, it is interesting the evolutionary approach it adopts, encompassing both product and services features.

Barnes and Vidgen (2000)[4] based on 54 students' evaluations of British online bookstores, have extended the SERVQUAL scale of Parasuraman et al. (1988) to an online context, encompassing softer service related attributes by introducing 24 different measurement items under their index named WebQual. They focused on the following aspects: *reliability, competence, responsiveness, access, credibility, communication and understanding*. Later on, Loiacono et al. (2002)[5] proposed the WebQual™ scale which emphasised again the technical aspects of the website in the evaluation of its online quality, developing 12 web design features. This approach has been criticised by Zeithaml et al. (2002) and Parasuram et al. (2005), for having limited capabilities in capturing important quality dimensions (e.g., "fulfilment", customer service), since these scales have been produced by using convenience samples of students rather than actual online purchasers. A further drawback derives from the fact that the participating students have rated researcher specified categories that had not emerged through a qualitative study.

Parasuraman et al. (2005) recently have developed the well known E-S-QUAL model. Under the latter, e-service quality dimensions have been divided into 7 categories: *efficiency, availability, fulfilment, privacy, service recovery dimension, compensation and contact*. A recent application of the E-S-QUAL model has been undertaken by Kim et al. (2006) which evaluated the performance of 111 US apparel retail websites in providing on line service attributes that facilitate efficient and effective shopping, purchasing and delivery of garments. Such on line service attributes were examined by means of content analysis, by considering the E-S-QUAL categories, accommodated to include other dimensions: *personalisation, information and graphic style*, regarded as relevant for the specific retail context. Overall, it was found that the e-SQ level of the sample companies was unsatisfactory.

Previous studies have investigated tourism websites from three different perspectives: a) from a business, b) from a customer perspective and c) a combination of the previous two. The former implies that the on line quality is evaluated as superior according to where the business is in the transformation process: *if a site is only informative or whether it offers more advanced features such as on line booking services, etc.* (Larson and Ankomah, 2005; Hart et al., 2000[6]; O' Connor, 1999[7]; Doolin et al., 2002). Representatives of this strand: Doolin et al. (2002), extended and applied an internet commerce adoption metric (eMICA) developed by Burgess and Cooper (2000)[8] for benchmarking the relative maturity of 26 New Zealand's Regional Tourism Organizations (RTO) websites and concluded that the majority of them displayed moderate to high levels of interactivity. The customer perspective encompasses two different approaches: the first assesses the websites according to their level of customer support during the information searching process, thus following a "consumer behavior theory"; whereas the second according to their level of design features superiority. Finally, under the last approach the business and customer perspectives are combined together, within different contingent evaluation frameworks, ranging from technical approaches, such as the Balanced Scorecard (Morrison et al., 1999; Ismail et al., 2002; Feng et al., 2002; So and Morrison, 2004), to more theoretical ones, such as the Marketspace model (Blum and Fallon, 2002), which emphasized the marketing mix and the customer relationships.

Moreover, so far, research in assessing websites effectiveness in the tourism sector, has been mainly focused on either a) opinions of experts of tourist services providers (Chung and Law, 2003; Hudson and Lang, 2002; Jung and Butler, 2000) or b) end users (tourists) evaluations (e.g. Jeong et al., 2003, Tierney 2000)[9] or c) by applying quantitative measures (e.g., Scharl et al., 2004, Wöber, 2003). Regardless of whether the end users or the tourist experts have been focused upon, both directions' research findings seem to converge in one common admittance: *the importance of the online content* in terms of richness of information, features and services (Huizingh, 2000; Scharl et al., 2004; Cai et al., 2004b) and *content quality* (Aladwani and Pavia, 2002) as critical success factor of tourism websites. In particular, as far as destination portals are concerned, their content has been broadly recognised (Doolin et al., 2002, Cano and Prentice, 1998) as being responsible for creating the perceived image of the destination. Finally, there is also a recent research stream (Skadberg et al., 2005; Chen and Wells, 1999, Hoffman and Novak, 1996)[10] which supports that since tourism is mainly experiential, the overall web site effectiveness depends on the flow experience of the online visitors in tourism destination websites.

Recently, Feng et al. (2002), Ismail et al. (2002) and So and Morrison (2004), in three papers, by means of content analysis, compared the performance of DMO websites of different countries, based on the Balanced Scorecard (BSC) approach, developed by Kaplan and Norton (1996)[11]. These studies acknowledge tourism website performance in a holistic way, encompassing four different perspectives. The first study compared 36 Chinese DMO websites to 30 US DMO websites and concluded that the latter were superior in terms of marketing strategies and destination information provided. The second study examined website's information content and photos from a cultural point of view, while the third one compared 15 East Asian NTO sites, concluding that none of them had been particular effective as an online marketing tool.

Finally, Mich et al. (2003, 2002) have developed a meta-model 2QCV3Q, to compare the regional tourist boards (RTB) websites in the area of Alps. In their approach, quality of web site has been identified as the ability to satisfy the needs and objectives of all the online users involved. Their model, by asking a set of questions, identifies seven dimensions of quality, according to which the tourism websites' overall quality was assessed, revealing a poor performance in terms of dissemination of information and use of modern technology.

From the above e-SQ and DMO literature, it can be concluded that regardless of the numerous different approaches developed through the last years, there still does not exist a detailed framework that provides a comprehensive understanding of e-SQ which could be used for the evaluation of websites and portals *independently* of sector of belonging. A common practice instead has been to tailor the different e-SQ models to the specific study under investigation.

DETERMINANTS OF NTO PORTALS SERVICE QUALITY ACROSS THE EU

The main objective of this study is to examine the characteristics of the NTO online offerings and to analyse which factors can explain the level of service quality observed. Our sample consists of the 25 EU official NTO portals, evaluated between June and July 2006. The latter organizations have been chosen, due to their unquestionable importance as primary suppliers of online information and services to market a destination and as coordinators of the other local/regional tourism authorities initiatives (Ismail et al., 2002; Cai et al., 2004a). By observing the global tourism statistics (United Nations Conference on Trade and Development, UNCTAD, 2005; World Tourism Organization, WTO, 2005), in terms of international arrivals and volume of tourist receipts, it was decided to focus on the whole population of EU states NTO portals since it was confirmed that the majority of the most significant tourism markets (e.g., France, Italy, UK, Spain, Germany, Austria, etc.) are found among those.

To the extent of our knowledge, no empirical study has defined and tested, through empirical analysis, any variables which could be particularly relevant to explain NTO portal service quality. Under the recognition that important regional differences do exist, four main country variables have been examined: affluence, tourism popularity, e-readiness and cultural richness.

It is widely believed that the extent of e-business adoption is associated with a country's economic development. For example, Di Gregorio et al. (2005) provide empirical evidence of e-business activity differences between high income nations and emerging markets. This disparity could support the initial claims that developing countries would benefit from the wide diffusion of the Internet and e-business. Different definition may be used to classify developed and emerging countries (e.g., the International Monetary Fund classification, the World Bank, the World Economic Outlook Report, etc.), this paper uses the 2005 Gross Domestic Product (GDP) per capita of the EU states, at purchase power parity, expressed in international $ (Euro monitor, 2006) to detect the "level of affluence" of each country. In this way it is possible to avoid that the results are dependent up on a specific definition. Based on the average GPD the EU states were dived into two different groups: affluent (less affluent) countries (see Table 1).

Along with the economic factor, a country's tourism industry and its popularity will likely influence NTO portals offerings. Buhalis and Deimezi (2004), explain that the inadequacy of the national planning process and the lack of infrastructures have affected the development of a comprehensive portal to promote Greek tourism. The popularity of a destination has been used as a proxy to enable a *first* appreciation of tourism industry. The popular (less popular) destinations (see Table 1) were identified by using the average number of tourist arrivals in the EU states for the year 2004 (WTO, 2005).

Certain academics (e.g., Di Gregorio et al., 2005), and consulting companies (e.g., Economic Intelligence Unit, Forester Research, etc.) have examined the extent to which "e-readiness" could be associated with the development of e-business adoption. Similarly, it could be the case that the "state of play" of a country's Information and Communication Technology (ICT) and the ability to use the latter, will explain difference in the on line offering of NTO portals. To examine this relation, the EU member states were divided into two groups: e-advanced (e-early stages) destinations (see Table 1) according to their e-readiness rankings, as emerged from the 2005 Economist Intelligence Unit study (Economist, 2005).

Apart from the country's e-readiness, "cultural richness" is a further variable that is supposed to have an impact on the present NTO offerings. In our case, the number of world heritages listed by the United Nations Education, Scientific and Cultural Organization (UNESCO) has been used as a proxy (http://whc.unesco.org/en/list/) of "cultural richness". According to the average number of listed sites, the 25 EU states were divided into two groups: cultural rich (less cultural rich) destinations (see Table 1).

As no one of the empirical literature on DMO has examined the effects of the above factors on the e-quality of NTO portals and because there

Table 1. Proxy measures used to cluster the 25 EU states

EU member state	International tourist arrivals (1000) for 2004[a]	Destination tourism popularity above the EU average	GDP per capita at ppp in $ (2005)[b]	Levels of affluence above the EU average	Economist E-readiness classification 2005	2005 E-readiness classification above average	No of UNESCO heritages	Cultural richness
Austria	19.400	1	33.822	3	8	5	8	8
Belgium	6.710	2	31.196	3	8	5	9	8
Cyprus	2.349	2	21.602	4	n.a	7	3	8
Czech Republic	6.061	2	18.404	4	6	7	12	8
Denmark	3.358	2	34.673	3	9	5	4	8
Estonia	1.750	2	16.452	4	6	5	2	8
Finland	2.840	2	31.237	3	8	5	7	8
France	75.100	1	30.356	3	8	5	30	7
Germany	20.100	1	30.489	3	0	5	32	7
Greece	14.000	1	23.314	4	6	5	16	7
Hungary	12.200	2	16.852	4	6	7	8	8
Ireland	6.982	2	41.767	3	8	5	2	8
Italy	37.100	1	28.597	3	7	5	41	7
Latvia	1.080	2	12.666	4	5	7	2	8
Lithuania	1.491	2	14.236	4	5	7	4	8
Luxembourg	874	2	68.869	3	8	5	1	8
Malta	1.156	2	19.708	4	n.a	7	3	8
Netherlands	9.600	2	30.784	3	8	5	7	8
Poland	14.300	1	12.864	4	6	7	13	7
Portugal	11.600	2	19.387	4	7	7	13	7
Slovakia	1.401	2	16.168	4	6	7	5	8
Slovenia	1.499	2	21.846	4	6	5	1	8
Spain	53.600	1	26.642	3	0	5	39	7
Sweden	3.003	2	30.049	3	9	5	14	7
UK	27.800	1	30.648	3	9	5	27	7
mean	13.414		26.505		6		12	

Notes: 1 (2) means popular tourism (less popular tourism) countries; 3 (4) means affluent (less affluent) countries; 5 (6) means e-advanced (e-early stages) countries; 7 (8) means rich cultural (less cultural rich) countries; a) source: WTO, 2005; b) source: Euromonitor database, 2006.

may be different competing explanations, the hypotheses have been stated in the null from:

- **Affluence levels:** The online offerings performance of NTO portals' is equal, in affluent destinations and in less affluent destinations, within the EU;
- **Tourism popularity:** The online offerings performance of NTO portals' is equal in popular tourist destinations and in less popular tourist destinations, within the EU;
- **E-readiness:** The online offerings performance of NTO portals' is equal in e-advanced destinations and less e-advanced destinations, within the EU;
- **Cultural richness:** The online offerings performance of NTO portals' is equal in cultural rich destinations and in less cultural rich destinations within the EU.

While the two control variables associated with H_1 and H_4 contribute to the assessment of a positive relationship between institutional factors (economic development and country's cultural richness) and online NTO performances, the variables associated with H_2 and H_3 might explain the extent to which tourism infrastructures and e-readiness, including Internet and ICTs infrastructure, are factors that contribute to the development of NTO tourism portals, providing clear implications for policy makers.

Figure 1. Balance scorecard (BSC) framework (adapted from Ismail et al., 2002)

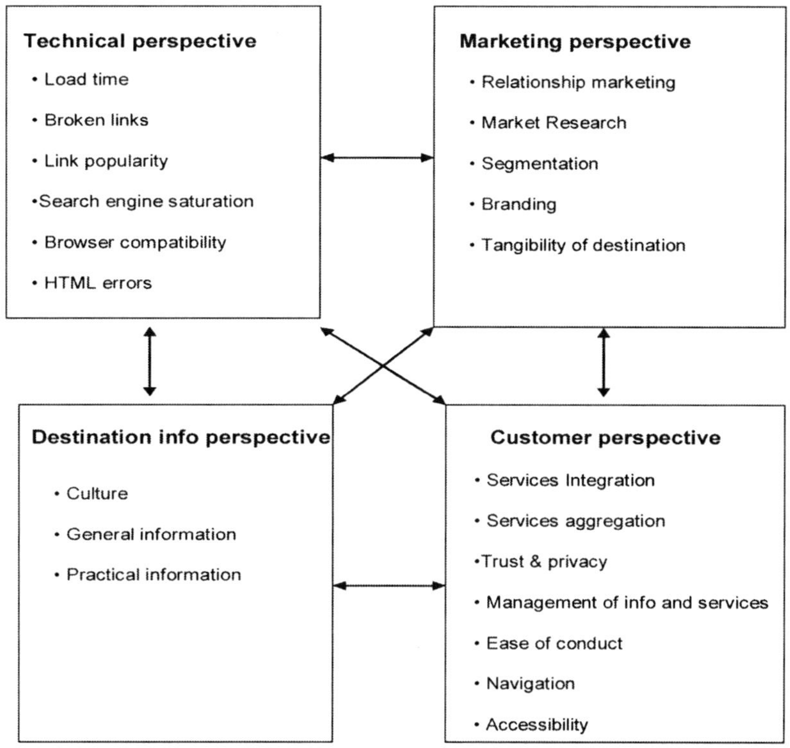

RESEARCH METHOD AND PERFORMANCE MEASUREMENT

In order to carry out the comparative analysis of the online offerings of the NTO portals in EU, content analysis was used to capture and quantify both the richness of the NTOs' information content and the number of useful services provided to the customers, which in turn shape important e-SQ dimensions, from a customer perspective. According to Weber (1985: 21–25), content analysis is process of creating and testing a coding instrument to identify the characteristics of a written message.

A prior-research driven approach (Boyatzis, 1998: 99) was followed in order to define the coding categories. The developed conceptual framework has emerged after taking into account the e-SQ literature discussed above (e.g., Kim et al., 2006), previous empirical studies on website evaluation (Mich and Franch, 2007), and best practices recommended by the World Tourist Organization (WTO, 2005). Together, it was generated a list of 129 attributes which were accommodated into 4 qualitative categories: *destination information, marketing, customer and technical perspective*, following the framework of the modified Balance Scorecard (BSC), as applied by So and Morrison (2004). The latter, was chosen due to its strong emphasis on customer service and marketing, both important features in evoking high levels of perceived e-SQ in tourism portals. Figure 1 and Table 2 illustrate the four categories and the full list of items, respectively.

Contrary to web evaluation based on a Likert type scale (Davidson and Yu, 2004; Morrison et al., 1999), a binary code was followed where a score of 1 was given if the item was available, and 0 if not[12]. According to the coding instrument's rules, multiple references of the same item were ignored. Following coding, the overall score

Table 2. List of performance items

		Frequency in percentage
Marketing perspective (43)		***51***
Segmentation		*51*
	No hotel lodging alternatives	88
	Spa	92
	Fitness	60
	Dining per categories	48
	Nightlife	44
	Kids corner	36
	Youth section	32
	Business tourism	84
	City break	52
	Gay/lesbian	32
	Religious tours	32
	Wedding organisations	20
	Educational courses	36
	Thematic forms of tourism	52
Tangibility of destination		58
	Photos different landscapes, all regions	88
	Maps	100
	Photo gallery	76
	Virtual tours	40
	Video clips	52
	Web cams	12
	E-cards	40
Branding		59
	Environment statements	20
	Quality certification	28
	Logo in homepage	100
	Logo in other webpages	84
	Information behind public entity	96
	URL among the first 5 findings	76
	Site popularity	60
	Data on use	4
Relationship marketing		34
	Customised research	32
	Feedback forms	44
	Sharing of imformation to counterpaters	52
	News letters	72
	Send comments	8
	View reviews	12
	Travel plans favourites	36
	Memory settings	12
Marketing research, customer database		55
	Links to lower level toursit organisations	84
	Tracking country of origin	52
	Portal versions according to country of choi-	44
	Registration within the site	76
	Online surveys	24
	On line competitions	48
Customer perspective (45)		***47***
Privacy and trust		24
	Identification of information source	24
	Un registration option	24
	Statements of personal data privacy	36
	Terms of use	44
	Security certification	8
	Last update date	8
Service integration		12
	Accomodation booking on line	32
	Holiday package on line	8
	Air plane ticket on line	4
	Other facilities on line	12
	Track state of orders	8
	Virtual community	8
Service aggregation		47
	Native language expression	28
	Press office	60
	List of articles, books, guides	24
	Weather forecast	60
	Exchange convertor	64

		Frequency in percentage
Management of information		61
	Option to search for lodging by type (e.g. stars)	72
	Directions of how to reach destinations	36
	List of "highlights" (e.g. main attractions)	56
	Option to request material on line	56
	Option to download on line	84
	Printing options (e.g. full page, some areas etc.)	80
	Audio	28
	Route planner	40
	Interactive maps	92
	Information updated	52
	FAQ section	40
	Advanced search engine	100
Ease of contact		61
	NTO address	80
	NTO operating hours	28
	Web-master e-mail	84
	NTO telephone number	88
	NTO fax number	76
	Call centre	12
Navigability		73
	Graphic design changes for each different section	76
	Site map	68
	Advanced search engine	40
	Link avoiding homepage	84
	Link to homepage from all pages	80
	Principal elements visible before entire loading	84
	Web site visible without images loaded	80
Accessibility		28
	Information for disabled accessability in hotels	68
	Portal version in "bigger fonts"	8
	Seperate specialised accessibility section	8
Destination information (35)		***67***
Culture		76
	Artistic heritage	100
	Local culinary traditions	100
	Local handicraft/trades	64
	Local famous people	68
	UNESCO listed sites	76
	Local events	84
	Food recipes	40
General information		66
	Popular sports	96
	Dining facilities	56
	Natural assets	92
	Political information	64
	Religion	68
	Economic information	40
	information	76
	Geographical information	96
	Highlights for the next year	8
Practical information		65
	Public transportation	100
	Car rental	72
	National public holidays	88
	Opening/business hours	76
	Pricing and payment methods	80
	Currency information	76
	Discounts	40
	Custom/taxes information	68
	Immigration/work permit	24
	Entry requirements	84
	Real estate information	4
	Traffic & parking rules	68
	Regulations for pets	52
	Taxis	64
	Voltage	72
	Embassies and consulates	36
	International phone acess code	76
	Climate	84
	Emergency numbers	68

(*Score*) for each of the three categories (j) was quantified as follows:

$$Score_j = S_k / TOTS \qquad (1)$$

where: j = the perspective category, j = 1, 2, 3; k = the item subscript, k = 1, ….129; s_k = the number of items found in each NTO portal (answered as "yes"); TOTS = the total maximum number of possible items for each perspective (i.e. 45 for customer perspective). Based on this score, each portal, within each of the 3 perspectives (marketing, destination information and customer), was ranked in a descending order from 1 to 25, with means assigned to ties. In the case of the technical perspective, each portal has been ranked within each of the 6 technical criteria used, as illustrated in Table 3.

Kendall's Coefficient of Concordance (W) was calculated to test the degree of association

Table 3. Technical rankings

NTO EU member state	HTML errors[a]		Compatibility Problems[b]		Link Popularity[c]		Search Engine Saturation[d]		Down loaded time at 56K[e]		Broken Links[f]		Sum of Rankings
Netherlands	0	1	0	1	12.105	18	230.900	4	0,2	3	8	3	30,0
Poland	1	2	3	2	10.834	19	153.895	9	3,09	4	1	2	38,0
Czech Republic	3	4	8	7	76.155	7	96.028	12	0,02	1	21	8	39,0
Austria	1	2	14	12	101.019	3	145.404	10	19,37	13	17	6	46,0
Cyprus	2	3	3	2	17.937	15	58.818	14	18	11	0	1	46,0
Italy	6	7	12	10	56.231	8	2.492.975	2	17,76	10	26	11	48,0
Malta	1	2	7	6	31.427	11	177.388	8	26,98	14	25	10	51,0
France	2	3	4	3	86.426	6	58.169	15	14,73	6	72	19	52,0
Finland	2	3	0	1	33.628	10	98.689	11	39,69	17	26	11	53,0
UK	16	12	3	2	163.552	1	3.318.441	1	48,65	21	38	16	53,0
Lithuania	0	1	0	1	6.262	22	30.201	18	0,06	2	27	12	56,0
Denmark	11	10	6	5	154.463	2	186.448	6	74,12	23	26	11	57,0
Slovenia	0	1	10	8	6.283	21	36.699	16	7,2	5	17	6	57,0
Estonia	5	6	4	3	43.130	9	22.289	20	16,87	9	33	15	62,0
Germany	0	1	16	14	90.997	5	77.148	13	35,39	16	31	14	63,0
Slovakia	0	1	0	1	10.522	20	23.030	19	47,57	20	12	4	65,0
Greece	2	3	3	2	3.453	23	819	24	14,76	7	22	9	68,0
Portugal	4	5	5	4	12.205	17	230.330	5	45,84	19	67	18	68,0
Spain	48	16	29	16	93.293	4	177.489	7	42,55	18	18	7	68,0
Sweden	19	13	11	9	22.384	13	2.287	22	16,74	8	14	5	70,0
Latvia	2	3	8	7	523	25	59	25	18,61	12	8	3	75,0
Luxembourg	27	15	7	6	13.510	16	255.001	3	194,12	24	64	17	81,0
Belgium	9	9	13	11	23.522	12	1.180	23	34,56	15	29	13	83,0
Ireland	8	8	23	15	1.718	24	32.096	17	54,13	22	0	1	87,0
Hungary	24	14	15	13	21.189	14	5.650	21	241,22	25	38	16	103,0

among the 4 different rankings as follows (Siegel and Castellan, 1988: 271):

$$W = \frac{\sum_{i=1}^{N} (\overline{R}_i - \overline{R})^2}{N(N^2 - 1)/12} \qquad (2)$$

where: N = the number of portals to be ranked; = the average of the ranks assigned to the *ith* portal, = the average (or grand mean) of the ranks assigned to a portal across all the categories. Since the sample consisted of 25 EU NTO portals, this coefficient can be approximated by a chi-square distribution (X^2) with 24 degrees of freedom. Inter-coder reliability test (Krippendorff's *alpha* coefficient) has been performed in order to assess the consistency of the coding process.

FINDINGS AND ANALYSIS: DESTINATION INFORMATION CATEGORY

The results of the BSC approach to evaluate the EU NTO portals are summarised in Table 4. It emerges that Denmark achieved the best overall ranking (4.8), implying that currently the Danish portal is the most customer led, whereas the Latvian (19.9) and the Greek portal (22.1) occupy the last positions, with the latter being the worst of all in terms of the marketing perspective.

Kendall's coefficient of concordance was found W=0.410, considering the four rankings of the BSC approach, adjusted for ties, and equal to 0.647 excluding the technical ranking. It is evident that this value is not satisfactory, however X^2 (39.35) is statistically significant at 5 per cent level and it can support the conclusion that the Danish portal has the best performance in terms of the four perspectives combined.

Table 4. Overall rankings through the BSC framework

EU Member state	URL	Marketing Ranking	Customer Ranking	Destination Info Ranking	Technical Ranking	Total
Denmark	http://www.visitdenmark.com	3	1	2,5	12,5	4,8
UK	http://www.visitbritain.com	1	2,5	7	9,5	5,0
Netherlands	http://www.holland.com	7,5	12,5	1	1	5,5
Austria	http://www.austria.info	9,5	5	7	4,5	6,5
Spain	http://www.spain.info	2	2,5	7	18	7,4
France	http://franceguide.com	4,5	8,5	18	8	9,8
Malta	http://www.visitmalta.com	4,5	15	13,5	7	10,0
Sweden	http://www.visit-sweden.com	9,5	8,5	7	20	11,3
Slovenia	http://www.slovenia.info	6	4	24	12,5	11,6
Czech Republic	http://www.cheztourism.com/	14	10	23	3	12,5
Ireland	www.discoverireland.com	11	11	4	24	12,5
Finland	http://www.visitfinland.com	16,5	18	7	9,5	12,8
Cyprus	www.visitcyprus.org.cy	16,5	22	10	4,5	13,3
Germany	http://www.germany-tourism.de	7,5	15	16	15	13,4
Hungary	http://www.hungary.com/	12	6	16	25	14,8
Belgium	http://www.visitbelgium.com	14	21	2,5	23	15,1
Estonia	http://www.visitestonia.com	20	12,5	16	14	15,6
Luxembourg	http://www.ont.lu	20	7	13,5	22	15,6
Slovakia	www.slovakiatourism.sk	20	17	11,5	16	16,1
Portugal	http://www.visitportugal.com	14	15	19,5	18	16,6
Poland	http://www.poland-tourism.pl	20	24	21,5	2	16,9
Italy	http://www.enit.it	20	19,5	25	6	17,6
Lithuania	http://www.travel.lt	24	19,5	19,5	11	18,5
Latvia	http://www.latviatourism.com	23	24	11,5	21	19,9
Greece	http://www.visitgreece.gr	25	24	21,5	18	22,1

Table 5 presents the descriptive statistics of our sample. The average scores in the three categories indicate that the NTOs' performance was higher in terms of Destination information in comparison to the Marketing and Customer categories of the BSC approach. Of the overall sub-categories of the scoring list, "culture" and "navigability" are the ones with the highest performances averaging 76 and 73 per cent respectively (see Table 2 for the sub-totals and frequencies of the single items).

Figure 2 shows the distribution of Destination information scores across the 25 portals. It reveals that the NTO portals are performing quite similarly, implying high degrees of standardisation in the levels of information provided online. This pattern may be further investigated by considering Table 2. For example, as expected, the vast majority of NTO sites provide practical advices covering basic useful travelling information (e.g. transportation, public holidays, entry requirements, etc.). However, less than half of them

Table 5. Descriptive statistics

Perspectives	Minimum	Maximum	Mean	Std. Deviation
Marketing	0.28	0.77	0.507	0.146
Customer	0.29	0.73	0.478	0.130
Information	0.17	0.86	0.674	0.143
Technical	30.00	103.00	60.760	16.741

Figure 2. Distribution of BSC scores across portals

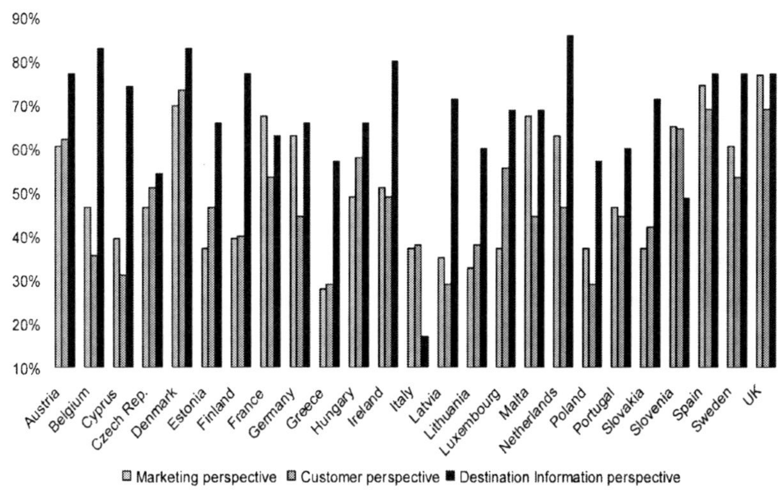

(40%) show increased sensitivity for the tourists' needs by including useful tips, such as information regarding tourist discounts, or information regarding foreign embassies and consulates in their country (36%).

The Dutch portal manages better to promote Holland through the provision of an impressively rich and well organised content. The practical advices provided go beyond the "typical" basic practical information before visiting the destination, covering aspects such as immigration and work permit regulations. The last place in this category is occupied by the Italian NTO portal since the latter fails completely to transmit a comprehensive picture about the diversity of the different Italian regions and it pays very limited attention to the Italian cultural assets such as local events. In addition, its content is poor and sometimes even outdated. By consulting the sub-category *Culture* (Table 2), it appears that EU members have understood the power of internet for marketing their own culture. All the websites maintain separate sections where the artistic heritage of the destination such as castles, churches, museums, as well as the local culinary traditions are thoroughly described. Moreover, the majority of them (21 portals) is in the position to provide an updated database, which covers the main incoming local events, with a particular emphasis on the small characteristic local festivals. Although it is evident that some destinations put more effort in marketing online their culture more extensively (e.g., Belgium, Netherlands, etc.), again it can be argued that the cultural cues used to promote a destination are characterised by relatively high degrees of standardisation. Only when it comes to examining the promotion of local handicrafts, trades and local food recipes, some higher degrees of individualism arise, with only 64% of them promoting the former and 40% of them providing the latter. Finally, interestingly enough, the relatively low destination information percentages of countries possessing rich cultural heritage such as Italy, France, Greece and Spain imply that the latter do not appear to leverage particularly successfully their NTO portals to promote it. Thus, it is confirmed the realisation of the Ismail et al., (2002: 175), that there is no evidence of particular effectiveness of NTO websites from destinations with high number of cultural attractions and resources. The latter statement has been tested statistically in section 6.

CUSTOMER PERSPECTIVE FINDINGS

Among the 25 portals, Denmark and UK scored higher within this category with the former having 33 out of the 45 identified items (73.3%) and the later having 31 (68.9%) respectively. Both these NTO have realised the importance of "one site shop" as a driver of superior customer service for the contemporary demanding and time sensitive visitors. Both of them are offering direct online booking for accommodation, holiday packages and even more specialised vacation items, such as theatre and other attraction tickets. In addition, the British portal supports the acquisition of airplane tickets and it is offering a well organised online shop, where buyers can track the state of their orders.

By consulting the sub-category *Privacy and trust* (Table 2), it emerges that a) a "terms of use" section, b) a "privacy statement" for the collection of personal data and c) a "security certification" are often missing. In particular, the lack of the above, combined with: "neglecting to mention the source of information provided" in 19 out of 25 portals (76%), and to "guarantee any last updating date for the site's content, antecedent of the last 2 months" in a stunning: 23 out of 25 portals, definitely influence the building of trust between the entity behind the website and its online visitors. Since trust and control of online users have been regarded as key components of e-SQ (Parasuraman et al., 2005; Nysveen et al., 2003) there is an emerging margin for improvement.

The three web sites with the most disappointing performance in the customer perspective are the Latvian, the Polish and the Greek one (Figure 2). These portals can be regarded as "product driven" ones, where emphasis is given on the presentation of as much as possible information about the country, failing to organise this information and to "empower" their visitors, through the provision of advanced search engines which allow them to discover on their own *only* that kind of information they are mostly interested about.

Disappointing is the picture regarding the measures undertaken by the portals for assuring *accessibility*, accommodating different users' needs and capabilities. More specifically, while the majority of the websites under examination (17) include sufficient information regarding accessibility for travellers with special needs, only 2 of them (the Spanish and the British NTO) declare that their portals are adhering with the legal imperatives for accessibility according to the web content accessibility guidelines (http//w3.org). This is consistent with the findings of Williams et al. (2004) who found discouraging low levels of accessibility for tourism related websites in Germany and UK. A further category where the sample portals are performing particularly weakly is *service integration*, averaging 12% across the total sample. Virtual communities are recognised as value added services (Nysveen et al., 2003; Hjalager, 2001) however, only 2 NTO websites (the Slovenian and the Irish one) are making use of them. As far as it concerns the category *management of information* the majority of portals (23 portals, or 92%) make extensive use of modern internet applications such as interactive maps, whereas less than half of them (9 portals or 36%) offer a complete value added service including the provision of directions of *how* to reach different destinations and/or a route planner (10 portals, or 40%) and even fewer are providing directions for alternative ways of transporting. Finally, it is worthy mentioning that, regardless of the portals' large size, the majority of them (73%) include functions which enhance navigability.

MARKETING AND TECHNICAL PERSPECTIVE FINDINGS

As Figure 2 reveals, the UK NTO website has scored higher in the marketing category, with 33 out of the 43 examined items (76,7%) being present. It appears as highly interactive with strong brand identity and satisfactory information customisation and personalisation features. Moreover, its design effectively supports market research and targeted marketing activities, and finally it assists the tangibility of destination through the provision of a wide variety of helping cues. On the other hand, the Greek and the Lithuanian portal have the poorest on line presence in terms of marketing functions (27.9% and 32.6% respectively) and need urgently to improve their efforts in marketing segmentation, tangibility of destination and market research. Finally, many websites such as the NTO portals of Estonia, Italia, Poland, Luxembourg and Slovakia have scored equally low (37,2%) implying the existence of significant margins for improvement.

A closer examination of the single items highlights some specific features within the *relationship marketing* category. First of all, it can be argued that the websites employ relatively low levels of interactivity, with only 11 or 44% of them supporting online feedback forms, and only two of them (Slovenia and Portugal) including users' ratings on: a) price offers and/or b) usefulness of the information received. Once more, very few of them (only 3) seem to have realised the importance of "word of mouth" and provide the possibility to browse other users' experiences and comments on certain issues. Similarly, there have been detected varying levels of customisation and personalisation of information. In terms of personalisation items, the sample websites did not perform well since only 36% of them (9 portals) are allowing online visitors to select, organise, and store personal interest information into a "favourites section" and even less (12% or 3 portals) maintain in memory previous settings such as "choice of language".

As far as it concerns the *segmentation category*, the vast majority of them (23), in conformity with one of the strongest trends of the recent years, are providing extensive information for spas and fitness centres, in an attempt not only to satisfy better the needs of their online users, but also to target more effectively the most valuable market segments. To a further extent, slightly more than half of these portals (52%) are including a city break section, another important trend gaining popularity among the time sensitive tourists of nowadays. On the other hand, segmentation according to lifestyle is not extensively used. Indeed the provision of a separate nightlife section, with information regarding entertainment options shows a less strong trend (only: 44% or 11 portals). The other emerged targeted segment is business tourism, with 21 portals (84%), providing separate, specialised web-sites within their main portal.

In terms of the number and kind of cues used to enhance the *tangibility of the destination*, despite that almost every portal makes use of tools such as maps (100%) and photographs of landscapes of different regions (88%), other more sophisticated and advanced tools such as virtual tours (10 portals or 40%) or video clips (13 portals or 52%), and webcams (3 portals or 12%) are not yet fully employed.

Eight items have been used to examine whether the NTO are *branding* their site sufficiently. Among these: a logo is included in the homepage of all the portals (100%), as well as in the rest of pages (84%). However, the sites often miss a quality certification (only 7 out of 25 portals do have one), failing to assure their visitors for the content of the information provided. Finally, they hardly include data on their use, such as number of registered users, number of hits, etc. (1 out of 25 portals only). By consulting the *marketing research and customer database* category, it emerges that the majority of the NTO portals (76%) are maintaining a customer database since they allow their visitors to register online. A less popular way to gather personal data regarding their visitors is through online competitions (12 portals or 48%). In terms of market research and targeting: 52% of the websites (in total 13 portals) track the country of origin of the different visitors and 11 portals

Table 6. Wilcoxon-Mann Whitney test

Perspectives Groups		N	Mean Rank	Sum of Ranks	Z
Marketing	Affluent	13	16.31	212.0	-2.352**
	Less affluent	12	9.42	113.0	
Customer	Affluent	13	15.85	206.0	-2.017**
	Less affluent	12	9.92	119.0	
Information	Affluent	13	16.96	220.5	-2.817***
	Less affluent	12	8.71	104.5	
Technical	Affluent	13	13.31	173.0	-0.218
	Less affluent	12	12.67	152.0	

Notes: ** and *** indicate statistical significance levels of 5 percent and 1 per cent, respectively, in two-tailed tests.

provide multiple versions of their website, with content adjusted to reflect the local tourist market conditions of each country.

As Table 3 reveals, the Dutch NTO portal was the one which scored higher in the technical perspective. Indeed, the latter portal gained the highest ranking position in terms of Hypertext Markup Language (HTML) errors and browser compatibility problems, an equally high classification in terms of broken links and overall downloaded time at a 56K speed connection (3rd position), and the 4th position in terms of search engine saturation (Table 3). On the other hand, the Hungarian website was rated as the least technically sound NTO portal with serious delays in downloading time. Finally, the high positions of some of the accession states, such as the 2nd position of Poland, the 3rd position of Czech Republic in contrast to the lower classifications of more e-advanced nations such as Sweden and Ireland (Economist, 2005) support the claim that Internet empowers new players and boosts competitiveness regardless the smaller internet penetration rates of the latter.

HYPOTHESIS TESTING

The Wilcoxon-Mann Whitney has been calculated to test whether the online performance were equal in the 8 groups of countries defined in section 3. It emerged that the variable affluence (see Table 6), has a significant influence on the online performance in terms of marketing, destination information and customer perspective. On the contrary, the "affluence" variable does not have any significant influence on the online performance of the NTO portals in terms of technical perspective. The remaining three independent variables were not found to have a statistically significant influence on the NTO portals' online performance.

Finally, a univariate correlation analysis was performed to assess the relationship between the four perspectives. All correlation coefficients were positive, except between customer and technical and between technical and destination information perspectives. Marketing was the most significant contributor to the total score at 0.907 ($p<0.01$) followed by the customer category at 0.765 ($p<0.01$). Moreover, a positive and high correlation (0.749) was found between the Marketing and the Customer perspective ($p< 0.01$), a realistic result since e-marketing excellence by definition is closely related to customer orientation. The correlation among the other perspectives was low and insignificant.

CONCLUSION AND FURTHER RESEARCH

This study analyses the online offerings of 25 EU NTOs using a framework that captures four e-quality categories. It is found that NTOs have realised that by just including basic information on their websites and waiting for online visitors to arrive is not a viable solution anymore. However, even if the vast majority of them demonstrates "acceptable" levels of online performances significant margins for improvements do exist. In particular, relatively high degrees of standardisation were observed in the areas of: content of information and cultural cues used to promote the destination. This implies that the NTOs are failing, up to a certain extent, to create a "unique sales proposition" to promote their destination. In most of the cases, some basic features necessary to promote "trust" for the online users were missing, and basic features enhancing accessibility for *all* online users were almost absent. It can be argued that the use of a simple binary code offers a partial valuation of the on line service quality and uniqueness[13]. In particular, neither differences in the content itself nor accessibility of selected features are always captured by the presence of different attributes.

Nevertheless, this research is a necessary *first step* in order to make inferences about the current level of online offerings and e-quality provided by the NTO web sites and to investigate possible determinants of on line performances in terms of marketing, destination information and customer perspective. Moreover, *customer perceptions* of e-quality need to be explored in order to form a complete picture of online quality. Thus, future research could concentrate on increasing our understanding of: a) *which of the information and services present here contribute the most* in achieving a high level of overall service quality, as perceived by the end users and b) if the latter perceptions are *culturally sensitive*. A survey could be addressed to online users with the scope to capture which of the identified online services are rated as most important by prospect tourists when seeking tourism information on line and in what order of importance. The latter would be of particular value to the NTO, since it would reveal eventual gaps between their current offerings and customers preferences of on line value added services. A further interesting direction would be: to examine if these findings can be generalized in *other categories of tourism websites* more profit oriented.

REFERENCES

Aladwani, A. M., & Pavia, P. C. (2002). Developing and validating an instrument for measuring user perceived web quality. *Information & Management*, *39*(6), 457–476. doi:10.1016/S0378-7206(01)00113-6

Blum, V., & Fallon, J. (2002). Welsh visitor attraction websites: multipurpose tools or technological tokenism? *Journal of Information Technology and Tourism*, *4*(34), 191–201.

Boyatzis, R. E. (1998). *Transforming qualitative information: thematic analysis and code development*. Thousand Oaks, CA: Sage Publications.

Buhalis, D., & Deimezi, O. (2002). E-tourism developments in Greece: information communication technologies adoption for the strategic management of Greek tourism industry. *Tourism and Hospitality Research*, *5*(2), 103–128. doi:10.1057/palgrave.thr.6040011

Buhalis, D., & Licata, M. (2002). The future of eTourism intermediaries. *Tourism Management*, *23*(3), 207–220. doi:10.1016/S0261-5177(01)00085-1

Cai, L. A., Card, J. A., & Cole, S. T. (2004a). Content delivery performance of world wide web sites of US tour operators focusing on destinations in China. *Tourism Management*, *25*(2), 219–227. doi:10.1016/S0261-5177(03)00095-5

Cai, L. A., Feng, R., & Breiter, D. (2004b). Tourism purchase decision involvement and information preferences. *Journal of Vacation Marketing*, *10*(2), 138–148. doi:10.1177/135676670401000204

Cano, V., & Prentice, R. (1998). Opportunities for endearment to place through electronic "visiting" WWW homepages and the tourism promotion of Scotland. *Tourism Management, 19*(1), 67–73. doi:10.1016/S0261-5177(97)00092-7

Chen, Q., & Wells, W. D. (1999). Attitude towards the site. *Journal of Advertising Research, 39*(5), 27–38.

Chung, T., & Law, R. (2003). Developing a performance indicator for hotel websites. *International Journal of Hospitality Management, 22*(1), 119–125. doi:10.1016/S0278-4319(02)00076-2

Davidson, A. P., & Yu, Y. (2004). The internet and the occidental tourist an analysis of Taiwan's tourism websites from the perspective of western tourists. *Journal of Information Technology and Tourism, 7*(2), 91–102. doi:10.3727/1098305054517318

Di Gregorio, D., Kassicieh, S. K., & De Gouveva, R. (2005). Drivers of e-business activity in developed and emerging markets. *IEE Transactions on Engineering Management, 52*(2), 155–166. doi:10.1109/TEM.2005.844464

Doolin, B., Burgess, L., & Cooper, J. (2002). Evaluating the use of web for tourism marketing: a case study from New Zeland. *Tourism Management, 23*(4), 557–561. doi:10.1016/S0261-5177(02)00014-6

Economist Intelligence Unit. IBM Institute for Business value (2005). *The 2005 e-readiness rankings*. White Paper. Retrieved June 23, 2006, from http://www.eiu.com/site_info.asp?info_name=eiu_2005_e_readiness_rankings.

Feng, R., Morrison, A. M., & Ismail, J. A. (2002). East versus West: a comparison of online destination marketing in China and the US. *Journal of Vacation Marketing, 10*(1), 43–56. doi:10.1177/135676670301000105

Garvin, D. A. (1984). What does "product quality" really mean? *Sloan Management Review,* Fall, *26*(1), 25-43.

Hjalager, A. (2001). Research and concepts: quality in tourism through the empowerment of tourists. *Managing Service Quality, 11*(4), 287–295. doi:10.1108/09604520110397995

Hudson, S., & Lang, N. (2002). A destination case study of marketing tourism on line: Banff, Canada. *Journal of Vacation Marketing, 8*(2), 155–166. doi:10.1177/135676670200800205

Huizingh, E. K. R. E. (2000). The content and design of web sites: an empirical study. *Information & Management, 37*(3), 123–134. doi:10.1016/S0378-7206(99)00044-0

Ismail, J. A., Labropoulos, T., Mills, J. E., & Morrison, A. M. (2002). A snapshot in time: the marketing of culture in European Union NTO websites. *Tourism Culture and Communication, 3*(3), 165–179.

Jeong, M., Ohand, H., & Gregoire, M. (2003). Conceptualizing Web quality and its consequences in the lodging industry. *International Journal of Hospitality Management, 22*(2), 161–175. doi:10.1016/S0278-4319(03)00016-1

Jung, T. H., & Butler, R. (2000). Perceptions of marketing managers of the effectiveness of the Internet in tourism and hospitality. *Journal of Information Technology and Tourism, 3*(3-4), 167–176.

Kim, M., Kim, J., & Lennon, S. (2006). Online service attributes available on apparel retail web sites: an E-S-QUAL approach. *Managing Service Quality, 16*(1), 51–77. doi:10.1108/09604520610639964

King, J. (2002). Destination marketing organizations-connecting the experience rather than promoting the place. *Journal of Vacation Marketing, 8*(2), 105–108. doi:10.1177/135676670200800201

Krippendorff, K. (1980). *Content analysis: an introduction to its methodology*. Beverly Hills, CA: Sage Publications.

Larson, C., & Ankomah, P. (2005). Evaluating tourism web site complexity. The case of international tourism in the U.S. *Services Marketing Quarterly*, *26*(2), 23–37. doi:10.1300/J396v26n02_02

Lexhagen, M. (2004). The importance of value-added services to support the customer search and purchase process on travel websites. *Journal of Information Technology and Tourism*, *7*(2), 119–135. doi:10.3727/1098305054517336

Liu, C., & Arnett, K. P. (2000). Exploring the factors associated with website success in the context of electronic commerce. *Information & Management*, *38*(1), 23–33. doi:10.1016/S0378-7206(00)00049-5

Madu, C. N., & Madu, A. A. (2002). Dimensions of e-quality. *International Journal of Quality & Reliability*, *19*(3), 246–258. doi:10.1108/02656710210415668

Mich, L., & Franch, M. (2007). *Un approccio multi-step per la valutazione dell'usabilità del sito web di una destinazione turistica*. Paper presented at the 4th Annual Conference of the Italian Marketing Academy: Il Marketing dei Talenti, Roma, 5-6 October.

Mich, L., Franch, M., & Gaio, L. (2002). *Evaluating and designing the quality of web sites*, Working paper, 70, DISA, University of Trento.

Mich, L., Franch, M., & Cilione, G. (2003). The 2QCV3Q quality model for the analysis of web site requirements. *Journal of Web Engineering*, *2*(1-2), 115–127.

Morgan, N., Pritchard, A., & Pride, R. (2002). *Destination branding. Creating the unique destination preposition*. Oxford: Butterworth-Heinemann.

Morrison, A. M., Taylor, S., Morrison, A. J., & Morrison, A. D. (1999). Marketing small hotels on the world wide web. *Journal of Information Technology and Tourism*, *2*(2), 97–113.

Nysveen, H., Methlie, L. B., & Pedersen, P. E. (2003). Tourism web sites and value added services: the gap between customer preferences and web sites' offerings. *Journal of Information Technology and Tourism*, *5*(3), 165–174. doi:10.3727/109830503108751117

O'Neill, M., Wright, C., & Fitz, F. (2001). Quality evaluation in online service environments. *Managing Service Quality*, *11*(6), 402–417. doi:10.1108/EUM0000000006519

Parasuraman, A., Zeithaml, V. A., & Berry, L. L. (1988). SERVQUAL: a multi-item scale for measuring consumer perceptions of the service quality. *Journal of Retailing*, *64*(1), 12–40.

Parasuraman, A., Zeithaml, V. A., & Malhotra, A. (2005). E-S-QUAL: A multiple-item scale for assessing electronic service quality. *Journal of Service Research*, *7*(3), 213–233. doi:10.1177/1094670504271156

Sainaghi, R. (2006). From contents to processes: versus a dynamic destination management model. *Tourism Management*, *27*(5), 1053–1063. doi:10.1016/j.tourman.2005.09.010

Santos, J. (2003). E-service quality: a model of virtual service quality dimensions. *Managing Service Quality*, *13*(3), 233–246. doi:10.1108/09604520310476490

Scharl, A., Wober, W. K., & Bauer, C. (2004). An integrated approach to measure web site effectiveness in the European hotel industry. *Journal of Information Technology and Tourism*, *6*(4), 257–271. doi:10.3727/1098305032781157

Siegel, S., & Castellan, N. J., Jr. (1988). *Nonparametric statistics for behavioral sciences*, Second edition, McGraw-Hill international editions.

Sigala, M. (2004). Measuring ASP service quality in Greece. *Managing Service Quality, 14*(1), 103–104. doi:10.1108/09604520410513703

Skadberg, Y. X., Skadberg, A. N., & Kimmel, J. R. (2005). Flow experience and its impact on the effectiveness of a tourism website. *Journal of Information Technology and Tourism, 7*(34), 147–156. doi:10.3727/109830505774297238

So, S., & Morrison, A. M. (2004). Internet marketing in tourism in Asia: an evaluation of the performance of East Asian National Tourism Organization web sites. *Journal of Hospitality & Leisure Marketing, 11*(4), 93–118. doi:10.1300/J150v11n04_07

Turban, E., King, D., & Viehland, D. (2004). *Electronic commerce 2004: a managerial perspective*, Upper Saddle River, New Jersey: Pearson education, Inc.

UNCTAD. (2005), *Taking off: E-tourism opportunities for developing countries*, Chapter 4, United Nations Conference on Trade and Development, e-commerce and development information economy report 2005. Retrieved April 01, 2006, from http://www.unctad.org/en/docs/sdteecb20051ch4_en.pdf.

Weber, R. P. (1985). *Basic Content Analysis, 49 Beverly Hills*. CA: Sage Publications.

Williams, R., Rattray, R., & Stork, A. (2004). Website accessibility of German and UK tourism information sites. *European Business Review, 16*(6), 577–589. doi:10.1108/09555340410565404

Wöber, K. W. (2003). *Evaluation of DMO web sites through interregional tourism portals: a European cities tourism case example*. Paper submitted for the 2003 ENTER Conference, January 29-31, Helsinki. Retrieved April, 10, 2006, from http://tourism.wuwien.ac.at/lehrv/lven/03ws/vk5/EuropeanCitiesTourismPortal.pdf.

World Tourism Organization. (2005). *Evaluating and improving websites*. The Tourism Destination Web Watch' Report. Retrieved March, 22, 2006, from http://www.world-tourism.org.

Yoo, B., & Donthu, N. (2001). Developing a scale to measure perceived quality of an internet shopping site (SITEQUAL). *Quarterly Journal of Electronic Commerce, 2*(1), 31–46.

Zeithaml, V. A., Parasuraman, A., & Malhotra, A. (2002). Service quality delivery through websites: a critical review of extant knowledge. *Journal of the Academy of Marketing Science, 30*(4), 362–375. doi:10.1177/009207002236911

Zhu, F. X., Wymer, W., & Chen, I. (2002). IT-based services and service quality in consumer banking. *International Journal of Service Industry Management, 13*(1), 69–90. doi:10.1108/09564230210421164

ENDNOTES

1. NTO is defined by WTO, (1996)as: "*An autonomous body of public, semi-public or private status, established or recognised by the state as the body with competence at the national level for the promotion and in some cases, marketing of inbound international tourism*" as cited in Law *et al.*, 2004:100
2. cited in Santos, 2003:236
3. cited in Santos, 2003:235
4. cited in Sigala, 2004: 105
5. cited in Zeithmal *et al.*, 2002: 366
6. cited in Blum and Fallon, 2002:193
7. cited in UNCTAD, 2005:159
8. cited in Doolin *et al.*, 2002:558
9. cited in Scharl *et al.*, 2004: 258
10. cited in Skadberg *et al.*, 2005: 148
11. cited in So and Morison, 2004:101
12. The material analyzed consisted of the English homepage including links, pictures and text information. However, links as hyper-

texts within a unique resource locator (URL) that would lead to a separate and independent web page, were not further considered. Neither it was analyzed information accessible to registered users.

13 We thank one of the reviewers for this observation.

This work was previously published in International Journal of Information Systems in the Service Sector (IJISSS), edited by John Wang, pp. 65-82, copyright 2009 by IGI Publishing (an imprint of IGI Global).

Section 4

Chapter 16
Performance Modeling and Analysis of Surgery Patient Identification Using RFID

Byungho Jeong
Chonbuk National University, Korea

Chen-Yang Cheng
Tunghai University, Taiwan

Vittal Prabhu
The Pennsylvania State University, USA

ABSTRACT

This paper proposes a workflow and performance model for surgery patient identification using RFID (Radio Frequency Identification). Certain types of mistakes may be prevented by automatically identifying the patient before surgery. The proposed workflow is designed to ensure that both the correct site and patient are engaged in the surgical process. The performance model can be used to predict patient waiting time and service duration time with RFID implementation. A proof-of-concept system is developed to understand the information flow and to use information in RFID-based patient identification. Performance model indicates the response time to patients can be reduced to 38% after four hours using the proposed RFID based workflow.

INTRODUCTION

Improvement in patient safety in medical care continues to be a very important issue in the medical care community. According to an Institute of Medicine (IOM) report, 44,000 to 98,000 people die each year as a result of preventable medical errors (Kohn, Corrigan, & Donaldson, 1999). The percentage of hospital inpatient admissions experiencing adverse events has been estimated at 3.7% in the U.S., 16.6% in Australia, and 10% in the UK (MF & JD, 2004). Various types of medical errors occur during the course of healthcare delivery, such as improper transfusions, wrong-site surgery, and mistaken patient identities. High error rates with serious consequences are most likely to occur in intensive care units, such as operating rooms and emergency departments ("What an unbelievable

DOI: 10.4018/978-1-60960-138-6.ch016

surgery!-Perform an operation with exchanged charts," 2006). Many of these medical errors are due mainly to avoidable human errors that can be potentially eliminated by proper design and error-proofing of the associated workflow. Surgery generally involves the execution of many complex tasks and each task is composed of multiple steps. The most common human error in the medical process is unintentional omission of one or more steps, especially when there are a large number of steps (Reason, 2002).

Patient identification is one of the necessary processes performed prior to anesthesia and surgery. Errors in this process can lead to unrecoverable medical accidents and there are numerous such accidents reported ("What an unbelievable surgery!-Perform an operation with exchanged charts," 2006). One instance of such an error involved intake nurses and surgery doctors: two patients—one with thyroid cancer and one with stomach cancer—had their identities exchanged in the surgery. As a result, the thyroid of the patient with stomach cancer was removed and the stomach of the patient with thyroid cancer was removed. There are other instances where medical doctors have reported performing invasive procedures on the wrong patients (Mark R. Chassin & Elise C. Becher, 2002).

The IOM report revealed that the majority of medical errors are not caused by individual recklessness or the actions of a particular group (Kohn, et al., 1999). More commonly, faulty systems, processes, and conditions lead people to make mistakes or fail to prevent them. Therefore there is a need to design and error-proof workflow systems that render human error essentially impossible or at least extremely difficult (Etchells, O'Neill, & Bernstein, 2003). Barcode system such as the Global Service Relation Number (GSRN) from GS1, which is used to identify patients and the services provided to them, may be helpful in addressing some of these needs (http://www.gs1.org/docs/patient_safety). However, use of such a barcode system may impose awkward constraints on the surgery team because a bar code must be within the line of sight of the scanner. Ideally, patient identification technology should be simple and reliable so that the overall activities and associated workflow of the surgical team is smooth and efficient. In this context, RFID technology offers an attractive solution because it does not need a line of sight and its reading range is greater than that involved with a barcode system. RFID technology is one potential solution in resolving occurrences of patient misidentification (Fisher, 2006; MF & JD, 2004).

We suggest a model that applies RFID technology to the patient identification process prior to entry into the operating room, and a prototype system for the application model. Automatic recognition eliminates the possibility of misidentification error by displaying the patient's identification information on the computer monitor of the operating room as s/he is being rolled into the room. This research is extended from the previous result, reliability model in the same problem(Jeong, Cheng, & Prabhu, 2009). A performance model is used to show that the probability of patient identification error can be reduced by the proposed RFID based workflow. Section 2 provides a literature review on the RFID application in medicine and an overview of current costs. In section 3 a typical workflow process for identifying a surgery patient is described and a process involving the RFID identification system is suggested. Section 4 evaluates the suggested process according to workflow process performance model. The prototype system developed to serve as a proof-of-concept of the proposed workflow process is discussed in section 5.

RFID TECHNOLOGY IN THE MEDICAL AREA

RFID technology may dramatically improve an organization's capability to obtain real-time information on the location and properties of tagged moving objects, such as people, materials, or equipment. It has been utilized in many areas, such as luggage tracking, security keys, toll collection, and supply chain management (SCM) (Angeles, 2005; Srivastava, 2004). The healthcare area is regarded as promising application area for RFID technology (Ericson, 2004; "RFID in the Hospital," 2004).

A limited number of hospitals are reportedly testing RFID. Most began with tracking and managing equipment. One hospital installed an RFID equipment tracking system to monitor 12,000 pieces of medical equipment. The hospital estimated that it had gained a $200,000 benefit per year over and above the cost of the RFID system's installation and maintenance costs ("Patient Safety Applications of Bar Code and RFID Technologies,"). Another hospital utilized inventory RFID tags, cutting inventory losses in half ("Patient Safety Applications of Bar Code and RFID Technologies,"). RFID technology has also been used in tracking sponges in surgery (Alex Macario, Dean Morris, & Sharon Morris, 2007; Schwaitzberg, 2006). Tagging equipment or materials may be simpler than tagging people as proven in its uses in the manufacturing and retail sectors.

RFID technology has rarely been used in tracking and managing people, such as patients, physicians and nurses. A location-based Medicare service project with a hospital-wide RFID system was conducted in a university hospital in Taiwan (Wang, Chen, Ong, Liu, & Chuang, 2006). Two Singaporean hospitals implemented a RFID system for tracking visitors, patients and staff in the Accident and Emergency Department. These systems were used to identify and trace the contact history of Severe Acute Respiratory Syndrome (SARS) infected patients ("Singapore Fights SARS with RFID," 2003).

Tagging people, however, is more challenging and requires more circumspection because of other technical and organizational problems. Many medical electronic devices use radio waves in a hospital. The presence of these devices raises the possibility of interference with RFID radio waves. Although the range of its operating frequency is restricted to free ISM (industrial, scientific, medical) bands, these frequencies can be a source of interference, too, and can interfere with RFID devices (Srivastava, 2004). Cost issues are another major obstacle to hospital-wide use of RFID technology. An RFID company estimated that it could cost between $500 and $2,000 per hospital bed to install its RFID system ("Health Care RFID Startup Scores $9 Million in Venture Funding," 2004). Like most electronic devices, even though RFID unit cost has fallen dramatically over the past few years, it is still too expensive for hospital-wide use. Unless these obstacles, such as unit price and device interference issues are resolved, application of RFID is likely to be limited to restricted areas of the hospital. Thus, it may be more efficient to deploy the RFID system in a specific area and for a specific function, such as patient identification in operating rooms. Such targeted uses may help to eliminate the possibility of unrecoverable and serious medical errors, such as performance of surgery on the wrong patient or at the wrong site.

RFID FOR SURGERY PATIENT IDENTIFICATION

A medical doctor decides to perform surgery on in- or outpatients, based upon the results of the patient's medical examination. A patient's surgery schedule is usually developed according to the schedule of the surgery doctor in charge. The patient, if an outpatient, is required to check into the hospital one day prior to the operating day if the operating schedule has been set. An operating room and an anesthetist are assigned to the patient on the previous afternoon of the operating day. The preoperative setting for the next day's operation usually begins in an operating room after finishing the scheduled surgical operations for the day. The

Figure 1. The original workflow diagram

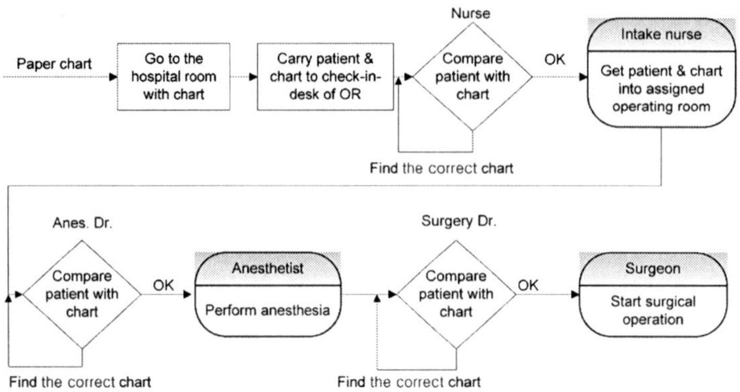

anesthetist in charge checks the medical status and physical constitution of the patient during rounds and determines the anesthetic method to be used in the next day's operation. The results of the anesthetic round must be recorded on the patient's chart and the hospital's information system. The workflow process involving the movement and identification of a surgery patient begins after completion of the necessary preoperative setting.

Figure 1 describes the typical workflow process around the movement of a surgery patient who is scheduled for an operation, focusing on consultation of a paper chart on the day of the surgery. A nurse or commensurate employee brings the patient to the designated surgery according to the surgery schedule. The worker takes the patient to the check-in desk in the operating room and turns him and the paper chart over to a nurse in charge. At that time, patient identification is confirmed by the nurse and the worker who brought the patient in. The nurse could ask for the name and compare it on the wristband and chart of the patient. After confirming the identity of the patient and presence of the correct chart, the patient moves into the assigned operating room. The nurse and anesthetist in charge of the operation confirm again identify of the patient and the chart before performing anesthesia. The surgeon then checks the identification of the patient by comparing

Figure 2. Conceptual diagram of an operating room with RFID system

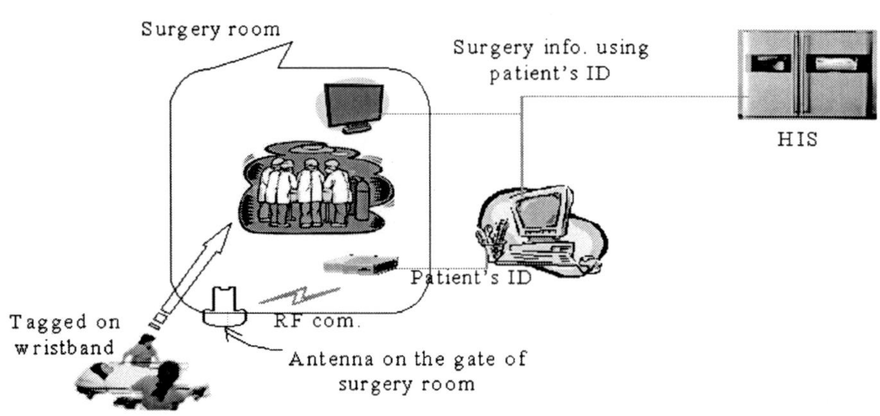

the wristband and the chart of the patient before beginning the operation.

In order to eliminate the possibility of human errors in confirming the patient's identification, it is necessary for any automatic error-free process to be introduced in parallel to the current confirmation process relied upon by a surgical team. We suggest a workflow process that prevents human error by deploying the characteristics of an RFID system. Figure 2 contains a conceptual diagram for an automatic identification system using RFID technology. RFID antennae may be placed at the entrance of each operating room and check-in room. An RFID reader may be connected to the existing information system through an RFID server. An RFID tag is attached to a surgery patient's wristband. The hospital information system is used in tandem with the prototype described in this paper. We assume the existence of a hospital information system and ability to retrieve necessary information from the system using the patient's ID.

Figure 3 shows a diagram of the suggested workflow process for identifying a surgery patient using an RFID reader in each confirming step of the current identification process. The possibility of human error in the confirmation process may be reduced by adapting RFID technology to identification of a moving object. In the proposed process, a patient is wearing a wristband with an RFID tag on his wrist. The surgeon confirms the patient's identity during rounds the morning of the surgery. When the patient is brought to the check-in area of the operating room, the identification is confirmed by the intake nurse and the worker who took the patient into the operating room. At this time, the patient's identification information is recognized by an RFID reader and displayed on a computer screen, allowing the intake nurse to again compare the displayed patient's name to the name on the paper chart. After the confirmation and check-in processes are complete, the patient is rolled into the surgery. As he passes through the entrance of the surgery, an RFID antenna at the entrance reads the RFID tag within the wristband and uploads information into the computer system in the operating room. The computer immediately queries the scheduling system about surgical operation to confirm that the patient is indeed scheduled to be in that specific operating room and then uploads the patient's identification information and other necessary information from the electronic medical record, including allergies, blood type, and laboratory reports, including laterality from radiology studies. If the RFID system indicates that the wrong

Figure 3. New workflow diagram using RFID in patient identification

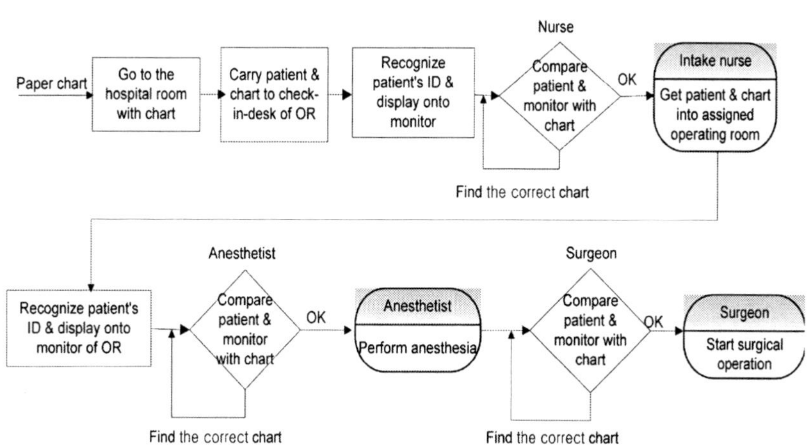

patient has entered the room, a warning is provided (e.g., beeping sound) and a warning sign is displayed on the monitor. At the instant the patient wearing an RFID tag enters the operating room, the computer system confirms that the right surgeon and right patient are in the right place before the surgical procedure begins.

Although the RFID technology contributes to patient safety and traceability, it may increase the complexity of processes and decrease hospital performance. In the next section, we analyze the performance of the workflow process and compare it with a paper-based process.

Performance Modeling using Queuing Theory

In a surgery process, patients move between the check-in desk and the operation room in a hospital. A patient with a surgery request may have to wait in a queue if nurses or doctors in the hospital cannot serve multiple patients at the same time; moreover, the surgery processing time is greater than the inter-arrival time (Figure 4). "Arrival" is defined as the moment a new patient reaches. The end-to-end response time – the total duration starting when a patient enters the check-in desk until the patient leaves – is the most important performance measure to the patients. From hospital providers' point of view, the utilization of surgery room and the number of patients served per unit time are more important aspects.

Figure 4. The queuing network model of the patient surgery

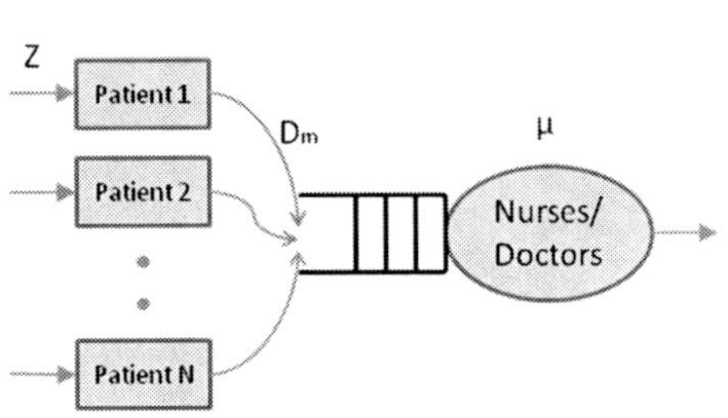

Therefore, this study proposes a queuing network model to estimate the performance index of service process time. Since the medical resource can perform one patient at a time, the model can be seen as a single server process. The processing time and patient inter-arrival rate are estimated to be exponentially distributed due to the diversity of patients seeking surgery. The solution technique proposed in this study is the mean value analysis (MVA) algorithm that relies on three important equations:

Little's formula

$$Q_m = XR_m \qquad (1)$$

Where Q_m is the queue length of patients at the queue m. R_m is the response time for the patient at the queue m.

Mean waiting time

$$R_m = D_m(1 + Q_m) \qquad (2)$$

Where D_m is the mean of processing time for the patient to finish the surgery.

Throughput rate

$$X = \frac{n}{\sum_{m=1}^{M} R_m + Z} \qquad (3)$$

Where X is the throughput of the patients with n patients and z is the time spent in a hospital before a new patient comes in.

The iteration continues until successive estimates of time averaged queue lengths are sufficiently close. The solution model yields values for performance measures such as utilization, throughput, response time, and queue length.

The pseudo code of iterative algorithm is as given below.

For m=0 to M do $Q_m = 0$

For n=1 to N do begin

For m=1 to M do $R_m = D_m(1 + Q_m)$

$$X = \frac{n}{\sum_{m=1}^{M} R_m + Z}$$

For m=1 to M do $Q_m = XR_m$

End

Where M is the number of patients in the queue and N is the number of patients

DEVELOPMENT OF A PROOF-OF-CONCEPT RFID SYSTEM

A. Design of the Proof-of-Concept System

In this study, a prototype system has been developed to show that an RFID system can be used in the identification process of a surgery patient. The hardware component of the RFID system is an RFID tool kit, manufactured by Alien, which includes an ALR-9800 Enterprise RFID reader and an ALR-9610-BC antenna. The ALR-9800 model uses an electromagnetic wave of 900 MHz band and the ALR-9610-BC model has a standard antenna. To investigate the identification ratio of this RFID system, an experiment was conducted in an open space with an object moving at working speed. Results of this experiment revealed an identification ratio of 99.9% within 4-m distance, and these results may correspond to a reliability prediction model.

The data capturing front-end plays a major role in initiating the patient identification process with the use of associated RFID readers, antennas, and tags. The RFID tag of each patient records patient information, such as patient name, gender, and age; surgery information, such as schedule, operation room, operation time, and operation position; and chart ID. While RFID middleware functions as the communication channel between hardware and software, RFID tagging and patient identification – the important processing modules – perform the main tasks. In the RFID tagging module, all basic information about a patient is mentioned on a wristband RFID tag that would be worn by the respective patient. The patient identification module drives the verification of the patient by displaying all basic information from the wristband tag of the patient onto a monitor while the surgery is performed. Both modules can be easily associated with possible legacy systems so that important data about the patient and surgery performed on that patient can be retrieved. This results in eliminating possible potential errors while performing different critical tasks, such as data entry, patient identification, and patient surgery. Once the patient's identity has been validated, the workflow engine for patient identification implements the defined logistics to trigger the activities of associated medical application systems, including the surgery scheduling system, medicine management system, and hospital information system. Figure 5 shows the framework of the RFID-aided patient identification process.

Based on the patient information, RFID tags can be grouped into either active or passive type. The three memory systems that each group however can support include: read-only memory (ROM), read/write (R/W), and write once/read many (WORM). Depending on the workflow characteristics of healthcare application, patients with R/W RFID tags with passive type information are selected. In this case, the jobs assigned may autonomously get completed depending on specific medical instructions reported on the RFID tags. The entire data structure of the RFID tag can fall under two different categories as shown in Figure 6 pre-allocated data and flexible data. Pre-allocated data is written by RFID middleware

Figure 5. RFID-aided patient identification framework

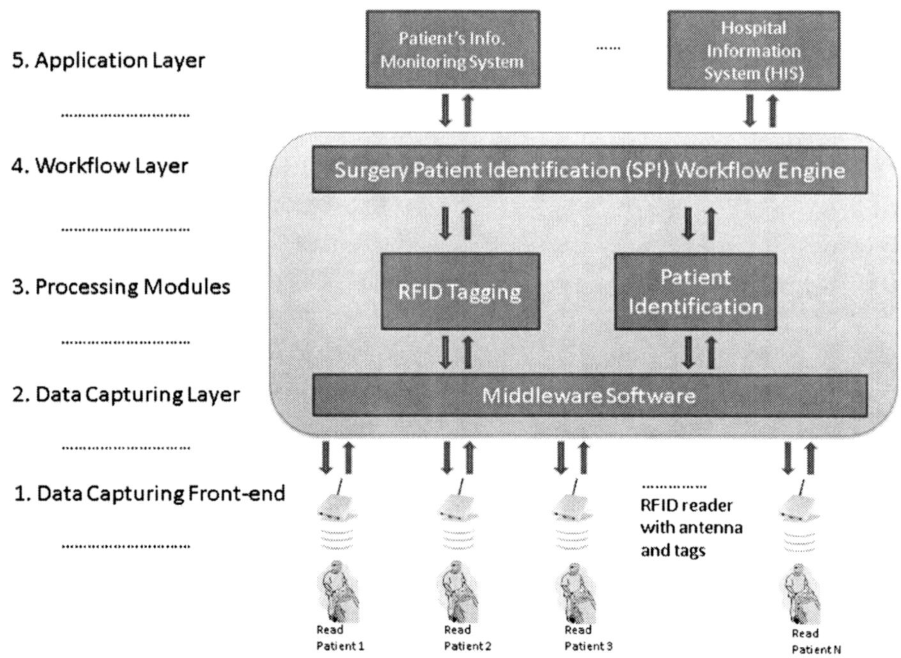

software that is applied to read/write information from/to RFID tags. The flexible data category in the data structure is updated with information provided by the nurse or surgeon based on the patient's activities in the hospital. The data model of patient identification system is depicted in Figure 7. For example, the RFID tagging system retrieves the basic information, such as the patient's ID, name, diagnostic department, hospital room number, and surgery room number, from the legacy database and records the information on the RFID tag that is attached to the wristband of that patient.

B. Implementation of the Prototype

In this study, a prototype module for middleware is developed that may be used to enable an information interchange between the RFID module and the legacy system. Figure 8 shows a form that may be used to display information about a patient who is being rolled into an operation room. Once a patient's surgical schedule has been finalized, the patient is hospitalized to prepare for preliminary procedures and is attached a wristband with RFID tag information. At this time, the tag information is assigned to the patient. An RFID antenna that sends radio waves continuously communicates whether a patient with an RFID tag is approaching or not. If a patient passes through the entrance of an operation room, the RFID reader recognizes the patient's RFID tag and displays basic information on the monitor of the operation room. The information may be retrieved from the hospital's legacy system using the tag information recognized by the RFID system. Surgical team members, such as surgery doctors and nurses in charge of the operation, may then again verify the identity of the patient by matching the patient's name on the monitor and paper chart while the patient is under effect of anesthesia. This prototype system displays only basic information about the patient as recognized on the RFID system. In real applications, however, other important medical information required for an operation may be easily retrieved

Figure 6. Data structure of RFID tag and operation process affecting tag information

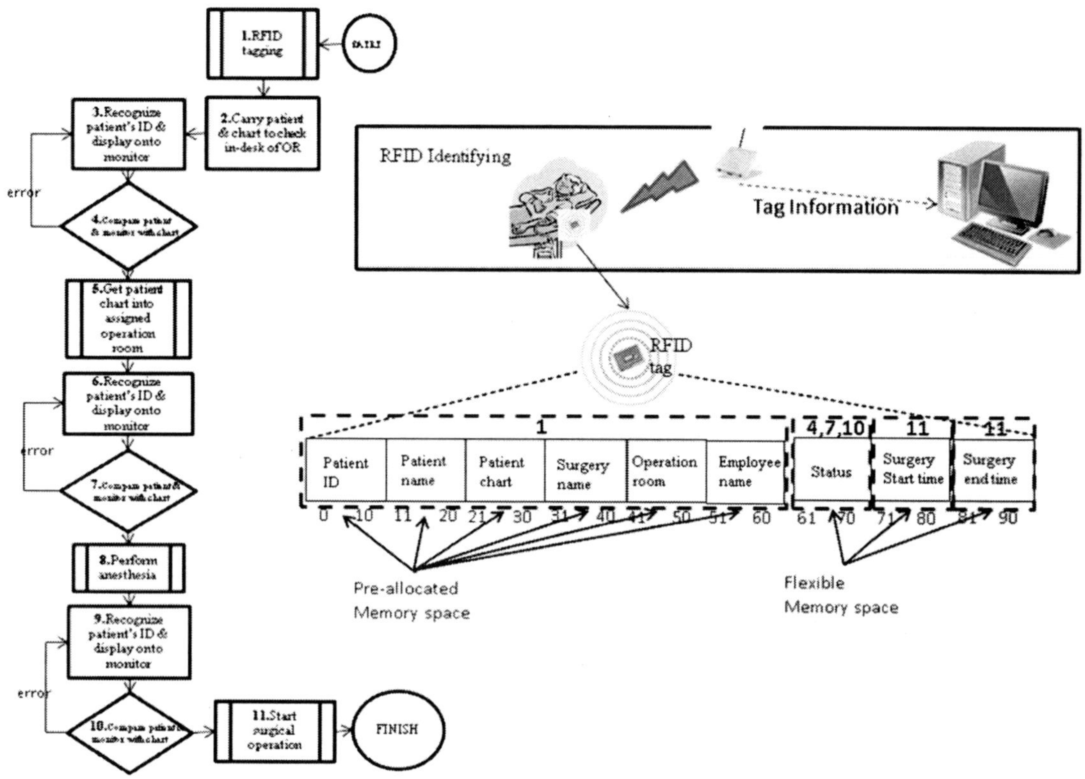

Figure 7. Data model of the patient identification system

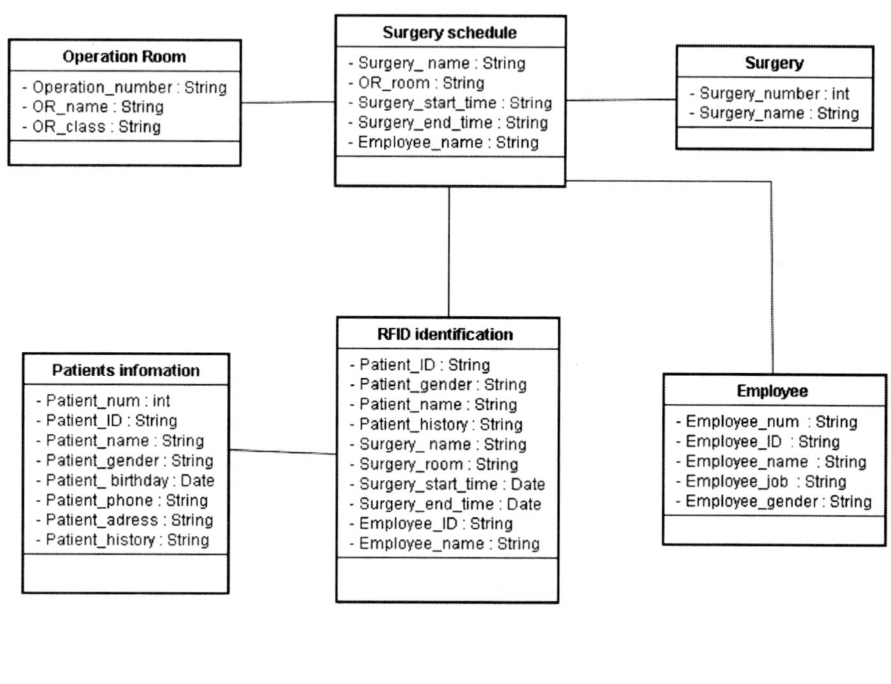

Figure 8. Process flow with two modules

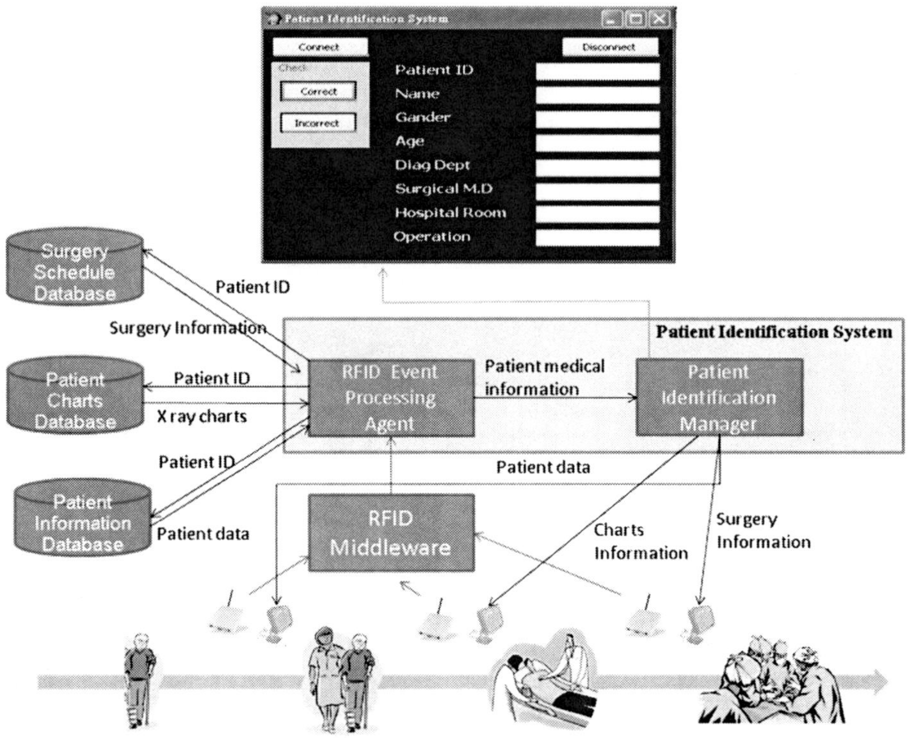

through the existing hospital information system. For example, the module immediately queries the surgery's scheduling module in the legacy system to confirm that the patient is indeed scheduled to be in the operation room. The module then uploads information about the electronic medical record from the legacy database. The system confirms that the right patient is in the right room before the surgery procedure begins.

C. Proof of Concept

In order to verify the application of RFID technology, this study considered one teaching hospital in Taiwan as an example. Usually, the surgical operation room is scheduled. However, the operation room in the emergency room cannot be scheduled in advance. A patient is sent to the emergency room and waits for the urgent operation. In this hospital, a total of 75 beds were allowed in the emergency room, and the maximum capacity of patients to be allowed was defined. For each hour, an average 8 patients were sent to the emergency room. The centralized ambulance system in this area arranged the next patient to various hospitals based on the available medical resource and the current status of each emergency room. Therefore, the model can be seen as a closed-loop queuing model with the number of patients defined.

RFID technology was used for aiding patient identification before surgical operation. Queue occurred at three different steps in the entire process. The first queue occurred when patients arrived at check-in desk or entered the emergency room outside the hospital. While the check-in desk remained occupied, other patients entering the hospital had to wait in the queue until the patient at the check-in desk was taken to the assigned operating room. The second queue occurred at the anesthesia station. The nurse and anesthetist who were in charge of the operation confirmed the identity of the patient before applying anesthesia.

Figure 9. Surgical patient in the emergency room

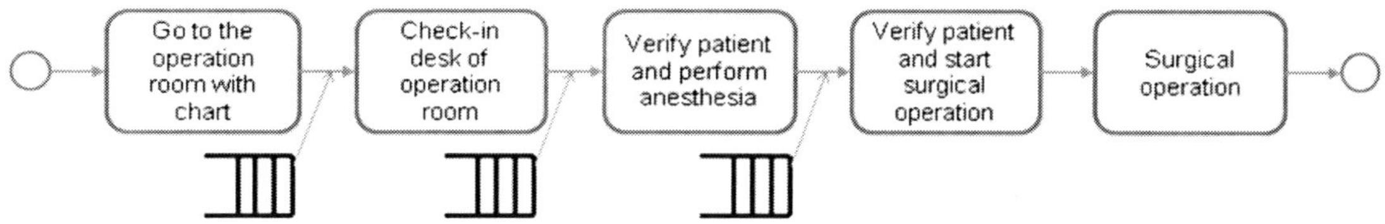

The third queue occurred at the surgery station. The surgeon verifies the identity and the report chart of the patient before beginning the operation. This entire procurement process consumed the maximum time in the surgical process (Figure 9).

An estimation model was built to analyze the queuing model with the mean value analysis (MVA) approach. Since queues happened only at three activities within the entire surgical process, rest of the activities were estimated to be using the average processing time as shown in Table 1. This processing time was collected from the teaching hospital directly. Table 2 shows the response time obtained from the analytical model in multiple groups each containing different number of patients. The data illustrates the relationship between number of patients and mean response time. It was observed that with an increase in the number of patients, the response time also increases. According to the performance model, the average of the estimated total process service time with 32 patients is 241.76 min. The RFID-aided process performed better in serving patients when patients entered the emergency room.

C. Preliminary Evaluation

In order to examine the impact of RFID in information accuracy and productivity improvements by reducing the keyboard entry, we had a preliminary evaluation in three scenarios. Each scenario contains two tests, user entry from the keyboard and RFID-based data collection. The user entry data mix with different data type including text, numerical, and date. The average length of a single record input data is 6.56 characters. Table 1 presents the preliminary evaluation result. The detail of the experiment is studied in (Cheng & Prabhu, 2007). Based on three-scenario evaluation processes, the accuracy of RFID data collection enables the end-to-end process automation that reduces the processing time and eliminates potential data entry errors. The evaluation result shows we can improve the accuracy of data acquisition, which is the main objective in this study.

CONCLUSION

In this paper a workflow model is suggested that utilizes RFID technology to improve patients' safety during a surgical operation. A workflow

Table 1. The average processing time for each activity

No.	Activity	Mean processing time without RFID (min)	Mean processing time with RFID (min)
1	Go to the operation room with chart	15	15
2	Check-in desk of the operation room	10	10
3	Verify patient and perform anesthesia	12	3.5
4	Verify patient and start surgical operation	15	5
5	Surgical operation	60	60

Table 2. The estimated model with different scenarios

Value	Activity	Number of Patients =1		Number of Patients =8		Number of Patients =16		Number of Patients =24		Number of Patients =32	
		Without RFID	With RFID	Without RFID	With RFID	Without RFID	With RFID	Without RFID	With RFID	Without RFID	With RFID
Q	Check-in desk of the operation room	0.07	0.09	0.70	1.30	1.50	5.62	1.70	7.77	1.94	15.13
	Verify patient and perform anesthesia	0.08	0.03	0.95	0.28	2.40	0.50	2.92	0.50	3.66	0.54
	Verify patient and start surgical operation	0.10	0.04	1.41	0.44	5.14	0.89	8.32	0.90	15.01	1.00
R	Check-in desk of the operation room	10.00	10.00	15.98	20.34	24.24	58.38	26.40	80.43	29.22	151.41
	Verify patient and perform anesthesia	12.00	3.50	21.44	4.34	38.70	5.19	45.35	5.22	55.17	5.38
	Verify patient and start surgical operation	15.00	5.00	32.07	6.88	82.85	9.27	129.25	9.35	226.48	9.97
Total response time (mins)		112	93.5 (-17%)	144.49	106.56 (-17%)	220.79	147.84 (-26%)	276	170 (-38%)	385.87	241.76 (-37%)

process that involves RFID technology in the identification process is proposed and a prototype system for RFID middleware is developed here. Some obstacles to RFID use remain hospital-wide, but it is becoming a promising option for some areas in healthcare. Furthermore, the suggested process offers the potential to reduce human errors by reducing/eliminating data entry. Performance model indicates the response time to patients can be reduced to 38% after four hours using the proposed RFID based workflow. In conclusion, this paper shows that using RFID can be expected to reduce patient identification errors significantly, thereby reducing potential harm to patients in terms of injury or death. A major caveat is that these results are theoretical and must be considered preliminary therefore no assertions can be made about eventual reductions in injuries or deaths

Table 3. The evaluation model of keyboard and RFID test

Scenario	Evaluation Process	Time	Accuracy
Scenario 1	Manual Entry process	2.1 min	98%
	RFID-based automated process	1 min	100%
Scenario 2	Manual Entry process	2.5 min	95%
	RFID-based automated process	0.8 min	100%
Scenario 3	Manual Entry process	3-5 days	99%
	RFID-based automated process	5 min	100%

with further research. Experimental research can also be used for assessing some of the technical challenges such as interference of RFID and other medical instruments, and assessing changes in workflow complexity caused by introduction of RFID. Future work could also consider changes in the workflow complexity by introducing RFID technology and applying RFID for monitoring patient flow through healthcare systems.

REFERENCES

Alex Macario, M., MBA, Dean Morris, M., & Sharon Morris, R., BSN, CNOR. (2007). Initial clinical evaluation of a handheld device for detecting retained surgical gauze sponges using radiofrequency identification yechnology. *Archives of Surgery*, *141*, 659–662. doi:10.1001/archsurg.141.7.659

Alex Macario, M., MBA, Dean Morris, M., & Sharon Morris, R., BSN, CNOR. (2007). Initial Clinical Evaluation of a Handheld Device for Detecting Retained Surgical Gauze Sponges Using Radiofrequency Identification Technology. *Archives of Surgery*, *141*, 659–662. doi:10.1001/archsurg.141.7.659

Angeles, R. (2005). RFID technologies: supply chains applications and implementation issues. *Information Systems Management*, *22*, 51–56. doi:10.1201/1078/44912.22.1.20051201/85739.7

Angeles, R. (2005). RFID technologies: Supply Chains Applications and Implementation Issues. *Information Systems Management*, *22*, 51–56. doi:10.1201/1078/44912.22.1.20051201/85739.7

Cheng, C. Y., & Prabhu, V. (2007, May 19 - 23). *Applying RFID for Cutting Tool Supply Chain Management.* Paper presented at the the 2007 Industrial Engineering Research Conference, Nashville, USA.

Cheng, C. Y., & Prabhu, V. (2007). Applying RFID for cutting tool supply chain management. In *Proceedings of the 2007 Industrial Engineering Research Conference*, Nashville, TN.

Ericson, J. (2004). *The RFID for Hospital Care.* The E-Business Executive Daily.

Ericson, J. (2004). *The RFID for hospital care.* The E-Business Executive Daily.

Etchells, E., O'Neill, C., & Bernstein, M. (2003). Patient Safety in Surgery: Error Detection and Prevention. *World Journal of Surgery*, *27*(8), 936–941. doi:10.1007/s00268-003-7097-2

Etchells, E., O'Neill, C., & Bernstein, M. (2003). Patient safety in surgery: error detection and prevention. *World Journal of Surgery*, *27*(8), 936–941. doi:10.1007/s00268-003-7097-2

Fisher, J. A. (2006). Indoor Positioning and Digital Management:Emerging Surveillance Regimes in Hospitals. *Technological Politics and Power in Everyday Life T. Monahan, Ed*, 77-88.

Fisher, J. A. (2006). Indoor positioning and digital management: emerging surveillance regimes in hospitals. *Technological Politics and Power in Everyday Life T. Monahan, Ed*, 77-88.

Health care RFID startup scores $9 million in venture funding. (2004, July 12, 2004). *Dow Jones Reuters Business Interactive.*

Health Care RFID Startup Scores $9 Million in Venture Funding. (2004, July 12, 2004). *Dow Jones Reuters Business Interactive.* Retrieved from http://www.gs1.org/docs/patient_safety Jeong, B., Cheng, C.-Y., & Prabhu, V. (2009). Modeling and Analysis of Surgery Patient Identification Using RFID. *International Journal of Information Systems In the Service Sector, 1*(4), 1-14.

http://www.gs1.org/docs/patient_safety. GS1 standards in healthcare.

Kohn, L. T., Corrigan, J. M., & Donaldson, M. S. (1999). *To Err Is Human: Building A Safer Health System.* Washington, D.C.: Institute of Medicine, National Academy Press.

Kohn, L. T., Corrigan, J. M., & Donaldson, M. S. (1999). *To err is human: building a safer health system*. Washington, D.C.: Institute of Medicine, National Academy Press.

Kuo, W., & Zuo, M. J. (2002). *Optimal reliability modeling: principles and applications*. Wiley.

Mark, R. Chassin, M., MPP, MPH, & Elise C. Becher, M., MA. (2002). The wrong patient. *Academia & Clinic, 136*(11), 826–833.

Mark, R. Chassin, M., MPP, MPH, & Elise C. Becher, M., MA. (2002). The wrong patient. *Academia & Clinic, 136*(11), 826–833.

MF, M., & JD, K. (2004). Patient Identification: Problems and Potential Solutions. *Vox Sanguinis, 87*, 197–202. doi:10.1111/j.1741-6892.2004.00482.x

MF, M., & JD, K. (2004). Patient identification: problems and potential solutions. *Vox Sanguinis, 87*, 197–202. doi:10.1111/j.1741-6892.2004.00482.x

Park, K. (1997). Human error. In G. Salvendy (Ed.), *Handbook of Human Factors and Ergonomics*, 150-171. New York: John Wiley & Sons.

Patient Safety Applications of Bar Code and RFID Technologies. *A Zebra Black & White Paper*.

Patient safety applications of bar code and RFID technologies. *A Zebra Black & White Paper.*

Reason, J. (2002). Combating omission errors through task analysis and good reminders. *Quality & Safety in Health Care, 11*(1), 40–44. doi:10.1136/qhc.11.1.40

Reason, J. (2002). Combating omission errors through task analysis and good reminders. *Quality & Safety in Health Care, 11*(1), 40–44. doi:10.1136/qhc.11.1.40

RFID in the Hospital. (2004, July 15, 2004). *RFID Gazette*.

RFID in the hospital. (2004, July 15, 2004). *RFID Gazette*.

Schwaitzberg, S. D. (2006). The emergence of radiofrequency identification tags: applications in surgery. *Surgical Endoscopy, 20*(8), 1315–1319. doi:10.1007/s00464-006-2050-8

Schwaitzberg, S. D. (2006). The emergence of radiofrequency identification tags: applications in surgery. *Surgical Endoscopy, 20*(8), 1315–1319. doi:10.1007/s00464-006-2050-8

Singapore Fights SARS with RFID. (2003, June 4). *RFID Journal*. Retrieved from http://www.rfidjournal.com/article/articleview/446/1/1

Singapore fights SARS with RFID. (2003, June 4, 2003). *RFID Journal*.

Srivastava, B. (2004). Radio frequency ID technology: The next revolution in SCM. *Business Horizons, 47*(6), 60–68. doi:10.1016/j.bushor.2004.09.009

Srivastava, B. (2004). Radio frequency ID technology: The next revolution in SCM. *Business Horizons, 47*(6), 60–68. doi:10.1016/j.bushor.2004.09.009

Wang, S.-W., Chen, W.-H., Ong, C.-S., Liu, L., & Chuang, Y.-W. (2006). RFID Application in Hospitals: A Case Study on a Demonstration RFID Project in a Taiwan Hospital. *8*, 184a - 184a.

Wang, S.-W., Chen, W.-H., Ong, C.-S., Liu, L., & Chuang, Y.-W. (2006). RFID application in hospitals: a case study on a demonstration RFID project in a Taiwan hospital. *8*, 184a - 184a.

What an unbelievable surgery!-Perform an operation with exchanged charts. (2006, 2006 Jan 15). *Donga News*.

What an unbelievable surgery!-Perform an operation with exchanged charts. (2006, 2006 Jan 15). *Donga News*.

Yoo, D.-S. K., Kim, S. K., Chang, H. O., Bae, B. C., Kim, H. S., & S.J. (2007). Location based blood bag management using active RFID and ubiquitous sensor network. *This paper appears in: Information Technology Applications in Biomedicine, 2007. ITAB 2007. 6th International Special Topic Conference on ITAB, Tokyo, 2007.*, 320-322.

Chapter 17
Does the Internet Increase Fundraising Revenues of Nonprofit Organizations?
An Economic Analysis

Yasin Ozcelik
Fairfield University, USA

ABSTRACT

Nonprofit organizations have been using the Internet for disseminating information about themselves, interacting with potential donors, and fundraising. In this chapter, we focus on online service providers for nonprofits (OSPNs) that bring donors and nonprofits together in an electronic environment to help them find a suitable match. We investigate the effects of OSPNs on the outcomes of fundraising markets by developing an economic model. We compare the total net revenues of nonprofits competing for donations in two different settings: while nonprofits in the first market use both the traditional fundraising techniques and the services provided by OSPNs, those in the second market implement the traditional method only. We derive analytical conditions under which the first setting provides better outcomes than the second one can generate.

INTRODUCTION

Nonprofit organizations constitute one of the largest economic sectors in the United States. It is larger than banking and electronics sectors with accumulated assets of almost $1 trillion (Jansen & Katz, 2002). Total donations to an estimated 1.3 million nonprofits in the United States rose to $240.72 billion in 2003 (Silverman, 2004), and they are projected to reach $25 trillion over the next 50 years (Lowell et al., 2001). Most nonprofits are small-sized institutions with annual budgets of less than $100,000. Nearly 700,000 of them are public charities and the remaining are private schools, foundations, hospitals, and religious organizations. The nonprofit sector is generally characterized by mission-driven services. Each nonprofit differentiates itself through its mission statement, which identifies the nature of people's needs that the nonprofit attempts to serve, such as education, hunger, homelessness, or unemployment. Moreover, the mission statement embodies

DOI: 10.4018/978-1-60960-138-6.ch017

certain beliefs about the management culture of the organization (Hackney & Pillay, 2002).

Traditionally, nonprofits have been using various forms of fundraising techniques, including on-site visits, direct-mail appeals, or phone calls to reach donors. However, many donors and nonprofits using these traditional methods are not able to make informed decisions since they cannot easily access comprehensive and accurate data about one another due to information asymmetry inherent in traditional fundraising environments (Tempel, 2003). Moreover, the cost of information exchange between the parties is high (Meehan, 2001). By offering a source of complete and transparent information, the Internet is evolving into a ubiquitous digital platform for allocating and optimizing resources throughout the nonprofit sector. The Internet enables nonprofits to reach and serve more people without barriers of distance and national borders, decreasing traditional advantages of location in a global market. Moreover, it enables donors to access more comprehensive financial and performance data on nonprofits, leading to better evaluations by prospective donors. In this chapter, we focus on online service providers for nonprofits (OSPN), which bring donors and nonprofits together in an electronic environment to help them find a suitable match. An OSPN maintains an online database of nonprofits and prospective donors. Nonprofits upload into this database all of their relevant information such as mission, location, expenses, assets, and liabilities. Donors, on the other hand, may specify the reason for their donation and indicate the maximum amount of donation they wish to make on the OSPN website. Donors and nonprofits can search this database and find a suitable match according to their needs and specifications. The OSPN may also facilitate the transactions between the parties by offering digital payment systems.

Given all the promises of OSPNs discussed so far, our goal in this chapter is to investigate possible effects of OSPNs on fundraising markets by developing a nonprofit duopoly model based on spatial competition. Using this model, we compare the total net revenues of nonprofits in two different market settings: nonprofits in the first market use both the traditional method and the services provided by OSPNs, while those in the second market employ only the traditional method. We then find analytical conditions where the first market setting generates better outcomes. Our analytical setup utilizes all of the following well-known economic models: (i) duopolistic spatial competition model based on Hotelling's (1929) classical linear city model, (ii) informative advertising model developed by Grossman & Shapiro (1984), and (iii) implicit price of a public good adopted from Okten & Weisbrod (2000).

A BRIEF SURVEY OF ONLINE SERVICE PROVIDERS FOR NONPROFITS

Many different forms of OSPNs exist (Ozcelik, 2008). For instance, GuideStar (www.guidestar.org) maintains an online database with financial and program information of more than a million nonprofits. Global Giving (www.globalgiving.com) provides an online platform that allows nonprofits to post their social projects on the website for funding. The posted projects are categorized according to their theme or region so that potential donors can browse and make an instant donation using their credit cards. Donors Choose (www.donorschoose.org) is another online medium where teachers can post a school project that needs funding.

In order to help nonprofits comply with government regulations and assist donors to make informed decisions, several online evaluation, accreditation, and seal programs for nonprofits were also launched recently. These programs evaluate and rate nonprofits by using different standards as explained below, leaving it up to donors to choose their own criteria when deciding on a donation. For instance, the online certification program offered by the Standards for Excellence Institute (www.standardsforexcellenceinstitute.org) enforces about 55 governance and operation standards. The institute's criteria include overhead limits (e.g., fundraising expenditure of the applicant organization should not exceed one fourth of its revenue), frequency of board meetings (e.g., at least four times a year), and financial oversight (e.g., financial reports for organizations with $300,000 or more annual revenue should be verified by a certified public accountant). Nonprofits satisfying these criteria are granted a "Seal of Excellence". The Better Business Bureau's Wise Giving Alliance (www.give.org) also offers a similar evaluation system and a seal of approval according to 20 financial and governance standards. The financial standards include (i) spending no more than 35% of contributions on fundraising, (ii) avoiding accumulating funds that could be used for current program activities, and (iii) making available complete annual financial statements that clearly show what portions of the total budget are allocated to program, fundraising, and administrative expenses. The governance standards include (i) having a board of directors with a minimum of five voting members to provide adequate oversight of the organization's operations, (ii) a minimum of three annual meetings with a majority in attendance, and (iii) not more than one or 10% (whichever is greater) compensated person(s) serving as voting members of the board. Accredited nonprofits in this program need to pay a fee to use the seal, which may be as much as $15,000 for large nonprofits. The Wise Giving Alliance also issues online reports on the evaluated nonprofits. The American Institute of Philanthropy (www.charitywatch.org) grades more than 500 large nonprofits according to their financial statements. The grading mechanism is based on several financial criteria, such as the cost of raising $100 by the organizations, which is calculated using the IRS filings, audited financial statements, and annual reports of the organizations. Similarly, the Charity Navigator (www.charitynavigator.org) rates nearly 3,700 nonprofits according to their financial health. The rating method depends on several metrics such as fundraising efficiency, which is the amount spent to raise $1 in charitable contributions. Finally, the Evangelical Council for Financial Accountability (www.ecfa.org) accredits and offers a seal to Christian ministries by examining their governance, financial transparency, and fundraising practices according to similar criteria utilized by the aforementioned institutions.

LITERATURE REVIEW

Our study draws upon four main areas of research in the literature: (i) competition in the nonprofit sector, (ii) certification of quality, (iii) online marketplaces, and (iv) spatial differentiation. In this section, we provide a brief survey of pertinent studies in each area from the literature.

Due to a rapid expansion both in the number and diversity with relatively constant resources (funds, donors, and volunteers), the nonprofit sector has witnessed an increasing competition and a more performance-driven approach over the years (Porter & Kramer, 1999). Weisbrod & Dominguez (1986) find that competition is indeed a disciplinary device for nonprofits promoting their efficiency. Posnett & Sandler (1989), Khanna et al. (1995), and Callen (1994) provide empirical support for the hypothesis of market competition as a driving force for the economic efficiency of nonprofits. Ritchie et al. (1999) argue that if a new technology offers more effective and cost-efficient solutions to the nonprofit sector, competition among nonprofits intensifies. Indeed, nonprofits have started using the Internet strategically for disseminating information, interacting with donors, and fundraising (Lee et al., 2001; Pollach et al., 2005). They have also leveraged it to differentiate themselves from competition by having their qualities certified and communicating this information to potential donors (Quinn, 2006).

Capozzi et al. (2003) emphasize that nonprofit foundations are knowledge-intensive bodies, and most of their processes from identifying innovative organizations to evaluating grants and publishing reports depend on the use of human and intellectual capital. Therefore, it is important for foundations to manage and disseminate their knowledge properly. Among the solutions for effective knowledge management for foundations are creating a searchable database of grant reports, establishing standards for documents, and building institutional memory to support future operations.

Quality certification through seals of approval by third-party institutions has been a common practice in many industries for years. It was argued that such certifications significantly affect consumer perception because they are considered to be useful mechanisms for communicating a threshold level of quality to consumers (Bennett & McCrohan, 1993). Due to consumers' perceived risk of online transactions (Bailey & Bakos, 1997), the use of similar seals of certification has been found to be especially important for e-commerce companies (Hoffman et al., 1999; Kim, 2003; Rees et al., 2003). For example, Miyazaki & Krishnamurthy (2002) empirically find that participation in online seals of approval programs by e-commerce companies positively affects consumer perception on the Internet. Ba et al. (1999) demonstrate that disseminating information on quality through the use of online intermediaries is a stable strategy for e-commerce companies in equilibrium, suggesting that it will be eventually adopted by most e-commerce companies. Finally, Palmer et al. (2000) empirically investigate the role of online intermediaries offering seals of approval services in the development of trust on the Internet. They find that websites that have a large number of incoming links tend to obtain seals of approval.

In one of the earliest studies on online marketplaces, Malone et al. (1987) recognized the potential of information technology in reducing the costs of coordination and predicted that economic activity would shift more toward electronic markets than electronic hierarchies. Bakos (1998) later argued that the ability of Internet marketplaces to reduce search costs for price and product information would increase competition in prices and reduce the monopoly power enjoyed by sellers in markets for differentiated goods. Campbell et al. (2005), however, show that such competitive gains may be difficult to realize if the same technology that eases consumer search also allows firms to monitor each other's prices more easily and thereby facilitates collusion. Some of the more recent research examines the implications of network effects in online markets. Parker & Van Alstyne (2005) pioneer the emerging literature on two-sided markets. They develop an analytical model to explain how a firm can rationally invest in a product it intends to give away into perpetuity. Bakos & Katsamakas (2008) show that ownership of an online intermediary by one side of the market (buyer or seller) is often optimal in terms of maximizing profits and total surplus, compared to ownership by an independent intermediary. This result is corroborated by Yoo et al. (2002). Bhargava & Choudhary (2004) focus on information intermediaries under network effects and find that they should offer quality differentiated versions of their services.

The literature on spatial differentiation originates from Hotelling's classical linear city model, where it is shown that competition for a market share between duopolists results in the minimum differentiation (Hotelling, 1929). In a slightly modified version of the original Hotelling model, D'Aspremont et al. (1979) demonstrate that profit maximizing firms should choose the maximum differentiation. Extensive research on the linear city model has emerged since then (De Palma et al., 1987; Bockem, 1994; Nero, 1999; Kim & Serfes, 2006). These papers typically examine the strategies of profit-maximizing firms that sell differentiated products. In this study, we develop a modified version of the linear city model in a context where nonprofits contact potential donors to maximize their total net fundraising revenues.

Figure 1. Fundraising market A

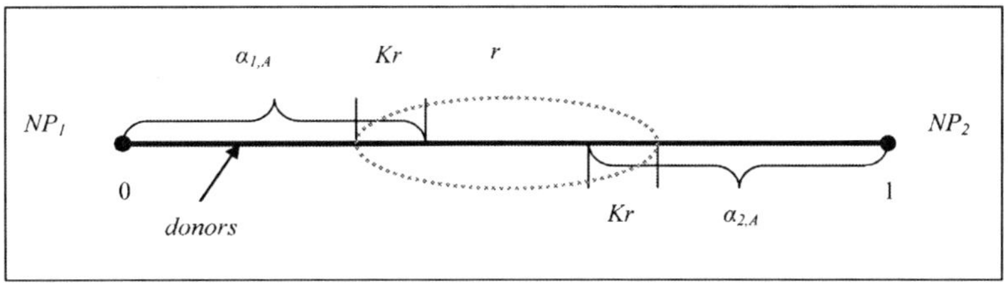

ECONOMIC MODEL

Our model is an application of the classical linear city model of Hotelling (1929) to fundraising markets. There is a continuum of donors distributed uniformly according to their preferred missions along the real line [0,1]. There are two nonprofits, denoted by NP_1 and NP_2, with fixed strategic missions located at points 0 and 1, respectively. Both nonprofits need to contact donors to receive a donation, and each of them tries to maximize its own total net revenue from all donations. Each contacted donor has an incentive to donate $\$z$ to one of the nonprofits if she receives a positive net utility from her donation. Nonprofits can contact donors by using any or both of the following methods: (i) the traditional method such as on-site visits, direct-mail appeals, or phone calls with an average unit cost denoted by v, and (ii) the online method by using services provided by OSPNs for which they have to pay a fixed fee, p, to the OSPN. This type of fixed pricing scheme is actually being adopted by most OSPNs on the Internet. For example, *GuideStar.org* offers an online search service called *Grant Explorer* priced at $499 as a yearly subscription by which nonprofits can find prospective donors according to their criteria, and apply for grants.

In order to develop an appropriate model to analyze the possible effects of OSPNs on fundraising markets, we consider two different market settings denoted by A and B. In market A, each nonprofit uses both the traditional method of contacting donors and the services of OSPNs. By using the traditional method, NP_1 contacts $\alpha_{1,A}$ fraction of donors while NP_2 contacts $\alpha_{2,A}$ fraction of donors, where $0 < \alpha_{1,A}, \alpha_{2,A} < 1$. Moreover, r fraction of donors use the OSPN to obtain information about both NP_1 and NP_2, where $0 < r < 1$. It is possible that some donors contacted by NP_1 or NP_2 through the traditional method also use the OSPN, implying an overlapping region between r and $\alpha_{i,A}$ $(i = 1, 2)$. We consider this situation by defining a new variable K such that the fraction of donors using both channels is Kr for each nonprofit, $0 \leq K \leq 1$ (see Figure 1). In market B, NP_1 contacts $\alpha_{1,B}$ fraction of donors while NP_2 contacts $\alpha_{2,B}$ fraction of donors by using the traditional method only, where $0 < \alpha_{1,B}, \alpha_{2,B} < 1$ (see Figure 2).

Figure 2. Fundraising market B

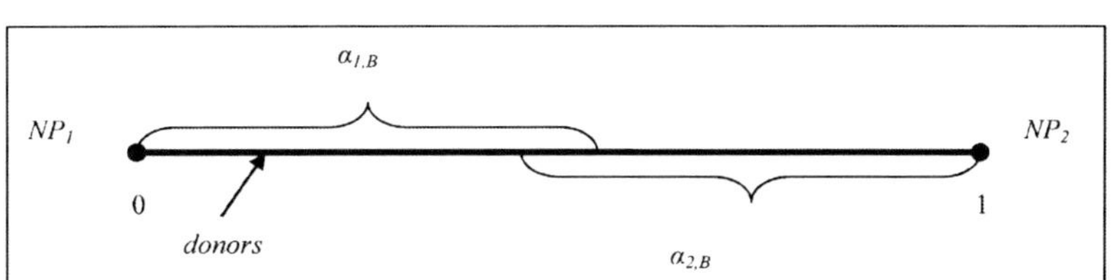

Since donors are the "buyers" of services provided by nonprofits, the utility function of a donor plays a central role in our model. A donor's utility from her donation depends on two different aspects of a nonprofit: (i) the social monetary output of the nonprofit, and (ii) the closeness of the preferred mission of the donor to the actual mission of the nonprofit. The social monetary output of a nonprofit is the net amount of a donation that is used to create a public service by the nonprofit. Given that the structures of markets *A* and *B* are different, the social monetary outputs of nonprofits in these markets will differ. We denote the social monetary outputs of NP_1 and NP_2 generated from a $\$z$ donation by $O_{1,A}$ and $O_{2,A}$ in market *A* and by $O_{1,B}$ and $O_{2,B}$ in market *B*, respectively. To calculate these values, we use the following formula for the implicit price of a public good, which is the amount of donation that should be given to a nonprofit to generate $1 worth of charitable output (Okten & Weisbrod, 2000).

$$\textit{implicit price of a public good} = \frac{1-\gamma}{1-f}$$

Here, γ is the income tax rate facing a donor, and f is the fraction of a donation spent by the nonprofit on fundraising expenditures, $0 < \gamma, f < 1$. Other variants of this formula were also used by Weisbrod & Dominguez (1986), Posnett & Sandler (1989), and Khanna et al. (1995). Using this formula, we obtain:

$$O_{1,A} = \frac{z(1-f_{1,A})}{1-\gamma} \quad \textit{and} \quad O_{2,A} = \frac{z(1-f_{2,A})}{1-\gamma},$$

where $f_{1,A}$ and $f_{2,A}$ $(0 < f_{1,A}, f_{2,A} < 1)$ are the fractions of the $\$z$ donation spent by NP_1 and NP_2 on fundraising expenditures in market *A*, respectively.

The second factor affecting a donor's utility is the misfit between the preferred mission of the donor and the actual mission of a nonprofit, which creates a psychological cost borne by the donor. If t denotes the unit cost of misfit between the preferred mission of the donor located at point $x_A \in [0,1]$ and the actual mission of a nonprofit, the disutility of the donor from her donation to NP_1 will be $-tx_A$. On the other hand, if the same donor donates to NP_2, rather than NP_1, then her disutility will be $-t(1-x_A)$. Combining both of the above utility factors, we find the utilities of the donor located at point $x_A \in [0,1]$ from donating $\$z$ to NP_1 or NP_2 in market *A* as follows:

$$U_{1,A} = O_{1,A} - tx_A = \frac{z(1-f_{1,A})}{1-\gamma} - tx_A$$

or

$$U_{2,A} = O_{2,A} - t(1-x_A) = \frac{z(1-f_{2,A})}{1-\gamma} - t(1-x_A)$$

Now, if all donors are fully informed about both NP_1 and NP_2, the donor located at $x_A \in [0,1]$ will be indifferent between donating $\$z$ to NP_1 or NP_2 in market *A* if $U_{1,A} = U_{2,A}$, i.e.,

$$\frac{z(1-f_{1,A})}{1-\gamma} - tx_A = \frac{z(1-f_{2,A})}{1-\gamma} - t(1-x_A)$$

Solving the above equality for x_A gives us the fraction of donors in market *A* who prefer to donate $\$z$ to NP_1 under full information as follows:

$$x_A = \frac{1}{2} + \frac{z(f_{2,A} - f_{1,A})}{2t(1-\gamma)} \tag{1}$$

Similarly, the fraction of donors who prefer to donate \$$z$ to NP_2 in market A under full information is $1 - x_A$. We now calculate the optimum total net revenues of nonprofits in market A under imperfect information, i.e., when each nonprofit needs to decide on the fraction of donors to be contacted using both methods. Since contacting donors either through the traditional method or the OSPN is the only source of expenditure for nonprofits in our model, there is a functional relationship among the variables $f_{1,A}$, $\alpha_{1,A}$, and r, as well as among $f_{2,A}$, $\alpha_{2,A}$, and r. In order to find these relationships in market A, we proceed as follows. Given the amount of donation \$$z$ to NP_1 by a donor, NP_1 uses some of this money for contacting donors through the traditional method as well as for paying the service fee charged by OSPN, p. Following Tirole (1997), we assume that the total cost of contacting $\alpha_{1,A}$ fraction of donors through the traditional method by NP_1 in market A is $v\alpha_{1,A}^2 / 2$, where v is the average unit cost of contacting a donor via the traditional method. Hence, per-donor cost of fundraising for NP_1 using the traditional method in market A is $v\alpha_{1,A}$. The per-donor cost of fundraising for NP_1 when she uses OSPN is found from dividing p by the fraction of donors using OSPN, r. Combining these two factors of fundraising costs for NP_1 in market A, we obtain:

$$f_{1,A} = \frac{v\alpha_{1,A} + \frac{p}{r}}{z} \tag{2}$$

Similarly, the formula for $f_{2,A}$ is calculated as:

$$f_{2,A} = \frac{v\alpha_{2,A} + \frac{p}{r}}{z} \tag{3}$$

Inserting equations (2) and (3) into equation (1) and simplifying leads to:

$$x_A = \frac{1}{2} + \frac{v\left(\alpha_{2,A} - \alpha_{1,A}\right)}{2t\left(1-\gamma\right)} \tag{4}$$

We calculate the total net revenues of NP_1 and NP_2 in market A under imperfect information, denoted by $TNR_{1,A}$ and $TNR_{2,A}$ respectively, from the following formulas:

$$TNR_{1,A} = \left[\alpha_{1,A} + \left(1-K\right)r\right]\left[1 - \left(\alpha_{2,A} + \left(1-K\right)r\right)\left(1-x_A\right)\right]z - \frac{v\alpha_{1,A}^2}{2} - p \tag{5}$$

$$TNR_{2,A} = \left[\alpha_{2,A} + \left(1-K\right)r\right]\left[1 - \left(\alpha_{1,A} + \left(1-K\right)r\right)x_A\right]z - \frac{v\alpha_{2,A}^2}{2} - p \tag{6}$$

Equations (5) and (6) follow from the informative advertising model of Grossman & Shapiro (1984). The total fraction of donors contacted by NP_1 is equal to $\left[\alpha_{1,A} + \left(1-K\right)r\right]$, in which $\alpha_{1,A}$ of them are contacted through the traditional method and $\left(1-K\right)r$ of them are contacted via the OSPN. The second term in square brackets in equation (5) corresponds to the probability of donation to NP_1, which decreases as a result of competition for donations from NP_2. The impact of the level of competition from NP_2 is calculated by multiplying the total fraction of donors contacted by NP_2, which is $\left(\alpha_{2,A} + \left(1-K\right)r\right)$, by the amount of donors who prefer donating to NP_2 under full information, which is $1 - x_A$. The gross total revenue of NP_1 is calculated by multiplying the three factors: (i) the total fraction of donors contacted by NP_1, (ii) the probability of donation to NP_1, and (iii) the donation amount. Finally, the total net revenue of NP_1 is found by subtracting from the gross total revenue the two factors of cost for NP_1, which are the total cost of traditional contact, $v\alpha_{1,A}^2 / 2$, and the service fee charged by the OSPN, p. The calculations for $TNR_{2,A}$ in equation (6) are similar to those of $TNR_{1,A}$. Now, inserting equation (4) into (5) and (6) leads to the following formulas for market A:

$$TNR_{1,A} = \left[\alpha_{1,A} + (1-K)r\right]\left[1 - \left(\alpha_{2,A} + (1-K)r\right)\left(\frac{1}{2} - \frac{v\left(\alpha_{2,A} - \alpha_{1,A}\right)}{2t(1-\gamma)}\right)\right]z - \frac{v\alpha_{1,A}^2}{2} - p$$

$$TNR_{2,A} = \left[\alpha_{2,A} + (1-K)r\right]\left[1 - \left(\alpha_{1,A} + (1-K)r\right)\left(\frac{1}{2} + \frac{v\left(\alpha_{2,A} - \alpha_{1,A}\right)}{2t(1-\gamma)}\right)\right]z - \frac{v\alpha_{2,A}^2}{2} - p$$

The calculations for market B are similar to those for market A, producing the following formulas:

$$f_{1,B} = \frac{v\alpha_{1,B}}{z} \quad and \quad f_{2,B} = \frac{v\alpha_{2,B}}{z}$$

$$x_B = \frac{1}{2} + \frac{z(f_{2,B} - f_{1,B})}{2t(1-\gamma)}$$

$$TNR_{1,B} = \alpha_{1,B}\left[1 - \alpha_{2,B}\left(\frac{1}{2} - \frac{v\left(\alpha_{2,B} - \alpha_{1,B}\right)}{2t(1-\gamma)}\right)\right]z - \frac{v\alpha_{1,B}^2}{2}$$

$$TNR_{2,B} = \alpha_{2,B}\left[1 - \alpha_{1,B}\left(\frac{1}{2} + \frac{v\left(\alpha_{2,B} - \alpha_{1,B}\right)}{2t(1-\gamma)}\right)\right]z - \frac{v\alpha_{2,B}^2}{2}$$

ANALYTICAL RESULTS

In this section, we first find the optimum values of the decision variables and the total net revenue of each nonprofit in markets A and B. We then derive analytical results by comparing these optimum values. In order to focus on the variables of interest and to make the model tractable, we normalize the variables z and t to unity and look for a symmetric equilibrium in each market. These normalizations lead to the following maximization problems in market A:

$$TNR_{1,A}^* = \underset{\alpha_{1,A}}{Max}\left[\alpha_{1,A} + (1-K)r\right]\left[1 - \left(\alpha_{2,A} + (1-K)r\right)\left(\frac{1}{2} - \frac{v\left(\alpha_{2,A} - \alpha_{1,A}\right)}{2(1-\gamma)}\right)\right] - \frac{v\alpha_{1,A}^2}{2} - p \quad (7)$$

$$TNR_{2,A}^* = \underset{\alpha_{2,A}}{Max}\left[\alpha_{2,A} + (1-K)r\right]\left[1 - \left(\alpha_{1,A} + (1-K)r\right)\left(\frac{1}{2} + \frac{v\left(\alpha_{2,A} - \alpha_{1,A}\right)}{2(1-\gamma)}\right)\right] - \frac{v\alpha_{2,A}^2}{2} - p \quad (8)$$

The simultaneous solution of equations (7) and (8) in symmetric equilibrium gives the optimum fractions of donors that NP_1 and NP_2 contacts by using the traditional method in market A as follows:

$$\alpha_{1,A}^* = \alpha_{2,A}^* = \frac{\sqrt{A_\alpha} - (1-\gamma)(1+2v) - 2vr(1-K)}{2v},$$

where

$$A_\alpha = (1-\gamma)^2\left(1 + 4v(v+1)\right) + 8v(1-\gamma)\left(1 + vr(1-K)\right)$$

Inserting $\alpha_{1,A}^*$ and $\alpha_{2,A}^*$ back into equations (7) and (8), and simplifying leads to the following optimum total net revenue of each organization in market A:

$$TNR^*_{1,A} = TNR^*_{2,A} = \frac{A_{T1}\sqrt{A_{T2}} - A_{T3} - A_{T4} - 4pv^2}{4v^2},$$

where

$$A_{T1} = 2v\left(1 + vr\left(1 - K\right)\right) + \left(1 - \gamma\right)\left(1 + v\right)\left(1 + 2v\right)$$

$$A_{T2} = \left(1 - \gamma\right)\left[8v\left(1 + vr\left(1 - K\right)\right) + \left(1 - \gamma\right)\left(1 + 2v\right)^2\right]$$

$$A_{T3} = 2v^2 r\left(1 - K\right)\left[vr\left(1 - K\right) + \left(1 - \gamma\right)\left(4v + 3\right)\right]$$

$$A_{T4} = \left(1 - \gamma\right)\left[\left(1 + 4v\right)^2 + \left(3 + 4v^2\right)v - \gamma\left(1 + v\right)\left(1 + 2v\right)^2\right]$$

Similarly, we have the following maximization problems in market B:

$$TNR^*_{1,B} = \underset{\alpha_{1,B}}{Max}\ \alpha_{1,B}\left[1 - \alpha_{2,B}\left(\frac{1}{2} - \frac{v\left(\alpha_{2,B} - \alpha_{1,B}\right)}{2\left(1 - \gamma\right)}\right)\right] - \frac{v\alpha^2_{1,B}}{2} \qquad (9)$$

$$TNR^*_{2,B} = \underset{\alpha_{2,B}}{Max}\ \alpha_{2,B}\left[1 - \alpha_{1,B}\left(\frac{1}{2} + \frac{v\left(\alpha_{2,B} - \alpha_{1,B}\right)}{2\left(1 - \gamma\right)}\right)\right] - \frac{v\alpha^2_{2,B}}{2} \qquad (10)$$

Simultaneous solution of the equations (9) and (10)leads to the following optimum values in market B:

$$\alpha^*_{1,B} = \alpha^*_{2,B} = \frac{\sqrt{B_\alpha} - \left(1 - \gamma\right)\left(1 + 2v\right)}{2v}$$

$$TNR^*_{1,B} = TNR^*_{2,B} = \frac{B_{T1}\sqrt{B_{T2}} - B_{T3}}{4v^2},$$

where

$$B_\alpha = \left(1 - \gamma\right)^2\left[1 + 4v\left(v + 1\right)\right] + 8v\left(1 - \gamma\right)$$

$$B_{T1} = 2v + \left(1 - \gamma\right)\left(1 + v\right)\left(1 + 2v\right)$$

$$B_{T2} = \left(1 - \gamma\right)\left[8v + \left(1 - \gamma\right)\left(1 + 2v\right)^2\right]$$

$$B_{T3} = \left(1 - \gamma\right)\left[\left(1 + 4v\right)^2 + \left(3 + 4v^2\right)v - \gamma\left(1 + v\right)\left(1 + 2v\right)^2\right]$$

Nonprofits benefit from the existence of an OSPN if its services enable them to decrease the fraction of donors contacted through the traditional method, i.e., the following condition must besatisfiedinourmodel $\alpha^*_{1,A} = \alpha^*_{2,A} < \alpha^*_{1,B} = \alpha^*_{2,B}$. The solution of this inequality gives us the following condition:

$$r > \frac{2v\left(1 - \gamma\right) - \sqrt{\left(1 - \gamma\right)^2\left[1 + 4v\left(v + 1\right)\right] + 8v\left(1 - \gamma\right)}}{v\left(1 - K\right)} \qquad (11)$$

Indeed, the inequality in (11) always holds because the right hand side is always negative and $0 < r < 1$. Another issue to be checked is whether the use of symmetric equilibrium restricts our model. The symmetric equilibrium implies that neither NP_1 nor NP_2 has an incentive to contact potential donors located beyond the point ½ using the traditional method in each market. Having the situation $\alpha^*_{1,A} = \alpha^*_{2,A} < \alpha^*_{1,B} = \alpha^*_{2,B}$ already satisfied, it remains to find conditions under which $\alpha^*_{1,B} = \alpha^*_{2,B} < 1/2$ holds. The solution of this inequality leads to:

Figure 3. Plots of the difference between the optimum total net revenues of nonprofits in markets A and B

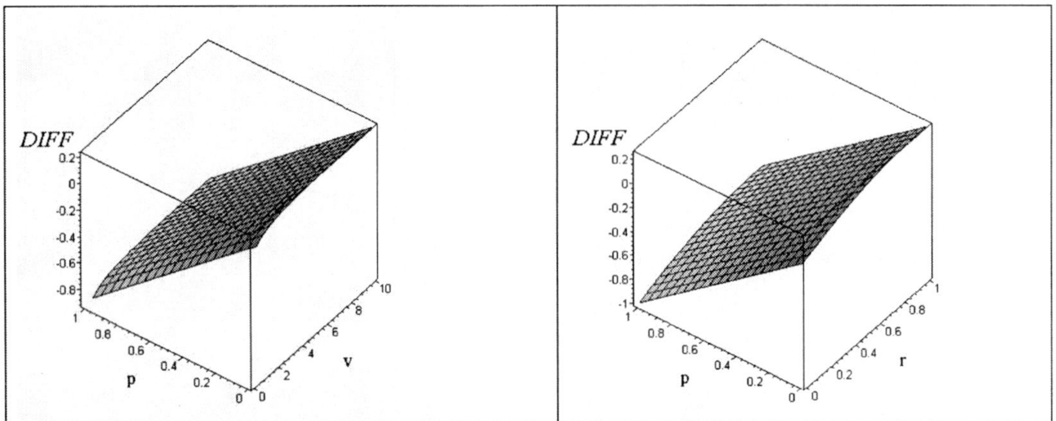

DIFF as a function of *p* and *v* ($r = 0.6$, $K = 0.5$, $\gamma = 0.3$)	*DIFF* as a function of *p* and *r* ($v = 1$, $K = 0$, $\gamma = 0.3$)

$$v > \frac{6(1-\gamma)}{1+4(1-\gamma)}$$

As a result, the findings of our model will be valid only when the average unit cost of contacting a donor through the traditional method is above a threshold value.

We now compare the optimum total net revenues of nonprofits in each market, and find analytical conditions under which the outcomes of market *A* are better than those of market *B*. Defining $TNR_A^* = TNR_{1,A}^* = TNR_{2,A}^*$ and $TNR_B^* = TNR_{1,B}^* = TNR_{2,B}^*$ we calculate the difference between these two values from $DIFF = TNR_A^* - TNR_B^*$. Hence, TNR_A^* is higher than TNR_B^* if the following condition holds:

$$DIFF = \frac{A_{T1}\sqrt{A_{T2}} - A_{T3} - B_{T1}\sqrt{B_{T2}} - 4pv^2}{4v^2} > 0 \tag{12}$$

It is easy to see from (12) that if the service price charged by the OSPN increases, then *DIFF* decreases. This implies that there must be an upper bound for price. Solving the inequality in (12) for p gives us the maximum price that the OSPN can charge nonprofits in market *A* as follows:

$$p < \frac{A_{T1}\sqrt{A_{T2}} - A_{T3} - B_{T1}\sqrt{B_{T2}}}{4v^2} \tag{13}$$

It is possible to find more intuitive results from the conditions in (12) and (13) by plotting the graphs of the variables of interest for some reasonable values to mimic the real-world situations, as in Figure 3 and Figure 4. The graphs in Figure 3 are drawn with the assumptions that 60% of donors use the services provided by the OSPN ($r = 0.6$), half or none of those donors are also contacted through the traditional method ($K = 0.5$ and $K = 0$, respectively), and the income tax rate facing a donor is 30% ($\gamma = 0.3$). Both of the graphs in Figure 3 show that increasing the price charged by the OSPN deteriorates the total net revenues of nonprofits in market *A* as compared to *B*. Moreover, the outcomes of market *A* become completely inferior beyond a threshold value of p, which was analytically shown in equation (13) above. On the other hand, if either the average unit cost of contact in the traditional method, v, or the fraction of donors using the OSPN, r,

Figure 4. Plot of the maximum service price for different values of v and r ($K = 0.1$, $\gamma = 0.3$)

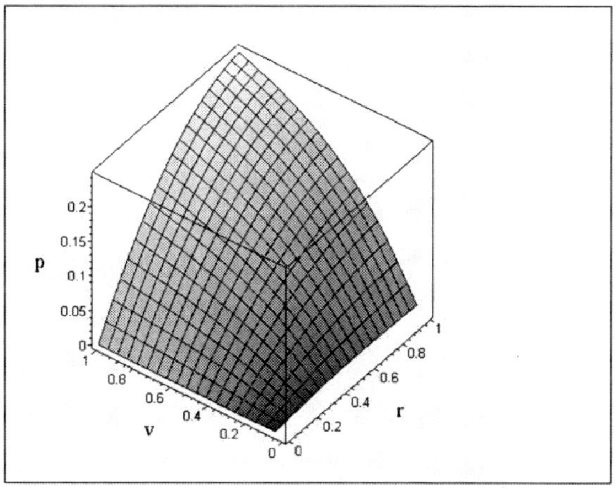

increases, then the nonprofits become better off in market A. The graph in Figure 4 below plots the maximum value of p as a function of v and r with the assumption that the amount of donors using the OSPN who are also contacted by the traditional method is 10% ($K = 0.1$), and the income tax rate facing a donor is 30% ($\gamma = 0.3$). Figure 4 implies that if the value of v or r increases, then it is possible for the OSPN to charge higher prices without deteriorating the total net revenues of the nonprofits in market A as compared to B.

CONCLUSION AND MANAGERIAL INSIGHTS

In this chapter, we developed a nonprofit duopoly model based on Hotelling's (1929) classical linear city model of horizontal differentiation. Using our model, we investigated the effects of online service providers for nonprofits (OSPNs) on the outcomes of fundraising markets. We compared the total net revenues of nonprofits competing for donations in two different settings: while nonprofits in the first market use both the traditional method of contacting donors and the services provided by OSPNs, those in the second market implement the traditional method only. We derived analytical conditions under which the first setting provides better outcomes than the second one can generate, and found the following results. First, online services provided by OSPNs can be a substitute for traditional methods of fundraising as the use of these services leads to a decrease in the fraction of donors contacted by using the traditional method. Second, the OSPNs can benefit nonprofits when the average unit cost of contacting a donor through the traditional method is above a certain level. Third, there must be an upper bound on the price charged by the OSPNs in order for nonprofits to generate higher net revenues when they use these services. Finally, if either the average unit cost of contact in the traditional method or the fraction of donors using the OSPN increases, then nonprofits become better off in markets where both the traditional methods and the services provided by OSPNs are available. Such increases also enable OSPNs to charge higher prices without deteriorating the relative benefits of their services. This implies that it is in OSPNs' best interest to encourage adoption of their services by nonprofits and potential donors. Similar to other service-related innovations in the area of information systems, a wide acceptance of OSPN services by donors and nonprofits will depend on several factors, including effective pricing of the services and the perception of the market participants about these services, such as usefulness and attitude (Kargin et al., 2009). Our study is indeed an attempt to shed some light on the pricing problem of the OSPNs. Once the use of these services becomes popular in the nonprofit sector, the usefulness and attitude problem can be addressed through industry surveys, and the service offerings can be adjusted according to user demands. From a social point of view, the diffusion of the OSPNs in the nonprofit sector may change the way fundraising markets operate by providing a cost-effective national reach. The wide acceptance of such a new fundraising model certainly requires establishing cohesive online platforms, creating exclusive databases, and offering innovative services with a reasonable price. It also important for the OSPNs to address key success factors necessary for a smooth execution of its services, such as reliability, confidentiality, integrity, and authentication of parties (Adamson, 2009).

There are several directions for future research on this topic. First, fundraising markets generally show characteristics of an oligopoly where more than two nonprofits compete for funds. Therefore, one can better capture features of fundraising markets by using Salop's (1979) circular city model. Second, OSPNs offer different types of services, including online databases and certification services for nonprofits that can complement each other. Incorporating the range of services offered by OSPNs in to our model can help us observe the degree of complementarities as well as their marginal effects on fundraising markets. Third, most nonprofits offer heterogeneous services even if they serve the same market. Analytical models examining such markets may also help managers in the nonprofit sector. Finally, examining potential effects of the certification criteria utilized by the OSPNs on market outcomes would be an interesting research area.

REFERENCES

Adamson, G. (2009). Portals and the challenge of simplifying internet business use. *International Journal of Web Portals*, *1*(1), 16–33.

Ba, S., Stinchcombe, M., Whinston, A. B., & Zhang, H. (1999). Trusted third parties in the electronic marketplace: An evolutionary game approach. In *Proceedings of the 5th Americas Conference on Information Systems* (pp. 238-240).

Bailey, J., & Bakos, Y. (1997). An exploratory study of the emerging role of electronic intermediaries. *International Journal of Electronic Commerce*, *1*(3), 7–20.

Bakos, Y. (1998). The emerging role of electronic marketplaces on the Internet. *Communications of the ACM*, *41*(8), 35–42. doi:10.1145/280324.280330

Bakos, Y., & Katsamakas, E. (2008). Design and ownership of two-sided networks: Implications for Internet platforms. *Journal of Management Information Systems*, *25*(2), 171–202. doi:10.2753/MIS0742-1222250208

Bennett, J. T., & McCrohan, K. F. (1993). Public policy issues in the marketing of seals of approval for food. *The Journal of Consumer Affairs*, *27*(2), 397–415. doi:10.1111/j.1745-6606.1993.tb00755.x

Bhargava, H. K., & Choudhary, V. (2004). Economics of an information intermediary with aggregation benefits. *Information Systems Research*, *15*(1), 22–36. doi:10.1287/isre.1040.0014

Bockem, S. (1994). A generalized model of horizontal product differentiation. *The Journal of Industrial Economics*, *42*(3), 287–298. doi:10.2307/2950571

Callen, J. L. (1994). Money donations, volunteering and organizational efficiency. *Journal of Productivity Analysis*, *5*, 215–228. doi:10.1007/BF01073908

Campbell, C., Ray, G., & Muhanna, W. A. (2005). Search and collusion in electronic markets. *Management Science*, *51*(3), 497–507. doi:10.1287/mnsc.1040.0327

Capozzi, M. M., Lowell, S. M., & Silverman, L. (2003). Knowledge management comes to philanthropy. *The McKinsey Quarterly*, *2*, 89.

D'Aspremont, C., Gabszewicz, J. J., & Thisse, J. F. (1979). On Hotelling's stability in competition. *Econometrica*, *47*(5), 1145–1150. doi:10.2307/1911955

De Palma, A., Ginsburgh, V., & Thisse, J. F. (1987). On existence of location equilibria in the 3-firm Hotelling problem. *The Journal of Industrial Economics*, *36*(2), 245–252. doi:10.2307/2098416

Grossman, G. M., & Shapiro, C. (1984). Informative advertising with differentiated products. *The Review of Economic Studies*, *51*(1), 63–81. doi:10.2307/2297705

Hackney, R., & Pillay, J. (2002). Organisational mission statements: A postmodernist perspective on the management of the IS/IT function. *Information Resources Management Journal*, *15*(1), 28–37.

Hoffman, D. L., Novak, T. P., & Peralta, M. (1999). Building consumer trust online. *Communications of the ACM*, *42*, 80–85. doi:10.1145/299157.299175

Hotelling, H. (1929). Stability in competition. *The Economic Journal*, *39*(153), 41–57. doi:10.2307/2224214

Jansen, P. J., & Katz, D. M. (2002). For nonprofits, time is money. *The McKinsey Quarterly*, (1): 124–133.

Kargin, B., Basoglu, N., & Daim, T. (2009). Adoption factors of mobile services. *International Journal of Information Systems in the Service Sector*, *1*(1), 15–34.

Khanna, J., Posnett, J., & Sandler, T. (1995). Charity donations in the UK: New evidence based on panel data. *Journal of Public Economics*, *56*, 257–272. doi:10.1016/0047-2727(94)01421-J

Kim, D. (2003). Short arguments for seals of approval and portal affiliation: Building consumer trust in online shopping. In *Proceedings of the 9th Americas Conference on Information Systems* (pp. 2194-2198).

Kim, H., & Serfes, K. (2006). A location model with preference for variety. *The Journal of Industrial Economics*, *54*(4), 569–595. doi:10.1111/j.1467-6451.2006.00300.x

Lee, T. D., Chen, J. Q., & Zhang, R. (2001). Utilizing the Internet as a competitive tool for non-profit organizations. *Journal of Computer Information Systems*, *41*(3), 26–31.

Lowell, S., Silverman, L., & Taliento, L. (2001). Not-for-profit management: The gift that keeps on giving. *The McKinsey Quarterly*, *1*, 147.

Malone, T. W., Yates, J., & Benjamin, R. I. (1987). Electronic markets and electronic hierarchies. *Communications of the ACM*, *30*(6), 484–497. doi:10.1145/214762.214766

Meehan, W. F. (2001). Reinventing philanthropy. *The McKinsey Quarterly*, 1.

Miyazaki, A. D., & Krishnamurthy, S. (2002). Internet seals of approval: Effects on online privacy policies and consumer perceptions. *The Journal of Consumer Affairs*, *36*(1), 28–49. doi:10.1111/j.1745-6606.2002.tb00419.x

Nero, G. (1999). Full or partial market coverage? A note on spatial competition with elastic demand. *Managerial and Decision Economics*, *20*(2), 107–111. doi:10.1002/(SICI)1099-1468(199903)20:2<107::AID-MDE921>3.0.CO;2-C

Okten, C., & Weisbrod, B. A. (2000). Determinants of donations in private nonprofit markets. *Journal of Public Economics*, *75*, 255–272. doi:10.1016/S0047-2727(99)00066-3

Ozcelik, Y. (2008). Globalization and the Internet: Digitizing the nonprofit sector. *Journal of Global Business Issues*, *2*(1), 149–152.

Palmer, J. W., Bailey, J. P., & Faraj, S. (2000). The role of intermediaries in the development of trust on the WWW: The use and prominence of trusted third parties and privacy statements. *Journal of Computer-Mediated Communication*, *5*(3). Retrieved October 1, 2008, from http://jcmc.indiana.edu/vol5/issue3/ palmer.html

Parker, G. G., & Van Alstyne, M. W. (2005). Two-sided network effects: A theory of information product design. *Management Science*, *51*(10), 1494–1504. doi:10.1287/mnsc.1050.0400

Pollach, I., Treiblmaier, H., & Floh, A. (2005). Online fundraising for environmental nonprofit organizations. In *Proceedings of the 38th Hawaii International Conference on System Sciences*, 178b.

Porter, M. E., & Kramer, M. R. (1999). Philanthropy's new agenda: Creating value. *Harvard Business Review*, *77*(2), 121–130.

Posnett, J., & Sandler, T. (1989). Demand for charity donations in private nonprofit markets: The case of the UK. *Journal of Public Economics*, *40*, 187–200. doi:10.1016/0047-2727(89)90002-9

Quinn, J. B. (2006). Giving freely and wisely. *Newsweek*, December 18, 51.

Rees, J., Koehler, G. J., & Ozcelik, Y. (2003). Information privacy and e-business activities: Key issues for managers. In Sharma, S. K., & Gupta, J. N. D. (Eds.), *Managing e-Business in the 21st Century* (pp. 139–151). Heidelberg Press.

Ritchie, R. J. B., Swami, S., & Weinberg, C. B. (1999). A brand new world for nonprofits. *International Journal of Nonprofit and Voluntary Sector Marketing*, *4*(1), 26–42. doi:10.1002/nvsm.54

Salop, S. (1979). Monopolistic competition with outside goods. *The Bell Journal of Economics*, *10*, 141–156. doi:10.2307/3003323

Silverman, R. E. (2004). Charities start to grade themselves. *The Wall Street Journal*, August 18, D1.

Tempel, E. (2003). Operation accountability. *Philanthropy Matters*, *13*(1), 4–5.

Tirole, J. (1997). *The Theory of Industrial Organization*. Cambridge, MA: The MIT Press.

Weisbrod, B. A., & Dominguez, N. D. (1986). Demand for collective goods in private nonprofit markets: Can fundraising expenditures help overcome free-rider behavior? *Journal of Public Economics*, *30*, 83–95. doi:10.1016/0047-2727(86)90078-2

Yoo, B., Choudhary, V., & Mukhopadhyay, T. (2002). A model of neutral B2B. *Journal of Management Information Systems*, *19*(3), 43–68.

APPENDIX

Table 1. Notation used in the chapter

NP_1, NP_2	nonprofit organizations 1 and 2 to which donors may donate money, respectively.
$\alpha_{1,A}, \alpha_{2,A}$	fractions of donors that NP_1 and NP_2 contacts through the traditional method in the fundraising market *A*, respectively, $0 < \alpha_{1,A}, \alpha_{2,A} < 1$.
$\alpha_{1,B}, \alpha_{2,B}$	fractions of donors that NP_1 and NP_2 contacts through the traditional method in the fundraising market *B*, respectively, $0 < \alpha_{1,B}, \alpha_{2,B} < 1$.
r	fraction of donors who obtain information about NP_1 and NP_2 by using the services provided by OSPNs in market *A*, $0 < r < 1$.
K	factor used to quantify the fraction of donors using the services provided by OSPNs in addition to the traditional contact by NP_1 or NP_2 in market *A*, $0 \leq K \leq 1$.
z	amount of money that each donor wants to donate to either NP_1 or NP_2.
$O_{1,A}, O_{2,A}$	social monetary outputs that are generated by NP_1 and NP_2 if they receive $\$z$ from a donor in market *A*, respectively.
γ	income tax rate facing a donor, $0 < \gamma < 1$.
t	unit cost of misfit between the preferred mission of a donor and the actual mission of a nonprofit.
$f_{1,A}, f_{2,A}$	fractions of a $\$z$ donation spent by NP_1 and NP_2 on fundraising expenditures in market *A*, respectively, $0 < f_{1,A}, f_{2,A} < 1$.
$f_{1,B}, f_{2,B}$	fractions of a $\$z$ donation spent by NP_1 and NP_2 on fundraising expenditures in market *B*, respectively, $0 < f_{1,B}, f_{2,B} < 1$.
x_A	fraction of donors who prefer to donate $\$z$ to NP_1 in market *A* under full information.
x_B	fraction of donors who prefer to donate $\$z$ to NP_1 in market *B* under full information.
$1 - x_A$	fraction of donors who prefer to donate $\$z$ to NP_2 in market *A* under full information.
$1 - x_B$	fraction of donors who prefer to donate $\$z$ to NP_2 in market *B* under full information.

continued on following page

Table 1. continued

$U_{1,A}, U_{2,A}$	utilities of a donor from donating $\$z$ to NP_1 or NP_2 in market *A*, respectively.
$U_{1,B}, U_{2,B}$	utilities of a donor from donating $\$z$ to NP_1 or NP_2 in market *B*, respectively.
p	service price charged by the OSPN to NP_1 and NP_2 in market *A*.
v	average unit cost of contacting a donor through the traditional method.
$TNR_{1,A}, TNR_{2,A}$	total net revenues of NP_1 and NP_2 in market *A*, respectively.
$TNR_{1,B}, TNR_{2,B}$	total net revenues of NP_1 and NP_2 in market *B*, respectively.
$DIFF$	difference between the optimum total net revenues of nonprofits in markets *A* and *B*.

Chapter 18
Perceived Risk for Multiple Services in the Consumer Buying Cycle

Lawrence F. Cunningham
University of Colorado Denver, USA

James Gerlach
University of Colorado Denver, USA

Michael D. Harper
University of Colorado Denver, USA

Deborah L. Kellogg
University of Colorado Denver, USA

ABSTRACT

This study compares consumer perceived risk between five e-service delivery systems and their traditional (non-Internet) counterparts over each stage of the buying cycle. Using a survey methodology, the authors find that in general consumers perceive e-services as riskier than traditional services. The difference in perceived risk, which the authors define as the Internet risk premium, is significant for each service and each stage of the buying cycle. There is a spike in perceived risk at the purchase stage in the buying cycle for each of the five services. This pattern is also evident in the four services with traditional delivery systems. Perceived risk affects the consumer throughout the buying cycle and is not alleviated in the information search stage. Different risk factors drive perceived risk at various stages in the buying cycle. The authors provide both research and managerial implications of these findings.

INTRODUCTION

In 2007, annual e-commerce U.S. sales reached \$136.4 billion, accounting for 3.4% of all retail activity (U.S. Department of Commerce, 2008). The slow adoption in online retail sales is perplexing given the early reports on the many advantages of and favorable consumer attitudes towards Internet shopping (Lohse, Bellman & Johnson, 2000). Of the many possible reasons that explain the slow growth of Internet retailing, consumer

DOI: 10.4018/978-1-60960-138-6.ch018

perceptions of risk for Internet shopping is one of the primary issues (e.g. Cases, 2002; Forsythe & Shi, 2003; Jarvenpaa & Todd, 1997; Liebermann & Stashevsky, 2002; Tan, 1999; Vijayasarathy & Jones, 2000).

Marketing academics have traditionally focused on perceived risk in the information search stage of the consumer buying process (e.g., Cox 1967; Dowling & Staelin 1994; Murray 1991). Typically, perceived risk declines during the information search stage because of consumer information seeking behavior from formal and informal sources (Zeithaml & Bitner 2003). However, researchers devote little effort to understanding the role of perceived risk in the consumer buying process subsequent to information search (e.g., Chen & Dubinsky 2003; Moriarty & Spekman 1984; Teo & Yeong, 2003; Erdem & Swait, 2004; Mitchell, 1998).

There are two important and notable exceptions; Cunningham, Gerlach, Harper and Young (2005) demonstrate the importance of measuring perceived risk by stage. Using a survey research approach, the study finds that perceived risk levels for Internet airline reservation services are greater for the Internet option than for the traditional service delivery system. They define this as an Internet risk premium. This study also indicates that perceived risk levels for Internet airline reservation services show more radical fluctuations across the stages of the consumer buying process. Second, Cunningham, Gerlach, and Harper (2005) examine the issue of risk and e-banking services over the consumer buying process. Like Internet airline reservation services, e-banking services show more radical changes in risk levels than traditional banking services over the consumer buying process.

This research continues the investigation into the nature of Internet shopping by examining the dynamics of perceived risk throughout the various stages of the consumer buying process in multiple services. Unlike most previous studies on perceived risk that typically examine the role of perceived risk at one or two stages, this study examines perceived risk levels and risk factors across all stages. The objective is to learn if this phenomenon is limited to airline reservations and e-banking, or if it is pervasive in Internet services in general.

This article reports on a survey of consumers that measures perceived risk for Internet delivered services as opposed to services distributed in a more traditional fashion. Within the context of airline reservations, banking, gifts, catalog, and library services, the study examines the presence and intensity of perceived risk at each stage of the consumer buying process.

This research focuses on a wide range of services rather than a single service to investigate the dynamics of perceived risk. By utilizing a wide range of services, this research attempts to understand perceived risk in the consumer buying process.

The first section of this article provides a review of literature regarding the perceived risk of Internet shopping. The second section presents several hypotheses regarding perceived risk and risk perception between Internet consumers and traditional shoppers. The third section presents the research methodology. The fourth section deals with data analysis and results and the last sections present a summary of the findings and an in-depth discussion of their research and managerial implications.

LITERATURE REVIEW

Perceived Risk and the Consumer Buying Process

A substantial body of past research shows that consumer perceptions of risk are known to influence purchase decisions to varying degrees, and in doing so influence consumer behavior (e.g., Bauer, 1960; Bettman, 1973; Chaudhuri, 1997; Cunningham, 1967; Mitchell, 1992, 1999). Risk exists when the consequences connected to a decision are uncertain and some are less desirable than others (Kogan & Wallach, 1964, 1967; MacCrimmon & Wehrung, 1986; Pollatsck & Tversky, 1970; Rapoport & Wallsten, 1972). Kogan & Wallach (1964) describe the concept of risk as having two dimensions: (a) the chance aspect where the focus is on probability and, (b) the danger aspect where the emphasis is on severity of negative consequence. Risk is a subjectively determined expectation of loss by the consumer (Stone & Winter, 1987); thus the term, perceived risk.

In theory, perceived risk only affects a consumer when it rises above an individual's acceptance limit (Greatorex & Mitchell, 1993). Perceived risk is measured as a multidimensional construct possessing aspects of physical risk, financial risk, psychological risk, time risk, performance risk, and social risk (Jacoby & Kaplan, 1972; Roselius, 1971).

Generally, researchers consider perceived risk as a factor in the early stages of the consumer buying process (e.g., Cox, 1967; Dowling & Staelin, 1994; Murray, 1991). The consumer buying process is described as a five-stage linear process (Blackwell, Miniard, & Engel, 2003; Hawkins, Coney, & Best, 2003): (stage one) need recognition, (stage two) information search, (stage three) alternatives evaluation, (stage four) purchase decision, and (stage five) post-purchase behavior.

Consumers first perceive risk when they recognize the need for a product or service (stage one). In the presence of high perceived risk levels, consumers apply risk reduction strategies during stages two and three.

Perceived risk may have a more pronounced effect on the evaluation of services (Guseman, 1981; Murray, 1991; Murray & Schlater, 1990). Services are difficult to evaluate prior to being experienced. Often consumers find themselves trying to evaluate virtually indistinguishable service alternatives and providers. Consequently consumers rely more on personal information sources and recommendations and less on brand loyalty (Mitra, Reiss, & Capella, 1999).

Internet Shopping and Perceived Risk

The majority of prior research on perceived risk occurs before the Internet reached maturity and focuses on traditional purchasing situations. There are some notable exceptions. Vijayasarathy and Jones (2000) show that perceived risk is a significant factor affecting Internet shoppers. Other researchers find a relationship between perceived risk and frequency of use (Liebermann & Stashevsky 2002; Forsythe & Shi 2003); supporting the contention that perceived risk is likely to have the greatest impact on infrequent Internet shoppers. This contention is supported by Tan (1999) who finds that less risk-averse consumers are more likely to shop through the Internet.

Researchers generally agree upon the sources of perceived risk for Internet shopping. For example, Cases (2002) identifies four potential risk sources: risk associated with the product, risk ensuing from a remote transaction, risk associated with the use of the Internet as a mode of purchase, and risk related to the site on which the transaction takes place.

Other researchers study tactics for mitigating these risks. Tan's (1999) research suggests the use of endorsement, retailer reputation, and established brand name as risk relievers for wary Internet shoppers. Biswas and Biswas (2004) suggest increased advertising expense sends a signal to cautious e-customers of the e-retailer's efforts and financial strength, which in turn implies a higher level of consumer confidence with the retailer and the product. Cases (2002) provides the most extensive study on risk mitigators. Cases adds viewing the product, exchange policy, money back guarantee, web site reputation, sales promotion, personal references, payment security, price information, and advertising to this growing list of risk relievers.

Lately, research attention focuses on the issue of trust. For instance, Corbitt, Thanasankit, and Yi (2003) find that people with a higher level of perceived web site quality have a higher level of perceived market orientation and trustworthiness towards e-commerce. They also find that positive personal recommendations, money back warranties, and partnerships with well-known business partners, rank as the top three effective risk reduction tactics.

Research also suggests that the influence of perceived risk is not likely to dissipate naturally as web experience accrues (Corbitt, Thanasankit, & Yi, 2003). Although risk relievers are somewhat effective, compiling a comprehensive risk mitigation strategy is not likely to be simple or inexpensive. Therefore, the solution to the Internet risk problem needs to come from a better understanding of the nature of the risk.

HYPOTHESES

Specifically, there are many academic studies dealing with Internet services. However, the authors believe they are the only researchers examining the issue of perceived risk in services over the consumer buying process. The authors examine if perceived risk intensifies after the information search stage of the consumer buying process. If risk level does intensify, the antecedents of perceived risk may be dynamic and depend upon the stage of the consumer buying process. Thus, the present research is a methodical analysis of the types of perceived risk that influence the consumer during each stage of the consumer buying process under the Internet versus traditional shopping contexts.

Hypothesis 1 (H1) proposes the existence of an Internet risk premium at each consumer buying stage. The Internet risk premium is defined as the mathematical difference between the subject's perception of risk for the Internet service and the subject's perception of risk for the tradition service. If H1 is supported, the Internet delivery method introduces a risk premium throughout the entire consumer buying process.

H1: The level of perceived risk is higher for Internet purchases than for traditional purchases at each stage of the buying process, that is, there exists an Internet risk premium.

Hypotheses 2 (H2) and 3 (H3) are based on the premise that perceived risk fluctuates significantly stage-to-stage for both Internet and traditional services. But depending upon type of delivery method and stage of consumer buying process, the level of perceived risk differs. Specifically, Hypothesis 2 (H2) tests whether there is a difference in the perceived risk, either traditional or Internet, across buying stages. Hypothesis 3 (H3) tests the Internet risk premium across buying stages. If H3 holds, then it supports the supposition that the effect of the Internet on perceived risk is magnified, reflecting the possible occurrence of additional risk factors or greater perceived risk for Internet consumers that is not shared by consumers of traditional services.

H2: The level of perceived risk is different at adjacent buying stages.

H3: The Internet risk premium is different at adjacent buying stages.

Lastly, this study examines whether the types of perceived risk consumers experience depend upon the stage as well. This study looks beyond financial risk, which is regarded as the predominant factor for explaining overall risk (Forsythe & Shi, 2003; Stone & Gronhaug, 1993), by measuring financial, performance, physical, psychological, social, and time risk, and explores the extent to which these are predictors of overall risk at the various buying stages.

Hypothesis 4 (H4): Overall perceived risk in Internet services is influenced by underlying factors of risk: financial, performance, physical, psychological, social, and time risk.

Hypothesis 5 (H5): The relative influence of the underlying factors of Internet risk is different at different buying stages.

RESEARCH DESIGN AND METHODS

Service Selection

The hypotheses are tested using five services: airline reservation systems, banking, catalog, gift, and library. In each case, the study uses services that are representative of e-services in general, cover a wide range of risk perceptions, and are likely to be familiar to the respondents.

This study uses Internet catalog service because it is a highly important e-service and it mirrors a traditional service purchase in which perceived risk research has occurred. In many ways gift services are similar to catalog service; however, gifts are necessarily purchased for others, whereas a catalog purchase is not. Gift buying may carry additional social and psychological risks as any failure is necessarily noticed by others, notably the gift recipient.

In Internet airline reservation sites, the consumer is responsible for searching multiple carriers for fares, comparing prices, and proper booking (Law & Leung; 2000). The consumer has very limited recourse for correcting errors. Wirtz, Kum, and Lee (2000) find perceived unfairness of pricing in airline reservation systems generates perceptions of financial risk.

The study also uses banking service because it incorporates privacy and security issues. Previous consumer surveys support the premise that e-banking offers convenience and time savings (Pew, 2002); however, security and privacy risks are major impediments (Bhimani 1996; Cockburn & Wilson, 1996; Quelch & Klein, 1996; Tan & Teo, 2000).

The study also uses library service because it is a relatively low risk e-service. Browsing for information on the Internet is one its major uses, even by those who do not purchase on the Internet. It is also a service that is most familiar to the respondents who are students at a major university.

Research Methods

This study uses a field survey of respondents' perceptions of perceived risk. The questionnaire gives definitions of the five risk types and the five stages of the consumer buying process. Respondents are encouraged to reflect on their own consumer behavior in these terms. A pretest demonstrated that respondents are able to differentiate risks based on buying stages.

The final instrument collects data on multiple levels, which is required for the five hypotheses. To address H1, H2, and H3, the survey instrument collects data on overall perceived risk for each of the aforementioned Internet services and traditional services. For each delivery method, respondents are asked for levels of perceived risk at each stage. Perceived risk is measured by a single indicator, level of risk. At the problem recognition stage, for example, the respondent is asked, "What is your level of risk when you recognize the need for gift buying services?" The respondent then assesses their perceived risk along a seven-point, Likert-type scale from low risk to high risk. Similar to the present study, previous studies rely on single item measures for perceived risk (e.g., Cases, 2002; Chen & He, 2003; Cho & Lee, 2006; Forsythe & Shi, 2003; Kanwar & Pagiavlas, 1992; Mitchell & Boustani, 1993).

To address H4 and H5, respondents are asked to evaluate the level of overall risk and the level of risk types (financial, performance, physical, psychological, social, and time) for each service delivered via the Internet. For example, respondents are asked, "What level of financial risk is involved in using an online gift buying service?"

Table 1. Means (Standard Deviations) of the Internet Risk Premium

	Airline	Bank	Catalog	Gift	Library
Stage 1	0.72(1.46)*** n=152	0.93(1.46)*** n=151	0.55(1.22)*** n=146	0.77(1.54)*** n=148	0.42(0.91)*** n=144
Stage 2	0.21(1.40)* n=147	0.40(1.10)*** n=151	0.39(1.20)*** n=147	0.28(1.10)** n=146	0.28(1.08)** n=141
Stage 3	0.26(1.33)** n=145	0.37(1.06)*** n=147	0.26(1.19)** n=143	0.24(1.06)** n=144	0.23(0.91)** n=139
Stage 4	0.87(1.59)*** n=150	0.89(1.30)*** n=151	0.71(1.54)*** n=146	1.01(1.59)*** n=147	0.55(1.18)*** n=142
Stage 5	0.87(1.42)*** n=151	0.91(1.37)*** n=152	0.70(1.34)*** n=149	0.77(1.54)*** n=146	0.42(1.18)*** n=140

* significant at p=.05, ** significant at p=.01, *** significant at p=.001

Although H5 deals with buying stages, statistical techniques provide a mechanism to use the data gathered for H1-H3, thus it is not necessary to collect risk assessments by risk type for each stage of the buying process.

One hundred fifty nine volunteer mid-career undergraduate and graduate business school students at a major urban university completed the survey with a response rate of 99%. The respondents are 79 males, 80 females, the average age is 26 years, and there are 103 undergraduates and 56 graduates. Almost all respondents are employed at least halftime, 112 fulltime with a median household income is $62,000 and 97 respondents are single.

The majority of the respondents indicate that they used traditional services and/or Internet services within one year of the date of the survey. In addition, given the theory-application nature of the study, homogeneous respondents are desirable (Calder, Phillips, & Tybout, 1981).

DATA ANALYSIS AND RESULTS

To address the first three hypotheses, Table 1 presents the mean differences, standard deviations, and significance levels for each stage of the buying process. Figure 1 presents a sample plot of these statistics for gift buying service. According to Table 1, the risk associated with the Internet service is always significantly greater than the risk for traditional service; hence, the plots of the other services resemble the plot for gift buying which shows that the Internet risk premium is consistently greater than zero throughout the buying process.

H1 suggests that the perceived risk for Internet is greater than for traditional purchases. The study performs a paired-difference t-test to determine if the means of the Internet data are significantly different from the means of the traditional data at each buying stage. Table 1 shows that the means are significantly different for each of the five

Figure 1. Descriptive Statistics for Gift Service (●Internet, ■Traditional, ○Internet Risk Premium)

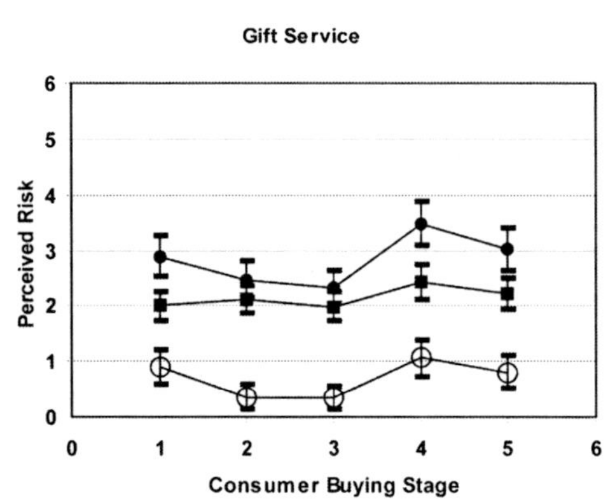

Table 2. Two-Way ANOVAs

	Internet	Traditional	Internet Risk Premium
Airline	$F_{4,444}$ =20.20 ***	$F_{4,444}$ =7.04 ***	$F_{4,444}$ =7.68 ***
Bank	$F_{4,412}$ =17.43 ***	$F_{4,412}$ =9.63 ***	$F_{4,412}$ =7.07 ***
Catalog	$F_{4,412}$ =25.59 ***	$F_{4,412}$ =14.23 ***	$F_{4,412}$ =4.67 **
Gift	$F_{4,376}$ =15.94 ***	$F_{4,376}$ =4.32 **	$F_{4,376}$ =11.10 ***
Library	$F_{4,384}$ =4.02 **	$F_{4,384}$ =1.73	$F_{4,384}$ =1.44

* significant at *p*=.05, ** significant at *p*=.01, *** significant at *p*=.001

services. Bank and catalog services are significant at the $p<.001$ level with the minor exception of catalog services in stage three, which is significant at the $p<.01$ level. Airline, gift and library are also significantly different at the $p< .001$ level for stages one, four, and five; $p < .01$ for stage three; and $p < .01$ for all but airline at stage two, which is significant at $p< .05$. Hence, the data supports H1 and demonstrates an Internet risk premium at each stage of the buying process.

H2 proposes that the level of risk differs between buying stages and H3 suggests that the Internet risk premium also differs between buying stages. For each of the three sets of means (traditional, Internet, and Internet risk premium) the study performs a two-way ANOVA, across stages, blocking on subjects, for each of the five services. The results are reported in Table 2. Each set of means shows significant difference at the $p < .01$ level with the exception of the traditional library. The Internet risk premium is also insignificant for library services. Thus, the data suggests initial support for H2 and H3; there are significant differences in risk between stages in the buying process.

However, to fully support the hypothesis, perceived risk also needs to fluctuate differently for Internet services than for traditional services. Given the significant differences among stages, the study conducts a post-hoc test to determine

Table 3. Summary of Fisher's Least Significant Difference Test for Adjacent Stages

	Adjacent Stages	Airline	Bank	Catalog	Gift	Library
Internet						
	1 to 2	0.50*	0.58**	0.67***	0.42**	0.10
	2 to 3	0.08	0.01	0.04	0.14	0.10
	3 to 4	1.19***	1.22***	1.38***	1.15***	0.42**
	4 to 5	0.28	0.43*	0.51**	0.45**	0.31*
Traditional						
	1 to 2	0.14	0.12	0.45**	0.12	0.01
	2 to 3	0.05	0.07	0.13	0.13	0.05
	3 to 4	0.65***	0.74***	0.88***	0.43***	0.23
	4 to 5	0.31*	0.37*	0.41**	0.20	0.23
Internet Risk Premium						
	1 to 2	0.36*	0.46***	0.22	0.54***	0.09
	2 to 3	0.03	0.08	0.09	0.01	0.05
	3 to 4	0.54***	0.48***	0.50***	0.72***	0.20
	4 to 5	0.04	0.07	0.10	0.25	0.08

*Significant at *p*=.05, ** significant at *p*=.01, *** significant at *p*=.001

where those fluctuations occur (Anderson, Sweeney, & Williams, 2005). Specifically, the study conducts Fisher's least significance difference tests on adjacent stages to determine at which stages there is a significant change in the perceived risk or perceived risk premium. Table 3 presents the results.

For Internet services, statistically significant decreases are observed in the means between stages one and two for airline ($p < .05$), bank ($p < .01$), catalog ($p < .001$), and gift ($p < .01$). Only the traditional catalog service shows a significant change between stages one and two ($p < .01$).

In moving between stages three and four, all Internet services experience a statistically significant increase in perceived risk: airline, bank, catalog, and gift ($p < .001$) and library ($p < .01$). This same pattern is seen in traditional services, with the exception of the library service, which does not show a significant change.

For stages four to five, all of the Internet services except airline show significant decreases: catalog and gift ($p < .01$), bank and library ($p < .05$). When moving between stages four to five in traditional services, statistically significant decreases occur for airline and bank ($p < .05$), and catalog ($p < .01$).

Moreover, for the Internet risk premium, statistically significant decreases occur at stages one to two for bank and gift ($p < .001$), and airline ($p < .05$).

The results provide mixed support. There are clearly significant fluctuations in perceived risk when moving between stages in the consumer buying process. In some cases the fluctuation is different when considering Internet versus traditional services; in other cases the fluctuation is similar. When moving between need recognition and information search, more Internet services show decreases. Both Internet and traditional services show a similar increase in perceived risk when moving between alternative evaluation and the purchase decision and a decrease in perceived risk when moving from the purchase decision and post-purchase behavior.

H4 suggests that in an Internet environment, specific risk factors influence overall perceived risk. The data in the study supports this, but differently than in previous research. For each Internet service, subjects are asked to assess their overall risk and specific risks: financial, performance, physical, psychological, social, and time. Cronbach's Alphas for the six specific risks range from 0.798 to 0.877. Clearly, these six specific risks are measuring a single construct. However, when looking at the coefficient of determination when overall risk is regressed onto those six risks, we find very low numbers, ranging from 0.09 to 0.45, finding only significance without magnitude. This differs from previous studies that have found that specific risk types account for as much as 88.8% of the variance in the overall risk measure (Stone & Gronghaug, 1993). The Stone and Gronhaug (1993) study is done considering the purchase of a personal computer. Perhaps, the analysis, although using the six common risk types to explain 9% and 45% of overall risk, misses other major risk types when Internet purchases are primarily services. Some researchers add risk types specific to Internet purchases, for example, privacy risk, security risk, and the risk of credit card misuse (Bhatnagar & Ghose, 2004; Featherman & Pavlou, 2003; Garbarinoa & Strahilevitz; 2004).

H5 suggests that the influence of the six risk types differs at various stages of the consumer buying process. To assess these, the study uses the assessment of overall risk and general assessments for each risk type for each service. It does not assess risk types for each stage of the buying process as we can infer possible relationships of risk type to overall risk at different buying stages with statistical analysis.

To identify the factors of perceived risk by stage, this study completes a separate stepwise regression for each stage. In each regression, we regress the subject's overall risk assessments for each of the five risk types and demographics

Table 4. Stepwise regression results of the impact of perceived risk on risk factors and control variables for Internet services. The values in the tables are standardized regression coefficients. All regressions are at a 5% level of significance.

			Dependent Variables					
Type	**Independent Variables**	**Service**	**Overall Risk**	**Risk at Stage 1**	**Risk at Stage 2**	**Risk at Stage 3**	**Risk at Stage 4**	**Risk at Stage 5**
Risk	Financial	Airline	0.009				0.018	
Risk	Financial	Bank	0.021	0.018	0.017	0.017	0.027	0.026
Risk	Financial	Catalog	0.021	0.018	0.016	0.017	0.024	
Risk	Financial	Gift	0.027	0.019	0.015		0.029	0.022
Risk	Financial	Library	0.034	0.024			0.032	0.034
Risk	Performance	Airline	0.028	0.015	0.012	0.009	0.019	0.022
Risk	Performance	Catalog						0.029
Risk	Performance	Gift						0.023
Risk	Physical	Airline			0.012	0.011		0.009
Risk	Physical	Bank			0.019	0.019		
Risk	Physical	Catalog	0.012		0.012	0.012		
Risk	Physical	Gift	0.013		0.018	0.028		
Risk	Physical	Library			0.035	0.040		
Risk	Psychological	Bank	0.014	0.015				
Risk	Psychological	Gift		0.018			0.013	
Risk	Social	Airline				0.009	0.004	
Risk	Social	Library	0.023	0.027				
Risk	Time	Bank						0.009
Demographics	Age	Library	0.001		0.001			0.001
Demographics	Education	Airline		-0.078				
Demographics	Gender	Airline					0.008	
Demographics	Gender	Gift	-0.092				-0.155	-0.167
Demographics	Income	Gift				-0.002		-0.002
Statistics	Adjusted R^2	Airline	0.40	0.12	0.14	0.15	0.35	0.27
Statistics	Adjusted R^2	Bank	0.40	0.33	0.23	0.26	0.34	0.34
Statistics	Adjusted R^2	Catalog	0.26	0.10	0.15	0.17	0.19	0.23
Statistics	Adjusted R^2	Gift	0.45	0.30	0.21	0.32	0.37	0.45
Statistics	Adjusted R^2	Library	0.29	0.21	0.18	0.24	0.09	0.14

onto the subject's overall risk assessment for that stage. Table 4 gives the results of the 30 stepwise regressions needed to predict the presence of risk factors overall and by stage. The table lists only the significant standardized regression coefficients and adjusted coefficients of determination.

The predominant risk factor for explaining overall perceived risk based on the standardized coefficient, is financial risk. However, performance, physical, psychological and social risks occur for some services (e.g., psychological risk is present for bank services.)

The regression analyses reveals that risk types drive perceived risk differently at each stage of the consumer buying process and supports H5. The adjusted R^2 values for perceived risk vary by stage, ranging from .09 to .45. The regression analyses of risk factors on perceived risk, as measured at each stage of the consumer buying process, is more revealing. For stage one, financial risk is significant for all five services, except airline service, which is the only service to include performance risk. Psychological risk is significant for bank and gift services; and social risk is significant for library service. Education is significant for airline service. At stage two, financial risk is significant for all services but airline and library; performance risk is significant for airline service; physical risk is significant for all services; age is significant for library service. At stage 3, financial risk is significant for bank and catalog services; performance risk is significant for airline service; physical risk is significant for all services; social risk is significant for airline service; and income is significant for gift service. At stage 4, financial risk is significant for all five services; performance risk is significant for airline service; psychological risk is significant for gift service; social risk is significant for airline service; and gender is significant for both gift and airline services. At stage 5, financial risk is significant for bank, gift, and library services; performance risk is significant for airline, catalog and gift services; physical risk is significant for airline service; time risk is significant for bank service; age is significant for library service; and gender and income are significant for gift services.

Overall, the analyses indicate that financial risk drives the Internet risk premium, while performance, physical, psychological, social and time risk play ancillary roles as risk drivers at certain stages. The one exception is airline service, which lists performance risk as the dominant risk factor. Selective demographic variables affect perceived risk significantly but the low standardized coefficients for age suggest the influence is minimal, which is similar to the findings of Liebermann and Stashevsky (2002). Female gender has a strong influence on risk at stages four and five for gift service; male gender has a strong influence at stage four and education has a strong influence at stage one for airline service.

LIMITATIONS

A significant limitation of this study is that the study used self-reported recall data that required respondents to recall feelings of risk perception. The study is based on correlations that are insufficient for establishing a causal influence on perceived risk. However, in the authors' opinions, the risk factors highlighted in this study are indeed real.

A final limitation is the use of single measures for each of the perceived risk variables, types of risk, and overall perceived risk at each stage. Thus, we are unable to provide measures of reliability for our constructs. The success of this research provides reason to investigate the issue more fully using multiple measures.

DISCUSSION

Statistical evidence from this study of five services demonstrates that perceived risk permeates the entire consumer buying process for both traditional and Internet services. There is a general pattern to the perceived risk fluctuations for traditional services. For airline, bank and gift, perceived risk levels remain flat during the need recognition stages, information search and evaluation of alternatives stages, but dramatically increase at the purchase stage. Although perceived risk levels slightly drop off at the post-purchase stage, the perceived risk level remains relatively high. In stark contrast to these services, traditional library services reveal no significant fluctuations in perceived risk and traditional catalog services reveals a pattern that is distinctive of Internet services.

Our findings indicate that perceived risk follows a different pattern for Internet services. Compared to traditional services, perceived risk levels for Internet services fall more rapidly during need recognition and information search and increase more quickly between the alternatives evaluation and purchase stages.

This study also shows that an Internet risk premium occurs at each stage of the consumer buying process for the services considered in this article. Hence, the Internet risk premium reflects the volatility of risk perceptions related to delivery method and stage.

The pattern of perceived risk fluctuations for traditional catalog services exactly matches that of Internet services, possibly reflecting a strong similarity in customers' risk perceptions. Resembling Internet customers, customers who purchase by catalog are unable to physically examine the product, are uncertain about product value, and are concerned about service quality and shopping experience. A spike in the Internet risk premium at the point of purchase that is driven solely by financial risk strongly suggests that the Internet imposes additional financial risks beyond those of traditional services.

Financial risk is the predominant factor since it is both significant and influential at nearly all stages of the consumer buying process for all of the Internet services, except airline services. Although airline consumers are aware of financial risk, performance risk is their dominant risk factor. However, risk factors other than financial risk play roles depending upon stage and service type.

Regardless of delivery method, perceived risk appears elevated during the actual purchase of a service for all services except traditional library services. This finding is important since it indicates that perceived risk is an issue that needs to be addressed in the purchase and post-purchase stages.

Similar consideration should be given to perceived risk at the post-purchase stage. While financial risk remains a significant factor, performance risk is just as significant and just as influential for airline, catalog and gift services. In contrast, bank services exhibit both a financial risk and a time risk at the post-purchase stage, but not performance risk. Due to the individual nature of perceived risk by service, general risk reduction strategies are likely to be less effective than ones that target specific risk concerns.

This exploratory study produces an intriguing picture of perceived risk in the consumer buying process. These initial findings suggest that perceived risk is of continuing research importance, not only because of the evolution of delivery methods, but also because it is a dynamic influence in the consumer buying process.

CONCLUSION

The process of converting traditional shoppers to Internet shoppers will continue to experience only moderate growth unless e-service providers take a more in-depth approach to understanding consumer behavior. Towards that end, this study offers insights into the problems that need to be addressed to accelerate the adoption and expansion of Internet shopping.

The results of this study raise interesting questions about the process of information search for online services. Online consumers experience a dramatic drop in risk as they move from problem recognition to information search. The differences in risk reduction may result from better information search tools, buyers with more experience in gathering information, or it may also derive from the extensive structure and immediacy of service specific information sources. In the case of online services, the information search process is an area ripe for additional inquiry.

The analyses suggest that risk rises rapidly for traditional and online services during the evaluation of alternatives and the purchase stages. We speculate that this acceleration of risk occurs for all goods and services. Further studies may indicate that the very nature of services may contribute to a more rapid rise in risk for services during these stages of the consumer buying process.

The analyses also suggest that risk rises more rapidly during the purchasing process for online services than traditional services. We hypothesize that in traditional services consumers have access to physical surrogate cues as well as an overall servicescape for evaluation purposes. Technology may give consumers the ability to have a similar experience online, for example, through streaming video.

The overall study offers some insights into the perceptions of consumers subsequent to the purchase of the service. While consumers experience a reduction in risk after purchase, the levels of risk remain relatively high in relation to original perceptions of risk. Many of the services in the study have credence-like characteristics. Their outcome is difficult to judge until long after the purchase decision. Finding ways to mitigate this post-purchase risk in an online environment is important.

Online services are by their very nature Self-Service Technologies (SSTs). They are purposely designed so that an employee is not present, sparsely present or not a part of the process. This heightens risk perceptions on the part of consumers during the purchase process. For example, who answers last minute questions for the consumer to alleviate the residual risk that can potentially terminate the purchase intention? The consumer is often left to his or her own devices to resolve any remaining issues. This may not be the best design choice, perhaps a hybrid model is necessary – one that connects the self-service consumer with a service representative for swift problem resolution.

Furthermore, the nature of the SSTs creates a separability between the consumer buying process and the service or product purchased. For example, the airline reservation system is obviously separated from the actual flight experience. We assume that the bank does actually pay the bill after our online request. But how and when does the consumer know if problems occur? When they arrive at the airport? When they receive past due notices? The authors contend that the separability of SSTs often creates the potential for risk premiums in the purchase stage and post purchase stages of SSTs. The connection between the concept of separability and risk deserves further research.

ACKNOWLEDGMENT

The authors wish to express their appreciation to the Business School at the University of Colorado at Denver for financial support and to Ms. Nancy Reed and Ms. Rachael DeMers at the Business School at the University of Colorado at Denver for their editorial assistance.

REFERENCES

Anderson, D. R., Sweeney, D. J., & Williams, T. A. (2005). *Statistics for Business and Economics* (9th ed.). Mason, OH: Thomson South-Western.

Bauer, R. A. (1960). Consumer behavior as risk taking. In R. Hancock (Ed.), *Dynamic Marketing for a Changing World, Proceedings of 43rd Conference* (pp. 389-398). Chicago, IL: American Marketing Association.

Bettman, J. R. (1973). Perceived risk and its components. *JMR, Journal of Marketing Research, 10*(2), 84–90. doi:10.2307/3149824

Bhatnagar, A., & Ghose, S. (2004). Segmenting consumers based on the benefits and risks of Internet shopping. *Journal of Business Research, 57*(12), 1352–1360. doi:10.1016/S0148-2963(03)00067-5

Bhimani, A. (1996). Securing the commercial Internet. *Communications of the ACM*, *39*(6), 29–35. doi:10.1145/228503.228509

Biswas, D., & Biswas, A. (2004). The diagnostic role of signals in the contest of perceived risks in online shopping: Do signals matter more on the web? *Journal of Interactive Marketing*, *18*(3), 30–45. doi:10.1002/dir.20010

Blackwell, R. D., Miniard, P. W., & Engel, J. F. (2003). *Consumer Behavior*. Orlando, FL: Harcourt.

Calder, B. J., Phillips, L. W., & Tybout, A. M. (1981). Designing research for application. *The Journal of Consumer Research*, *8*(2), 197–207. doi:10.1086/208856

Cases, A. (2002). Perceived risk and risk-reduction strategies in Internet shopping. *International Review of Retail, Distribution and Consumer Research*, *12*(4), 375–394. doi:10.1080/09593960210151162

Chaudhuri, A. (1997). Consumption emotion and perceived risk: A macro-analytic approach. *Journal of Business Research*, *39*(2), 81–92. doi:10.1016/S0148-2963(96)00144-0

Chen, R., & He, F. (2003). Examination of brand knowledge, perceived risk and consumers' intention to adopt an online retailer. *TQM & Business Excellence*, *14*(6), 677–693. doi:10.1080/1478336032000053825

Chen, Z., & Dubinsky, A. J. (2003). A conceptual model of perceived customer value in e-commerce: A preliminary investigation. *Psychology and Marketing*, *20*(4), 323–347. doi:10.1002/mar.10076

Cho, J., & Lee, J. (2006). An integrated model of risk and risk-reducing strategies. *Journal of Business Research*, *59*(1), 112–120. doi:10.1016/j.jbusres.2005.03.006

Cockburn, C., & Wilson, T. D. (1996). Business use of the world wide web. *International Journal of Information Management*, *16*(2), 83–102. doi:10.1016/0268-4012(95)00071-2

Corbitt, B. J., Thanasankit, T., & Yi, H. (2003). Trust and e-commerce: a study of consumer perceptions. *Electronic Commerce Research and Applications*, *2*(3), 203–215. doi:10.1016/S1567-4223(03)00024-3

Cox, D. (1967). *Risk Taking and Information Handling in Consumer Behavior*. Boston, MA: Harvard University, Division of Research, Graduate School of Business Administration.

Cunningham, L. F., Gerlach, J. H., & Harper, M. D. (2005). Perceived risk and e-banking services: An analysis from the perspective of the consumer. *Journal of Financial Services Marketing*, *10*(2), 165–178. doi:10.1057/palgrave.fsm.4770183

Cunningham, L. F., Gerlach, J. H., Harper, M. D., & Young, C. E. (2005). Perceived risk and the consumer buying process: Internet airline reservations. *International Journal of Service Industry Management*, *16*(4), 357–372. doi:10.1108/09564230510614004

Cunningham, S. M. (1967). Perceived risk and brand loyalty. In Cox, D.F. (Ed.), *Risk-Taking and Information Handling in Consumer Behavior* (pp. 507-523). Boston, MA: Boston University Press.

Dowling, G. R., & Staelin, R. (1994). A model of perceived risk and intended risk-handling activity. *The Journal of Consumer Research*, *21*(1), 119–134. doi:10.1086/209386

Erdem, T., & Swait, J. (2004). Brand credibility, brand consideration, and choice. *The Journal of Consumer Research*, *31*(1), 191–198. doi:10.1086/383434

Featherman, M., & Pavlou, P. (2003). Predicting e-services adoption: A perceived risk facets perspective. *International Journal of Human-Computer Studies*, *59*(4), 451–474. doi:10.1016/S1071-5819(03)00111-3

Forsythe, S., & Shi, B. (2003). Consumer patronage and risk perceptions in Internet shopping. *Journal of Business Research*, *56*(11), 867–875. doi:10.1016/S0148-2963(01)00273-9

Garbarino, E., & Strahilevitz, M. (2004). Gender differences in the perceived risk of buying online and the effects of receiving a site recommendation. *Journal of Business Research*, *57*(6), 768–775. doi:10.1016/S0148-2963(02)00363-6

Greatorex, M., & Mitchell, V. W. (1993). Developing the perceived risk concept: Emerging issues in marketing. In M. Davies et al. (Eds.), *Proceedings, Marketing Education Group Conference* (pp. 405-415). Loughborough.

Guseman, D. S. (1981). Risk perception and risk reduction in consumer services. In J. H. Donnelly & W. R. George (Eds.), *Marketing of Services*. Chicago, IL: American Marketing Association.

Hawkins, D. I., Coney, K. A., & Best, R. J. (2003). *Consumer Behavior: Building Marketing Strategy*, Chicago, IL: Irwin.

Jacoby, J., & Kaplan, L. B. (1972). The components of perceived risk. In M. Venkatesan, (Ed.), *Proceedings of the 3rd Annual Conference of the Association for Consumer Research* (pp. 382-393). College Park, MD: Association for Consumer Research.

Jarvenpaa, S. L., & Todd, P. A. (1997). Consumer reactions to electronic shopping on the world wide web. *International Journal of Electronic Commerce*, *1*(2), 59–88.

Kanwar, R., & Pagiavlas, N. (1992). When are higher social class consumers more and less brand loyal than lower social class consumers? The role of mediating variables. *Advances in Consumer Research. Association for Consumer Research (U. S.)*, *19*, 589–595.

Kogan, N., & Wallach, M. A. (1964). *Risk Taking, a Study in Cognition and Personality*, New York, NY: Holt, Rinehart, and Winston.

Kogan, N., & Wallach, M. A. (1967). Group risk taking as a function of members' anxiety and defensiveness levels. *Journal of Personality*, *35*(1), 50–63. doi:10.1111/j.1467-6494.1967.tb01415.x

Law, R., & Leung, R. (2000). A study of airlines' online reservation services on the Internet. *Journal of Research*, *39*(2), 202–211.

Liebermann, Y., & Stashevsky, S. (2002). Perceived risks as barriers to internet and e-commerce usage. *Qualitative Market Research: An International Journal*, *5*(4), 291–300. doi:10.1108/13522750210443245

Lohse, G. L., Bellman, S., & Johnson, E. J. (2000). Consumer buying behavior on the internet: findings from panel data. *Journal of Interactive Marketing*, *14*(1), 15–29. doi:10.1002/(SICI)1520-6653(200024)14:1<15::AID-DIR2>3.0.CO;2-C

MacCrimmon, K. R., & Wehrung, D. A. (1986). *Taking Risks: The Management of Uncertainty*. New York, NY: The Free Press.

Mitchell, V. W. (1992). Understanding consumers' behavior: Can perceived risk theory help? *Management Decision*, *30*(3), 326–331. doi:10.1108/00251749210013050

Mitchell, V. W. (1998). Buy-phase and buy-class effects on organizational risk perceptions and risk reduction in purchasing professional services. *Journal of Business and Industrial Marketing*, *13*(6), 461–478. doi:10.1108/08858629810246779

Mitchell, V. W. (1999). Consumer perceived risk: Conceptualizations and models. *European Journal of Marketing*, *33*(1/2), 163–195. doi:10.1108/03090569910249229

Mitchell, V. W., & Boustani, P. (1993). Market development using new products and new customers: A role for perceived risk. *European Journal of Marketing*, *27*(2), 17–32. doi:10.1108/03090569310026385

Mitra, K., Reiss, M. C., & Capella, L. M. (1999). An examination of perceived risk, information search, and behavior intentions in search, experience and credence services. *Journal of Services Marketing*, *13*(3), 208–228. doi:10.1108/08876049910273763

Moriarty, R., & Spekman, R. (1984). An empirical investigation of the information buying sources used during the industrial buying process. *JMR, Journal of Marketing Research*, *21*(2), 137–147. doi:10.2307/3151696

Murray, K. B. (1991). A test of service marketing theory: Consumer information acquisition activities. *Journal of Marketing*, *55*(1), 10–25. doi:10.2307/1252200

Murray, K. B., & Schlater, J. L. (1990). The impact of services versus goods on consumers' assessment of perceived risk. *Journal of the Academy of Marketing Science*, *18*(1), 51–65. doi:10.1007/BF02729762

Pew Internet & American Life Project. (2002). Online banking: A Pew Internet project data memo. http://www.pewinternet.org/pdfs/PIP_Online_Banking.pdf (November).

Pollatsck, A., & Tversky, A. (1970). A theory of risk. *Journal of Mathematical Psychology*, *7*(3), 540–553. doi:10.1016/0022-2496(70)90039-8

Quelch, J. A., & Klein, L. R. (1996). The Internet and international marketing. *Sloan Management Review*, *37*(3), 60–75.

Rapoport, A., & Wallsten, T. S. (1972). Individual decision behavior. *Annual Review of Psychology*, *23*, 131–176. doi:10.1146/annurev.ps.23.020172.001023

Roselius, T. (1971). Consumer ranking of risk reduction methods. *Journal of Marketing*, *35*(1), 56–61. doi:10.2307/1250565

Stone, R. N., & Gronhaug, K. (1993). Perceived risk: Further considerations for the marketing discipline. *European Journal of Marketing*, *27*(3), 39–50. doi:10.1108/03090569310026637

Stone, R. N., & Winter, F. W. (1987). Risk: Is it still uncertainty times consequences? In R. W. Belk et al. (Eds.), *Proceedings of the American Marketing Association* (pp. 261-265). Chicago, IL: Winter Educators Conference.

Tan, M., & Teo, T. S. H. (2000). Factors influencing the adoption of Internet banking. *Journal of the Association for Information Systems*, *1*(5), 1–38.

Tan, S. J. (1999). Strategies for reducing consumers' risk aversion in Internet shopping. *Journal of Consumer Marketing*, *16*(2), 163–180. doi:10.1108/07363769910260515

Teo, T., & Yeong, Y. (2003). Assessing the consumer decision process in the digital marketplace. *Omega*, *31*(5), 349–363. doi:10.1016/S0305-0483(03)00055-0

U.S. Department of Commerce, U.S. Census Bureau News, Feb 15th 2008, Washington, D.C.

Vijayasarathy, L. R., & Jones, J. M. (2000). Print and Internet catalog shopping: Assessing attitudes and intentions. *Internet Research: Electronic Networking Applications and Policy*, *10*(3), 191–202. doi:10.1108/10662240010331948

Wirtz, J., Kum, D., & Lee, K. S. (2000). Should a firm with a reputation for outstanding service quality offer a service guarantee? *Journal of Services Marketing*, *14*(6), 502–512. doi:10.1108/08876040010347615

Zeithaml, V. A., & Bitner, M. J. (2003). *Services Marketing: Integrating Customer Focus Across the firm* (3rd ed.). New York, NY: McGraw-Hill.

This work was previously published in International Journal of Information Systems in the Service Sector (IJISSS), edited by John Wang, pp. 33-49, copyright 2009 by IGI Publishing (an imprint of IGI Global).

Chapter 19
Modeling and Governance of Procurement as a Service Responsive to Business Events

Darko Galinec
Ministry of Defense, Croatia

Ksenija Klasić
K & K LLC, Croatia

ABSTRACT

The procurement as business discipline and function of equipping process has started the process of transformation from an administrative competence and necessity to a strategic capability (Kyte, 2006). To be efficient its processes have to be interoperable in the processing, semantic and technological way with other functions and processes of the business system; end-to-end process integration of the business system should be obtained. It is important to fully understand and document user requirements before development of the procurement (business) process. This results in the need for the development of a defined, articulated, communicated and managed model of procurement process. On the level of conceptual system modeling (business process owner's perspective) (ZIFA, 2010) this article shapes a new procurement model, in form of business service with appertaining processes, activities and other services necessary forits accomplishment. At logical and physical modeling level (designer's and builder's perspective) (ZIFA, 2010) service oriented perspective (SOA) has been considered, as well as Web services as technological concept for the implementation of the shaped procurement service model at the conceptual level of the system. Application of the shaped model requires organizational, process and system changes of the business system, that is, procurement function must develop the culture of service provider, avoiding the role of corporate purchasing controller. Event-Driven Business Process Management (EDBPM) is nowadays an enhancement of BPM by new concepts e.g. Event Driven Architecture (EDA). In this paper The position and the role of business service modeling within entire business process management (BPM) discipline has been established as well.

DOI: 10.4018/978-1-60960-138-6.ch019

INTRODUCTION

Part of the reason that business system's processes, including procurement, are complex is that persons who own these processes are accountable for different outcomes than those responsible for specific projects. The individuals who own the procurement process are bound by procurement laws, policies and procedures. These policies may have an unintended consequence related to the needs of particular projects. In many cases, procurement managers are tasked with ensuring that bad things do not happen, rather than enabling successful outcomes (Kyte, 2006).

Procurement function becomes more service oriented and less command and control oriented. The procurement as business discipline and function of equipping process has started the process of transformation from an administrative competence and necessity to a strategic capability (Kyte, 2006). The focus of this article is on procurement process transformation, aiming to investigate the ways and means for its successful achievement. In that regard defined, articulated, communicated and managed model of procurement process as a service is to be developed. For its implementation a service oriented perspective (SOA) is to be considered, BPM orchestration layer is needed to facilitate a relationship between procurement and other services, and rigorous change management processes are mandatory to guarantee availability, reliability, and scalability of the procurement process as a service.

Project managers usually are responsible for successfully implementing a project on time and on budget. Few project managers have significant control over the processes that are used to acquire what they will implement. Procurement managers, however, generally are not directly accountable for the success of projects in which they participate. Their performance metrics involve reducing costs and risks in procurement processes. Being forced to adhere to such processes, policies and procedures (even when they lead to the wrong outcome) indicates that the wrong performance metrics are being used.

Thus, procurement must be more tightly linked to the achievement of business system's policy and operational goals, rather than process goals. To achieve the aforesaid it is necessary to perform organizational and process changes in a business system. It is necessary to create new procurement process models adjusted to the needs of complex inside and outside business system environment. Procurement business function should be modeled in a way which will render possible providing of services to the other parts of business system, those which need them i.e. those which are authorized by common superior level on the basis of existing business rules within the system.

PROCESS OF PROCUREMENT FUNCTION AS A SERVICE

Procurement professionals must increasingly be viewed and used as partners, with shared objectives and accountability for project (procurement) success. Although these professionals may not report directly to the project manager, they should be, like the project manager, accountable to the same people and for the project's success.

Procurement professionals, based on training and good judgment, must be empowered to exercise discretion to ensure a successful outcome, rather than adhere to rigid processes. Rigid processes will make the job of procurement professionals more difficult because they will no longer rely on the process to make decisions. Professionals will need to be well-trained and render expert judgments, often altering processes to ensure that a good outcome is achieved.

Methodology

The methodology of the article used is the one based on Gartner's BPM Maturity model. Through the six phases of BPM Maturity the reason why business process management (BPM) is gaining the attention of many enterprises and identify the key elements to achieve success is explored (Rosser, 2007).Phase 0 begins with the BPM process with awareness that things could be better in your organization if you paid more attention to the performance of various business activities. This leads to measuring and monitoring relevant activities.

Phase 1: Process-Aware

The data generated in Phase 0 will lead to the process-aware phase, where process analysis occurs. The responsibility to act on this analysis is created by establishing process owners who develop a joint means of making decisions and overseeing results through a governance mechanism.

The majority of organizations are still in these first two phases of BPM maturity.

Phase 2: Intra Process Automation and Control

In Phase 2, organizations generate new process models and rule extraction methods, leading to enhanced control over process execution. This control often employs the use of optimization techniques and a more refined approach to cost analysis, using activity-based costing methods. In addition, automation is introduced, which incrementally improves processes.

Phase 3: Inter Process Automation and Control

In Phase 3, process efforts are aligned with the primary business strategy and expanded beyond individual processes to look more broadly at end-to-end processes across the organization. The continuation of this phase will lead to processes that extend to external partners and customers to fully gain larger process benefits for the organization.

Phase 4: Enterprise Valuation Control

In Phase 4, the BPM approach becomes more sophisticated as the organization moves toward automatically making dynamic process changes to attain overall goals. In this phase, processes are directly linked to specific outcomes.

Phase 5: Agile Business Structure

Phase 5, which is the most advanced level of agility, allows for the rapid change of prior capabilities and innovation. Processes are faster, smarter and more goal-directed, and enable organizations to compete in real time.

Process Owners

A variety of individuals with different skill sets and needs play different roles in the business systems. In some business systems more than one individual may share a role, while in others one individual may perform more than one role. One of the roles is business process owner. This individual owns the business process and therefore is responsible for the overall design and specifications that dictate the behaviour of the process. These include performance requirements that the automated process is expected to achieve (Khan, 2004, p. 195). Because processes cross functions and territories, each needs an owner - a senior manager with authority over the process. The process owner's role is to:

- Oversee the execution of the process, set goals and act as arbitrator in the event of serious disagreements
- Ensure that systems and applications supporting the process provide process users and managers with the services needed to do their jobs
- Sponsor continuous improvement

- Recognize relevant internal and external changes and sponsor the necessary process changes
- Recognize when major process change has become desirable and lead the change effort. In general, the process owners are responsible for (Melenovsky, 2006, p. 13):
- Strategy and business case development
- Business performance metrics
- Process discovery
- Functional process design
- Simulation, optimization and scenario creation
- Business change management and communication
- Business rules and event discovery
- Policy management.

The process owner may have a small team which works with business system analysts and designers, as well as other specialists, to support the process owner. The closer process modelling and analysis to the process owner is the more engaged the process owner becomes.

Command and Control vs. Service

Business systems have many functions that are a command and control or service function or both (Kost, 2003). Procurement function generally is expected to acquire services and goods on behalf of users. However, it often plays a role in telling users what they can buy and how they must buy it. If a procurement function dictates what and how something may be bought, users will be less inclined to seek its advice to improve achieving of their objectives. Under these circumstances, procurement function personnel are perceived as antagonists, and they become less useful to the organization. Instead of making procurement part of a command and control function, business system should rely on other functions, to the extent they are necessary, to control behavior. The task of acquiring needed services and goods is complex enough. Procurement personnel should have their performance objectives aligned with the needs of their users. They should be considered as part of the (project) team, especially regarding the acquisition of complex technology as they should be asked to provide the best advice about processes and techniques to ensure the success of the project.

Procurement function should become more service oriented and less command and control oriented. It needs to become more proactive, creating contracting processes that enable project managers and other process users to accomplish their tasks more quickly. Service orientation is a way of integrating business processes as linked services, and the outcomes that these services bring (IBM Corporation Software Group, 2005, p. 3). The roots of service orientation can be found in three different areas: programming paradigms, distribution technology, and business computing. The development of different programming language paradigms has not only contributed to the implementation platform for the different elements of an SOA but also has influenced the interfacing techniques used in an SOA, as well as the interaction patterns that are employed between service providers and service consumers.

Many of the concepts originally found in programming languages have also made their way into the distribution technology that is presently used to offer remote access to services provided by different applications on different technical platforms. The evolution of business computing has resulted in a large number of proprietary as well as packaged applications such as Enterprise Resource Planning (ERP), Customer Relationship Management (CRM), and Supply Chain Management (SCM), which today are providing the content, the data and the business logic that brings an SOA to life.

Because of the closeness of services to concrete business functionality, service orientation has the potential to become the first paradigm that truly brings technology and business together on a level where people from both sides can equally understand and talk about the underlying concepts. SOA aims to leverage the business logic and data that resides in the many applications, databases, and legacy systems of business systems, offering them a sustainable strategy for flexibly adapting their information systems to changes in functional requirements and business strategy (Krafzig & Banke & Slama, 2004).

SOA has strong architectural focus (e.g., SOA governance, development processes, service and data modeling, and tool support) and is ideal for creating long-term strategic value. Services provide an ideal level of abstraction for aligning business needs and technical capabilities (compared to procedures, objects, or components). Services provide an ideal level of abstraction for creating reusable, coarse-grained business functionality (compared to procedures, objects, or components). Loosely coupled services reduce vendor lock-in and simplify application migration and application consolidation. Well-defined service contracts clearly separate the service interface from the underlying details of the service implementation. Service-level data model defines documents to be exchanged among service requesters and service providers in a manner that is aligned with a particular business domain and that is independent of a specific application or technology platform.

Web services are open standards for distributed computing and document exchange. Web services are more pervasive and extensible than earlier distributed computing technologies such as COM/DCOM, CORBA, Java RMI, DCE/RPC and message oriented middleware (MOM). They are supported by all major independent software vendors (ISVs), including platform vendors. Tool support for Web services and related technologies is thriving and growing. Extended Web services standards hold the promise of providing most of the elements of a Web services platform. Enterprise application integration (EAI) products (Galinec & Vidović, 2007) relied on proprietary data formats and message buses, which hampered interoperability with other products and created vendor lock-in. Extensible markup language (XML) and Web services allow the same open, standards-based technologies to be applied across all business domains, thus simplifying future interoperability. XML is widely accepted standard for defining business documents and exchanging information. Extensible so that business domain-specific schemas can be defined, but they are still based on the same core technologies. XML is supported by all major ISVs, including platform vendors. Tool support for XML and related technologies is thriving and growing. EAI products defined proprietary data formats and provided proprietary tools for data transformation. XML is supported by open, standards-based technologies such as XML Schema, validating parsers, XPath, XSLT, XQuery, and XHTML that support data validation, data transformation, and displaying XML data. Earlier standards for data exchange (e.g., EDI, HL7, SWIFT, and FIX) tended to be focused on a particular problem domain or business domain and were only supported by ISVs focused on that domain. XML is extensible so that business domain-specific schemas can be defined, but they are still based on the same core technologies. SOA and BPM are more commonly initiated by business managers than IT managers. BPM's initial goal is usually cost reduction, but other goals grow in importance. Different levels of SOA and BPM activity and maturity may exist across the organization; an assessment is valuable for planning. Factors important to BPM's success exist, but the critical ones vary depending on the maturity level (Rosser, 2007).

Manufacturing vs. Service Oriented Paradigm

According to Allen (2005), the manufacturing paradigm focuses on transformation of:

- Raw materials into finished goods

- Raw data into finished information and knowledge.

The main assumptions for that are:

- Initiating inputs and outputs are "given"
- The emphasis is on how best to transform the material or data, much less on how the inputs and outputs might change
- The processes are highly predictable. Characteristics are:
- Internal focus
- End-to-end value chain
- Decomposition
- Procedural
- Agility is important
- Data are "stored"
- IT is a support function.

In this connection, the main goal is to optimize the flow of work along the production line in a way that brings value to the customer. On the other hand, the service oriented paradigm (Allen, 2005) focuses on the marketplace where organizations collaborate together consuming and offering services.

Assumptions:

- Service providers offer commodity functionality better, faster and cheaper
- Contracts between providers and consumers are clearly understood
- The processes change with market conditions.

Characteristics:

- Cross organization focus
- Business capability
- Collaboration
- Contractual
- Agility is vital
- Data are "shared"
- IT is an enabler.

The main goal becomes to provide customer value by concentrating on core competencies and by contracting others to do what a company has to do just to get by.

SOA and Web-Services in Service Providing

Complexity is a fact of life in information technology (IT). Dealing with the complexity while building new applications, replacing existing applications, and keeping up with all the maintenance and enhancement requests represents a major challenge (Lomow & Newcomer, 2005). The leading architectural constructs of SOA are Web services, portal frameworks and application servers. Its most anticipated benefit is faster and more flexible reconfiguration of business processes. Those who plan to deploy SOA expect to reconfigure business processes more easily than with traditional methods of integration (Austvold & Carter, 2005, p. 2).

Service companies are more likely to evaluate and implement SOA technology and components than are manufacturers and retailers, because most of them haven't standardized on an Enterprise Resource Planning (ERP) backbone – they have a mishmash of systems. This becomes worse through Mergers and Acquisitions (M & As) (Austvold & Carter, 2005, p. 7). But in both companies procurement function can be modelled as business service based on SOA since communication with other parts of business system (functions, processes, services) on the basis of request/respond principle is its peculiarity.

SOA's greatest shortcoming is the burden of complexity (Austvold & Carter, 2005, p. 2). Even though the biggest expected benefit of SOA is reconfigurable business processes, a resulting burden of complexity has appeared post-implementation of SOA. Those that have deployed SOAs find that most of their software applications are not yet modularized to work in an SOA, that highly modular software services need a common repository to manage the services, that a BPM orchestration layer is needed to facilitate a relationship between services, and rigorous change management processes are mandatory to guarantee service availability, reliability, and scalability.

MODELING OF PROCUREMENT AS A BUSINESS SERVICE AND PROCESS MANAGEMENT

Process design is the conscious (re-)evaluation and organization of the tasks that a business process is composed of. Designing a process that improves current performance and/or conformance is a challenging task that requires a plethora of inputs (for example, organizational strategies, goals, constraints, and IT capabilities, to name a few). Process modeling, which is a heavily researched aspect of the business process lifecycle, is also an important pre-requisite of process design. However, it is the actual act of process improvement that is the most value-adding step in the process lifecycle. Unlike the comprehensive body of research on process modeling, process design – the "white space" between the "as-is" and the "to-be" - has so far attracted limited academic contributions. As a result, practical process improvement exercises rely heavily on tacit knowledge, inspiration and personal experiences, with a lack of guidance and best practice approaches. This situation can result in inconsistent results that undermine the true potential of Business Process Management (BPM) initiatives in organizations (Indulska & Limam Mansar & Rosemann, 2010).

Model designing phase begins by gathering and analyzing business requirements needed to model, simulate and optimize business processes. The most critical skills required for modeling are process design and change management.

The resulting business processes are used to design associated software services and service levels to support these processes. During this phase, model is being used to establish a common understanding between business and IT of business processes, objectives and outcomes, as well as to help ensure that the resulting application meets business requirements defined by process owners and users. This model also provides a base line from which to measure business performance. After the model is designed services are created out of existing assets, such as ERP and financial systems and other applications and solutions that run the business. In many cases, a library of existing services can be used to find services that already exist in business system. If no functionality exists a services can be created and tested to deliver the functionality required for a particular business process. After the required services are available, the services are orchestrated to implement a business process.

The Model of Procurement as a Service

The focus of a Service Oriented Architecture is on the functional infrastructure and its business services, not the technical infrastructure and its technical services. A business-oriented service in an SOA is typically concerned with one major aspect of the business, be it a business entity, a business function, or a business process.

A business process is a set of activities that is initiated by an event, transforms information or materials and produces an output. Value chains produce outputs that are valued by customers. Other processes produce outputs that are valued by other processes (Allen, 2005). A service is functionality that works as a family unit that offers business capability. It is specified in terms of contracts between the provider of the functionality and its consumers. It is akin to a reusable chunk of a business process that can be mixed and matched with other services (Allen, 2005). It's a repeatable business task (IBM Corporation Software Group, 2005, p. 3). Asoftware service is a type of service (Allen, 2005). A Web service is a software service that complies with certain standards (Allen, 2005).

Figure 1. Procurement business service model

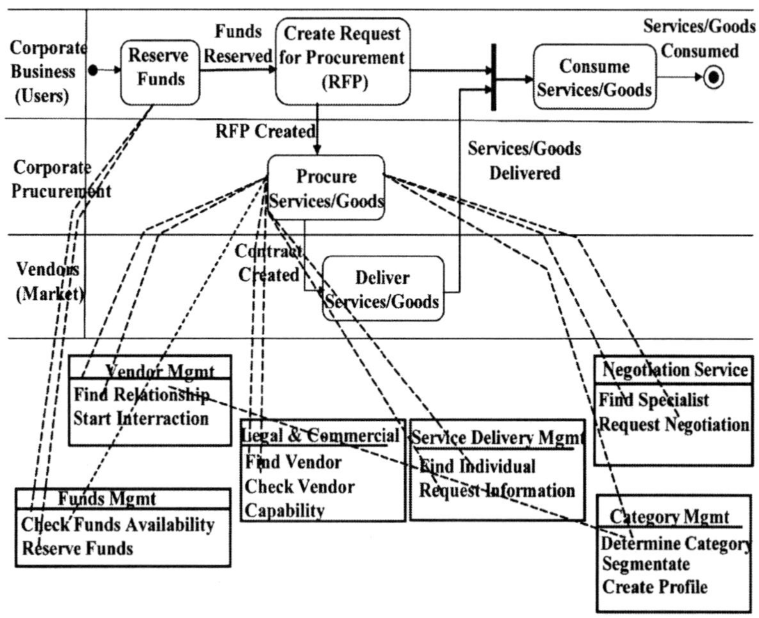

It is self-describing, self-contained, modular unit of software application logic that provides defined business functionality.

Web service is consumable software service that typically includes some combination of business logic and data. Web services can be aggregated to establish a larger workflow or business transactions. Inherently, the architectural components of Web services support messaging, services description, registries and loosely coupled interoperability.

Composite application is a set of related and integrated services that support a business process built on SOA (IBM Corporation Software Group, 2005, p. 3).

Figure 1 shows the procurement of services/goods process as business service initiated by another processes: funds reservation and request of procurement creation (creating tactical study, drawing up the characteristics sheet with tactical requirements and technical specifications, performing functional analysis, creating feasibility study and implementation program). Through the execution, procure services/goods service is followed by other processes and invokes other services (negotiation, legal & commercial etc.) to complete its function: approving of the request, making a contract with vendor, procuring (with governance, tracking, quality control) and finally delivering the services/goods to the customer, which then can be consumed (fielding and operational use). The contractor shall evaluate the design of any new or modified equipment to provide cost, schedule and technical impact statement

(Adler, 2004). Enabling public finance and public procurement by Internet, governments are not only reducing own expenditures, but improving transparency and democratic development as well (Novotny & Sabati, 2007). Other services can also invoke each other independently for other business purposes, when needed (vendormanagementand categorymanagement). The system which orchestrates and ties multiple processes and services together into a process flow of execution resides at BPM layer. BPM is set of software systems, tools and methodologies that addresses how organizations identify, model, develop, deploy, and manage business processes.

BPM systems are designed to help align business processes with desirable business outcomes and ensure that the information systems support those business processes. They let business process owners and users model their business processes graphically, and they separate business process logic from other application code.

Business rules technologies are BPM complimentary technology. They enable business systems to define rules (using graphical interfaces), apply, reuse, modify and manage the rules, decision points and criterions (according to business requirements or process changes) for business process flow and execution. With business rules technologies in place business systems can centralize their business process logic (business rules repository) and thus eliminate multiple definitions of the same rule, while allowing distributed rules creation and modifications and updates. Separating business process logic (represented by business rules) from other application code helps increase productivity, reduce operational costs, and improve agility. When implemented correctly (for example, using BPM as a consumer of an SOA with Web services), business systems can more quickly respond to changing market conditions and seize opportunities for gaining a competitive advantage.According to (Lomow & Newcomer, 2005) BPM simplifies the problem of how to combine the execution of multiple Web services to solve a particular business problem. By taking the process flow out of the application-level code, the business process can be more easily changed and updated for new application features and functions such as a change in suppliers, inventory management, or the procurement process. The convergence of BPM, SOA, Web services, and XML promises to significantly improve corporate agility, reduce time-to-market for new products and services, reduce costs, and improve operational efficiency of IT systems (Lomow & Newcomer, 2005).

Event-Driven Business Process Management (EDBPM) is nowadays an enhancement of BPM by new concepts of SOA, Event Driven Architecture (EDA), Software as a Service (SaaS), Business Activity Monitoring (BAM) and Complex Event Processing (CEP). In this context BPM means a software platform which provides companies the ability to model, manage, and optimize these processes for significant gain. As an independent system, CEP is a parallel running platform that analyses and processes events. The BPM- and the CEP-platform correspond via events which are produced by the BPM-workflow engine and by the - if distributed - IT services which are associated with the business process steps. Also events coming from different event sources in different forms can trigger a business process or influence the execution of the process or a service, which can result in another event. Even more, the correlation of these events in a particular context can be treated as a complex, business level event, relevant for the execution of other business processes or services. A business process - arbitrarily fine or coarse grained - can be seen as a service again and can be choreographed with other business processes or services, even between different enterprises and organisations. Loosely coupled event-driven architecture for BPM provides important benefits:

- Responsiveness. Events can occur at any time from any source and processes respond to them immediately, whenever they happen and wherever they happen.
- Agility. New processes can be modeled, implemented, deployed, and optimized more quickly in response to changing business requirements.
- Flexibility. Processes can span heterogeneous platforms and programming languages. Participating applications can be upgraded or changed without breaking the process model (Stevens Institute of Technology, 2010).

Service Governance, Metrics and Risk

IT management must have a vision of how to organize for the successful adoption of IT service management processes. Process management success requires a framework. A governing community affords a solid starting point. Via this forum, documented policies institute a set of procedures to regulate and control asset processes. It establishes a system of authorizations by which various persons or groups coordinate their efforts and take on specialized roles and functions.

The IT organization constructs a network of appropriate dependencies based on a realistic appraisal of what it and others can provide. This approach yields a vehicle that enables the IT organization to control where it is going, not where it has been. Governance will require cross-departmental collaboration. It will offer a forum where policies can be agreed to and grievances can be aired. In addition to the application development team, the operational change group, service desk and operations, the governance committee should include stakeholders from the lines of business. The lines of business will provide some of the vision - expectations for new business objectives, new employee growth and merger-and-acquisition activity.

Successful organizations typically have well-defined and -articulated goals and objectives. Translating these goals and objectives into quantifiable metrics is a way to motivate people to try and achieve them. However, metrics can be a doubleedged sword. People will modify their behavior to do what they think will help achieve a particular metric on which they are being judged. If the metrics aren't carefully selected, the behavior that is encouraged may actually hinder the organization from achieving its goals. For instance, if service desk agents are measured by the number of calls they handle, they will naturally attempt to keep each call as short as possible to rack up the numbers. This can be damaging to customer service. At the other extreme, if the same service desk agents are judged on the percentage of calls that are resolved without having to escalate, they will keep the customer on the phone for excessive time in the hopes they can solve the problem. By creating a balanced set of metrics, you can ensure that people better understand the desired behavior. They will find ways to avoid either extreme. Metrics are powerful, but tricky. They should be monitored to ensure they are serving as a means of measuring something you want to achieve (Govekar, 2010).

Governance alignment refers to ensuring correct accountabilities and responsibilities in the service delivery life cycle, from:

- Regulatory, policy and technology perspectives
- Oversight of implementation/compliance - that is, the coordination of assurance functions
- Instituting more-comprehensive risk management process and procedures with a broader scope
- Focusing on operational and IT risk, not just information security risk.

The service delivery life cycle refers to actively integrating warranty design and control - risk and security control points in the RACI (meaning responsible, accountable, consulted and informed) charts; formalizing and improving risk and business impact assessment with consistent processes and documentation requirements, and with agreement on the scope of risk assessment (RA) and business impact analysis (BIA) - technology, information security, compliance and business. Architecture relates to the taxonomy of relevant service platform functions; the principles of common services vs. integrated functions; multibaseline choices lined to Service Level Agreements (SLAs); and a common requirements definition - deriving governance, risk management and compliance (GRC) requirements from actual business drivers, imperatives and needs. Metrics must link GRC metrics and reporting to service-and-operations-level agreements. Portfolio of security services should follow service portfolio templates, for example, identity and access management (IAM) services, compliance services, risk management services and infrastructure protection services (Scholtz, 2010).

CONCLUSION

Business process is between business requirements and IT. Service orientation is a way of representing IT capability of business services. Service is what business requires, it is not defined by IT. Business is defining the services because business is defining the processes, and services implement the processes. Business systems are working to streamline and improve their procurement process in order to become closer to the users. Users need adequate end-to-end process and (composite) application support through services to assure operation utility of process crossing several functional or business units.

Business systems that adopt service orientation can dynamically change processes to align them for users, according to their intentions and needs for the business which continues to change. Therefore, procurement function within business system needs to develop the culture of service provider, not the process controller. This requires a well established and accepted change management process based on changing needs of both the user and the business system, followed by all users.

SOAs are all about the sharing and management of services and data, as well as processes and orchestrations that exist on top of those services. The technology employed should be appropriate for business requirements. BPM involves integrating systems, processes and services with human workflow, which enables business systems to model and modify their business processes and services in response to changing business needs. In this connection, the new model of procurement as a business service with appertaining processes, data, activities and other services necessary for its accomplishment in this article is presented.

In this article the new service model of specific business process (procurement as a part of equipping system) is presented. Model takes place in the beginning of overall BPM discipline of modeling, automating, managing and optimizing of business process through its lifecycle. Presented service model should be exposed as a service within the BPM system, its execution should be initiated by an event and it should be performed according to the business rules created. Thus, it is appropriate for linkage with other services in value chain. Events can occur at any time from any authorized source and procurement service with its processes is capable to respond to them immediately. In that sense the presented model fits well into the event-driven SOA (EDSOA).

REFERENCES

Adler, R. T. (2004). An exploratory study of team perceptions of trust and distrust in a contract negotiation setting.The Institute of Behavioral and Applied Management. *Journal of Behavioral and Applied Management*, *5*(3), 245–278.

Allen, P. (2005). *Service-oriented business process redesign. In Proceedings of Business Process Management Conference Europe 2005*. Business Process Management Group.

Austvold, E., & Carter, K. (2005). *Service-oriented architecture: survey findings on deployment and plans for the future*. AMR Research Market Analytix Report: Market Trends Series.

Galinec, D., & Vidović, S. (2007). Methodology framework for process integration and service management. [Faculty of Organization and Informatics Varaždin - University of Zagreb.]. *Journal of Information and Organizational Sciences*, *31*(1), 37–49.

Govekar, M. (2010). *Making ITIL a Reality: Pitfalls and Strategy. Gartner local briefing in Zagreb*. Gartner, Inc.

IBM Corporation Software Group. (2005). *IBM SOA foundation: providing what you need to get started with SOA*. Service oriented architecture solutions: white paper. IBM.

Indulska, M., Limam Mansar, S., & Rosemann, M. (2010). *Business Process Design*. Retrieved June 15th, 2010 from http://www.bpm2010.org/conference-program/workshops/bpd10/. 6th International Workshop on Business Process Design.

Khan, R. N. (2004). *Business process management a practical guide*. Meghan-Kiffer Press.

Kost, J. (2003). *Government procurement reform is a strategic imperative*. Gartner, Inc.

Krafzig, D., Banke, K., & Slama, D. (2004). *Enterprise SOA: service-oriented architecture best practices*. Prentice Hall PTR.

Kyte, A. (2006). *Procurement governance, organization, strategies and systems. Gartner local briefing in Zagreb*. Gartner, Inc.

Lomow, G., & Newcomer, E. (2005). *Understanding SOA with web services*. Addison-Wesley Professional.

Melenovsky, M. J. (2006). *Case study: BPM organizational staffing and structure*. Gartner, Inc.

Novotny, D., & Sabati, Z. (2007). Internet enabled public services as a driver of economic growth - case study ECroatia 2006. Faculty of Organization and Informatics Varaždin - University of Zagreb. *Journal of Information and Organizational Sciences*, *31*(1), 141–156.

Rosser, D. (2007). *Toolkit tactical guideline: how to determine the right time to launch a BPM program*. Gartner, Inc.

Scholtz, T. (2010). *Integrating Security Management into ITIL v.3 Strategies: Case Study and Best Practices*. Gartner local briefing in Zagreb. Gartner, Inc.

Stevens Institute of Technology. (2010). *Event-driven Business Process Management*. Retrieved June 14th, 2010 from http://www.bpm2010.org/conference-program/workshops/edbpm10/. 8th International Conference on Business Process Management.

ZIFA. (2010). *Zachman framework*. Retrieved June 16th, 2010 from http://www.zachmaninternational.com/index.php/the-zachman-framework. Zachman International Enterprise Architecture.

Chapter 20
Staying Competitive in the Political Unrest and Global Financial Crisis:
Perspective of a Thai Healthcare Organization

William Wall
Shinawatra University, Thailand

ABSTRACT

Global competition today is a complex dimension to add in the success of a healthcare organization. Providing state of the art technology along with the manpower and management skills to bridge boundaries and cultures, confronts today's healthcare organizations with challenges that, while on the surface may appear simple, may also prove to be a bigger challenge to their success and survival than the medical care they are actually providing. This study is a follow up to an earlier study conducted on a major healthcare organization in Thailand posing the question of how the current political unrest in Thailand and the global financial crisis has affected their global competitiveness. An inductive approach was utilized for a method of determining competitiveness. The resulting qualitative analysis of that data addresses issues of threats to maintaining global competitiveness, providing superior quality care with competitive and reasonable pricing of sub-specialty and high acuity services and work effectively through strategic alliances. In the case of the healthcare organization in this study, their global competitiveness is threatened potentially by the global recession and most recently, the political instability in Thailand. Reputation and the ability to provide comfort and hospitality at the same time as providing excellent medical care and facilities give them both economy of scale to provide reasonable pricing and a uniqueness in the medical care provided. This uniqueness and quality in service attracts strategic alliances and allows for retention of competitiveness in global markets.

DOI: 10.4018/978-1-60960-138-6.ch020

INTRODUCTION

With recent global economics changing, the competitive pressure on organizations becomes more intense. This is never more evident that in the current political and economic environment that is seen today in Thailand. The main question to be answered today is, from the perspective of this healthcare organization, what impact have these factors had on their global competitiveness?

The private healthcare organization in this case study is one of a total of 344 hospitals with 35,086 beds in Thailand. Of these hospitals, 102 are private hospitals with a total of 15,000 beds located in Bangkok. 43% of the entire country's facilities are concentrated mainly in Bangkok (Kasikorn Research, 2007). Thailand as a destination for medical treatment has rocketed in recent years. As an example, over 60,000 United Arab Emirates citizens a year come to Thailand to receive treatment (Tourism Authority of Thailand, 2007). Tourism Authority of Thailand (TAT) is planning to promote health and wellness tourism online by launching a new Arabic-language web site for medical tourism, www.thailandmedtourism.com. Together with more than 70 Thai private hospitals, plastic surgery clinics and spas in Thailand, TAT will provide information on all their respective health and wellness services. Thailand continues to be the largest health and wellness destination globally with more than 1.5 million medical tourists last year according to the Tourism Authority of Thailand (2009). Medical tourism is quickly becoming one of Asia's fastest growing industries. It is projected by 2012 to be worth a minimum of $4 billion USD. Why? Tourists get the promise of low cost quality healthcare in countries like Thailand where the average medical tourist spends on average $362 USD per day, compared to the average traveler spending $144 USD. In addition those costs are five to ten times less expensive than in Europe and the US as in the following examples:

- Cardiac surgery – India $4,000 vs. United States $30,000 (Stokes, 2007)
- Hip Replacement – Thailand, Singapore $13,000-$13,500 vs. United States $44,500 - (Global Doctor Options Guide, 2008)
- Knee Replacement - India $7,000 vs. United States $45,000 (Wockhardt Hospitals, 2008)

The main reasons for this influx of medical travelers are lack of health insurance and the high cost of healthcare (Bernheim, 2008).

But to retain global competitiveness in healthcare, do quality of care, low prices and easy travel offset the uncertainty of the political unrest and global economic crisis? According to official data from the Tourism Authority of Thailand, international passengers arriving at Suvarnabhumi International Airport fell by an average of 20% over May 2009 and by 30% over May 2008. In the period of 18-24 May, 2010, alone, daily arrivals declined by an average of 12,000 – 14,000 over normal. Some countries from the Middle East instructed their citizens not to come to Thailand or even hosted charter flights to return citizens back home soon after the protests began to produce casualties. (Tourism Authority of Thailand, 2010).

By the middle of April 2010, medical tourism had begun to feel the pressure of the prolonged political strife in Thailand. Bangkok Dusit Medical Services (BGH), the country's largest private hospital operator, said foreign patient visits decreased by 20% compared with the same period of 2009 (Wiriyapong, 2010). Phyathai Hospital saw a 7-10% decline of international patients arriving compared with last April.

Regardless of what might be occurring in the streets, the second quarter of the year is typically low season for the health-care industry, since it is the off-peak tourism season which means less international patient traffic. However, if the situation improves before the third quarter, the impact from political unrest on the health-care service sector might be minimal (International Medical Travel Journal, 2010).

Even as Bangkok has been hit by political unrest, Thailand's medical tourism industry has been surprisingly resilient. Since demonstrations began in March 2010, the stock price of Bumrungrad Hospital, one of the premier hospitals in Thailand for international patients, is down less than 8 percent. Bangkok Dusit Medical Center is actually up by 0.8 percent (KGI Securities, 2010).

So how will healthcare organizations overcome the challenges to come? These questions must be continually addressed if today's healthcare system is to be effectively and efficiently competitive on a global scale (Cortez, 2008).

If an organization is to be profitable it needs to focus on three major areas of operation: quality service, competitive and reasonable pricing, and the effective and efficient delivery of that service. Today's hospital must also be a strong financial institution.

METHODOLOGY

The research was conducted by way of a survey. To gather the required data to address the research questions, the main survey technique used was a questionnaire. While other instruments may be used to collect this data, it was found that the questionnaire is relatively inexpensive to administer and reasonably easy to analyze the data collected.

The construction of the questionnaire was accomplished by reviewing prior examples (Bowling, 2005). The procedure of the questionnaire construction is explained here addressing the subjects, the development of the questionnaire, components of the questionnaire, administration, collection and validity and reliability.

The objective of this research was to determine what impact the political unrest in Thailand and the global financial crisis has had on the global competitiveness of this healthcare organization.

Thirty subjects were investigated in this study: Senior Management (4); Administrators (10); Medical Personnel (8); and, Staff (8). These 30 subjects were chosen because it was believed that they represented the most significant subjects working in their respective divisions at the present time. The highest level of education among the subjects was a Doctor degree (37%) followed by a Master degree (57%) and all with Bachelor degrees with 13 subjects being male and 17 being female.

The questionnaire used in this research consisted of 6 questions written in English and was given to all 30 subjects. Closed-end and open-ended questions were used and the questionnaire was designed to relate to the purpose of the research and obtain relevant information from subjects (Appendix A). The administration of this questionnaire and the resulting clarification interviews were conducted by the researcher. Of the subjects given questionnaires, 26 were interviewed. These interviews were used as a means to expand and allow subjects to discuss openly and freely some of their responses to the questionnaire. From the data collected and from the information obtained, some irrelevant items were excluded and some ambiguities were clarified.

Questionnaire construction and subsequent interviews were conducted with no predetermined outcome in an effort to avoid any type of bias. Bias may arise in quantitative analysis, where quantitative researchers sometimes use it, for example in discussions of significance levels (Levine, 1993). It may also be used by qualitative researchers. Becker argued that sociological analysis is always from someone's point of view, and is therefore partisan (Becker, 1967). In this **qualitative research**, every effort was made to avoid biases and therefore, as stated in the previous paragraph, subjects were allowed to discuss their responses in the interviews openly and freely. The researcher also had no predetermined agenda or result in mind in the construction of the questionnaire or the resulting information derived from the questionnaire or the subsequent interviews.

Every effort was made to assure the validity of the research instrument. Development and construction of the questionnaire was based on literature and research reviews and preliminary discussions with subjects used in this research. Comments and suggestions were then incorporated into the final instrument to reflect a reasonable claim of face validity as justification of the questionnaire produced. The reliability value of the questionnaire was calculated using Cronbach's Alpha Method revealing the reliability coefficient of the questionnaire was .9693

The questionnaire (Appendix A) used in this study included 'open' questions that resembled interview scripts. Written responses were more likely to be one of conscious effort and not repetitive, while in an interview interesting responses could be explored interactively in great depth. Categories derived from the questionnaire responses were combined with categories derived from interviews in grounded theory analysis.

Grounded Theory (Strauss & Corbin, 1998) and Porter's Diamond (Porter, 1990) was used in the qualitative analysis (Ezzy, 2002) of this study to discover patterns, aspects and importance of global competitiveness as well as the interrelationship of those factors from the data collected. Qualitative analysis was used also since it was not the objective of this study to compile the data collected numerically (Miles, 1994). The field of inquiry was limited to areas, subjects, people and questions that would directly relate to data necessary to be analyzed (Wolcott, 1994). Qualitative conclusions also lent themselves to communicating the vision, mission and support of the organization's current plans and those of the future.

Porter's Diamond (Porter, 1990) was used to identify key areas of competitiveness utilized by the healthcare organization in this study addressing four broad attributes - factor conditions, demand conditions, related and supporting industries and firm strategy, structure and rivalry - of an organization that shape the environment in which firms compete and either promote or impede the creation of competitive advantage. Porter's Model for Competitive Advantage was utilized addressing cost leadership, differentiation and focus (Porter, 1998).

With cost leadership through economies of scale, the company has a better ability to manage growth and hold off competition. For instance, by establishing a hospital facility where little or no hospital services or medical care exist, distributed fixed costs can remain fairly stable and services can be priced to be more profitable (Bushe, 1995).

Differentiation is achieved by concentrating on specific specialties or sub-specialties creating a service that is perceived as unique by the patient. This is perceived as superior value by the patients and therefore, since the patient sees the service as unrivaled unequaled, the price value can be adjusted to be more flexible. This also tends to develop more brand loyalty and helps insulate the organization against the competition.

The focus is important because the organization seeks to be more competitive by being more effective than efficient. Hence the focus to specialty and sub-specialty practice to set the organization apart as being the best in a certain segment of the business within a group of businesses.

This competitive advantage is key for organizations such as the one studied here to perform well and survive in today's highly globalized and intensely competitive healthcare market.

An inductive approach (Thomas, 2006) for analysis of data was initially used to consolidate and refine that data followed by a more concise triangulation of information as a qualitative process to specifically determine conclusions of this study.

Background of the Healthcare Organization

Established in 1972, started by a group of doctors and pharmacists with five specialists and 30 full time nurses, this healthcare organization became the largest hospital in Thailand with more than 400 fulltime consultant physicians and 600 nurses. One hospital has now turned into 12 hospitals, 16 specialty centers and 15 clinics at home and eight other facilities in Cambodia, Vietnam, Burma and Bangladesh.

Specialized centers come completely equipped with the latest treatment and diagnostic methods and tools that cover a range of services from pediatrics to geriatrics, neurology, cardiology and ophthalmology and treatments for sports related injuries.

Patient's requirements for different cultural and personal needs are attended to through specially designed outpatient clinics. Each clinic has unique facilities such as International, Japanese and Arabic services and is broken into four groups: Internal medicine; Surgery; Obstetric and Gynecology; and, a special clinic to deal with psychiatric disorders such as insomnia, depression and behavioral problems of children.

Investment is made in the latest technology, medical expertise and support facilities and is in continuous development contributing to the hospital's reputation and current status as one of the top medical organizations in Southeast Asia. A state-of the-art videoconferencing system links all of its hospitals, clinics and medical professionals in Thailand enabling the sharing of medical images while minimizing time for treatment administration and discussion of cases by specialists and physicians in different centers throughout the country. This allows the group to operate its branches as a single entity and is currently being developed for Southeast Asian inclusion.

This organization is dedicated to maintaining the highest international standards of medical practice by delivering quality patient care to each and every patient. Their vision statement tells it all – "our patients' complete satisfaction."

Maintaining Global Competitiveness

Two major questions for this healthcare organization are how does the current global economic crisis affecting their business and what affect has the current political crisis in Thailand had on their competitiveness? While the healthcare market in Thailand has not yet saturated, to maintain growth, this Thai healthcare organization looked outside the country. Due to the increasing cost of travel, eventually foreigners, especially in the Middle East, will not be able to afford to travel. The main reason for this is in examples found in long term care. Traditionally, in the Middle East relatives typically accompany the patient. Not just the cost of health care, but accommodation, plane ticket, extra expenses and pocket money are increasing to the point of making a trip abroad prohibitive. The Middle East is also trying to discourage people from seeking health care outside the country. For instance, there is only one hospital in Saudi Arabia that has long term care. Rich people can still afford to travel, but the poor may not be able to afford the care outside the country.

Currently, medical travelers from Bahrain who are financially able still travel to this healthcare organization's facilities in Thailand for treatment, while government staff that used to be supported for medical travel and treatment from the Bahrain government now have lost those privileges as a direct response due to the current global economic crisis (Anonymous, 2010).

Global expansion to maintain competitiveness for this healthcare organization is answered by addressing location and planning. Being a pioneer in healthcare in Thailand, this organization has served both local and foreign patients and their communities with prompt professionalism in world-class facilities at reasonable prices for more than 26 years making it difficult for its closest competitors to follow.

It has positioned itself as a convenient, integrated solution to often complex healthcare. This is due largely to a well established differentiation in its infrastructure where Positioning (convenient and integrated healthcare solutions), Differentiation (wide network, wide range of services) and Brand working in conjunction with Brand Integrity, Image and Identity all work together to create a winning situation for both patient and healthcare organization (Porter, 2006).

This healthcare organization has recently opened a hospital in Abu Dhabi. Abu Dhabi is a wealthy country and still underdeveloped in the areas of medical care and their economy. Conversely, Dubai is saturated with medical facilities and a multitude of hospitals, the population growth is slowing down. Abu Dhabi is now working on a plan to catch up with Dubai. There has been a population explosion in Abu Dhabi and they currently have produced a 22 year plan regarding growth and population planning.

Abu Dhabi is a modern society shaped by an ancient culture. The strategic policies in this Urban Structure Framework Plan, "Plan Abu Dhabi 2030", provide a way of reversing sometimes inappropriate development trends and of satisfying the needs of a growing population (Abu Dhabi Plan 2003, 2007). These policies are grounded by the three basic elements of sustainability: the natural environment, economic development and cultural heritage. Abu Dhabi is only the beginning of this active search for expandable locations. Doha, Qatar and Saudi Arabia are the next areas that may be looked at. Saudi Arabia has a population of more than 30 million people and the healthcare structure there is still underdeveloped.

Investment is not the only answer. Establishing and maintaining that global competitiveness can be focused into three main areas:

1. Expanding the reach as a healthcare provider into key strategic locations such as urban and industrial areas where patients reside as well as specific tourist destinations.
2. Providing quality with sub-specialty and high acuity services with global and national patient care quality standards together with state-of-the-art medical technologies.
3. Efficiency of shared services among network hospitals, sharing resources, consolidating back offices and decreasing monitoring and administrative work.

In addition, by utilizing this network approach the duplication of services can be avoided while concentrating on providing the best possible service to the customer at a reasonable cost.

So while patient numbers may be slightly reduced in Thailand from inbound patients, the establishment of local hospitals such as the one in Abu Dhabi has helped this healthcare organization in combating the global financial crisis by providing the same level of quality care and service with competitive pricing at the local level as is offered in Thailand.

The recent political unrest that was seen the Thailand in the past few months has been something that has been out of the control of this healthcare organization. They are fortunate to be located away from the downtown area of protests and in other provinces where little or no unrest was seen. Other hospitals more centrally located in the city of Bangkok saw an increase in patient numbers from casualty treatments, but reduction in the numbers of foreign patients.

Superior Quality Care, Reasonable Cost

The biggest factor in determining global competitiveness of all the issues covered in this research is assurance to the patient of quality care. The organizational growth and improvement of the quality of services is clearly linked to an organization's commitment to improvement (Spulber, 2007). How this improvement process is driven, the use of performance measurement, external verification and the difficulties in accessing relevant data is a constant challenge. In healthcare today the pursuit of excellence is no longer an option (Asch, et al., 2006). It is essential.

Encouraged by the government's drive to make Thailand a regional hub for healthcare, this organization raised its bed capacity and looked beyond the local market, currently serving over 10,000 outpatients and 1,000 in-patients per day. The International division is now staffed with an international team who is culturally aware of the needs of patients and the need to provide those patients with a comfortable and reassuring environment and ambiance to make their stay as pleasant as possible. Hotel-style rooms and specially catered meals suiting every dietary requirement are provided to patients as well as access to the hospital's language translation service covering 26 different languages to help patients in making inquires and to explain medical conditions as well as instructions for treatment and maintenance. In-patient care is prompt and professional with care taken for consideration of special cultural, personal and religious needs and the tension of medical treatments is eased by specially selected services like Thai massage or personal grooming.

What standards are provided to assure the patient of safety and reliability in treatment? In the case of this health care organization, quality care is determined based on American standard practices of medicine as well as accreditation by the Joint Commission International (JCI).

JCI's mission is to continuously improve the safety and quality of care in the international community through the provision of education and consultation services and international accreditation. As the largest accrediting agency of health care organizations in the United States, it surveys nearly 20,000 health care programs through a voluntary accreditation process. (Joint Commission International, 2007).

Specific services for sub-specialty and high acuity services are not only targeted demographically, but are coordinated with state of the art technology to provide a standard of quality that patients can rely on time after time. Customer relationship management (CRM) (Buttle, 2003) helps to develop and improve Key Performance Indicators (KPI) (Shahin, 2007). Key Performance Indicators help a healthcare organization to define and measure progress toward organizational goals. Once the healthcare organization has analyzed their mission, identified all their stakeholders and defined their goals, they need a way to measure progress toward those goals. Key Performance Indicators are those measurements.

Faster availability of data is beginning to becoming more and more a concern. Delays of a month or two may provide unreliable information as demographics change. So technology is needed to blend with organizational goals.

Cost efficiency is accomplished through a network of shared services among network hospitals sharing services and resources, consolidating back offices and decreasing monitoring and administrative work and Key Performance Indicators (KPI) are watched closely and once the network has been established a number of issues are addressed. The main areas of analyses are:

1. Volume numbers related to patients (new patients, existing status and patient attrition).
2. Patient turnover by market segment (demographic studies).
3. Analysis of individuals demographically who may be potential patients.
4. Profitability by demographic segments and segmentation of customers by profitability.

This combination of cost control to provide reasonably priced health services in areas that are lacking not only in the quality but availability of healthcare allows this healthcare organization to be competitive in the market outside Thailand. It is important to note that a company must be explicit about its choice of strategy with regard to value creation (differentiation) and low cost (Porter, 1996).

Strength through Strategic Alliances

Alliances and contractual relations between collaborating partners in the healthcare market are shifting rapidly, therefore the need to be adaptive to the changing environment and be competitive both domestically and internationally are critical. Strategic alliances have allowed this healthcare organization to have revenue with a diversified base with a different environment, currency, nationality and behavior. The challenge is to manage those factors and get a positive result.

Today's healthcare industry is characterized by new and often problematic, opportunities and challenges in greatly expanding markets that can change overnight by research findings, a financial report, new legislation, new regulations, or the introduction of new technology. The healthcare industry is a "turbulent environment where companies worldwide and across many industries are turning to alliances as a cooperative, inter-organizational mechanism for adaptation" (Zuckerman, 2002). Strategic alliances enable participating organizations to extend their operations and expand toward desirable strategic goals. They can help to be more than a convenient arrangement to help healthcare providers to get through a tough period or resolve a major problem. Strategic alliances are now used in the healthcare field as a viable operational and strategic consideration. In today's environment of continual change and unpredictable developments, organizations may many times face circumstances where strategic alliance is necessary to stay timely and competitive. Strategic alliances are designed to achieve strategic purposes not attainable by one single organization. They provide flexibility and the ability to be responsive while retaining the basic structure of participating organizations (Lieberman, 1987).

The rationale to form these alliances is to recognize their value in engendering flexibility and allow them to access to a broadening array of resources and markets. These are essential considerations of any corporation that hopes to continue to remain relevant and vibrant (Stein, 1992). In the case of this Thai healthcare organization, a strategic alliance in Abu Dhabi tends to be particularly important in an unfamiliar market. While this provider has dealt with the Middle Eastern client base for a number of years, trying to enter the local market through a strategic alliance was a sound practice to build local alliances since local knowledge and connections are extremely valuable. It also enabled them to network ties outside their traditional boundaries and to possibly expand global resources of materials, capital, and/or expertise.

More enhanced operational capabilities and higher strategic goals are not achieved automatically. Management issues can be continual and difficult to resolve. These issues must be met by experienced, capable businesspersons, if an alliance is to be workable, productive and beneficial. Some alliances come apart; and some do not fulfill their purposes. Management complexities are enormous. To justify all the short term, extra costs, the rewards to both the hospital as well as the community must be enormous (Size, 1995).

Strategic alliances currently have been formed by this healthcare organization in Cambodia and Abu Dhabi and the 30 bed facility recently opened in Abu Dhabi is in negotiation to expand to a 60 bed facility (Anonymous, 2010). Abu Dhabi, however, presents a diverse challenge.

Issues such as cross-cultural communication present reoccurring problems that must be resolved on a daily basis. The Health Authority in Abu Dhabi (HAAD) has mandated that all health care facilities' staff need to be culturally sensitive and deliver culturally competent health care for the population residing in the Emirate of Abu Dhabi (Health Authority - Abu Dhabi, 2007). They have also identified five specific elements that are expected if the staffing and service delivery system is to become more culturally competent:

1. value diversity
2. have the capacity for cultural self-assessment
3. be conscious of the dynamics inherent when cultures interact
4. institutionalize cultural knowledge
5. develop programs and services that reflect an understanding of diversity between and within cultures

A strong source of competitive advantage can come from understanding and proactively managing these cultural differences. If the management is poor, it can create a source of poor team performance and divided patient/provider relationships. Cultural norms in one country can differ greatly from those of another country making a seemingly minor incident into something of extraordinary proportion.

Being an effective and trusted global healthcare services provider requires not only a network of competent healthcare professionals, but a genuine understanding by all key administrators, doctors, nurses and support staff of the cultural issues that affect the core of the healthcare process in another country. This healthcare organization has addressed active steps to generate value from the diversity of their internal talent to help them be best placed to compete in the increasingly international healthcare environment.

CONCLUSION

Competitive strategy has been experiencing a dramatic transformation from a situation where one competitor gains at the expense of another, to one that is a mutually beneficial collaborative effort, where that joint effort creates more economic value for all parties. This new competition involves looking forward and positioning oneself in future and possibly still undefined markets and developing these markets with collaborative efforts. In today's competitive global economy with its intensively interconnected business environment, a major challenge faced by healthcare organizations is how to maximize shareholder value and sustain growth, while at the same time creating economic value for all. Added to this challenge are the current global financial crisis and the political unrest facing Thailand. As this Thai healthcare organization looks at the future of global competitiveness, two necessary strategic ingredients are needed to achieve the long range organizational objectives:

1. To set up and be the central focal point of a cluster of partners with whom a new and continuous stream of attractive and innovative services with value are developed and offered to customers, and
2. Identifying unique combinations of these services by actively engaging customers in the development of those customized services to meet their continuously unique and changing needs.

The conclusion drawn from this follow up research is that if a company wants to attain a competitive advantage and remain profitable, the strategy, operations and organization must be consistent with each other coupled with unique service. Markets must be sought out that lack sufficient medical care to service their population. The most often sited reason for the global competitiveness of this healthcare provider using triangulation of data received was the ability to provide comfort and hospitality or "Thainess" (90% response) at the same time as providing excellent specialty and sub-specialty medical care and facilities (82% response) giving the organization both economy of scale to provide reasonable pricing and uniqueness in the medical care provided. In turn, that uniqueness and quality in service has attracted strategic alliances that provide further inroads to a wider base of patients in the global community.

It is in this venue that this Thai healthcare organization competes not to maximize their market share, but to maximize the **value of service** offered to the customer, those providing them with a stable position in the competitive global healthcare industry.

While in the short term, the current plans for this healthcare organization will not change appreciably, the continual cross-cultural management of good doctors, good nurses, improved information technology and assessment of the improvement of services continue to affect the strategy, operations and organization of the company. This constant self-assessment is seen as the main stabilizing force in keeping the Thai healthcare organization competitive while combating the uncertainty of current political unrest in Thailand and the global financial crisis.

ACKNOWLEDGMENT

The author acknowledges the Editor-in-Chief of the Journal, Professor John Wang, and the anonymous reviewers for their indispensible input that improved this paper significantly.

REFERENCES

Abu Dhabi Health Authority. (2007). *Policy on Cultural Sensitivity and Awareness in Health Care Facilities*. Reference Number: PPR/HCP/P0004/07 Issue Date: May 2007 Revision Date: May 2009 Version: II. Abu Dhabi, UAE: Author.

Abu Dhabi Urban Planning Council (UPC). (2007). *Abu Dhabi Plan 2003*. Abu Dhabi, UAE: Author.

Asch, S. M., Kerr, E. A., Keesey, J., Adams, J. L., Setodji, C. M., Malik, S., & McGlynn, E. A. (2006). Who is at greatest risk for receiving poor - quality health care? *The New England Journal of Medicine*, *354*(11), 1147–1156. doi:10.1056/NEJMsa044464

Becker, H. S. (1967). Whose side are we on? *Social Problems*, *14*, 239–247. doi:10.1525/sp.1967.14.3.03a00010

Bernheim, (2008). Influence of patients' socioeconomic status on clinical management decisions: A qualitative study. *Annals of Family Medicine*, *6*, 53–59. doi:10.1370/afm.749

Bowling, A., & Ebrahim, S. (2005). *Handbook of health research methods*. Buckingham: Open University Press.

Bushe, G. R. (1995). Organization development. Faculty of Business Administration, Simon Fraser University. *Organization Development Journal*, *13*(3), 14–22.

Buttle, F. (2003). *Customer relationship management: Concepts and tools*. Oxford: Elsevier Butterworth-Heinemann.

Cortez, N. (2008). Patients without Borders: The Emerging Global Market for Patients and the Evolution of Modern Health Care. *Indiana Law Journal, 83*; SMU Dedman School of Law Legal Studies Research Paper No. 00-24.

Ezzy, D. (2002). *Qualitative analysis: Practice and innovation*. Crows Nest, New South Wales, AU: Allen & Unwin.

Global Doctor Options. (2008). *Global Doctor Options Guide*. Las Vegas, NV: Author.

International Medical Travel Journal. (2010). *2010 Medical Tourism Climate Survey*. London, UK: Author.

Joint Commission International. (2007). *Joint Commission International Accreditation: Getting Started*. Oak Brook, IL: Author.

Kasikorn Research. (2007, October). Thailand Hospital Statistics. *Medical Tourism News*.

Levine, J. H. (1993). *Exceptions are the Rule: An Inquiry into Methods in the Social Sciences*. Boulder, CO: Westview Press.

Lieberman, M. B. (1987). The learning curve, diffusion, and competitive strategy. *Strategic Management Journal*, *8*(5), 441–452.

Miles, M. B., & Huberman, A. M. (1994). *Qualitative data analysis: An expanded sourcebook*. Thousand Oaks, CA: Sage Publications.

Porter, M. E. (1990). *The competitive advantage of nations*. New York: Free Press.

Porter, M. E. (1996). What is Strategy? *Harvard Business Review*, (November-December): 61–78.

Porter, M. E. (1998). *Competitive advantage: Creating and sustaining superior performance*. New York: Free Press.

Porter, M. E., & Teisberg, E. O. (2006). *Redefining health care: Creating value-based competition on results*. Boston, MA: Harvard Business School Press.

Shahin, A., & Mahbod, M. A. (2007). Prioritization of key performance indicators: An integration of analytical hierarchy process and goal setting. *International Journal of Productivity and Performance Management*, *56*(3), 226–240. doi:10.1108/17410400710731437

Size, T. (1995). *Strategic alliances: Some lessons from experience*: A Commentary, from Partners for the Dance: Forming Strategic Alliances in Health Care, edited by Arnold D. Kaluzny, Howard S. Zuckerman, and Thomas C. Ricketts, III. (1995). Foundation of the American College of Healthcare Executives. Ann Arbor, MI: Health Administration Press, pp. 40-52.

Spulber, D. F. (2007). *Global competitive strategy*. Cambridge, MA: Cambridge University Press.

Stein, B. (1992). *Strategic alliances: Some lessons from experience*. New York: Simon & Schuster.

Stokes, B. (2007). Bedside India. *National Journal*, *39*(18), 36–40.

Strauss, A., & Corbin, J. (1998). *Basics of qualitative research: grounded theory and procedures and techniques*. Newbury Park, CA: Sage Publications.

Thomas, D. R. (2006). A general inductive approach for analyzing qualitative evaluation data. *The American Journal of Evaluation*, *27*, 237–246. doi:10.1177/1098214005283748

Tourism Authority of Thailand, (2010). *Thailand tourism overview for 2009 and tourism goals and trends for 2010*.

Wiriyapong, N. (2010, April 30). Medical tourism operators want political healing. *Bangkok Post*. Retrieved from http://www.bangkokpost.com

Wockhardt Hospitals. (2008). *Wockhardt Hospitals*. Retrieved November 14, 2008 from http://www.companionglobalhealthcare.com/agents/providernetwork/wockhardthospitalsmumbai.aspx

Wolcott, H. F. (1994). Transforming qualitative data: Description, analysis, and interpretation. *Journal of Phenomenological Research*, *14*, 197–242.

Zuckerman, H. S. (2002). *Strategic alliances: A worldwide phenomenon comes to health care*. Washington, D.C.: Beard Books.

APPENDIX A

Questionnaire Used in the Paper

Questionnaire on Affect of the Political Unrest and Global Financial Crisis on Global Competitiveness?

Please answer the following questions as clearly and concisely as possible. Thank you for your cooperation in this questionnaire.

1. What is your administrative position?
2. Has the global financial crisis had an effect on your healthcare organization?
3. What steps is your healthcare organization taking to retain competitiveness?
4. Has the recent political unrest in Thailand affected foreign patient inflow?
5. What is your healthcare organization doing to counter the effects of the political unrest?
6. In addition to current plans, is your healthcare organization planning any additional strategies to remain competitive?

Thank you for your participation in this questionnaire.
All information provided here will be kept strictly confidential.

Compilation of References

Abbot, A. (2001). *Chaos of Disciplines*. Chicago, IL: University of Chicago Press. 14 (3 8)

Abu Dhabi Health Authority. (2007). *Policy on Cultural Sensitivity and Awareness in Health Care Facilities*. Reference Number: PPR/HCP/P0004/07 Issue Date: May 2007 Revision Date: May 2009 Version: II. Abu Dhabi, UAE: Author.

Abu Dhabi Urban Planning Council (UPC). (2007). *Abu Dhabi Plan 2003*. Abu Dhabi, UAE: Author.

Accabi, R., & Lopez, L. (1995). Outsourcing estremo per situazioni complesse. *L'Impresa,10*.

Ackoff, R. (1971). Towards a system of systems concepts. *Management Science*, *17*(11), 661–671. doi:10.1287/mnsc.17.11.661

ACM/AIS/AITP Joint Task Force on Computing Curricula. (2002). *IS 2002: Model Curriculum Guidelines for Undergraduate Degree Programs in Information Systems*. New York: Association for Computing Machinery.

ACM/AIS/IEEE The Joint Task Force on Computing Curricula. (2005). *Computing Curricula 2005: The Overview Report*. New York: Association for Computing Machinery.

ACM/IEEE The Joint Task Force on Computing Curricula. (2000). *Computing Curricula 2000: Graduate IS Curricula*. New York: Association for Computing Machinery.

Adams, J. (1995/2000). *Risk*. London, UK: Routledge. 1 (12 15)

Adamson, G. (2009). Portals and the challenge of simplifying internet business use. *International Journal of Web Portals*, *1*(1), 16–33.

Adler, R. T. (2004). An exploratory study of team perceptions of trust and distrust in a contract negotiation setting. The Institute of Behavioral and Applied Management. *Journal of Behavioral and Applied Management*, *5*(3), 245–278.

Afuh, A. (2004). *Business Models: A Strategic Management Approach*. New York, NY: McGraw-Hill Irwin. 1, (12)

Agarwal, R., & Prasad, J. (1997). The Role of Innovation Characteristics and Perceived Voluntariness in the Acceptance of Information Technologies. *Decision Sciences*, *28*(3), 557–581. doi:10.1111/j.1540-5915.1997.tb01322.x

Agarwal, R., & Prasad, J. (1998). A Conceptual and Operational Definition of Personal Innovativeness in the Domain of Information Technology. *Information Systems Research*, *9*(2), 204–215. doi:10.1287/isre.9.2.204

Ahituv, N., Munro, M. C., & Wand, Y. (1981). The value of information in information analysis. *Information & Management*, *4*(3), 143–150. doi:10.1016/0378-7206(81)90041-0

AIEA & CLUSIT. (2006). *The IT outsourcing: best practice and auditing*. Milano: Aiea-Clusit.

Ajzen, I. (1991). The Theory of Planned Behaviour. *Organizational Behavior and Human Decision Processes*, *50*(2), 179–211. doi:10.1016/0749-5978(91)90020-T

Ajzen, I., & Fishbein, M. (1980). *Understanding Attitudes and Predicting Social Behaviour*. Englewood Cliffs, NJ: Prentice-Hall.

Al Najjari, N. (2005). Le Pmi tra delocalizzazione e neo protezionismo: quali opzioni per chi va, quali scelte per chi resta. [Electronic version]. *PMI*, *4*, 31–37.

Aladwani, A. M., & Pavia, P. C. (2002). Developing and validating an instrument for measuring user perceived web quality. *Information & Management*, *39*(6), 457–476. doi:10.1016/S0378-7206(01)00113-6

Albrecht, K., & Zemke, R. (1985). *Service America!* New York, NY: Warner Books. 12 (3)

Alex Macario, M., MBA, Dean Morris, M., & Sharon Morris, R., BSN, CNOR. (2007). Initial clinical evaluation of a handheld device for detecting retained surgical gauze sponges using radiofrequency identification yechnology. *Archives of Surgery*, *141*, 659–662. doi:10.1001/archsurg.141.7.659

All, A. (2008). ITIL's Popularity Continues to Grow. http://www.itbusinessedge.com/blogs/tve/?p=286 [On-line].

Allen, G., Dramlitsch, T., Foster, I., Karonis, N., Ripeanu, M., Seidel, E., and Toonen, B. (2001). Supporting Efficient Execution in Heterogeneous Distributed Computing Environments with Cactus and Globus. Supercomputing 2001.

Allen, P. (2005). *Service-oriented business process redesign. In Proceedings of Business Process Management Conference Europe 2005*. Business Process Management Group.

Allport, G., Vernon, P., & Lindzey, G. (1951). *Study of values. Manual of directions*. Boston, MA: Houghton Mifflin.

Alter, S. (2003). 18 Reasons Why IT-Reliant Work Systems Should Replace "The IT Artifact" as the Core Subject Matter of the IS Field. *Communications of AIS*, *12*, 366–395.

Alter, S. (2002). *Information Systems: The Foundations of e-Business*. Upper Saddle River, NJ: Prentice Hall. 10, (12)

Alter, S. (2006). *The Work System Method: Connecting People, Processes, and IT for Business Results*. Larkspur, CA: Work Systems Press. 2 (10 15)

Alter, S. (2008). Service Systems Fundamentals: Work systems, value chains and life cycle. *IBM Systems Journal*, 47(1). 1 (11)

Anckar, B., Carlsson, C., & Walden, P. (2003). Factors Affecting Adoption Decisions and Intents In *Mobile Commerce: Empirical Insights, 16th Bled eCommerce Conference. eTransformation*, 886- 900.

Anderson, C. (2006). *The Long Tail: Why the Future of Business Is Selling Less of More*. New York, NY: Hyperion. 12 (4)

Anderson, D. R., Sweeney, D. J., & Williams, T. A. (2005). *Statistics for Business and Economics* (9th ed.). Mason, OH: Thomson South-Western.

Anderson, J. C., Narus, J. A. Narus, & van Rossum, W. (2006). Customer Value Propositions in Business Markets. *Harvard Business Review,* 84(3), 90-99. 1 (4 15)

Andrews, K. R. (1987). *The concept of corporate strategy*. Homewood, IL: Irwin.

Angeles, R. (2005). RFID technologies: Supply Chains Applications and Implementation Issues. *Information Systems Management*, *22*, 51–56. doi:10.1201/1078/44912.22.1.20051201/85739.7

Anonymous.(2008). Improving education outcomes. *OECD Economic Surveys,* 2008(7), 93-132.

Ansoff, H. I. (1965). *Corporate strategy*. New York: McGraw-Hill.

Anthes, G. H. (2008). ITIL v3: Five ways to make it work for you. http://www.computerworld.com/action/article.do?command=printArticleBasic&articleId=9077960 [On-line].

Arambewela, R., & Hall, J. (2006, July). A comparative analysis of international education satisfaction using Servqual. *Journal of Service Research*, *6*(special issue), 141–163.

Argote, L. (2005). *Organizational Learning: Creating, Retaining and Transferring Knowledge*. New York, NY: Springer. 11 (1 15)

Argyris, C. (1992/1999). *On Organizational Learning*. Second Edition. Malden, MA: Blackwell. 11 (8 12)

Argyris, C., & Schon, D. A. (1996). Organizational *Learning II: Theory, Method, Practice*. New York, NY: Addison-Wesley. 11 (12)

Arnold, V. (1995). Discussion of an experimental evaluation of measurements of information system effectiveness. *Journal of Information Systems*, *9*(2), 85–91.

Arnold, D., Casanova, H., and Dongarra, J. (2003). Innovation of the NetSolve Grid Computing System. Concurrency and Computation: Practice and Experience.

Arrow, K. J. (1974). *The Limits of Organization*. New York, NY: W.W. Norton & Company. 3 (6)

Arthur, W. B. (1994). *Increasing Returns and Path Dependence in the Economy.* Ann Arbor, MI: University of Michigan Press. 3 (1)

Asch, S. M., Kerr, E. A., Keesey, J., Adams, J. L., Setodji, C. M., Malik, S., & McGlynn, E. A. (2006). Who is at greatest risk for receiving poor - quality health care? *The New England Journal of Medicine*, *354*(11), 1147–1156. doi:10.1056/NEJMsa044464

Associated Press. (2003). U.S. tops the world in school spending but not test scores. *USA Today,* September 16.

Austvold, E., & Carter, K. (2005). *Service-oriented architecture: survey findings on deployment and plans for the future*. AMR Research Market Analytix Report: Market Trends Series.

Ba, S., Stinchcombe, M., Whinston, A. B., & Zhang, H. (1999). Trusted third parties in the electronic marketplace: An evolutionary game approach. In *Proceedings of the 5th Americas Conference on Information Systems* (pp. 238-240).

Baden-Fuller, C., Targett, D., & Hunt, B. (2000). Outsourcing to outmanoeuvre: outsourcing re-defines competitive strategy and structure. *European Management Journal*, *18*(3), 285–295. doi:10.1016/S0263-2373(00)00010-4

Bailey, J. E., & Pearson, S. W. (1983). Development of a tool for measuring and analyzing computer user satisfaction. *Management Science*, *29*(5), 530–546. doi:10.1287/mnsc.29.5.530

Bailey, J., & Bakos, Y. (1997). An exploratory study of the emerging role of electronic intermediaries. *International Journal of Electronic Commerce*, *1*(3), 7–20.

Bakos, Y. (1998). The emerging role of electronic marketplaces on the Internet. *Communications of the ACM*, *41*(8), 35–42. doi:10.1145/280324.280330

Bakos, Y., & Katsamakas, E. (2008). Design and ownership of two-sided networks: Implications for Internet platforms. *Journal of Management Information Systems*, *25*(2), 171–202. doi:10.2753/MIS0742-1222250208

Baldwin, C. Y., & Clark, K. B. (2000). *Design Rules: Volume 1. The Power of Modularity.* Cambridge, MA: MIT Press. 7 (3)

Barki, H., & Hartwick, J. (1994). Measuring user participation, user involvement, and user attitude. *Management Information Systems Quarterly*, *18*(1), 59–82. doi:10.2307/249610

Barley, S. R., & Orr, J. E. (1997). Introduction: The Neglected Workforce. In S. R. Barley & J. E. Orr (Ed.), *Between Craft and Science: Technical Work in U.S. Settings.* Ithaca, NY: Cornell University Press. 8 (3)

Barlow, S., Parry, S., & Faulkner, M. (2005). *Sense and Respond: The Journey to Customer Purpose*. New York, NY: Palgrave/MacMillan. 4 (11)

Barn, B., Dexter, H., Oussena, S., & Sparks, D. (2007). SOA-MDK: Towards a method development kit for service oriented system development. In Magyar, G., Knapp, G., Wojtkowski, W., Wojtkowski, W. G., & Zupančič, J. (Eds.), *Advances in information systems development: New methods and practice for the networked society* (pp. 191–201). Berlin: Springer.

Barnard, C. I. (1938/1968). *The Functions of the Executive*. Thirtieth Anniversary Edition. Boston, MA: Harvard University Press. 1 (11 12)

Barnes, S. J., & Vidgen, R. T. (2000, July 3-5). *WebQual: An Exploration of Web-Site Quality.* Paper presented at the Proceedings of the 8th European Conference on Information Systems, Trends in Information and Communication Systems for the 21st Century, ECIS 2000, Vienna, Austria.

Baroudi, J. J., Olson, M. H., & Ives, B. (1986). An empirical study of the impact of user involvement on system usage and information satisfaction. *Communications of the ACM*, *29*(3), 232–238. doi:10.1145/5666.5669

Baroudi, J. J., & Orlikowski, W. J. (1988). A short-from measure of user information satisfaction: A psychometric evaluation and notes on use. *Journal of Management Information Systems*, *4*(4), 44–60.

Barthélemy, J., & Dominique, G. (2004). The determinants of total IT outsourcing: An empirical investigation of French and German firms. *Journal of Computer Information Systems*, *44*(3), 91–98.

Barthélemy, J. (2001). The hidden costs of IT outsourcing. *Sloan Management Review, Spring.*

Bastiat, F. (1848/1964). *Selected Essays on Political Economy*, Patrick S. Sterling, trans, G. B. de Huzar (Ed.). Princeton, NJ: D. Van Nordstrand. 3 (6 8 11)

Bastiat, F. (1850/1979). Economic *Harmonies.* Irvington-on-Hudson, NY: The Foundation for Economics Education. 3 (6 8 11)

Bateson, J. E. G. (1979). Why We Need Service Marketing. In Ferrell, O. C., Brown, S. W., & Lamb, C. W. (Eds.), *Conceptual and Theoretical Developments in Marketing* (pp. 131–146). Chicago: American Marketing Association.

Bauer, R. A. (1960). Consumer behavior as risk taking. In R. Hancock (Ed.), *Dynamic Marketing for a Changing World, Proceedings of 43rd Conference* (pp. 389-398). Chicago, IL: American Marketing Association.

Baumol, W. J. (2002). Services as Leaders and the Leader of the Services. In J. Gadrey, & F. Gallouj (Ed.), *Productivity, Innovation and Knowledge in Services: New Economic & Socio-Economic Approaches,* (pp. 147-163). Cheltenham, UK: Edward Elgar, 3 (1)

Baumol, W. J., Litan, R. E., & Schramm, C. J. (2007). *Good Capitalism, Bad Capitalism, and the Economies of Growth and Prosperity*. New Haven, CT: Yale University Press. 11 (3)

Bausch, K. C. (2001). *The Emerging Consensus in Social Systems Theory*. New York, NY: Kluwer. 14 (1)

Beachboard, J., Conger, S., Galup, S., Venkataraman, R., Probst, J., & Hernandez, A. (2007). *A roadmap*. IT Service Managementin the IS Curriculum.

Beachboard, J., Conger, S., Galup, S., Hernandez, A., Probst, J., & Venkataraman, R. (2007). AMCIS 2007 Panel on IT Service Management: IT Service Management in the IS Curriculum. *CAIS,* 20(35).

Beatty, S. E., & Smith, S. M. (1987). External search effort: An investigation across several product categories. *The Journal of Consumer Research*, *14*(June), 83–95. doi:10.1086/209095

Beatty, S. E., Kahle, L. R., Homer, P., & Misra, S. (1985). Alternative measurement approaches to consumer values: The list of values and the Rokeach value survey. *Psychology and Marketing*, *2*(3), 181–200. doi:10.1002/mar.4220020305

Becker, H. S. (1967). Whose side are we on? *Social Problems*, *14*, 239–247. doi:10.1525/sp.1967.14.3.03a00010

Becker, G. S. (1976/1990). *The Economic Approach to Human Behavior*. Chicago, IL: University of Chicago Press. 3 (8 15)

Beer, S. (1981). *Brain of the Firm*. Chichester: John Wiley & Sons.

Beinhocker, E. D. (2006). *The Origin of Wealth: Evolution, Complexity, and the Radical Remaking of Economics*. Cambridge, MA: Harvard Business School Press. 3 (8 1 14 15)

Beldona, S., Morrison, A. M., & O'Leary, J. (2005). Online shopping motivations and pleasure travel products: A correspondence analysis. *Tourism Management*, *26*, 561–570. doi:10.1016/j.tourman.2004.03.008

Bell, D. (1976). *The Coming of Post-Industrial Society*. New York: Basic Books.

Bell, D. (1973/1999). The *Coming of the Post-Industrial Society: A Venture in Social Forecasting*. New York, NY: Basic. 12 (3)

Bell, D. (1981). The Social Framework of the Information Society. In Forester, T. (Ed.) *The Microelectronics Revolution*. Cambridge, MA: the MIT Press, 500-549.

Beniger, J. R. (1986). *The Control Revolution: Technological and Economic Origins of the Information Society.* Cambridge, MA: Harvard University Press. 9 (3 10)

Benkler, Y. (2007). *The Wealth of Networks: How Social Production Transforms Markets and Freedom*. New Haven, CT: Yale University Press. 3 (10 8)

Bennett, J. T., & McCrohan, K. F. (1993). Public policy issues in the marketing of seals of approval for food. *The Journal of Consumer Affairs*, *27*(2), 397–415. doi:10.1111/j.1745-6606.1993.tb00755.x

Benson, D. H. (1982). A field study of end-user computing: Findings and issues. *Management Information Systems Quarterly*, *6*(2), 11–31.

Berger, P. L., & Luckmann, T. (1967). *The Social Construction of Reality: A Treatise in the Sociology of Knowledge*. New York, NY: Anchor. 8 (1 15)

Berman, F., Fox, C. G., & Hey, A. (2003). *Grid Computing: Making the global infrastructure a reality*. Wiley Press.

Bernheim, (2008). Influence of patients' socioeconomic status on clinical management decisions: A qualitative study. *Annals of Family Medicine*, *6*, 53–59. doi:10.1370/afm.749

Bernstein, P. L. (1998). *Against the Gods: The Remarkable Story of Risk*. New York, NY: Wiley. 12 (3)

Berry, L. L. (1995). *On Great Service: A Framework for Action*. New York, NY: Free Press. 4 (12)

Bertion, E., Castano, S., Ferrari, E., & Mesiti, E. (1999). Controlled access and dissemination of xml documents. In *Processings of the second international workshop on Web information and data management* (pp. 22–27). ACM Press. doi:10.1145/319759.319770

Bertion, E., & Ferrari, E. (2002). Secure and selective dis-semination of xml documents. *ACM Transactions on Information and System Security*, *5*(3), 290–331. doi:10.1145/545186.545190

Bertion, E. (2002). Protecting XML documents. In *Proceedings of Computer Software and Applications Conference* (pp.132-133), Taiwan.

Bettman, J. R. (1973). Perceived risk and its components. *JMR, Journal of Marketing Research*, *10*(2), 84–90. doi:10.2307/3149824

Bhalla, A., Sodhi, M. S., & Son, B. (2008). Is more IT offshoring better? An exploratory study of western companies offshoring to South East Asia. *Journal of Operations Management*, *26*, 322–335. doi:10.1016/j.jom.2007.02.005

Bhargava, H. K., & Choudhary, V. (2004). Economics of an information intermediary with aggregation benefits. *Information Systems Research*, *15*(1), 22–36. doi:10.1287/isre.1040.0014

Bhatnagar, A., & Ghose, S. (2004). Segmenting consumers based on the benefits and risks of Internet shopping. *Journal of Business Research*, *57*(12), 1352–1360. doi:10.1016/S0148-2963(03)00067-5

Bhimani, A. (1996). Securing the commercial Internet. *Communications of the ACM*, *39*(6), 29–35. doi:10.1145/228503.228509

Bianculli, D., & Ghezzi, C. (2007). *Monitoring conversational web services*. Paper presented at the 2nd International Workshop on Service Oriented Software Engineering (IW-SOSWE'07), Dubrovnik, Croatia. Retrieved 21.1., 2008, from http://www.selab.isti.cnr.it/IW-SOSWE07/program.html.

Bieberstein, N., Sanjay, B., Fiammante, M., Jones, K., & Shah, R. (2006). *Service-Oriented Architecture Compass: Business Value, Planning, and Enterprise Roadmap*. Upper Saddle River, NJ: IBM Press.

Bieberstein, N., Bose, S., Walker, L., & Lynch, A. (2005). Impact of service-oriented architecture on enterprise systems, organizational structures, and individuals. *IBM Systems Journal*, *44*(4), 691–708. doi:10.1147/sj.444.0691

Biswas, D., & Biswas, A. (2004). The diagnostic role of signals in the contest of perceived risks in online shopping: Do signals matter more on the web? *Journal of Interactive Marketing*, *18*(3), 30–45. doi:10.1002/dir.20010

Bitner, M. J., & Brown, S. W. (2006). The Evolution and Discovery of Services Science in Business Schools. *Communications of the ACM*, *49*(7), 73–78. doi:10.1145/1139922.1139952

Bitner, M. J., Ostrom, A. L., & Morgan, F. N. (2007). Service Blueprinting: A Practical Tool for Service Innovation. Working Paper, Center for Services Leadership, Arizona State University.

Blackwell, R. D., Miniard, P. W., & Engel, J. F. (2003). *Consumer Behavior*. Orlando, FL: Harcourt.

Blake, M. B. (2007). Decomposing composition: Service-oriented software engineers. *IEEE Software*, *24*(6), 68–77. doi:10.1109/MS.2007.162

Blum, V., & Fallon, J. (2002). Welsh visitor attraction websites: multipurpose tools or technological tokenism? *Journal of Information Technology and Tourism*, *4*(34), 191–201.

Bockem, S. (1994). A generalized model of horizontal product differentiation. *The Journal of Industrial Economics*, *42*(3), 287–298. doi:10.2307/2950571

Bohn, R., & Jaikumar, R. (2005). *From Filing and Fitting to Flexible Manufacturing*. Hanover, MA: Now Publishers Inc. 3 (9 5)

Boisot, M. H. (2002). *Knowledge Assets: Securing Competitive Advantage in the Information Economy*. Oxford, UK: Oxford University Press. 1 (10 15)

Bouch, A., Kuchinsky, A., & Bhatti, N. (2000, April 1-6). *Quality is in the Eye of the Beholder: Meeting Users' Requirements for Internet Quality of Service*. Paper presented at the Proc. of CHI'00, The Hague, The Netherlands.

Bourret, R. (2003). XML Database Products.

Bouwman, H., Carlsson, C., Moline-Castillo, F., Walden, P. (2006). Barriers and drivers in the adoption of current and future mobile services in Filland, Telematics and Informatics.

Bowen, D. E. (1990a). Interdisciplinary Study of Service: Some Progress, Some Prospects. *Journal of Business Research*, *20*(1), 71–79. doi:10.1016/0148-2963(90)90044-E

Bowen, D. E., Chase, R. B., Cummings, Th. G., & Associates. (Edts). (1990). *Service Management Effectiveness, Balancing Strategy, Organization and Human Resources, Operations, and Marketing*. San Francisco: Jossey-Bass Publishers.

Bowling, A., & Ebrahim, S. (2005). *Handbook of health research methods*. Buckingham: Open University Press.

Boyatzis, R. E. (1998). *Transforming qualitative information: thematic analysis and code development*. Thousand Oaks, CA: Sage Publications.

Brambilla, M., Ceri, S., Comai, S., & Fraternali, P. (2006). A CASE tool for modelling and automatically generating web service-enabled applications. *Int. J. Web Engineering and Technology*, *2*(4).

Brambilla, M., Ceri, S., Facca, F. M., Celino, I., Cerizza, D., & Della Valle, E. (2007). Model-driven design and development of semantic web service applications. *ACM Transactions on Internet Technology*, *8*(1), 3:1-3:31.

Brandes, H., Lilliecreutz, J., & Brege, S. (1997). Outsourcing: success or failure? *European Journal of Purchasing & Supply Management*, *3*, 63–75. doi:10.1016/S0969-7012(97)00001-4

Bray, T., Paoli, J., Sperberg, M., & Maler, E. (2000). Extensible Markup Language (XML) 1.1 (Second Edition). World Wide Web Consortium (W3C), Cambridge, MA, USA.

Breitenbach, C. S., & Van Doren, D. C. (1998). Value-added marketing in the digital domain: enhancing the utility of the Internet. *Journal of Consumer Marketing, 15*(6), 558–575. doi:10.1108/07363769810241436

Breivik, E., Troye, S. V., & Olsson, U. H. (1998). *Dimensions of Intangibility and Their Impact on Product Evaluation,* working paper presented at the annual conference (October) of the Association for Consumer Research, Montreal, Canada.

Broadbent, M., & Kitzis, E. S. (2005). *The New CIO Leader*. Harvard Business School Press.

Brodie, C., Karat, C.-M., & Karat, J. (2004). Creating an e-Commerce Environment Where Consumers are Willing to Share Personal Information. In Karat, C.-M., Blom, J. O., & Karat, J. (Eds.), *Designing Personalized User Experiences in eCommerce* (pp. 185–206). Kluwer Academic Publishers. doi:10.1007/1-4020-2148-8_11

Brown, M. A. (1976). Values - a necessary but neglected ingredient of motivation on the job. *Academy of Management Review, 1*(4), 15–23. doi:10.2307/257721

Bruton, N. (2004). *Managing the IT services process.* Oxford: Butterworth-Heinemann.

Bryson, J. R., Daniels, P. W., & Warf, B. (2004). *Service Worlds: People, Organizations, and Technology.* New York, NY: Routledge. 3 (8 9 10 11)

Buchanan, M. (2001). *Ubiquity: Why Catastrophes Happen.* New York, NY: Three River Press. 14 (3)

Buchanan, M. (2007). *The Social Atom: Why the rich get richer, cheaters get caught, and your neighbors usually look like you.* New York, NY: Bloomsbury. 8 (14)

Buhalis, D., & Deimezi, O. (2002). E-tourism developments in Greece: information communication technologies adoption for the strategic management of Greek tourism industry. *Tourism and Hospitality Research, 5*(2), 103–128. doi:10.1057/palgrave.thr.6040011

Buhalis, D., & Licata, M. (2002). The future of eTourism intermediaries. *Tourism Management, 23*(3), 207–220. doi:10.1016/S0261-5177(01)00085-1

Buhler, P. A., & Vidal, J. M. (2005). Towards Adaptive Workflow Enactment Using Multiagent Systems. *Information Technology Management, 6*(1), 61–87. doi:10.1007/s10799-004-7775-2

Bureau of Economic Analysis. (2008). htpp//www.bea.gov/national, Retrieved 4-28-2008.

Bush, V. (1945). As We May Think. *The Atlantic Monthly,* 176(1), 101-108 (July). 10 (12)

Bushe, G. R. (1995). Organization development. Faculty of Business Administration, Simon Fraser University. *Organization Development Journal, 13*(3), 14–22.

Buttle, F. (2003). *Customer relationship management: Concepts and tools.* Oxford: Elsevier Butterworth-Heinemann.

Cabral, L., Domingue, J., Motta, E., Payne, T. R., & Hakimpour, F. (2004). *Approaches to semantic web services: An overview and comparisons.* Paper presented at the ESWS'04.

Cai, L. A., Card, J. A., & Cole, S. T. (2004a). Content delivery performance of world wide web sites of US tour operators focusing on destinations in China. *Tourism Management, 25*(2), 219–227. doi:10.1016/S0261-5177(03)00095-5

Cai, L. A., Feng, R., & Breiter, D. (2004b). Tourism purchase decision involvement and information preferences. *Journal of Vacation Marketing, 10*(2), 138–148. doi:10.1177/135676670401000204

Calder, B. J., Phillips, L. W., & Tybout, A. M. (1981). Designing research for application. *The Journal of Consumer Research, 8*(2), 197–207. doi:10.1086/208856

Callen, J. L. (1994). Money donations, volunteering and organizational efficiency. *Journal of Productivity Analysis, 5*, 215–228. doi:10.1007/BF01073908

Campbell, C., Ray, G., & Muhanna, W. A. (2005). Search and collusion in electronic markets. *Management Science, 51*(3), 497–507. doi:10.1287/mnsc.1040.0327

Canavesio, M., & Martinez, E. (2007). Enterprise modeling of a project-oriented fractal company for SMEs networking. *Computers in Industry*, *58*(8-9), 794–813. doi:10.1016/j.compind.2007.02.005

Cano, V., & Prentice, R. (1998). Opportunities for endearment to place through electronic "visiting" WWW homepages and the tourism promotion of Scotland. *Tourism Management*, *19*(1), 67–73. doi:10.1016/S0261-5177(97)00092-7

Cao, J., Sun, L., & Wang, H. (2005). Towards secure XML document with usage control, *Proceedings of The 7th Asia Pacific Web Conference, Lecture Notes in Computer Science, Springer* (pp.296-307), Shanghai, China.

Capozzi, M. M., Lowell, S. M., & Silverman, L. (2003). Knowledge management comes to philanthropy. *The McKinsey Quarterly*, *2*, 89.

Carlsson, C., Carlsson, J., Hyvönen, K., Puhakainen, J., & Walden, P. (2006). *Adoption of Mobile Devices/Services – Searching for Answers with the UTAUT *Institute for Advanced Management Systems Research.* Finland: Åbo Akademi.

Carlsson, Christer, Hyvönen, Kaarina, Repo, Petteri and Walden, Pirkko, Asynchronous Adoption Patterns of Mobile Services. IAMSR/Abo Akademi University and National Consumer Research Centre, 2005

Casaló, L. V., Flavián, C. & Guinalíu, M. (in press). Determinants of the intention to participate in firm-hosted online travel communities and effects on consumer behavioural intentions. *Tourism Management*, 2010, doi: 10.1016/j.tourman.2010.04.007.

Cases, A. (2002). Perceived risk and risk-reduction strategies in Internet shopping. *International Review of Retail, Distribution and Consumer Research*, *12*(4), 375–394. doi:10.1080/09593960210151162

Castells, M. (2004). *The Network Society: A Cross-cultural Perspective.* Cheltenham, UK: Edward Elger. 8 (3 10 11 12)

Cater-Steel, A., & Toleman, M. (2007). Education for IT service management standards. *International Journal of IT Standards and Standardization Research*, *5*, 27–41.

Cater-Steel, A. P., & McBride, N. (2007). *IT Service Management Improvement – an Actor Network Perspective.* Paper presented at the European Conference on Information Systems.

Cater-Steel, A. P., & Pollard, C. (2008). *Conflicting views on ITIL implementation: managed as a project – or business as usual?* Paper presented at the International Conference on Information Resources Management (Conf-IRM).

Cater-Steel, A. P., Tan, W., & Toleman, M. (2009). itSMF Australia 2009 Conference: Summary of Report of ITSM Standards and Frameworks Survey.

Cavalcanti, M. C., Targino, R., Baião, F., Rössle, S. C., Bisch, P. M., & Pires, P. F. (2005). Managing structural genomic workflows using Web services. *Data & Knowledge Engineering*, *53*(1), 45–74. doi:10.1016/S0169-023X(04)00112-0

Cerf, V. G. (1991). Networks. *Scientific American*, *265*(3), 42–51. doi:10.1038/scientificamerican0991-72

Chan, J., Leung, M., & Wang, Z. (2006). Impact of school facilities on working behavior of teachers. *International Journal of Strategic Property Management*, *10*(2), 79–91.

Chandler, A. D. (1977). *The Visible Hand: The Managerial Revolution in American Business.* Cambridge, MA: Belknap/Harvard University Press. 3 (11 12)

Chang, M. K., Waiman, C., & Lai, V. S. (2005). Literature derived reference models for the adoption of online shopping. *Information & Management*, *42*, 543–559. doi:10.1016/S0378-7206(04)00051-5

Chappell, D. (2007). *Introducing sca.* Chappell & Associates.

Chase, R. B., Jacobs, F. R., & Aquilano, N. J. (2004). *Operations Management for Competitive Advantage.* Instructor's Edition. Tenth Edition. New York, NY: McGraw Hill Irwin. 2 (5 15)

Chaudhuri, A. (1997). Consumption emotion and perceived risk: A macro-analytic approach. *Journal of Business Research*, *39*(2), 81–92. doi:10.1016/S0148-2963(96)00144-0

Checkland, P. (2000). Soft Systems Methodology: a 30-year Retrospective. In Checkland, P. (Ed.), *Systems Thinking, Systems Practice* (pp. A1–A65). Chichester: Wiley.

Checkland, P., & Holwell, S. (1998/2005). *Information, Systems, and Information Systems: Making Sense of the Field.* Chichester, UK: Wiley. 10 (1 14 15)

Chen, Z., & Dubinsky, A. J. (2003). A conceptual model of perceived customer value in e-commerce: A preliminary investigation. *Psychology and Marketing*, *20*(4), 323–347. doi:10.1002/mar.10076

Chen, T. Y. (2008). Knowledge sharing in virtual enterprises via an ontology-based access control approach. *Computers in Industry*, *59*(5), 502–519. doi:10.1016/j.compind.2007.12.004

Chen, Q., & Wells, W. D. (1999). Attitude towards the site. *Journal of Advertising Research*, *39*(5), 27–38.

Chen, R., & He, F. (2003). Examination of brand knowledge, perceived risk and consumers' intention to adopt an online retailer. *TQM & Business Excellence*, *14*(6), 677–693. doi:10.1080/1478336032000053825

Chen, Z., & Dubinsky, A. J. (2003). A conceptual model of perceived customer value in e-commerce: A preliminary investigation. *Psychology and Marketing*, *20*(4), 323–347. doi:10.1002/mar.10076

Chen-Burger, Y. H. (2003). A Semantic Based Workflow Management in a Virtual Organization. E-Science Workflow Workshop.

Cheng, C. Y., & Prabhu, V. (2007, May 19 - 23). *Applying RFID for Cutting Tool Supply Chain Management.* Paper presented at the the 2007 Industrial Engineering Research Conference, Nashville, USA.

Cheng, C. Y., & Prabhu, V. (2007). Applying RFID for cutting tool supply chain management. In *Proceedings of the 2007 Industrial Engineering Research Conference*, Nashville, TN.

Chesbrough, H., & Spohrer, J. (2006). A Research Manifesto for Services Sciences. *Communications of the ACM*, *49*(7), 35–40. doi:10.1145/1139922.1139945

Chesbrough, H., & Spohrer, J. (2006). A Research Manifesto for Services Science. *Communications of the ACM*, *49*(7), 35–40. doi:10.1145/1139922.1139945

Chesbrough, H. (2005). Toward a science of services (in Breakthrough Ideas of 2005). *Harvard Business Review*, 83(2), 17-54. 1 (14)

Chesbrough, H. (2006). *Open Business Models: How to thrive in the New Innovation Landscape*. Boston, MA: Harvard Business School Press. 7 (12)

Chesbrough, H., & Spohrer, J. (2006). A research manifesto for services science. *Communications of the ACM*, 49(7), 35-40. 1 (14)

Childe, V. G. (1936/2003). *Man Makes Himself.* Nottingham, UK: Spokesman/Watts. 3 (8)

Chiou, J.-S. (2004). The antecedents of consumers' loyalty toward internet service providers. *Information & Management*, *41*(6), 685–695. doi:10.1016/j.im.2003.08.006

Cho, J., & Lee, J. (2006). An integrated model of risk and risk-reducing strategies. *Journal of Business Research*, *59*(1), 112–120. doi:10.1016/j.jbusres.2005.03.006

Christopher, M., Payne, A., & Ballantyne, D. (1991). *Relationship Marketing: Bringing quality, customer service, and marketing together.* London, UK: Butterworth-Heinemann. 4 (12)

Christopher, W. F. (2007). *Holistic Management: Managing What Matters for Company Success.* Hoboken, NJ: Wiley-Interscience. 14 (1 11 12 15)

Chung, T., & Law, R. (2003). Developing a performance indicator for hotel websites. *International Journal of Hospitality Management*, *22*(1), 119–125. doi:10.1016/S0278-4319(02)00076-2

Clark, C. (1940). *The Conditions of Economic Progress*. London: Macmillan.

Clark, C. (1940/1957). *Conditions of Economic Progress*. Third Edition. New York, NY: Macmillan. 3 (11)

Clippinger, J. H., III. (1999). *The Biology of Business: Decoding the Natural Laws of Enterprise*. Jossey-Bass. 14 (3 11)

Coase, R. H. (1937). The Nature of the Firm. *Economica*, 4, 386-405. 3 (11)

Coase, R. H. (1990). *The Firm, the Market, and the Law*. Chicago, IL: University of Chicago Press. 3 (6 11)

Cockburn, C., & Wilson, T. D. (1996). Business use of the world wide web. *International Journal of Information Management*, *16*(2), 83–102. doi:10.1016/0268-4012(95)00071-2

Codd, E. F. (1970). A Relational Model of Data for Large Shared Data Banks. *Communications of the ACM*, *13*, 377–387. doi:10.1145/362384.362685

Cohen, L., & Young, A. (2006). *Multisourcing: Moving Beyond Outsourcing to Achieve Growth and Agility*. Boston, MA: Harvard Business School Press. 11 (6 12 15)

Cohen, S. S., & Zysman, J. (1988). *Manufacturing Matters: The Myth of the Post-Industrial Economy*. New York, NY: Basic. 3 (10 13)

Collins, H., & Kusch, M. (1999). The *Shape of Actions: What Humans and Machines Can Do*. Cambridge, MA: MIT Press. 8 (10 Collins, J (2005). Why Business Thinking is Not the Answer: Good to Great and the Social Sector: A monograph to Accompany *Good to Great. Why Some Companies Make the Leap ... and Others Don't*. ISBN-10: 0-9773264-0-3. 12 (13)

Collins, H., Evans, R., & Gorman, M. (2007). Trading zones and interactional expertise. *Studies in History and Philosophy of Science*, 39(1). 13 (8)

Conger, S. (2008). *Tech 7370 Requirements and Sourcing Course (Rep. No. Unit 4)*. Irving, TX: University of Dallas.

Conger, S., & Schultze, U. (2008). *IT Governance and Control: Making sense of Standards, Guidelines, and Frameworks*. Chicago, IL: The Society for Information Management Advanced Practices Council.

Conger, S., Venkataraman, R., Hernandez, A., & Probst, J. (2008). (Forthcoming). Market Potential for ITSM Students. *Survey (London, England)*.

Cook, D., Goh, C., & Chung, C. (1999). Service Typologies: a State of the Art Survey. *Production and Operations Management*, *8*(3), 318–338. doi:10.1111/j.1937-5956.1999.tb00311.x

Cooper, R. G., & Edgett, S. J. (1999). *Product Development for the Service Sector: Lessons from Market Leaders*. Cambridge, MA: Basic Books. 7 (12)

Corbitt, B. J., Thanasankit, T., & Yi, H. (2003). Trust and e-commerce: a study of consumer perceptions. *Electronic Commerce Research and Applications*, *2*(3), 203–215. doi:10.1016/S1567-4223(03)00024-3

Cortez, N. (2008). Patients without Borders: The Emerging Global Market for Patients and the Evolution of Modern Health Care. *Indiana Law Journal, 83*; SMU Dedman School of Law Legal Studies Research Paper No. 00-24.

COSEPUP. (2007). Rising Above the Gathering Storm: Energizing and Employing America for a Brighter Economic Future. Committee on Science, Engineering, and Public Policy (COSEPUP), US National Academies Press. 13 (14)

Cotte, J., Chowdhury, T. G., Ratneshwar, S., & Ricci, L. M. (2006). Pleasure or utility? Time planning style and web usage behaviours. *Journal of Interactive Marketing*, *20*(1), 45–57. doi:10.1002/dir.20055

Cox, D. (1967). *Risk Taking and Information Handling in Consumer Behavior*. Boston, MA: Harvard University, Division of Research, Graduate School of Business Administration.

Creemers, B. (2006, December). The importance and perspectives of international studies in educational effectiveness. *Educational Research and Evaluation*, *12*(6), 499–511. doi:10.1080/13803610600873978

Crossley, M. (2007, November). The political economy of cross-cultural educational research. *Comparative Education*, *43*(4), 469–470. doi:10.1080/03050060701611862

Csikszentmihalyi, M. (1990). Flow: *The Psychology of Optimal Experience: Steps Toward Enhancing The Quality of Life.* New York, NY: Harper/Perennial. 7 (4 8 13)

Cunningham, L. F., Gerlach, J. H., & Harper, M. D. (2005). Perceived risk and e-banking services: An analysis from the perspective of the consumer. *Journal of Financial Services Marketing, 10*(2), 165–178. doi:10.1057/palgrave.fsm.4770183

Cunningham, L. F., Gerlach, J. H., Harper, M. D., & Young, C. E. (2005). Perceived risk and the consumer buying process: Internet airline reservations. *International Journal of Service Industry Management, 16*(4), 357–372. doi:10.1108/09564230510614004

Cunningham, S. M. (1967). Perceived risk and brand loyalty. In Cox, D.F. (Ed.), *Risk-Taking and Information Handling in Consumer Behavior* (pp. 507-523). Boston, MA: Boston University Press.

D'Aspremont, C., Gabszewicz, J. J., & Thisse, J. F. (1979). On Hotelling's stability in competition. *Econometrica, 47*(5), 1145–1150. doi:10.2307/1911955

Dabholkar, P. A. (1994). *Technology-based Service Delivery, A Classification Scheme for Developing Marketing Strategies. Advances in Service Marketing and Management* (*Vol. 3*, pp. 241–271). Greenwich, CT: JAI Press.

Dabholkar, P. A. (1996). Consumer Evaluation of New Technology-Based Self-Service Options: An investigation of alternative models of service quality. *International Journal of Research in Marketing, 13*(1), 29–51. doi:10.1016/0167-8116(95)00027-5

Damiani, E., Paraboschi, S., & Samarati, P. (2002). A fine-grained access control system for XML documents. *ACM Transactions on Information and System Security, 5*(2), 169–202. doi:10.1145/505586.505590

Damiani, E., & Samarati, S., Vimercati, di., & Paraboschi, S. (2001). Controlling access to XML documents. *IEEE Internet Computing, 5*(6), 18–28. doi:10.1109/4236.968827

Damiani, E., Capitani, S., & Samarati, P. (2002). Towards securing xml web services. *In Proc. of the 2002 ACM Workshop on XML Security,* Washington, DC, USA.

Darr, A. (2006). *Selling Technology: The Changing Shape of Sales in an Information Economy.* Ithaca. NY: Cornell University Press. 8 (3 9)

Date, C. J. (1999). *An Introduction to Database Systems* (8th ed.). NY: Addison-Wesley Longman.

Davidson, A. P., & Yu, Y. (2004). The internet and the occidental tourist an analysis of Taiwan's tourism websites from the perspective of western tourists. *Journal of Information Technology and Tourism, 7*(2), 91–102. doi:10.3727/1098305054517318

Davis, F. D., Bagozzi, R. P., & Warshaw, P. R. (1989). User Acceptance of Computer Technology: A Comparison of Two Theoretical Models. *Management Science, 35*(8), 982–1003. doi:10.1287/mnsc.35.8.982

Davis, R. D. (1989). Perceived Usefulness, Perceived Ease of Use, and User Acceptance of Technology. *Management Information Systems Quarterly, 13*(3), 319–340. doi:10.2307/249008

Davis, F. D. (1989). Perceived usefulness, perceived ease of use, and user acceptance of information technology. *Management Information Systems Quarterly, 13*(3), 319–339. doi:10.2307/249008

Davis, F. D., Bagozzi, R. P., & Warshaw, P. R. (1989). User acceptance of computer technology: A comparison of two theoretical models. *Management Science, 35*(8), 982–1004. doi:10.1287/mnsc.35.8.982

Davis, F. D. (1986). Technology acceptance model for empirically testing new end-user information systems: Theory and results. Dissertation abstracts international. (umi no. Aat 0374529). MA, USA: Massachusetts Institute of Technology.

Davis, F.D., Bagozzi, R.P., & Warshaw, P.R., Extrinsic and intrinsic motivation to use computers in workplace, Journal of Applied Social Psychology, 1992

Davis, M. M., & Heineke, J. (2005). *Operations Management: Integrating Manufacturing and Services.* Fifth Edition. Boston, MA: McGraw-Hill Irwin. 2 (5 15)

Dawson, R. (2005). Developing Knowledge-Based Client Relationships: Leadership in Professional Services. New York, NY: Elsevier. 12 (4 8 10)

De Marco, T. P. P. J. (1979). *Structured Analysis and System Specification*. Prentice Hall.

De Palma, A., Ginsburgh, V., & Thisse, J. F. (1987). On existence of location equilibria in the 3-firm Hotelling problem. *The Journal of Industrial Economics*, *36*(2), 245–252. doi:10.2307/2098416

Deacon, T. W. (1997). *The Symbolic Species: The Co-Evolution of Language and the Brain*. New York, NY: Norton. 10 (3)

DeLone, W. H., & McLean, E. R. (1992). Information system success: The quest for the dependent variable. *Information Systems Research*, *3*(1), 60–95. doi:10.1287/isre.3.1.60

DeLone, W. H., & McLean, E. R. (2003). The DeLone and McLean model of information systems success: A ten-year update. *Journal of Management Information Systems*, *19*(4), 9–30.

Dertouzos, M. L. (1991a). Communications, Computers and Networks. *Scientific American*, *265*(3), 30–37. doi:10.1038/scientificamerican0991-62

Dertouzos, M. L. (Ed.). (1991b). *Scientific American* (*Vol. 265*, p. 3). Special Issue on Communications, Computers, and Networks.

Dexter, H., Petch, J., & Powley, D. (2007, 11-12 Jan). *Establishing an SOA composite applications development process for work-based learning and competency progression management.* Paper presented at the 2nd TENCompetence Open Workshop, Manchester, UK. Retrieved 20.1., 2008, from http://www.medicine.manchester.ac.uk/helm/TENCompPaper.pdf

Dhamija, R., Tygar, J. D., & Hearst, M. (2006). *Why Phishing Works*. Paper presented at the Proc. of CHI'06, Montreal, Canada.

Di Gregorio, D., Kassicieh, S. K., & De Gouveva, R. (2005). Drivers of e-business activity in developed and emerging markets. *IEE Transactions on Engineering Management*, *52*(2), 155–166. doi:10.1109/TEM.2005.844464

Di Renzo, B., Barafort, B., Lejeune, V., Prime, S., & Simon, J. M. (2005, April). *ITIL based service management measurement and ISO/IEC 15504 process assessment: A win-win opportunity.* Paper presented at the SPICE 2005 Conference, Klagenfurt, Austria.

Di Romualdo, A., & Gurbaxani, V. (1998). Strategic intent for IT outsourcing. *Sloan Management Review, Summer*.

Diamond, J. (2005). *Collapse: How Societies Choose to Fail or Succeed.* New York, NY: Viking. 3 (12)

Dishaw, M.T, Strong, D.M, Extending The Technology Acceptance Model With Task-Technology Fit Constructs, Information Management, 1998.

Dixit, A. K. (2004). *Lawlessness and Economics: Alternative Models of Governance.* Princeton, NJ: Princeton University Press. 6 (1 3 11 12 15)

Dodds, W. B., Monroe, K. B., & Grewal, D. (1991). Effects of price, brand and store information on buyers' product evaluations. *JMR, Journal of Marketing Research*, *28*(3), 307–319. doi:10.2307/3172866

Doll, W., & Torkzadeh, G. (1988). The measurement of end-user computing satisfaction. *Management Information Systems Quarterly*, *12*(2), 259–274. doi:10.2307/248851

Doll, W. J., & Torkzadeh, G. (1991). The measurement of end-user computing satisfaction: Theoretical and methodological issues. *Management Information Systems Quarterly*, *15*(1), 5–9. doi:10.2307/249429

Doll, W. J., Xia, W., & Torkzadeh, G. (1994). A confirmatory factor analysis of the end-user computing satisfaction instrument. *Management Information Systems Quarterly*, *18*(4), 453–461. doi:10.2307/249524

Domberger, S. (1998). *The contracting organization. A guide to strategic outsourcing. Oxford.* UK: Oxford University Press.

Doolin, B., Burgess, L., & Cooper, J. (2002). Evaluating the use of web for tourism marketing: a case study from New Zeland. *Tourism Management, 23*(4), 557–561. doi:10.1016/S0261-5177(02)00014-6

Dossani, R., & Kenney, M. (2004). *The next wave of globalization: Exploring the relocation of service provision to India.* Working paper. Stanford, CA: Asia Pacific Research Center, Stanford University.

Dourdas, N., Zhu, X., Maiden, N., Jones, S., & Zachos, K. (2006). Discovering remote software services that satisfy requirements: Patterns for query reformulation. In Dubois, E. & Pohl, K. (Eds.): *Advanced Information Systems Engineering, 18th International Conference*, CAiSE 2006, Luxembourg, June 5-9, 2006, Proceedings. Lecture Notes in Computer Science 4001 (pp. 239-254), Berlin: Springer.

Dowling, G. R., & Staelin, R. (1994). A model of perceived risk and intended risk-handling activity. *The Journal of Consumer Research, 21*(1), 119–134. doi:10.1086/209386

Doz, Y., Santos, R., & Williamson, O. (2004). *Da globale a metanazionale.* Bologna: Il Mulino.

Drucker, P. (1969). *The Age of Discontinuity.* New York: Harper & Row.

Drucker, P. F. (1993). *Post-Capitalist Society.* New York, NY: Harper Business. 12 (3)

Dubie, D. (2008). ITIL adoption increases in U.S., proficiency still lacking. *NetworkWorld.com.*

Duman, T., & Mattila, A. S. (2005). The role of affective factors on perceived cruise vacation value. *Tourism Management, 26*, 311–323. doi:10.1016/j.tourman.2003.11.014

Durgee, J. F., O'Connor, G. C., & Veryzer, R. W. (1996). Translating values into product wants. *Journal of Advertising Research, 36*(6), 90–101.

Durkheim, E. (1893/1997). *The Division of Labor in Society.* New York, NY: Free Press. 3 (8)

Durvasula, S., Guttmann, M., Kumar, A., Lamb, J., Mitchell, T., Oral, B., et al. (2008). *SOA Practitioners Guide Part 2: SOA Reference Architecture*http://www.soablueprint.com/whitepapers/SOAPGPart2.pdf.

Dustmann, C., Fitzenberger, B., & Machin, S. (2007). The economics of education and training. *Empirical Economics, 32*(2), 255–260. doi:10.1007/s00181-006-0113-2

Dyer, J. K., Kale, P., & Singh, H. (2001). How to make strategic alliances work. *Sloan Management Review*, (Summer): 37–44.

Dyer, J. K., & Singh, H. (1998). The relational view: cooperative strategy and sources of interorganizational competitive advantage. *Academy of Management Review, 23*(4), 660–679. doi:10.2307/259056

Eastlick, M. A., & Lotz, S. (1999). Profiling Potential Adopters and Non-adopters of an Interactive Electronic, Shopping Medium. *International Journal of Retail and Distribution Management, 26*(6), 209–223.

Economist Intelligence Unit. IBM Institute for Business value (2005). *The 2005 e-readiness rankings.* White Paper. Retrieved June 23, 2006, from http://www.eiu.com/site_info.asp?info_name=eiu_2005_e_readiness_rankings.

Elenius, D., Denker, G., Martin, D., Gilham, F., Khouri, J., Sadaati, S., et al. (2005). The OWL-S editor: A development tool for semantic web services. In Gómez-Pérez, A. & Euzenat, J. (Eds.): *The Semantic Web: Research and Applications*, Second European Semantic Web Conference, ESWC 2005, Heraklion, Crete, Greece, May 29 - June 1, 2005, Proceedings. Lecture Notes in Computer Science 3532 (pp. 78-92). Berlin: Springer.

Ellram, L. M., Tate, W. L., & Billington, C. (2008). Offshore outsourcing of professional services: A transaction cost economics perspective. *Journal of Operations Management, 26*, 148–163. doi:10.1016/j.jom.2007.02.008

Emmanouilides, C., & Hammond, K. (2000). Internet usage: predictors of active users and frequency of use. *Journal of Interactive Marketing, 14*(2), 17–32. doi:10.1002/(SICI)1520-6653(200021)14:2<17::AID-DIR2>3.0.CO;2-E

Erdem, T., & Swait, J. (2004). Brand credibility, brand consideration, and choice. *The Journal of Consumer Research*, *31*(1), 191–198. doi:10.1086/383434

Ericson, J. (2004). *The RFID for Hospital Care*. The E-Business Executive Daily.

Ericson, J. (2004). *The RFID for hospital care*. The E-Business Executive Daily.

Erl, Th. (2004). *Service-oriented Architecture: A Field Guide to Integrating XML and Web Services*. Upper Saddle River, NJ: Prentice Hall.

Erl, T. (2005). *Service-oriented architecture: Concepts, technology, and design*. Upper Saddle River, NJ: Prentice-Hall.

Etchells, E., O'Neill, C., & Bernstein, M. (2003). Patient Safety in Surgery: Error Detection and Prevention. *World Journal of Surgery*, *27*(8), 936–941. doi:10.1007/s00268-003-7097-2

Etchells, E., O'Neill, C., & Bernstein, M. (2003). Patient safety in surgery: error detection and prevention. *World Journal of Surgery*, *27*(8), 936–941. doi:10.1007/s00268-003-7097-2

Etezadi-Amoli, J., & Farhoomand, A. F. (1991). On end-user computing satisfaction. *Management Information Systems Quarterly*, *15*(1), 1–5. doi:10.2307/249428

EXIN. (2008). ISO/IEC 20000 Certification Exams. Examination Board Ref Type: Internet Communication

Ezzy, D. (2002). *Qualitative analysis: Practice and innovation*. Crows Nest, New South Wales, AU: Allen & Unwin.

Fagin, R., Halpern, J. Y., Moses, Y., & Vardi, M. Y. (2003). *Reasoning About Knowledge*. Cambridge, MA: MIT Press. 1 (10 15)

Feather, N. T. (1967). An expectancy-value model of information-seeking behavior. *Psychological Review*, *74*(5), 242–360. doi:10.1037/h0024879

Feather, N. T. (1975). *Values in education and society*. New York, NY: The Free Press.

Featherman, M., & Pavlou, P. (2003). Predicting e-services adoption: A perceived risk facets perspective. *International Journal of Human-Computer Studies*, *59*(4), 451–474. doi:10.1016/S1071-5819(03)00111-3

Featherman, M. S., Valacich, J. S., & Wells, J. D. (2006). Is That Autentic or Artificial? Understanding Consumer Perceptions of Risk in e-Service Encounters. *Information Systems Journal, 16*(2), pgs. 107-134.

Felipe, L. (2005). *Web Services Architecture and Its Specifications: Essential for Understanding WS (Pro-Developer)*. Redwood, WA: Microsoft Press.

Feng, R., Morrison, A. M., & Ismail, J. A. (2002). East versus West: a comparison of online destination marketing in China and the US. *Journal of Vacation Marketing*, *10*(1), 43–56. doi:10.1177/135676670301000105

Ferguson, D. F., & Stockton, M. L. (2005). Service-Oriented Architecture: Programming Model and Product Architecture. *IBM Systems Journal*, *44*(4), 753–780. doi:10.1147/sj.444.0753

Fishbein, M., & Ajzen, I. (1975). *Belief, attitude, intention and behavior: an introduction to theory and research*. Reading, MA: Addison-Wesley.

Fisher, J. A. (2006). Indoor Positioning and Digital Management:Emerging Surveillance Regimes in Hospitals. *Technological Politics and Power in Everyday Life T. Monahan, Ed*, 77-88.

Fisher, J. A. (2006). Indoor positioning and digital management: emerging surveillance regimes in hospitals. *Technological Politics and Power in Everyday Life T. Monahan, Ed*, 77-88.

Fisteus, J. A., Fernández, L. S., & Kloos, C. D. (2005). Applying model checking to BPEL4WS business collaborations. ACM Symposium on Applied computing, 826- 830.

Fitzsimmons, J. A., & Fitzsimmons, M. J. (2004). *Service Management: Operations*. Strategy, and Information Technology.

Fitzsimmons, J. A., & Fitzsimmons, M. J. (2007). *Service management: Operations, Strategy, Information Technology.* Sixth Edition. New York, NY: McGraw-Hill Irwin. 2 (5 12 15)

Fleming, W. (2005). *Using Cost of Service to Align IT* Presentation at itSMF-USA, Chicago, IL.

Fogg, B. J., Marshall, J., Laraki, O., Osipovich, A., Varma, C., Fang, N., et al. (2001, Mar 31-Apr 5). *What Makes Web Sites Credible? A Report on a Large Quantitative Study.* Paper presented at the Proc. of CHI'01, Seattle, Washington.

Forsythe, S., & Shi, B. (2003). Consumer patronage and risk perceptions in Internet shopping. *Journal of Business Research, 56*(11), 867–875. doi:10.1016/S0148-2963(01)00273-9

Foster, I., & Kesselman, C. (2003). *Grid 2: Blueprint for a New Computing Infrastructure.* The Elsevier Series in Grid Computing.

Foster, I., Kesselman, C., & Tuecke, S. (2001). The Anatomy of the Grid: Enabling Scalable Virtual Organizations. *International Journal of High Performance Computing Applications, 15*(3), 200–222. doi:10.1177/109434200101500302

Foster, I., & Tuecke, S. (2005). The different faces of IT as a Service. *ACM Queue; Tomorrow's Computing Today, 3*(6), 27–34.

Foster, I., Kesselman, C., Nick, J., & Tuecke, S. (2002). The Physiology of the Grid: An Open Grid Services Architecture for Distributed Systems Integration. Open Grid Service Infrastructure WG, Global Grid Forum, [on line] http://www.ggf.org/

Foster, I., Kesselman, C., & Tuecke, S. (2001). The Anatomy of the Grid: Enabling Scalable Virtual Organizations. *International J. Supercomputer Applications,* 15(3). 10 (6 11)

Freiden, J., Goldsmith, R., Takacs, S., & Hofacker, Ch. F. (1998). Information as a Product: Not Goods, Not Services. *Marketing Intelligence & Planning, 16*(Fall), 210–220. doi:10.1108/02634509810217327

Freidson, E. (2001). *Professionalism: The Third Logic/ On the Practice of Knowledge.* Chicago, IL: University of Chicago Press. 14 (13)

Friedman, D. (1996/2007). A little manifesto on Learning and Economics. URL http://leeps.ucsc.edu/leeps/manifesto. 3 (12)

Friedman, T. L. (2005). *The World is Flat.* Farrar Straus & Giroux. 11 (3)

Fuerst, W. L., & Cheney, P. H. (1982). Factors affecting the perceived utilization of computer-based decision support systems in the oil industry. *Decision Sciences, 13*(4), 554–569.

Gabillon, A. (2004) An authorization model for xml databases. *In Proceedings of the 11th ACM conference on Computer Security.*

Gadrey, J., & Gallouj, F. (2002). *Productivity, Innovation and Knowledge in Services: New Economic & Socio-Economic Approaches.* Cheltenham, U.K: Edward Elgar. 3 (5 7)

Galinec, D., & Vidović, S. (2007). Methodology framework for process integration and service management. [Faculty of Organization and Informatics Varaždin - University of Zagreb.]. *Journal of Information and Organizational Sciences, 31*(1), 37–49.

Galletta, D. F., & Lederer, A. L. (1989). Some cautions on the measurement of user information satisfaction. *Decision Sciences, 20*(3), 419–439. doi:10.1111/j.1540-5915.1989.tb01558.x

Ganz, W. (2006). Germany: service engineering. *Communications of the ACM,* 49(7), 79. 9 (2)

Garbarino, E., & Strahilevitz, M. (2004). Gender differences in the perceived risk of buying online and the effects of receiving a site recommendation. *Journal of Business Research, 57*(6), 768–775. doi:10.1016/S0148-2963(02)00363-6

Garner, C.A. (2004). Offshoring in the service sector: economic impact and policy issues. *Federal Reserve Bank of Kansas City Economic Review, third-quarter.*

Garud, R., Kumaraswamy, A., & Langlois, R. N. (2003). *Managing in the Modular Age: Architectures, Networks, and Organizations*. New York, NY: Blackwell Publishing. 14 (10 11)

Garvin, D. A. (1984). What does "product quality" really mean? *Sloan Management Review,* Fall, *26*(1), 25-43.

Gefen, D., & Ragowsky, A. (2005). A multi-level approach to measuring the benefits of an erp system in manufacturing firms. *Information Systems Management, 22*(1), 18–26. doi:10.1201/1078/44912.22.1.20051201/85735.3

Gefen, D., & Carmel, E. (2008). Is the world really flat? A look at offshoring at an online programming marketplace. *Management Information Systems Quarterly, 32*(2), 367–384.

Gelderman, M. (1998). The relation between user satisfaction, usage of information systems and performance. *Information & Management, 34*(1), 11–18. doi:10.1016/S0378-7206(98)00044-5

Gelman, O., & Garcia, J. (1989). Formulation and axiomatization of the concept of general system. *Outlet of the Mexican Institute of Planning and Systems Operation, 19*(92), 1–81.

Gelman, O., Mora, M., Forgionne, G., & Cervantes, F. (2005). *Information Systems and Systems Theory. Encyclopedia of Information Science and Technology* (pp. 1491–1496). Hershey, PA: Idea Group.

Gershuny, J. (2000). Changing *Times: Work and Leisure in Postindustrial Society*. Oxford, UK: Oxford University Press. 3 (8)

Gersuny, C., & Rosengren, W. R. (1973). *The Service Society*. Cambridge, MA: Schenkman.

Ghayekhloo, G., Sedighi, M., Nassiri, R., Latif Shabgahi, G., & Khodadadi Tirkolaei, H. (2009). *Pathology of organizations currently implementing ITIL in developing countries*. Paper presented at the Second International Conference on Computer and Electrical Engineering.

Gilbert, A. Lee, Han, Hilda, Understanding mobile data services adoption: Demography, attitudes or needs?, 2004

Gilbert, T. F. (1978). *Human Competence: Engineering Worthy Performance*. New York, NY: McGraw Hill. 9 (8)

Ginzberg, M. J. (1981). Early diagnosis of MIS implementation failure: Promising results and unanswered questions. *Management Science, 27*(4), 459–478. doi:10.1287/mnsc.27.4.459

Glaser, B. G. (1978). *Theoretical sensitivity – advances in the methodology of grounded theory*. San Francisco: The Sociology Press.

Glass, R. L., Ramesh, V., & Vessey, I. (2004). An analysis of research in computing disciplines. *Communications of the ACM, 47*(6), 89–94. doi:10.1145/990680.990686

Glass, R., Armes, V., & Vessey, I. (2004). An Analysis of Research in Computing Disciplines. *Communications of the ACM, 47*(6), 89–94. doi:10.1145/990680.990686

Global Doctor Options. (2008). *Global Doctor Options Guide*. Las Vegas, NV: Author.

Global Education Digest. (2007). UNESCO Institute for Statistics, Retrieved July 1, 2008, from www.uis.unesco.org/publications/GED2007

Glushko, R. J. (2008). Design a Service Science Discipline with Disciple. *IBM Systems Journal, 47*(1), 15–27. doi:10.1147/sj.471.0015

Glushko, R., & McGrath, T. (2005). *Document Engineering: Analyzing and Designing Documents for Business Informatics and Web Services*. Cambridge, MA: MIT Press. 10 (9 15)

Goldratt, E. M. (1990). *Theory of Constraints*. Great Barrington, MA: North River Press. 11 (14)

Goldsmith, R. E. (2002). Explaining and predicting consumer intention to purchase over the Internet: An exploratory study. *Journal of Marketing Theory and Practice*, Spring, 22-28.

Gomez-Perez, A., & González-Cabero, R. (2004, 22-24 Mar). *A framework for design and composition of semantic web services*. Paper presented at the First International Semantic Web Services Symposium, Palo Alto, CA. Retrieved 22.4., 2007, from http://www.daml.ecs.soton.ac.uk/SSS-SWS04/44.pdf

Gonzales, P., Guzman, J. C., & Jocelyn, L. (2004). Highlights from the Trends in International Mathematics and Science Study (TIMSS 2003). *United States Department of Education*. Retrieved July 1, 2008 from http://nces.ed.gov/pubs2005/2005005.pdf

Gonzalez, R., Gasco, J., & Llopis, J. (2006). Information Systems Outsourcing: a literature analysis. *Information & Management*, *43*(7), 821–834. doi:10.1016/j.im.2006.07.002

Govekar, M. (2010). *Making ITIL a Reality: Pitfalls and Strategy. Gartner local briefing in Zagreb*. Gartner, Inc.

Goyal, B., & Lawande, S. (2007). *Grid Revolution: An Introduction to Enterprise Grid Computing*. McGraw-Hill.

Grant, R., Clarke, R. J., & Kyriazis, E. (2010). Research needs for assessing online value creation in complex consumer purchase process behaviour. *Journal of Retailing and Consumer Services*, *17*, 53–60. doi:10.1016/j.jretconser.2009.09.004

GRASP. (2008). Grid Application Service Provision Project Web Site. [on line] www.eu-grasp.net.

Greatorex, M., & Mitchell, V. W. (1993). Developing the perceived risk concept: Emerging issues in marketing. In M. Davies et al. (Eds.), *Proceedings, Marketing Education Group Conference* (pp. 405-415). Loughborough.

Greaver, M. F. (1999). *Strategic outsourcing. A structured approach to outsourcing decisions and initiatives*. New York: Amacom.

Greiner, L. (2007). ITIL: The international repository of it wisdom. *Business: the 8th layer,* 9-11.

Grewal, D., Iyer, G. R., Krishnan, R., & Sharma, A. (2003). The Internet and the price-value- loyalty chain. *Journal of Business Research*, *56*, 391–398. doi:10.1016/S0148-2963(01)00227-2

Grinter, R. E., & Eldridge, M. (2001). *Y do tngrs luv 2 txt msg? K. Schmidt and V. Wilf. Dordrecht* (pp. 219–238). Dordrecht: Kluwer Academic Publishers.

Grossman, G. M., & Shapiro, C. (1984). Informative advertising with differentiated products. *The Review of Economic Studies*, *51*(1), 63–81. doi:10.2307/2297705

Grover, V., Seung, R. J., & Segars, A. H. (1996). Information systems effectiveness: The construct space and patters of application. *Information & Management*, *31*(4), 177–191. doi:10.1016/S0378-7206(96)01079-8

Gu, Q., & Lago, P. (2007). *A stakeholder-driven service life cycle model for soa.* Paper presented at the 2nd International Workshop on Service Oriented Software Engineering (IW-SOSWE'07), Dubrovnik, Croatia. Retrieved 21.1., 2008, from http://www.selab.isti.cnr.it/IW-SOSWE07/program.html.

Guba, E. G., & Lincoln, Y. S. (1989). *Fourth Generation Evaluation*. London, UK: Sage. 2 (3 4 5 6 7 8 9 12)

Guex, V. (2010). A sociological view of the cybertourists. In Gretzel, U., Law, R. & Fuchs, M. (Eds.) *Information and Communication Technologies in Tourism 2010* (417-428). Proceedings of the ENTER conference Wien: Springer-Verlag.

Guile, B. R., & Quinn, J. B. (1988). *Technology in Services: Policies for Growth, Trade, and Employment*. Washington, DC: National Academy Press. 9 (6)

Gummesson, E. (2001). Are current research approaches in marketing leading us astray? *Marketing Theory,* 1(1), 27-48. 2 (4 11 13 14)

Gummesson, E. (2003). All research is interpretive! *Journal of Business & Industrial Marketing*, (18)6/7, 482-492. 2 (4 11 13 14)

Gummesson, E. (2006). Many-to-many marketing as grand theory In Lusch, R. F. & Vargo S. L. (Eds.) *The service-dominant logic of marketing – dialogue, debate, and directions* (339-353). New York: M.E. Sharpe.

Gummesson, E. (2007). Exit Services Marketing – Enter Service Marketing. *The Journal of Customer Behaviour,* 6(2), 113-141. 4 (12)

Gummesson, E. (2007). Case study research and network theory: birds of a feather. *Qualitative Research in Organizations and Management: An International Journal,* 2(3), 226-248. 2 (4 11 14)

Gunasekaran, A., Lai, K., & Cheng, T. C. (2008). Responsive supply chain: Acompetitive strategy in a networked economy. *The International Journal of Management Science*, *36*(4), 549–564.

Guseman, D. S. (1981). Risk perception and risk reduction in consumer services. In J. H. Donnelly & W. R. George (Eds.), *Marketing of Services*. Chicago, IL: American Marketing Association.

Gustafsson, A., & Johnson, M. D. (2003). *Competing in a Service Economy: How to Create Competitive Advantage Through Service Development and Innovation*. San Francisco, CA: Wiley/Jossey-Bass. 7 (12)

Gutek, B., & Welsh, Th. (2000). *The Brave New Service Strategy*. New York: AMA.

Gutek, B. A. (1995). *The Dynamics of Service: Reflections on the Changing Nature of Customer/Provider Interactions*. San Francico, CA: Jossey-Bass Publishers. 1 (3 4 8 10 11 12 15)

Gutek, B., & Welsh, T. (2000). *The Brave New Service Strategy – Aligning Customer Relationships, Market Strategies, and Business Structure*. New York, NY: AMACOM. 12 (3 4 8 11)

Hackney, R., & Pillay, J. (2002). Organisational mission statements: A postmodernist perspective on the management of the IS/IT function. *Information Resources Management Journal*, *15*(1), 28–37.

Hahn, E. D., & Bunyaratavej, K. (2010). Services cultural alignment in offshoring: The impact of cultural dimensions on offshoring location choices. *Journal of Operations Management*, *28*, 186–193. doi:10.1016/j.jom.2009.10.005

Hakimpour, F., Sell, D., Cabral, L., Domingue, J., & Motta, E. (2005). *Semantic web service composition in IRS-III: The structured approach.* Paper presented at the 7th IEEE International Conference on E-Commerce Technology (CEC'05).

Hall, A. D. (1962). *A Methodology for Systems Engineering*. Princeton, NJ: D. Van Nostrand Company. 14 (9 15)

Hall, G. (1999), Presentation at the OECD Business and Industry Policy Forum on *Realizing the Potential of the Service Economy*, 28 September.

Hammond, L. (2008, February). How they do it abroad. *Time*, *171*(8), 34.

Handy, C. (2000). *Understanding Organizations*. Penguin.

Handy, C. (1989). *The Age of Unreason*. Cambridge, MA: Harvard Business School Press. 12 (8 11)

Hansen, T., Jensen, J. M., & Solgaard, H. S. (2004). Predicting online grocery buying intention: a comparison of the theory of reasoned action and the theory of planned behaviour. *International Journal of Information Management*, *24*, 539–550. doi:10.1016/j.ijinfomgt.2004.08.004

Hanushek, E. A., Jamison, D. T., Jamison, E. A., & Woessmann, L. (2008, Spring). Education and economic growth: it's not just going to school, but learning something while there that matters. (Research). *Education Next*, *8*(2), 62–70.

Harkness, S., Blom, M., Oliva, A., Moscardino, U., Zylicz, P., & Bermudez, M. (2007). Teachers' ethno theories of the 'ideal student' in five western cultures. *Comparative Education*, *43*(1), 113–135. doi:10.1080/03050060601162438

Hawkins, D. I., Coney, K. A., & Best, R. J. (2003). *Consumer Behavior: Building Marketing Strategy*, Chicago, IL: Irwin.

Hawley, A. H. (1986). *Human Ecology: A Theoretical Essay*. Chicago, IL: University of Chicago Press. 14 (3 8 11)

Head, K., Mayer, T., & Ries, J. (2009). How remote is the offshoring threat? *European Economic Review*, *53*, 429–444. doi:10.1016/j.euroecorev.2008.08.001

Health care RFID startup scores $9 million in venture funding. (2004, July 12, 2004). *Dow Jones Reuters Business Interactive.*

Health Care RFID Startup Scores $9 Million in Venture Funding. (2004, July 12, 2004). *Dow Jones Reuters Business Interactive*. Retrieved from http://www.gs1.org/docs/patient_safety Jeong, B., Cheng, C.-Y., & Prabhu, V. (2009). Modeling and Analysis of Surgery Patient Identification Using RFID. *International Journal of Information Systems In the Service Sector, 1*(4), 1-14.

Heizer, J., & Render, B. (2004). *Principles of Operations Management.* Upper Saddle Creek, NJ: Pearson Education. 5 (2)

Helpman, E. (2004). *The Mystery of Economic Growth.* Cambridge, MA: Harvard University Press. 3 (5)

Hendrickson, A. R., Glorfeld, K., & Cronan, T. P. (1994). On the repeated test-retest reliability of the end-user computing satisfaction instrument: A comment. *Decision Sciences, 25*(4), 655–668. doi:10.1111/j.1540-5915.1994.tb01864.x

Heritage, J. (1984/1989). *Garfinkel and Enthnomethodology.* Cambridge, UK: Polity Press. 8 (2 11)

Herzenberg, S. A., Alic, J. A., & Wial, H. (2000). *New Rules for a New Economy: Employment and Opportunity in Postindustrial America.* Ithaca, NY: ILR Press Books, Cornell University Press. 3 (6 12)

Heskett, J. L., Sasser, W. E., & Schlesinger, L. A. (1997). *The Service Profit Chain: How Leading Companies Link Profit and Growth to Loyalty, Satisfaction, and Value.* New York: Free Press.

Heskett, J. (1987). Lessons in the service sector. *Harvard Business Review,* (Mar-Apr): 118–126.

Heskett, J. L. (1990). Rethinking Strategy for Service Management.in Bowen, D. E., Chase, R. B., Cummings, Th. G. and Associates (Eds). (1990). *Service Management Effectiveness, Balancing Strategy, Organization and Human Resources, Operations, and Marketing.* San Francisco: Jossey-Bass Publishers.pp. 17-40.

Heskett, J. L., Sasser, W. E., Jr., & Schlesinger, L. A. (1997). *The Service Profit Chain.* New York, NY: The Free Press. 2 (12)

Heß, A., Johnston, E., & Kushmerick, N. (2004). *Assam: A tool for semi-automatically annotating semantic web services.* Paper presented at the International Semantic Web Conference (ISWC04), Hiroshima, Japan.

Hevner, A. R., March, S. T., Park, J., & Ram, S. (2004). Design Science in Information Systems Research. *Management Information Systems Quarterly, 28*(1), 75–105.

Hidaka, K. (2006). Trends in services sciences in Japan and abroad. *Science & Technology Trends: Quarterly Review,* 19, 35-47 (April). 1 (10)

Hinterhuber, H. & Stuhec, U. (1996). Competenze distintive e outsourcing strategico. *Finanza, Marketing e Produzione, 4.*

Hitt, M., Dacin, M. T., Levitas, E., Arregle, J. L., & Borza, A. (2000). Partner selection in emerging and developed market contexts: resource-based and organizational learning perspective. *Academy of Management Journal, 43,* 449–467. doi:10.2307/1556404

Hjalager, A. (2001). Research and concepts: quality in tourism through the empowerment of tourists. *Managing Service Quality, 11*(4), 287–295. doi:10.1108/09604520110397995

Hochstein, A., Tamm, G., & Brenner, W. (2005). *Service-Oriented IT Management: Benefit, Cost and Success Factors.* Paper presented at the 15th European Conference on Information Systems.

Hoffman, D. L., & Novak, T. P. (1996). Marketing in hypermedia computer-mediated environments: Conceptual foundations. *Journal of Marketing, 60*(July), 50–68. doi:10.2307/1251841

Hoffman, D. L., Novak, T. P., & Peralta, M. (1999). Building consumer trust online. *Communications of the ACM, 42,* 80–85. doi:10.1145/299157.299175

Höflich, J. R., & Rössler, P. (2001). Mobile schriftliche Kommunikation oder: E -Mail für das Handy. *Medien & Kommunikationswissenschaft*, *49*, 437–461.

Hofstede, G. H. (2001). *Culture's consequences: Comparing values, behaviors, institutions and organizations across nations*. CA: Thousand Oaks.

Holbrook, M. B. (1999). *Consumer value – A framework for analysis and research*. London: Routledge. doi:10.4324/9780203010679

Holbrook, M. B. (1996). Customer value – A framework for analysis and research. In Corfman, K. P., & Lynch, J. G. Jr., (Eds.), *Advances in Consumer Research, 23 (138-42)*. Provo, UT: Association for Consumer Research.

Holbrook, M. B. (1994). Defining service quality. In Rust, R. T. & Oliver, R. L. (Eds.) *Service Quality – New Directions in Theory and Practice* (21-71). Thousand Oaks, CA: Sage Publications.

Holcomb, R. T., & Hitt, M. A. (2007). Toward a model of strategic outsourcing. *Journal of Operations Management*, *25*, 464–481. doi:10.1016/j.jom.2006.05.003

Honebein, P. C., & Cammarano, R. F. (2005). *Creating Do-It-Yourself Customers: How Great Customer Experiences Build Great Companies*. Mason, OH: Thomson. 4 (7)

Hong, Se-Joon, Tam, Kar Yan, Kim, Jinwoo, Mobile Data Service Fuels the Desire for Uniqueness, Communication of the ACM, 2006

Hoopes, J. (2003). *False Prophets: The Gurus Who Created Modern Management and Why Their Ideas are Bad for Business Today*. Cambridge, MA: Perseus Books. 3 (12)

Hopp, W. J., & Spearman, M. L. (1996). *Factory Physics: Foundations of Manufacturing Management*. Boston, MA: Irwin McGraw-Hill. 5 (2 14)

Horn, P. (2005). The New Discipline of Services Science. *BusinessWeek*, January 21, 2005. 14 (10)

Hotelling, H. (1929). Stability in competition. *The Economic Journal*, *39*(153), 41–57. doi:10.2307/2224214

Howard, R., & Kerschberg, L. (2004). A framework for dynamic semantic web services management. *International Journal of Cooperative Information Systems*, *13*(4), 441–485. doi:10.1142/S0218843004001024

Hsu, C. (Ed.). (2007) "Models of Cyberinfrastructure-based Enterprises and their Engineering"*Service Enterprise Integration: an Enterprise Engineering Perspective*, Springer Science, 2007

Hsu, Chin-Lung, Lu, His-Peng, Hsu, Huei-Hsia, Adoption f the mobile Internet: An empirical study of multimedia message service (MMS), Omega, 2006

http://www.gs1.org/docs/patient_safety. GS1 standards in healthcare.

Huang, C.-Y., Chour, C.-J., & Lin, P.-C. (2010). Involvment theory in constructing bloggers' intention to purchase travel products. *Tourism Management*, *31*, 513–526. doi:10.1016/j.tourman.2009.06.003

Huang, P., Lurie, N. H., & Mitra, S. (2009). Searching for experiences on the web: An empirical examination of consumer behavior for search and experience goods. *Journal of Marketing*, *73*(March), 55–69. doi:10.1509/jmkg.73.2.55

Huang, Y.-C., Backman, S. J., & Backman, K. F. (2010). The impacts of virtual experiences on people's travel intentions. In Gretzel, U., Law, R. & Fuchs, M. (Eds.) *Information and Communication Technologies in Tourism 2010* (555-566). Proceedings of the ENTER conference Wien: Springer-Verlag.

Hudson, S., & Lang, N. (2002). A destination case study of marketing tourism on line: Banff, Canada. *Journal of Vacation Marketing*, *8*(2), 155–166. doi:10.1177/135676670200800205

Huizingh, E. K. R. E. (2000). The content and design of web sites: an empirical study. *Information & Management*, *37*(3), 123–134. doi:10.1016/S0378-7206(99)00044-0

Hung, Shin-Yuan, Ku, Cheng-Yuan, Chang, Chia-Ming, Critical Factors of Wap Services Adoption: an empirical study, 2003

Hunt, S. D. (2000). *A General Theory of Competition: Resources, Competences, Productivity, Economic Growth*. Thousand Oaks, CA: Sage Publications. 3 (1 11)

Huntzinger, J. R. (2007). *Lean Cost Management: Accounting for Lean by Establishing Flow.* Fort Lauderdale, FL: Ross Publishing. 12 (2 9)

IBM Corporation Software Group. (2005). *IBM SOA foundation: providing what you need to get started with SOA*. Service oriented architecture solutions: white paper. IBM.

IBM. (2006). IBM RUP for service-oriented modeling and architecture v2.4. Retrieved 2.4., 2008, from http://www.ibm.com/developerworks/rational/downloads/06/rmc_soma/

Iden, J., & Langeland, L. (2010). Setting the Stage for a Successful ITIL Adoption: A Delphi Study of IT Experts in the Norwegian Armed Forces. *Information Systems Management*, (27): 103–112. doi:10.1080/10580531003708378

IfM & IBM. (2007). Succeeding through Service Innovation: A Discussion Paper. Cambridge, United Kingdom: University of Cambridge Institute for Manufacturing. ISBN: 978-1-902546-59-8. 1 (14)

Indulska, M., Limam Mansar, S., & Rosemann, M. (2010). *Business Process Design*. Retrieved June 15th, 2010 from http://www.bpm2010.org/conference-program/workshops/bpd10/. 6th International Workshop on Business Process Design.

International Medical Travel Journal. (2010). *2010 Medical Tourism Climate Survey*. London, UK: Author.

Internet World Stats. (n.d.). *Internet World Stats.* Retrieved June 24th, 2010, from Keen, C., Wetzels, M., de Ruyter, K. & Feinberg, R. (2004). E-tailers versus retailers: Which factors determine consumer preferences. *Journal of Business Research*, 57, 685-695. http://www.internetworldstats.com/stats.htm.

Ismail, J. A., Labropoulos, T., Mills, J. E., & Morrison, A. M. (2002). A snapshot in time: the marketing of culture in European Union NTO websites. *Tourism Culture and Communication*, *3*(3), 165–179.

ISO/IEC. (2003). *ISO/IEC 15504.5:2004 Information technology - Process assessment - an exemplar Process Assessment Model o*. Document Number.

ISO/IEC. (2005). ISO/IEC 20000:2005 Information technology - Service management - Part 2: Code of practice [Electronic Version]

ITGI. (2007). *Control Objectives for IT and related Technologies 4.1. Rolling Meadows, IL: IT Governance Institute (ITGI). itSMF (2007). An Introductory Overview of ITIL V3*. London: IT Service Management Forum.

itSMF. (2010). Certified Organisations. Retrieved 8 March, 2010, from http://www.isoiec20000certification.com/lookuplist.asp?Type=9

itSMFI. itSMF International: the IT Service Management Forum. Retrieved 31 October, 2008, from http://www.itsmfi.org/content/chapters

Ives, B., Olson, M. H., & Baroudi, J. J. (1983). The measurement of user information satisfaction. *Communications of the ACM*, *26*(10), 785–793. doi:10.1145/358413.358430

Jacobson, I., & Booch, G. Rumbaugh, & James (1998). *Unified Software Development Process*. (Unified Software Development Process ed.) Addison Wesley Longman.

Jacoby, J., & Kaplan, L. B. (1972). The components of perceived risk. In M. Venkatesan, (Ed.), *Proceedings of the 3rd Annual Conference of the Association for Consumer Research* (pp. 382-393). College Park, MD: Association for Consumer Research.

Jaeger, M. C., Engel, L., & Geihs, K. (2005). *A methodology for developing OWL-S descriptions.* Paper presented at the Workshop on Web Services and Interoperability at First International Conference on Interoperability of Enterprise Software and Applications, Geneva, Switzerland.

Jansen, P. J., & Katz, D. M. (2002). For nonprofits, time is money. *The McKinsey Quarterly*, (1): 124–133.

Janssen, M., & Joha, A. (2008). Emerging shared service organizations and the service-oriented enterprise: critical management issues. *Outsourcing: an International Journal*, *1*(1), 35–49. doi:10.1108/17538290810857466

Jarvenpaa, S. L., & Todd, P. A. (1997). Consumer reactions to electronic shopping on the world wide web. *International Journal of Electronic Commerce, 1*(2), 59–88.

Jenkins, A. M., & Ricketts, J. A. (1979). *Development of an instrument to measure user information satisfaction with management information systems* (pp. 1–27). Bloomington: Indiana University.

Jeong, M., Ohand, H., & Gregoire, M. (2003). Conceptualizing Web quality and its consequences in the lodging industry. *International Journal of Hospitality Management, 22*(2), 161–175. doi:10.1016/S0278-4319(03)00016-1

Jilovec, N. (2005). L'offshoring delle risorse IT. *I-Series News, marzo* 22-26.

Johansson, F. (2006). *The Medici Effect: What Elephants and Epidemics Can Teach Us About Innovation*. Boston, MA: Harvard Business School Press. 13 (7)

Johnson, M. W., Hately, A., Miller, B. A., & Orr, R. (2007). Evolving standards for IT service management. *IBM Systems Journal, 46*(3), 583–597. doi:10.1147/sj.463.0583

Johnson, S. (2001). *Emergence: The connected lives of ants, brains, cities, and software*. New York, NY: Scribner. 14 (11)

Johnston, D. C. (2007). *Free Lunch: How The Wealthiest Americans Enrich Themselves At Government Expense (And Stick You With The Bill)*. New York, NY: Portfolio. 6 (3)

Johnston, S. (2005). UML 2.0 profile for software services. Retrieved 4.4., 2008, from http://www-128.ibm.com/developerworks/rational/library/05/419_soa/

Joint Commission International. (2007). *Joint Commission International Accreditation: Getting Started*. Oak Brook, IL: Author.

Jones, S. V., Maiden, N. A. M., Zachos, K., & Zhu, X. (2005). *How service-centric systems change the requirements process*. Paper presented at the 11th International Workshop on Requirements Engineering: Foundation for Software Quality (REFSQ'05), Porto, Portugal, 13-14 Jun.

Jung, T. H., & Butler, R. (2000). Perceptions of marketing managers of the effectiveness of the Internet in tourism and hospitality. *Journal of Information Technology and Tourism, 3*(3-4), 167–176.

Kahle, L. R., & Kennedy, P. (1988). Using the list of values lov to understand consumers. *Journal of Services Marketing, 2*(4), 49–56. doi:10.1108/eb024742

Kahn, R. E., & Cerf, V. G. (1988). *The Digital Library Project, volume I: The World of Knowbots*.Unpublished manuscript, Reston, VA.

Kakeshita, T., & Murata, M. (2003). *A declarative manipulation for OODB and XML DB having cyclic schema*. IEEE.

Kakihara, M., & Sorensen, C. (2001). Expanding the 'Mobility' Concept. *SIGGROUP Bulletin, 22*(3), 33–37.

Kanwar, R., & Pagiavlas, N. (1992). When are higher social class consumers more and less brand loyal than lower social class consumers? The role of mediating variables. *Advances in Consumer Research. Association for Consumer Research (U. S.), 19*, 589–595.

Kao, C. (1994). Evaluation of Junior Colleges of Technology: The Taiwan Case. *European Journal of Operational Research, 72*, 43–51. doi:10.1016/0377-2217(94)90328-X

Karat, C.-M., Blom, J. O., & Karat, J. (Eds.). (2004). *Designing Personalized User Experiences in eCommerce*. Kluwer Academic Publishers. doi:10.1007/1-4020-2148-8

Karat, J., Karat, C.-M., Brodie, C., & Feng, J. (2005). Privacy in Information Technology: Designing to Enable Privacy Policy Management in Organizations. *International Journal of Human-Computer Studies, 63*, 153–174. doi:10.1016/j.ijhcs.2005.04.011

Karat, J., Karat, C.-M., & Brodie, C. (2004). Personalizing Interaction: Directions for HCI Research. In Karat, C.-M., Blom, J. O., & Karat, J. (Eds.), *Designing Personalized User Experiences in eCommerce* (pp. 7–17). Kluwer Academic Publishers. doi:10.1007/1-4020-2148-8_2

Kargin, B., Basoglu, N., & Daim, T. (2009). Adoption factors of mobile services. *International Journal of Information Systems in the Service Sector, 1*(1), 15–34.

Kaseniemi, E.-L. (2003). *Mobile Messages: Young People and a New Communication Culture*. Tampere: Tampere University Press.

Kasikorn Research. (2007, October). Thailand Hospital Statistics. *Medical Tourism News.*

Kaufmann, D., Kraay, A., & Mastruzzi, M. (2003). Governance Matters III: Governance Indicators for 1996–2002. World Bank, World Bank Policy Research Working Paper 3106. Available at: http://www.worldbank.org/wbi/governance/pubs/govmatters2001.htm 6 (12)

Kedia, B. L., & Lahiri, S. (2007). International outsourcing of services: A partnership model. *Journal of International Management, 13*, 22–37. doi:10.1016/j.intman.2006.09.006

Kedia, B. L., Lahiri, S., & Lovvorn, A. (2005). Seeking competitive advantage on distant shores. *European Business Forum, 21*, 37–40.

Kedia, B. L., & Mukherjee, D. (2009). Understanding offshoring: A research framework based on disintegration, location and externalization advantages. *Journal of World Business, 44*, 250–261. doi:10.1016/j.jwb.2008.08.005

Keel, A. J., Orr, M. A., Hernandez, R. R., Patrocinio, E. A., & Bouchard, J. (2007). From a technology-oriented to a service-oriented approach to IT management. *IBM Systems Journal, 46*(3), 549–564. doi:10.1147/sj.463.0549

Keeney, R. L. (1999). The value of internet commerce to the customer. *Management Science, 45*(4), 533–542. doi:10.1287/mnsc.45.4.533

Keeney, R. L., & Raiffa, H. (1993). *Decisions with multiple objectives: Preferences and value tradeoffs*. Cambridge, MA: Harvard University Press.

Kessler, A. (2005). *How We Got Here: A Slightly Irreverent History of Technology and Markets.* New York, NY: Harper Collins. 3 (6 9 11 12)

Kettinger, W. J., & Lee, C. C. (1994). Perceived service quality and user satisfaction with the information systems. *Decision Sciences, 25*(5/6), 737–767. doi:10.1111/j.1540-5915.1994.tb01868.x

Kettinger, W., & Lee, C. (1997). Pragmatic Perspectives on the Measurement of Information Systems Service Quality. *Management Information Systems Quarterly, 21*(2), 223–240. doi:10.2307/249421

Kettinger, W., & Lee, C. (2005). Zones of Tolerance: Alternatives Scales for Measuring Information Systems Service Quality. *Management Information Systems Quarterly, 29*(4), 607–623.

Khalil, T. (2000). *Management of Technology: The Key to Competitiveness and Wealth Creation.* Boston, MA: McGraw-Hill. 9 (7 12)

Khan, R. N. (2004). *Business process management a practical guide*. Meghan-Kiffer Press.

Khanna, J., Posnett, J., & Sandler, T. (1995). Charity donations in the UK: New evidence based on panel data. *Journal of Public Economics, 56*, 257–272. doi:10.1016/0047-2727(94)01421-J

Kim, H. W., Chan, H. C., & Gupta, S. (2007). Value-based adoption of mobile Internet: An empirical investigation. *Decision Support Systems, 43*, 111–126. doi:10.1016/j.dss.2005.05.009

Kim, K. K. (1989). User satisfaction: A synthesis of three different perspectives. *Journal of Information Systems, 4*(1), 1–12.

Kim, M., Kim, J., & Lennon, S. (2006). Online service attributes available on apparel retail web sites: an E-S-QUAL approach. *Managing Service Quality, 16*(1), 51–77. doi:10.1108/09604520610639964

Kim, H., & Serfes, K. (2006). A location model with preference for variety. *The Journal of Industrial Economics, 54*(4), 569–595. doi:10.1111/j.1467-6451.2006.00300.x

Kim, D. (2003). Short arguments for seals of approval and portal affiliation: Building consumer trust in online shopping. In *Proceedings of the 9th Americas Conference on Information Systems* (pp. 2194-2198).

Kim, J., & Gil, Y. (2004). *Towards interactive composition of semantic web services.* Paper presented at the First International Semantic Web Services Symposium.

Kim, W. C., & Mauborgne, R. (2005). *Blue Ocean Strategy: How to Create Uncontested Market Space and Make the Competition Irrelevant.* Boston, MA: Harvard Business School Press. 7 (12)

King, W. R. (1985). Information Technology and Corporate Growth. *The Columbia Journal of World Business, 20*, 29–34.

King, J. (2002). Destination marketing organizations-connecting the experience rather than promoting the place. *Journal of Vacation Marketing, 8*(2), 105–108. doi:10.1177/135676670200800201

Kitchenham, B. (2004). *Procedures for performing systematic reviews* (Technical Report No. TR/SE-04-01). Keele, Staffordshire, UK: Keele University.

Kleijnen, M., de Ruyter, K., & Wetzels, M. (2007). An assessment of value creation in mobile service delivery and the moderating role of time consciousness. *Journal of Retailing, 83*(1), 33–46. doi:10.1016/j.jretai.2006.10.004

Kleijnen, M., & de Ruyter, K. Factors Influencing the Adoption of Mobile Gaming Services, Mobile Commerce: Technology, Theory, and Applications, Hershey, Pennsylvania, Idea Group Publishing, 2003 Knutsen, Lars, Constantiou, Ioanna D., Damsgaard, Jan, Acceptance and Perceptions of advanced mobile services: Alterations during a field study

Klein, M., & Koenig-Ries, B. (2003). *A process and a tool for creating service descriptions based on DAML-S.* Paper presented at the 4th International Workshop Technologies for E-Services (TES 2003).

Kleinrock, L., Nomadicity: anytime, anywhere in a disconnected world, Mobile Networks and Applications, 1, 4, 1996, 351-357

Klir, J. A. (1985). *Architect of System Problem Solving.* New York: Plenum Press.

Kluckhohn, C. (1951). Values and value-orientations in the theory of action. In Parsons, T., & Shils, E. (Eds.), *Towards a general theory of action.* Cambridge, MA: Harvard University Press.

Kogan, N., & Wallach, M. A. (1967). Group risk taking as a function of members' anxiety and defensiveness levels. *Journal of Personality, 35*(1), 50–63. doi:10.1111/j.1467-6494.1967.tb01415.x

Kogan, N., & Wallach, M. A. (1964). *Risk Taking, a Study in Cognition and Personality*, New York, NY: Holt, Rinehart, and Winston.

Kohn, L. T., Corrigan, J. M., & Donaldson, M. S. (1999). *To Err Is Human: Building A Safer Health System.* Washington, D.C.: Institute of Medicine, National Academy Press.

Kohn, L. T., Corrigan, J. M., & Donaldson, M. S. (1999). *To err is human: building a safer health system.* Washington, D.C.: Institute of Medicine, National Academy Press.

Kontogiannis, K., Lewis, G., Smith, D., Litoiu, M., Müller, H., Schuster, S., & Stroulia, E. (2007). The Landscape of Service-Oriented Systems: A Research Perspective. In: *International Workshop on Systems Development in SOA Environments* ((SDSOA'07: ICSE Workshops 2007). IEEE, 1-6.

Kost, J. (2003). *Government procurement reform is a strategic imperative.* Gartner, Inc.

Kotabe, M., & Murray, J. Y. (2004). Global sourcing strategy and sustainable competitive advantage. *Industrial Marketing Management, 33*, 7–14. doi:10.1016/j.indmarman.2003.08.004

Krafzig, D., Banke, K., & Slama, D. (2004). *Enterprise SOA: service-oriented architecture best practices.* Prentice Hall PTR.

Krippendorff, K. (1980). *Content analysis: an introduction to its methodology.* Beverly Hills, CA: Sage Publications.

Krueger, A. B. (2003). Economic considerations and class size. *The Economic Journal, 113*(485), F34–F63. doi:10.1111/1468-0297.00098

Kudo, M., & Hada, S. (2000). Xml access control. Retrieved October 24, 2000, from http://www.trl.ibm.com/projects/xml/xacl/xmlac-proposal.html

Kudo, M., & Hada, S. (2000) XML document security based on provisional authorization. *In Proc. 7th ACM Conference on Computer and Communications Security* (pp.87-96).

Küngas, P., & Matskin, M. (2006, 19-25 Feb). *Web services roadmap: The semantic web perspective.* Paper presented at the AICT/ICIW'06.

Kuo, W., & Zuo, M. J. (2002). *Optimal reliability modeling: principles and applications.* Wiley.

Kuper, G., Massacci, F., & Rassadko, N. (2005). Generalized xml security views. In *Proceedings of the 10th ACM sysposium on Access control models and technologies* (pp. 77-84). ACM Press.

Kwan, S. K., & Freund, L. (2007). Developing a Service Science, Management and Engineering (SSME) Program at SJSU. 13 (14)

Kyte, A. (2006). *Procurement governance, organization, strategies and systems. Gartner local briefing in Zagreb.* Gartner, Inc.

Lacity, M., & Willcocks, L. (1998). An empirical investigation of information technology sourcing practices: lessons from experience. *Management Information Systems Quarterly*, (September): 363–409. doi:10.2307/249670

Ladd, H., & Fiske, E. (2008). *Handbook of research in education finance and policy.* New York: Routledge.

Lampel, J., & Bhalla, A. (2008). Embracing realism and recognizing choice in IT offshoring initiatives. *Business Horizons, 51*, 429–440. doi:10.1016/j.bushor.2008.03.007

Langlois, R. N., & Robertson, P. L. (1995). *Firms, Markets, and Economic Change.* London, UK: Routledge. 3 (6 11)

Laroche, M., Bergerson, J., & Goutaland, Ch. (2001). A Three-Dimentional Scale of Intangibility. *Journal of Service Research, 4*(1), 26–38. doi:10.1177/109467050141003

Larson, C., & Ankomah, P. (2005). Evaluating tourism web site complexity. The case of international tourism in the U.S. *Services Marketing Quarterly, 26*(2), 23–37. doi:10.1300/J396v26n02_02

Laszlo, E. (2002). *The Systems View of the World.* Cresskill, NJ: Hampton Press. 14 (13)

Laszlo, E. (2007). *Science and the Akashic Field: An Integrated Theory of Everything.* Rochester, VT: Inner Traditions. 14 (13)

Latour, B. (2007). *Reassembling the Social: An Introduction to Actor-Network-Theory* (Clarendon Lectures in Management Studies). Oxford, UK: Oxford University. 8 (11)

Laudon, K. C., & Laudon, J. P. (2010). *Management Information Systems: Managing the Digital Firm* (11 ed.). Upper Saddle River, New Jersey: Prentice Hall.

Laurel, B. (1991). *Computers as Theatre.* Reading, Massachusetts: Addison-Wesley.

Law, R., & Leung, R. (2000). A study of airlines' online reservation services on the Internet. *Journal of Research, 39*(2), 202–211.

Lawkobkit, M. (2008). *Thailand IT Service Management Adoption.* Thailand: itSMFo. Document Number)

Lederer, A. L., Maupin, D. J., Sena, M. P., & Zhuang, Y. (2000). The Technology Acceptance Model and the World Wide Web. *Decision Support Systems*, (29): 269–282. doi:10.1016/S0167-9236(00)00076-2

Lee, J., Siau, K., & Hong, S. (2003). Enterprise integration with ERP and EAI. *Communications of the ACM, 46*(2), 54–60. doi:10.1145/606272.606273

Lee, S. M., Kim, Y. R., & Lee, J. (1995). An empirical study of the relationships among end-user infor. *Journal of Management Information Systems, 12*(2), 189–203.

Lee, J. N. (2001). The impact of knowledge sharing, organizational capability and partnership quality in IS outsourcing success. *Information & Management, 38*, 323–335. doi:10.1016/S0378-7206(00)00074-4

Lee, J. N., & Kim, Y. G. (1999). Effects of partnership quality on IS outsourcing success: conceptual framework and empirical evidence. *Journal of Management Information Systems*, (Spring): 15, 29–61.

Lee, T. D., Chen, J. Q., & Zhang, R. (2001). Utilizing the Internet as a competitive tool for non-profit organizations. *Journal of Computer Information Systems*, *41*(3), 26–31.

Leitheiser, R., & Wheteber, J. (1986). Service-Support Levels: an Organized Approach to End-user Computing. *Management Information Systems Quarterly*, (December): 337–349. doi:10.2307/249187

Leonard, J. (2006). Offshoring of information technology jobs: myths and realities. *American Sentinel University, May.*

Leung, L., & Wei, R. (2000). More than just talk on the move: Uses and gratifications of the cellular phone. *J&MC Quarterly*, *77*, 308–320.

Levina, N., & Vaast, E. (2008). Innovating or doing as told? Status differences and overlapping boundaries in offshore collaboration. *Management Information Systems Quarterly*, *32*(2), 307–332.

Levine, J. H. (1993). *Exceptions are the Rule: An Inquiry into Methods in the Social Sciences*. Boulder, CO: Westview Press.

Levinson, M. (2006). *The Box: How the Shipping Container Made the World Smaller and the World Economy Bigger.* Princeton, NJ: Princeton University Press. 5 (3 9 11)

Levitt, T. (1972). Production-line approach to service. *Harvard Business Review*, (Sep-Oct): 41–52.

Levitt, T. (1976). The Industrialization of Service. *Harvard Business Review*, (Sep-Oct): 63–74.

Levitt, T. (1976). The Industrialization of Service. *Harvard Business Review*. 54(5), 63-74. 12 (9)

Levy, F., & Murnane, R. J. (2005). *The New Division of Labor: How Computers Are Creating the Next Job Market*. Princeton, NJ: Princeton University Press. 3 (11)

Lewin, A. Y., & Peeters, C. (2006). The top-line allure of offshoring. *Harvard Business Review*, *84*, 22–24.

Lewin, A. Y. & Couto, V. (2007). *Next generation offshoring: The globalization of innovation*. Durkham: Duke University Ciber/Booz Allen Hamilton Report.

Lewis, L. (1976). Service level: a concept of the user and the computer center. *IBM Systems Journal*, *4*, 328–357. doi:10.1147/sj.154.0328

Lewis, W. W. (2004). *The Power of Productivity: Wealth, Poverty, and the Threat to Global Stability.* Chicago, IL: University of Chicago Press. 5 (3 6)

Lexhagen, M. (2009). E-marketing and customer perceived value in travel and tourism. [Östersund, Sweden: ETOUR.]. *ETOUR*, *2009*, 20.

Lexhagen, M. (2004). The importance of value-added services to support the customer search and purchase process on travel websites. *Journal of Information Technology and Tourism*, *7*(2), 119–135. doi:10.3727/1098305054517336

Lieberman, M. B. (1987). The learning curve, diffusion, and competitive strategy. *Strategic Management Journal*, *8*(5), 441–452.

Liebermann, Y., & Stashevsky, S. (2002). Perceived risks as barriers to internet and e-commerce usage. *Qualitative Market Research: An International Journal*, *5*(4), 291–300. doi:10.1108/13522750210443245

Liu, J., Zhang, S., & Hu, J. (2005). A case study of an inter-enterprise workflow-supported supply chain management system. *Information & Management*, *42*(3), 441–454. doi:10.1016/j.im.2004.01.010

Liu, C., & Arnett, K. P. (2000). Exploring the factors associated with website success in the context of electronic commerce. *Information & Management*, *38*(1), 23–33. doi:10.1016/S0378-7206(00)00049-5

Lohse, G. L., Bellman, S., & Johnson, E. J. (2000). Consumer buying behavior on the internet: findings from panel data. *Journal of Interactive Marketing*, *14*(1), 15–29. doi:10.1002/(SICI)1520-6653(200024)14:1<15::AID-DIR2>3.0.CO;2-C

Loiacono, E. T., Watson, R. T., & Goodhue, D. L. (2007). WebQual: An Instrument for Consumer Evaluations of Web Sites. *To appear in the Internation Journal of Electronic Commerce*.

Lomow, G., & Newcomer, E. (2005). *Understanding SOA with web services*. Addison-Wesley Professional.

Lovelock, Ch. H. (1983). Classifying Services to Gain Strategic Marketing Insights. *Journal of Marketing*, *47*(Summer), 9–20. doi:10.2307/1251193

Lovelock, Ch. H. (2001). *Services Marketing: People, Technology, Strategy*. Upper Saddle River, NJ: Prentice Hall.

Lovelock, C. H., & Wirtz, J. (2004). *Services Marketing: People, Technology, Strategy* (5th ed.). Upper Saddle River, N.J.: Pearson/Prentice Hall.

Lovelock, C., & Gummesson, E. (2004). Whither services marketing? In search of a new paradigm and fresh perspectives. *Journal of Service Research*, *7*(1), 20–41. doi:10.1177/1094670504266131

Lovelock, C. (2007*). Services Marketing: People, Technology, Strategy*. Sixth Edition. Upper Saddle River, NJ: Pearson Education. 4 (2 8 9 10 11 12 15)

Lovelock, C., & Gummesson, E. (2004). Whither service marketing? In search of a new paradigm and fresh perspectives. *Journal of Service Research*, 7(1), 20-41. 4 (12)

Lovelock, Ch. And J. Wirtz. (2007). *Service Marketing, People, Technology, Strategy*. Upper Saddle River, NJ: Pearson-Prentice Hall.

Lowell, S., Silverman, L., & Taliento, L. (2001). Not-for-profit management: The gift that keeps on giving. *The McKinsey Quarterly*, *1*, 147.

Luo, Y. (2007). A coopetition perspective of global competition. *Journal of World Business*, *42*, 129–144. doi:10.1016/j.jwb.2006.08.007

Lusch, R. F., & Vargo, S. L. (2006). *The Service-Dominant Logic of Marketing: Dialog, Debate and Directions*. Armonk, NY: M.E. Sharpe. 4 (12 15)

Lusch, R., & Vargo, S. (2006). (Eds.). *The Service-Dominant Logic of Marketing: Dialog, Debate, and Directions*. M.E. Sharpe: New York.

MacCrimmon, K. R., & Wehrung, D. A. (1986). *Taking Risks: The Management of Uncertainty*. New York, NY: The Free Press.

Madhoc, A. (2006). How much does ownership really matter? Equity and trust relations in joint venture relationship. *Journal of International Business Studies*, *37*, 4–11. doi:10.1057/palgrave.jibs.8400182

Madu, C. N., & Madu, A. A. (2002). Dimensions of e-quality. *International Journal of Quality & Reliability*, *19*(3), 246–258. doi:10.1108/02656710210415668

Mäenpää, K. (2006). Clustering the consumer on the basis of their perceptions of the internet banking services. *Internet Research*, *16*(3), 304–322. doi:10.1108/10662240610673718

Maglio, P. P., & Spohrer, J. (2006). (in press). SSME. *Production and Operations Management*, *14*(13).

Maglio, P. P., Kreulen, J., Srinivasan, S., & Spohrer, J. (2006). Service systems, service scientists, SSME, and innovation. *Communications of the ACM*, 49(7), 81 – 85. 14 (1)

Magni, M., Taylor, M. S., & Venkatesh, V. (2010). To play or not to play: A cross-temporal investigation using hedonic and instrumental perspectives to explain user intentions to explore a technology. *International Journal of Human-Computer Studies*, *68*, 572–588. doi:10.1016/j.ijhcs.2010.03.004

Mahnke, V. (2001). The process of vertical dis-integration: an evolutionary perspective on outsourcing. *Journal of Management and Governance*, *5*, 353–379. doi:10.1023/A:1014003229386

Mahnke, V., Overby, M. L., & Vang, J. (2003). Strategic IT outsourcing: what do we know and need to know? *Paper presented at the Druid Conference 2003 on Creating, sharing and transferring knowledge*. Copenhagen, June 12-14.

Malhotra, Yogesh, Galletta, Dennis F., Extending the Technology Acceptance Model to Account for Social Influence: Theoretical Bases and Emprical Validation, 1999

Mallat et al., The Impact of Use Situation and Mobility on the Acceptance of Mobile Ticketing Services, 2006

Malone, T. W., Yates, J., & Benjamin, R. I. (1987). Electronic markets and electronic hierarchies. *Communications of the ACM*, *30*(6), 484–497. doi:10.1145/214762.214766

Malone, T. W. (2004). *The Future of Work: How the New Order of Business Will Shape Your Organization, Your Management Style, and Your Life*. Cambridge, MA: Harvard Business School Press. 11 (3 6 8 10 12)

Mandelbaum, A., & Zeltyn, S. (2008). Service engineering of call centers; Research, Teaching, and Practice. In Hefly, B., & Murphy W. (Ed.), *Service Science Management and Engineer: Education for the 21st Century*, (pp. 317-328). New York, NY: Springer. 9 (10)

March, S., & Smith, G. (1995). Design and natural science research on information technology. *Decision Support Systems*, *15*, 251–266. doi:10.1016/0167-9236(94)00041-2

March, J. G. (1988). *Decisions and Organizations*. New York, NY: Basil Blackwell. 6 (11 12)

March, J. G. (1991). Exploration and exploitation in organizational learning. *Organizational Science*, 2(1), 71-87. 11 (5 7 12)

March, J. G. (1999). *The Pursuit of Organizational Intelligence*. Malden, MA: Blackwell. 11 (14)

March, J., & Simon, H. (1958/2003). *Organizations*. Second Edition. Cambridge, MA: Blackwell. 11 (6 8 12 14)

Marcussen, C. H. (n.d.). *Marcussen*Retrieved June 20th, 2010, from http://wwwcrt.dk/UK/staff/chm/trends.htm.

Mark, R. Chassin, M., MPP, MPH, & Elise C. Becher, M., MA. (2002). The wrong patient. *Academia & Clinic*, *136*(11), 826–833.

Marks, E. A., & Bell, M. (2006). *Service-Oriented Architecture: A Planning and Implementation Guide for Business and Technology.* Hoboken, NJ: Wiley. 10 (12)

Marshall, A. (1890/2006). *Principles of Economics.* Abridged Edition. New York, NY: Cosimo. 3 (6 8)

Martin, D., Paolucci, M., McIlraith, S., Burstein, M., McDermott, D., McGuinness, D., et al. (2004). *Bringing semantics to web services: The OWL-S approach.* Paper presented at the First International Workshop on Semantic Web Services and Web Process Composition.

Martin, E., Basu, S., & Xie, T. (2007). WebSob: A tool for robustness testing of web services. *29th International Conference on Software Engineering* (ICSE 2007), Minneapolis, MN, USA, May 20-26, 2007, *Companion Volume* (pp. 65-66). Los Vaqueros, CA: IEEE Computer Society.

Mathwick, C., Malhotra, N., & Rigdon, E. (2001). Experiential value: conceptualization, measurement and application in the catalogue and Internet shopping environment. *Journal of Retailing*, *77*, 39–56. doi:10.1016/S0022-4359(00)00045-2

Mathwick, C., Malhotra, N., & Rigdon, E. (2002). The effect of dynamic retail experiences on experiential perceptions of value: an Internet and catalogue comparison. *Journal of Retailing*, *78*, 51–60. doi:10.1016/S0022-4359(01)00066-5

May, P. (2001). *Opportunities, Applications, and Technologies of Wireless Business*. Mobile, Commerce: Cambridge University Press. doi:10.1017/CBO9780511583919

McFarlan, F. W. (1981). Portfolio Approach to Information Systems. *Harvard Business Review*, (September-October): 142–150.

McGahan, A. M. (2004). *How Industries Evolve: Principles for Achieving and Sustaining Superior Performance*. Boston, MA: Harvard Business School Press. 7 (3 11)

McHaney, R., & Cronan, T. P. (1998). Computer simulation success: On the use of the end-user computing satisfaction instrument: A comment. *Decision Sciences*, *29*(2), 525–537. doi:10.1111/j.1540-5915.1998.tb01589.x

McHaney, R., Hightower, R., & Pearson, J. (2002). A validation of the end-user computing satisfaction instrument in Taiwan. *Information & Management*, *39*(6), 503–511. doi:10.1016/S0378-7206(01)00119-7

McKenna, C. D. (2006). *The World's Newest Profession: Management Consulting in the Twentieth Century* (Cambridge Studies in the Emergence of Global Enterprise). Cambridge, UK: Cambridge University Press. 13 (8 11 12 14 15)

Meehan, W. F. (2001). Reinventing philanthropy. *The McKinsey Quarterly*, 1.

Melenovsky, M. J. (2006). *Case study: BPM organizational staffing and structure*. Gartner, Inc.

Mendelson, H., & Ziegler, J. (1999). *Survival of the Smartest: Managing Information for Rapid Action and World-Class Performance*. New York, NY: Wiley. 12 (10 11)

Mennecke, B., & Strader, T. (2003). *Mobile Commerce Technology, Theory and Applications*. Hershey, Pennsylvania: Idea Group.

Mertler, C. A., & Vannatta, R. A. (2001). *Advanced and multivariate statistical methods: Practical application and interpretation*. Los Angeles, CA: Pyrczak Publishing.

Metters, R. (2008). A case study of national culture and offshoring services. *International Journal of Operations & Production Management*, *28*(8), 727–747. doi:10.1108/01443570810888616

MF, M., & JD, K. (2004). Patient Identification: Problems and Potential Solutions. *Vox Sanguinis*, *87*, 197–202. doi:10.1111/j.1741-6892.2004.00482.x

Mich, L., Franch, M., & Gaio, L. (2002). *Evaluating and designing the quality of web sites*, Working paper, 70, DISA, University of Trento. Mich, L., Franch, M., & Cilione, G. (2003). The 2QCV3Q quality model for the analysis of web site requirements. *Journal of Web Engineering*, *2*(1-2), 115–127.

Mich, L., & Franch, M. (2007). *Un approccio multi-step per la valutazione dell'usabilità del sito web di una destinazione turistica*. Paper presented at the 4th Annual Conference of the Italian Marketing Academy: Il Marketing dei Talenti, Roma, 5-6 October.

Miles, M. B., & Huberman, A. M. (1994). *Qualitative data analysis: An expanded sourcebook*. Thousand Oaks, CA: Sage Publications.

Milgrom, P., & Roberts, J. (1992). *Economics, Organization, and Management*. Upper Saddle River, NJ: Prentice Hall. 3 (11 12)

Mill, J. S. (1929). *Principles of the Political Economy*. London, UK: Longmans Green. (Available on Google Books) 3 (6 8)

Mintzberg, H., Ahlstrand, B., & Lampel, J. (1998). *Strategy safari: A guide through the wilds of strategic management*. New York: The Free Press.

Mitchell, V. W. (1992). Understanding consumers' behavior: Can perceived risk theory help? *Management Decision*, *30*(3), 326–331. doi:10.1108/00251749210013050

Mitchell, V. W. (1998). Buy-phase and buy-class effects on organizational risk perceptions and risk reduction in purchasing professional services. *Journal of Business and Industrial Marketing*, *13*(6), 461–478. doi:10.1108/08858629810246779

Mitchell, V. W. (1999). Consumer perceived risk: Conceptualizations and models. *European Journal of Marketing*, *33*(1/2), 163–195. doi:10.1108/03090569910249229

Mitchell, V. W., & Boustani, P. (1993). Market development using new products and new customers: A role for perceived risk. *European Journal of Marketing*, *27*(2), 17–32. doi:10.1108/03090569310026385

Mitra, K., Reiss, M. C., & Capella, L. M. (1999). An examination of perceived risk, information search, and behavior intentions in search, experience and credence services. *Journal of Services Marketing*, *13*(3), 208–228. doi:10.1108/08876049910273763

Mittal, K. (2007). Service oriented unified process. Retrieved 3.3., 2008, from http://www.kunalmittal.com/html/soup.shtml

Miyazaki, A. D., & Krishnamurthy, S. (2002). Internet seals of approval: Effects on online privacy policies and consumer perceptions. *The Journal of Consumer Affairs*, *36*(1), 28–49. doi:10.1111/j.1745-6606.2002.tb00419.x

Mohamed, M. S., Ribière, V. M., O'Sullivan, K. J., & Mohamed, M. A. (2008). The re-structuring of the information technology infrastructure library (ITIL) implementation using knowledge management framework. *Vine*, *38*(3). doi:10.1108/03055720810904835

Mol, M. J., van Tulder, R. J. M., & Beije, P. R. (2005). Antecedents and performance consequences of international outsourcing. *International Business Review*, *14*, 599–617. doi:10.1016/j.ibusrev.2005.05.004

Monahan, B., Pym, D., Taylor, R., Tofts, C., & Yearworth, M. (2006). Grand Challenges for Systems and Services Sciences. Paper prepared for FET/FP7 Workshop, Brussels (January 31, 2006). Available as HP Labs Technical Report, HPL-2006-99, from http://www.hpl.hp.com/techreports/2006/HPL-2006-99.pdf 14 (9 10)

Moore, G., & Benbasat, I. (1991). Development of an Instrument to Measure the Perceptions of Adopting an Information Technology Innovation. *Information Systems Research*, *2*(3), 192–222. doi:10.1287/isre.2.3.192

Moore, G. (2005). *Dealing with Darwin: How Great Companies Innovate at Every Phase of Their Evolution.* New York, NY: Portfolio/Penguin Group. 7 (11 12)

Mora, M., Gelman, O., Forgionne, G., Petkov, D., & Cano, J. (2007). Integrating the Fragmented Pieces of Is research Paradigms and Frameworks: A systems Approach. *Information Resources Management Journal*, *20*(2), 1–12.

Mora, M., Gelman, O., Frank, M., Cervantes, F., & Forgionne, G. (2008a). Toward an Interdisciplinary Engineering and Management of Complex IT-intensive Organizational Systems: a Systems View. *International Journal of Information Technologies and Systems Approach*, *1*(1), 1–24.

Mora, M., Gelman, O., O'Connor, R., Alvarez, F., & Macias-Luevano, J. (2008b). A Conceptual Descriptive-Comparative Study of Models and Standards of Processes in SE, SwE and IT disciplines using the Theory of Systems. *International Journal of Information Technologies and Systems Approach*, *1*(2).

Mora, M., Gelman, O., & Cervantes, F. (2003). A systemic approach for the formalization of the information system concept: why information systems are systems? In Cano, J. (Ed.), *Critical reflections of Information systems: a systemic approach* (pp. 1–29). Hershey, PA: Idea Group.

Mora, M., Gelman, O., Paradice, D., & Cervantes, F. (2008). The Case for Conceptual Research in Information Systems. In: Janczewski, L. & Gutierrez, J.: *Proceedings of the 2008 International Conference in Information Resources Management* (pp 1-10), Hershey, Pennsylvania: IRMA.

Mora, M., Gelman, O., Paradice, D., & Cervantes, F. (2008c). The Case for Conceptual Research in Information Systems. In: G. Grant & F. Tan (Eds), e-Proceedings of the 2008 International Conference on Information Resources Management (Conf-IRM), May 18-20, 2008, Niagara Falls, Ontario, Canada, 1-10.

Morgan, G. (1997). *Images of Organization.* Thousand Oaks, CA. *Sage (Atlanta, Ga.)*, *11*(8).

Morgan, N., Pritchard, A., & Pride, R. (2002). *Destination branding. Creating the unique destination preposition.* Oxford: Butterworth-Heinemann.

Moriarty, R., & Spekman, R. (1984). An empirical investigation of the information buying sources used during the industrial buying process. *JMR, Journal of Marketing Research*, *21*(2), 137–147. doi:10.2307/3151696

Morrison, A. M., Taylor, S., Morrison, A. J., & Morrison, A. D. (1999). Marketing small hotels on the world wide web. *Journal of Information Technology and Tourism*, *2*(2), 97–113.

Moulton Reger, S. J. (2006). *Can Two Rights Make a Wrong? Insights from IBM's Tangible Culture Approach*. Upper Saddle River, NJ: Pearson/IBM Press. 8 (10 11)

Mulgan, G. (2006). The Process of Social Innovation. Innovations, 145-162 (Spring). URL: http://www.youngfoundation.org 13 (6 7)

Mummalaneni, V. (2005). An empirical investigation of web site characteristics, consumer emotional states and on-line shopping behaviours. *Journal of Business Research*, *58*, 526–532. doi:10.1016/S0148-2963(03)00143-7

Murmann, J. P. (2006). *Knowledge and Competitive Advantage: The Coevolution of Firms, Technology, and National Institutions* (Cambridge Studies in the Emergence of Global Enterprise). Cambridge, UK: Cambridge University Press. 3 (6 7 8 9 10 11)

Murray, K. B. (1991). A test of service marketing theory: Consumer information acquisition activities. *Journal of Marketing*, *55*(1), 10–25. doi:10.2307/1252200

Murray, K. B., & Schlater, J. L. (1990). The impact of services versus goods on consumers' assessment of perceived risk. *Journal of the Academy of Marketing Science*, *18*(1), 51–65. doi:10.1007/BF02729762

Murray, S. (2008, January). Youthful force for change in society. FT.com, 1. Retrieved July 1, 2008, from ABI/INFORM Global database. (Document ID: 1418621681).

Musson, D., & Jordan, E. (2006). *The Benefits of IT Governance.* Paper presented at the European Conference on Information Systems Goteborg, Sweden.

Nagle, T. T., & Holden, R. K. (1987/2002). *The Strategy and Tactics of Pricing: A Guide to Profitable Decision Making*. Third Edition. Upper Saddle River. NJ: Prentice Hall. 12 (4)

Nah, F. F.-H., & Davis, S. (2002). HCI Research Issues in Electronic Commerce. *Journal of Electronic Commerce Research*, *3*(3), 98–113.

Nambisan, S., & Sawhney, M. (2008). *The Global Brain: Your Roadmap for Innovating Faster and Smarter in a Networked World.* Saddle River, NJ: Pearson Education, Wharton School Publishing. 7 (6 11 12)

Neftci, S. N. (2004). *Principles of Financial Engineering*. New York, NY: Elsevier. 9 (12 15)

Nelson, R. R., & Winter, S. G. (1982). *An Evolutionary Theory of Economic Change*. Cambridge, MA: Harvard University Press. 3 (8 14)

Nero, G. (1999). Full or partial market coverage? A note on spatial competition with elastic demand. *Managerial and Decision Economics*, *20*(2), 107–111. doi:10.1002/(SICI)1099-1468(199903)20:2<107::AID-MDE921>3.0.CO;2-C

Neudorfer, R. (2004). *Critical Success Factors for the Management of Innovative Mobile Business Models*. Evolaris Research Lab.

New Media, E. T. C. (n.d.). *ETC New Media.* Retrieved June 24th, 2010, from http://www.newmediatrendwatch.com/world-overview/91-online-travel-market.

New Media, E. T. C. (n.d.). *ETC New Media. ETC New Media*, (n.d.). Retrieved June 8th, 2007, from http://www.etcnewmedia.com/review/default.asp?SectionID=3&uID=962&nnID=20/1173#1173.

Newnan, D. G., Lavelle, J. P., & Eschenbach, T. G. (2003). *Essentials of Engineering Economics*. Second Edition. Oxford, UK: Oxford University Press. 9 (3 12)

Nickerson, G. T., & Kritsonis, W. A. (2006). A global prospective: A comparison of Asian and American educational systems that impact student academic achievement. *National Journal for Publishing and Mentoring Doctoral Student Research*, *3*(1), 1–4.

Nielsen, J. (2000). *Designing Web Usability: The Practice of Simplicity*. Indianapolis, Indiana: New Riders Publishing.

Nieves, M., & Iqbal, M. (2007). *ITIL v3 Core Practice Book 1: Service Strategy* (3rd ed.). London, UK: The Stationary Office of the Office of Government Commerce.

Nilsson, A. G. (2005). Information Systems Development (ISD): Past, Present, Future. Information Systems Development: Advances in Theory, Practice and Education Edited by O. Vasilecas et al., Springer, 29-40. Open Grid Services Architecture (OGSA), [on line] http://www.ggf.org/ogsa-wg/

Noble, S. M., Griffith, D. A., & Weinberger, M. G. (2005). Consumer derived utilitarian value and channel utilization in a multi-channel retail context. *Journal of Business Research, 58*(12), 1643–1651. doi:10.1016/j.jbusres.2004.10.005

Nonoyama-Tarumi, Y. (2008, January). Cross-national estimates of the effects of family background on student achievement: A sensitivity analysis. *International Review of Education, 54*(1), 57–82. doi:10.1007/s11159-007-9069-5

Norman, D. A. (1988). *The Psychology of Everyday Things*. New York, New York: Basic Books.

Norman, D. A. (1993). *Things That Make Us Smart: Defending Human Attributes in the Age of the Machine.* New York, NY: Addison Wesley. 7 (8 9)

Norman, D. A. (2006, Sep+Oct). Words Matter. Talk About People -- Not Customers, Not Consumers, Not Users. *Interactions, 13,* 49,63.

Normann, R. (2001). *Reframing Business: When the Map Changes the Landscape.* Chichester, New Sussex: Wiley. 1 (2 4 6 7 8 12 13 14 15)

North, D. C. (2005). *Understanding the process of economic change.* Princeton, NJ: Princeton University Press. 1 (3 6 11 15)

Novotny, D., & Sabati, Z. (2007). Internet enabled public services as a driver of economic growth - case study ECroatia 2006. Faculty of Organization and Informatics Varaždin - University of Zagreb. *Journal of Information and Organizational Sciences, 31*(1), 141–156.

Nysveen, H., Methlie, L. B., & Pedersen, P. E. (2003). Tourism web sites and value added services: the gap between customer preferences and web sites' offerings. *Journal of Information Technology and Tourism, 5*(3), 165–174. doi:10.3727/109830503108751117

O'Neill, M., Wright, C., & Fitz, F. (2001). Quality evaluation in online service environments. *Managing Service Quality, 11*(6), 402–417. doi:10.1108/EUM0000000006519

OECD. (2000). *The Service Economy. Paris: OECD. Rathmell, John M. (1974), Marketing in the Service Sector.* Cambridge, MA: Winthrop.

OECD. (2007). Education at a glance 2007: OECD indicators. Retrieved July 1, 2008, from http://www.oecd.org/dataoecd/4/55/39313286.pdf

Offutt, J., & Xu, W. (2004). Generating test cases for web services using data perturbation. *ACM SIGSOFT Software Engineering Notes, 29*(5), 1–10. doi:10.1145/1022494.1022529

OGC. (2007). *Service Strategy*. London: TSO for the Office of Government Commerce.

OGC. (2007). *The Official Introduction to the ITIL Service Lifecycle*. London: TSO.

OGC. (2008). ITIL. http://www.itil.co.uk/ [On-line].

Okten, C., & Weisbrod, B. A. (2000). Determinants of donations in private nonprofit markets. *Journal of Public Economics, 75*, 255–272. doi:10.1016/S0047-2727(99)00066-3

Oliva, R., & Sterman, J. D. (2001). Cutting Corners and Working Overtime: Quality Erosion in the Service Industry. *Management Science, 47*(7), 894–914. doi:10.1287/mnsc.47.7.894.9807

Olson, M., & Chervany, N. (1980). The relationship between organizational characteristics and the structure of the information service function. *Management Information Systems Quarterly*, (June): 57–68. doi:10.2307/249337

OMG. (2006). Ontology definition metamodel. Retrieved 3.4., 2008, from http://www.omg.org/cgi-bin/doc?ad/06-05-01.pdf

Open Grid Services Architecture (OGSA) Glossary of Terms v. 1.5 (2006). [on line] http://www.ogf.org/documents/GFD.81.pdf

Open Grid Services Architecture Web Services Reference Framework (OGSA WSRF). (2006) [on line] http://www.ogf.org/documents/GFD.72.pdf

Ormerod, P. (2005). *Why Most Things Fail: Evolution, Extinction, and Economics*. London, UK: Faber and Faber. 3 (11 12)

Overby, J. W., & Lee, E. J. (2006). The effects of utilitarian and hedonic online shopping value on consumer preferences and intentions. *Journal of Business Research*, *59*, 1160–1166. doi:10.1016/j.jbusres.2006.03.008

Ozcelik, Y. (2008). Globalization and the Internet: Digitizing the nonprofit sector. *Journal of Global Business Issues*, *2*(1), 149–152.

Pagani, Margherita, Determinants of Adoption of Third Generation Mobile Multimedia Services Journal of Interactive Marketing Volume 18, Number 3, 2004

Palmer, J. W., Bailey, J. P., & Faraj, S. (2000). The role of intermediaries in the development of trust on the WWW: The use and prominence of trusted third parties and privacy statements. *Journal of Computer-Mediated Communication, 5*(3). Retrieved October 1, 2008, from http://jcmc.indiana.edu/vol5/issue3/ palmer.html

Palmisano, S.J. (2006). The Globally Integrated Enterprise. *Foreign Affairs*, 127-136 (May/June). 11 (12)

Palvia, P. C. (1996). A model and instrument for measuring small business user satisfaction with information technology. *Information & Management*, *31*(3), 151–163. doi:10.1016/S0378-7206(96)01069-5

Papazoglou, M. P., & van den Heuvel, W.-J. (2006). Service-oriented design and development methodology. *International Journal of Web Engineering and Technology*, *2*(4), 412–442. doi:10.1504/IJWET.2006.010423

Papazoglou, M. P., & van den Heuvel, W.-J. (2007). Service-oriented architectures: Approaches, technologies and research issues. *The VLDB Journal*, *16*, 389–415. doi:10.1007/s00778-007-0044-3

Parasuraman, A., & Zinkhan, G. M. (2002). Marketing to and service customers through the Internet: An overview and research agenda. *Journal of the Academy of Marketing Science*, *30*(4), 286–295. doi:10.1177/009207002236906

Parasuraman, A., Zeithaml, V. A., & Berry, L. L. (1988). SERVQUAL: A multiple-item scale for measuring consumer perceptions of service quality. *Journal of Retailing*, *64*(1), 12–40.

Parasuraman, A., Zeithaml, V. A., & Berry, L. L. (1985, Fall). A Conceptual Model of Service Quality and Its Implications for Future Research. *Journal of Marketing*, *49*, 41–50. doi:10.2307/1251430

Parasuraman, A., Zeithaml, V. A., & Malhotra, A. (2005). E-S-QUAL: A Multiple-Item Scale for Assessing Electronic Service Quality. *Journal of Service Research*, *7*(3), 213–233. doi:10.1177/1094670504271156

Parasuraman, A., Zeithaml, V., & Berry, L. (1988). SERVQUAL: a Multiple-item Scale for Measuring Consumer Perceptions in Service Quality. *Journal of Retailing*, *64*(1), 12–40.

Parasuraman, A., Zeithaml, V. A., & Berry, L. (1994). Alternative Scales for Measuring Service Quality: A Comparative Assessment Based on Psychometric and Diagnostic Criteria. *Journal of Retailing*, *70*(3), 201–229. doi:10.1016/0022-4359(94)90033-7

Parasuraman, A., Zeithaml, V. A., & Malhotra, A. (2005). E-S-QUAL: A multiple-item scale for assessing electronic service quality. *Journal of Service Research*, *7*(3), 213–233. doi:10.1177/1094670504271156

Park, C. S. (2004). *Fundamentals of Engineering Economics*. Upper Saddle River, NJ: Pearson. 9 (2 3 12)

Park, J., & Sandhu, R. (2002). Towards usage control models: beyond traditional access control. In *Proceedings of the seventh ACM symposium on Access control models and technologies* (pp. 57-64). ACM Press.

Park, J., Sandhu, R., & Schifalacqua, J. (2003). Security architectures for controlled digital information dissemination. *In Proceedings of 16th Annual Computer Security Application Conference.*

Park, K. (1997). Human error. In G. Salvendy (Ed.), *Handbook of Human Factors and Ergonomics*, 150-171. New York: John Wiley & Sons.

Parker, G. G., & Van Alstyne, M. W. (2005). Two-sided network effects: A theory of information product design. *Management Science*, *51*(10), 1494–1504. doi:10.1287/mnsc.1050.0400

Parsons, A. G. (2002). Non-functional motives for online shoppers: Why we click. *Journal of Consumer Marketing*, *19*(5), 380–392. doi:10.1108/07363760210437614

Patient safety applications of bar code and RFID technologies. *A Zebra Black & White Paper.*

Patient Safety Applications of Bar Code and RFID Technologies. *A Zebra Black & White Paper.*

Paul, L., Ingham, J., & Collerette, P. (2003). Why do people use information technology? A critical review of the technology acceptance model. *Information & Management*, *40*, 191–204. doi:10.1016/S0378-7206(01)00143-4

Pedersen, Per E., Nysveen, Herbjørn, Thorbjørnsen, Helge., Adoption of Mobile Services. Model Development and Cross-Service Study, 2004

Penrose, E. (1959/1995). *The Theory of the Growth of the Firm.* Third Edition. Oxford, UK: Oxford University Press. 3 (8 11 12)

Penta, M. D., Canfora, G., Esposito, G., Mazza, V., & Bruno, M. (2007). *Search-based testing of service level agreements.* In Thierens, D. et al. (Eds.), *GECCO'07 - Genetic and Evolutionary Computation Conference*, (pp. 1090-1097), New York: ACM Press.

Peter, J. P., & Olson, J. C. (2002). *Consumer Behaviour and Marketing Strategy* (6th ed.). New York: McGraw-Hill.

Petrie, C. (1995). Using Pareto optimality to coordinate distributed agents, *Stanford.* Retrieved July 1, 2008, from http://www-cdr.stanford.edu/nextlink/papers/pareto/pareto.html

Pew Internet & American Life Project. (2002). Online banking: A Pew Internet project data memo. http://www.pewinternet.org/pdfs/PIP_Online_Banking.pdf (November).

Pfannenstein, L. L., & Tsai, R. J. (2004). Offshoring outsourcing: Current and future effect on American IT industry. *Information Systems Management*, *21*(4), 72–80. doi:10.1201/1078/44705.21.4.20040901/84190.9

Phocuswright.com. (2010) *Phocuswright.com. Phocuswright*, (2010). FYI Newsletter., Retrievedreceived on the 5th of April 2010 from http://www.phocuswright.com.

Phocuswright.com. (n.d.) *Phocuswright.com.* Retrieved June 20th, 2010, from http://www.phocuswright.com.

Pine, B. J., II, & Gilmore, J. H. (1999). *The Experience Economy: Work is Theatre and Every Business a Stage.* Boston, MA: Harvard Business School Press. 7 (3 4 8 12)

Pinhanez, C. (2007, July 10-13). *Ubiquitous Services.* Paper presented at the Proc. of IEEE Services Computing Conference - SCC'07, Salt Lake City, Utah.

Pinhanez, C. (2008). *Service Systems as Customer-Intensive Systems and its Implications for Service Science and Engineering.* Paper presented at the Proc. of Hawaiian International Conference on System Sciences, HICSS-41, Big Island, Hawaii.

Pitt, L. F., Watson, R. T., & Kavan, C. B. (1995). Service quality: A measure of information systems effectiveness. *Management Information Systems Quarterly*, *19*(2), 173–187. doi:10.2307/249687

Pitt, L., Watson, R., & Kavan, C. (1997). Measuring Information Systems Service Quality: Concerns for a Complete Canvas. *Management Information Systems Quarterly*, *21*(2), 209–221. doi:10.2307/249420

Pitt, L., Berthon, P., & Lane, N. (1998). Gaps within the IS department: barriers to service quality. *Journal of Information Technology, 13*(3), 191–200. doi:10.1080/026839698344837

Plouffe, C. R., Hulland, J. S., & Vandenbosh, M. (2001). 2001a. Richness versus parsimony in modeling technology adoption decisions, understanding merchant adoption of a smart card-based payment system. *Information Systems Research, 12*, 208–222. doi:10.1287/isre.12.2.208.9697

Pollach, I., Treiblmaier, H., & Floh, A. (2005). Online fundraising for environmental nonprofit organizations. In *Proceedings of the 38th Hawaii International Conference on System Sciences*, 178b.

Pollatsck, A., & Tversky, A. (1970). A theory of risk. *Journal of Mathematical Psychology, 7*(3), 540–553. doi:10.1016/0022-2496(70)90039-8

Popoli, P., & Popoli, A. (2009). Old and new paradigms for IT services offshoring. *International Journal of Information Systems in the Service Sector, 1*(3), 47–64.

Poppo, L., & Zenger, T. (2002). Do formal contracts and relational governance function as substitutes or complements? *Strategic Management Journal, 23*, 707–725. doi:10.1002/smj.249

Porat, M. U. (1977). The Information Economy: Definition and Measurement. US Department of Commerce, Office of Telecommunications, OT Special Publication, 77-12(1). 3 (8 10 11)

Porter, M. E. (1991). Toward a dynamic theory of strategy. *Strategic Management Journal, 12*(1), 95–117. doi:10.1002/smj.4250121008

Porter, M. E., & Kramer, M. R. (1999). Philanthropy's new agenda: Creating value. *Harvard Business Review, 77*(2), 121–130.

Porter, M. E. (1990). *The competitive advantage of nations*. New York: Free Press.

Porter, M. E. (1996). What is Strategy? *Harvard Business Review*, (November-December): 61–78.

Porter, M. E. (1998). *Competitive advantage: Creating and sustaining superior performance*. New York: Free Press.

Porter, M. E., & Teisberg, E. O. (2006). *Redefining health care: Creating value-based competition on results*. Boston, MA: Harvard Business School Press.

Posnett, J., & Sandler, T. (1989). Demand for charity donations in private nonprofit markets: The case of the UK. *Journal of Public Economics, 40*, 187–200. doi:10.1016/0047-2727(89)90002-9

Praeg, C.-P., & Schnabel, U. (2006, 4-7 Jan). *IT-Service Cachet - managing IT-service performance and IT-service quality.* Paper presented at the 39th Annual Hawaii International Conference on System Sciences (HICSS'06), Kauai.

Prahalad, C. K., & Hamel, G. (1990). *The core competence of the corporation*. Harvard Business Review, May-June.

Prahalad, C. K. (2004). *The Future of Competition. Co-Creating Unique Value with Customers*. Boston, MA: Harvard Business School Press. 7 (4)

Prencipe, A., Davies, A., & Hobday, M. (2005). *The Business of Systems Integration.* Oxford, UK: Oxford University Press. 9 (3 11 12)

Prescott, S., & Hopkins, G. (1984). The value and attitude structure of special educators. *College Student Journal, 18*(2), 56–59.

Preus, B. (2007). Educational trends in China and the United States: proverbial pendulum or potential for balance? *Phi Delta Kappan, 89*(2), 115–118.

Quelch, J. A., & Klein, L. R. (1996). The Internet and international marketing. *Sloan Management Review, 37*(3), 60–75.

Quinn, J. (1992). *Intelligent Enterprise*. New York: The Free Press.

Quinn, J. B., & Hilmer, F. G. (1994). Strategic outsourcing. *Sloan Management Review*, 35.

Quinn, J. B. (2006). Giving freely and wisely. *Newsweek*, December 18, 51.

Quinn, J. B., & Paquette, P. C. (1990). Technology in services: Creating organizational revolutions. *Sloan Management Review*, 31(2), 67-78. 11 (4 9 10 12)

Quinn, J. B., Baruch, J. J., & Paquette, P. C. (1987). Technology in Services. *Scientific American*, 257(2) (December). 9 (4 10 11 12)

Quinn, J.B. (1999). Strategic outsourcing: leveraging knowledge capabilities. *Sloan Management Review, Summer.*

Rabitti, F., Bertino, E., Kim, W., & Woelk, D. (1991). A model of authorization for next-generation database systems. *ACM Transactions on Database Systems*, *16*(1), 88–131. doi:10.1145/103140.103144

Rafaeli, S., & Raban, D. (2003). Experimental investigation of the subjective value of information in trading. *Journal of the AIS*, *4*(5), 119–137.

Ragowsky, A. (1995). Ranking the benefits of IS applications for manufacturing. *Journal of Systems Management*, *46*(2), 56–60.

Ragowsky, A., Somers, T. M., & Adams, D. A. (2005). Assessing the value provided by erp applications through organizational activities. *Communications of AIS*, *16*(18), 1–50.

Ragowsky, A., Stern, M., & Adams, D. A. (2000). Relating benefits from using IS to an organization's operating characteristics: Interpreting results from two countries. *Journal of Management Information Systems*, *16*(4), 175–195.

Ramollari, E., Dranidis, D., & Simons, A. J. H. (2007). *A survey of service oriented development methodologies.* Paper presented at the 2nd European Young Researchers Workshop on Service Oriented Computing, Leicester, UK. Retrieved 3.2., 2008, from http://www.dcs.shef.ac.uk/~ajhs/research/papers/soasurvey.pdf

Rao, J., & Su, X. (2004). A survey of automated web service composition methods. In J. Cardoso & A. Sheth (Eds.), *Semantic web services and web process composition* (pp. 43-54): Springer (LNCS 3387).

Rapoport, A., & Wallsten, T. S. (1972). Individual decision behavior. *Annual Review of Psychology*, *23*, 131–176. doi:10.1146/annurev.ps.23.020172.001023

Rau, Pei-Lun Patrick, Chen, Duye, Effects of watermark and music on mobile message advertisements, International Journal of Human-Computer Studies, 2006

Reason, J. (2002). Combating omission errors through task analysis and good reminders. *Quality & Safety in Health Care*, *11*(1), 40–44. doi:10.1136/qhc.11.1.40

Rees, J., Koehler, G. J., & Ozcelik, Y. (2003). Information privacy and e-business activities: Key issues for managers. In Sharma, S. K., & Gupta, J. N. D. (Eds.), *Managing e-Business in the 21st Century* (pp. 139–151). Heidelberg Press.

Reibstein, D. J. (2002). What attracts customers to online stores, and what keeps them coming back? *Journal of the Academy of Marketing Science*, *30*(4), 465–473. doi:10.1177/009207002236918

Reichheld, F and Teal, T. (1996)., *The Loyalty Effect.* Boston: Harvard Business School Press.

Renard, I. (2003, December 8). L'outsourcing vers les low cost. L'angle Juridique. [Electronic version]. *Edhec Business et Technologie – Télécom Bretagne – Club France Amériques.*

Research, I. B. M. (2004). "Services science: a new academic discipline?" A 120-page report of a two-day summit entitled Architecture of On-Demand Business, May 17-18, 2004. 14 (10 11 12)

Rettie, R. (2001). An exploration of flow during Internet use. *Internet Research: Electronic Networking Applications and Policy*, *11*(2), 103–113. doi:10.1108/10662240110695070

Reynolds, T. J., & Gutman, J. (1988). Laddering theory, method, analysis and interpretation. *Journal of Advertising Research*, *28*(February/March), 11–31.

RFID in the hospital. (2004, July 15, 2004). *RFID Gazette.*

Ricardo, D. (1817/2004). *The Principles of Political Economy and Taxation*. Mineola, NY: Dover Publications. 1 (3 6 8 9 12)

Richardson, P. J., & Boyd, R. (2005). *Not By Genes Alone: How Culture Transformed Human Evolution*. Chicago, IL: University of Chicago Press. 8 (3 10)

Riordin, J. (1962). *Stochastic Service Systems*. New York, NY: Wiley. 14 (1 5 9)

Ritchie, R. J. B., Swami, S., & Weinberg, C. B. (1999). A brand new world for nonprofits. *International Journal of Nonprofit and Voluntary Sector Marketing*, *4*(1), 26–42. doi:10.1002/nvsm.54

Roberts, J. (2004). *The Modern Firm: Organizational Design for Performance and Growth*. Oxford, UK: Oxford University Press. 11 (3 6 8 12 15)

Roberts, Keith, James B. Pick G., Technology Factors in Corporate Adoption Mobile Cell Phones: A Case Study, 2004

Rogers, E. M., Diffusion of Innovations, 3rd edition, New York/London, 1993

Rokeach, M. (1969). *Beliefs, attitudes, and values*. San Francisco, CA: Jossey-Bass Inc. Publishers.

Rokeach, M. (1973). *The nature of human values*. New York, NY: The Free Press.

Rokeach, M. (1979). *Understanding human values*. New York, NY: The Free Press.

Roselius, T. (1971). Consumer ranking of risk reduction methods. *Journal of Marketing*, *35*(1), 56–61. doi:10.2307/1250565

Rosenfeld, L., & Morvile, P. (2006). *Information Architecture for the World Wide Web: Designing Large-Scale Web Sites*. Sebastopol, CA: O'Reilly Media, Inc.

Roshan, K. T., & Ravi, S. S. (1993). Discretionary access control in Object-Oriented databases issues and research directions. *Proc. Of the 16th NIST_NCSC National Computer Security conference* (pp. 63-74).

Ross, J., Weill, P., Ross, J., & Robertson, D. C. (2006). *Enterprise Architecture as Strategy*. Harvard Business School Press.

Rosser, D. (2007). *Toolkit tactical guideline: how to determine the right time to launch a BPM program*. Gartner, Inc.

Rottman, J., & Lacity, M. (2004). Twenty practices for offshore sourcing. *MIS Quarterly Executive*, *3*(3), 117–130.

Roughgarden, T. (2005). *Selfish Routing and the Price of Anarchy*. Cambridge, MA: MIT Press. 1 (3 5 6 8 9 10 11)

Rouse, W. B. (2006). *Enterprise Transformation: Understanding and Enabling Fundamental Change*. Hoboken, NJ: Wiley. 14 (2 8 9 10 11 12)

Rust, R. T., Zahorik, A. J., & Keiningham, T. L. (1996). *Service Marketing*. New York: HarperCollins.

Rust, R. T., & Kannan, P. K. (2003). E-service: a new paradigm for business in the electronic environment. *Communications of the ACM*, *43*(6), 37–42.

Rust, R. T., & Miu, C. (2006). What Academic Research Tells us about Service. *Communications of the ACM*, *49*(7), 49–54. doi:10.1145/1139922.1139948

Rust, R., Zeithaml, V., & Lemon, K. (2000). *Driving Customer Equity: How Customer Lifetime Value is Reshaping Corporate Strategy*. New York, NY: Free Press. 4 (12 15)

Ruth, M. E. (2008). *Concurrency in a decentralized automatic regression test selection framework for web services*. Paper presented at the 15th ACM Mardi Gras conference (MG'08), Baton Rouge, LA.

Ryan, G., & Valverde, M. (2006). Waiting in Line for Online Services: a Qualitative Study of the User's Perspective. *Information Systems Journal, 16*(2), pgs. 181-211.

Saeed, K. A., Hwang, Y., & Grover, V. (2002). Investigating the impact of web site value and advertising on firm performance in electronic commerce. *International Journal of Electronic Commerce*, *7*(2), 119–141.

Sainaghi, R. (2006). From contents to processes: versus a dynamic destination management model. *Tourism Management*, *27*(5), 1053–1063. doi:10.1016/j.tourman.2005.09.010

Salop, S. (1979). Monopolistic competition with outside goods. *The Bell Journal of Economics*, *10*, 141–156. doi:10.2307/3003323

Sambamurthy, V., & Zmud, R. (2000). Research commentary: the organizing logic for an enterprise's IT activities in the digital era. A prognosis of practice and a call for research. *Information Systems Research*, *11*(2), 105–114. doi:10.1287/isre.11.2.105.11780

Sampson, S. E. (2001). *Understanding Service Businesses* (2nd ed.). John Wiley & Sons.

Sampson, S. E., & Froehle, C. M. (2005). (Submitted to). [*Production and Operations Management*.]. *Foundations and Implications of a Proposed Unified Services Theory.*

Sampson, S. E., & Froehle, C. M. (2006). Foundations and Implications of a Proposed Unified Services Theory. *Production and Operations Management*, *15*(2), 329–343. doi:10.1111/j.1937-5956.2006.tb00248.x

Sampson, S. E. (2001) "Understanding service businesses". John Wiley: New York Serving the Services, *ORMS Today* June 2006.

Sampson, S. E. (2001). *Understanding Service Businesses: Applying Principles of the Unified Services Theory.* Second Edition. Wiley. 2 (4 5 12 14 15)

Sampson, S. E., & Froehle, C. M. (2006). Foundations and Implications of a Proposed Unified Services Theory. *Production and Operations Management*, 15(2), 329-343. 14 (4 5 12)

Sandhu, R., & Park, J. (2003). Usage control: A vision for next generation access control. In *MMM-ACNS 2003* (pp. 17-31). Springer-Verlag Berlin Heideberg.

Santos, J. (2003). E-service quality: a model of virtual service quality dimensions. *Managing Service Quality*, *13*(3), 233–246. doi:10.1108/09604520310476490

Sargent, R. (1999). Validation and Verification of Simulation Models. In: P. A. Farrington, H. B. Nembhard, D. T. Sturrock, and G. W. Evans (Eds), *Proceedings of the 1999 Winter Simulation Conference,* Phoenix, Arizona, USA, 39-48.

Sawyer, R. K. (2005). *Social Emergence: Societies as Complex Systems*. Cambridge, UK: Cambridge University Press. 14 (6 8 11)

Say, J. B. (1821). *A Treatise on the Political Economy*. Boston, MA: Wells and Lilly. (In Google Books) 6 (3)

Scharl, A., Wober, W. K., & Bauer, C. (2004). An integrated approach to measure web site effectiveness in the European hotel industry. *Journal of Information Technology and Tourism*, *6*(4), 257–271. doi:10.3727/1098305032781157

Scheer, A., & Spath, D. (2004). *Computer-Aided Service Engineering*. Berlin, Germany: Springer. In German 9 (7)

Schlesinger, L., & Heskett, J. (1991). The Service-driven Service Company. *Harvard Business Review*, (Sep-Oct): 71–81.

Schlosser, A. E., Barnett-White, T., & Lloyd, S. M. (2006). Converting web site visitors into buyers: How web site investment increases consumer trusting beliefs and online purchase intentions. *Journal of Marketing*, *70*(April), 133–148. doi:10.1509/jmkg.70.2.133

Schmenner, R. W. (1986). How Can Service Businesses Survive and Prosper? *Sloan Management Review*, 27(3). 2 (4 5 12)

Schmidt, J. B., & Spreng, R. A. (1996). A proposed model of external consumer information search. *Journal of the Academy of Marketing Science*, *24*(3), 246–256. doi:10.1177/0092070396243005

Schmitt, B. H. (2003). *Customer Experience Management: A Revolutionary Approach to Connecting With Your Customers*. Hoboken, NJ: Wiley. 4 (7 12)

Schneider, B., & White, S. S. (2004). *Service Quality: Research Perspectives*. Thousand Oaks, Calif.: Sage Publications.

Schneider, B., & Bowen, D. E. (1995). *Winning the Service Game*. Boston, MA: Harvard Business School Press. 4 (8 11 12)

Schneider, B., & White, S. S. (2003). *Service Quality: Research Perspectives*. Thousand Oaks, CA: Sage. 4 (8 11 12)

Scholtz, T. (2010). *Integrating Security Management into ITIL v.3 Strategies: Case Study and Best Practices.* Gartner local briefing in Zagreb. Gartner, Inc.

Schwaitzberg, S. D. (2006). The emergence of radio-frequency identification tags: applications in surgery. *Surgical Endoscopy*, *20*(8), 1315–1319. doi:10.1007/s00464-006-2050-8

Scicluna, J., Abela, C., & Montebello, M. (2004). *Visual modeling of OWL-S services.* Paper presented at the IADIS International Conference WWW/Internet, Madrid, Spain.

Scott, J. E. (1995). The measurement of information systems effectiveness: Evaluating a measuring instrument. *The Data Base for Advances in Information Systems*, *26*(1), 43–61.

Scott, W. R. (1981/2003). *Organizations: Rational, Natural, and Open Systems*. Fifth Edition. Upper Saddle River, NJ: Prentice Hall. 11 (6 12)

Seabright, P. (2005). *The Company of Strangers: A Natural History of Economic Life.* Princeton, NJ: Princeton University. 3 (8 11)

Seddon, P., & Yip, S. K. (1992). An empirical evaluation of user information satisfaction (UIS) measures for use with general ledger accounting software. *The Journal of Information Systems*, *6*(1), 75–93.

SEI. (2006). *CMMI for Development 1.2*. Pittsburgh, PA: Software Engineering Institute (SEI), Inc.

Sen, A. (2000). *Development As Freedom*. New York, NY: Anchor/Random House. 3 (6 8 11 13 15)

Sepulveda, J. A., Souder, W. E., & Gottfried, B. S. (1984). *Theory and Problems of Engineering Economics.* New York, NY: McGraw Hill/Schaum's Outline Series. 9 (2 3 12)

Shahin, A., & Mahbod, M. A. (2007). Prioritization of key performance indicators: An integration of analytical hierarchy process and goal setting. *International Journal of Productivity and Performance Management*, *56*(3), 226–240. doi:10.1108/17410400710731437

Shannon, C. E., & Weaver, W. (1949). *The mathematical theory of communication*. Urbana, IL: University of Illinois Press.

Shardanand, U., & Maes, P. (1995, May 7-11). *Social Information Filtering: Algorithms for Automating Word of Mouth.* Paper presented at the Proc. of CHI'95, Denver, Colorado.

Sheehan, J. (2006). Understanding Service Sector and Innovation. *Communications of the ACM*, *49*(7), 43–47. doi:10.1145/1139922.1139946

Shneiderman, B. (1987). *Designing the User Interface: Strategies for Effective Human-Computer Interaction.* Reading, Massachusetts: Addison-Wesley.

Shneiderman, B. (2000). Designing Trust into Online Experiences. *Communications of the ACM*, *43*(12), 57–59. doi:10.1145/355112.355124

Shostack, G. L. (1977). Breaking Free from Product Marketing. *Journal of Marketing*, *41*(April), 73. doi:10.2307/1250637

Shostack, G. L. (1984). Designing Services that Deliver. *Harvard Business Review*, *62*(1), 133–139.

Shostack, G.L. (1982). How to Design a Service. *European Journal of Marketing,* 16(1), 49-63. 7 (2 4 8 15)

Siegel, S., & Castellan, N. J., Jr. (1988). *Non parametric statistics for behavioral sciences*, Second edition, McGraw-Hill international editions.

Sigala, M. (2004). Measuring ASP service quality in Greece. *Managing Service Quality*, *14*(1), 103–104. doi:10.1108/09604520410513703

Sigala, M. (2004). Designing experiential web sites in tourism and hospitality: A customer-centric value approach. In Frew, A. (Eds.) *Information and Communication Technologies in Tourism 2004* (161-171). Proceedings of the ENTER conference. Vienna: Springer.

Silverman, R. E. (2004). Charities start to grade themselves. *The Wall Street Journal*, August 18, D1.

Simon, H. A. (1945/1997). *Administrative Behavior: A study of decision-making processes in administrative organizations.* New York, NY: Free Press. 11 (3 6 8 10 12 14)

Sindre, G., Conradi, R., & Karlsson, E.-A. (1995). The reboot approach to software reuse. *Journal of Systems and Software*, *30*(3), 201–212. doi:10.1016/0164-1212(94)00134-9

Singapore fights SARS with RFID. (2003, June 4, 2003). *RFID Journal.*

Singapore Fights SARS with RFID. (2003, June 4). *RFID Journal.* Retrieved from http://www.rfidjournal.com/article/articleview/446/1/1

Sinha, A., & Paradkar, A. (2006). *Model-based functional conformance testing of web services operating on persistent data.* In *Proceedings of the 2006 workshop on Testing, analysis, and verification of web services and applications* (TAV-WEB'06), Portland, Maine (pp. 17-22). New York: ACM.

Sirin, E., & Parsia, B., & J., H. (2004). Filtering and selecting semantic web services with interactive composition techniques. *IEEE Intelligent Systems*, *19*(4), 42–49. doi:10.1109/MIS.2004.27

Sismeiro, C., & Bucklin, R. E. (2004). Modeling purchase behavior at an e-commerce web site: A task-completion approach. *JMR, Journal of Marketing Research*, *XLI*(August), 306–323. doi:10.1509/jmkr.41.3.306.35985

Size, T. (1995). *Strategic alliances: Some lessons from experience*: A Commentary, from Partners for the Dance: Forming Strategic Alliances in Health Care, edited by Arnold D. Kaluzny, Howard S. Zuckerman, and Thomas C. Ricketts, III. (1995). Foundation of the American College of Healthcare Executives. Ann Arbor, MI: Health Administration Press, pp. 40-52.

Skadberg, Y. X., Skadberg, A. N., & Kimmel, J. R. (2005). Flow experience and its impact on the effectiveness of a tourism website. *Journal of Information Technology and Tourism*, *7*(34), 147–156. doi:10.3727/109830505774297238

Slywotzky, A., Wise, W., & Weber, K. (2003). *How to Grow When Markets Don't.* New York, NY: Warner Business Books. 7 (4 11 12)

Smith, P. (2006). Building a world of learning for all. *Prospects*, *36*, 5–7. doi:10.1007/s11125-006-8205-5

Smith, D. N., & Sivakumar, K. (2004). Flow and Internet shopping behaviour: A conceptual model and research propositions. *Journal of Business Research*, *57*, 1199–1208. doi:10.1016/S0148-2963(02)00330-2

Smith, A. (1977). *The Wealth of Nations.* New York: Dutton. (Original work published 1776)

Smith, A. (1776/1904). *An Inquiry into the Nature and Causes of the Wealth of Nations.* London, UK: W. Strahan & T, Cadell, 3 (1 5 8 11)

Smyth, J. A. (2008). The origins of the international standard classification of education. *Peabody Journal of Education*, *83*, 5–40.

So, M. W. C., & Sculli, D. (2002). The role of trust, quality, value and risk in conducting e-business. *Industrial Management & Data Systems*, *102*(9), 503–512. doi:10.1108/02635570210450181

So, S., & Morrison, A. M. (2004). Internet marketing in tourism in Asia: an evaluation of the performance of East Asian National Tourism Organization web sites. *Journal of Hospitality & Leisure Marketing*, *11*(4), 93–118. doi:10.1300/J150v11n04_07

Solow, R. (1956). A Contribution to the Theory of Economic Growth. *Quarterly Journal of Economics*, February. 3 (5 6 7 8 9 10 11 12)

Spath, D. (2007). *Advances in Services Innovations*. New York, NY: Springer. 7 (2 9)

Spitzer, D. R. (2007). *Transforming Performance Measurement: Rethinking the Way We Measure and Drive Organizational Success*. New York, NY: American Management Association. 1 (4 5 6 7 8 11 12)

Spohrer, J. (2008). (in press). [Draft version provided from author by email.]. *The Service Systems as the Basic Abstraction of Service Science.*

Spohrer, J., & Kwan, S. K. (2008forthcoming). Service Science, Management, Engineering, and Design (SSMED): Outline & References. In Ganz, W., & Spath, D. (Eds.), *The Future of Services – Trends and Perspectives*. Stuttgart, Germany: Frunhofer-Institut Arbeitswirtschaft und Organisation.

Spohrer, J, Maglio, P. P., Bailey, J., & Gruhl, D. (2007). Towards a Science of Service Systems. *Computer*, 40(1), 71-77. 1 (14 15)

Spohrer, J., & Maglio, P. P. (In Press). The emergence of service science. *Production and Operations Management*. 14 (13)

Spohrer, J., & Riecken, D. (Eds.). (2006). *Communications of ACM: Special Issue on Services Science* (Vol. 49:7).

Spohrer, J., & Riecken, D. (2006). Special Issue: Services science. *Communications of the ACM*. 49(7), 30 – 87 (July). 14 (3 4 5 6 7 8 9 10 11 12 13)

Spohrer, J., Anderson, L., Pass, N., & Gruhl, D. (Submitted). Service Science. *The Journal of Grid Computing*. 10 (1)

Spohrer, J., Maglio, P. P., Bailey, J., & Gruhl, D. (2007). Steps Toward a Science of Service Systems. *IEEE Computer*, 71-77.

Spohrer, J., Maglio, P., Bailey, J., & Gruhl, D. (2007). Steps Toward a Science of Service Systems, *IEEE Computer*, January, 71-77.

Spohrer, J., Maglio, P. P., McDavid, D., & Cortada, D. (2006). NBIC Convergence and Coevolution: Towards a Services Science to Increase Productivity Capacity. In W. S. Bainbridge & M. C. Roco (Ed.), *Managing Nano-Bio-Info-Cogno Innovations*. The Netherlands: Springer. 14 (3 9)

Spohrer, J., Vargo, S., Maglio, P. M., & Caswell, N. (submitted). The service system is the basic abstraction of service science. HICSS Conference. 1 (14)

Spulber, D. F. (2007). *Global competitive strategy*. Cambridge, MA: Cambridge University Press.

Srinivasan, A. (1985). Alternative measures of system effectiveness: Associations and implications. *Management Information Systems Quarterly*, *9*(3), 243–253. doi:10.2307/248951

Srivastava, B. (2004). Radio frequency ID technology: The next revolution in SCM. *Business Horizons*, *47*(6), 60–68. doi:10.1016/j.bushor.2004.09.009

Srivastava, B., & Koehler, J. (2003). *Web service composition - current solutions and open problems.* Paper presented at the ICAPS 2003 Workshop on Planning for Web Services, Trento, Italy.

Stacey, R. D. (2003). *Strategic Management and Organizational Dynamics: The Challenge of Complexity*. Fourth Edition. Harlow, England: Prentice Hall/Pearson Education. 12 (11 14)

Stangle, B., & Dickinger, A. (2010). How communication modes determine website satisfaction In Gretzel, U., Law, R. & Fuchs, M. (Eds.) *Information and Communication Technologies in Tourism 2010* (273-284). Proceedings of the ENTER conference. Wien: Springer-Verlag.

Steenkamp, J. B. E. M., & Geyskens, I. (2006). How country characteristics affect the perceived value of web sites. *Journal of Marketing*, *70*(July), 136–150. doi:10.1509/jmkg.70.3.136

Stein, B. (1992). *Strategic alliances: Some lessons from experience*. New York: Simon & Schuster.

Steinberg, R. A. (2005). *Implementing ITIL: adapting your organization to the coming revolution in IT service management*. Victoria, BC: Trafford.

Sterman, J. D. (2000). *Business Dynamics: Systems Thinking and Modeling for a Complex World*. Irwin Boston, MA: McGraw-Hill. 13 (1 2 3 4 5 6 7 8 9 10 11 12 14 15)

Stevens Institute of Technology. (2010). *Event-driven Business Process Management*. Retrieved June 14th, 2010 from http://www.bpm2010.org/conference-program/workshops/edbpm10/. 8th International Conference on Business Process Management.

Stockinger, H. (2007). Defining the grid: a snapshot on the current view. *The Journal of Supercomputing*, *42*, 3–17. doi:10.1007/s11227-006-0037-9

Stojanovic, Z., & Dahanayake, A. (2005). Service-oriented software system engineering: Challenges and practices: Preface. In Stojanovic, Z., & Dahanayake, A. (Eds.), *Service-oriented software system engineering: Challenges and practices* (pp. vii–xv). Hershey, PA: Idea Group.

Stojanovic, Z., Dahanayake, A., & Sol, H. (2004). *Modeling and design of service-oriented architecture*. In International Conference on Systems, Man and Cybernetics (pp. 4147 - 4152), IEEE.

Stokes, B. (2007). Bedside India. *National Journal*, *39*(18), 36–40.

Stone, D. N. (1990). Assumptions and values in the practice of information system evaluation. *The Journal of Information Systems*, *5*(1), 1–17.

Stone, R. N., & Gronhaug, K. (1993). Perceived risk: Further considerations for the marketing discipline. *European Journal of Marketing*, *27*(3), 39–50. doi:10.1108/03090569310026637

Stone, R. N., & Winter, F. W. (1987). Risk: Is it still uncertainty times consequences? In R. W. Belk et al. (Eds.), *Proceedings of the American Marketing Association* (pp. 261-265). Chicago, IL: Winter Educators Conference.

Straus, A., & Corbin, J. (1990). *Basics of Qualitative Research: Grounded Theory Procedures and Techniques*. Newbury Park: SAGE Publications.

Stringfellow, A., Teagarden, M., & Nie, W. (2008). Invisible costs in offshoring services worl. *Journal of Operations Management*, *26*, 164–179. doi:10.1016/j.jom.2007.02.009

Subramanian, K. (Subbu) (2000). *The System Approach: A Strategy to Survive and Succeed in the Global Economy*. Cincinnati, OH: Modern Machine Shop/Hanser Gardner Publications. 14 (12)

Sun, L., & Li, Y. (2006). DTD level authorization in xml documents with usage control. In. *International Journal of Science Network Security*, *6*, 244–250.

Sun. (2006). SOA RQ methodology: A pragmatic approach. Retrieved 2.4., 2008, from http://www.sun.com/products/soa/soa_methodology.pdf

Szymanski, D. M., & Hiseb, R. T. (2000). E-satisfaction: An Initial Examination. *Journal of Retailing*, *76*(3), 309–322. doi:10.1016/S0022-4359(00)00035-X

Taleb, N. N. (2004). *Fooled by Randomness: The Hidden Role of Chance in Life and in the Markets*. Second Edition. New York, NY: Texere/Thomson. 12 (8)

Tan, M., & Teo, T. S. H. (2000). Factors influencing the adoption of Internet banking. *Journal of the Association for Information Systems*, *1*(5), 1–38.

Tan, S. J. (1999). Strategies for reducing consumers' risk aversion in Internet shopping. *Journal of Consumer Marketing*, *16*(2), 163–180. doi:10.1108/07363769910260515

Tapscott, D. (2003). *The Naked Corporation: How the Age of Transparency Will Revolutionize Business*. New York, NY: Free Press. 11 (2 6 10 12)

Tapscott, D., & Williams, A. D. (2006). *Wikinomics: How Mass Collaboration Changes Everything*. New York, NY: Portfolio/Penguin. 6 (3 4 8 10 11 12)

Targowski, A. (1990). *The Architecture and Planning of Enterprise-wide Information Management Systems*. Harrisburg, PA: Idea group Publishing.

Targowski, A. (2003). *Electronic Enterprise*. Harrisburg, PA: The IRM Press.

Taylor, R. (1999), "Microsoft to Rent Software on the Internet", *WSJ Interactive*, 30 September.

Taylor, S. (2007). *ITIL Service Management Practices: V3 Qualifications Scheme* London, UK: Office of General Commerce (OGC).

Teboul, J. (2006). *Service Is Front Stage: Positioning Services for Value Advantage*. INSEAD Business Press, Palgrave MacMillan. 2 (4 5 12 15)

Teece, D. J., Pisano, G., & Shuen, A. (1990). *Firm capabilities, resources and concept of strategy: four paradigms of strategic management*. Berkeley: University of California, Center for Research in Management.

Tempel, E. (2003). Operation accountability. *Philanthropy Matters*, *13*(1), 4–5.

Teo, T., & Yeong, Y. (2003). Assessing the consumer decision process in the digital marketplace. *Omega*, *31*(5), 349–363. doi:10.1016/S0305-0483(03)00055-0

Teo, T.S.H, Pok, Siau Heong, Adoption of WAP-enabled mobile phones among Internet users, 2003

Terveen, L., & McDonald, D. W. (2005). Social Matching: A Framework and Research Agenda. *ACM Transactions on Computer-Human Interaction*, *12*(3), 401–434. doi:10.1145/1096737.1096740

The Joint Task Force. (2005). *Computing Curricula 2005* New York: Association for Computing Machinery (ACM).

The Joint Task Force. (2008). *Computing Curricula: Information Technology Volume* New York: Association for Computing Machinery (ACM).

Thomas, D. R. (2006). A general inductive approach for analyzing qualitative evaluation data. *The American Journal of Evaluation*, *27*, 237–246. doi:10.1177/1098214005283748

Thong, James Y.L., Hong, Se-Joon, Tam, Kar Yan, The effects of post-adoption beliefs on the expectation-confirmation model for information technology continuance, International Journal of Human-Computer Studies, 2006

Tien, J. M., & Berg, D. (2007). A Calculus for Services Innovation. *J Sys Sci Syst Eng*, 16(2), 129-165. 7 (13 14)

Tien, J. M., & Berg, D. (under review). On Services Research and Education. *Journal of Systems Science and Systems Engineering*. 14 (13)

Timm, J. T. E., & Gannod, G. C. (2005, 11-15 Jul). *A model-driven approach for specifying semantic web services*. Proceedings of the IEEE International Conference on Web Services (pp. 313-320), Los Vaqueros, CA: IEEE Computer Society Press.

Tirole, J. (1997). *The Theory of Industrial Organization*. Cambridge, MA: The MIT Press.

Torkzadeh, G., & Doll, W. J. (1991). Test-retest reliability of the end-user computing satisfaction instrument. *Decision Sciences*, *22*(1), 26–38. doi:10.1111/j.1540-5915.1991.tb01259.x

Tourism Authority of Thailand, (2010). *Thailand tourism overview for 2009 and tourism goals and trends for 2010*.

Trends in Services Sciences in Japan and Abroad *Science and Technology Trends Quarterly Review*, April 2006

Triplett, J. E., & Bosworth, B. P. (2004). *Productivity in the U.S. Services Sector: New Sources of Economic Growth*. Washington, DC: The Brookings Institute. 5 (3 8 11)

Trocchia, P. J., & Janda, S. (2003). How Do Consumers Evaluate Internet Retail Service Quality? *Journal of Services Marketing*, *17*(3), 243–253. doi:10.1108/08876040310474800

Troman, G., & Jeffery, B. (2007). Qualitative data analysis in cross-cultural projects. *Comparative Education*, *43*(4), 511–525. doi:10.1080/03050060701611904

Tsai, W. T., Malek, M., Chen, Y., & Bastani, F. (2006, May 27-28). *Perspectives on service-oriented computing and service-oriented system engineering.* In Proceedings International Workshop on Service Oriented Software Engineering (pp. 3-10), IEEE.

TSO. (2007). *ITIL® V3 Glossary v01*. London: Office of Government Commerce.

Turban, E., King, D., & Viehland, D. (2004). *Electronic commerce 2004: a managerial perspective*, Upper Saddle River, New Jersey: Pearson education, Inc.

Turel, Ofir, Serenko, Alexander, Satisfaction with mobile services in Canada: An empirical investigation, Telecommunications Policy, 2006

U.S. Bureau of The Census. (1999), *North American Industry Classification System*, http://www.census.gov/ epcd/ www/naics.html.52

U.S. Council of Economic Advisers And The Us Department of Labor. (1999), "20 Million Jobs: January 1993 – November 1999", December, http://www.dol.gov.

U.S. Department of Commerce, U.S. Census Bureau News, Feb 15th 2008, Washington, D.C.

U.S. Department of Education (2000). International comparisons of educational expenditures. Retrieved April 12, 2008, from Academic Search Premier. (Document ID: 3029268)

U.S. Department of Education. (2008). Budget Office — U.S. Department of Education. Retrieved July 1, 2008, from https://www.ed.gov/about/overview/budget/index.html?scr=gu

UNCTAD. (2005), *Taking off: E-tourism opportunities for developing countries*, Chapter 4, United Nations Conference on Trade and Development, e-commerce and development information economy report 2005. Retrieved April 01, 2006, from http://www.unctad.org/en/docs/sdteecb20051ch4_en.pdf.

UNICEF. (2002, November). A league table of educational disadvantage in rich nations. Innocenti Report Card No.4. UNICEF Innocenti Research Centre, Florence.

Unni, R., & Harmon, R. Location Based Services: Models for Strategy Development in M-Commerce. Portland/ usa, 2005]

Van Bon, J. (2007). *IT Service Management based on ITIL v3*. Saltbommel: Van Haren.

van Bon, J., Pieper, M., & van deer Veen, A. (2006). *Foundations of IT service management, based in ITIL.* San Antonio, TX: Van Haren.

Vanderhaeghen, D., & Loos, P. (2007). Distributed model management platform for cross-enterprise business process management in virtual enterprise networks. *Journal of Intelligent Manufacturing, 18*, 553–559. doi:10.1007/s10845-007-0060-6

Vargo, S. L. (In Press). On A Theory of Markets And Marketing: From Positively Normative To Normatively Positive. *Australasian Marketing Journal*. 4 (3)

Vargo, S. L., & Lusch, R.F. (2004). Evolving to a New Dominant Logic for Marketing. *Journal of Marketing*, 68, 1-17. 1 (3 4)

Vargo, S. L., & Lusch, R. F. (2006). Service-Dominant Logic: What It Is, What It Is Not, What It Might Be. In R.F. Lusch & S. L. Vargo, S. L. (Ed.) *The Service-Dominant Logic of Marketing: Dialog, Debate, and Directions*. Armonk, NY: M.E. Sharpe. 4 (1 3)

Vargo, S. L., & Lusch, R. F. (In Press a). From Goods To Service(s): Divergences And Convergences Of Logics. *Industrial Marketing Management*. 4 (1 3)

Vargo, S. L., & Morgan, F. W. (2005). An Historical Reexamination of the Nature of Exchange: The Service-Dominant Perspective. *Journal of Macromarketing*, 25 (1), 42-53. 4 (1 3)

Venkatesh, V., Morris, M. G., Davis, G. B., & Davis, F. D. (2003). User Acceptance of Information Technology: Toward a Unified View. *Management Information Systems Quarterly*, *27*(3).

Venkatraman, N. (1997). Beyond outsourcing: managing IT resource as a value center. *Research Policy*, *26*, 51–63.

Verma, R., Iqbal, Z., & Plaschka, G. (2004). Understanding customer choices in e-financial services. *California Management Review*, *46*(4), 43–67.

Vijayasarathy, L. R., & Jones, J. M. (2000). Print and Internet catalog shopping: Assessing attitudes and intentions. *Internet Research: Electronic Networking Applications and Policy*, *10*(3), 191–202. doi:10.1108/10662240010331948

Vivek, S. D., Glenn Richey, R., & Dalela, V. (2009). A longitudinal examination of partnership governance in offshoring: A moving target. *Journal of World Business*, *44*, 16–30. doi:10.1016/j.jwb.2008.03.017

Vivek, S. D., Shankar, R., & Banwet, D. K. (2008). Analysis of interactions among core, transaction and relationship-specific investments: The case of offshoring. *Journal of Operations Management*, *26*(2), 180–197. doi:10.1016/j.jom.2007.02.010

von Bertalanffy, L. (1976). *General System Theory: Foundation, Development, Applications*. George Braziller. 14 (11)

von Mises, L. (1998). *Human Action: A Treatise on Economics* (Scholars Edition). Ludwig Von Mises Institute. 3 (1 8 15)

Voss, C. (2003). Rethinking Paradigms of Service: Service in a Virtual Environment. [IJOP]. *International Journal of Operations & Production Management*, *23*(1), 88–104. doi:10.1108/01443570310453271

Votis, K., Vassiliadis, B., Alexakos, Ch., Likothanassis, S., & Tsakalidis, A. (2004). Workflow Coordination in Grid Networks for Supporting Enterprise-wide Business Solutions. IADIS International Conference on E-Commerce, 253-260.

Walker, J. (1990). Through the Looking Glass. In Laurel, B. (Ed.), *The Art of Human-Computer Interface Design*. Reading, Massachusetts: Addison-Wesley.

Walkerdine, J., Hutchinson, J., Sawyer, P., Dobson, G., & Onditi, V. (2007). *A faceted approach to service specification*. Paper presented at the Second International Conference on Internet and Web Applications and Services (ICIW'07).

Wallin, J. (2006). *Business Orchestration: Strategic Leadership in the Era of Digital Convergence*. Hoboken, NJ: Wiley. 12 (6 9 10 11)

Wang, Y., & Fesenmaier, D. R. (2004). Towards understanding members' general participation in and active contribution to an online travel community. *Tourism Management*, *25*, 709–722. doi:10.1016/j.tourman.2003.09.011

Wang, Y. D., & Emurian, H. H. (2005). An Overview of Online Trust: Concepts, Elements, and Implications. *Computers in Human Behavior*, *21*, 105–125. doi:10.1016/j.chb.2003.11.008

Wang, H., Zhang, Y., & Cao, J. (2006). Ubiquitous computing environments and its usage access control. *The First International Conference on Scalable Information Systems (INFOSCALE 2006)*, IEEE CS Society, Hong Kong.

Wang, J., & Osborn, S. L. (2004) A role-based approach to access control for XML databases. *SACMAT'04*.

Wang, S.-W., Chen, W.-H., Ong, C.-S., Liu, L., & Chuang, Y.-W. (2006). RFID Application in Hospitals: A Case Study on a Demonstration RFID Project in a Taiwan Hospital. *8*, 184a - 184a.

Wang, Y., & Tan, K. (2001). A scalable xml access control system. In *Proceedings of the 10th international WWW conference*, Poster.

Watts, D. J. (2003). *Six Degrees: The Science of a Connected Age*. New York, NY: W.W. Norton & Company. 14 (1 15)

Webb, H. W., & Webb, L. A. (2004). SiteQual: An Integrated Measure of Web Site Quality. *Journal of Enterprise Information Management*, *17*(6), 430–440. doi:10.1108/17410390410566724

Weber, R. P. (1985). *Basic Content Analysis, 49 Beverly Hills*. CA: Sage Publications.

Weber, M. (1978). *Economy and Society*. Berkeley, CA: University of California Press. 3 (6 8 11)

Weber, S. (2004). *The Success of Open Source*. Cambridge, MA: Harvard Business Press. 6 (10)

Webster, J., & Hackley, P. (1997). Teaching effectiveness in technology-mediated distance learning. *Academy of Management Journal*, *40*(6), 1282–1310. doi:10.2307/257034

Weidong, L., Gaishan, Z., Hailiang, W., Xianghui, X., Yujing, W., Huiqing, Z., (2006). Application of Grid Computing in Petroleum Exploration. Grid and Cooperative Computing Workshops, 27 – 34.

Weill, P., & Ross, J. (2004). *IT Governance*. Harvard Business School Press.

Weinberg, G. M. (1975/2001). *An Introduction to General Systems Thinking* (Silver Anniversary Edition). Dorset House Publishing. 14 (13 15)

Weisbrod, B. A., & Dominguez, N. D. (1986). Demand for collective goods in private nonprofit markets: Can fundraising expenditures help overcome free-rider behavior? *Journal of Public Economics*, *30*, 83–95. doi:10.1016/0047-2727(86)90078-2

Wells, A. J. (2008). *Grid Application System Design*. CRC Press.

What an unbelievable surgery!-Perform an operation with exchanged charts. (2006, 2006 Jan 15). *Donga News*.

Wieczorek, C. C. (2008). Comparative analysis of educational systems of American and Japanese schools: views and visions. (Author abstract)(Report). *Educational Horizons*.

Williams, R., Rattray, R., & Stork, A. (2004). Website accessibility of German and UK tourism information sites. *European Business Review*, *16*(6), 577–589. doi:10.1108/09555340410565404

Williams, R. M. (1979). Change and stability in values and value system: A sociological perspective. In Rokeach, M. (Ed.), *Understanding human values*. New York, NY: The Free Press.

Williamson, O. E. (1986). *Economic organization. Firms, markets and policy control*. London: Harverster Wheatsheaf.

Williamson, O. E. (1985). *The Economic Institutions of Capitalism*. New York, NY: Free Press. 6 (3 8 12)

Williamson, O. E. (1999). *The Mechanisms of Governance*. Oxford, UK: Oxford University Press. 6 (1 3 11 12 15)

Wilson, E. O. (1998). *Consilience: The Unity of Knowledge*. New York, NY: Borzoi/Knopf. 14 (8)

Wiriyapong, N. (2010, April 30). Medical tourism operators want political healing. *Bangkok Post*. Retrieved from http://www.bangkokpost.com

Wirtz, J., Kum, D., & Lee, K. S. (2000). Should a firm with a reputation for outstanding service quality offer a service guarantee? *Journal of Services Marketing*, *14*(6), 502–512. doi:10.1108/08876040010347615

Wöber, K. W. (2003). *Evaluation of DMO web sites through interregional tourism portals: a European cities tourism case example*. Paper submitted for the 2003 ENTER Conference, January 29-31, Helsinki. Retrieved April, 10, 2006, from http://tourism.wuwien.ac.at/lehrv/lven/03ws/vk5/EuropeanCitiesTourismPortal.pdf.

Wockhardt Hospitals. (2008). *Wockhardt Hospitals*. Retrieved November 14, 2008 from http://www.companionglobalhealthcare.com/agents/providernetwork/wockhardthospitalsmumbai.aspx

Woessmann, L. (2002). How central exams affected educational attainment: International evidence from TIMSS and TIMSS-repeat. *Harvard University Program on Education Policy and Governance Working Paper* No. PEPG.-02-10.

Wolcott, H. F. (1994). Transforming qualitative data: Description, analysis, and interpretation. *Journal of Phenomenological Research*, *14*, 197–242.

Wolfinbarger, M., & Gilly, M. C. (2003). eTailQ: Dimensionalizing, Measuring and Predicting etail Quality. *Journal of Retailing*, *79*(3), 183–198. doi:10.1016/S0022-4359(03)00034-4

Womack, J. P., & Jones, D. T. (2005). *Lean Solutions: How Companies and Customers Can Create Value and Wealth Together*. New York, NY: Free Press. 5 (2 4 8 11 12 15)

Woodruff, R. B. (1997). Customer Value: The next source for competitive advantage. *Journal of the Academy of Marketing Science, 25*(2), 139–153. doi:10.1007/BF02894350

Woodruff, R. B., & Gardial, S. F. (1996). *Know your customer – New approaches to understanding customer value and satisfaction*. Malden, MA: Blackwell Publishing.

Woodruff, R. B., & Flint, D. J. (2006). Marketing's service-dominant logic and customer value. In Lusch, R. F. & Vargo S. L. (Eds.) *The service-dominant logic of marketing – dialogue, debate, and directions* (183-195). New York: M.E. Sharpe.

Woods, B. M., & Degarmo, E. P. (1953/1959). *Introduction to Engineering Economy.* Second Edition. New York, NY: Macmillan. 9 (2 3 12)

Wooldridge, M. (2002). *An Introduction to MultiAgent Systems*. Chichester, UK: John Wiley. 10 (1 2 6 8 11 13 14 15)

World Services Congress 99 (1999), "Recommendations of the Global Services Network and Business Policy Forums for Services 2000 Trade Negotiations", November, http://www.worldservicescongress.com/home.cfm.

World Tourism Organization. (2005). *Evaluating and improving websites*. The Tourism Destination Web Watch' Report. Retrieved March, 22, 2006, from http://www.world-tourism.org.

Wright, R. (2000). *Non-Zero: The Logic of Human Destiny*. New York, NY: Vintage/Random House. 3 (6 1)

Yadav, M. S., & Varadarajan, P. R. (2005). Understanding product migration to the electronic marketplace: A conceptual framework. *Journal of Retailing, 81*(2), 125–140. doi:10.1016/j.jretai.2005.03.006

Yang, Z., & Peterson, R. T. (2004). Customer perceived value, satisfaction, and loyalty: The role of switching costs. *Psychology and Marketing, 21*(10), 799–822. doi:10.1002/mar.20030

Yang, M., Liang, H., & Xu, B. (2005). S-WFMS: A Service-Based Workflow Management System in Grid Environment. 19th International Conference on Advanced Information Networking and Applications, 293 – 297.

Yoo, B., & Donthu, N. (2001). Developing a Scale to Measure the Perceived Quality of an Internet Shopping Site (SITEQUAL). *Quarterly Journal of Electronic Commerce, 2*(1), 31–47.

Yoo, B., & Donthu, N. (2001). Developing a scale to measure perceived quality of an internet shopping site (SITEQUAL). *Quarterly Journal of Electronic Commerce, 2*(1), 31–46.

Yoo, B., Choudhary, V., & Mukhopadhyay, T. (2002). A model of neutral B2B. *Journal of Management Information Systems, 19*(3), 43–68.

Yoo, D.-S. K., Kim, S. K., Chang, H. O., Bae, B. C., Kim, H. S., & S.J. (2007). Location based blood bag management using active RFID and ubiquitous sensor network. *This paper appears in: Information Technology Applications in Biomedicine, 2007. ITAB 2007. 6th International Special Topic Conference on ITAB, Tokyo, 2007.*, 320-322.

Young, H. P. (1998/2001). *Individual Strategy and Social Structure: An Evolutionary Theory of Institutions.* Princeton, NJ: Princeton University Press. 11 (1 3 6 8 12 14 15)

Yourdon, E. (1988). *Modern Structured Analysis*. Prentice Hall.

Yu, H., Bai, X., & Marinescu, D. C. (2005). Workflow management and resource discovery for an intelligent grid. *Parallel Computing, 31*(7), 797–811. doi:10.1016/j.parco.2005.04.009

Yuthas, K., & Eining, M. M. (1995). An experimental evaluation of measurements of information system effectiveness. *The Journal of Information Systems, 9*(2), 69–84.

Zachos, K., Maiden, N. A. M., Zhu, X., & Jones, S. (2007, Jun 11-15). *Discovering web services to specify more complete system requirements.* In Opdahl, A.L., Sindre, G. & Krogstie, J.: 19th Conference on Advanced Information Systems Engineering (CAiSE'07), Proceedings [Berlin: Springer.]. *Lecture Notes in Computer Science, 4495*, 142–157. doi:10.1007/978-3-540-72988-4_11

Zeithaml, V. A. (1988). Consumer perceptions of price, quality, and value: A means-end model and synthesis of evidence. *Journal of Marketing, 52*(July), 2–22. doi:10.2307/1251446

Zeithaml, V. A., Bitner, M. J., & Gremler, D. D. (2006). *Services Marketing: Integrating Customer Focus Across the Firm* (4th ed.). Boston: McGraw-Hill/Irwin.

Zeithaml, V. A., Parasuraman, A., & Malhotra, A. (2002). Service quality delivery through websites: a critical review of extant knowledge. *Journal of the Academy of Marketing Science*, *30*(4), 362–375. doi:10.1177/009207002236911

Zeithaml, V. A., & Bitner, M. J. M. J. (2000), *Services Marketing: Integrating Customer Focus across the Firms.* New York: McGraw-Hill.

Zeithaml, V. A., & Bitner, M. J. (2003). *Services Marketing: Integrating Customer Focus Across the firm* (3rd ed.). New York, NY: McGraw-Hill.

Zeithaml, V. A., Bitner, M. J., & Gremler, D. D. (2006). *Services Marketing: Integrating Customer Focus Across the Firm*. 4th Edition. New York, NY: McGraw-Hill Irwin. 4 (2 15)

Zhang, X., Park, J., & Parisi-Presicce, F. (2004). A logical specification for usage control. In *SACMAT'4*. ACM Press.

Zhang, L. (2007). Modern *Technologies in Web Services Research.* Hershey, PA: IGI Publishing. 10 (9 15)

Zhang, X., Park, J., & Sandhu, R. (2003). Schema based xml security: Rbac approach. In *Proceedings of the IFIP WG*. ACM Press.

Zhao, J., Hsu, C., Jain, H., Spohrer, J., & Tanniru, M. (2007). Panel on: Bridging service computing and service management: how MIS contributes to service orientation. *Twenty Eighth International Conference on Information Systems*, Montreal, CA, 1-4.

Zhu, F. X., Wymer, W., & Chen, I. (2002). IT-based services and service quality in consumer banking. *International Journal of Service Industry Management*, *13*(1), 69–90. doi:10.1108/09564230210421164

Zhu, L., Gorton, I., Liu, Y., & Bui, N. B. (2006). *Model driven benchmark generation for web services.* In *International Workshop on Service Oriented Software Engineering* (pp. 33-39), IEEE.

Zhu, W., & Fui-Hoon, N. (2002). Factors Influencing Adoption of Mobile Computing. In *Proceedings of the Conference on Issues and Trends of IT Management in Contemporary Organizations* (IRMA). Hershey, PA: Idea Publishing Group.

ZIFA. (2010). *Zachman framework*. Retrieved June 16th, 2010 from http://www.zachmaninternational.com/index.php/the-zachman-framework. Zachman International Enterprise Architecture.

Zimmermann, O., Schlimm, N., Waller, G., & Pestel, M. (2005). Analysis and design techniques for service-oriented development and integration. *GI Jahrestagung*(2), 606-611.

Zuboff, S., & Maxmin, J. (2002). *The Support Economy: Why Corporations are Failing Individuals and the Next Episode of Capitalism*. New York, NY: Penguin. 3 (4 8 12)

Zuckerman, H. S. (2002). *Strategic alliances: A worldwide phenomenon comes to health care*. Washington, D.C.: Beard Books.

Zviran, M., & Erlich, Z. (2003). Measuring IS user satisfaction: Review and implications. *Communications of the Association for Information Systems*, *12*(1), 81–103.

Zysman, J. (2006). The Algorithmic Revolution –The Fourth Service Transformation. *Communications of the ACM*, *49*(7), 48–48. doi:10.1145/1139922.1139947

About the Contributors

John Wang is a professor in the Department of Management and Information Systems at Montclair State University, USA. Having received a scholarship award, he came to the USA and completed his Ph.D. in operations research from Temple University. He has published over 100 refereed papers and six books. He has also developed several computer software programs based on his research findings. He is the Editor-in-Chief of Int. J. of Information Systems in the Service Sector, Int. J. of Information Systems and Supply Chain Management. Furthermore, he is the Editor of Data Warehousing and Mining: Concepts, Methodologies, Tools, and Applications (six-volume) and the Editor of the Encyclopedia of Data Warehousing and Mining, 2e (four-volume). His long-term research goal is on the synergy of operations research, data mining and cybernetics.

* * *

Marina Avgeri received her MS in international marketing from the University of Strathclyde, MS in finance from Lancaster University and BA in business administration from the University of Thessaloniki. After maturing a two year experience in the International Markets Department of Bank 121, she moved to the Foreign Department of the Monte dei Paschi di Siena Bank where she is currently working.

Nuri Basoglu is a Professor in Department of Management Information Systems, Bogazici University, Istanbul, Turkey. His current interests are customer-focused product development, information technology adaptation and wireless service design, adaptive human computer interfaces. He has published articles in journals such as Technology Forecasting and Social Change, Journal of High Technology Management, Technology in Society, International Journal of Services Sciences, Computers in Human Behavior and Foresight. He received his BS in Industrial Engineering at Bogazici University and MS and PhD in Business Administration at Istanbul University.

Aileen Cater-Steel is an Associate Professor in Information Systems at the University of Southern Queensland (USQ). She leads a research team investigating the adoption and benefits of IT Service Management frameworks such as the IT Infrastructure Library (ITIL). The team has achieved funding from the Australian Research Council for two ITSM projects to research the return on investment from ITIL implementation and to develop a tool for software-mediated ITSM process assessment. Her current research interests include IT governance and assessment, software process improvement, doctoral supervision, research methodologies and gender issues in IS/IT. She has also published research related to software engineering standards, organisational and national culture, and electronic commerce. From a teaching perspective, she applies authentic learning principles and has incorporated ITSM certification into USQ's Information Systems curriculum. Prior to her academic appointment, Aileen worked in private sector and government organisations where her career progressed from programmer, systems analyst and project manager to IT Manager.

Chen-Yang Cheng received his Ph.D. in Industrial and Manufacturing Engineering at Penn State University. He is currently an Assistant Professor in Department of Industrial Engineering and Enterprise Information at Tunghai University. His research interests include Computer Integrated Manufacturing, Human Computer Interaction, Distributed Systems and Control, Intelligent Systems.

Sue Conger has a Ph.D. in computer information systems from the Stern School of Management at New York University. She is on the faculty of University of Dallas where she manages both Information Technology and IT Service Management (ITSM) programs. Professor Conger is Vice President of Chapters for the Association of Information Systems (AIS), President of special interest group on IT Services (AIS SIGSVC), manages the ITSMF-USA Relationship Subcommittee, and hosts the ITSMF-USA Academic Forum. She is on five editorial boards and the program and planning committees for several conferences. She authored two books and is working on two others.

Lawrence Cunningham is a Professor of Marketing at the Business School at the University of Colorado Denver and a Distinguished Research Professor and Fellow at the EDHEC School of Business in Lille/Nice France. Professor Cunningham has served as the Joseph and Martha Davis Term Professor of Marketing at the University of Colorado Denver (2003-2007) and as a Fulbright Distinguished Professor at the University of Linz in International Business in the 2006-2007 Fulbright Program. Professor Cunningham is a member of the Editorial Boards of the Journal of Business Research, International Journal of Service Industry Management, the Services Industries Journal, Chinese Marketing Review, Journal of Chinese Marketing, International Journal of Information Systems and Services, International Journal of Information Systems and Decision Sciences, Journal of Air Transportation and World Review of Inter-model Transportation Research. He also serves as an ad hoc reviewer for the Journal of the Academy of Marketing Science and Psychology and Marketing. His main areas of research are services, international services marketing and international marketing.

Tugrul Daim is an Associate Professor of Engineering and Technology Management at Portland State University. Previously, he worked at Intel Corporation where he had held management positions ranging from technology planning to new product development. He received his BS in Mechanical Engineering from Bogazici University in Turkey, MS in Mechanical Engineering from Lehigh University in Pennsylvania, another MS in Engineering Management from Portland State University and a PhD in Systems Science-Engineering Management from Portland State University.

Darko Galinec was born in Zagreb, 1967. He obtained PhD (2009) and MSc degree (program and information engineering, 2000) in Information Science from Faculty of Organization and Informatics at University of Zagreb. His research interests include appliance of fuzzy logic, service modeling, enterprise application integration (EAI) and command and control information systems (C2IS) interoperability. His work has appeared in such scientific books and journals as Encyclopedia of Multimedia Technology and Networking 2nd Edition (Information Science Reference, USA), Journal of Information and Organizational Sciences (University of Zagreb, Croatia), Journal of Behavioral and Applied Management (The Institute of Behavioral and Applied Management, USA), International Journal of Information Systems in the Service Sector, International Journal of Human Capital and Information Technology Professionals (IGI Publishing, USA) and in refereed conference proceedings as well. He completed specialized training programs at Oxford Saïd Business School: CIO Academy (2008) and NATO Communications and Information Systems School: Communications and Information Systems Orientation for Cooperation Partners Course (2001). As senior lecturer, he teaches enterprise application integration at Polytechnic of Zagreb. Also, he serves as editorial board member for International Journal of Society Systems Science (Inderscience Publishers, UK) and International Journal of Human Capital and Information Technology Proffesionals (IGI Publishing, USA).

Ovsei Gelman-Muravchik is a Senior Researcher at the Center of Applied Sciences and Technology Development (CCADET) of the National Autonomous University of Mexico (UNAM). He holds a BS, MS and PhD in Physics and Mathematics from the University of Tbilisi, Georgia. In the last 35 years he has contributed to the advance of the Systems Science discipline and Interdisciplinary Research through the publication of approximately 250 research papers in books, national and international journals and conference proceedings, as well as by the participation as an advisor in the Engineering Graduate Program at UNAM and by the consulting for governmental and private organizations.

James Gerlach is a professor of information systems at the The Business School, University of Colorado at Denver. He holds a M.S. in computer science and a Ph.D. in management, both from Purdue University. His research interests include e-commerce and management of information systems technology. His work appears in such notable journals as Management Information Systems Quarterly, IEEE Computer, IEEE Software, Communications of the ACM, Information & Management, Decision Support Systems, and The Accounting Review. He currently serves on the editorial boards of International Journal of Information Systems in the Service Sector and International Journal of Information and Decision Sciences.

Peijun Guo received the BE, ME and PhD in 1990, 1993 and 1996, respectively, all from Dalian University of Technology and the PhD in 2000 from Osaka Prefecture University. He was an Assistant Professor (2000–2001) and aan Associate Professor (2001–2007) in Faculty of Economics, Kagawa University. Since 2007, he has been an Associate Professor of Decision Sciences in Faculty of Business Administration, Yokohama National University. His papers appear in IEEE Transactions on SMC-Part A: Systems and Humans, European Journal of Operational Research, Fuzzy Sets and Systems, Computational Statistics and Data Analysis, Information Sciences, etc.

Michael Harper is a senior instructor of Operations Management and Statistics in the Business School at the University of Colorado at Denver. The courses he teaches include operations management, statistics, supply chain management, and project management. He received a Ph.D. in operations research and statistics from Rensselaer Polytechnic Institute in Troy, New York. He has worked as a staff member at Los Alamos Scientific Laboratory and as a consultant in the oil industry. He has published in government research publications, Journal of Air Transportation, Journal of Financial Services Marketing, and Geophysics.

Byung Ho Jeong is a professor of Industrial and Information Systems Engineering at the Chonbuk National University, KOREA. He obtained his Ph.D degree and master's degree in Industrial Engineering, Korea Advanced Institute of Science and Technology. His research interests include Multi-attribute decision making, Simulation modeling analysis in service sector and Supply Chain Management. His articles appeared in the International Journal of Operational Research and International Journal of Production Research.

Kimberly Hollister, Ph.D. is an Associate Professor in the Department of Management & Information Systems at Montclair State University, Upper Montclair, New Jersey. Dr. Hollister's research falls into two main categories: Applied Operations Management and Educational Program Assessment of Management Information Systems and Operations Management curriculums. Dr. Hollister's research has been published in many peer-reviewed journals including: European Journal of Operational Research, Journal of Informatics and Education Research, Journal of Accountancy, Journal of Business & Economic Studies. Dr. Hollister is actively engaged in sharing her work with the greater academic community at regional, national, and international conferences.

Banu Kargin graduated from the Department of Management Information Systems of Bogazici University in 2002. She earned her MA in MIS Department of Bogazici University. Now, she is a Senior Specialist in the Department of Value Added Services of the leading GSM operator, Turkcell in Turkey. She has experience in the area of database marketing, customer analytics and mobile services. Her research areas of interest include database marketing and value added services, especially messaging services, locationbased services (LBS) and mobile advertising.

Deborah Kellogg, Ph.D., is an Associate Professor of Operations Management in the Business School at the University of Colorado Denver. She received her Ph.D. in Operations Management from the University of Southern California, a M.S. in Information Systems from University of Colorado Denver, and her B.S. in Nursing from Pacific Lutheran University. Her research interests include service delivery systems, service quality, healthcare operations, and service quality. Her research articles include publications in Management Science, Journal of Operations Management, International Journal of Service Industry Management, and Interfaces.

Soo Kim is currently an Assistant Professor in the Department of Management & Information Systems, School of Business, Montclair State University. Dr. Kim received her Ph.D. in Organizational Behavior from the School of Hospitality Management, The Pennsylvania State University. Her research interests include leadership (leader-member exchange), emotion at work, counterproductive work behavior, and self-control theory in the service industry. Her works appeared in International Journal of Business Research, Review of Business Research, Journal of Academy of Business and Economics, Journal of Human Resources in Hospitality & Tourism, Encyclopedia of Data Warehousing and Mining - 2nd Edition, and The Encyclopedia of Human Resource Management and Workplace Policy.

Ksenija Klasić (Zagreb, 1955) took her BSc in theoretical physics at the University of Zagreb. After several years of professorial experience in system engineering, she became specialist for data organization in the SOUR-Rade Koncar. She obtained her Ph.D. in Information Science at the Faculty of Organization and Informatics at the University of Zagreb. She has worked as an independent consultant for development and management of business processes, organization and IT. Until 2009, she worked as the permanent court expert for IT industry. She also worked in insurance business, most notably Croatia Insurance Ltd, and Allianz Zagreb. Since 2000 she teaches information science and insurance at various polytechnic schools and universities. She is a professor of information science and assistant professor for economics. She wrote a series (56) of articles in information science and insurance as well as three textbooks used in various universities, some of which have been translated to several languages. She currently works in K & K Insurance Broker Ltd as a licensed insurance broker and a board member.

Stephen Kwan is a professor of Management Information Systems at the College of Business, San José State University. He was the founding chair of the department and had served as the Senior Associate Dean of the College. He is currently working on the development of a Service Science, Management and Engineering (SSME) program at his university, and the promotion of education and research about standardization in US universities. He received a B.S. and M.S. in Computer Science from the University of Oregon, and a Ph.D. in Management from UCLA.

Yair Levy is an associate professor at the Graduate School of Computer and Information Sciences at Nova Southeastern University. He earned his Bachelor's degree in Aerospace Engineering from the Technion, Israel. He received his MBA and Ph.D. from Florida International University. His current research interests include effectiveness of IS and cognitive aspects of IS. His research publications appear in the IS journals, conference proceedings, invited book chapters, and encyclopedias. He is the editor-in-chief of the International Journal of Doctoral Studies and serving as an editorial review board member of several other refereed journals. He has been serving as a referee reviewer for numerous scientific journals.

Maria Lexhagen, PhD, is a senior lecturer and researcher at the European Tourism Research Institute at Mid Sweden University in Östersund, Sweden. Her teaching and research interests are in the area of marketing, customer behaviour, and information and communication technology, applied to the field of travel and tourism. More specifically research has in recent years been focused on customer perceived value when information and communication technology is used for marketing purposes in travel and tourism. Currently she is involved in research on the topics of "Destination knowledge management", "Customer-based innovation", "Data mining in tourism", and "Popular culture tourism and the use of social media". She has published papers in journals such as, Scandinavian Journal of Hospitality and Tourism, Journal of Information Technology and Tourism, and Event Management. Furthermore, for 10 years she has been a member of the International Federation for Information Technology and Tourism which regularly organizes the ENTER conference where she has also published several articles in the conference proceedings.

Yan Li received her PhD degree from the Flinders University of South Australia, Australia in March 2003. She is currently an Associate Professor in the Department of Mathematics and Computing at the University of Southern Queensland, Australia. Her research interests lie in the areas of artificial intelligent, Neural Networks, Computer Communications and Internet Technologies, Blind Signal Separation, Signal/Image Processing technologies and their applications on medical bioinformatics etc.

Manuel Mora-Tavarez is an Associate Professor of Information Systems in the Autonomous University of Aguascalientes (UAA), Mexico, since 1994. Dr. Mora holds a BS in Computer Systems Engineering (1984) and a MSc in Artificial Intelligence (1989) from Monterrey Tech (ITESM), and an EngD in Systems Engineering (2003) from the National Autonomous University of Mexico (UNAM). He has published around 35 research papers in international top conferences, books and/or journals. His main research interest is the development of a common management and engineering body of knowledge for software engineering, systems engineering and information systems underpinned in the Systems Approach.

Kenneth Murphy (Ken) is an Associate Professor of Information Systems in the Atkinson Graduate School of Management at Willamette University. Dr. Murphy's recent research focuses on business integration, knowledge sharing and enterprise resource planning systems implementation strategies, methodologies and management in global organizations. He has also published in the areas of scheduling and organizational learning. Dr. Murphy has published in Operations Research, Naval Research Logistics, Communications of the ACM and Information Systems Journals. He is currently an active member of The Institute for Operations Research and Management Science (INFORMS), the Decision Sciences Institute (DSI), and the Association of Information Systems (AIS). He holds a B.A in Mathematics from Reed College, M.S. in Statistics from Oregon State University and a M.S. and Ph.D. from Carnegie Mellon University in Operations Research.

Rory O'Connor is a Senior Lecturer in Software Engineering at Dublin City University and a Senior Researcher with Lero, The Irish Software Engineering Research Centre. He is also Chairperson of the Irish Software Testing Board and an Irish representative to ISO/IEC JTC1/SC7. He has published more that 60 referred articles in journals and conference, and has edited 8 books. His research interests are centered on the processes whereby software intensive systems are designed, implemented and managed, in particular the methods and techniques for supporting the work of software project managers and software developers in relation to software process improvement and management of software development projects.

Yasin Ozcelik is an Assistant Professor of Information Systems and Operations Management at the Dolan School of Business, Fairfield University, Connecticut, USA. He obtained his Ph.D degree in Management Information Systems and master's degree in Economics both from Purdue University. His research interests include economics of information systems, business models in electronic commerce, business value of information technology, and strategic use of information technology to improve firm performance. He presented his research at several international conferences, including Americas Conference on Information Systems (AMCIS), European Conference on Information Systems (ECIS), INFORMS, and Workshop on Information Systems and Economics (WISE). His articles appeared in the following journals: Journal of Management Information Systems, Information Systems and E-Business Management, International Journal of Project Management, International Journal of E-Business Research, International Journal of Business Information Systems, International Journal of Services and Operations Management, International Journal of Information Systems in the Service Sector, and Journal of Global Business Issues. He also published several book chapters. He taught courses at Fairfield University and Purdue University, and received three awards for distinguished teaching.

Marco Papa received his PhD in business administration from the University of Bari, MA in Accounting and Finance from Lancaster University, and BA in economics and commerce from the University of Bari. Throughout the academic year 2005-2006, he worked at the Department of Accounting and Finance of the University of Glasgow as visiting researcher. He is currently lecturer in business administration at the Faculty of Economics of the University of Bari. His research interests concern e-tourism and business reporting.

Claudio Pinhanez is a computer scientist, a service scientist, and a media artist. He has been a research scientist at the IBM Thomas J. Watson Research Center since 1999, where he currently conducts research on service science (theory, tools, methodology, and applications); and in ubiquitous computing and advanced computer interfaces. Claudio was born in Brazil, where he received a Bachelor's degree in Mathematics and a M.Sc. in Computer Science from the University of São Paulo. He obtained his Ph.D. in Media Arts and Sciences in 1999 from the MIT Media Laboratory. Claudio has more than 90 international publications, including 3 best paper awards, and several patents in the US, Japan, and EU.

Paolo Popoli is Associate Professor on "Business Management" at "Parthenope" University of Naples, Italy. He is member of "Accademia Italiana di Economia Aziendale" (AIDEA) and "Society for Global Business and Economic Development" (SGBED), Montclair State University, Montclair, NJ. His main area of interest is Management both in public and private sectors, with a special focus on firm's theoretical analysis. He is author of scientific publications on several themes: managerial control, privatization, deregulation, marketing management. In the recent years he is been focusing his researches on the outsourcing processes and decisions, deepening strategic and operational aspects of outsourcing risk management.

Vittal Prabhu received his Ph.D. in mechanical engineering from the University of Wisconsin-Madison. He is currently a professor of industrial engineering at the Pennsylvania State University. His research interests include distributed control systems, sensing and control of machines, and high-performance computing for manufacturing systems. He teaches courses in robotics, information technology, and manufacturing systems. He is the founder and codirector of the Center for Manufacturing Enterprise Integration at Penn State.

Mahesh Raisinghani is an associate professor in the Executive MBA program at the TWU School of Management. He is a Certified E-Commerce Consultant (CEC) and a Project Management Professional (PMP). Dr. Raisinghani was awarded the 2008 Excellence in Research & Scholarship award and the 2007 G. Ann Uhlir Endowed Fellowship in Higher Education Administration. He was also the recipient of TWU School of Management's 2005 Best Professor Award for the Most Innovative Teaching Methods; 2002 research award; 2001 King/Haggar Award for excellence in teaching, research and service; and a 1999 UD-GSM Presidential Award. His research has been published in several academic journals such as IEEE Transactions on Engineering Management, Information & Management, Information Resources Management Journal, International Journal of Innovation and Learning, Journal of IT Review, Journal of Global IT Management among others and international/national conferences. Dr. Raisinghani is included in the millennium edition of Who's Who in the World, Who's Who among Professionals, Who's Who among America's Teachers and Who's Who in Information Technology.

Guttorm Sindre is professor in Information Systems at the Department of Computer and Information Science, Norwegian University of Science and Technology. His main research interests are information systems development methods, conceptual modeling, model quality, and requirements engineering, specifically focusing on early stage elicitation techniques for safety and security requirements. He has participated in several EU and Norwegian research projects and was manager of the WISEMOD project, in which this work was done. He has published more than 50 papers in refereed international journals and conferences, and was program co-chair of CAiSE'07 and posters and demos chair of RE'08.

Jim Spohrer is Director of Service Research at IBM's Almaden Research Center in San José, CA, where he directs efforts to develop systematic approaches to service innovation. Jim is a founding member of the SRII (Service Research and Innovation Initiative - http:/www.thesrii.org). Previously, he was CTO of IBM's Venture Capital Relations Group. In the 1990's he was a Distinguished Engineer Scientist and Technologists in Apple Computer's Advanced Technology Group. Jim has a PhD in Computer Science from Yale University, and a BS Physics from MIT.

Lili Sun received her PhD degree in computer science from the University of Southern Queensland (USQ), Australia in 2010. She is currently a research assistant at the University of Southern Queensland. Her research interests include databases, Web service and access control for Electronic service system. She has published about 15 articles in international journals and conferences.

Andrew Targowski was engaged in the development of social computing in totalitarian Poland (INFOSTRADA and Social Security # for 38 million citizens - PESEL-1972) and received political asylum in the U.S. during the crackdown on Solidarity in 1981. He has been a professor of Computer Information Systems at Western Michigan University since 1980. He published 21 books on information technology, history, and political science (Red Fascism-1982) in English and Polish. During the 1990s he was a Director of the TeleCITY of Kalamazoo Project, one of the first digital cities in the U.S. He investigates the role of info-communication in enterprise, economy, and civilization. He is a President of the International Society for the Comparative Study of Civilizations and a former Chairman of the Advisory Council of the Information Resources Management Association (1995-2003).

Bill Vassiliadis obtained his diploma and PhD from the Department of Computer Engineering and Informatics of the University of Patras (1995 and 2003, respectively). He is currently work¬ing as a post-doctoral research fellow at the Digital Systems and Media Computing Lab of the Hellenic Open University. His current research interests include information systems design and information management. He has published more than 50 papers in international conferences and journals.

Terje Wahl was a PhD student at the Department of Computer and Information Science, Norwegian University of Science and Technology, while most of the work with this paper was done. His main research focus during his PhD studies was semantic web and software engineering methods for developing service-oriented systems. He was also the PhD students' representative in the university's executive board. Wahl is now in the R&D department of Intrapoint in Trondheim, Norway, a company which develops incident and crisis management solutions, in particular automated real-time decision support systems.

William Wall is the Manager of International Business Development and Contract Agreement for Thai Polycons Public Company Limited, Bangkok Thailand and International Advisor for Civil Tech Design and Consultants Co., Ltd., Bangkok, Thailand. He holds a Master degree in International Communication and a PhD in International Business Management. He has lectured at Columbia, Yale, and New York University, Pratt Institute, School of Architecture and Fashion Institute of Technology in the United States and at Chulalongkorn University, University of the Thai Chamber of Commerce and Ramkhamhaeng University in Thailand. His research has been presented at numerous conferences in Thailand and the UAE and he has been published in International Journals such as the Language Forum in India and the International Journal of Information Systems in the Service Sector in the United States of America. His first book, "Ten Things Thai Business People Should Know" is to be published in the near future.

Yawei Wang is currently an Assistant Professor in the Department of Marketing at Montclair State University, NJ. She holds a Ph.D. in Recreation & Tourism from Clemson University, SC. Her research focuses on travel and tourism - with emphasis on mature tourism and aging issues. Her teaching interests include introduction to marketing, introduction to leisure & tourism, behavioral concepts in leisure & tourism, research methods in leisure & tourism. Prior to joining Montclair State University, Yawei worked with the Gerontology Research Interdisciplinary Team in the College of Health Education & Human Development at Clemson, SC.

Hua Wang is an associate professor in the University of Southern Queensland. Dr Wang awarded a PhD degree in Computer Science from the University of Southern Queensland in 2004. He has been active in the areas of Information Systems Management, Distributed Database Management Systems, Access Control, Software Engineering and Electronic Commerce. He has participated in research projects on mobile electronic system, Web service, and role-based access control for Electronic service system, and has already published over 100 research papers. He is the co-editor-in-chief for ICST Transaction on Scalable Information Systems and was an editor of the special issue for International Journal of Security and Networks (IJSN) as well as an Editorial Board Member of The Open Cybernetics and Systemics Journal. He is also a member of the Australian Research Council Network in Enterprise Information Infrastructure.

John Wang is a full professor at Montclair State University. Having received a scholarship award, he came to the USA and completed his PhD in operations research from Temple University. He has published more than 100 refereed papers and six books. He has also developed several computer software programs based on his research findings. He is the Editor of the Encyclopedia of Data Warehousing and Mining, 1st and 2nd Edition. Also, he is the Editor-in-Chief of International Journal of Applied Management Science, International Journal of Information Systems and Supply Chain Management, International Journal of Data Analysis Techniques and Strategies. He has served as a guest editor and referee for many other highly prestigious journals. His long-term research goal is on the synergy of operations research, data mining and cybernetics.

Jun Xia is Assistant Professor of Management and International Business at Montclair State University, New Jersey, U.S. A. He holds a Ph.D. degree in Management from Texas Tech University. His research interests include foreign entry strategies, institutional change, and transition economies.

Stelios Zanakis is Professor of Decision Science & Information Systems at Florida International University. He served as associate editor for Decision Sciences and as guest editor for Management Science and the European Journal of Operational Research. His articles have appeared in major academic journals, mainly on multicriteria decision support systems, multivariate data analysis, and knowledge discovery in databases. His latest book "Decision Making: Recent Developments & Worldwide Applications" (Kluwer 2000) includes papers drawn from the 5th International Conference of the Decision Sciences Institute, Athens, Greece, 1999, for which he was the program chair. He has been a consultant to several industrial, hospital, governmental and service organizations, and an expert witness on statistical audits in legal disputes. Degrees include a PhD in Management Science, MS in Statistics and MBA, all from The Pennsylvania State University, and a BS in Mechanical/ Electrical Engineering from the National Technical University of Athens, Greece.

Index

D

E

J

K

Q

R

S

T

U

Breinigsville, PA USA
04 February 2011
254635BV00004BA/3/P

9 781609 601386